human resource MANAGEMENT

third edition

human resource MANAGEMENT

third edition

DIPAK KUMAR BHATTACHARYYA

EXCEL BOOKS

ISBN: 978-93-5062-010-6

First Edition: New Delhi, 2002
Reprint: 2005
Second Edition: New Delhi, 2006
Reprint: 2008, 2009, 2010, 2011
Third Edition: New Delhi, 2012

EXCEL BOOKS
A-45, Naraina, Phase I,
New Delhi - 110 028

INDIA SALES OFFICES
2/8, Ansari Road, Darya Ganj, New Delhi-110002
No. 10, Kalidasa Marg, Gandhi Nagar, Bengaluru-560009
1st Floor, 19/150, Anand Nagar, Vakola, Santacruz (East), Mumbai-400056
2-2-1167/2H, Near Railway Bridge, Tilaknagar, Nallakunta, Hyderabad-500044
S-3/21-23, Shastri Market, Near "B" Block Circle, Indira Nagar, Lucknow-226016

AFRICA SALES OFFICES
71 Burg Street, Cape Town-8000, South Africa
211 Pietermaritz Street, Pietermaritzburg, South Africa
27/31 Field (Joe Slovo) Street, Durban, 4000, KZN, South Africa
43 Biccard Street, Braamfontein, Johannesburg-2000, South Africa

Published by Anurag Jain for Excel Books, A-45, Naraina, Phase-I, New Delhi - 110 028
and printed by him at Excel Printers Pvt. Ltd., Plot No. 317, Sector-7, Phase-II, IMT Manesar, Gurgaon - 122 050

Dedicated to my wife
SUTAPA
and sons
SUDIP and TAPODEEP
to indulge me in this nerve testing task.

BRIEF CONTENTS

DETAILED CONTENTS

PREFACE TO THE THIRD EDITION

Third, revised and enlarged edition of this book is primarily based on the feedback and suggestions received from readers from different Institutes and Universities, including the faculty members and professional managers. Many of my HR colleagues also inspired me to enlarge the book to increase its appeal to students. Meanwhile, syllabi of various Institutes and Universities have also been enriched to keep pace with the requirements of the corporate world. Keeping view of all these, the third edition has been thoroughly changed and enriched with new content, almost in every chapter. Two new chapters have been added in this edition-one chapter on Work Environment and another chapter on Human Resource Control. Additionally, in this edition, each chapter starts with an opening case or vignette and ends with a case study. At the end, Appendices for Skill Development has been added to help the students practice their learned knowledge through various HR games, role plays, decision-making, multiple choice questions, case studies, situation analysis, simulations, etc. I am quite sure this book will be able to position itself as a quality book on human resource management, and may even be preferred over others for its student-friendly approach, quality inputs, industry examples, case studies, and pedagogy.

I sincerely acknowledge the support and help that I have received from my faculty colleagues of Camellia Business Schools, Mr. N.R. Datta, Chairman of Camellia Group; Shri Partha Pal, Dy. Director; Prof. S. Banerjea, University of Calcutta; all my family friends; and especially from my wife and my children. Finally, I acknowledge with gratitude the support of Mr. Anurag Jain and his team members of Excel Books, New Delhi.

DIPAK KUMAR BHATTACHARYYA

PREFACE TO THE FIRST EDITION

One management discipline which perhaps suffers most from the crisis of a proper name is HRM. Even the name 'HRM' which I have used, does not hold global consensus. But it has now become more common, at least for the time being. Two new names have already been accepted by some organisations. They are very cute and trendy - Human Capital Management and Knowledge Management. Knowledge Management, however, becomes more generic. Everybody feels like using the term 'knowledge', either as prefix or suffix to their discipline, to make it a Fast Moving Product. One example is 'e-enabled Knowledge Management.' This may be viewed by the critics as a possible identity crisis for the profession. But let me assure you that this is because the subject of HRM is becoming more humanised, like our children, who may have several nicknames, but one core name, which is recorded in his birth certificate.

For the present book also, I was thinking to select a trendy nickname. However, considering its academic and professional bent, I thought I must not confuse my reader. I have used the term 'Human Resource Management'.

This book covers all the contemporary issues in Human Resource Management.

The balanced academic and professional bent of the book serves the dual purpose of learning and practice. This book is divided into 21 chapters to meet the requirements of management students of ISTD, NIPM, AIMA, IMT, ICFAI, IIMs and all the institutes and universities, where this subject is taught, either as a core paper or as a specialisation paper. The book is also important for the professionals, who wish to learn the HRM process for better utilisation of their human resources.

I am grateful to Mr. Anurag Jain of Excel Books, who has agreed to publish the book.

I also acknowledge with gratitude the contribution of my colleagues at AIMA. Dr. Raj Agrawal, Prof. Nitin Balwani, Prof. Rupesh Goel, Prof. Vinod Dumblekar, Dr. Vigya Garg, and Prof. M. Washid have all immensely supported me in this venture. I would be failing in my duty without mentioning the role of my secretary, Mr N.S. Rawat, who had painstakingly typed this manuscript within the shortest possible time.

Finally, my wife Sutapa and my child Sudip also deserve special mention, as they have managed during the time I developed this manuscript.

DIPAK KUMAR BHATTACHARYYA

ABOUT THE AUTHOR

Dipak Kumar Bhattacharyya is PhD from the University of Calcutta and is engaged in teaching and research at Post Graduate level Management Programmes for more than 20 years. He has over 15 years of industry experience in HR-related functions. At present, he is working as a Professor, Xavier Institute of Management, Bhubaneswar. Earlier, he was the Corporate Director, Camellia Group. He has also served as Dean of the Indian Institute of Social Welfare and Business Management (IISWBM), Kolkata; and as Director of the Institute of Engineering and Management, Kolkata, and All India Management Association - Centre for Management Education, New Delhi. He has been a visiting professor at XLRI, Jamshedpur and IIFT, Kolkata. He is actively involved in teaching, research, training, and consulting activities.

Dr. Bhattacharyya has authored several books on HR and management and also published more than 100 research papers in various journals of national and international repute.

BLOCK ONE

INTRODUCTION

UNIT 1

Introduction to Human Resource Management and Human Resource Development

Learning Objectives

After completion of this unit, the students will be aware of the following topics:

- *Introduction*
- *History of HRM*
- *Development Process*
- *Human Resource Development as a Separate Personnel Discipline*
- *Human Resource Management (HRM) and Human Resource Development (HRD)*
- *HRM versus Personnel Management*
- *HRD Concepts*
- *Objectives of HRD*
- *Role and Significance of HRD*
- *Management of HRD Unit*
- *Focus of the HRD System*
- *Structure of HRD System*
- *Roles of HRD Manager*
- *Role of Consultants in HRD*
- *Line Managers and HRD*
- *HRD Culture*

INTRODUCTION

Any discussion on Human Resource Management (HRM) would be incomplete, without an overview on the process of its development. Hence we have to take a brief note on HRM, especially its different phases of development, conceptual issues, objectives, importance and linkages with other organisational roles. With this backdrop, we then have to understand HRM and appreciate why HRM has now become so important for the successful management of an organisation.

Particularly at a stage when we all confine our attention to downsizing or rightsizing of manpower, organisational restructuring, process re-engineering, cost minimisation, etc., to address to the problem of an organisation, HRM, per se, has assumed more importance. While employment practices differ from country to country, we find the experiences of industrially advanced nations also by and large converge on HRM issues. Almost everyday, newspapers and business magazines carry news items on VRS, job-cuts, downsizing or rightsizing, early retirement, retrenchment and manpower pruning. And this is not limited to only those organisations who are operating on a smaller scale, even globally visible multinationals are also in the fray. Thus HRM issues are globally relevant, although their magnitude may differ from country to country at the macro level and organisation to organisation at the micro level.

Before we discuss structured HRM systems and processes, as was mentioned above, let us take a brief overview of the HRM history and understand its present status.

HISTORY OF HRM

Management of human resources, as a subject of study even though of relatively recent origin – the concept upon which the theory is based – dates back to 400 B.C. (Chaldeans Inventive wage plans). Minimum wage and incentive wage plans were in Babylonian Codes or Hammurabi around 1800 B.C. The Chinese as early as 1650 B.C. had originated the Principle of Division of Labour (Specialisation). The 'Span of Management' and the related concepts of organisation were well understood by Moses around 1200 B.C. In India, Kautilya observed a sound base for systematic management of human resource, as early as 4th century B.C.

Prior to Industrial Revolution, the status of labour was extremely low and the human relationships between the employer and the employees were characterised by slavery, serfdom and the guild system. Slavery was based on negative incentive system and serfdom was based on positive incentive system. However, both these systems have been replaced with the growth of manufacturing and commercial enterprises by the guild system involving master craftsman (the owner), the journeyman (the travelling worker) and the apprentice. Guild System marked the beginning of Human Resource Management for selection, training and development of workers and emergence of collective bargaining for wages and working conditions.

The Industrial Revolution followed the new economic doctrine of laissez faire. New industrial organisations were characterised by the factory system (a change from cottage system or home centered production system), which deteriorated the employer-employee relationship due to unhealthy work environment, long working hours, fatigue, monotony, strain, increased likelihood of accidents, etc.

Reviewing the history, it is observed that great thrust had been given to personnel management functions by business expansion, labour strategies and higher wage rates during the first World War (1917). Many of these activities had been initiated for welfare and paternalism. The great depression of 1920-21 threw many personnel men out of jobs and this created a disillusion for this profession. A number of literatures came up worldwide during 1920-22, dealing with different areas of personnel administration. By 1923, the profession had reached the stage of maturity, as organisations started giving importance to it like other core functions, viz., production and marketing.

Development Process

Tracing the history, we find that personnel function derived from the introduction of welfare and charitable activity. Initially, it was perceived as a moral duty and later it was considered as the precondition for industrial efficiency. The second development sprung from the employers' endeavours to cope with the challenges of trade unionism. The third phase could be attributed to the development of the concept of humanisation of work.

Factors which are responsible for development of this profession in a phased manner can be listed as follows:

- Technological changes are taking place at a rapid pace throughout the world. Such changes have a great bearing upon personnel functions because they fundamentally changed the relationship between people and work. From an overall point of view, they induced a major change in the economic system and the structure of the society.
- The rising competition both at home and abroad (in cases of International Trade), virtually reduces the profit to the level of production cost (unless the industry is monopolist). The free movement of technology from one country to another does not allow any production process to monopolise a particular technology for their use.
- The rise of consumerism, government protection, so also international competition, developed the necessity to maintain quality and price, which completely redress the opportunity to follow the traditional production method.
- Social changes are also taking place at a fast pace. Business function is no longer a mere profit multiplying one. Organisation being a part of the society, also owes something to it.
- The political development also restructured trade unionism. Trade unionists are no longer mere wage bargainers.
- The structural changes in employment (more oriented towards white collared jobs, gradual decline of unskilled jobs) and changes in sectoral distribution of employment (more geared to tertiary or service sectors) also bought a great challenge to the employers.

For the personnel profession, all these challenges have a great impact on their functions.

Alienating and dehumanising effect of repetitive and monotonous tasks, in the wake of technological advancement is a universal phenomenon. Effective utilisation of human resources under this technological environment is the prime challenge before today's personnel profession. Even in the United States of America (USA) at the present level of production, particularly for workers in the service industries, it is estimated only 50 per cent of the potential is available from existing human skills, initiative and energy. About 50 million employees are now considered obsolete in the USA, which includes a considerable number of engineers, IT professionals and technical people. Manpower obsolescence is also being faced by Japanese industries. Other industrially advanced countries are also facing a similar crisis.

The history of evolution and growth of Personnel Management in India is not very old. The Royal Commission on Labour in 1931 for the first time recommended the abolition of Jobbers System and appointment of Labour Officers to deal with recruitment and to settle their grievances. The Factories Act, 1948, statutorily made it obligatory for the industries to appoint Labour Welfare Officers. Today Personnel Management function in India encompasses all the professional disciplines like; Welfare, Industrial Relations, Personnel Administration, Human Resource Development (HRD), etc.

The general functional areas of personnel vis-á-vis HRD professionals can be grouped under five major heads as:

- Determining and staffing for employment needs,
- Measuring performance and developing employee potential,
- Preserving effective employee-management relationships,
- Uncovering and resolving employee problems,
- Anticipating and coping with organisational change.

The new changes have extended the functional horizon to many. From a legalistic approach it extended to human relations. From a mere passive factor of production, employees are now perceived as human resources. The functional demand, therefore, encompasses many areas like; management by anticipation, more use of work teams by small group activities/ quality circles, practising total quality management culture, etc.

Human Resource Development as a Separate Personnel Discipline

So far, our discussion centres around personnel functions. At this stage we will delineate Human Resource Development (HRD) as a separate discipline of Personnel Management. But before we go into the details of HRD functions, brief understanding of the historical process is considered necessary to appreciate the importance of HRD functions in today's organisation.

It is believed that Kurt Lewin's (1947) studies of behaviour of small groups and setting up of National Training Laboratories laid the foundation for HRD profession, which till late 1940 was the domain of psychiatrists, psychologists, counsellors, nurses, and furthered the concept of human relations training and the experiential approach. Participants in training groups (T-groups) effectively identified problems, acquired the skills and also actively collaborated in the problem solving process. Training group leaders, unshackling their traditional role of instructors, became facilitators and focussed on how the individual relates to and interacts with other individuals and with groups and trained on leadership and its influence, handling conflicts, expressing feelings, giving and receiving feedback, competition and cooperations, problem-solving and increasing awareness of oneself and ones impact on others.

In 1969, the Handbook of Structured Experiences for Human Relations Training was published by University Associates giving structured experiences with guidelines for training and development. Subsequent publication of handbooks for Group Facilitators in 1972 and 1973, furthered the process of developing Training and Organisation Development vis-à-vis Human Resource Development as a recognised area of professional endeavour, delineating HRD as a new profession, encompassing the personnel function.

Human Resource Management (HRM) and Human Resource Development (HRD)

In the introductory submission, we have discussed the development process of HRD, delineating it from traditional Personnel Management functions and Human Resource Management. Before we begin with the definitions and objectives of HRD, it is necessary to study the factors which developed the concept of HRM by replacing the traditional concept of Labour Welfare and Personnel Management. These factors are:

Search for Competitive Advantage

The competitive advantage school of thought (pioneered by Beer, 1985; Tricky, Fombrun and Devenna, 1982) argued that better utilisation of human resources by an organisation or by any nation is necessary to achieve competitive advantage.

Models of Excellence

Study of Successful Organisations as Models of Excellence by Peters and Waterman (1982) and Kanter (1984) evinced the interest of HRM, as models of excellent companies, isolating it from traditional Personnel Management Functions.

Failure of Personnel Management

Management of human resources as a mainstream management activity has been advocated by Skinner (1981) and many others as their studies show Personnel Management has failed to promote potential benefits of effective management of people.

Decline in Trade Union Pressure

Changing economic and political climate around the world resulted in decline in trade union pressure on management. This necessitated switch in emphasis from collective issues (traditional Industrial Relations Approach) to individual and cooperative issues, i.e., the Human Resource Management Approach.

Changes in Workforce and the Nature of Work

Structural change in the occupational pattern is now a worldwide phenomenon. Technology, increased requirement of skill and knowledge, occupational shifts, restructuring of production, new quality systems requirement, etc., are now demanding better educated, new generation of workers, who obviously have higher expectations from their organisations. Such a trend calls for redefining the employer-employee relationship associated with Human Resource Management.

All these factors listed above revolutionised the concept of traditional Personnel Management, which is restricted to utilisation of human resources complying with mainly statutes and coping with the challenges of trade unions; and led to the development of HRM as another form of response for sustaining better employer-employee relation.

HRM is a subsystem of the total management system and is the responsibility of all managers, irrespective of their functions, disciplines and levels. It is primarily concerned with the management of people, individuals or groups at work, as also their interrelationships. HRD, OD and IR are separate aspects of the broader concept of HRM. However, in reality each of this concept overlaps and cannot be viewed in isolation. HRM practices, to succeed, must go concurrently with HRD, OD interventions. Sound IR systems cannot be visualised without good HRD practices.

HRM VERSUS PERSONNEL MANAGEMENT

HRM is a distinctive approach and it is possible to distinguish it from traditional Personnel Management in three different ways as follows:

- The first approach is by simple retitling of Personnel Management, as many companies did by renaming their Personnel Department as HR Department.
- The second approach is by reconceptualising and reorganising personnel roles in line with the conceptual framework of Harvard Business School (1985), i.e., subsuming personnel and labour relation activities in four policy areas, like employee influence, human resource flow, reward systems and work systems, differentiating HRM from Personnel Management concepts pioneered by Institute of Personnel Management, UK i.e., employee relations, employee resourcing and employee development. Thus, it is apparent that HRM concept categorises employee relations (industrial relations) as a separate strategic function, which falls under the traditional Personnel Management function.

- The third approach designates HRM as a distinctively different and new approach for Management. This approach integrates HRM into Strategic management and emphasises on full utilisation of human resources.

At this stage, it is necessary to develop a definition of HRM. Let us now define the term human resources first. Human resource is the total knowledge, skills, creative abilities, talents, aptitudes, values, attitudes and beliefs of the people of an organisation. There are, however, differences of opinion among many experts as some of them consider that human resource is not only the people, who are part of the organisation, i.e., the direct employees, it includes customers (TQM concepts) and others who are having a variety of other relationships with the organisation. Integrating the concept of human resource with management, we can define HRM as an approach to identify right people for the right job. It also includes the process of socialising such identified people to integrate them with the organisation, train them for increasing their functional skill, develop them for both identified and unidentified future roles, place them in right tasks and roles, motivate them to perform well and inculcate in them a sense of belongingness.

Within the HRM, there are two major activities; the first is concerned with the recruitment, selection, placement, compensation and appraisal of the human resources (personnel functions), more commonly termed as Human Resource Utilisation (HRU) function. The other group of functions are directed towards working with the existing human resources in order to improve their efficiency and effectiveness. Such activities are also designed to enable the existing members of the organisation to assume new roles and functions. These activities are concerned with Human Resource Development (HRD).

HRD Concepts

HRD is concerned with an organised series of learning activities, within a specified time limit, designed to produce behavioural change in the learner (Naddler, 1969). From the organisational context, therefore, HRD is a process which helps employees of an organisation to improve their functional capabilities for their present and future roles, to develop their general capabilities, to harness their inner potentialities both for their self and organisational development and, to develop organisational culture to sustain harmonious superior-subordinate relationships, teamwork, motivation, quality, and a sense of belongingness.

There are a lot of misconceptions about training, education and development functions vis-à-vis HRD. Essentially, HRD activities are designed to make people effective in their present job position, which is a part of the training function. But when the focus is on a future identifiable job it becomes a part of the education function. For future unidentifiable jobs, i.e., to develop capabilities for a future position or new activities within the organisation, which are not very specific at the present stage, it becomes a part of the development function.

Without precisely knowing the functions of training, education and development, it would further make it difficult for us to appreciate the objectives, roles and significance of HRD in an organisation. In the succeeding paragraphs we will take a cursory view of these functions before we elaborate on other issues of HRD.

Training

Training concerns people already employed with the organisation and whose jobs are so defined that we are able to identify what should be the desired job behaviours. The focus on training programmes should be such, so as to enable the individual to perform more effectively in his present job position. Training is also needed when a person is hired without the requisite skills, attitude or knowledge or after putting the person on the job, we are able to identify deficiencies that are possible to rectify through training. Even in cases, where an employee may be performing very well, changes in procedures, materials, processes may stimulate the need for further training. Total Quality Management (TQM), Small Group Activities (SGA) or Quality Circles (QC) concepts are now calling for new areas of training for employees to make them functionally more effective in their restructured jobs. We have discussed these issues in a separate supplementary note. For effective results, the responsibility for training should be on the immediate supervisor of the trainee. As the payoff of training is verified on the job, the supervisor is expected to see the results and therefore, he is the right person to allocate physical and financial resources to improve his human resources. However, in most of the organisations, supervisors are made responsible for identification of training needs and their role is restricted to imparting technical skill enriching training. For conceptual and human skills, training is given by a specialised group of trainers. Training can either be conducted through in-house programmes or by retaining professional trainers/consultants.

The evaluation of training is done in direct relation to the job. At the end of the training, it is expected that there should be some identifiable changes in job behaviour. Where no such changes in job behaviour could be identified, we expect there may be one or more of the following problems; ineffective training programme, lack of linkage between the training programme and the job or negative reinforcements in the work situation. Evaluation of training is easy because of its job relatedness.

Education

Educational experiences benefit those who are employed and who are required to be gradually equipped for other positions in the organisation. Thus, the education component of HRD is future oriented for identifiable job positions. Since return on investment from education is unclear or unascertainable, very few organisations are prepared to invest on employee education programmes unless future needs or manpower plan of the organisation substantiates the possibility of redeployment of employees after completion of educational programmes.

Many organisations allow their employees to go on study leave for pursuing institutional studies in areas like, Management, Accounting and Finance, Quality, Engineering or even for Research, which are relevant to organisational needs. Employees are allowed to draw their pay and get reimbursement of actual cost for study during this period and such leave is not debited against employees' leave account.

Some organisations encourage their employees to get enrolled in part-time evening programmes and allow them reimbursement of actual cost. In India a number of institutes are encouraging sponsored candidates to pursue studies as full-time students.

However, education within the organisation is considered as a better alternative as it simultaneously ensures employees on-the-job activities and learning of new techniques for their future roles. For example, some organisations with their in-house talents run professional programmes for their employees like, Engineering Degree Courses of Institute of Engineers, Indian Institute of Metals, Management Degree Courses of All India Management Association, National Institute of Personnel Management, ICFAI Business School, International Institute of Management Science, Professional Programmes of Indian Society for Training and Development, National HRD Network, Academy of HRD, etc. This is considered more cost-effective than the earlier two methods and this also reduces the time-lag between the time of education experience and its application on the new job.

Employee education calls for attitudinal changes of corporate leaders as they should be prepared at the outset to invest in the future of individuals who may or may not remain with the organisation. It is also necessary to identify individuals who are future oriented. Evaluation of employee education is difficult when there is considerable time-lag between learning and its actual on-the-job application.

Development

The development component of HRD is to conduct learning experiences for a future undefined job. The focus being on a future undefined job an organisation, before going ahead with employee development, the organisation must be able to identify individuals who enjoy high risk and new undefined challenging jobs. Such risk takers may not necessarily be confined to the higher levels of an organisation, even though conventionally, development function rests with the higher levels only since decisions on investment in employee development are taken at higher levels and, people at higher levels are considered to be more knowledgeable (both by virtue of experience and educational background) than people at lower levels. Hardly a few organisations consider it right to risk the investment to develop employees at lower levels. However, experience shows, carefully planned development experiences can be helpful in realising human potential, irrespective of the hierarchical levels and functional areas.

Before the introduction of computers in Indian organisations, computer literacy was considered as a development function. At present, however, TQM, business process re-engineering, benchmarking, ISO:9000 quality systems, value engineering, etc., are considered as new areas of development.

Valuation of employee development programmes is extremely difficult both in terms of return on investment and application of learned experiences, for obvious time-lag, in the organisation.

However, success of training, i.e. HRD efforts of an organisation in the form of education and development programmes, largely depends on simultaneous changes in the organisation, which is known as Organisational Development (OD). Changes in the employee behaviour (for training, education and development programmes) is reinforced by changes in the organisation by OD process, which uses many strategies and interventions. Hence, HRD efforts should be in congruence with OD investments.

Objectives of HRD

From the foregoing discussion, objectives of HRD can be listed as follows:

1. To develop capabilities of all individuals working in an organisation in relation to their present role.
2. To develop capabilities of all such individuals in relation to their future role.
3. To develop better interpersonal and employer-employee relationships in an organisation.
4. To develop team spirit.
5. To develop coordination among different units of an organisation.
6. To develop organisational health by continuous renewal of individual capabilities (averting manpower obsolescence) keeping pace with the technological changes.

Objectives of HRD can be made clear when we highlight the importance of human resources in line with the examination process of the 'Baldridge Award', which is given at an international level to a quality organisation. Objectives of HRD practices in an organisation should be to put efforts to develop/and realise the full potential of the workforce, including management and to maintain an environment conducive to total participation, quality leadership and personal and organisational growth. In an organisation there are six units which are concerned with HRD, namely person, role, dyad, team, inter-team and organisation. The effectiveness of one contributes in turn to the effectiveness of the others.

HRD objectives can also be couched in line with W. Edward Deming's fourteen principles for quality improvement in an organisation. Here we won't discuss the fourteen principles but we will focus on only those points which are related to HRD objectives. There are:

1. Institute training on the job.
2. Breakdown barriers between departments to build teamwork.
3. Drive fear out of the workplace.
4. Create conditions to enable employees to take pride in their workmanship.
5. Institute programme of education and self-improvement.

At this stage for better appreciation, we will review the HRD objectives of two leading companies in India.

EXHIBIT 1.1

HRD OBJECTIVES OF SIEMENS LIMITED

- Development of employees is the primary task of the company.
- It is the policy of Siemens to recruit, train, develop and advance employees within the company.

To achieve these objectives Siemens have laid down their policies as under:

- Recruitment of quality manpower and their retention.
- Recruitment mainly at entry level.
- Plan and monitor career development staff to perform effectively in their present jobs; groom potential managers for higher responsibilities.
- To introduce and sustain an objective system of evaluation of performance based on result.
- Performance as the sole criterion for increments and promotion.
- Use of training as the strategic factor for competitive advantage.
- To nurture a spirit of entrepreneurship among employees.
- Work in close collaboration for fostering the spirit of openness.
- To ensure transparency in decision-making.
  - Self-motivated employees
  - Employee commitment
  - Commitment of results.

EXHIBIT 1.2

HRD OBJECTIVES OF W.S. INDUSTRIES INDIA LIMITED

- To plan and induct appropriate manpower in terms of knowledge, skill and attitude.
- To provide opportunities for growth to employees in terms of remuneration, career and skill endowment.
- To practice equity and fairness in all its dealings with employees.
- To continuously enhance knowledge, skill of employees for the performance of their present and future tasks through education and training.
- To create an organisational climate which encourages a highly motivated workforce.
- To prepare employees for easy and faster adaptation to change.

ROLE AND SIGNIFICANCE OF HRD

For any dynamic and growth-oriented organisation to survive in a fast-changing environment, HRD activities play a very crucial role. Recent economic restructuring in India at the macro-level influenced the need for production restructuring at unit (micro) level and production restructuring necessitated labour restructuring vis-à-vis restructuring of HRD activities in organisations. Training, retraining and redeployment have now become buzzwords in corporate circles as market globalisation (which is an outcome of the economic restructuring programme), delicensing and free flow of technology (as per New Industrial Policy of July, 1991), and intensified competition are rendering traditional skills and knowledge redundant.

Many organisations in India are now threatened with manpower obsolescence. To withstand this, HRD activities have now received prime importance.

Increased morale and motivation of employees no doubt are necessary to achieve productivity and functional effectiveness. But these alone cannot sustain a dynamic organisation, unless effort and competencies of human resource are renewed constantly, developing an enabling organisational culture. An enabling organisation culture is possible when employees of an organisation are found to use their initiative, take risks, experiment, innovate and make things happen.

Hence, role and significance of HRD in an organisation can be appreciated when we consider the fast-changing environment coupled with technological change and intensified competition. This has necessitated the need for renewal of capabilities of people working in the organisation which are simultaneously reinforced by changes in the organisation by the Organisational Development (OD) process.

The role and significance of HRD can further be appreciated when we consider different systems of HRD like performance appraisal, career planning and development, manpower planning, management succession and development, training (which includes the role of education and development discussed earlier), Organisational Development (OD), Quality of Work Life (QWL), etc.

Management of HRD Unit

It is pertinent to mention that Indian organisations, by and large, have personnel functions integrated with HRD functions, except for a few who have separate HRD department, exclusively for HRD functions. Most of the organisations, therefore, merely retitled the designation of their core personnel people by either calling them Human Resource Manager or Human Resource Development Manager. Yet there are some organisations, who have isolated their HRD as training function, entrusting the responsibility to Management Development Officers or Principals of their Management Development Centres. Public sector giants like Steel Authority of India Ltd. (SAIL), Indian Oil Corporation (IOC), NTPC, ONGC, Coal India, have set up their own management development institutions/centres. Departmental undertakings like Indian Ordinance Factories, Indian Railways also have their separate management development centres. Many commercial banks, Reserve Bank of India, Regional Rural Banks, Industrial Financial Corporation of India (IFCI), Industrial Credit and Investment Corporation of India (ICICI), insurance companies like, Life Insurance Corporation of India, General Insurance Corporation of India, have set up their own staff training colleges for developing their human resources. Similarly private companies like TISCO, Kirloskar Group, Reliance, Lakshmi Group, Hinduja Group, Modern Group, Lalbhai Group, have their own management development centres to develop and train their human resources.

We have shown three different organisational charts for personnel/human resources/HRD functions for a large company, for a company where personnel/HRD functions are integrated and for an organisation where HRD is shown as a separate department. But before we review the organisation charts, it is important to discuss the principles pertaining to focus, structure and functioning, which we should consider while designing an integrated HRD organisation.

Focus of the HRD System

Reviewing the definition, role, significance, purpose and objectives of HRD it is evident that HRD department of an organisation focuses on the following important areas:

1. Increasing the 'enabling' capabilities by developing human resources, organisational health, team spirit and increasing employee motivation and productivity.

2. Focus on balanced organisational culture by conducting periodic surveys, workshops, discussions stimulating openness, mutual trust, team spirit, creativity, initiative, mutuality, collaboration, delegation, autonomy, respect, management of mistake, management of conflict, etc.

3. Focus on learning contextual factors from different professional bodies like NIPM, ISTD, HRD Network, AIMA, etc. These professional bodies, through their publications, seminars and workshops, share the experiences of the corporate world.

4. Focus on periodic reviewing of HRD system which may call for redesigning performance appraisal, job-rotation, reward systems, career planning, promotion, selection, induction, training and development programme, etc.

5. Focus on integrating HRD with other corporate functions like production, marketing, finance, material, corporate planning, etc. Such integration will strengthen the development of an 'enabling' organisation.

6. Focus on diffusion of HRD function involving line managers in various HRD aspects like training of subordinates, performance appraisal, promotion, placement, selection, career planning, etc. Line people by virtue of their rich experience may effectively contribute to these HRD areas. Moreover, their active association will accentuate the process of developing an integrated HRD system in an organisation.

7. Focus on working with unions by taking them into confidence and collaborating with them. That unions can also play a positive role in furthering the organisation is evident from a number of examples. Syndicate Bank Employees Union very recently collaborated with the management to reduce the Non-performing assets (i.e. bad debt realisation).

Structure of HRD System

The precise organisational plan for an HRD department depends on the type of organisation and the size of organisation. Here we are giving hypothetical examples of organisation structure for three different organisations to appreciate the functioning of HRD departments in different organisations.

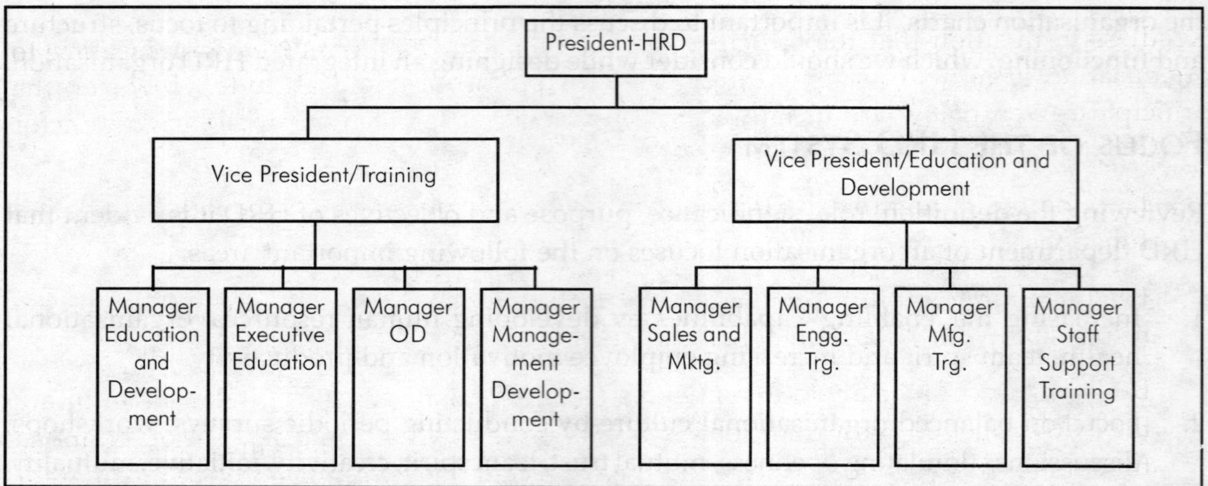

Figure 1.1: Organisation Chart No. 1 for a Large Company

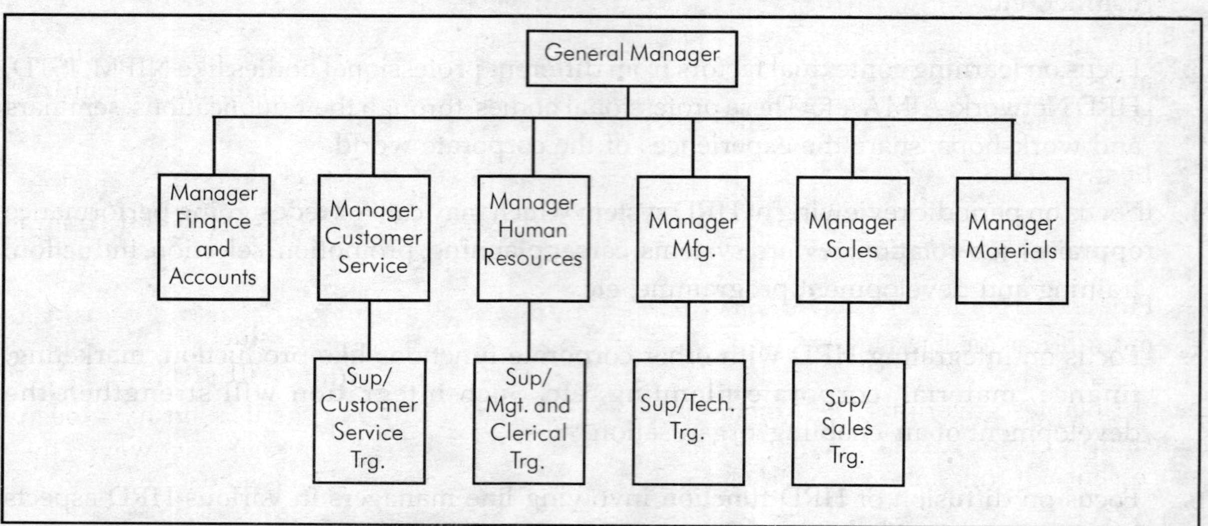

Figure 1.2: Organisation Chart No. 2 Integrated HRD

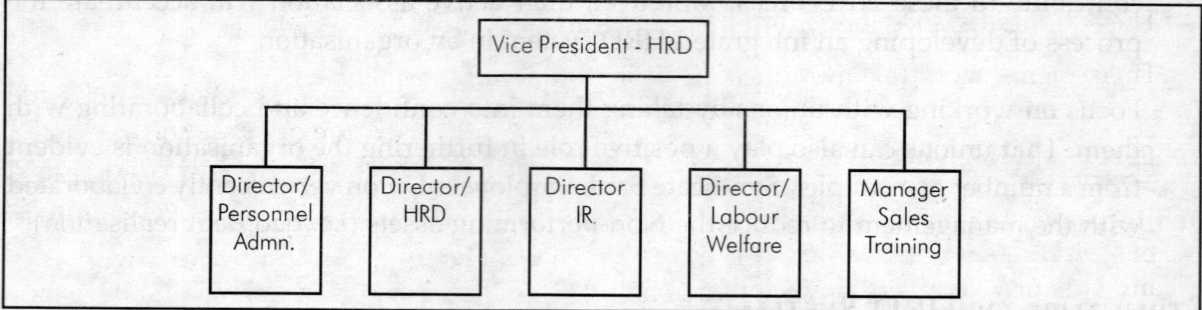

Figure 1.3: Organisation Chart No. 3 HRD as a Separate Department

The structure of HRD system organisations was briefly discussed in the introductory part of this unit, duly illustrating an integrated HRD structure and HRD as a separate functional identity in an organisation. Here we will discuss the basic principles while structuring the HRD department of an organisation.

Needless to mention that the structure of HRD department differs from organisation to organisation in terms of size, nature of activity, philosophy and attitude. However, the principles given below are usually followed in every organisation, while it goes in for structuring the HRD Department.

1. Developing an identity of HRD which may or may not encompass other personnel functions.
2. Establishing credibility for the HRD function, which is possible by entrusting the responsibility for HRD at a higher level in an organisational hierarchy.
3. Balancing integration and differentiation. Differentiation can be ensured by not diluting the HRD function with traditional Personnel Management and Industrial Relations function, which is possible by entrusting the functional responsibilities to different department heads as illustrated in the organisation Chart No. 3. Similarly, integration can be achieved by diffusion of HRD function with other major corporate functions like; marketing, production (as explained earlier) and line functions, as inputs from these areas can enrich the functioning of the HRD department, the structure of which has been illustrated in Organisation Chart No. 2.
4. Likewise, while structuring an HRD department of an organisation, it should be ensured that it has linkages with external and internal systems, i.e. HRD department should represent various task groups, adhoc committees, etc.
5. Finally, structure of HRD department should be developed so that it can sustain a monitoring mechanism.

Basic principles governing the functioning of HRD systems in an organisation have been made amply clear by ASTD, while describing different roles of HRD managers. However, the basic essence of functioning principles of HRD systems can be listed as follows:

1. HRD systems should develop a strong feedback and re-enforcing mechanism.
2. They should balance qualitative (subjective) and quantitative (objective) decisions.
3. They should balance the requirement of internal and external expertise.
4. The systems should be introduced in a phased manner.

Roles of HRD Manager

From the foregoing discussions, it is apparent that the primary goal of HRD is to increase a worker's productivity and a firm's profitability as investment in HRD improves a worker's skill and enhances motivation. The other goal of HRD is to prevent obsolescence at all levels. To achieve these two goals, the HRD manager of any organisation plays the following two important roles:

1. To assist people in obtaining the knowledge and skills they need for present and future jobs and to assist them in attaining their personal goals.
2. To play the 'enabling' role by providing the right context in which human performance occurs and the organisation reaches its stated objectives.

The American Society for Training and Development (ASTD, 1998) identified eleven roles of the HRD manager, which can be enumerated as follows:

1. *Administrator:* The role of providing coordination and support services for the delivery of HRD programmes and services.
2. *Evaluator:* The role of identifying the impact of an intervention on individual or organisational effectiveness.
3. *Individual Career Development Advisor:* The role of helping individuals to assess personal competencies, values and goals and to identify, plan and implement development and career actions.
4. *HRD Manager:* The role of supporting and leading a group's work and linking that work with the total organisation.
5. *Instructor/Facilitator:* The role of presenting information, directing structured learning experiences and managing group discussions and group process.
6. *Marketer:* The role of marketing and contracting from HRD viewpoints, programmes and services.
7. *Material Developer:* The role of producing written and/or electronically mediated instructional materials.
8. *Needs Analyst:* The role of identifying ideal and actual performance and performance conditions and determining causes of discrepancies.
9. *Organisational Change:* The role of influencing and supporting changes in organisational behaviour.
10. *Programme Designer:* The role of preparing objectives, defining content and selecting and sequencing activities for a specific intervention.
11. *Researcher:* The role of identifying, developing or testing new information (theory, concepts, technology, models, hardware) and translating these two implications for improved individual or organisational performance.

R. Wayne Pace, Philip C. Smith and Gordon Mills (1991) after reviewing the eleven roles of HRD, as indicated by ASTD, grouped all these roles into four major areas, as given below:

1. *Analytic*
   (a) Needs Analyst
   (b) Researcher
   (c) Evaluator
2. *Developmental*
   (a) Programme Designer
   (b) Materials Developer

3. ***Instrumental***

   (a) Instructor/Facilitator

   (b) Organisation Change Agent

   (c) Marketer

4. ***Mediational***

   (a) HRD Manger

   (b) Individual Career Development Advisor

   (c) Administrator

ROLE OF CONSULTANTS IN HRD

In HRD, consultants play a very crucial role, particularly in the following areas:

1. In designing a career plan for the employees, many organisations prefer to retain the services of consultants. Career planning is a very complicated function of the organisation as faulty career planning may ultimately lead to dissatisfaction among the employees, who may leave the present organisation to get employed elsewhere. Many Indian organisations are facing the crisis of mid-career shift for not adopting suitable career plans for their employees. SAIL, the public sector giant very recently lost 400 of their key and middle level executives who left to join the newly formed private steel manufacturing companies. The chairman of SAIL in a recent press briefing lamented such large-scale exodus of executives from SAIL will cost heavily to the organisation, as developing an executive requires 10 to 15 years time. All such executives who have left SAIL attributed reasons which, inter alia, include absence of better career progression in SAIL and more financial benefits in private steel manufacturing companies. Banks and other financial institutions are also facing similar unpleasant situations due to the recent liberalisation of financial markets vis-á-vis emergence of private banks/foreign banks/global financial institutions, etc. Very recently the State Bank of India retained the services of world famous management consultant, McKinsey for restructuring the organisation, which inter alia includes developing suitable career plans for their employees.

2. Manpower planning has also become a crucial function for HRD consultants, especially in the wake of increasing manpower obsolescence for technological changes in Indian industries.

3. Similarly in training and development, performance appraisal, recruitment, selection and placement, developing suitable promotional policies, management succession and management development, etc., HRD consultants are playing a very crucial role.

Before engaging HRD consultants, it is necessary to consider the following important points:

1. When an organisation needs to expand its capabilities on 'Crash Basis' it cannot afford to rely solely on the untried competence of internal resources. It needs to hire the services of consultants, who have the required expertise.

2. Similarly an organisation may require to avail the services of specialised experts in some areas, where it does not have the requisite internal skill and knowledge. This is particularly relevant in cases like training and management development programmes where we find many organisations retaining consultants to impart training on TQM, ISO:9000, quality circles, value engineering, business process re-engineering, benchmarking, Just in-Time, total productive maintenance, etc.

3. HRD consultants are also engaged in cases where objectivity or corporate strategy leverage to a job done needs to be given.

Whatever may be reasons for retaining the services of HRD consultants, we find their increasing use in the corporate sector for efficient results, cost benefit, less time-lag, etc.

Line Managers and HRD

Udai Pareek and T.V. Rao (1991) also emphasised the role of line managers in realising the HRD objective of an organisation. Since, line managers translate the objectives in to action, they are responsible to develop and utilise the manpower. In all the components of HRD, i.e., career planning, training, performance appraisal and organisation development, line managers have certain specific responsibilities, which precede development of certain congenial conditions for employees. Line managers need to ensure that, they create such conditions in the workplace which enable employees to:

1. Acquire and develop new capabilities;
2. Perceive possible outcome of acquiring such new capabilities;
3. Assess the self-growth; and
4. Enjoy the growth process.

Since line managers are in close proximity with the operations people, it is their responsibility to create and develop such conditions in the organisation, which can reinforce the HRD objectives of the organisation as a whole. Creating the above conditions in the workplace, is a precondition in realising the HRD objectives by line managers, which, inter alia, also require them to play a proactive role in the following area:

1. Line managers need to define the capabilities of employees. By developing such capability profiles of employees, they can facilitate skill and competency mapping for other strategic decisions of the organisations, like; HRM, etc. This input also helps an organisations to identify shortage in critical skill areas and accordingly organisation can initiate required action plan through training and development programmes. Apart from the above

strategic functions, this also helps in developing skill inventory, deciding about redundancy, transfer, promotion, relocation, restructuring, redeployment, etc.

2. Line managers facilitate identification of training needs. Being in close proximity to the operational people, they observe and understand the performance of employees better. This requirement is important even for documentation of quality standards, i.e., ISO: 9000. All the ISO certified organisations have documented systems in this respect.

3. Line managers also play other developmental roles to motivate people to learn and take responsibility by continuous coaching and developing problem solving skills, by recommending them for further training, etc. They encourage employees to promote small group activities like; Quality Circles, TQM club, value engineering team, etc. Many organisations prefer to involve line managers in in-house training programmes, rather than outsourcing training experts.

4. Line managers also play a role in identification and clarification of KRAs/KPAs. Setting KRAs/KPAs alone cannot set the ball rolling. It requires continuous support and sustaining of an environment of mutual trust and openness. Line managers by extending their help and support, enable the subordinates to realise their goals. This inculcate a sense of achieving, which has tremendous motivational benefit.

5. In OD intervention also, line managers play an important role by identifying required initiatives, by participating in organisational diagnosis surveys and finally by implementing the suggestive action plan.

6. Line managers also reinforce teamwork and collaboration, suggest rewards for good performance and foster total participation culture by involving subordinates in decision-making. These together reinforce HRD climate in an organisation.

7. Finally in career planning and development also, line managers play a crucial role in identification of career opportunities and encourage subordinates to develop the required potential to grab such opportunities.

Internationally, it is now being debated whether HRM or HRD should continue as a separate support function or be integrated with line functions. Since organisational structure also is getting changed (from traditional functional system to strategic or independent business units), it is bound to get cognizance. HR as a core management knowledge is already recognised. However, for Indian organisations, this requires a major attitudinal change.

The threat is also from the profession itself, as it may culminate into an identify crisis.

HRD Culture

HRD facilitates development of an enabling culture in an organisation. In a changing environment, organisations are required to go for frequent restructuring and redesigning of activities. Without an enabling culture it is difficult for the organisation to withstand the change requirements. Enabling culture is creating an environment where employees are motivated to take initiative and risk, they feel enthused to experiment, innovate and they make things happen. Thus HRD culture, which develops an enabling culture in an organisation, is characterised by the following practices:

- Openness
- Confrontation
- Trust
- Autonomy
- Proactiveness
- Authenticity
- Collaboration

HRD Climate

HRD climate is the perception of the employees about the prevailing HRD culture in the organisation. To understand the HRD climate, organisations often institute a survey with a structured questionnaire. Analysing survey responses, it is possible to map the HRD climate, covering all the enabling practices mentioned earlier. Necessary remedial action, if any, can be initiated by the organisation to address the gap. Some of the elements of the questionnaire, can be listed as follows:

1. Does the organisation consider employees as the most important resource?
2. Does the organisation believe in developing competencies of all cross-sections of employees and initiate action in that direction?
3. To what extent the organisation is transparent in communication?
4. Are the employees encouraged to take risks?
5. Is there a climate of collaboration, team spirit, mutual trust and confidence?
6. Are the personnel policies supportive in nature?
7. To what extent HRD activities are development-oriented?

HRD Matrix

HRD matrix is the interrelationship between HRD practices and organisational effectiveness. HRD practices generate HRD processes, which result in HRD outcomes that contribute to organisational effectiveness. T.V. Rao (1990) developed such a matrix, which is presented below:

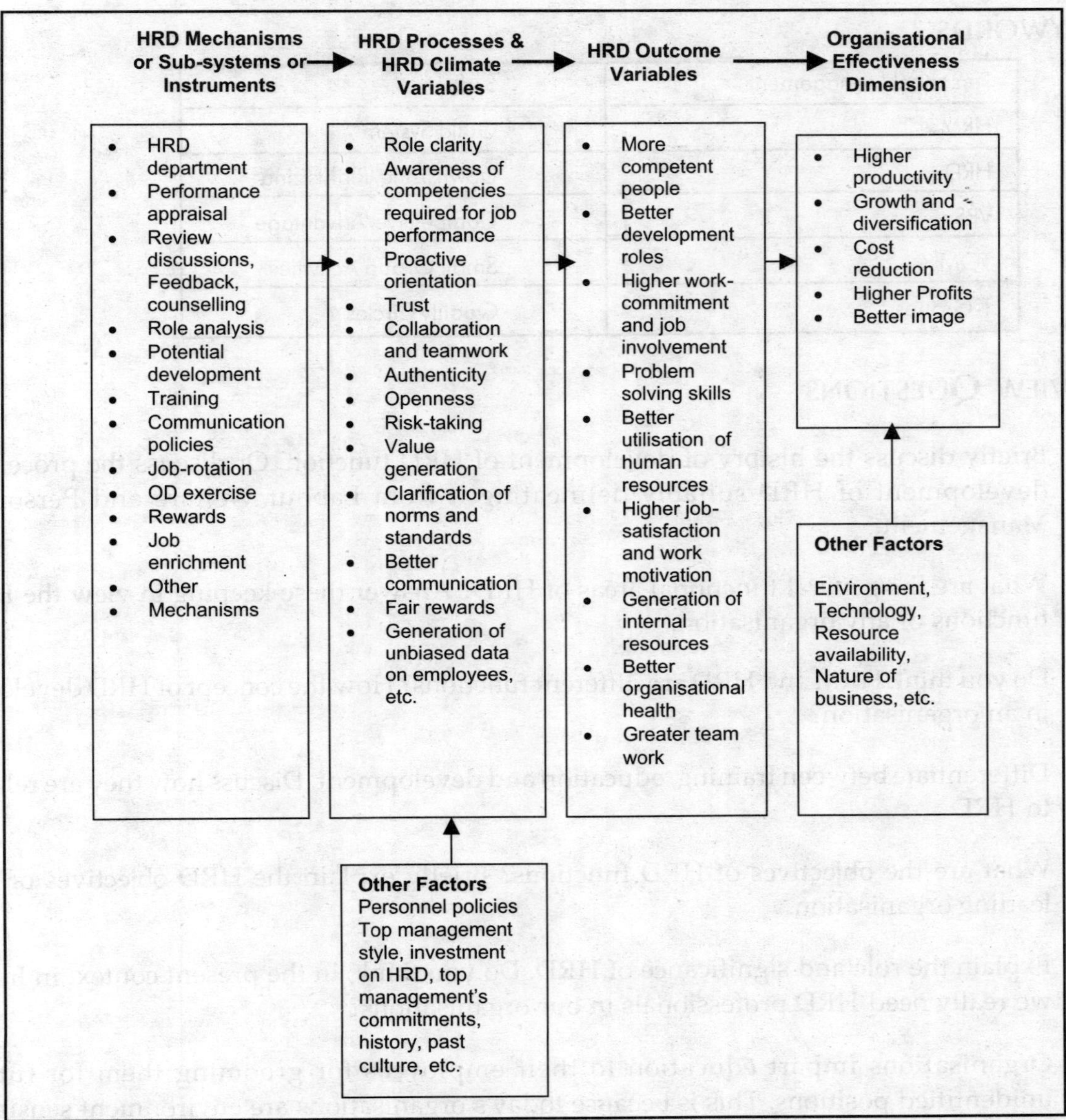

Figure 1.4: HRD Matrix

SUMMARY

HRM, per se, cannot be understood without appreciating its process of development, suitably delineating it from the traditional labour welfare and Personnel Management concepts. Even though, we still suffer from the crisis of a suitable title for the profession; HRM or HRD and there obviously exists a difference of opinion, we should not unnecessarily drag this debate and leave it to the organisations to name it as it suits them. Whether it is utilisation or development, strategic or operational, HRM and HRD can really be not separated as one reinforces the other. For the purpose of this book we have used both the terms without bothering much about its etymological connotation. HRM is an integrated part of HRD and without successful HRM, organisations cannot remain competitive.

KEYWORDS

Personnel Management	Serfdom
HRM	Guild System
HRD	Downsizing/Rightsizing
VRS	Competitive/Advantage
TQM	Small Group Activities
T-Groups	Quality Circles

REVIEW QUESTIONS

1. Briefly discuss the history of development of HRD function. Or discuss the process of development of HRD suitably delineating it from Labour Welfare and Personnel Management.
2. What are the general functional areas of HRD? Answer these keeping in view the HRD functions of any organisation.
3. Do you think HRM and HRD are different functions? How the concept of HRD developed in an organisation?
4. Differentiate between training, education and development. Discuss how they are related to HRD.
5. What are the objectives of HRD functions? Briefly explain the HRD objectives of any leading organisation.
6. Explain the role and significance of HRD. Do you think, in the present context in India, we really need HRD professionals in our organisations?
7. Organisations impart education to their employees for grooming them for future unidentified positions. This is because today's organisations are environment sensitive. Elucidate this statement.
8. What should be your focus areas for designing an effective HRD system? Which focus would you consider more important than others?
9. What important factors should be considered while structuring the HRD unit of an organisation? Illustrate your answer with an organisation chart of HRD department of any organisation.
10. Briefly discuss the principles for functioning of HRD system of an organisation. What are the important roles of a HRD manger?

11. Do you think for an organisation it is necessary to retain an HRD consultant? What are the possible advantages and disadvantages in retaining HRD consultants?

12. Write short notes on:

    (a) Guild System

    (b) Structural Change in Employment

    (c) Kurt Lewin

    (d) T-Groups

    (e) Competitive Advantage

    (f) Human Resource Utilisation (HRU)

    (g) Integrated HRD Functions

    (h) Enabling Organisation

    (i) Analytic Role

    (j) Instrumental Role

CASE STUDY
ROLE PLAY

Do this role play, writing the dialogues both for the Manager and for the Graduate. The focal theme is "PRAISE AND DEVELOP".

Brief for the Manager

You are the manager of a design department, whose task is to plan, organise and control layout and equipment changes in the manufacturing division of the company. One of your staff, a graduate aged 25, has just completed a project to install a new layout of conveyors, sorters and packing machines at the end of a line, producing small plastic bottles. This has been highly successful. The manager of the line and the staff working on it are all pleased with it and prefer it to the original layout.

Now is the time to talk to your young graduate, show how pleased you are with this project and try to discover which areas are ones in which further help, training and development of skills are required.

Brief for the Graduate

You have been working for one year in this design department, whose task is to plan, organise and control layout and equipment changes in the manufacturing division of the company. You have just completed a project to install a new layout of conveyors, sorters and packing machines at the end of a line, producing small plastic bottles. This has been highly successful. The manager of the line and the staff working on it are all pleased with it and prefer it to the original layout.

Your boss has asked to see you. You hope he is as pleased as you are with the outcome of this project. If you get the chance, you would like to become involved in an automation and computerisation project next. You have heard that the main line producing the shrink wrapped 6-pack of half-litre bottles is due to be automated further later this year. You would like to do that. The most difficult issue during this last project was negotiating with several different companies for the purchase of the conveyor equipment; their salesmen were fairly aggressive and you found it difficult to deal with them.

UNIT 2

Human Resource Policies and Strategies

Learning Objectives

After completion of this unit, the students will be aware of the following topics:

- *Introduction*
- *Role of HR Strategy in Strategic Management*
- *What is Policy?*
- *HR Policies and Procedures*
- *Framing Strategy*
- *Strategic Control*
- *Functional and Grand Strategies*

INTRODUCTION

HR strategy is the pattern of decisions concerning policies and practices associated with the HR system. Each organisational system encompasses all functional area of an organisation and thereby helps in formulation of organisation-wide strategies. Strategic Human Resource Management (SHRM) is a competency-based approach for management of HR. It focuses on developing HR for sustainable competitive advantage.

ROLE OF HR STRATEGY IN STRATEGIC MANAGEMENT

There are a number of theories which define the role of HR strategy. Behavioural role theory, pioneered by Katz & Khan (1978), Jackson & Schuler (1995), considers employee behaviours as key to successful strategy implementation. By aligning HR policies and practices with organisation-wide strategy, employees can fulfil their role expectations within the organisation. Resource-based theory of Barney (1991) and Prahalad & Hamel (1990) suggests HR has the sustainable competitive advantage for the organisation. This is because HR is characteristically rare, inimitable and non-substitutable source for achieving competitive advantage. Other resources do not have such characteristic features. The human capital theory of Becker (1964) suggests strategic importance to HR like other economic assets as knowledge, skills and abilities of the people have also economic values. This concept later developed the human resource accounting by Flamholtz (1981) and others. Transaction cost theory of Williamson (1981) suggests that strategic HR approach can ensure cost minimization as this will enhance periodic monitoring and governance. Agency theory of Eisenhardt (1989) suggests, strategic approach to HR aligns agents (employees) and principals (employers) interests and thereby ensures streamlining of employment relations and systems within the organisation.

All the above theories justify alignment of HR with organisation-wide strategy and therefore, they are grouped under rational choice theories of HR. Institutional (Meyer & Rowen, 1977; Powell & DiMaggio, 1991) and dependency (Pfeffer & Salancik, 1977) theories on HR strategy, however, focus on constituency-based interest. This is because the strategic approach to HR is not empirically proved as a contributor to organisational performance. While institutional theory argues strategic approach to HR should emanate from legitimacy and acceptance from stakeholders, dependency theory argues, this will unduly enhance the level of influence over the organisations (from HR) and thereby will defeat the purpose.

Prima facie, environmental, organisational, institutional and technological factors are potential influencers in strategy. The relative importance of each such factor will depend on organisational characteristics. However, for HRP, we need to give cognizance to each such factor, or else this will not be a strategic decision for sustaining organisational growth and profitability. Any redundancy decision without considering the possible reaction of unions may transpire as defeating. Similarly for an FMCG organisation, product life cycle being short, employees with multiple skill-sets would always be better than those who are having specialised skill sets. We have discussed strategy in this unit as an organisation-wide initiative with policies and procedures. At the end, examples of HR strategy have been given duly linking it with organisational strategy.

Strategy is the direction and scope of an organisation over long-term, matching its resources to its changing environment and in particular its markets, customers or clients, so as to meet stakeholders' expectations.

Strategy is primarily concerned with:

- The scope of an organisation's activities
- Matching the activities of an organisation to that environment in which it operates
- Resource implication
- Operational decisions
- The values and expectations of stakeholders
- Long-term direction.

Levels of Strategy

1. ***Corporate Level:*** Corporate level strategy addresses the following issues:

   (a) Overall scope of an organisation

   (b) How to run in structural and financial terms

   (c) How resources are allocated to different operations.

   Corporate level strategy is influenced by the mission of the organisation.

2. ***Competitive or Business Strategy:*** These strategies are adopted in order to strengthen the position of the organisation in the market. It explains:

   (a) How to compete in a market

   (b) Which products or services should be developed and offered to which markets

   (c) To what extent it meets customers' needs

   (d) Does it achieve the objective of the organisations, viz., long-term profitability, market growth and efficiency.

3. ***Operational Strategies:*** Operational strategies are adopted at the functional level and the success at the functional or operational level ultimately enables an organisation to achieve the corporate level and competitive strategies.

Strategy therefore is either the plans made or the actions taken to help an organisation to fulfil its intended purposes. Strategic plans for the future are called intended strategy and strategic actions are known as realised strategy. Strategic means are plans and policies while strategic ends may be either broad (vision and mission) or focussed (goals and objectives).

WHAT IS POLICY?

A policy is a predetermined established guideline towards the attainment of accepted goals and objectives. Such guidelines facilitate properly designed efforts to accomplish the strategic intent. Policy is not a strategy or tactic. Strategy is a proposed course of action to exert a far-reaching impact on the ability of the enterprise to attain its goals. Strategy relates to means.

Policy can be differentiated from objective, programmes and procedures. Policy relates to the fundamental framework of principles and rules which are used as reference information for decision-making and provide a constant pattern of decisions and structured thought processes. Objectives are specific goals or aims, preferably in quantitative terms and can be considered as something which an individual or group seeks to accomplish. Hence an objective is something to accomplish, while a policy is a guide to accomplish it.

Again policy is different from procedure, as procedure defines the manner or way of accomplishing something, i.e., it is the process and method. While policy forms part of a framework of general principles, a procedure necessarily indicates how to do something and direct employees towards the accomplishment of goals. Policies are also differentiated from programmes. Programmes are developed on the basis of policies with a view to implementing them and accordingly programmes involve one additional step beyond policies to simplify the decisions. The execution of programmes leads to specific actions including practices and procedures.

HR POLICIES AND PROCEDURES

Policies in the management of HR cover a wide variety of subjects. A comprehensive coverage of policies embrace any action or decision, taken by either employees or management in relation to the working environment, the rights and responsibilities of employees and management and the action of both parties. Thus one policy may be a statement of standards for employee attendance and another a statement of management obligations in grievance administration. One policy may explain conditions under which loans will be granted whereas another may indicate conditions under which an employee is subjected to discharge.

Procedures prescribe the details for carrying out policies. They spell out the specific rules and regulations, the steps, time, place, and personnel responsible for implementing policies. Procedures also clarify what is to be done in particular circumstances.

HR Programme

HR programme consists of the entire broad course of action governing employees at all levels (including management) in a firm. Like any other programme of management, it can be thought of as a "stable plan of action that continues over an extensive period of time." It is the end product of philosophy, values, concepts, principles, policies and procedures.

Some universal elements in an HR programme are:

1. Employment – Selection and job change,
2. Training and development,
3. Communication,
4. Grievances and discipline,
5. Wages and salary,
6. Health and safety,
7. Benefits and services,
8. Labour relations,
9. Research.

Considerations in Developing HR Policies

Statements of policy constitute criteria for making decisions. They render decision-making easier, more routine. They permit decisions on problems without detailed analysis and thus facilitate saving of precious time.

Policies provide a clear idea of what management and employees can expect. Therefore, policies promote consistency and fairness of action under conditions that are similar in character and eliminate any bias in employee related decisions. This way, policies help to avoid confusion and misunderstanding.

Policies may originate from anywhere inside an organisation or from external sources – the community, state and national legislation, changes in the economy, and even international forces, such as war-time or defence conditions. Internally, policies have their inception in employees' suggestions or complaints, in collective bargaining, and at any level of management – staff or line.

The approval of new or changed HR policies ultimately come from top management. However, the responsibility for administration rests with the line. An effective HR department recommends policies and policy changes that it considers appropriate for the benefit of the organisation. The HR department also has to assist in communicating policies to those who should know about them. There are many ways of communicating the policies, like; standing orders, house journals, circulars or through a documented policy manuals. HR department interprets policies, exercises control over policy administration and periodically reviews the same in order to ensure fairness and uniformity.

In formulating policies, the first consideration is the objective or purpose. Operationally, it is also necessary to consider the economics (costs) and benefits in relation to the size and complexity of the organisation. Then comes the need for determining the policies acceptability to management and to employees, and this depends to a great extent on their administrative feasibility and fairness to employees.

Because of an unfortunate tendency to think of policies as formulae that obviate the need for careful thought, it is necessary to anticipate circumstances that may arise subsequently in administration. Imagination is required here, as well as knowledge of operating problems. Supervisors are in a good position to aid in projecting exigencies that can arise under a particular policy.

Unions have had a tremendous impact on policy formulation. They seek certain policies; they seek to alter management policies (e.g., in overtime payment); and they cause concerns without unions to change policy as a defence against unions. Some unions' influence on policy administration appears to be beneficial whereas some is harmful to employee relations.

Guidelines for Policy Formulation

A number of guidelines for policy writing have been well established and are worth enumerating.

1. ***Purpose:*** A statement of purpose or rationale helps to understand the policy and ensures acceptance of it.
2. ***Semantics:*** Choice of words should be geared to the educational level of the group for whom the policy is intended. Wording should avoid irritating expressions that antagonise, denote inferiority, or cast aspersion, e.g., "You are forbidden."
3. ***Tone:*** A warm, understanding tone will help to show the interest and concern of management. This means avoidance of legalistic language as much as possible.
4. ***Form:*** A outline form may be useful for management reference and application. But outlines are difficult for employees to follow, they repel reading, and they are cold and lifeless. Relatively short paragraphs, some use of underlinings, and adequate spacing (double rather than single) – encourage reading.
5. ***Clarity:*** Short sentences are better than long ones linked together with "whereas", "provided", etc., and simple sentences are easier to read and comprehend than complex or compound sentences.

Communicating the Policies

Management has a definite responsibility to see that employees become familiar with any policies that affect them. Written explanations of changes in policy, reinforced by oral discussion, are minimal for policy communication. All of the written media found in organisations may be used employee hand books, bulletin boards, company periodicals, etc. In orientation sessions for new and old employees, oral explanation can be accompanied by visual aids such as film strips, placards and funnel boards.

Administering Policies

Uniformity in administration is desirable when circumstances are similar among the various individuals and groups concerned. Customs amongst various groups, practices that have been in operation for sometime and needs of different groups of employees, etc., influence decisions in regard to degree and extent of uniformity. Also to be weighed the questions of fairness, and of employees' attitudes toward concession in specific cases. Long-standing policy differences between office and shop, for example, are under constant fire from unions.

Questions of rigidity of administration and consistency or flexibility of interpretation must also be faced. In weighing special consideration to an employee or penalty for a violation, many factors must be taken into account, work record, demonstrated capability, history of relationships, impact on other and on future situations, knowledge at the individual's disposal, past practices, responsibility of management, nature and frequency of the request or act, obligations to the organisation, to the employee and to society, respective values, reasons, ameliorating circumstances, etc.

Framing Strategy

Strategic plans in the process of thinking through the current mission of the organisation with due cognizance to current environmental conditions – both external and internal. Such plans, therefore, set guidelines for future decisions and results.

Vision

- It is the category of intensions that are broad, all inclusive and forward thinking.
- It describes aspirations for the future.
- It does not specify the means that are used to achieve the desired ends.
- It must be inspirational.
- Visions are often unwritten.
- It must be communicated.

Communication of vision can be done in two ways: (i) in the form of mission statement, (ii) through personal selling (e.g. behaviour of the visionary). Attitude towards quality, customers' complaints handling are examples of vision or intentions of an organisation.

Mission

- A vision in tangible form is a mission statement.
- Mission statements verbalise the vision.

A mission statement attempts to answer the following questions:

- Basic purpose
- Unique or distinctiveness of the organisation
- Likely difference in business, three to five years into the future
- Principal customers, clients or key market segments
- Principal goods and services, present and future
- Principal economic concerns
- Basic beliefs, values, aspirations and philosophical priorities of the firm.

Key Elements of Mission Statement

1. *View of the future*
    - The anticipated regulatory, competitive and economic environment.
2. *Competitive arenas*
    - The business and geographic business arenas where the company will compete.
3. *Sources of competitive advantage*
    - The skills that the company will develop; a description of how the company intends to succeed.
4. *Benefits*
    - Establish boundaries to guide strategy formulation.
    - Acknowledge responsibilities to various stakeholders and establish standards for organisational performance.
    - Suggest standards of individual behaviour.
5. *Goals*

    A mission statement tries to make a vision more specific, while goals are attempts to make a mission statement more concrete. Goals have several features as under:

    - They address both financial and non-financial issues.
    - They facilitate reasoned trade-off (range of goals should be perfectly consistent with one another).
    - They can be reached with a stretch.
    - They cut across functional areas.

6. ***Objectives***

- They are the operational definitions of goals.
- They describe what the organisations hopes to accomplish.
- They can be measured.
- They indicate time dimension.
- They reduce conflict (misunderstandings).

7. ***Policy***

- Policies are general statements or understandings.
- Policies guide managers' thinking in decision-making.
- Policies ensure that decisions fall within certain boundaries.

8. ***Strategy***

- It is the direction.
- It concerns with deployment of human and material resources.
- It increases the chance of achieving selected objectives.

Strategies and policies are put into practice by means of plans. Tactics are the action plans, through which strategies are executed.

Strategic Control

Strategy is selected and implemented over time. But strategies being forward looking, and designed to accomplish the objectives in future, it is necessary to enforce control over strategy.

Strategic controls, which can be enforced by certain operational controls, are designed to answer the following questions:

1. Are we moving in right direction?
2. Are key things falling into place?
3. Are our assumptions about major trends and changes correct?
4. Are the critical things we need to do, being done?
5. Do we need to adjust or abort this strategy?
6. How are we performing?
7. Are we meeting objectives and schedules?

8. How are costs, revenues and cash flows matching projections?

9. Do we need to make operational changes?

To establish strategic control:

1. Allow the time between initial implementation and achievement of intended results.

2. Steer the organisation through different actions (like undertaking of project, investment, etc.) environmental situation and firm's internal situation.

3. Correct the actions and directions of the firm as required by certain developments and chances in external environment and internal situation.

Types of Strategic Control

There are four basic types of strategic control:

1. Premise Control

2. Implementation Control

3. Strategic Surveillance

4. Special Alert Control

Premise Control is designed to check systematically and continuously whether or not the premises set during the planning and implementation process are still valid. For example, a bank may adopt an aggressive marketing strategy to achieve 15 per cent annual growth, establishing a planning premise that not more than 10 per cent would be their non-performing assets. Premise Control should be ensured by monitoring the non-performing assets at the branch level on a regular basis.

Implementation Control is designed to assess whether the overall strategy results associated with incremental steps and actions that implement the overall strategy. For example, an internationally known fast food centre decided to maintain 3 to 1 company-owned franchise ratio as part of their expansion strategy, to ensure control over quality of foods, rates, etc. But growing competition in this business later forced them to reverse the ratio to accelerate its ability to open new locations.

Strategic Surveillance is designed to monitor a broad range of events inside and outside the company that are likely to threaten the course of the firm's strategy. For example, in the early years of its attempt to sell the PGDBA CFA course. ICFAI made its course more finance-oriented, covering all conceivable finance laden papers, targeting the financial services sector as the prospective employers of their students. The financial services sector being highly unstable in terms of market volatility, ICFAI felt the need to target other sectors as prospective employers of their students with adequate shift in focus to PGDBA papers like; Marketing, HRD, Information Technology, Strategic Management, etc. Similar shift in focus was adopted by IBM in marketing their large expensive mainframe computers from corporate houses to libraries, worldwide.

Special Alert Control is the need to thoroughly, and often rapidly, reconsider the firm's basic strategy based on a sudden, unexpected event. A likely political coup or home war in Afganistan will put pressure on exporters to these countries, who may have to thoroughly reconsider their export market strategy. A sudden air crash could have a devastating effect on a major airline.

Operational Control Systems

Strategic controls are useful to top management in monitoring and steering the basic strategic direction of the company. But operating managers also need control methods appropriate to their level of strategy implementation. The primary concern at the operating level is allocation and use of the company resources. Operational control systems guide, monitor and evaluate progress in meeting annual objectives. Usually, the following steps are taken for operational control:

1. Set standards of performance
2. Measure actual performance
3. Identify deviations from standards
4. Initiate corrective action or adjustment.

There are three types of operational control systems. Those are budgets, schedules and key success factors.

FUNCTIONAL AND GRAND STRATEGIES

Functional strategies guide functional actions to implement grand strategies, which provide general direction. Functional strategies give specific guidance to managers for accomplishing annual objectives. Functional strategies, therefore, translate grand strategies at the business level into action plans for the organisation. Operating or functional managers develop such strategies taking into cognizance the policy guidelines. Therefore, time horizon for such strategies may be a year or less. Grand strategies, on the other hand, are framed with a long-term perspective at the corporate level.

Formulating functional strategies at each operational level, at the outset, requires identification of critical success factors. For example, marketing strategies need to focus on product, price, marketplace and promotion. Finance strategies may focus on capital acquisition, allocation, dividend, working capital management. Research and Development strategies focus on basic research, commercial development, time horizon, organisational fit, basic R&D posture (defensive, offensive, innovation, development, etc.).

For evaluating strategy, we consider its internal and external consistency, its appropriateness in terms of available resources, its degree of risk (which should be reasonable), its time horizon (not too long to face the risk of obsolescence) and its workability.

Operations Strategy Factors

From the operations manager's point of view, it is important to study the following factors while adopting an operations strategy.

1. The number, type, size and location of operations facilities.
2. Type of equipment that will be utilised (focused and specific or general-purpose and flexible, automated or principally manual).
3. Make or buy decision.
4. Organisation structure – weather it is suitable to accomplish and coordinate all the necessary efforts.
5. The workforce selection, employment security, compensation methods and management style.
6. The information systems that will be used to collect, analyse and distribute information on production, purchasing, inventory, quality, personnel, etc.
7. Production planning, scheduling and control, system and inventory policy.
8. The quality control and improvement methods that will be used.
9. The productivity improvement methods – machine/manpower.

HR Strategy Factors

HR strategy factors encompass those areas which are instrumental for the success of an organisation. We can classify such factors as under:

1. ***Recruitment and Selection:*** Outsourcing or direct recruitment, contractual or on permanent payroll, multi-skill attributes or specialisation are some of the issues considered at this level.
2. ***Career Development:*** Career mapping, succession planning and management development, integrating career development with OD initiatives are the factors considered in this area.
3. ***Performance Appraisal:*** Designing appropriate tools and aligning such appraisal with training needs, promotion, transfer and relocation are the issues that deserve attention at this stage.
4. ***Training and Development:*** Developing in-house training, ROI models for evaluating training, training budgets, etc., are considered at this level.
5. ***Compensation Designing:*** Designing compensation and incentive schemes, suitable to attract talent and retain them, NWLC aspects, etc., are the crucial factors.
6. ***HRP:*** Developing an Human Resource Information System, aligning HRP with corporate strategies, skill and competence mapping are important aspects of strategic HRP.

Example of Strategy and Action Plan for HRM

The strategy and action plan for HRM for a hypothetical organisation has been discussed here, first by listing the details in the light of vision, mission, goals, objectives, strategies and action plan and secondly by presenting the same in a structured manner in Exhibit 2.1.

Vision

1. We are committed to provide an enjoyable work environment to our employees to promote team work, quality improvement and excellence.
2. Our employees are our valued customers and most important stakeholders.

We are committed to achieve financial growth of our organisation fostering growth and creativity for our valued employees.

Mission

To achieve excellence in human resource management, fostering growth and creativity.

Goals

1. To promote teamwork
2. To ensure quality improvement
3. To foster growth and creativity.

Objectives

Goal 1	• Achieve group cohesiveness by inculcating participative management • Reduce dissonance in managerial decisions • Reduce conflict and grievances to achieve • Zero man-days loss and increased productivity
Goal 2	• Achieve increased quality consciousness in the organisation • Reduce costs of quality to zero by next 5 years • Provide error-free product and services to customers to increase their retention and to increase further market share
Goals 3	• Promote creativity in the organisation • Provide opportunities for growth of the employees • Increase retention of employees so as to reduce current employee turnover by 80 per cent in the next 5 years.

Strategies

1. Improve participative management.
2. Initiate organisation-wide quality improvement
3. Develop culture to promote growth and creativity

Action Plan

Strategy 1	• Establish small group forums like; Quality Circles (QC), Self-managed Teams (SMTs), value engineering teams, Total Quality Management (TQM) clubs, etc., in the organisation. • Shift focus from statutory participation to total participation. • Empower employees by involving them in decision-making process. • Implement organisation-wide transparent communication network.
Strategy 2	• Implement quality awareness programmes through regular training and development. • Develop TQM culture by increasing formal and informal interaction with all cross-sections of employees. • Practice TQM philosophy through personal selling (reflected through the behaviour of all).
Strategy 3	• Encourage directed creativity culture and practices with clear documented policy. • Emphasise on in-house talent rather than outsourcing. • Implement reward system for focussed and need-based creative ideas. • Implement documented promotion policy to provide growth opportunities for employees.

EXHIBIT 2.1

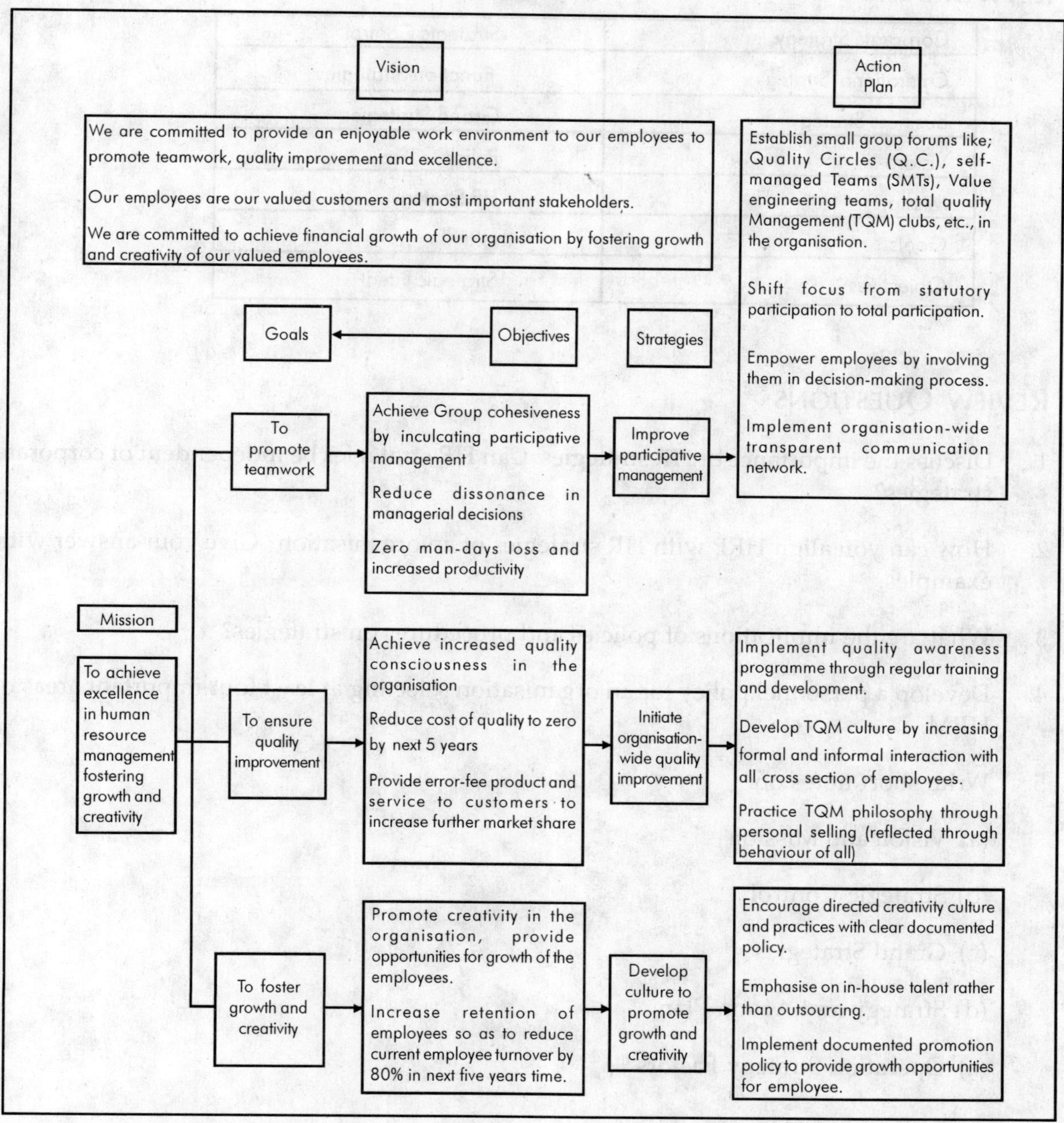

SUMMARY

HR strategy and its alignment with organisation-wide strategies are still debatable, obviously due to inadequate empirical research. However, organisations are now practising such alignment. Strategies and policies are interdependent. While strategies are direction, policies are guidelines. Any forward looking organisation needs to enforce control over strategy, which is best achieved by operational control. Because strategies are put to use at different operations, HR strategy factors, among others, give more emphasis on HRP.

KEYWORDS

Corporate Strategy	Strategic Control
Operational Strategy	Function Strategies
Business Strategy	Grand Strategies
Vision	Policy
Mission	HR Strategy
Goals	HRP
Objectives	Strategic Intent

REVIEW QUESTIONS

1. Discuss the importance of HR strategies. Can HR strategies be independent of corporate strategies?
2. How can you align HRP with HR strategies of an organisation? Give your answer with examples.
3. What are the implications of policies and procedures on strategies?
4. Develop a personnel policy for an organisation selecting at least four important areas of HRM.
5. Write short notes on:
   (a) Vision and Mission
   (b) Strategic Control
   (c) Grand Strategies
   (d) Strategy and Action Plan
   (e) Operation Strategy Factors

CASE STUDY

DISSONANCE

Vinod was the Works Manager of Lakshmi Engg. Rahul was with the company as Finance Manager and head of the Accounts and Finance Division reporting to the Works Manager.

Rahul's general attitude was to be tightfisted with financial matters. He was always conscious of the need to conform to company policy and procedures and he firmly opposed any deviation from policy, but was often willing to explain the reasons for his view. He prided himself as a man of principles. Vinod, the Works Manager, was the type who wanted to take action regardless of past practice or policy. He considered himself a result-oriented manager.

The differing attitudes of the Works Manager and the Finance Manager had led to conflicts on past occasions and Vinod had warned Rahul on two occasions that if Rahul could not carry out his instructions he was free to search for a job elsewhere.

Rahul had argued his case with a measure of success stating that his approach was proper and that in financial matters the policy guidelines had to be observed.

One afternoon, Vinod approached Rahul and said, "Here is an incentive plan for the maintenance group. I am notifying it today and introducing it from tomorrow. Have a look at it." Rahul appeared to be surprised. He had not known that an incentive plan was being contemplated for maintenance workers as the company's policy till then was to pay incentives only to direct production workers. Nevertheless, he took the plan and returned it to Vinod a couple of hours later, saying "You can't introduce this plan straightaway. We have to give this some more thought. Our maintenance costs are too high mainly due to lack of adherence to norms on consumption of spare parts. Further, it will only add to maintenance costs without any real benefit to the company."

Vinod's reaction was one of anger. "You understand nothing of incentive plans", he retorted, and added, "spare parts consumption is high due to poor quality of spares bought by the Materials Department. Anyway, I do not intend to waste time on this with you. I am notifying this incentive plan today."

An altercation followed and the arguments of both Rahul and Vinod became so loud that it attracted the attention of others in the hall, outside Vinod's office. "I am the boss here", screamed Vinod and added, "if you can't work with me and obey my instructions, you are free to leave your job and go elsewhere."

A few moments later Rahul was back in his office, tired and sullen. He called his secretary and dictated his letter of resignation.

Questions

1. Discuss the problem in this case with specific reference to strategic management.
2. What kind of organisational climate is created?

The CEO's Parlour – HR Joke

CEO	:	Can I issue a policy that no women should be hired for the position of a receptionist?
Secretary	:	How about waiting until next week?
CEO	:	Why delay an issue which can be declared right now?
Secretary	:	I feel the legal defence funds are slightly weak now.
Secretary	:	Can you lower my salary while I am going through my divorce proceedings? I don't want to have my child-support payments based on this high salary.
CEO	:	If it would help, we will be delighted to stop paying you at all.
Secretary	:	Our HR Controller wants to have a serious meeting with you regarding the growing absenteeism.
CEO	:	Ask him to meet me in the afternoon.
Secretary	:	I am afraid he is not there today, his maternal uncle's wife's brother-in-law's niece has bruised her toe nail.
CEO	:	I am so sorry to hear that, ask him to see me tomorrow.
Secretary	:	Tomorrow, I presume he will not be coming, they might have to call a doctor, how about day after tomorrow.
CEO	:	You forgot, I am going on my quarterly vacation from day after tomorrow. Schedule the appointment sometime next month.
Secretary	:	No problem, a month's time will help our HR Department have some more numbers on their list.
CEO	:	I was walking down the corridor, and found many not in their seats.
HR Controller	:	Of late we have found many spending time in the bathroom.
Secretary	:	A policy should be issued at once on this.
CEO	:	You are right, let's issue a policy that an employee should only spend as much time in the bathroom as he needs to.

UNIT 3

Strategic Human Resource Management (SHRM)

Learning Objectives

After completion of this unit, the students will be aware of the following topics:

- *Introduction*
- *Definition and Concept of SHRM*
- *Integration of HR with Business Strategy*
- *Two Approaches to Strategic Management*
- *HRM and Organisational Strategic Decisions*
- *Strategic HR Planning*
- *Strategic Manpower Planning*
- *Strategic Performance Management*
- *Strategic Compensation Management*
- *HRD and Strategic HRM*
- *HRD Strategy: Key Targets*

Introduction

Planning and strategy have a long history (Mintzberg, 1994). Writing in 1916, Henri Fayol (1916) supported the maxim that 'managing means looking ahead'. Thus foresight is an essential part of management. Strategic thinking can occur at a number of levels. Chaffee (1985) considers that (academically) strategy is viewed in three distinct but sometimes conflicting ways: linear strategy, adaptive strategy, and interpretive strategy. The linear model focuses on planning and forecasting. The second model is described as adaptive and most closely associated with 'strategic management'. This model 'tends to focus the manager's attention on means' and is largely concerned with 'fit'. The third, interpretative model sees strategy as a metaphor and, therefore, it is not something which can be measured but is viewed in qualitative terms.

Mintzberg et al. (1998) identified 10 schools of strategic management thought which has emerged as a field of study during the 1960s:

1. ***The Design School*** - strategy as a process of conception
2. ***The Planning School*** - strategy as a formal process
3. ***The Positioning School*** - strategy as an analytical process
4. ***The Entrepreneurial School*** - strategy as a visionary process
5. ***The Cognitive School*** - strategy as a mental process
6. ***The Learning School*** - strategy as an emergent process
7. ***The Power School*** - strategy as a process of negotiation
8. ***The Cultural School*** - strategy as a collective process
9. ***The Environmental School*** - strategy as a reactive process
10. ***The Configuration School*** - strategy as a process of transformation.

Definition and Concept of SHRM

The role of personnel department conventionally was to screen resumes, interview the prospective employees and to do paper work for routine events, like; enforcing discipline in conformance to a policy, decide on promotions, transfer, demotion, annual increments, retirements, etc. But the role of personnel department has now changed. Personnel function is now known as human resources management. Even though human resource management department still performs traditional administrative tasks, they are even more responsible for managing the function in strategic way, aligning with corporate strategy of the organisation. To keep pace with the changing requirements of the organisation, personnel department now requires to manage wide range of skills and needs, enable downsizing, accommodate flexible schedules and administer a host of new programmes for compensation, benefits, training and development. With IT interface (human resource information systems), personnel department is now able to play strategic role more effectively collaborating on enterprise-wide client/server-based-systems that are designed to provide management with critical information about workforce issues.

In our introductory discussions, we have discussed on the process of development of HR functions. Traditional Personnel Administration jobs used to focus on keeping files, processing of papers and forms, administering payroll, etc. It was then considered as supplementary task. With the development of Personnel Management concept, the scope of HR activities extended and HR continued to get professionalised and became a specialised function. The concept of Strategic Human Resource Management (SHRM) became important once it was thought of aligning HR with the business strategy of the organisation. This was possible, however, after it was established internationally that HR can generate competitive advantage for an organisation.

Strategy is the direction and scope of an organisation over long term, matching its resources to its changing environment and in particular its markets, customers or clients, so as to meet stakeholders' expectations.

Strategic Human Resource Management (SHRM) is a competency-based approach for management. There are many definitions on SHRM, including:

'A human resource system that is tailored to the demands of the business strategy' (Miles and Snow 1984).

'The pattern of planned human resource activities intended to enable an organisation to achieve its goals' (Wright and McMahan 1992).

"The pattern of planned human resource actions and deployments intended to enable the firm to achieve its goals" (Wright/McMahan 1992: 298).

"All those activities affecting the behavior of individuals in their efforts to formulate and implement the strategic needs of the business" (Schuler 1992: 30).

"Our definition of SHRM includes the following characteristics: a long termed focus, linkage between HRM and strategy process, and the expectation that effective HRM policies should produce organisational performance benefits. Line managers, as well as HRM professionals, may play a role in transforming the HRM function to become more strategic" (Martell/Carroll 1995: 254).

Reviewing such definitions we can relate SHRM as a 'reactive' management field, where human resource management is a tool to implement strategy, a more proactive function in which HR activities can actually create and shape the business strategy (Sanz-Valle et al, 1998) of HR. It focuses on developing HR for sustainable competitive advantage. Strategic human resource management requires formulation of HR objectives, strategies and policies. These enable the provision of the skills and abilities needed to meet the requirements of an organisation's overall objectives. In other words, they provide the framework, which ensures that an organisation's people needs are met.

The range of activities and themes encompassed by SHRM can be seen, for example, in Mabey et al (1998) which looks at the subject from four perspectives:

1. The social and economic context of SHRM - including the internal (corporate) and external environments that influence the development and implementation of HR strategies.

2. The relationship between SHRM and business performance, emphasizing the measurement of performance.

3. Management style and the development of new forms of organisation.

4. The relationship between SHRM and the development of organisational capability, including knowledge management.

Other authors have attempted to provide more analytical frameworks for SHRM. Delery and Doty (1996), for example, make distinctions between three different theoretical frameworks:

- ***Universalistic***, where some HR practices is believed to be universally effective.
- ***Contingent***, with the effectiveness of HR practices supposed to be dependent on an organisation's strategy.
- ***Configurational***, where it is believed to have synergistic effects between HR practices and strategy that are crucial for enhanced performance.

Wright and Snell's (1998) model of SHRM aims to achieve both fit and flexibility. They emphasise a distinction between HRM practices, skills and behaviour in their relation to strategy on the one hand, and the issue of tight and loose coupling of HR practices and strategy on the other.

Integration of HR with Business Strategy

Reviewing various definitions of SHRM, we can classify SHRM into four different models. The first model, pioneered by Fombrun, Trichy and Devanna (1984), although known as 'the human resource management cycle', it emphasises on strategic focus on five variables of HR, like; selection, performance, appraisal, rewards and human resource development. The model suggests to focus more attention on the characteristics of tasks and functions of HR.

A second well-known model is the 'Harvard model of HRM' by Beer (1984). In this model, situational factors (among which strategy, laws and societal values, labour market) together with stakeholders' interests influence HR policies and HR outcomes: high commitment and high individual performance leading to a cost effective performance of the organisation as a whole. In turn, HR outcomes lead also to long-term consequences (individual well-being, organisational effectiveness and societal well-being) that feed back on the situational factors and the stakeholders' interests. No doubt the Harvard model is attractive from an analytical point of view.

However, it concentrates on high commitment as a preferred state of the work force and is rather abstract. Further, it does not differentiate between the HR-consequences of different strategies, types of organisation, situational factors and the like.

The third model of HRM by Guest (Guest, 1987, 1997) also states that HRM can help to achieve better performance. Guest stresses the integration of HR-practices such as selection, training, appraisal, rewards, job design, involvement and status and security. Guest states that his model performs better in 'organic' organisations. This is quite understandable as the model defines performance outcomes in terms of productivity, quality and innovation that are produced by motivation, cooperation, involvement and organisational citizenship. Therefore, performance is linked to high commitment HRM only.

Of the four models discussed here the so-called Warwick model by Hendry and Pettigrew (1990) is the one most oriented to processes of change. The authors take the position that the 'outer context of HRM' – i.e. socio-economic, technical, political legal and competitive influences – affects the 'inner context': culture, structure, politics and leadership, task technology and business outputs. High performance levels of organisations are explained by the degree to which organisations manage to adapt their inner contexts to the outer ones. In the Warwick model the 'business strategy content' (objectives, product-market combinations, strategy and tactics) directly influences the HR-content of HR-flows, work systems, reward systems and employee relations. In turn, strategy formulation is affected by the inner context. However, the model fails to make clear how and in what ways HR-instruments like recruitment, selection, appraisal and rewarding as part of the HR-content contribute to strategy formulation and performance.

Reviewing the four models, four conclusions can be drawn. First, with the exception of the Fombrun, Tichy & Devanna model, all models link HR-processes to business strategy and performance although it is not made clear how these processes exactly function. Secondly, there is no attention paid to business strategy as a variable on HR processes. Only the Warwick model emphasises the relation between the HRM-content and the business strategy content, but the nature of this link remains obscure. Nevertheless it is the only one with a strategic HRM orientation. Thirdly, two of the models, i.e. Beer's and Guest's, consider high commitment. HRM as a prerequisite to high levels of performance; the main mission of HR-instruments is to enhance the commitment required. Fourthly, except in the case of Fombrun, Tichy & Devanna, the nature of the work to be done (work system, job design) is an element in all models. However, similar to other social scientific theories of SHRM, the social and technical organisation of work itself is considered as given. Consequently, HR-policies are aimed to change people by the application of HR-instruments.

Two Approaches to Strategic Management

Formal-Rational Approach

Strategy is deliberately set up and a realised plan and it requires comprehensive planning. This approach separated strategy formulation and implementation and consider organisation as rational actor. Since this approach believes strategic decisions flow from the top, it believes also to manage implementation of strategy, it is important to follow the structure of the organisation. It states structure follows strategy.

Informal-Incremental Approach

This approach considers strategy as pattern of realised decision on important and urging problems. Decision-making being informal and iterative, vision of the organisation largely serves as a decision premises.

Yet in another way we can divide the approaches to strategic human resource management in two parts, i.e., complementarities (Warwick) and bundled approaches. Complementary approaches uses several HR practices at the same time to complement and reinforce each other. This is quite common in the USA and in some large organisations of UK. Bundled HR practices believe that improvements in one area enhances other HR practices as well.

HRM and Organisational Strategic Decisions

Integration of HR in strategic decisions may be direct or indirect, formal or informal. The formal approach requires strategy formation and strategy implementation. The informal approach on the contrary involves HR managers and HRM become the initiator of strategic decisions. Yet in another way also we can interpret HR integrated organisational strategic decisions, i.e., deliberate and emergent. If it is deliberate, HR exerts specific influence on strategic decision makers. In emergent cases, HR practices being influence organisational culture, HR by default become the strategic decision maker.

Strategic HR Planning

Strategic HR planning establishes link between organisation's strategic planning and HRM like other managerial functions; marketing, production, finance, etc. Formally strategic HR planning decides how to acquire, develop, utilise and maintain human resources of an organisation with active involvement and support from the top management. Strategic HR planning sets basic goals for various HR functions like recruitment, compensation designs, training and development, disciplinary approach by proper horizontal integration with various HR functions. Therefore, it plans for basic HR objectives and HR strategies.

Craft (1988) identifies following HR inputs to strategic HR planning:

1. *Availability Analysis:* These inputs consist of HR inventory (internal) and labour market analysis data, which facilitates HR supply forecasts and HR mobility patterns.

2. *Environmental Analysis:* These inputs highlight on complexity and stability issues and also on external trends like, technical social, legal, political and economic.

3. *HR Competitive Analysis:* Here inputs include competence profile, strategy/competence fit assessment reports, competitive advantage factors and various HR strategic initiatives.

4. *Feasibility and Impact Analysis:* Under this head HR costs and potential strategic alternatives for reducing it, assessment of HR's impact in organisational growth, employment and distribution, etc. are compiled for strategic HR planning.

Levels of Strategic HR Planning

Like corporate strategic plan, strategic HR planning also has three levels; corporate, business and department (operations) levels. Corporate level HR strategic plan deals with corporate HR staff and corporate HR management group. At this level organisation wide HR strategies and policies are drawn to fit the corporate mission and business portfolio plans. At Business or divisional level, divisional HR staff and divisional HR management group are involved. Here HR strategies and policies are drawn within the ambit of corporate HR strategies and policies to meet specific product/market/customer segments. At department or operation level, departmental HR staff members are involved who draw HR programmes and policies for each functional area (e.g. recruitment, staffing, compensation, career development, etc.).

The Process of Strategic HR Planning

Strategic HR planning process requires to follow certain steps sequentially as under:

- Environmental Analysis
- Internal HR Analysis
- HR Threats and Opportunities
- HR Strengths and Weaknesses
- Strategic HR Issues
- HR Objectives and Strategies
- HR Functional Programmes
- Operational HR Plans
- Business Strategies

Emulating the example of Balanced Score card, here also HR Scorecard is drawn to facilitate measurement of HR initiatives and to understand how far such initiatives meet various perspectives. For HR scorecard, strategic perspective put thrust on achieving five strategic HR intents to meet the requirements of organisational strategies. These are – talent, leadership, customer service and support, organisational integration and HR capability. Operational perspective measures HR's success in operational excellence, especially staffing, technology, and HR processes and transactions. Financial perspective for HR scorecard helps to assess how far HR adds measurable financial value to the organisation in terms of ROI in training, technology, staffing, cost of service delivery, etc. Customer perspective, on the other hand, assesses HR from key customer segments (internal or external) through surveys, employee involvement, and employee capability and productivity data. We have illustrated separately HR Scorecard in Performance Management unit.

Once HR scorecard is developed, it adequately facilities strategic HR planning process, as all HR initiatives become measurable.

HR Portfolios

The term HR portfolio is used in strategic HRM and it denotes strategically relevant HR information. Such information may be basic or critical. Basic HR portfolio information included company, strategic business units, departments, functional areas, work force segments, single employees, HR practices, etc. Critical HR portfolio information includes employee performance/employee potential, strategic relevance/HR quality of SBUs, external supply/internal stocks of skilled labour, employee motivation/employee qualification, etc. The process of information compilation for HR portfolios is to first select units and the criteria of analysis, visualise the present condition and plan for the future (in the form of targets) and then develop HR strategies in more specific and quantifiable terms. HR portfolios analysis helps in identification of HR strengths and weakness, opportunities and threats in more concrete terms. Thus it supports formulation of HR strategies, integration of HR with the strategic decision-making process of the organisation and finally it enhances HR utilisation, charting specific action plans.

5-P Model of HR Strategy

Schuler (1992) advocated this model to highlight HR's strategic relevance in an organisation. His model outlines 5-P as under:

- ***HR Philosophy:*** Expressed in statements defining business value and culture
- ***HR Policies:*** Expressed as shared values (guidelines)
- ***HR Programmes:*** Articulated as HR strategies
- ***HR Practices:*** For leadership, managerial, and operational roles
- ***HR Processes***

The Model explains, for formulation and implementation of HR strategies, it is necessary to spell out how we treat and value people in the organisation. The model establishes guidelines for action on people-related business issues and HR programmes, how to coordinate efforts to facilitate change to address major people related business issues and motivate the desired role behaviours.

STRATEGIC MANPOWER PLANNING

Strategic Manpower Planning is a dynamic, proactive, ongoing process of systematically attracting, identifying, developing, mentoring and retaining employees to support current and future organisational goals. Strategic manpower Planning focuses specifically on proactive planning to meet anticipated or unanticipated vacancies due to retirement and other factors.

Successful Strategic Manpower Planning:

- Requires a team approach and must be viewed as a process, not a single act.
- Must have support of senior management.
- Must have line management ownership and be involved in the process with support from Human Resources personnel.
- Must align strategic manpower plan programme with the department's culture, services, and vision.
- Necessitates creative thinking that may challenge and change the status quo.
- Must ensure that the most qualified candidates move into positions of greater responsibility.
- Influences the decision makers on future appointments/promotions.
- Must be tailored to each department's needs and structure.
- Requires the employee to take ownership of his/her individual development with strong management support.

Thus, strategic manpower planning requires development of strategy of appropriate recruitment, development and retention as well as timeliness to address gaps and surpluses to ensure that the organisation gets appropriate manpower to meet its future functional requirements.

Benefits of Strategic Manpower Planning

Strategic Manpower Planning can benefit an organisation in following ways:

- Engages senior management in a disciplined review of leadership talent.
- Guides development activities of key executive, managerial, and professional employees.
- Assures continuity of leadership and management support.
- Avoids transition problems by having candidates who are fully prepared to assume positions of greater responsibility.
- Prevents premature promotion.
- Audits the current workforce and thereby influences resources and development strategies.
- Identifies the competencies needed by the current and future workforce.

- Fosters a culture of viewing employees as a valuable resource who are worth developing.
- Supports the overall mission of the department to provide superior service and improve efficiency by maximizing the human capital potential.

A Strategic Manpower Plan requires considering following important aspects:

- *Departmental Priorities:* Which requires assessment of departmental priorities duly examining the department's mission and objectives and identifying how they are being met.
- *Departmental Structure:* Relates the priorities of the department to its actual structure, programmes, classifications, organisational charts and budgets.
- *Workload:* Examines the department's workload to create a picture of future needs as the workload increases or decreases in the department.
- *Workforce:* Involves using the information gathered to determine current and future workforce needs.

Strategic Performance Management

Performance Management (PM) is one of the most important HR strategy factors. HR strategy factors largely encompass six areas like; recruitment and selection, career development, performance appraisal, training and development, compensation designing and human resource planning. Career development and performance appraisal have direct linkage with PMS. While career development considers career mapping, succession planning and management development, integrating career development with OD initiatives; performance appraisal designs appropriate tools and aligns such appraisal with training needs, promotion, transfer and relocation.

PMS involves thinking through various facets of performance, identifying critical dimensions of performance, planning, reviewing and developing and enhancing performance and related competencies.

Performance has many dimensions:

- Output or result dimension;
- Input dimension;
- Time dimensions;
- Focus dimension;
- Quality dimensions; and
- Cost dimension.

Performance is what is expected to be delivered by an individual or a set of individuals within a time frame. What is expected to be delivered could be stated in terms of results or effort, tasks and quality, with specification of conditions under which it is to be delivered.

Therefore, PMS reinforces strategic human resource management principles as it helps an organisation to achieve the strategic intent, i.e., goals and objectives by ensuring and developing the desired set of competencies among people in the organisation through various strategic interventions, as explained above.

Performance Management is the day-to-day management of the performance of an individual or a workgroup, by both the immediate manager and the individual employees themselves. Having an established framework and set of condition, which takes care of these aspects is called as system, and having such a system completes the term - Performance Management System (PMS). The new economy today has identified 'people' of the organisation as the sole competitive advantage, which on being leveraged in the proper way can lead the firm to a favourable position. It is exactly here where the concept of performance management takes up a strategic role.

Effective performance management can only be ensured when the top management is committed towards employee development and believes in discussing with the employees about the performance parameters in order to arrive at an agreement regarding the performance standards.

Strategic Compensation Management

The strategic use of rewards to regulate behaviour and performance has led to the concept of 'compensation management' or 'reward systems' – terms, which belong in the HRM, rather than the Industrial relations, framework. 'Remuneration' refers to monetary rewards, which are seen as one arm of total compensation.

A total reward or compensation system would have a number of components based on the distinctions between Intrinsic Rewards and Extrinsic Rewards.

Intrinsic rewards are non-monetary and include rewards of three types:

1. ***Job Satisfaction:*** Included in this category are the interest, variety and autonomy of the job, and its capacity to respect the dignity and creativity of the worker.
2. ***Social Aspects of the Job:*** These aspects include the companionship and friendship networks which people derive from coming to work and the recognition that they are accorded, both through doing a fulfilling job and through social interaction.
3. ***Career Paths:*** Career progression is an indirect form of monetary reward, achieved over time. Alternatively it is a means of enhancing job satisfaction.

Extrinsic rewards are monetary rewards. They are of two types – Direct and Indirect.

1. Indirect benefits include:

   (a) Benefits that may be mandated by legislation. e.g. employer contributions to provident/superannuating funds.

   (b) Minimum leave entitlements.

   (c) Benefits that are provided by or bargained with the employer, e.g. fringe benefits:

      - expenses on account of lunches

      - health club membership

      - child care fees

2. Direct benefits

The three strategic aims of reward management HRM are to:

1. Attract employees

2. Retain employees

3. Motivate employees

Pay relativities are an important factor in attracting the desired employee. External relativities need to be correctly established between the jobs in question and similar jobs offered by other employers. Higher than average rates will attract a range of suitable applicants. Lower than average rates will leave jobs unfilled, even in a climate of high overall unemployment.

Pay equity is the key to retaining staff. Adams' Equity Theory of Motivation from *Organisational Behaviour* - employees engage in a continual process of comparison between their own situation and those of others whom they see as in a similar situation in the organisation. How one's ratios of outcomes (pay, conditions, position) to inputs (effort, experience) compare with those of other employees in similar situations?

HR Management therefore needs to monitor internal relativities among grades within the organisation. A compressed salaries range will not retain people interested in career advancement. Gender-based pay inequities will discourage women from staying.

Pay equity is also a key to motivation. Establishing pay systems in which relativities are appropriate and pay levels are seen as equitable, it is necessary to establish:

- Job grades,

- Pay points, and

- Career paths.

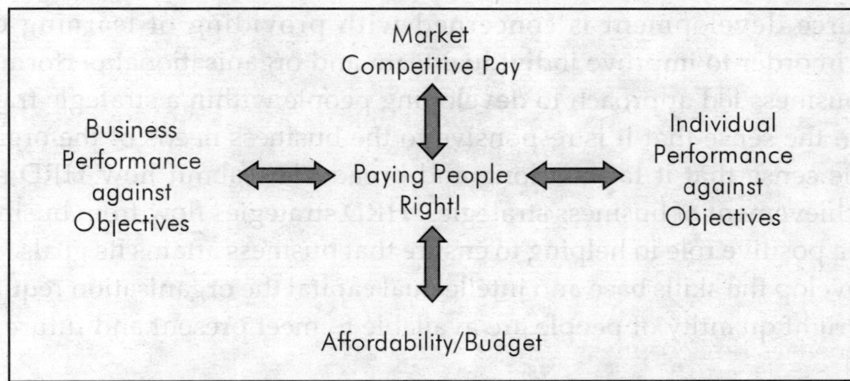

Figure 3.1: A Strategic Reward Management Model

To conclude a strategic reward management is essential to enhance organisational capability to cope with the competition as people is now considered only sustainable competitive advantage for an organisation.

HRD and Strategic HRM

The resource based approach to strategic human resources (SHRM) described by Frank Muller recognises the value of informal, incidental learning in the workplace and stresses on the activation of this reservoir of skills and accumulated knowledge for competitive advantage.

Learning and Development promotes exchange of information between employees hence creating a more knowledgeable workforce. This produces a very flexible organisation where people will accept and adapt to new ideas and changes through a shared vision. Learning organisation is defined as *an* organisation that learns and encourages learning among its people. Tracing history we find that in the 1980's, organisation worldwide discovered time as a new source of competitive advantage. This leads to *'capabilities-based competition'*, which included the capability of learning.

It is therefore, well established that learning and development processes are central to the achievement of SHRM.

The Strategic HR Framework Approach, pioneered by Ulrich and Lake (1990) aims to leverage and/or align HR practices to build critical organisational capabilities that enable an organisation to achieve its goals. This framework offers specific tools and paths to identify how a firm can leverage its HR practices. Business strategy, organisational capabilities and HR practices are the three important elements in this framework. Developing organisational capabilities is best possible through learning and development process.

Even the Integrative Framework of HR, among others focus on building organisational capabilities.

The strategic HR frame work aims to leverage or align the HR practices to build critical capabilities that enable an organisation to achieve its goals. The integrative framework of SHRM, pioneered by Yeung and Berman identifies three paths through which HR practices can contribute to business performance by building original capabilities, by improving employee satisfaction and by shaping the shareholder and customer satisfaction.

Human resource development is concerned with providing of learning development opportunities in order to improve individual team and organisational performance. HRD is essentially a business led approach to developing people within a strategic framework. It is business led in the sense that it is responsive to the business needs of the organisation and strategic in the sense that it takes a long and broad view about how HRD strategies can support the achievement of business strategies. HRD strategies flow from business strategies but they have a positive role in helping to ensure that business attains its goals. To do this it is essential to develop the skills base and intellectual capital the organisation requires as well as ensuring that right quantity of people are available to meet present and future needs.

The overall aim of human resource development is to see that the organisation had the quality of people it needs to attain its goal for improved performance and growth. This aim is achieved by ensuring as far as possible that every one in the organisation has the knowledge and skills and reaches the level of competence required to carry out their work effectively, that the performance of individuals and teams is subject to continuous improvement and that people are developed in a way that maximises their potential for growth and promotion.

Human resource development strategy is business led. It is the strategic plans of the enterprises, which define where it is going, the resources it needs to get there and levels of performance required to achieve business goals initiate it.

These business plan forms the basis for human resource plans, which define the numbers of people, needed and the knowledge, skills and competencies they will require. The human resource plan flows from the business plan and contribute to it by spelling out how much more could be achieved making better use of organisational human resources.

Human resource development strategy is declaration of intent, which states in effect that we believe in strategy for investing in people and this is what we are going to do about. The strategy sets out how HRD processes, policies and programmes will contribute to the áchievement of the corporate goals contained in business plan.

The human resource development strategy should address the critical success factors of the business in the field of product-market development, innovation, quality and cost leadership. It should demonstrate the real links between learning, development and training activities and business performance and indicate how these activities will add value and contribute to achievement of competitive advantage. The HRD strategy should be designed to benefit all the stakeholders in the business enterprise, which not only include the shareholders but also employees' customers, suppliers and the community. That is why HRD strategy should be prepared with in the context of the employee development philosophy of the business, which should be determined at top level and communicated throughout the organisation.

Thus to promote strategic approach to human resource development through learning and development process in an organisation, we need to follow under mentioned principles:

Learning and Development process to help an organisation to develop HRD systems to increase their enabling capabilities. These capabilities include: development of human resources in all aspects, organisational health, improvements in problem solving capabilities, diagnostic skills, capabilities to support all the other systems in the organisation, etc. Learning and Development process also promotes HRD systems that can help individuals in an organisation to recognise their potential and help them to contribute their best towards the various organisational roles they are expected to perform. Learning and Development process also enhances the sense of responsibility of individuals and thereby promotes a culture, which is very important for strategic reasons, like; de-centralisation through delegation and shared responsibility. It facilitates and reinforces participative decision-making. Finally learning and development process also balances the current organisational culture with changing culture.

To conclude the strategic approach to human resource development can be promoted through learning and development integrating Human Resource Development Systems with the organisation.

HRD Strategy: Key Targets

Key Aims	Key Targets	Key Dates
RECRUITMENT & RETENTION		
To recruit and retain staff of the highest quality in order to provide outstanding services to customers, reducing response time to less than an hour (HR Policy No. RR.1.1: 2005)	To spend ₹ 25 million over over next three years on recruitment, reward and retention of employees in all groups, including improved promotion and up-gradation opportunities.	To attract increasing number of applicants for all advertised positions at least by 29% by January, 2007. To reduce the number of unfilled posts to 5% By June 2007. To reduce employee turnover to overall 5%. For service engineers and managerial staff, reduce such turnover to 1%. For manual staff and clerical employees reduce such turnover to 15%. Achieve such turnover rate by January, 2007. To provide career advancement opportunities to the employees, ensuring time-scale promotional scheme, adopting suitable HR policy by January, 2007.
STAFF TRAINING & DEVELOPMENT:		
To provide staff with training and educational opportunities to develop their competencies and periodically renew their skills, keeping pace with the changing requirement of the company. (HR Policy No. STD.1.1: 2005)	To create the In-house Training and Development Group by next one-year for co-ordinating the planning, budgeting, designing, delivering and monitoring of staff induction, training and development. To review and increase the frequency of training programmes for staff members from current 3 man-days to 6 man-days by next one year.	All service engineers and managerial employees have to be made aware about the career advancement scheme, which is linked with compulsory attendance in training programmes and clearing examinations as per HR Policy No. STD.1.1: 2005 by January, 2007.

SUMMARY

Like all other managerial functions HR has also become a strategic function for achieving organisational goals and objectives. Strategic relevance of HR has received worldwide attention, once it is established that ultimate source of competitive advantage for an organisation is its human resources because of its unique characteristics. In this unit we have discussed the how various HR functions can become strategically relevant. Today's HR manager has to understand HR more from business perspectives to appreciate its strategic significance. This we have substantiated citing various corporate examples and finally extracting some case examples from Indian and international perspectives. Basic strategy formulation and developing strategy map we have discussed in earlier unit.

KEYWORDS

Strategy	Decision-making Process
Manpower Planning	Performance Management
Pay Equity	

REVIEW QUESTIONS

1. Discuss SHRM concept and explain why HR should be strategic in today's organisation.
2. Discuss the different perspectives of SHRM and also explain how HR can be integrated with business strategy.
3. What are the various approaches to SHRM? Discuss various characteristics of SHRM.
4. What are the various HR strategy factors?
5. Discuss the concepts of strategic manpower planning and state what are its benefits.
6. What is strategic performance management and why performance management systems are now strategic?
7. Can compensation management be a strategic function! Elaborate your answer.
8. Write short notes on:
   (a) HR Portfolios
   (b) 5-P Model of HR Strategy
   (c) Strategic HR Framework
   (d) Integrative HR Framework
   (e) Analytic HR Framework
   (f) Formal Rational Approach
   (g) Informal incremental approach

CASE STUDY 1

ORGANISATIONAL SHRM PRACTICES

SHRM is a pursuit of a unique way of competing. Human resource practices are also aligned and integrated to business strategy. This ensures congruence and synergy within the organisation. Creating a response to a strategic business challenge e.g. developing greater international perspective among managers in an increasingly global business not only improves the cost-effectiveness of development and learning approaches but also benefits the organisation to get competitive edge. Using HP-Compaq Case study, we have explained how strategic approach to management of people is a viable option for senior managers of an organisation.

Stanford University classmates Bill Hewlett and Dave Packard founded HP in 1939. HP is a leading global provider of products, technologies, solutions and services to consumers and business. Compaq Computer Corporation was formed after a 1982 meeting in a Houston, Texas, in a pie shop. The May 2002 merger of Hewlett-Packard and Compaq Computer Corporation forged a dynamic, powerful team of 140,000 employees with capabilities in 160 countries and doing business in 43 currencies and 15 languages. Revenues for the combined companies were $72 billion for the fiscal year that ended October 31, 2002.

The successful merger of HP and Compaq is attributable to strategic human resource management practices by both the organisations. Together, employees in the new HP share a passion for customers, an intense focus on teamwork, speed and agility, and a commitment to trust and respect for all individuals.

Strategic approach to the management of people is evident from HP's diversity and inclusion philosophy. How HP makes use of such strategic approach can be understood from some of the examples. HP considers a diverse, high-achieving workforce is the sustainable competitive advantage that differentiates them from others. Strategic use of such diverse workforce is essential to win in the marketplaces, workplaces and communities around the world. An inclusive, flexible work environment at HP values differences and motivates employees to contribute their best. To better serve the customers, HP attracts, develops, promotes and retains a diverse workforce. Trust, mutual respect and dignity are fundamental beliefs that are reflected in behaviour and actions of HP's workforce. Accountability for diversity and inclusion goals drives HP's success. This is further reinforced by compliance, equal opportunity and affirmative action.

SHRM practices at HP is also evident from their policies and supporting practices which are built upon their core philosophy, as well as a set of values that include a strong belief that all employees should be treated with dignity and respect. HP does not discriminate against any employee or applicant for employment because of race, creed, colour, religion, gender, sexual orientation, gender identity/expression, national origin, disability and age. It is also HP's policy to comply with all applicable national and local laws pertaining to nondiscrimination and equal opportunity.

Strategically HP emphasises on the equity compensation plans and benefits programmes. HR at HP evaluates human resources and compensation strategies and oversee HP's total rewards programme, reviews the leadership development process, reviews and approves objectives relevant to performance and determines the compensation in accordance with those objectives, approves employment agreements for key executive officers, approves and amends HP's incentive compensation, stock appreciation rights and stock option programmes, etc. HR at HP also monitors global workforce management programmes. Such strategic focus to HR helps HP not only to recruit and retain diverse talented workforce globally but also to repose confidence in the minds of the HP's human resources.

According HP's CEO, HP's ......*'philosophy on rewards is refreshingly simple: when excellent performance is acknowledged and rewarded, people are motivated and work smarter.'* Strategic compensation and benefits programme at HP encourages and support actions that enable HP to build on market leadership. This helps to strive toward exceptional achievement - and when that achievement leads to increased profit, everyone shares in the rewards.

Another example of HP's strategic human resource management practice is evident from HP's aim to tailor working hours to employees' needs, depending on their personal and business roles, and actively support working from home.

Contd...

HP encourages employees to develop their work and life skills so as to help them to achieve personal as well as career goals. HP supports employees in acquiring additional relevant knowledge and skills, as well as ensures their work projects and assignments complement and accelerate their individual development. Sustaining a happy and stable working environment also motives HP's people to perform.

HP believes ideas thrive on teamwork. Thus all cross section of employees at HP is encouraged to have original ideas and to share them.

That HP practices SHRM is evident from the excerpts from new advertisement for a HR Specialist job at HP. 'hp invents. We make ideas happen. And we make great products. Our locations are state-of-the-art, cutting edge and all over the world. Our HR generalists provide all-round support to an assigned business entity by using their specialist skills to deliver customer focused HR programs, services and consultancy that will improve business and operational performance.'

Some of the models of SHRM, which relates to HP's way of managing the human resources and also the organisation as a whole can be best practice view, pioneered by Huselid, 1995; Becker and Gerhart, 1996. In this model 18 key practices are covered, bundles of which make one organisation to achieve sustainable competitive advantage over the other. David Guest and Angela Baron (2000) study indicates it pay to pursue best practice view of SHRM. Some of the best practices, like; feedback on performance, performance related pay, regular appraisals, multi-skilling, equitable HR policies, etc. are followed by HP.

Similarly we also find integration of 'best-fit' model of SHRM pioneered by Buller (1988) in HP's practices. For HP's global presence, they have integrated the global environment in their HR policy responses. In fact HP acclaims their diversity has helped them to better follow the inclusion strategy, which they have reflected in their HR practices to truly derive benefit from SHRM.

Reflection of resource-based approach to SHRM, pioneered by Prahalad and Hammond, 1990; Storey (1995); Muller (1998), etc. is also traceable to HP's practices. For HP their diverse global manpower is their best strength, as they leverage the competencies of this workforce for managing the organisation. HP leverages bundle of tangible and intangible resources around their products and services, integrates various skills, technologies and business process to get competitive advantage.

HR Strategy of Dell

Making HR strategy as an opportunity to fulfill mutual objectives of organisation and people require building and sustaining the HR Brand of an organisation; distinct and yet synchronous with its overall corporate brand. HR departments can ensure this by taking their functions to strategic spaces provided they rebuild their credibility and stature - the compulsions of business and the wisdom.

To ensure that HR objectives mutually fulfill both employees and organisational objectives, Dell Computers actively seeks and cultivates a certain type of employee mind-set. In fact with change of business focus from renting a computer to selling, Dell required an HR department that can partner with the company's business units. To achieve this Dell divided HR into two types; HR operations and HR management. While HR Operations supports Dell employees in general, HR management supports Dell's business. Dell's HR management team identifies personnel needs; work out lines of reporting and organisational charts, and defining training needs. HR management consults strategically with the business unit. This ensures zero confusion with strategy. Accountability and roles of the people at Dell are very clear, which makes speedy execution of the plan possible. At Dell strategy starts with an executive team that develops key objectives for the coming year, which are very quantitative and measurable. These objectives are articulated and circulated globally. In this way Dell creates a culture of ownership and develops 'shared visions' which give opportunity to mutually fulfill the organisational and employees' objectives.

Thus it is evident that human resource management strategy can significantly offer an organisation and its employees an opportunity to mutually fulfill their objectives.

CASE STUDY 2

HR STRATEGY – A CASE OF DABUR INDIA LIMITED

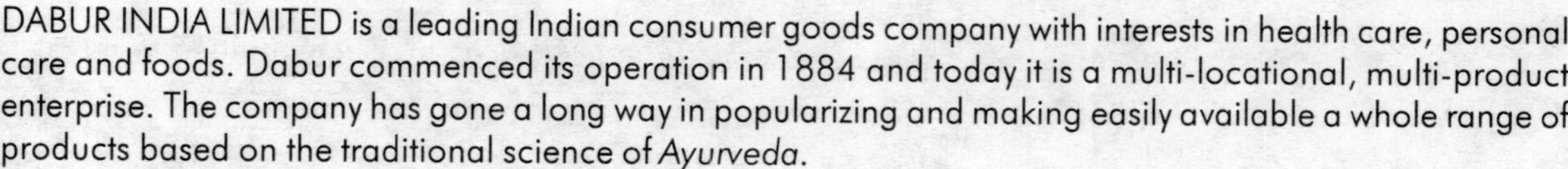

DABUR INDIA LIMITED is a leading Indian consumer goods company with interests in health care, personal care and foods. Dabur commenced its operation in 1884 and today it is a multi-locational, multi-product enterprise. The company has gone a long way in popularizing and making easily available a whole range of products based on the traditional science of *Ayurveda*.

Dabur's products are available for people in more than 50 countries including the Middle East, South-east Asia, Africa, the European Union and America. It has collaborated with leaders in their fields to set up joint ventures in India.

One of the important strategies of DABUR is to 'be the most sought out employer.' To achieve this strategy DABUR focuses on following action plan:

a. Career Development of the employees.

b. Career Mapping and management development with OD initiatives.

c. Delegation & De-centralization.

d. Identification of Training Needs of the employees to be done more frequently and followed more diligently.

e. Innovativeness and creativity of the employees to be given more weightage, given proper recognitions and suitably rewarded.

f. System of Flexible Rewards and choosing of Incentives to be introduced.

HR plays a vital role in strategy formulation. HR ensures the right amount of personnel at the right time. Through various tools HR ensures job-fit candidates and the required competencies required by the personnel in carrying out the job. It calculates the future manpower requirements thus ensuring the requisite strength of manpower for future assignments. It is able to visualize the future manpower's competency requirements.

BLOCK TWO

HUMAN RESOURCE PROCUREMENT

UNIT 4

Productivity, Technology and HRM

Learning Objectives

After completion of this unit, the students will be aware of the following topics:

- *Introduction*
- *History*
- *Productivity*
- *Productivity Measurements – Ratio Problem*
- *Technology and Human Resource Management Issues*
- *Technology Upgradation and Employment in India*

SETTING RIGHT THE ORGANISATIONS – A CASE OF CHEW FRESH

Technological change in life style product manufacturing is very high and takes place at a very short interval. In spite of their rapid technological reformations, Chew Fresh, a manufacturer of the state of art life style products, continues to believe that human resource remains their backbone. Being in new generation life style products business, Chew Fresh always needs to develop new products and generate demand for the same to strengthen their position in the market. In no time, Chew Fresh finds other competing organisations aping their product ideas and introducing matching substitutes at a much lesser price. For Chew Fresh, to establish a brand identity for new products requires a minimum incubating period of three to five years, while new competitors appear in the market in less than six months time. This means Chew Fresh cannot captivate customers, as they settle for price efficient substitutes, after their new product uses habit formation. Price band of their recently introduced chewing gum is almost 50% higher than other newly established competing organisations, leading to their significant market loss, after their initial surge in demand. Chew Fresh then, went for product differentiation through stepped up R&D activities. Chew Fresh repositioned their chewing gum with sweeteners, harmless for children and diabetic patient, without however, naming it as sugar free; else this will create only a niche market of diabetic patients. 'Healthy Chew' is their new brand name, which among others, reduces bad breathe, protects teeth and gum and even with fragrance of almond and chocolate, give the feeling to the customers, as if they are taking a bite of crispy candy. First thing, what Chew Fresh did was to get the name of 'Healthy Chew' patented.

Chew Fresh could do all these because of their highly motivated people who are innovative and always feel the need to change. Chew Fresh believes that their people are the key input for their continuous pursuit for product innovation. HRM at Chew Fresh systematically review the competencies of people and meet the gap through various interventions. For Chew Fresh, training and development is the last priority. They make use of job rotation, employee empowerment and career development as their major instruments to develop their human resources.

INTRODUCTION

HRM initiatives in any organisation, need to account for productivity trends and extent of technological changes. However, attributing productivity to labour efficiency alone is no longer tenable. In this unit, we have analysed the productivity issues and impact of technological changes on work or job content.

Traditionally, productivity was considered as an input-output relational measurement. Orthodox views, attribute productivity to labour efficiency as output quantification can immediately be related to labour efficiency. However, this hypothesis suffers from a major lacuna, as many organisations, despite achieving high labour efficiency (measured in terms of value added in manufacturing) suffer from overall dysfunction and become sick.

Organisations operate on team efforts, by distributing different functional areas to different departments. Ultimate success depends on effective joint efforts of different team groups. A lapse in single functional area or areas can offset the efficiency of other functional area or areas, so much so that it may ultimately affect corporate efficiency.

Even within the ambit of input-output relationship, the concept of input has widely changed under present circumstances. Inputs are no longer confined within the direct materials used for production but it also considers even the supportive functions in more abstract form. Thus knowledge, ideas, etc., have also been thought within the definitional context of inputs. In an organisation, the production section in reality transforms the physical inputs to outputs.

But other functional departments, though not engaged in direct material transformation, provide supportive inputs to production departments for efficient functioning.

Total factor productivity concept gives emphasis on quantification of such abstract inputs and like-wise enables us to measure the overall corporate efficiency more scientifically.

HISTORY

With the declaration of the International Year of Productivity in 1992, productivity consciousness has gained worldwide momentum. The concept of productivity was originally enunciated by classical economists like Adam Smith, David Ricardo, J.S. Mill in the 18th and 19th centuries in the form of law of diminishing return to all resources. However, in the 19th century, Frederick W. Taylor's thesis 'task study' gave a more reasonable slogan on the issue, i.e., human worth can be made infinitely more productive not by working harder but by working smarter. In India, the productivity movement and consciousness gained momentum with the establishment of National Productivity Council (NPC) in 1958.

Tracing history, we find that the productivity concepts originally emerged during the post-war period. After the World War II, the ravaged economy needed urgent reconstruction, renovation and rationalisation in all countries. Growth was then everybody's concern and in such a milieu the growth theory was advocated by the economists.

The interest in economic growth and focus on political, economic, social and cultural relations, anthropological, psychological, institutional, legal, managerial, administrative and host of other related aspects, are instrumental in furthering economic growth.

The following basic economic factors have been unanimously recognised as the crucial factors in economic growth:

1. Capital formation for the present and to combat uncertainties in future.
2. High productivity of all factors of production and inputs (including time and knowledge).

PRODUCTIVITY

From the economic point of view productivity means the yield from:

- each factor of production (land, labour, capital and organisation).
- each input (raw materials, fuel, time and knowledge).
- overall yield of the joint factors and resources enumerated above.

From the management perspective, productivity in its broadest sense is the quantitative relationship between what we produce and resources which we use. There is a distinct difference between production and productivity. In simple terms, production means a process of transformation of raw materials and other inputs into finished goods or services.

But productivity denotes surplus-generation. To define the term productivity in terms of input-output relationship, while production is transforming input into output, by adding values, productivity is to get higher output over given input. The excess output, therefore, tantamounts to surplus generation. Productivity can be increased by interchanging the input ratios, while in such changing process the outputs will proportionately increase more than the changes in input ratio.

Conventionally, productivity was understood as an inevitable outcome of labour efficiency, i.e., only efficient functioning of the workmen could contribute to productivity improvement. In complex corporate systems, this emphasis on a single factor gradually lost its importance as with single efficiency of workmen, productivity cannot be improved or corporate success cannot be achieved.

Thus functional efficiency of all other factors of production and all other subsystems of all such factors have finally been considered as the ultimate goal for overall corporate efficiency and, productivity thereafter has been considered as the efficiency of total factors instead of emphasis on efficiency of labour (single factor approach).

Production = value addition to new materials

Productivity = efficiency of production

= f (surplus efficiency of all points)

= f (Men, Materials, Management)

Improving Productivity

Positive actions can be summarised under six headings which have come to be known as the six lines of attack to improve productivity efficiency.

1.	Improve basic process by research and development	Long-term measures and will require capital
2.	Provide more and improved physical means of producing	
3.	Simplify and improve the product and reduce the variety	Intermediate measures and may require capital
4.	Improve methods of operation	Short-term measures and will require little or no capital
5.	Improve organisation, planning and control	
6.	Increase manpower effectiveness at all levels	

There exists an essential difference between the first two lines of attack on the others as they require considerable capital expenditure and are necessary for long-term projects. They require initial investment in highly trained technical staff and in buildings, plant and equipment as well as all those facilities which go with technical and engineering research and development, specially as applied to the creation of new products and the design of new plants.

The third line to attack, i.e., simplification and improvement of the product and reduction of varieties is considered as an intermediate one, and it may not require huge expenditure of capital to improve technical efficiency and/or to make other changes. The expenditure amounts, if any, depend on the particular circumstances in each case. Work study technique has a great role to play in this regard.

The other three lines of attack are the short-term measures which essentially concentrate on the operational fields and where work study can be widely and immediately applied. Since no capital expenditure as such is required for such exercises, these lines of technique are perceived as the most successful and solicited line of attacks for productivity improvement.

Method of operations can be improved by analytical and intensive study of the details of operations of existing plans. The industrial engineering approach (technique of work study) are to be adequately integrated with technical considerations. Improvement in planning and organsing is obvious and essential. To increase the manpower effectiveness at all functional levels, again, emphasis on systematic training as a continuous exercise is considered necessary. Thus, to increase the manpower effectiveness of executives and workers of an organisation, systematic training programmes should be broadly included.

Improvement of productivity through HRD has now become more important for manpower obsolescence, which is now gripping the industries for technological changes. Technology as lead factor cannot improve productivity unless simultaneous development has been renewed particularly for the current economic environment, which is characterised by liberalisation and globalisation. While innovations and developments in technology no doubt ensure increased productivity, human factors cannot be altogether ignored. Productivity improvement through increased employee motivation, commitment, satisfaction and efficiency at work reinforced by managerial policies and practices now contribute significantly to bring about the desired improvement.

Improving productivity through HRD intervention calls for in-depth knowledge of human behaviour at work, especially in the context of productivity-related issues – skills to diagnose the strengths and weaknesses of the people and the process of channelising these to productivity behaviour and awareness and assimilation of innovative approaches to man management.

In manufacturing, increasing introduction of NC, CNC and DNC systems have made the traditional skill and knowledge redundant and compelled the employers to renew their knowledge and skill.

Such skill and knowledge enriching training, despite having time-lag (between learning and actual application), effectively contributes to productivity improvement. Apart from training, good HRD practices ensure effective career planning and development, effective manpower planning, performance appraisal, management succession and development and all these have far-reaching impact on increasing productivity.

Six important factors thus have been identified, which affect productivity in an organisation. These factors are as follows:

1. *Nature and Quality of Raw Materials:* This factor demands better methods to eliminate the awful waste which is evident in the use of natural resources and provide for efficient handling.

2. *Basic Nature of Processes Employed:* Drive for better methods in using, what is possibly the most valuable of any nation's resources, demands that technologies should be used to the best advantage in constantly improved processes. Scientific research should continuously try to improve the processes and the procedures.

3. *Amount of Plant and Equipment Employed:* In India, physical effort of a workman is considerably less than many other countries of the world. Technically, it is highly uneconomical from the productivity point of view for a man to do work manually which could reasonably be done by mechanical equipment. Further it is also counter productive where a country's plant, equipment and buildings are obsolete and ill-designed. This is due to failure to plough back enough capital for modern equipment for future profit. In India, this is particularly evident. Technological obsolescence is one of the most important factors for non-achieving productive efficiency by the industries. Many industries are practically sluggish in growth and development and are retarding day by day. This virtually forces them to finally close down their operations. Thus it is necessary to ensure that capital resources are used to the best advantage for productive efficiency. What should be matching investments for plant and equipment, which also broadly includes periodic updating of existing technologies, vary from unit to unit.

4. *Efficiency of Plant and Equipment Employed:* This factor partly depends on adequate supply of technologies but it equally demands eagerness and action at all levels in a firm to obtain the best from existing resources. To make this eagerness effective, information on production, performance and cost must be made available to all concerned.

5. *Volume Continuity and Uniformity of Production:* Standardisation of products resulting in longer and more economical runs, depends upon finding out the best and most simple products to fill the market needs and the best method of making them. Sometimes customer's education may be necessary, but this should not be difficult if the products offered are cheap and satisfying.

   Productivity does not mean retrenchment or redundancy, in contrast, productivity in fact increases the employment potentiality.

   The national conference on the 'Role of Trade Union in Productivity Improvement', organised by the National Productivity Council during February, 1990 in collaboration with the Ministry of Labour, Government of India and the International Labour Organisation at New Delhi, has deliberated on certain important issues of productivity. For the first time at a national level conference, the significance of total factor productivity has been recognised and it was deliberated that productivity increases will inter alia improve the quality of working life of employees.

It was suggested that a national level productivity policy should be evolved to improve all aspects of production, such as skill improvement, education of workers, training for attitudinal changes, creation of participative culture and sharing the gains of productivity. The conference emphasised on the urgent need for attitudinal changes amongst managers towards workers and unions so that misconceptions could be cleared.

6. *Utilisation of Manpower:* Manpower is a fundamental resource. There is a real need to see that both general planning and detailed methods of work are not wasteful and avoid fatigue and frustration.

Finally, to understand the spirit of productivity from its true perspective, it is essential to clear some misconceptions, which are centered around the aim, scope and purpose of productivity.

(a) Productivity is not concerned with any group of people but that of every member of the society.

(b) Productivity does not signify just more production but stands for the functional optimisation.

(c) Productivity does not mean making the worker work harder.

(d) Productivity does not result in working longer hours or more number of days in the week.

(e) Productivity is not confined to factory and manufacturing organisations. It pervades all spheres of economic activities where human endeavour is involved.

The labour force should be involved at the planning stage for technological changes and productivity improvements. The increased emphasis on small group activities such as quality circles and other consultative mechanisms is thought as an inevitable outcome in the years to come to achieve improvement in productivity. While production improvements are important, equally important would be equitable distribution of productivity gains among different partners, namely, labourers, shareholders, consumers and the organisations themselves and the state.

The message of productivity should be percolated down the shopfloor level through necessary training sessions under the active guidance of local productivity councils and the National Productivity Council. Finally, the conference also stressed upon the necessity to get active cooperation from trade unions to spread the message of productivity improvements and to successfully achieve productivity in organisations for overall economic growth and development of the country.

Total Factor Productivity

In an organisation there are different functional departments to coordinate different activities. In the area of specialisation, independent alike functions have been grouped together and are assigned to competent men at the helm of affairs to coordinate and control the entire functions with active support from other down the line staff members. Each such functional department is assigned to accomplish a particular important function, any deficiency at any functional area either at the macro-level or at the micro-level is likely to affect the overall corporate efficiency.

To understand the problem better, it is appropriate at this stage to briefly introduce the functional areas of management in an organisation and to relate such separate functions to the overall corporate activities. As has been pointed out earlier, from the economist's point of view, total factor productivity means the efficiency and contribution of each factor of production like, land, labour, capital and organisation. Factor endowments of each such factor together contribute to the national income. Such factor endowments are rent, wages, interest and profit. Unless such endowments are realised to the optimum extent, they cannot effectively contribute to the country's overall economic activity and productive efficiency at the macro-level. At the macro-level, the productive efficiency is measured at each individual industrial unit, in which unit, the entire corporate function is divided into a number of managerial functions as stated below.

The marketing department of any particular industrial unit is doing/performing the most important managerial function. For analysing the task and functions of a marketing department, it is evident that the following common functions are performed by such a department.

Marketing department is assigned to arrange for selling the end-products or finished outputs of a unit. While the task of producing is entrusted with the production department, the task of selling lies with the marketing department. Marketing department books orders and in the form of a feedback mechanism, provides the input support to the production department to help it in successful production planning for manufacturing and effecting delivery as per the user's schedule. Recently, however, in a competitive environment, the role of marketing department has increased enormously and various new and challenging tasks have now been incorporated within their functional ambit. Such new functional areas are:

1. Developing the market for future growth and development of the organisation.
2. Keeping abreast of the changing user's demand in intimating the users? sentiments from time to time to production department to prepare it for product innovation, catering to user's demand.
3. Tapping the prospective potential users to increase the market share and thus to facilitate growth and expansion of the organisation.
4. Keeping abreast of competitors' strategies and implementing necessary changes from time to time in matters of line of attack.
5. Spreading the message of the organisation to wide spectrum of the population, selecting the appropriate advertisement media and attracting attention with catchy advertisements with the help of professional agencies.
6. Exploring the export potentiality, tapping foreign buyers.

7. Constant touch with users, maintaining the proper linkage through a network of service personnel.

8. Timely collecting the due bills to avert bad debts and consequential loss of the organisation.

9. Selecting the most cost-effective distribution channel for reaching the product to the widely dispersed users' segments.

10. Constantly reviewing mistakes and lapses with suitable statistical analysis for effective future guidance.

Most of the companies, unfortunately, assume that they will continue to enjoy the market share irrespective of any major or minor lapses on their part or irrespective of any changes in the business environment. Nurturing such notions truly reflects the inefficiency in marketing function and ultimately leads to corporate collapse. Marketing department, very often, due to over enthusiasm, books the orders, without taking into cognizance the available production facilities. This truly reflects the lack of coordination between marketing and production functions in an organisation. Unnecessary stockpiling of inventories, raw materials, anticipating future requirements, accumulating finished inventories, anticipating future demand to a great extent strain corporate liquidity and profitability. This is also squarely attributed to the lapse of the marketing department.

The next important functional area of management is production planning and control. With active computer support, production planning and control functions are now-a-days becoming more important for effectively contributing to corporate success. To understand the overall concept of production planning and control scientifically, it is necessary to introduce certain basic concepts and their influences on production planning and control functions.

The first such important concept is the product supply pipeline. This pipeline extends from the person extracting raw material from the natural resources to the ultimate consumers of the finished products. The entire pipeline may be broadly subdivided into:

1. The raw material pipeline

2. The manufacturing pipeline

3. The distribution pipeline

Throughout these whole pipelines, continuity is the key word. Managerial plans and policies influence the pipeline. Thus, it is necessary to understand the effectiveness of the pipelines relating these to the efficiency of the top management who are initiating plans and policies.

The second major influence of the management of production is lead time. Manufacturing lead-time is the time interval between the issue of production order and the shipment of the product. Thus, strict adherence to the delivery schedule to complete the production cycle in time is very important to gain consumers satisfaction and confidence. These uphold the corporate image on the goodwill. Committing unrealistic delivery schedules without taking into cognizance the manufacturing lead-time badly affects the corporate efficiency. Manufacturing lead-time *inter alia*, also depends on purchasing lead time. Thus, it becomes an uphill task for the production planning and control department to coordinate with the inventory management functions, keeping in close touch with materials management groups. For efficient evaluation of lead time which influences production planning and control function, a periodic review of the lead time should receive close attention, to achieve following objectives:

1. To ensure delivery of the products in time,
2. To maintain optimum supply of finished goods and work-in-progress,
3. To maintain flexibility in the manufacturing operation,
4. To develop and coordinate schedule and order to the production department to follow-up production schedule and finally,
5. To maintain optimum inventories.

Thus to attain the above noted objective, the basic function of production planning and control may be grouped under: planning, scheduling, dispatching, progressing and follow up.

Planning is concerned with deciding how the production should be carried out. Scheduling means the time-table of production. Dispatching deals with all aspects of giving the necessary authority to start and obtaining tools, materials and other requirements. Progressing and follow up enables us to find out whether work is carried out as planned.

From the total factor productivity perspective, therefore, an efficiency index can be prepared to understand the effectiveness of the individual sub-functions.

The next important functional area in corporate sector is personnel/human resources management. Although very recently, this function has received due importance and professional cognizance to deal with the manpower successfully so as motivate them for work and to achieve higher productivity, in most of the organisations, personnel function is still considered a formal ritualistic statutory compliance with the legal norms. People are considered as the most valuable asset for an organisation, because their efficiency can make the difference for an organisation. Hence personnel professionals are now gradually receiving importance in organisations. An inefficient personnel system badly affects corporate productivity. Necessary efforts have also been made to construct productivity indices for the personnel function in an organisation.

Labour productivity ratio, labour turnover rate, structure of industrial dispute, skill level for workers, human resource development programme, etc., fall under this category.

Material management function has now become an important functional area for the manager. Timely purchase of raw materials to ensure continuity of production uninterruptedly forms an important function under this department. Purchasing right materials at a reasonable price and keeping them arranged for use by production department at times of necessity, successfully depends on efficient materials management function. Overloading of raw materials not only strains liquidity of the organisation but also increases the possibility of pilferages, damages and losing of rent value of occupied godown space. From our experience, it is revealed that many procured raw materials by organisations are subsequently becoming non-moving or slow-moving items, for lying long in godown and even at times, raw material condition becomes so bad that they hardly retain the scrap value of the material.

Ordering optimum quantity, developing vendors/suppliers, following approach of just-in-time, material requirement planning are certain basic requirements of materials management functions. Efficiency index for material management function can also be prepared to relate this to the total factor productivity.

For understanding the efficiency of financial management, various ratios have been developed, variances of which can be related to the corporate success or otherwise. There are many ways and means to interpret financial data, which are brought out by the organisation through documented annual reports. The interpretation to understand their influence on total factor productivity is, therefore, not relevant here.

PRODUCTIVITY MEASUREMENTS – RATIO PROBLEM

Conventionally, productivity measurement is left to ratio analysis. Let me illustrate this with a small problem.

A company manufactures 50000 Desktops in a year. Each Desktop sells @ ₹ 25000/-. The company spends @ ₹ 5000 per Desktop in material inputs and 2,00,000 man hours to make the Desktops. Compute following productivity ratios from the above problem:

1. output/labour ratio
2. output value/labour ratio
3. value added/labour ratio

Solution:

1. Output/labour ratio (in terms of man hours) = 50000 Desktops/200000 man hours = 0.25 Desktop per man hour
2. Output value/labour ratio (50000 Desktops × 25000 per Desktop)/200000

   Man hours = ₹ 6250 per man hour
3. Value added/labour ratio – This is computed first by computing the value added, which is = (output value – material cost) = {(50000 × 25000) – (50000 × 5000) = 1000000

   So value added/labour (in man hours) = 1000000/200000 = ₹ 5 per man hour.

But this approach to productivity measurement and linking it straight to wages will neither benefit organisation nor it will benefit the workers in the long run for obvious reasons explained earlier.

In today's complex production system, overall productivity being important than labour productivity, for rational pricing of labour (i.e., linking wages), following two models can alternatively yield better results.

1. ***Omni Factor Model:*** This model gives a composite productivity index for all input and output costs of all the products. While input costs are taken for all, output costs are determined on Average Marginal Costs (AMC) method. Input costs are:
   i. Raw material costs
   ii. Manpower costs
   iii. Capital costs, viz., depreciation, interest, stock investment, etc.
   iv. Indirect production costs
   v. Cost of utilities

   Output costs on AMC method worked out as under:

   Assuming, we have three products, A, B & C.

$$\text{Aggregate Output} = \text{Output A} + \text{Output B} \times \left(\frac{\text{AMC of B}}{\text{AMC of B}}\right) + \text{Output C} \times \left(\frac{\text{AMC of C}}{\text{AMC of A}}\right).$$

$$\text{Where, AMC percentage of A} = \left(\frac{\text{Total input costs of A}}{\text{Total output costs of A}}\right) \times 100$$

   Productivity = Aggregate output/Input costs

2. ***Surrogate Models:*** This model primarily consider some qualitative factors to measure productivity. Factors like satisfaction of investors, employees, customers and suppliers are considered in qualitative terms. Quantification of these qualitative terms are done as under:

   Investors' satisfaction (S_i) = Net Profit/Total Investment

   Employees' satisfaction (S_e) = Total value added/Total number of man hours

   Customers' satisfaction(S_c) = Total Sales revenue/Total number of customers

   Suppliers satisfaction(S_s) = Total purchases/Total number of Suppliers

   Composite Productivity Index, therefore,

   $A.S_i + B.S_e + C.S_c + D.S_s$

   A, B, C and D are constants, which indicate relative weightage of four parameters.

Linking wages to productivity, based on these two models, yield better results as organisations can objectively price the labour and also labour could get their legitimate share of productivity gain.

Productivity Measurement Difficulty for Knowledge Workers

Measuring productivity for number of units produced by an worker using a machine is not difficult for obvious ease of quantification. But productivity of knowledge worker is difficult to measure. This is primarily because of difficulty to relate cost of capital in measurement. Other difficulties can be related to following factors:

1. Effects of strategic decision, both positive and negative, may not be immediately evident. Such time lag is therefore difficult to relate to a particular time period. Moreover, we can not directly relate every strategic decision to individual's efficiency and inefficiency. Outcome of some strategic decisions may depend on various external factors, which may be beyond the control of managers,
2. Knowledge workers' often extend services to other units of an organisation, which may have some effects on final output but it is difficult to quantify. For example an Advertising Manager's efforts in increasing sales is difficult to measure.
3. Knowledge workers often contribute indirectly to the achievement of the end result, which is difficult to measure. For example, a knowledge worker's contribution towards design and development directly attributable to final output. Yet his efforts are all the more important.

For all such difficulties, Total Factor Productivity (TFP) Study is a better approach, as it considers functional efficiency/performance of all departments of an organisation at aggregate level, without bothering for individual productivity. We have discussed this at length.

Productivity and Quality

When quality increases productivity also improves. This is because wastes and rework are reduced and inputs are optimally utilized. Higher productivity enables an organisation to reduce price and gain competitive advantage both in terms of price and quality. Customers also feel happy as they get value for their money. Since organisation's bottom line improves, it raises the satisfaction level of all stakeholders, including employees. Significance of cost of quality has been discussed, while explaining the ISO certification requirements. Saving the cost of quality will have immediate effect on enhanced productivity of an organisation. All these establish that quality and productivity are indirectly related.

Productivity, therefore, should not be misconstrued as labour performance alone. It is sum total efficiency. However, increased productivity requires less manpower is a tenable argument as with productivity rise, man hours requirement for a given output reduce.

Corporate Sickness and Productivity

Productivity is now considered as the effect of the sum-total efficiency of each and every functional area. Hence, corporate sickness can directly be studied in depth by using total factor productivity indices. In that respect, corporate sickness has a direct relationship with the productivity achievement figures of the company and the total factor productivity indices also help us to study the industrial sickness at the macro-level.

Among other things, industrial sickness in most of the cases is attributed to quality of management, impractical planning, lack of financial control, diversion of resources, inadequate attention to research and development, technological obsolescence and poor industrial relations. In fact, taking into account the above management related causes, when the sickness trend is analysed, it transpires that over 95 per cent of the total causes of sickness can be directly attributed to such reasons, which are more internal than external.

All such reasons being internal in nature can be considerably averted, provided early detection of such causes or reasons through analysis of total factor productivity indices is initiated on time. This is possible when such monitoring at the corporate level on a continuous basis, is introduced. Since total factor productivity analysis enables us to quickly identify the weak operational areas, immediate intervention can help in avoiding the situation, the culmination of which otherwise can prompt sickness for the unit.

Although an organisational level study to relate sickness to total factor productivity indices has not been initiated in India but such exercises to identify corporate dysfunction have already been initiated in many industrially advanced countries in the world. Such a study acts as an early signal to locate weak operational areas and it helps the industries to adopt quick remedial measures. Thus, instead of fully relying on financial performance indicators to understand the viability or otherwise of sample organisation, it is more appropriate to consider the productivity trend to study corporate health.

In the context of recent changes in the Indian economy, productivity analyses have assumed greater importance. The Board for Industrial and Financial Reconstruction (BIFR), to understand the viability prospect of sick industries, to a great extent relies on productivity indices. On such analyses, if BIFR finds that a particular industry has become sick due to inefficient operations in a number or cases and mere pumping of credit simply cannot help in averting such lapses, it recommends winding up.

Technology and Human Resource Management Issues

The concept of technology is different from automation or mass production techniques. Automation or mass production techniques leverage on engineering excellence and focus on replacing the operators in many cases. Hence technology makes the process of manufacturing-uniform, faster and cost effective. Technology, on the other hand, guides the process. It is more science and innovation driven, and is the result of combined efforts of scientists, engineers, and technologists. (Dayal, 1987) It is knowledge intensive process which complements the manufacturing or rendering of services. Therefore, with new technology, we require new set of skills, i.e., the compositional shift of skill base of employees and workers. Modern technology does not substitute manpower. Thus, we can define technology as the invention in science.

Because of globalisation, today, we find spurt in technology transfer. Technology transfer is the process of sharing knowledge, technologies, skills, methods of manufacturing and such facilities can be shared among the countries and so also among the organisations. Countries with conventional technology now find it easier to achieve cost-effectiveness, new products development, etc. for technology transfer. Technology being the more holistic term than automation, it is better construed as the knowledge transfer or sharing.

For development and so also for application of technology, human resources play the most important and crucial role. Today's organisation cannot sustain without continuous upgradation of technology. If any organisation fails, their competitor can match with the state-of-the art technology requirement, and accordingly can gain the competitive edge over others. Therefore for business imperatives, organisations feel compelled to embrace new technology. Cost effectiveness, quality, on time customer services, effective decision-making, monitoring and control, and economy of scale are some of the important benefits of technology. But implementation of technology requires skilled human resources. Therefore, from human resource management point of view, technology requires the support from people and also requires the knowledge and skill of workers. Also, HR department can benefit from technology, as technology enabled HR solutions facilitate in streamlining HR functions, and so also support in real time HR decisions.

Technology influences various people related issues. Some of the important areas of technological influence in organisations, which encompass human resource management and development issues are; leadership, talent management, performance management, motivation, reward systems and corporate culture.

Likewise, technology also influences talent management process in organisation. Talent management ensures achievement of performance targets through co-ordinated efforts of the human resources. Therefore, organisational leader has to emphasise on recruiting the right people, with right competencies, in the right position and at the right time. It has been established worldwide that people in an organisation can generate values, which can lead to upward performance achievement, varying from one to ten percent. There are organisations where such additional value generation through people can exceed even ten percent. However, reasons for such accentuated value due to people factor are difficult to identify and control. But organisational ability to attract, motivate and retain the best and most appropriate talent, certainly adds to this value factor. Organisations, which succeed in generating high value, categorise it as strategic value from people. They ensure such strategic value aligning behaviour of the people with the organisational strategy, understanding the set of competencies required to develop organisational capability, developing it and utilizing it, keeping in view the principle of best-fit.

In competitive business, organisation, no doubt, can sustain through stringent cost control. This primary objective essentially dominates the financial decisions. Through effective talent management, integrating dynamic people with matching talent achieves this objective. Thus, talent management is the central tenet of leadership. Jeffrey Immelt, Chairman and CEO of General Electric, believes that development and management of people are the key success factors, along with a lean cost structure and a clear strategy for market sector dominance.

Change of Occupational Pattern in India

Structural change in the economy can be measured in terms of change in relative shares of incomes of factors of production in the major sectors of the Indian economy. The Central Statistics Organisation (CSO) presents such estimates under the following five categories:

1. Compensation of employees,
2. Interest,

3. Rent,
4. Profits and dividends, and
5. Mixed income of self-employed.

In India wage-employment has substantially increased over the years, which is evident from increased income shares under the 'compensation of employees' head and decreased income share under the 'mixed income of self-employed' head over the decades.

Distribution of net domestic product, at factor-cost, over the decades for the three sectors, shows that share of primary sector (agriculture and allied activities) declined while the share of tertiary sector (service) and secondary sector have (manufacturing) increased over the decades. The increase in share of the tertiary sector is more significant than the increase in the share of the secondary sector.

Such structural changes in the economy are instrumental in bringing structural change in occupational pattern. Apart from the structural change in the economy, technological change also played a crucial role in bringing structural change in the occupational pattern in India. Technology is an important element in the distribution of the labour force amongst industries and sectors of the economy. The decrease of employment in agriculture over the decades and the virtual constancy in the proportion of the labour force employed in manufacturing are attributable primarily to technological change.

Usually, technological changes induce change in occupational structure through:

1. Creation of new functions,
2. Dilution of skills,
3. Substitution of manpower for technology, and finally
4. Variation in the range of existing functions.

Again from the economic point of view, technology brings changes in the labour market. It is widely believed, particularly by the Marxist school of thought, that with technology, production becomes increasingly capitalistic, which again leads to the emergence of wage earners. This for its far-reaching effect transforms labour as an item of competitive sale and purchase and labour units further become more and more specific. Interestingly this smoothened the path of development of the occupational labour market. All these factors together helped in the emergence of the educated white-collar working class.

Since technology significantly induces change in the production system, sectoral distribution of employment change is not considered as a better indicator to signify changes in occupational pattern. However, from the latest census report, we find that while sectoral distribution of employment in agriculture over decades shows a decreasing trend and secondary sector shows a marginal increase, the tertiary or service sector indeed shows a significant increasing trend in percentage share of employment.

Distribution of different occupational categories over the decades, shows that professional, technical and related workers have increased. A significant rise in clerical and related workers and workers in unclassifiable jobs, also indicates a major change in the pattern of occupational structure in India.

Technology Upgradation and Employment in India

During the post liberalisation era, macro-level economic restructuring vis-à-vis unit level production restructuring is taking place, which inter alia, displace a large section of the working population from employment. Macro-level change in employment levels due to economic liberalisation has already been focused earlier. What is more important to mention here is that Indian industries are now required to restructure their production by introducing technology and efficient systems to make their product qualitatively better to compete with international manufacturers. This, therefore, necessitates Indian industry to undertake redeployment programme of their existing workers by giving them suitable training. Government of India to counter this burden of unemployment started the National Renewal Fund (NRF), which will extend facilities for training and redeployment programmes, or for financing the voluntary retirement, production restructuring, displacement of labour forces, upon flexibilisation of labour, wages, working hours and even work allocation.

To make them globally competitive, Indian industries are required to upgrade their technology, which *inter alia*, will result in large-scale displacement, as discussed earlier. In addition, technology introduction will also change the occupational pattern by changing the job content of industrial employees.

Apart from change in occupational pattern, Indian industries are also likely to face wage flexibility (both in paid wages and non-paid wages). This trend is already evident as we now find wide wage disparity between organisations, even though they are operating in the same region and manufacturing the same items or providing the same services.

Flexible working hours (FWH) is also another important change at the organisation level. Although FWH in the form of staggered duty hours has been in vogue for certain categories of employment and industries (both for convenience and technical feasibility), customer-orientation is now forcing many organisations (more particularly those who render services) to adopt a more institutionalised approach to FWH. The present state-of-art-technology is more flexible. To produce as per customers' requirements is now compelling the organisations to change their prevalent practice of producing only some specific varieties. Such is also the trend in service organisations. Therefore, to accommodate the growing variety of products and to make organisations more transparent, flexible manufacturing systems are now increasingly being adopted. This technology is also instrumental in influencing the job content of workers and/or employees. Trade specific skills and even, if not in all cases, at least in some cases, industry-specific skills are now being diluted due to commonness of technology. To achieve better functional efficiency, jobs are now being restructured and workers are being trained to man such restructured positions in organisations. In most of the organisations, horizontal expansion of jobs (job enlargement) is making work allocation more flexible. Service organisations are also considering in principle to confer double designation to their workers to ensure more productive utilisation of human resources.

SUMMARY

Productivity and technology are two important constructs of HRM. Attributing productivity to labour efficiency alone, i.e., single factor approach, is a misnomer. Globally productivity is now considered as sum-total efficiency, i.e., total factor approach. Productivity trends have direct relationship to employment and manpower planning in an organisation. Achieving productivity is possible both by short-term and long inventions, which among others also encompass HRD. Technology offers occupational pattern and employment structure. Technology, organisational systems and productivity together influence manpower planning both at macro-and micro-level.

KEYWORDS

Single Factor Productivity	Total Factor Productivity
Work Study	Occupational Pattern
National Renewal Fund	BIFR
Corporate Sickness	Flexible Working Hours

REVIEW QUESTIONS

1. Briefly discuss the concept of productivity. What contributions have been made by the economists towards the development of productivity?
2. What are your suggestions to improve productivity? Answer this question relating your observation to the experience of an organisation.
3. What are the factors responsible for failure of productivity in an organisation? Give your answer with specific reference to the Indian industries.
4. Define total factor productivity. Explain how it relates to the study of each functional area of an organisation.
5. Do you think corporate sickness is primarily attributable to the failure of the organisation to achieve increased productivity? Justify selecting a sick unit (refer to the annual reports of a sick unit and then answer).
6. Do you think in India we are experiencing a change in the occupational pattern? Justify your answer.
7. In what way does technology upgradation influence employment in India?
8. Write short notes on:

   (a) BIFR

   (b) Total Factor Productivity Indices

(c) Financial Ratios

(d) National Renewal Fund

(e) Non-moving and Slow-moving Inventories

(f) Production Planning and Control

PRODUCTIVITY GAME

In the table below, we have presented the indices of Partial Labour Productivity, Partial Capital Productivity and Total Factor Productivity for the years 1985-86 to 1988-89, which are taken from the published documents (1997) of *Indian Labour Year Book*, 1995, Labour Bureau, Shimla.

(Base 1970-71 = 100)

S. No	Industry Type	Partial Labour Productivity Indices				Partial Capital Productivity Indices				Total Factor Productivity Indices			
		85-86	86-87	87-88	88-89	85-86	86-87	87-88	88-89	85-86	86-87	87-88	88-89
1.	Hydrogenated oils (vanaspati)	380	423	532	252	298	280	376	286	338	343	447	267
2.	Edible oils (other vanaspati)	286	167	261	332	186	104	167	130	222	126	201	180
3.	Tea processing	219	210	300	230	316	285	422	311	269	250	361	272
4.	Cotton textiles	130	135	278	90	130	142	336	122	130	137	288	90
5.	Tyres and tubes	223	240	249	279	190	222	322	540	201	228	289	396
6.	Petroleum refineries	1566	1386	1094	908	989	832	620	590	1090	922	696	646
7.	Chemicals & chemical products	476	520	562	619	393	350	385	444	420	400	439	500
8.	Cement lime & plaster	207	188	305	430	167	112	179	253	182	136	218	310
9.	Iron & steel	197	169	227	304	177	147	193	290	193	165	221	302
10.	Ship building and repairing	142	160	171	156	103	102	105	96	139	154	166	151

Study the productivity trends under different categories and argue whether different productivity measures have any interrelationship. Which measure(s) are more appropriate for HRM.

UNIT 5

Job Analysis and Job Design

Learning Objectives

After completion of this unit, the students will be aware of the following topics:

- *Introduction*
- *Job Analysis*
- *Job Questionnaire*
- *Job Descriptions*
- *Job Specifications*
- *Job Evaluation*
- *Job Design*
- *Job Assessment*
- *Work Measurement*
- *Concept and Definition of Ergonomics*
- *Motion Economy*
- *Human Engineering*
- *Value Analysis*

KELLOGG'S JOB ANALYSIS

Globally, many are facing huge employment related litigations. Analyses of such litigations indicate that most of these are for inconsistent human resource management practices, both in the case of recruitment and subsequent promotion of employees. Reasons for such inconsistencies can be attributed to improper job analysis. Realising such potential problem of employment related litigation, Kellogg, a multinational food services company based in the U.S.A. initiated the process of job analysis to redefine the numerous job titles and integrate the same with their HR practices. Globally, Kellogg employs more than 30,000 people. The company has manufacturing units in 18 countries and sells their products across the world (in more than 180 countries). Kellogg was established in 1906 and is now a Fortune 500 company. It is the largest producer of cereal and convenience foods and during the year 2007, the company could achieve sales to the tune of $11 billion.

The need for job analysis was initially envisaged by the company to mitigate possible employment related litigations. Subsequently, however, the company could realise, that job analysis helped them in effective HR decision making, including managing of talents and at the same time, developing the integrated people management practices.

To perform the job analysis, Kellogg involved the leaders and other stakeholders, and made the entire process participative. The holistic and systematic approach of performing job analysis could help the company with detailed job descriptions, requirements of qualifications and skills for the job performance, job families, career progression paths and approaches to career development, job-wise functional and technical competency models and finally, the documented competency based recruitment and selection process.

INTRODUCTION

For HRM in an organisation, effective information and documentation on job analysis, job description and job evaluation are important prerequisites. All these processes help in identifying job requirements and suitably describing the job and job-families, skill sets, skill mapping and developing skill inventories in an organisation. In HRM, these are critical inputs to decide about manpower requirement to meet present and future needs. Although we have briefly discussed these concepts in other units, here we will be discussing these in detail to understand their importance in HRM.

Job information is one essential input for effective HRP. It not only facilitates job evaluation for compensation designing but also helps in disseminating information to employees about their duties and responsibilities. Imperfect knowledge of employees about their duties and responsibilities due to inadequate job information also affect their performance and overall organisational productivity. Disseminating job information in the 'Letter of Appointment' may not be adequate. Proper documentation and communication in induction training is the right approach.

- The first objective of job information is to communicate duties and responsibilities attached to a job to the employees for their clear understanding. This also helps employees to understand organisational expectations from them.

- Another objective of job information is organisational analysis. It helps in work flow analysis with respect to a job and also helps in identification of redundant work elements in a job and thus facilitates in job restructuring.

- For HRP, job information helps in analysing the scope for internal hiring and the requirements of external hiring for staffing various positions in the organisation.
- In setting performance standards and establishing job objectives, job information is essential both in qualitative and quantitative terms. This also facilitates in appraising performance of an employee against such set standards more scientifically.
- For other HR related decisions like; promotion, transfer, relocation, redundancy and compensation designing, job information provides critical inputs.

JOB ANALYSIS

Job analysis is the process of gathering information about the job and evaluating such information in terms of what is necessary and relevant. Essentially, job analysis involves three questions: What is a job? What should be analysed? What methods of analysis should be used?

A job is a group of essentially similar activities or tasks performed by a person or a group of persons. These activities or tasks together become a job. Obviously tasks or activities of jobs need not be identical. They may be performed in different places, with different equipment, in a different sequence. Also, some employees may perform certain activities in addition to the main job. Or some employees may perform a job occasionally or temporarily, normally to fill in for persons who are absent or on vacation. This definition of a job is typically used in compensation designing and for other management practices. However, a more generic description of a job is used, which is identified by 'position' rather than 'job'. A position is a family of jobs in which specific duties vary but some interchangeability of work is possible and the functional nature of the work is similar. Examples include assemblers, clerk-cum-typists, and book-keepers. Broader definition of a job, facilitates development of accurate job information and this accurately reflects the work of each employee. While on the other hand, the more precise the job definition, the more difficult it is to identify the job differences, which further complicates the management of employees.

Another basic issue for job analysis is whether the organisation should measure work assigned or work actually performed. Some compensation designing experts argue that unless job analysis considers work performed, the organisation may not account for employees' credit for what they are actually doing. On the other hand, analysing work performed may imply that employees have been given latitude to assign work to themselves. While in reality it is the manager's responsibility to assign a job. The role of a analyst is essentially to gather job information and not to evaluate the logic of work assignments. He is primarily responsible for recording of those responsibilities that a manager has assigned to an employee.

What should be Analysed?

What should be the nature of job information for job analysis, depends upon a number of considerations. Whether the analysis is required for evaluation purposes or for other purposes as well; what job level is to be analysed; what type of evaluation plan is to be used; and what job knowledge is held by the analyst who is going to conduct the evaluation. Certain basic areas of information may include:

- Fundamental purpose of the job.
- Work elements in the job. It requires study of specific tasks, areas of responsibility, and examples of work.
- General importance of each job element and its relationship to the total operation. How it is integrated with the total job?
- Approximate time spent on each task or specific area of responsibility.
- Scope of the job and its impact on the operation.
- Inherent authority (not only formal delegation but also latitude of action) and formal or informal audits of work.
- Working relationships (including supervision).
- Specific methods, equipment or techniques, that are required for the job.
- Job climate, including objectives and work environment.
- Job conditions like physical effort, hazards, discomfort, chasing of deadlines, travel requirement, creativity and innovations required, etc.

What Methods of Analysis should be Used?

Job information can be obtained in various ways either by a staff analyst or by the individual line manager. Because of functional proximity, it is always better to involve the line managers in compiling job information. One relatively simple and inexpensive method of analysis is collecting of job information through the questionnaire response. Direct observation of work performed is another important method of job analysis. Observation of work is essential to understand the job role. However, it is more costly and time-consuming.

Valuable job information can also be obtained from organisation manuals, time-study reports, former job descriptions, and method studies.

JOB QUESTIONNAIRE

A job questionnaire is a special tool for consolidating job information. It is a printed form, in which essential information about the job may be listed either by the employee or by his supervisors. The major advantage of the job questionnaire is that it uses the knowledge of those who are proximate to the job. In addition, it gives each employee an opportunity to participate and contribute by giving responses to the questionnaire, which facilitates immediate compilation of job information.

Another important advantage of job questionnaire is that compiled information can be used as job descriptions. This, therefore, eliminates the requirement of further writing of job descriptions. Moreover, by using a job questionnaire, organisations also get the benefit of communicating the up-to-date job information to the employees.

However, the major disadvantages associated with job questionnaire are that, its success depends on the understanding and writing ability of individual employees and supervisors. For perceptual incongruence, inconsistencies in the response pattern may arise. Such inconsistencies in the response pattern may multiply further when more cross-section of people participate in the questionnaire response/survey. In addition, compiling job information from the questionnaire response again may suffer from the problem of exaggeration. These are the inherent problems of information quality through job questionnaire.

To eliminate such inherent problems of compiling job information through job questionnaire, it is always better to compile the information through a combination of direct observation and job questionnaire. This approach may be time consuming and involve huge cost, but is more scientific as it eliminates the chance of error by both accounting the perceptive differences between what they perceive and what they do.

The Position Analysis Questionnaire (PAQ)

Recently there has been increased concern about quantification of the process of job analysis. A structured Position Analysis Questionnaire (PAQ) can help the process. The PAQ was developed in the early 1970s through the efforts of McCormick and others. It consists of 194 job elements of a "worker-oriented" nature which are divided into six major categories. The job elements are normally rated by the analyst on a scale of 0 to 5. However, administering PAQ is not at all simple.

JOB DESCRIPTIONS

Compiled job information is translated to job descriptions. Job descriptions are written records of job duties and responsibilities and they provide a factual basis for job evaluation. Job descriptions are recorded on a standard form in a uniform manner.

For the obvious requirement of writing skill in the preparation of job descriptions, many organisations assign this task to trained and professional job analysts. However, this by itself cannot guarantee flawless job descriptions. This is because a professional job analyst may not have specific job knowledge. Therefore, despite engaging an analyst, it is always better to involve the in-house people for scientific description of jobs.

In terms of format, the job description should first name the job, using the title which accurately summarises duties assigned. While naming a job, it is always better to consider the job family. To illustrate, instead of naming a HR job as HR Manager, if the term 'Knowledge Manager' is used, it may give a contemporary or trendy job title but for the others (including members within the organisation) it may be a misnomer. Secondly, job description should then document in a single form (frequently with short sentences or phrases) a list of duties assigned. What is to be included, while listing the job duties and how those are to be written will depend on the level of the position and the purpose to be served by the description. For the top management level, a job description may be the description of the business goals and objectives. While, at the operational level, job descriptions may be limited to listing of specific duties performed, equipment used, and procedures followed. The broader the use of the job description information and the higher the functional level, the longer the job description.

Therefore for operational positions, job description may be about one page, while for higher management, it may run through pages.

Should Employees See their Job Descriptions?

Today's organisations are dynamic and every now and then require restructuring, which also necessitates redesigning of jobs. Therefore, it is widely believed that showing a job description to employees may cause controversy and in future employees may resist doing work which are not specifically listed in their job descriptions. However, if job descriptions are well developed, there is nothing wrong in sharing them with the employees, as it spells out the list of duties employees are expected to perform. To eliminate the problem, an all inclusive statement like 'in addition to the listed duties and responsibilities, your superior may ask you to perform other tasks from time to time' can be considered.

By sharing job descriptions with employees, organisations can make their job evaluation process participative and avoid any dissonance on job evaluation results. This is also important, as organisations are also laden with employees' dissatisfaction on job pricing. Communication of job descriptions enhance acceptance of the same, as employees are not left with any doubts about their duties and responsibilities. Such communication with the employees should be an on-going exercise, as employees also can understand their changed job duties and responsibilities, if any.

Objectives of Job Description

Job descriptions help in getting the things done through people and it helps management to accomplish following objectives:

1. Efficient organisation of jobs.
2. Proper recruitment or staffing in the organisation.
3. Assigning jobs to people by communicating to them their duties and responsibilities and by setting job standards.
4. Reviewing performance of the people.
5. Improving performance through appraisal and training.
6. Rewarding employees.

Therefore, job descriptions play a very crucial role in key management activities. However, it is very important for the manager to ensure that job descriptions are correct and whatever jobs have been assigned are essential. He must ensure that essential tasks have only been grouped into jobs. Since job descriptions have interconnectivity, he has to align it to recruitment, performance appraisal, training needs, promotion, transfer and relocation decisions. From employees' point of view, it should also show employees what is expected of them how to do the work assigned.

By listing assigned duties in a job description, a manager can determine reasonable performance standards. Identification of such performance standards facilitate benchmarking of performance of an employee against the best performer.

Job descriptions also facilitate proper manpower utilisation. By periodic reviewing of the listed duties, a manager can identify which jobs are time consuming but require lower skill-set. He can reassign such jobs accordingly to lower-paid employees. In addition, the manager can also study jobs in terms of workload and determine man-hours required. For low technology and low-skill jobs, he can consider the decision to off-load the job to subcontractors. Therefore, it has tremendous implication for effective HRP in an organisation. We may call this also an instrument for proper rightsizing of employees in an organisation.

Finally, job descriptions, as a basic management tool, also influence operating procedures by identifying duplication of work, indicating a scientific work flow, suggesting better allocation of jobs and by pointing out possible job bottlenecks.

A central peripheral relational model of job analysis is given below:

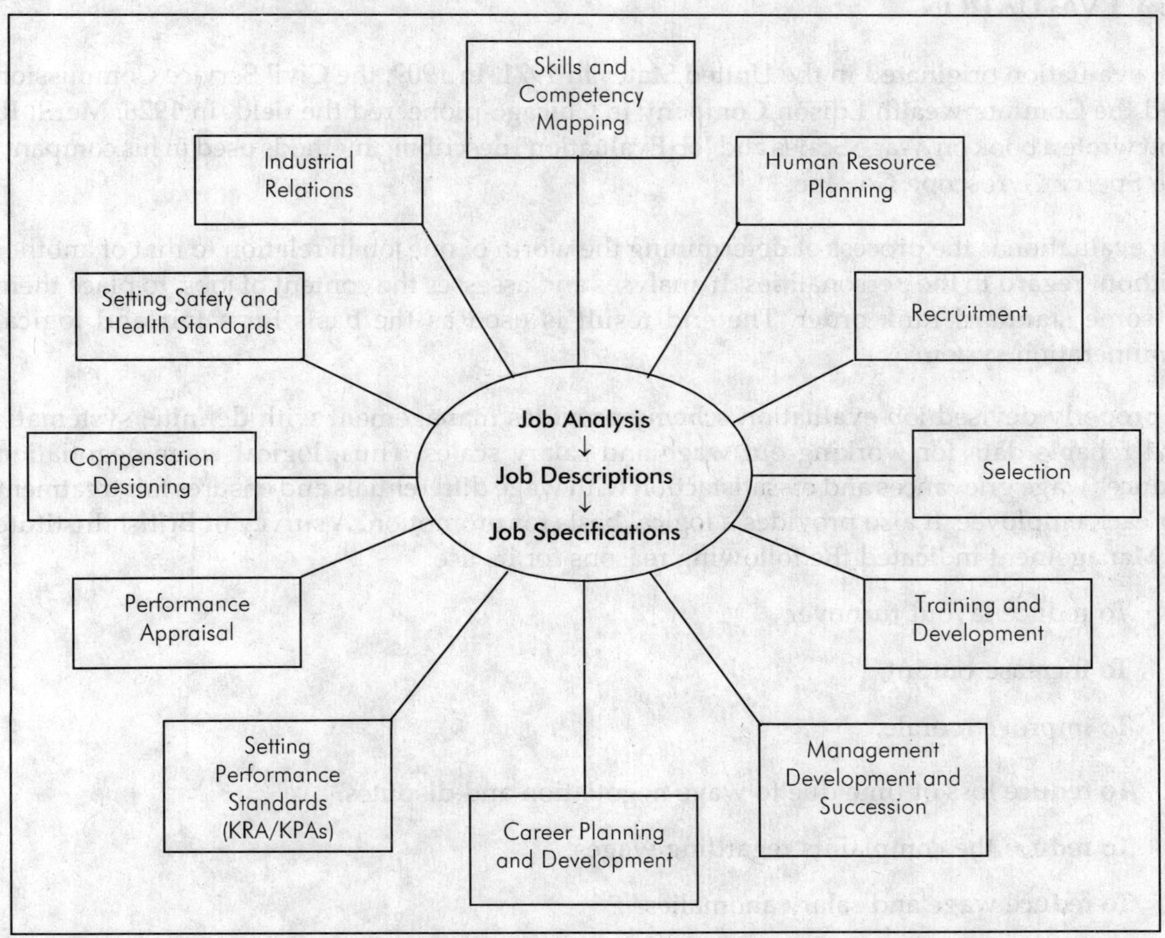

Figure 5.1: Peripheral Relational Model

JOB SPECIFICATIONS

In addition to providing information about duties associated with job assignments, job descriptions also outline basic specifications of the job. Such specifications include education or experience, required to do the job and special knowledge and skill set necessary to carry out the job. In addition, specifications also identify the soft skills like interpersonal skills, analytical ability, problem-solving skills or decision-making skill, etc., which are required to perform the duties assigned.

This exercise of processing job information is known as developing job specification. It helps in the evaluation of jobs and at the same time it defines the attributes required for a job position, which are required while going for recruitment. Therefore, job specifications list out all those attributes, like education, experience, age, physical fitness, etc., along with other soft skills required for performing a job. This also requires special skill of the analyst, as any judgemental mistake, may defeat the purpose, not only by selecting a wrong person for a job but also for wrongly evaluating a job, which is directly associated with job pricing.

JOB EVALUATION

Job evaluation originated in the United States in 1971. In 1909, the Civil Service Commission and the Commonwealth Edison Company in Chicago pioneered the field. In 1926, Merill R. Lott wrote a book on 'Wage Scales and Job Evaluation', describing methods used in his company, the Sperry Gyroscope Co., Inc.

Job evaluation is the process of determining the worth of one job in relation to that of another without regard to the personalities. It analyses and assesses the content of jobs, to place them in some standard rank order. The end result is used as the basis for a fair and logical remuneration system.

A properly devised job evaluation scheme provides management with definite, systematic and reliable data for working out wage and salary scales. Thus, logical wage negotiation reduces wage grievances and dissatisfaction with wage differentials and ensures fair treatment for each employee. It also provides a logical basis for promotion. A survey of British Institute of Management indicated the following reasons for its use:

1. To reduce layout turnover,
2. To increase output,
3. To improve morale,
4. To reduce loss of time due to wage negotiation and disputes,
5. To reduce the complaints regarding wages,
6. To reduce wage and salary anomalies.

Steps in Job Evaluation

1. Thorough examination of the job (job assessment),
2. Preparation of job description (recording its characteristics to suit assessment of method),
3. Preparation of job analysis to set out the requirements of the job under various factor headings,

4. Comparison of one job with another,
5. Arrangement of jobs in a progression,
6. Relating the progression of jobs to a money scale.

Types of Job Evaluation Schemes

There are four basic types of job evaluation, which can be enumerated as follows:

1. *Ranking:* This is a simple system to judge each job as a whole to understand its relative worth by ranking one whole job against another job. To start with, a job description is prepared in a narrative form, starting with duties, responsibilities and qualifications, required for the job. Jobs are then ranked in order of relative difficulty or value to the company and grade levels are then defined and wage levels are finalised. One of the disadvantages of this method is that the degree of difference between jobs cannot be indicated. Ranking, therefore, may be incorrect and unduly influenced. Relative value of the employees (currently occupying the jobs) may be ranked rather than the jobs. The method may be adequate for the easily defined jobs of a small number of workmen but it is regarded as impractical for complicated jobs and large number of workmen.
2. *Classification:* This is different from ranking as in this case grade and wage levels are predetermined before jobs are ranked and descriptions are written defining the type of job which should fall into each group. Under this method, usually a committee allocates jobs to each group using job description. The system is simple but suffers from limitations similar to the ranking system.
3. *Points Rating:* Under this system, to achieve a higher level of accuracy, each job is broken down into its component factors or characteristics and then evaluated separately rather than evaluating the job as a whole. A narrative job description is prepared and supplemented by a statement of the various requirements (present in the job). Characteristics like experience and training, mental and physical effort, common to the jobs are selected and a point value for each characteristic or factor is determined. Factors are defined objectively and points are given to each factors based on its estimated importance. Consolidated point values are finally converted into money terms.
4. *Factor Comparison:* This method is also similar to the points rating system as here also each job is broken into factors. The only difference, here five factors are used, i.e. mental requirements, skill requirements, physical requirements, responsibility and working conditions. After job descriptions, key jobs are judged and related to one another. The jobs are considered one by one and reviewed to understand how much of the current wage rate for the job is paid for each factor. Key jobs are arranged in a scale in order of their value for each factor.

Remaining jobs are compared with the key job factors and a comparative money value is determined for each factor in each individual job. The total of the factor values so determined for each job represents its rate. This is a complex system, however, higher degree of accuracy can be attained through this.

Limitations of Job Evaluation

Job evaluation alone cannot establish a wage scale. For wage fixation, we need to take into cognizance statutory requirements, like Minimum Wages Act, 1948. Similarly, other factors of wage fixation like, capacity to pay, inter-industry wage variation, inter-regional wage variation, collective bargaining agreement, if any, also need to be given importance. Job evaluation is highly subjective (being based on judgemental estimate). Similarly, it cannot take into account the cyclical effect of market value of occupations. For example, finance jobs were highly priced in the market at one point of time (now IT and marketing has taken its place). However, with the failure of NBFC, finance jobs are not that highly priced in the market, at least, at this point of time, even though no material change in the job profile of finance professionals has taken place in between. Despite such limitations, job evaluation technique is considered very useful for reasons explained earlier.

JOB DESIGN

Every work undergoes constant modification because of the impact of mechanisation and automation. Some jobs become redundant while others are created and still others are altered in content. This necessitates different types of education, experience and other attributes. Also for effecting job design, the organisation needs to respect the unions, who otherwise may stall the move on one ground or the other.

While designing a job, management must also be concerned with the practical considerations of quantity and quality of available personnel (both within the organisation and in the labour market). Personality conflict and friction, problem of human relations, boredom, obsessive thinking, etc., also need to be taken care of.

Thus the factors, which are likely to affect job design can be enumerated as follows:

1. Job specialisation and repetitive operations,
2. Changing technology,
3. Labour-union policies,
4. Abilities of present personnel,
5. Adequate availability of potential personnel,
6. Interaction among jobs with the system, and
7. Psychological and social needs that can be met by the job.

JOB ASSESSMENT

At this stage information about each job is made available to the assessors. Every job, whether manual or not, is closely observed and inspected in actual operation by the assessors. If required, assessors question the operators and their supervisors to collect further details about the job to clear doubts if any. To keep pace with the changing job content, due to technological changes, it is necessary to make periodic assessment of the job keeping in view the old job description.

Pricing Job Value

The purpose of job evaluation is to establish the relative job value within the organisation in terms of points or rankings and in terms of pay levels. The next step is to translate these data into a pay structure through job-co-relation. This, therefore, involves first deciding the pay grades and then developing pay ranges for each grade.

Steps in Job Pricing

The initial process of pricing the job and fitting them into a pay structure calls for translating the points into different job grades. Thereafter jobs have to be grouped as per different pay grades and the result is related with comparable jobs in other companies. However, this may not be possible for jobs which are unique in nature. When jobs are properly grouped, it is not difficult to price each such job group. After pricing each job group, pay structure can be developed on the mathematical principle that 'things which are equal to the same things are equal to each other'.

From the survey report of other companies, base salaries for each pay grade are established considering the average paid by the companies surveyed.

The next step in job pricing is to develop pay ranges around the base salaries. Once this is developed, individual compensation based on performance and other considerations can be worked out. Different pay ranges enable an organisation to adopt a flexible approach (within the range) in hiring new employees, taking into cognizance the labour market flexibility.

To illustrate, for a manufacturing organisation, a Fitter may have a pay grade ranging between ₹ 5,000-10,000 per month. This pay grade can be broken into different ranges, like, Fitter Grade-I ₹ 8,000-10,000 per month, Fitter Grade-II ₹ 6,000-8,000 per month, Fitter Grade-III ₹ 5,000-6,000 per month.

Other Methods of Job Assessment

There are various other methods of job assessment for pricing a job value, which is essential for compensation designing. At the same time such methods ensure job simplification and humanisation of jobs. Even though some of these method do not directly contribute to job pricing, these are still useful for achieving productivity and efficiency. In the subsequent part of this unit, we have discussed such methods briefly.

Work Study

Work study literally implies study of human work. British Standards Institute 3138 : 1969 defined work study as:

A management service based on those techniques, particularly method study and work measurement, which are used in the examination of human work in all its contexts and which lead to the systematic investigation of all the resources and factors which affect the efficiency and economy of the situation being reviewed, in order to effect improvement.

Thus it is a generic term for two interdependent techniques, i.e., method study and work measurement. In the said British standard, methods study has been defined as: "The systematic recording and critical examination of the factors and resources involved in existing and proposed ways of doing work, as means of developing and applying easier and more effective methods and reducing costs." Work measurement on the other hand is defined by the British Standards Institute as "the application of techniques designed to establish the time for a qualified worker to carry out a specified job at the defined level of performance."

Contextual analysis of the agreed definition of work study given by the British Standards Institute, therefore, enables us to define the subject as a procedure for understanding and determining the truth about the activities of the people, plant and machineries, identifying the factors which affect their efficiency and achieving economy through their optimum utilisation. Most of the productivity improvement techniques involve major capital expenditure in plant or equipment. Work study being a management technique, on the other hand, ensures productivity by using existing resources. In work study, human element is emphasised and importance is given to operation rather than to the technical process. This, therefore, assists management in following three major ways, which are actually its primary objectives:

1. Effective use of plant and equipment
2. Effective use of human effort
3. Evaluation of human work

Human Context of Work Study – Trade Union's Response

If work study techniques are not properly applied, they are likely to encounter resistance at all levels. Therefore, it is important to understand the human reactions and design the programme investigation and implementation accordingly. Most of the unions by now are aware that work study provides benefits to the workers by eliminating drudgery, frustration and unhealthy working environment. So also it gives an opportunity to the workers to increase their earnings at the micro-level and the nation as a whole at the macro-level.

However, to satisfy the unions the following three points need to be considered:

1. Workers should be consulted before the introduction of any scheme, which is likely to affect their interest, in one way or the other.
2. There should be a definite policy for those workers who will become redundant after implementation of the recommendations of the work study team.
3. The procedure to deal with the changes in the method of work and for measurement of work would be laid down and communicated to the workers.

International Labour Organisation (ILO) emphasised on the importance of such sharing of information with the workers in a resolution concerning consultation and cooperation between employers and workers at the level of the undertaking in the 35th session at Geneva in the year 1952.

Method Study

Method study is a productivity improvement step, which helps to produce same output using less resources or enables to produce more with a proportionately less increase in the inputs. Thus it reduces, the waste. Method study ensures creativity, innovativeness, optimal decision-making power, good organisational practices and better communication. It is essential to keep the following factors in mind while carrying out a method study:

1. Economic considerations
2. Technical considerations
3. Human reactions

Role of Method Study

Summarising, the above discussions, we can, therefore enunciate the role of method study as follows:

1. To appraise the purpose and objectives of the organisation
2. To asses the tasks of the organisation
3. To evaluate the communication and control structure of the organisation
4. To optimise the use of resources of the organisation
5. To improve the procedures, methods and processes of the organisation
6. To ensure individual and group effectiveness and at the same time satisfaction of work in the organisation.

Importance of Method Study

The objective of method study is to find better ways of doing things and to contribute to the improved efficiency by eliminating unnecessary work, avoidable delays and other forms of waste. Through systematic recording, analysis and critical examination of methods and movements involved in the performance of existing or proposed ways of doing work, it achieves the above stated objectives. However, importance or objectives of method study would be more clear once we review its contributions that flow from its above role. The contributions of method study could be indicated below:

1. Reorientation of the corporate objectives and mission
2. Review of the plans and programmes
3. Evaluation of the tasks, targets and available resources

4. Balancing the structure of the organisation
5. Introduction of a good communication system in the organisation
6. Better design of plant and equipment
7. Simplification of processes and methods
8. Standardisation of products and procedures
9. Improvement of work flow
10. Planning and control of work
11. Managing resources, inventory control and replacement of plant and machinery
12. Quality and cost control
13. Improving the layout of the shop floor
14. Betterment of working environment and working conditions
15. Optimum utilisation of resources
16. Higher standards of safety, security and health
17. Performance satisfaction.

Basic Procedure of Method Study

The method study technique is flexible enough to accommodate different given situations, however, a simple framework for its application in any given circumstances may be designed as follows:

Select	:	the work to be studied
Record	:	all the relevant facts of the present (or proposed method)
Examine	:	facts critically and in sequence
Develop	:	the most practical, economic and effective methods, with due regard to all contingent circumstances
Install	:	that method as a standard practice
Maintain	:	that standard practice by regular routine checks

Even though, we have indicated five basic steps in a particular order in the actual study, it does not necessarily follow that sequence or pattern. Selection of the subject of study may be preceded by the possibility of data collection. Similarly, preliminary critical examination (pilot study) may be needed in order to identify the problem area. During a pilot study, there may be need for more detailed data. Or, it may be revealed during preliminary critical examination that the real problem is something other than the selected one. Thus sticking to a rigid procedure of analysis may often mar the prospect of getting a productive solution.

In method study, there should not be any veil of secrecy. Discussion, exchange of views and efforts at mutual understanding are part of every basic step of method study. There are several undefined stages. Before implementation, the final plan has to be discussed with all concerned. Similarly, installing the new system has to be preceded by a plan to familiarise all concerned through reorientation programmes. After installation, the system has to be maintained to ensure that this becomes an accepted standard.

The steps of method study, therefore, may be enumerated as below:

1. Initial data collection
2. Preliminary/pilot survey and assessment
3. Identification of problem areas
4. Collection and assembly of data concerning the factors
5. Determining their interconnection
6. Finalising the subjects for study
7. Defining the problems/subject for study
8. Assessment of their impact/reaction
9. Evolving alternatives
10. Deciding optimal solutions
11. Testing the solutions
12. Preparation of the report
13. Presentation of recommendations
14. Decision on implementation
15. Preparation for implementation
16. Installation of the newly evolved system
17. Maintenance of the newly installed system
18. Evaluation of improvements achieved

Detailed Procedures Steps in Method Study

Procedures/steps in detail in any method study investigation may be enumerated as follows:

1. ***Selection of the Job:*** Once the method study idea is conceived, the first step is orientation and determination of objectives. The problem must be defined. The method study investigator faces the following types of problem:

   (a) Bottlenecks, which disrupt smooth flow of materials or processes.

(b) Products which may have to be produced economically by application of cost-reducing techniques.

(c) Economic utilisation of space, including land and buildings.

(d) Economic utilisation of labour, material and plant

(e) Elimination of idle item or non-value adding time caused due to problems of flow, queues and congestion.

While selecting the subjects for study, it is essential to keep in mind that the ultimate objective of the method study is to improve achievement by raising the level of productivity and increasing satisfaction at work. Secondly, the term 'select' should not be taken in a narrow sense, i.e., to choose from among others, but it must include a preliminary survey, which enables the investigator to decide on the continuity of the study. Similarly, select does not necessarily mean just selection of the job but also selection of the appropriate techniques to achieve the end-result.

2. *Record the Facts:* Before discarding the existing method or procedure, adequate facts about the present system must be collected. This is required to prepare an objective record of the way the job is carried out. To eliminate the change of bias, this record is not compiled from second hand accounts or on the manager's version as to how he thinks the job is done or an operator's description of how the job is done, but is based on direct observation by the concerned investigator.

3. *Critically Examine the Facts:* It is also an important stage of method study. Information collected is scrutinised in this stage and each part of the job critically examined to determine whether any part may be:

(a) Eliminated altogether

(b) Combined with any other part of the job

(c) Changed in sequence

(d) Simplified to reduce the content of the work involved.

For effective examination of the facts, following questions are generally asked:

(a) What is done and why is it done?

(b) What it does and what that person does?

(c) Where is it done and why it is done there?

(d) When is it done and why it is done then?

(e) How is it done and why is it done this way?

By rearranging, simplifying, combining, eliminating or modifying the facts or records, a basis is obtained for an improved method.

4. *Develop the New Method:* Alternatives selected are used to reshape and develop the new method, layout or procedure. These may require test runs to determine their

feasibility. Tests of this nature may be preferably carried out at a place, away from the work site, if possible. To ease the problems of acceptance for the new method in the department, it is good to involve the department. The end result must be an improved method and must be acceptable to the departmental staff and workers. It must meet all their practical requirements and technical specifications.

5. *Instal the Method:* To instal the method, decision must be taken on ordering of new plants or material (if any), phasing in changes in production process, deciding the extent of redeployment, training, introducing new documentation procedures, setting new quality standards and test procedures. It is good to have a detailed time-table for effecting such changes. The end product of the installation stage is that the new method is in operation at the work site, the line management is in complete control and finally that all members of the department are fully conversant with the method.

6. *Maintaining the Method:* When a method has been installed, it tends to change slowly for obvious small alterations made by the operators or supervisors. A reference standard (job instruction sheet) is needed against which the job can be compared to detect any alterations. Similarly, a corresponding document for an incentive scheme, which also contains details of the standard time for each job, called a job specification, is prepared. With these data, changes in method can be detected. If changes are considered to be useful, the instruction sheet can be amended to incorporate them and if they are thought undesirable, they can be removed through line management.

WORK MEASUREMENT

ILO defined work measurement "as the application of techniques designed to establish the work content of a specified task by determining the time required for carrying it out at a defined standard of performance by a qualified worker." Conventionally it is known as time study, which is primarily carried out to determine the standard time to perform a specific task. Such time standard is used for planning and scheduling work, for cost estimating or for labour cost control or it may serve as the basis for a wage incentive plan. But we find it has wide application in deciding a wage incentive plan.

There are different techniques of work measurement. However, the following are the principal techniques:

1. Time study
2. Ratio-delay study (statistical sampling technique)
3. Synthesis from standard data
4. Predetermined motion time standard
5. Analytic estimating

Out of all these, only time study technique is widely used, others being complicated in nature. Here also we will discuss in detail the time study only, while simply defining the other techniques.

Time Study

ILO defined time study as "a technique for determining as accurately as possible from a limited number of observations the time necessary to carry out a given activity at a defined standard of performance." For carrying out a time study, equipment like stopwatch, study board, pencils, slide rule, etc., are required. The stopwatches are of different types, like

1. Stopwatch which records one minute per revolution by intervals of 1/5th of a second with a small hand recording 30 minutes.
2. Stopwatch which records one minute per revolution, calibrated in 1/100th of a minute with a small hand recording 30 minutes.
3. Decimal-hour stopwatch recording 1/100th of an hour and a small hand records up to one hour in 100 divisions.

Following steps are necessary for carrying out a time study for measurement of work:

- To collect and complete all available information about the job, which should also include surrounding conditions and so also the attribute of the operators, which are likely to affect the work.
- To record the details of the method and also to break down different operations into elements.
- To record the time taken by the operators to perform the operation (element-wise) measuring preferably with a timing device like stopwatch.
- To assess the working speed of the operators comparing the same with a predetermined normal speed.
- To convert the observed time to normal time.
- To decide the rate of allowances which may be given over and above the normal time of the operation.
- To determine the allowed time for the operation.

Other Techniques of Work Measurement

Since carrying out time study for each job is a time-consuming task, statistical techniques, i.e., ratio-delay study is often carried out. Ratio-delay is a sampling technique. Instead of going for the complete job study under ratio-delay techniques, a sufficiently large number of readings are taken at random intervals. Like all other sampling techniques, under this method also there are bound to be some errors. However, the cost of such study being less, many organisations which are having the expertise may prefer this method. Moreover, under this method as rating is not done, the time is recorded directly using a stopwatch. This method encounters no resistance from the workers.

Synthesis from standard data method synthesise time standards that are built up or synthesised from element times previously obtained from direct time-study. Most of the organisations that have an independent work study department, build up a synthetic table converting the common elements. However, some units also use such time record of other organisations as standard data. For obvious non-commonality of technology, skill, process and working environments, this type of synthesis may not always be correct.

Predetermined motion time standards have been developed for different job elements based on elementary movement. Usually, for time measurement, work factor and basic motion times are recorded in any predetermined time standards. Work study analysts use such time standards as the basis for comparing the observed time of the present workers. This enables the work study men to quickly decide the efficiency or otherwise of the workers and to give decision accordingly.

Analytical estimating is normally used in plant maintenance and repair work. This is a compromise between straight rate fixing and time study. Since maintenance and repair jobs require adequate planning and also job nature calls for creativity and innovativeness, it is difficult to enforce straight rate fixing. Analytical estimating is difficult in nature and also not always foolproof due to inexperience of the work-study men.

Concept and Definition of Ergonomics

Ergonomics is derived from two Greek words; ergon, meaning work and enomos, meaning laws. It is the study of the effects of work system on workers and it aims at fitting the work to the men to increase their efficiency, comfort and satisfaction. ILO defined ergonomics as:

> *The application of human biological sciences in conjunction with engineering sciences to the worker and his working environment, so as to obtain maximum satisfaction for the work which, at the same time, enhances productivity.*

Contextual analysis of the ILO definition, therefore, provides a more meaningful basis for understanding ergonomics. An ergonomist for effective accomplishment of work tries to integrate the work system (which broadly includes the tasks, working equipment, working conditions and working space) with the capabilities and requirements of work. In this process, he therefore, tries to ensure job satisfaction for the workers, which, inter alia, increases their productivity.

In all schemes of human activity, ergonomics can be applied, be it in offices, factories, shops, ships, air and even in the space. Some of the areas where ergonomics has been successfully applied are as under:

1. Design of equipment, power and hand tools.
2. Design of displays and warning systems.
3. Design of furniture, seats, rests and steps for operators.
4. Design of tools, jigs and fixtures.
5. Plant layout.
6. Improvement in working conditions and environments.
7. Computation of relaxation allowances for workers.

8. Selection, training and placement of personnel.
9. Motivation of workers.

However, for better understanding, the areas of ergonomic investigation of a work system may be grouped as given below:

1. ***Human Characteristics:*** Health, physique, anthropometric data, personal background, education, training, experience, age, sex, intelligence, aptitude, reaction time, interest, personality characteristics, temperament, attitude towards work, motivation, etc.
2. ***Work:*** Physical loads, perceptual loads, mental loads, displays and warning systems, controls, compatibility of inputs and outputs.
3. ***Working Conditions:*** Workplace layout, postures, motion and movements, fatigue, monotony and relaxation allowances, comfort, safety and health, working hours and shift work conditions.
4. ***Environment:*** Illumination, ventilation, temperature and humidity, colour dynamics, fumes, dust, odour and smoke, landscape, scenery and garden, cleanliness and sanitation.

Many alternative terms like human engineering, human factors in engineering, engineering psychology, applied experimental psychology, applied and human engineering research, man-machine system analysis, etc., are used to designate the discipline. This subject has developed during the World War II with the coordinated efforts of physiologist, psychologists and the design engineers. Its earliest application can be traced to Frederick Winslow Taylor (1856-1915). Taylor's experiments were mainly to arrive at the optimum design of equipment for specific types of work and so also to train the workers to suit them for each type of task. Frank Bunker Gilberth (1869-1924) and his wife Lillian elaborated the principles of motion economy and introduced the rest pauses and spacing out of work to reduce the fatigue and eliminate stresses. Since then, with the advancement of experimental physiology, psychology and method study, the subject delved deeper into the human make-up for better and scientific understanding of the efforts of working conditions and environment on human body and mind.

Impact of Ergonomics on Work Study

Work study, which aims at scientific analysis of a work system to increase productivity and satisfaction at work, is dependent on ergonomics for the research data on many facets of human reaction to a given work situation. Such input information makes the task of the work study practitioner more scientific and result-oriented. These input information/data mostly relate to the following areas:

1. Limits of sustained physical endurance, normal speeds of movement and optimum method of handling of controls.
2. Receptivity to sensory inputs and time required for perception of deviations.
3. Reaction time for motion output and time required for evaluation and decision-making.

4. Anthropometric data to guide the design and layout of equipment, work place and furniture.
5. Effects of different types of environmental conditions on the human being in order to generate improvements.
6. Effects of working conditions so as to raise the standards of comfort, safety and health.
7. Qualitative and quantitative analysis of factors contributing to industrial fatigue for computation of 'relaxation allowances'.

Ergonomics and Management

Ergonomics is a discipline at the service of management from the very planning and design stage of a work system. In the organisation and control of human effort directed to specific ends, management needs to have an appreciation of the human factors involved in a work system.

The findings of ergonomic research, particularly in the field of perceptual and mental loading have a special bearing on the work situation confronting managerial performance in an organisation. The aim here will be to eliminate all perceptual and mental loading that may arise from the perusal and evaluation of reports on the normal activities of the organisation, thereby highlighting only the deviations from the equilibrium state. This will permit more effective application of the managerial talent to really important problems over a wide span. In other words, ergonomics can help in increasing the productivity of managerial brain power. This single improvement, by itself, without any changes in the methods on the shop floor will lead to a spectacular increase in overall productivity of the organisations.

Working Areas

The working area of an operator may be categorised into three groups; normal, immediate and maximum working areas. The normal working area is one that can be reached by the operator using any movement up to and inclusive of a class 3 movement. This area is bounded by two arcs made by the fingers using the elbow as the pivot. The immediate working area is the surface immediately in front of the operator where the two arcs of the normal working area overlap. The maximum working area is one that can be reached by the operator using arcs made by the fingers with the shoulders as the pivot.

The space between the normal and the maximum working areas is accessible through a class 4 movement. Anything beyond the maximum working area may be reached only through a class 5 movement, including body bending or stretching. The immediate working area is most suitable for bi-manual operation. If the various equipment, materials and tools are replaced within the normal working area, they can be reached without using the upper arm and shoulder muscles. It is not desirable to place anything outside the maximum working area.

The field of vision should also be taken into account while considering working areas. The normal cone of vision, without head movement, is restricted. Covering the whole perimeter of the normal working area would impose undue eye strain and sometimes involve excessive head movements. Due care must, therefore, be taken to position all the materials well within a worker's cone of vision. In inspection work, as much of the work as possible, must take place directly in front of the operator.

For better understanding, classes of movements can be grouped under the following five categories, based on the pivots around which the body members move:

Class	Pivot	Body member movement
1	Knuckle (finger joint)	Finger(s)
2	Wrist	Hand and fingers
3	Elbow	Forearm, hand and fingers
4	Shoulder	Upper arm, forearm, hand and fingers
5	Trunk (body apart from limbs)	Torso, upper arm, forearm, hand and fingers

A similar classification is available of the movements of corresponding members of the leg. For economy of motion, the movement should be of the lowest classification possible, compatible with the normal capacity of the body member affected.

MOTION ECONOMY

Motion economy is the process of minimising the physical and perceptual loads imposed on people engaged in any type of work; whether it be in the office, the shop floor, the kitchen or at the driving wheel. It leads to better design of equipment, jigs and fixtures, hand tools, furniture and labour-saving devices. Also it facilitates better layout of offices, warehouses, plants and operating areas like office desk, work bench, aircraft, cockpit and crew compartments of armoured fighting vehicles. Application of the principles of motion economy eliminates or minimises wasteful and fatiguing movements and increases the productivity of the workers. It considers minimising movements in respect of:

1. Number of movements
2. Length of movements
3. Classification
4. Number of parts of body used
5. Necessity for control
6. Muscular force
7. Complexity of movements
8. Distances between eye fixation
9. Time required for eye fixation

For achieving motion economy, following principles have been evolved by different specialists:

1. Principle of minimum movement
2. Principle of natural movement

3. Principle of simultaneous movement
4. Principle of rhythmic movement
5. Principle of habitual movement
6. Principle of continuous movement

Simultaneous movements reduce fatigue and increase the rate of output. More fatigue is caused when only one hand is working, the other is idle. Simultaneous movements include the movements of the feet while both the hands are operating as in driving a car. Application of this principle leads to the better design of jigs, fixtures and duplication of tools, so that both hands work at similar tasks simultaneously.

The principle of symmetrical movements should be applied in conjunction with simultaneous movements. Proper balance is achieved only when the movement of one hand is the 'mirror image' or eliminates fumbling. When movements of the hands are asymmetrical, there is a tendency on the part of the operators to interpolate additional, but non-productive, movements in order to achieve balance.

Rhythm is the regular repetition of a movement pattern. It often incorporates the accentuation of a specific part of a cycle. Rhythm contributes to speed, elimination of fumbling and reduction in fatigue. Examples of rhythmic movements are; boat rowing, hammering at the smithy and drawing water from a well using a see-saw lift.

The pattern of movement should be so designed as to facilitate habituation. When a cycle of activities is performed habitually, the movements are executed almost as a reflex action. Habitual movements eliminate hesitation and increase speed of performance. Rhythm helps in speed habit formation. Tools, materials, displays and controls must always be located in the same position. The pattern must be standardised for similar types of panels, work places and equipment. Continuous movements which are smooth and curved are superior to jerky straight line movements which involve sudden changes of direction and loss of momentum. Materials, tools and jigs must be so positioned as to incorporate smooth, curved and continuous movements and eliminate undue changes of direction.

The above principles should be treated merely as guides and not rigid rules. Quite often, one principle would be in conflict with another and a proper evaluation of the principles, in their totality, would be needed for optimisation. Conditions differ from job to job. It may sometimes be necessary to compromise load over the various muscles or to give due weightage to the principle of continuous movement. It is, therefore, essential that the principles are applied with flexibility.

HUMAN ENGINEERING

Method study seeks to determine the effective combination of the man, the machine and the working environment. In doing so, it is necessary to determine which functions are better performed by men and which functions are better performed by machines. Both men and machines can surpass each other in certain ways. The question of economy again influences the man-machine combination. The term human engineering is more appropriately used to solve man-machine problems in design, operation and maintenance of plants and machinery and in fact it broadly comes under the purview of ergonomics. It is therefore, not appropriate to designate human engineering as an independent discipline, separating it from ergonomics. However, to understand the context and meaning of human engineering, it is considered necessary to define it in the context and meaning of human engineering, in line with Ernest J. McCormick. McCormick defined it as the mechanism for the adaptation of human tasks and working environment to sensory, perceptual, mental, physical and other attributes of people. This adaptation for human use applies to such functions as the design of equipment, instruments, man-machine systems and consumer products and the development of optimum work methods and work environment.

Human Engineering and Machine Design

The designer of the machine should know the way the human being functions, his body dimensions, his physical limitations and so also the conditions under which a person performs perfectly. For performing a task, a person normally does the following three things:

1. Receiving the information (through different sense organs)
2. Making decisions (acting on perceived information)
3. Taking action (which results from decision)

Thus the basic control cycle for the human being consists of these parts – sense, decide and act. The power to reason inductively, exercise judgement, develop concepts, decide and create methods are unique to human beings. While quick performing of repetitive routine tasks, power to perform rapid computations, apply great force, simultaneous performance of many different functions, etc., are characteristic features of machines.

The designer of the machine, therefore, is required to consider all the above details before developing a better designed machine for productive use. Most of the Computer Numerically Controlled (CNC) machining centres developed by large industrial organisations in India are not performing well as they have been designed without considering the human factor. In fact the sophisticated machine centres, whenever introduced, have become instrumental for perpetual industrial relations problems as these adversely affect workers pay packets as cycle time printed in the machine literature is considerably less than the actual time taken by the workers. This complicates job correlation with the workers' payment, as technically they are supposed to get payment as per the printed cycle time.

Since, a badly designed machine may be responsible for poor performance of the workers, application of ergonomics/human engineering techniques is necessary to design the machine. Modern machines are ergonomically designed to prevent stress and fatigue of the workers, to make them work at ease and at the same time to gain an increased rate of production. We also find application of human engineering/ergonomic techniques even in designing consumer products, kitchen gadgets, furniture, etc. Recently, Blow Plast Ltd., under technical collaboration with Klober of Germany, designed office-chairs ergonomically.

VALUE ANALYSIS

Henry Erlicher of General Electric Company, in 1947, drawing lessons from the World War-II, observed that substitution of materials (as manufacturers were then compelled to go for substitution to encounter shortage of original materials) often led to cost reduction and better functionality. This has prompted further research in the field of alternative materials and processes and in fact L.D. Miles, another top executive of the company, was directed by him to go into the details which was later called as value analysis. By 1949, this approach in its more institutionalised form was used in General Electric Company and gradually in the US Department of Defence. By 1970, the value engineering concept received international attention.

Value engineering is an organised creative technique to analyse functions of a product or service or a system to achieve the required functions at the lowest cost ensuring its performance reliability and maintainability. It is also known as value analysis or value management.

Literally, value is the worth of an article/product/service. In terms of cost and function, value is determined. Value of product can be improved by:

1. Improving function (keeping function constant)
2. Reducing cost (keeping function constant)
3. Both by improving function as well as by reducing cost.

There are different types of values of an industrial product, which may be classified as follows:

1. ***Use Value:*** The properties and qualities which are useful and which enable to accomplish the work. Use value again may be either for primary use, secondary use or for auxiliary use.
2. ***Esteem Value:*** Aesthetic features or properties which attract a customer to own it.
3. ***Cost Value:*** The cost required to produce the item.
4. ***Exchange Value:*** The properties which enable the owner to exchange it for anything else, if he so desires, in the future.

However, for all practical purposes, in industrial situations, we are primarily concerned with use value and esteem value only.

In the backdrop of the above discussion, value analysis, therefore, can be defined as a "method of search, a systematic procedure resulting in the orderly utilisation of alternative materials and processes. It focuses on engineering, manufacturing and purchasing with attention on one objective, that of obtaining equivalent or even better performance for lower cost."

Steps in Value Analysis

Following steps are followed for value analysis:

1. Collect full facts and information about the product
2. Get the details of the cost break-up
3. Determine the function
4. Think creatively
5. Compare and evaluate the alternatives

To succeed in each step, it is necessary to take the following line of action:

1. Eliminate the redundant parts
2. Initiate action of cheaper substitutes without impairing the use value
3. Standardise the parts
4. Develop alternative methods
5. Redesign, if necessary.

Advantages of Value Analysis

We can get the following advantages from value analysis:

1. Lowering of cost
2. Better quality of product
3. Increased efficiency
4. High level of morale and team spirit
5. Increased customer satisfaction
6. Optimum resource utilisation
7. Improved methods of production
8. Increased job satisfaction and motivation to workers through use of their creative ability.

The term value analysis has now been replaced by value engineering in corporate circles. In most of the organisations, value engineering practices are followed, forming a value engineering team of workers (a small group activity like quality circles, etc.). This, therefore, provides the opportunity to workers to derive creative satisfaction and also to fulfil their intrinsic needs. At the same time, the organisation also gets active services from the workers.

SUMMARY

For HRM, critical inputs related to a job are necessary. This in one way helps in identifying the skill sets while hiring and on the other hand also helps in compensation designing.

Although job analysis and job evaluation are considered as important techniques for such purposes, we have discussed other important areas too for understanding a job from the holistic point of view.

KEYWORDS

Value Engineering	Method Study
Job Description	Time Study
Job Analysis	Motion Economy Ergonomics
Job Information	Machine Design
Job Assessment	Job Evaluation
Job Pricing	Factor Comparison

REVIEW QUESTIONS

1. What are the purposes of job evaluation? Discuss the steps involved in job evaluation.
2. Discuss different types of job evaluation technique. Which type do you consider more suitable and why?
3. In what ways are job analysis and job assessment different? Select any job and analyse its individual content.
4. Define job analysis and its role in the HRP process. Explain briefly the elements that constitute the job analysis process.
5. How is compensation structure linked with job evaluation?
6. Define work study. What are its important objectives? Why trade unions react to a work study programme? In what way can you combat such a reaction?
7. What are the important roles of method study? Identify the important contributions of method study and discuss at least five such contributions in detail.
8. Elaborately discuss the steps involved in a method study programme.
9. Define work measurement. What are its different techniques? Discuss at least three techniques elaborately.
10. What are the steps involved in a time study programme? How does it help work measurement programmes in an industrial unit?
11. What is ergonomics? How does it help to increase productivity? Discuss with examples.
12. What are the basic principles of motion economy? Discuss these principles in relation to a work area with which you are familiar.
13. Explain how human engineering techniques influence machine design. Select an advertisement of a furniture item and discuss its ergonomic features.
14. What are the steps involved in value analysis? What course of action can you suggest for a successful value analysis study? Elaborate your answer.
15. For HRM, why it is so important for us to study different job measurement techniques?

CASE STUDY

GOODEARTH FINANCIAL SERVICES

Goodearth Financial Services Limited, has grown considerably during the last 5 years. Mr Jashpal Bhatti started the company with two employees and business for ₹ 6,00,000 in gross sales. The company now employs 200 people and is expected to have business for ₹ 6,00,00,000 this year. During the early years, it was always clear what was expected from each employee. Everyone knew how to do everything and was often called upon to do exactly that. This is no longer true and it is apparent to Mr Jashpal Bhatti that each employee must be given a clear set of general guidelines as to what duties the employee must perform.

A number of new players are now in financial services who are the arch competitors for Mr Bhatti's company. The service-mix for Goodearth also has significantly changed to keep pace with the changing customers' expectation. The company, therefore, had to change its operation strategy.

In addition, it is becoming increasingly difficult to hire employees without having a clear understanding of exactly what the individual will be doing. Applicants seem reluctant to join the firm without some information about their probable job profile and it is difficult to know exactly what skills, the prospective applicants should have without knowing in some detail what they will be doing.

Mr Jashpal Bhatti decided to write job descriptions and job specifications for his employees. It is his belief that such documents will clear any misunderstandings among employees regarding responsibilities, help to organise better the work that must be done, inform prospective employees about their probable job duties, orient new employees and help to make better selection decisions.

You have been retained by Mr Bhatti to determine whose responsibility it will be to gather the data and write the descriptions and specifications, how the data will be gathered (observation, questionnaire or interview) and how detailed descriptions and specifications should be.

Mr Bhatti is currently considering these job analysis issues but has a number of questions about how each will affect the final results.

Questions

1. What recommendations would you make to him regarding the most appropriate individuals and methods to be used for data collection?
2. What approach to the design of jobs should be considered by you and why?
3. Keeping in mind the recent trends in financial services companies, design the job of different hierarchical levels for at least four operational areas with supporting background information, like; job analysis, job description, etc.

APPENDIX 1

JOB ANALYSIS DATA SHEET

Job Title ____________________ CODE:

Other Titles

Suggested Title ____________________

Department ____________ Dept. No. ________ Dept. Head ________

No. on Job ____________ Range ________ Supervised By ________

Persons Interviewed ____________________

Analysis ____________ Date ____________ Location of Job ________

Other Identification ____________________

Job Summary (Key phrases that cover job): ____________________

Relation To Others Jobs : ____________________

Promotion From : ____________________

Promotion To : ____________________

Transfer To And From : ____________________

Work Performed: What - How - Why (Use additional sheets if required)

Major Duties : ____________________

Other Tasks : ____________________

Equipment, Machines : ____________________

Skills Involved-Physical Demands : ____________________

Experience (type and amount) : ____________________

Education and training (specific skills required) : ____________________

Responsibility for product and material : ____________________

Responsibility for equipment and machinery : ____________________

Responsibility for work of others : ____________________

Other Jobs directly affected : ____________________

Resourcefulness : ____________________

Monetary : ____________________

Visual efforts : ____________________

Physical efforts : ____________________

Surroundings : ____________________

Hazards : ____________________

APPENDIX 2

JOB DESCRIPTION

FORM NO. 2

Job Identification Data :

Present Job Title :

Department/Section :

Suggested Job Title : Date:______

Job Code :

Employees Interviewed :

Job Summary

(A) Regular Tasks :

1.

2.

3.

4.

(B) Casual Tasks :

1.

2.

3.

(C) Equipment or Machine Used :

(D) Working Conditions And Hazards :

FORM NO. 3

Job Specifications :

Job Title (Existing) : Job Code No.:______

Job Title (Suggested) :

Department/Sec	Total Points	Classification
1. Education		Points
2. Experience		Points
3. Responsibility for Product or Materials		Points
4. Responsibility for Machinery & Equipment		Points
5. Responsibility for Works of Others		Points
6. Responsibility for Safety of Others		Points
7. Manual Skill		Points
8. Physical Effort		Points
9. Working Condition including Hazards		Points

UNIT 6

Human Resource Planning

Learning Objectives

After completion of this unit, the students will be aware of the following topics:

- *Introduction*
- *Defining HRP*
- *Activities Required for HRP/Manpower Planning*
- *Responsibilities of the HR Department*
- *Steps for HRP/Manpower Planning*
- *Objectives of HRP*
- *Manpower Demand Forecasting*
- *Analysis of Performance*
- *Analysis of Productivity*
- *Macro and Micro Human Resource Planning*
- *Macro-level Manpower Planning Models and Techniques*
- *Macro-level HRP Models*
- *Labour Economics*

HUMAN RESOURCE PLANNING AT NEHA, THE STAR HOTEL OF NEW DELHI

Human resource planning is now a strategic function in organisations, as effective human resource plans ensure cost optimisation. In a competitive market, every organisation seizes the opportunity of cost optimisation through technology, process re-engineering, six-sigma and lean management practices. The only alternative that the organisations now consider is manpower cost optimisation.

Neha, a star hotel in New Delhi is now facing acute price competition from its competitors. The restructuring process could identify at least 40% food wastage in room services and unnecessary electricity consumption in rooms, even when the guest is away. After addressing all these issues, keeping customer services in their top priority, Neha now started looking for opportunities to optimise manpower cost. Internal manpower restructuring could identify surplus manpower in room services, attendants, stewards, etc. For high skill interchangeability, Neha could redeploy such surplus manpower gainfully. Almost 80% of people at Neha are taken on daily rate basis from the pool of workers who queue outside the second gate of the hotel (not exposed to the guests). Using a Simulation model, Neha could optimise such manpower requirement, which led to 10% saving of manpower cost. All these initiatives, could ultimately put Neha back in to the competitive spree.

INTRODUCTION

Comparison of the present human resources to future needs of an organisation, duly identifying skill and competency gaps and subsequently developing plans for building the human resources needed in future is the basic process of Human Resource Planning (HRP). The process not only limits its focus on such assessment but also tries to ensure that the required competency is maintained in line with organisational mission, vision and strategic objectives. HRP provides strategic basis for taking HR decisions, and anticipating change. It is not merely concerned with manpower demographics, turnover projections, succession planning, etc. Therefore, HRP helps to plan replacements and changes in manpower competencies in a systematic manner. Of late HRP has become an important enterprise-wide strategic function not only to achieve goals and objectives but also to sustain the present level in organisations. Globally, skill shortages, competency gaps, redundancies, downsizing, rightsizing are the major issues in today's organisations. Such syndromes have become so acute in Indian organisations also that almost everyday we find newspapers carrying reports on job cut or manpower redundancies. These phenomena have changed the structure of employment relations in Indian organisations, not to talk about global organisations. All major Indian organisations like, SAIL, Keltrons, IBP, Tata Iron & Steel, etc., are going for manpower redundancies in a phased manner. Commercial banking organisations in India recently reduced 30 per cent of their workforce at a whopping cost of ₹ 10,000 crore.

There are many reasons for such manpower or human resource redundancies, although at the corporate level, the only possible reason attributed to such cause is skill obsolescence. Inadequate business planning, inflexibility of job descriptions, absence of training and development programmes are some of the identified causes. But the biggest problem lies with inadequate Human Resource Planning (HRP).

With labour percentage increasing at the rate of 1.09 per cent against job opportunities of 0.96 per cent (during the period from 1993-94 to 1999-2000), large-scale manpower redundancies are further adding fuel to the fire, causing a national problem.

John Bramham (1989-94) has distinguished between HRP and manpower planning (MP). He has defined HRP as a process in which costs, numbers, controls and systems interact and play a part. While manpower planning is more concerned with the numerical elements of forecasting of manpower. However, other authors like; Benni Son and Casson (1984), Thomason (1988) have discarded such perceptual differences, arguing that HRP and manpower planning are the same thing. For our purpose also we have not conceded any difference in HRP and MP and discussed the issues from a holistic approach.

Defining HRP

Human resource or manpower is a primary resource without which other resources, physical and financial, cannot be put into use. Even a fully automatic unit requires manpower to run it and also to plan for further improvement.

To achieve any goal, manpower requirement needs to be assessed, located and harnessed. HRP is not mere assessment of the number of men required. An organisation has to categorise men as per their knowledge and skills and also ensure their balanced allocation. Improper manpower planning may lead to over-staffing increasing direct cost (viz., salary), cost of training, amenities, apart from the cost of production. Under-staffing also affects production, morale and productivity.

Optimum manpower planning, therefore, aims at:

- Balancing demand, supply, distribution and allocation of manpower
- Controlling cost of human resources
- Formulating policies on transfer, succession, relocation of manpower.

HRP / manpower planning is essential wherever production of goods and services are involved. This may be done either by external agencies (consultants, suppliers of plant and machineries) or internal agencies. (Personnel Department, Industrial Engineering Department, Production Department, etc.)

HRP is a planning process by which an organisation can move from its current manpower position to its desired manpower position. Through manpower planning, an organisation strives to have the right number and the right kinds of people at the right places at the right time. However, this definition only focuses on assessment of manpower needs in an organisation. More appropriately manpower planning may be defined as a strategy for acquisition, utlisation, improvement and retention of human resources.

Activities Required for HRP/Manpower Planning

Manpower planning consists of a series of activities, which can be listed as follows:

- ***Forecasting Future Manpower Requirements:*** This is done either in terms of mathematical projections or in terms of judgemental estimates. Mathematical projections are done extrapolating factors like, economic environment, development trends in industry, etc.

Judgemental estimates, on the other hand, are done depending on the specific future plans of a company by managerial discretion, which is based on past experience.

- *Preparing an Inventory of Present Manpower:* Such inventory contains data about each employee's skills, abilities, work preferences and other items of information. Inventory of manpower resources helps in assessing the extent of deploying such resources optimally.

- *Anticipating Problems of Manpower:* This can be done by projecting present resources into the future and comparing the same with the forecast of manpower requirements. This helps in determining the quantitative and qualitative adequacy of manpower.

- *Meeting Manpower Requirements:* This can be achieved through planning, recruitment and selection, training and development, induction and placement, promotion and transfer, motivation and compensation to ensure that future manpower requirements are correctly met.

RESPONSIBILITIES OF THE HR DEPARTMENT

HR Department, as an internal agency, plays a crucial role in manpower planning. Its responsibilities in regard to manpower planning may be summed up as follows:

- The first responsibility is to put pressure on the operating management to plan and establish objectives. HR Department at this stage is required to assist and to give counsel to the operating management groups firm time to time.

- It has to collect data in total organisation terms and to ensure that manpower planning is carried out, keeping pace with the long-range objectives and the total business plan of the organisation.

- It has to measure and monitor performance against the plan and provide feedback to the top management.

- It has to carry out research for effective manpower and organisational planning.

STEPS FOR HRP/MANPOWER PLANNING

From the above discussions, it is evident that HRP/manpower planning should precede a number of steps. Such steps can be briefly discussed as follows:

Job Analysis

To start with, job analysis is done to differentiate one job from the other. Job is defined as collection or aggregation of tasks, duties and responsibilities, which are assigned to an individual employee. Job analysis, therefore, provides requisite information about a job. It is a process of determining the nature of a specific job through a detailed and systematic study.

Job analysis provides the following information:

- Job identification, which is done by providing a title or a code number for each job.
- Job characteristics, location, physical setting, hazards and discomforts of a job.
- Job assignment, specific operations and tasks which make an assignment, its importance, simplicity, complexity and the responsibility.
- Materials, tools and equipment required for a job.
- Job performance, nature of operations (lifting, handling, drilling, setting up, etc.)
- Personal attributes, like experience, training, physical strength, mental capabilities, aptitudes, other skills, etc., required for efficient performance of the job.
- Job relationship, scope for advancement, patterns of promotions, direction or leadership form, etc.

Sources of Information

Information on a job is usually obtained from following principal sources as follows:

- From those who are supervising the job, e.g., supervisors and foreman.
- From professional job analysts (consultants), who may be retained to study a job.
- From technology vendors, who define jobs in their literatures.

Purposes of Job Analysis

Apart from HRP, job analysis serves the following important purposes of Human Resource Management:

- Recruitment and selection
- Wage and salary administration
- Job re-engineering
- Industrial engineering activity
- Employees training and management development
- Performance appraisal
- Health and safety

Job Description and Job Specification

After the job analysis process is over, job description and job specification are developed before going into the successive steps of HRP. Job description is recording of duties, responsibilities and conditions needed for satisfactory performance of a particular job. Both the terms, job description and job specification are used interchangeably. However, it is appropriate to distinguish the term 'description' to cover job content (conditions, tasks and responsibilities) and 'specification to denote job requirements' (i.e. qualities necessary) in the worker for satisfactory performance of the job.

Thus job specifications translate job descriptions into human qualifications, required for successful performance of a job.

Developing Work Rules

Most of the organisations, after developing job descriptions and job specifications, develop work rules, which are some predetermined decisions about certain courses of action that may be taken when certain contingencies arise. Organisations develop such work rules in documented form and use the same as a control device to ensure predictability of behaviour. Starting and stopping of work, rest periods, time-keeping, insubordination, fighting or drinking on the job, smoking, report of injuries, etc., are normally incorporated in such work rules.

Application of Industrial Engineering Techniques

Work study, method study and work measurement techniques are also applied as a preceding step for HRP. These techniques provide opportunity for effective use of plant and equipment, effective use of human efforts, measurement of human work, better ways of doing things, developing predetermined standard time, etc.

Other Factors

Layout

Layout of a factory influences determination of manpower requirement. Some plants and equipment work in isolation (like lathe, drilling machine, etc.), while some others work in groups continuously (like excavators). When a group of machines work in union, the whole group may be attended by one or more persons. But when machines are not in continuous operation, a single person may look after more than one machines. Thus requirements of manpower may vary for the layout and machine arrangement in a shop floor or factory.

Statutory Requirements

For certain positions in mines, electrical installations, hazardous places (chemical plants, etc.), welfare amenities need to be provided as per statutory regulations. Positions like Welfare Officers, Safety Officers, Medical Officers fall under this category.

Shifts

Number of manpower required also depends on whether the work would be carried out in general shift or in shifts. Number of working shifts will decide the requirement of manpower.

Leave Reserve

Since no one can work all the days for one reason or the other, certain allowances need to be given while working out manpower requirement. Apart from unpredictable leave of absence, workers are allowed leave systematically for a certain period in a year. Conventionally, 20 per cent allowance for weekly off and leave reserves are allowed in factories while working out manpower requirements. In mines, however, rate of absenteeism being high, such allowance percentage is on the higher side.

OBJECTIVES OF HRP

The first objective of manpower planning is to integrate planning and control of manpower with organisational planning to ensure best possible utilisation of all resources.

The next objective is to coordinate manpower policies of the organisation. Requirement and selection, training and development programmes, placement and induction programmes, promotion and transfer policies, decisions on remuneration and rewards, etc., affect the future need of manpower. Without proper coordination of manpower policies with each such decision, it is difficult to achieve the corporate objectives. Therefore, it is necessary to harmonise such objectives (corporate) with the manpower planning system. Without coordination, a company's plans may get frustrated for not having the right people in the right place at the right time. Subsequent objectives of manpower planning are to:

- Achieve efficiency of work in all spheres of the corporate body,
- Ensure cost minimisation,
- Eliminate all types of wastages including waste of time,
- Maintain required levels of skill and competency, matching present and future needs of the organisation.

MANPOWER DEMAND FORECASTING

Manpower demand forecasting is influenced primarily by two important factors, i.e. volume of output and the level of productivity. Manpower requirement may change due to change in output volume or mix, which calls for analysis of performance.

Similarly, as the level of productivity alters over time, it also affects manpower requirements. This calls for analysis of productivity.

ANALYSIS OF PERFORMANCE

To derive the manpower demand, it is necessary to estimate the manpower requirements in relation to the workload. To start with, each unit of manpower (more conveniently defined in terms of man-hours or man-days) required for different categories of job to accomplish the job in its entirety, are determined. After such determination the total workload is related with the manpower units of different categories and then finally the total requirement of manpower of different categories is determined. Such analysis, therefore, calls for analysis of performance either through direct or indirect methods.

Direct analysis is to review past performance to derive a ratio between two variables (workload and manpower of certain category). This can be done either by relating to a particular point of time or by averaging figures over a period of time. To illustrate this, we may give the following hypothetical example:

Category A	Category B
Manufacturing	Manufacturing
1 tonne of saleable steel requires 10 skilled workers	1 tonne of saleable steel requires 10 skilled workers
2 tonnes require 20 skilled workers	2 tonnes require 15 skilled workers

Category A has a constant ratio, while Category B has a variable ratio, as it can double the rate of production, adding relatively less number of manpower and therefore, can achieve the economy of scale. The period over which such forecasts can be made depends on the organisation.

Indirect analysis is based on the estimates made on past experience. Thus it is less systematic than the direct analysis. However, for short-range forecasts, indirect analysis is more preferred, as experienced managers can make this analysis after considerable thought.

For making both direct and indirect analysis, interdependence of different factors need to be considered. The experience of Indian Ordnance Factories may be illustrated here to understand the importance of such interdependence. Very recently some Ordnance Factories have gone in for technological change over, installing NC, CNC, DNC machines and systems. Today most of the Ordnance Factories are facing acute crisis of operators and so also paucity of maintenance men to gain the advantage from such technology. Such short-sightedness, therefore, is resulting in idling crores of rupees of investment.

Analysis of Productivity

Productivity has two major components, technological change and manpower utilisation. As technological change requires huge capital investment, organisations look for better manpower utilisation to achieve increased productivity. With better human relations, productivity can be increased. Again rates of productivity substantially vary the level of performance. Manpower demand forecasting can be made more effective, once we consider both the variables, i.e., the performance and the productivity. Most of the public sector enterprises are over-staffed, presumably due to inadequate emphasis on both these two aspects simultaneously.

Macro and Micro Human Resource Planning

Organisation level manpower or human resource planning cannot be done in isolation of macro issues. In fact, the primary reason for rising importance of HRP are both macro-and micro-level issues. At the aggregative or macro-level, HRP is influenced by general environmental factors like employment-unemployment situation, demographic changes, legal control and institutional policies, policies on globalisation and opening of markets, etc. At organisational or micro-level, HRP is more influenced by technology changes, organisational restructuring, skill and competency gap, strategic objectives, trade unions pressure (though it is dwindling over the years), lead time for manpower procurement, i.e., recruitment and selection, training and development, etc. Macro-level issues are exogenous, i.e., uncontrollable, while micro-level issues are endogenous and, therefore, controllable by an organisation.

HRP at Macro-level

Development of human resources is one of the important objectives of any country for long-term economic growth. For a developing economy like India such importance is far more. This is more visible from our economic planning, as governments over the years have been giving increasing priority to population planning and control, education, health, social security, housing, etc. All planned efforts are now being initiated to augment institutional support for developing human resources at the national level. Following are the major issues before our Government to develop human resources at the national level:

1. ***Population Planning and Control:*** To enforce control over population explosion to avert economic imbalances, population planning and control measures have been initiated by the government. Unless such control is enforced in a planned manner, no amount of institutional support can sustain this, resulting in generation of unproductive population, which will remain a drain on our national resources. Recognising this, Government of India has adopted a National Population Policy (2000) to ensure population stabilisation. The policy emphasises on affordable reproductive health care, increased quality of life by enhancing services of primary and secondary education, sanitation, drinking water, housing, transport, communication and empowering women. Such planned efforts have helped us to achieve the goal, if not in absolute terms, at least in percentages, is evident from the decadal trend analysis on population growth in India. Birth rate from 3.99 per cent in 1951 has decreased to a level of 2.61 per cent in 1999. There is a significant rise in population control awareness among people, which is evident from the phenomenal increase in averting birth over the decades. In Table 6.1, such a trend is reproduced for better appreciation.

2. ***Literacy and Education:*** To develop human resources at the macro-level, the Government of India has also adopted a National Policy on Education in 1986. The policy provides a broad framework for complete eradication of illiteracy in the country by declaring basic primary level education up to standard V, free and compulsory. To strengthen institutional infrastructure for education, the policy emphasises on increased government and non-government expenditure. Allowing private participation in education is a right direction at this stage. From elementary education, the focus on secondary, university and higher education, and technical and vocational education, adult education are also increasing. A significant rise in literacy rate (37.26 per cent) authenticates the effort of our government in developing human resources at the macro-level.

Table 6.1: Trends in Vital Statistics

Parameter	1951	1981	1991	2001	2011
Birth Rate (per 1,000 population)	39.9	33.9 (SRS)	29.5 (SRS)	24.28	20.97
Total Fertility Rate	6.0	4.5 (SRS)	3.6 (SRS)	3.04	2.62
Infant Mortality Rate (per 1,000 live births)	146	110 (SRS)	80 (SRS)	63.19	47.57
Child Mortality Rate (0-4 yrs, per 1000 children)	57.3 (1972)	39.1 (1982)	26.5 (SRS)	19.3	14.1 (2009)
Couple Protection Rate (%)	10.4 (1971)	22.8	44.1	45.6	40.4
Life Expectation (M)	73.2	54.1	60.5		65.77
(F)	36.2	54.7	61.7 (1991-96)		67.95
Literacy Rate	18.33	43.57	52.21	65.38	74.04

Note: SRS = Sample Registration System, which is complied by the Registrar General, India.
Source: Economic Survey, Government of India and Ministry of Health and Family Welfare, Government of India

3. ***Health and Medical Care:*** Health sector reforms is another required initiative for developing human resources at the macro-level. In this respect, India has recorded disparity and regional imbalances. Although there is an increased allocation of 36.9 per cent in 2000-01 over 1999-2000 for Central Sector health services, at the state level, the situation is very depressive. Baring few positive changes in life expectancy ratio, infant mortality rate, child mortality rate, etc., we are still far away from improving general health indices for the nation. Core communicable and non-communicable diseases like, malaria, tuberculosis, leprosy, blindness, AIDS, cancer, etc., are still not under the expected level of control. Although, government statistically proves otherwise, still more than 50 per cent of our population is not having access to basic health care. In other heath related activities like water supply and sanitation, achievements are also not at its expected level to support total development of quality of life.

4. ***Housing:*** In housing, government have renewed its efforts by adopting the National Housing and Habitat Policy, 1998. The basic thrust of this policy is to achieve sustainable development of housing infrastructure through public-private partnership. Repealing of Urban Land Ceiling and Regulation Act, 1976 is also another positive direction in this respect. In building housing infrastructure, Housing and Urban Development Corporation (HUDCO) is playing a crucial role. Although achievement is falling far short of the requirement, positive attitude of the government in this direction would definitely contribute to the development of human resources and quality of life in years to come.

Plan and non-plan expenditure of the Central Government on the above social sector services increased by about 4 times over 1992-93. In GDP terms, it is now 10.7 per cent (in 2000-01). Following social sectors schemes of the government are in operation to enhance social security and overall 'quality of life'.

1. Jawahar Gram Samridhi Yojana (JGSY)

2. Employment Assurance Scheme (EAS)

3. National Social Assistance Programme

4. Swaran Jayanti Gram Swarozgar Yojana (SJGS)

5. Nehru Rozgar Yojana (NRY)

6. Prime Minister's Rozgar Yojana

In addition to the above centralized strategy for human resource planning and development, at the state level, state planning boards and at the district level, manpower planning generation councils have been set up. At the apex level, Planning Commission is very active in HRP related activities, which culminated in the setting up of the Institute of Applied Manpower Research (IAMR). So far, however, IAMR could come out with labour market information planning and forecasting of scientific manpower.

Macro-level HRP is a complex and dynamic process and it requires longitudinal study to understand the results of various policy measures and actions. In Table 6.2, annual growth of employment in organised sector, both public and private for the period 1991-99 is presented. The trend indicates hardly any growth in public sector and marginal growth in private sector employment. There is a tremendous structural change in the employment pattern, with more shift towards knowledge intensive jobs. Sectoral growth rates in GDP in the year 2000-01 is highest in services (8.3 per cent), followed by industry (6.6 per cent) and agriculture (0.9 per cent).

Table 6.2: Growth Rates of Employment in Organised Sector (Percentages)

Year	Public Sector	Private Sector	Total Organised
1991	1.52	1.24	1.44
1992	0.80	2.21	1.21
1993	0.60	0.06	0.44
1994	0.62	0.01	0.73
1995	0.11	1.63	0.55
1996	(-) 0.19	5.62	1.51
1997	0.67	2.04	1.09
1998	(-) 0.09	1.72	0.46
1999	0.00	0.11	0.04

Source: Economic Survey, Government of India.

From years 2000 to 2003, growth rates of employment in organized sector is negative, which indicates employment in organized is reducing.

There still exists an imbalance in supply and demand for human resources at the macro-level. While on the one hand the country is facing the mounting burden of unemployment, on the other, it is still in shortage of skilled manpower. Large scale migration of skilled manpower to other countries has further aggravated the situation.

HRP at Micro-level

We have discussed the micro or organisational level HRP in our initial notes. Major activities, objectives, steps and processes for micro-level HRP have been introduced in this chapter. However, the HRP process, in detail, is discussed in Chapter III.

Macro-level Manpower Planning Models and Techniques

Manpower planning models at macro level is concerned more with the demand for jobs than with the supply side of the employment equation. Labour market models are used both for labour market analysis and to design labour market information systems. Both are dependent on each other. It is essential for macro level manpower planning to understand how many people are coming to the labour market, what are their education and training levels, what is their age etc. These input information are essential for an organisation to determine the induction training needs to shape the labour supply to meet the demands of the economy. Thus macro level manpower planning cannot be carried out in isolation. We have detailed such inter relationships earlier. Some of the well known models and techniques are:

The Manpower Requirements Approach (MRA)

This is the dominant model of manpower planning (according to Youdi, 1985). The three major steps in his model are: (a) assessing the demand for manpower, (b) assessing the supply of manpower, and (c) balancing the supply and demand.

The Demand Side of the Model

There are five main steps to assess the demand of manpower in terms of level of educational level over a time frame:

1. Estimation of the future level of GDP or output (X).
2. Estimation of the structural transformation of the economy in terms of distribution of output by economic sector (X_i/X) over time.
3. Estimation on labour productivity by economic sector (L_i/X_i) and its evolution over time.
4. Estimation of occupational structure of the labour force within economic sectors and its evolution over time (L_{ij}/L_i).
5. Estimation of educational structure of the labour force in given occupations within economic sectors over time (L_{ijk}/L_{ij}).

Hence the demand function for educated labour looks something like:

$$L^D_{ijk} = f\,(X, X_i/X, L_i/X_i, L_{ij}/L_i, L_{ijk}/L_{ij}) \qquad \ldots (1)$$

Note: i = economic sector, j = occupation, k = educational level, a = age, s = sex;

The Supply Side of the Model

Like demand side, supply side of the model also requires four basic steps as under:

1. Estimation of population $P_{a,s,k}$ by age, sex and educational level.
2. Estimation of number of graduates, dropouts by age, sex and educational level, $E_{a,s,k}$.
3. Distribution labour force participants (L^S) with age, sex, educational level and then assessing labour force participation rates to the number of graduates, $l_{a,s,k}$.
4. Estimation of occupational supply based on the labour supply by education level using education to occupation matrix $M_{k,j}$

Hence the supply function for educated labour looks something like:

$$L^S_{j,k} = f(P_{a,s,k}, E_{a,s,k}, l_{a,s,k}, M_{k,j}) \quad \text{... (2)}$$

Balancing Labour Supply to Demand

Balancing is normally done in two ways. First, if $L^D_{.j}$ is very different from L^S_{j} due to poor data quality it then tends to use an *ad hoc* adjustment mechanism revising one or more of the key assumptions. To illustrate, while developing a manpower plan, if the planner is too optimistic about labour productivity, his forecasting may fall short of actual labour demand. While on the contrary optimistic labour force participation rate can increase the actual supply of labour For such paradoxical situations, therefore, it is imperative to reconcile labour supply and its demand using this model.

MACRO-LEVEL HRP MODELS

Macro-level manpower planning is reinforced through educational planning with the following two recognised approaches:

1. The Manpower Requirement Approach (MRA)
2. The Rate of Return Approach (RRA)

RRA is also known as Cost-Benefit Analysis of Human Capital.

Manpower Requirement Approach (MRA)

By establishing a linear relationship between the manpower category in different industry groups and their output, MRA helps us to project the demand for manpower at the macro-level. For the educational planning at the national level, this approach is much in use in our country. Let us understand how it works:

1. It establishes a linear relation between employment and output and then extrapolates manpower requirements in different categories for years to come.

2. Initially category-wise manpower coefficients are computed, based on past data, which then are applied on the hypothesised growth pattern of different industry groups.
3. Thereafter, aggregate manpower requirement of different categories are worked out.
4. These inputs are then converted to different type of educational requirements.

Even though it is a simple technique for macro-level manpower vis-à-vis educational planning, it is not a dynamic approach, as it does not cater for labour market flexibility. Perhaps this deficiency, is responsible for the critical skills shortage in our country, as our educational planning is reinforced by this approach. Similarly, technology-output relationship is considered as stable under this approach, which in reality is not. Moreover, inter-occupational job mobility, man-machine substitution, costs, etc., are also not considered, while computing aggregate manpower requirement of different categories. That such limitations defeat the purpose of macro-level manpower planning is evident from the fact that it took over a decade for us to respond to redesigning course curriculum in IITs and ITIs, matching the same to industry requirements.

Rate of Return Approach (RRA)

This is based on the calculation of the net returns on educational expenditure (ILO, 1984). It is measured considering the increase in net income that an individual will be able to earn in relation to the income that an individual would have earned had the individual not reached a given educational level. Therefore, the present value of the flow of future net income is calculated on the basis of the above definition. Educational programmes, which show positive returns are promoted, while programmes showing zero or negative Net Present Value (NPV) are reduced or even may be phased out. However, there is a difference between private and social rate of return. Private rate of return is current discounted rate of net income after tax and costs (both direct and indirect). Social rate of return is income before tax and costs.

The MACBETH Model

MACBETH model is a recursive simulation model of the labour market and the evolution of occupational mismatches. This model is robust to data inconsistencies but straightforward for quick application. Particularly in a developing country like India we have large scale labour related data inconsistencies. In such situations, therefore, this model can calibrate the switching between occupations providing insights into labour market analysis. This model is extensive used in developing countries.

Labour Market Signaling

Labour market signaling advocates guiding of schooling and training decisions based on the need for wage and employment trends. Thus this approach evaluates the functioning of the labour markets, estimating upward or downward pressure on the economic returns to investment in specific skills. This approach can also focus on those skill and knowledge sets, which are having strategic significance for the economic development of the country. The labour market signals are: wages, employment trends by education and training and occupational classifications, costs of specific education and training programs, enrolment data for institutions, programs of study, individual courses, 'help-wanted' advertisements in newspapers and professional journals, unemployment rates by education, skill, training, occupation.

Learning Curve

It is our common that people and organisations become more efficient over time. Such difference in efficiency rate over time is having a major impact on business decisions. To illustrate an organisation may estimate the production rate of a given product, and can determine from the same what would be the time and money resources requirement for future production. Such effect of increased efficiency with production volume is known as the "learning curve" effect. The "curve" is the idea that if we plot "production time per unit" over time, the amount will curve down.

There are three major assumptions in the learning curve effect:

1. The time required to complete a given task will decrease the more times the task is performed.
2. The decrease will decrease in a decreasing rate.
3. The decrease will follow a predictable pattern.

Calculations

The most common form of learning curve calculation is an exponential decay function (i.e. production rates decay — or decrease — following an exponential curve). The standard equation is as follows:

$$T_n = T_1 \, n^b$$

Where;

n = the unit number (1 for the first unit, 2 for the second unit, etc.)

T_1 = the amount of time to produce the first unit

T_n = the amount of time to produce unit n

b = the learning curve factor, calculated as ln(p)/ln(2), where ln(x) is the natural logarithm of x.

p = the learning percentage.

The learning percentage p is interpreted as follows:

Every time the cumulative production quantity doubles, the unit production rate will decrease by the percentage p. This is shown in the following calculation:

Imagine that we have $T_1 = 10$ hours and $p = 90\% = 0.90$. We can calculate the production time for the first 10 units as follows:

$b = \ln(0.90)/\ln(2) = -0.152.$

$T_1 = 10\ (1^{-0.152}) = 10$

$T_2 = 10\ (2^{-0.152}) = 9$

$T_3 = 10\ (3^{-0.152}) = 8.46$ (rounded to two decimal places)

$T_4 = 10\ (4^{-0.152}) = 8.10$

$T_5 = 10\ (5^{-0.152}) = 7.83$

$T_6 = 10\ (6^{-0.152}) = 7.62$

$T_7 = 10\ (7^{-0.152}) = 7.44$

$T_8 = 10\ (8^{-0.152}) = 7.29$

$T_9 = 10\ (9^{-0.152}) = 7.16$

$T_{10} = 10\ (10^{-0.152}) = 7.05$

This means that even though the 1st unit will take 10 hours, the 10th unit will only take 7.05 hours. Observe that the improvement from the 1st to the 2nd units was 10 – 9 = 1 hour of improvement. From the 9th to the 10th unit only showed 7.16 – 7.05 = 0.11 hour of improvement. Indeed we see a decreasing improvement rate. Also observe that when production doubles, the unit production time is reduced by p = 90%.

T_2 is 90 per cent of T_1.

T_4 is 90 per cent of T_2. (i.e. $8.10 = 9 \times 0.90$)

T_8 is 90 per cent of T_4. (i.e. $7.29 = 8.10 \times 0.90$) etc.

We would also observe that the 200,000th unit would take 90% of the time it takes to produce the 100,000th unit.

Example

A former construction company executive just started a new company called Cookie-Cutter Homes. The company only makes one home type, so as to maximize the learning curve effect. The entrepreneur assumes that his company will realize a 75 per cent learning curve effect. The first home took 200 days to complete. How long will it take to produce the 5th home? How about the 10th home? What about the 100th home? What about the 104th home?

First, we calculate the learning curve factor b = ln(p)/ln(2) = ln(0.75)/ln(2) = – 0.415.

$T_1 = 200$

$T_5 = 200\ (5^{-0.415}) = 102.56$ or about 103 days

$T_{10} = 200\ (10^{-0.415}) = 76.92$ or about 77 days

$T_{100} = 200\ (100^{-0.415}) = 29.58$ or about 30 days

$T_{104} = 200\ (104^{-0.415}) = 29.10$ or about 29 days

Thus we see that Cookie-Cutter Homes will realize dramatic learning curve benefits for the early homes, but reduced incremental benefits later on.

Cause and Effect Model in HRP

Reinhardt (2002) recommended a compact equation to describe surplus or shortage of manpower in future year t. The equation goes as under:

$$X_t = {}_{at\,ct}\,S_t - (D_t/Q_t)N_t$$

Here product ${}_{at\,ct}\,S_t$ denotes the projected supply of manpower in a year t. Component S_t denotes number of manpower projected to be alive in a year t, component ${}_{at}$ is the fraction of those manpower who are professionally active in year t, and component ${}_{ct}$ is the fraction of those manpower who are professionally active and available for service. The product $(D_t/Q_t)N_t$ represents the projected demand or requirements of manpower in a year t. Variable D_t denotes the projected average number of manpower services needed or demanded in year t. Q_t is the projected average number of manpower services produced in year t. N_t is the volume of jobs to be attended. This compact equation was basically used to predict the demand of physicians in USA. This can also be used at micro-level manpower planning by an organisation having large manpower for long-term HRP.

However, despite such deficiencies in both the estimation tools of manpower at the macro-level, these can at least help in approximation in setting priorities in education and skill development. Certain deficiencies are due to our in-built system of compiling labour market information. At least on two important counts, these are visible. Indian Labour Year Book and Annual Survey of Industries are two major publications of the Government of India, which can streamline the information inputs required for macro-level manpower planning. First of all both the publications are not available on time. There still exists a time lag of 5-6 years in their publications. The system of data compilation in such publications is age-old and not in relation to requirements. Here we will explain one major deficiency in Indian Labour Year Book of Labour Bureau, Shimla. This Year Book, among others, compiles data on the trend of industrial disputes in India, with their distribution of causal factors, like, wages and salaries, indiscipline and violence, bonus, etc., in percentage terms. There is no interrelation with 'mandays loss'. Therefore, it is difficult for us to understand the severity of individual causal factor, as mere percentage distribution is a misnomer. The Institute of Applied Manpower Research over the years studied the manpower requirements of different categories in the country. They have made some sectoral and occupational requirement analysis of manpower for engineers, nurses, scientific manpower, etc.

Apart from the above, Labour Economics as a subject for study is not yet properly integrated with major labour-management related courses, which again restricts our knowledge input about labour market trend and its analysis. For the primary understanding, we have briefly discussed the concepts of Labour Economics.

Labour Economics

Labour Economics studies the demand and supply for the important factor of production, i.e., human beings. Marshall and Smith are the two pioneering economists who first recognised that the study of market for labour is not possible without understanding the social relations of production, long-term contractual arrangement, problems of motivation, institutions like unions and internal labour markets, etc. All these characteristic requirements differentiate the market for labour from other markets.

The most important development in modern Labour Economics is the development of the concept of human capital. Human capital approach analyses the individual decision-making in regard to supply of labour and other behavioural areas which are more related with sociology rather than economics. Before the development of the concept of human capital, labour supply decisions were considered more as an economic rationality. By making such decision as in interrelational variable of education, skill, investment, wages, working hours, etc., the subject of labour economics has been demarcated from the traditional economic analysis.

Like labour supply, which emphasise on individual decision-making, as an outcome of different interrelational variables, labour demand and a firm's behaviour is influenced by internal labour markets, hiring, promotion, wage policies and the structure of wages in various markets, etc. Most of the firms maintain computerised personnel records to analyse their demand for labour. There are many techniques for analysis of labour demand. For example, a firm may study the likely response of workers to a particular wage and personnel policy (which optimises their profits). Some firms offer maximum compensation to match with the workers' expectations and then try to maximise the utility of workers, while other study the effect of deferred compensation, piece rates and others systems of rewards. The neo-classical model on study of labour demand examines the magnitude of elasticities and cross-elasticities of labour demand for workers of different skills and the effect of minimum wages on employment. Similarly, elasticities of substitution and complementarity are also studied to analyse the labour demand.

In the area of labour institutions, effects of unions on wages, wages in unionised and non-unionised industries and occupations, differences between union and non-union workers, etc., are studied.

Labour Markets

Demand, supply and institutions interact in labour markets and labour economics studies the operation of labour markets considering all these issues. Analysis of labour markets are carried out for different occupational segments, viz., markets for blue-collar workers, markets for white-collar workers, markets for professionals, etc. Investigating markets for knowledgeable and skilled workers, differentiating supply and demand forces in the markets, geographic and industrial mobilities, unemployment, wage pattern, etc., are the areas for studying the labour markets. Recently, however, macro changes in wages and unemployment over a given period of time, both within the country and across countries, are also studied to synthesize the facts of the labour markets with the basic principles of economics.

In India, pioneering studies in labour economics are institutionally being carried out by the Indian Society of Labour Economics (ISLE). ISLE organises national level conferences on different areas of labour economics and is trying to develop this as a distinct discipline having importance both in academic and professional research in understanding the trend of the most important factors of production, i.e., human beings. ISLE regularly publishes the *Indian Journal of Labour Economics*, which is considered as an international journal on the subject of Labour Economics.

SUMMARY

The basic concern of HRP is to identify skill and competency gaps and subsequently develop plans for development of deficient skills and competencies in manpower in order to remain competitive. It has now become an important enterprise-wide strategic function not only to achieve goals and objectives but also to sustain the present level in a globally competitive environment. Macro-level HRP is an important objective of the Government for long-term economic growth. Micro-level HRP is influenced by technological changes, organisational restructuring, skill and competency gap, strategic objectives, trade unions pressure, lead time for manpower procurement, etc.

KEYWORDS

HRP	Job Description
Competency Gap	Layout
Skill Gap	Leave Reserve
Job Analysis	Social Sector

REVIEW QUESTIONS

1. Define manpower planning. What are the activities involved in manpower planning?
2. What is optimum manpower planning? You have been retained by an organisation to develop a manpower planning system. What factors would you recommend them to consider for effective manpower planning?

3. Explain the importance of macro-level manpower planning in India.
4. Discuss the different models of macro-level manpower planning.
5. Write short notes on:
    (a) Judgemental Estimate of Manpower
    (b) Job Description
    (c) Work Rules
    (d) Industrial Engineering Techniques
    (e) Leave Reserve
    (f) Indirect Analysis of Manpower

Case Study

Right Payment

Human resources are among the most challenging inputs to manage because people are so much more complex than machines. Job design policies should recognise this humanness and foster satisfaction of higher-level needs. Work goals should be clear, moderately challenging, and accepted if they are to be useful.

A well-designed job should reflect both social (market) priorities and technical (organisational) capacities. Motivational techniques focus upon (1) variety (job enlargement adds more tasks, and job rotation adds variety because workers are rotated among tasks), (2) time (flexitime, 4-day work weeks, and job sharing), and (3) psychology (enrichment).

The Herzberg enrichment approach emphasises five motivational factors, and the Hackman-Oldham model stresses meaningfulness and responsibility. Hackman and Oldham have also developed a Job Diagnostic Survey, which measures skill variety, task identity, task importance, autonomy, and feedback. Finally, the socio-technical approach is a view of production systems which incorporate much of this psychological knowledge into a working system that blends both social and technical components.

Work methods can often be improved by conducting a scientific study of present methods using well-developed questioning techniques and principles of motion economy. In office systems, significant productivity improvements can come from better information flow and better used employee time.

Standards of performance should encourage the cooperation and participation of the workers to whom they will apply. Historical approaches, time studies, predetermined time methods, and work sampling are all useful ways of developing standards. Both time-study and work-sampling methods consist of sampling a worker's activities and subjectively rating the worker's performance level to determine a normal time. Allowances are then taken into consideration and a standard time is determined. Work sampling is particularly suitable for analysing less structured activities and group operations.

Every operations manager has opportunities to foster a favourable work climate among the employees by providing safe working conditions, just wages, and an environment that gives employees stake in what the organisation is doing. Many firms report favourable results from worker participation in problem solving teams, quality circles, and other involvement programmes.

Question

In the context of the above text, briefly discuss the significance of work study and method study and suggest the most appropriate tool for pricing a job in an organisation engaged in the manufacture of a ball point pen.

UNIT 7

Human Resource Planning Process

Learning Objectives

After completion of this unit, the students will be aware of the following topics:

- *Introduction*
- *HRP Process Outline*
- *Time-scale of HRP Forecasts*
- *Difficulties in Manpower Forecasts using Quantitative Tools*
- *Use of Qualitative Models for Better Managerial Judgement*
- *Analysis of Manpower Supply*
- *Different Methods of Wastage Analysis*
- *Manpower Planning Models*

SONO'S DILEMMA IN HUMAN RESOURCE PLANNING

Human resource planning is a process mapping the consequences of organisational strategy with respect to the availability of human resources. Every organisation adopts their business strategies keeping pace with their Strengths, Weaknesses, Opportunities and Threats (SWOT). While considering the strengths and weaknesses, organisation needs to account for the skill and competence and also, their manpower availability.

Sono India, a mid-sized manufacturing company of India does sub-contracting jobs of U.S. based multinational. With stable order bookings, the company is able to sustain with profitability and growth. For Sono, most of the sub-contracting jobs require them to recruit highly qualified tech-savvy mechanical and electrical engineers and technicians at least at the diploma level. Sono cannot perform the jobs retaining the outsourced employees for cost effectiveness, due to stringent labour laws, which prohibit such skill hiring on temporary basis. Further, the nature of work being highly skilled, Sono requires training of their workers after initial induction, putting them under mentors. The U.S. based multinational, as part of their agreement with Sono, can also alter the orders, including the size and variety which requires Sono to frequently go for changing the process and at times, even the skill and competency profile of engineers and technicians.

Sono performs its manpower requirement analysis based on the forecasted order booking positions of U.S. multinational. Sono's manufactured items being not a standard saleable item in the market, hardly gets opportunity for alternative disposal, when the U.S. major declines or refuses the consignment (even against confirmed order booking), on count of quality and bad workmanships. Of-late, Sono could realise their U.S. partner refusing their consignments at times on sluggish business trends which unnecessarily deplete their resources. To settle this impasse, Sono asked their U.S. partner to accept such dispatched items against price deviation, which the multinational gladly accepted. Gradually, the multinational started price negotiation, reducing it to almost ten percent less than earlier accepted price tags for Sono.

Sono now faces acute problem of cost optimisation to survive. The only alternative that Sono can now think of is optimisation of compensation cost through scientific manpower planning, training and productivity increase. Through a restructured process, Sono could identify some of the jobs that can be outsourced by them in smaller manufacturing units to achieve cost effectiveness. However, this requires Sono to ensure in-process quality checks at the suppliers' end to meet the stringent quality requirements. This also outweighs Sono's cost saving through outsourcing. At this juncture, Sono is unable to find a solution for effective manpower planning.

INTRODUCTION

In the earlier unit we have introduced the concepts of Human Resource Planning at macro- and micro-levels, suitably delineating its strategic role rather than mere head counts and extrapolation, keeping pace with budgetary requirements. We have also discussed that HRP at organisational or macro-level cannot be done without taking into account the micro-level issues. Almost all developed countries today are facing the crisis of quality manpower. The problem is so acute for them that they are now going for direct recruitment in developing countries instead of outsourcing from body shoppers. The United Kingdom is now finding them in a very awkward situation for non-availability of teachers. Nearly 2,00000 teachers need to be recruited by them from developing countries, including India, to man such posts. The situation is not so different in other developed countries for almost all trades like; computer scientists/engineers and systems analysts, physical and corrective therapy assistants and Aids, medical assistants, physical therapists, occupational therapy assistants, sales representatives, social and human service assistants, speech language pathologists and audiologists, health information technicians, dental hygienists, physician assistants, professional managers, engineers, etc. In explaining the trades, we have used the job titles as they prevail in their countries. Major reasons for such job vacancies in those countries can be attributed to total failure of their macro-level planning of human resources. Interestingly all these countries are also going for simultaneous curtailment of their manpower.

Almost every day in the newspapers we get news-clips on downsizing or job cuts, be it in IT industry or banking and finance or engineering. Such redundancy of manpower, once again vouches, that even at micro-level, they are equally not able to address to the problem of skill obsolescence. It is interesting to observe that even with acknowledged professionalism, they are not able to adopt a strategic approach to HRP, resulting in culmination of redundancy problems, after each annual performance results. It has now become their operational decision, every now and then to go for manpower redundancy. When we get news like, ABN Ambro reduces 2,000 jobs in the Netherlands or American Express announces 5,000 job-cuts worldwide or even Micro Systems asks 872 of their workers to find new jobs within the company or leave, or NEC Corporation, Japan, to cut 4,000 jobs, we ponder over, how come, such world-class and globally visible organisations could not get a signal well ahead! Are their business plans a total failure! Are their strategic plans minus people! The situation in India not quite different, but we still can boast, we are well ahead. Be it for the prevailing work culture (institutional employment relations rather than contractual) or for the ability to foresee the organisational dysfunctions, is a matter of debate. When Telco goes for axing 1,500 jobs through VRS or Balco offers VRS to their employees, or even commercial banking organisations to axe 30 per cent of their employee strength through VRS, we do not get surprised, as it is more for organisational restructuring rather than operational results. They are doing all this for a better tomorrow, as a part of their organisation-wide restructuring plan. And they give reasonable separation benefits. But when Daewoo Motors asks their employees to leave without compensation, we question their business practice!

Such detailed outlining of the global scenario is necessary to understand the problem of HRP across the world.

HRP process cannot be something like a thumb rule which is universally applicable. It varies from organisation to organisation. In this chapter, we have discussed the HRP process in general, which may merit the attention of practitioners. But what to adopt and what not, is left to the practitioners to identify, keeping pace with organisational requirements.

HRP Process Outline

Let us once again review a definition of HRP of HMSO, 1974. It is a strategy for the acquisition, utilization and retention of an enterprise's human resources. It seeks to link policy and practice in day to day decision-making. Thus inter-relationship of HRP with other HR functions is a established hypothesis, as evident from corporate practices.

We can broadly delineate the HRP process into four different stages as under:

1. ***Investigation:*** It is the primary stage of HRP in any organisation. In this stage, organisations try to develop their awareness about the detailed manpower scenario with a holistic view, looking at their current manpower. A SWOT analysis can reveal a better

picture with due consideration of the external environment, performance and productivity trends, working practices, operational and strategic plans. Scientific homework, at this stage itself can help to identify present and future skill gaps. For a better result, SWOT analysis can proceed a cause-effect diagram (fish-bone diagram), which is simple to comprehend. While doing external manpower review, macro level issues need to be understood with due cognizance to the relevant literatures like Annual Economic Survey, Year Book on Indian Labour, Survey of Indian Industries, ILO International Year Book on Labour, various reports of Planning Commission on manpower, etc. Internal manpower review has to be done with enterprise-wide current operational data, like; marketing, finance, performance data, current employment practices and methods, etc. Also internal manpower review is done with a futuristic view with due cognizance to strategic plans and objectives.

2. *Forecasting:* After adequate investigation, in the next phase of HRP process, analysis of demand and supply of manpower is done. There are different models of demand forecasting, which we have discussed later in this chapter. Manpower supply analysis is done considering both internal and external supply. While doing internal supply analysis, career planning and development, training and development and succession plan aspects are considered along with corporate policies and procedures. For example, 'promotion from within' as a corporate policy may or may not exist in a particular organisation. Where it exists, it has to be understood for which levels it is applicable, is it a time-scale (seniority) promotion or promotion on merit, is there any policy on this, etc. Interestingly promotional decision is a prerogative of management, hence an employee, prima facie cannot contest such a decision of management in a court of law, unless otherwise he or she can prove that such a decision has prejudiced his or her interest. The onus of proving this lies with the employee concerned. Many organisations have their documented promotion policy, to address to the problem of personal bias in promotional decision. External supply analysis is done considering macro-level issues to understand their availability. Since current employment practice is to employ people for a given time period, employment status also needs to be assessed in terms of availability. Demand forecasting helps in identifying requirements of manpower for various positions at different points of time. What should be the status of employment (permanent, temporary, part-time contract labour, sub-contracting, etc.) will depend to some extent also on the nature of position. While in abroad, they have the flexibility to hire for all positions from employee leasing companies on assignment basis, in our country the scope of such engagement is limited to some specific jobs only. Moreover, people are by nature sensitized for contractual employment terms. This practice however, is slowly catching up and since it is a total transition of attitude, it will take some time to settle down. May be in 5-10 years time, job mobility will increase and people of the new-age will consider it normal.

3. *Planning and Control of Manpower:* At this stage forecasts of manpower are translated into HR policies, which encompass all HRP related issues like recruitment, training and development. While going for recruitment, it is necessary to understand the job descriptions, which precede job analysis and job roles. Also it is necessary to document

the status of recruitment, i.e. the time period for which recruitment has to be made. Most of the organisations have their own documented recruitment system. What should be best, needs to be decided by the HR managers. Most of the organisations are besieged with the problem of restructuring. Hence extent and scope of internal hiring, i.e. redeploying in restructured jobs also need to be understood. Similar efforts should be made in planning and documenting the training and development policies of the organisation to address to the problem of knowledge and skill obsolescence in the context of changing technology. Hence the scope for redeployment through retraining also needs to be explored at this stage. While doing HRP, flexibility and interrelationship of all other policies also need to be considered. We must appreciate that manpower redundancy in India and abroad is not only for inadequate business planning but also for inadequate human resource planning, which among others, can be attributed to inflexible policies on redundancy, inflexible job descriptions (that restrict lateral job movement), inflexible employment conditions, absence of retraining and redeployment programmes. Mere planning and documenting the policies will not help. Control must be there to correct any observed deficiency in such plans. For example offering VRS with additional benefits may transpire to be a costly decision than skill renewal of manpower through training and re-training. Similarly outsourcing manpower through a body shopper may be costly than direct recruitment on contractual terms. Giving overtime to employees for sharing extra job load may be cheaper than recruiting an extra hand (obviously if extra job load is seasonal). Need for control can be understood, when manpower costs overshoot the budget.

4. ***Utilisation:*** In this final stage of HRP process, success is measured in terms of achievement trend, both quantitatively and qualitatively. While quantitative achievement is visible from productivity trend, manpower cost, etc., qualitative achievement is a subjective appraisal on achievement of organisational objectives. Reflection of qualitative achievement can also be studied in the context of prevailing industrial relations, level of motivation and morale, grievance pattern, etc.

TIME-SCALE OF HRP FORECASTS

Determining the time-scale of human resource forecasts is very important to decide about their availability and chart the possible action to meet the requirement. We have already explained that forecasts for the manpower or human resources are made at the organisational level, keeping in view demand and supply analysis, internal availability, external availability, employment practices, etc. Depending on the time-frame, which again depends on the basis of requirement, nature of analysis of the above factors, keeps on changing.

Thus it is evident that depending on the time-scale, human resource or manpower forecast pattern also changes. However, it is not out of place to mention that today's organisations are not catering to such requirement analysis beyond the time-frame of 1-2 years, as they take decisions on manpower redundancy based on their annual operational results.

For better appreciation, we have explained a tentative table for manpower forecasts, below:

Table 7.1: Manpower Forecasts

Time-frame	Requirement basis	Availability	Possible action plans to meet the requirement
Less than a year	Annual Budget (operational plans)	Existing manpower (by proper distribution of workload) + contractual manpower	Body shoppers/contractors, overtime, recruitment on contractual terms, restructuring, and layoffs.
1-2 years	Forecasted budget or forward budget (business plans)	Current manpower less projected attrition	Transfer, promotion, new recruitment, restructuring, redundancy, training and development
2-5 years	Long-term plans	Projected manpower (including those trainees who will be inducted during the period)	Succession plans, recruitment, training and development, restructuring, redundancy
More than 5 years	Perspective plans	Labour market, education system	Succession plans, management development, organizational development, redeployment, job restructuring

Forecasting HR or manpower requirements: Forecasting processes have been briefly discussed, while explaining steps in manpower planning in the next chapter. Here we have discussed various quantitative tools to reinforce the idea. Use of quantitative tools in manpower planning centres around the following areas given below. There are, however, many developed models for HRP, which we have discussed separately.

Analysis of Workload Factors

To forecast the manpower requirements at different points of time, workload analysis is extremely important. Analysis of present and future workload depends on the possibility of quantifying the work content in every area of an organisational activity. Following steps help in workload analysis.

1. ***Classification of Work:*** Classification of work is done by identifying the work or job content and time requirement for such job or work unit. Work or job content classification helps in breaking jobs in different components, which together completes an operation. Time requirement analysis for each such job component can be done by deciding the standard time, using work measurement techniques. In some cases, cycle time for each job component is mentioned in machine literatures. Extrapolating time requirement from such data can help in deciding time requirement. However, this may not help us for service jobs, like customers' query handling, administrative or managerial jobs, clerical jobs, etc. Approximation of time requirement for such jobs can be done for an existing organisation, based on past experience and benchmarking with others. While a new organisation can emulate others, there are certain limitations of job or work content analysis. First, for the reason that all jobs are not strictly quantifiable. Deciding the standard time of job scientifically, requires rigorous time study, which is not only costly but also

time-consuming. Secondly, normal fatigue allowance is not considered while developing such time requirement. However, during the process of developing standard time through time study, such problems can be addressed. Thirdly, with the pace of technological change, standard time required also varies, which means setting of job time at one point of time may not hold good subsequently. Moreover, technology also changes the job content and even the job family. For example, the job of a turner, who is using a lathe machine, may change to an operator, when he uses a computerised machining centre. Similarly, the job of a clerk who is doing the job manually, may change to a computer operator, when he is using computer systems.

Thus classification of job content and analysis of time requirement for each job component is a dynamic process.

2. *Forecasting Number the of Jobs:* After classification of jobs and work content and its time requirement, in the next phase of workload analysis, job forecasting in quantitative terms for a number of jobs is done for a time period. This is done based on the demand projection.
3. *Converting the Projected Jobs in Man-hours:* Multiplying the time requirement of each job with the number of projected jobs, man-hours for jobs are computed.
4. *Converting the Man-hours into Manpower Requirement:* In the final phase of workload analysis, aggregate man-hours are converted into manpower requirements. This is done considering leave reserve, normal fatigue allowance, etc.

Let us analyse workload factor to access manpower requirement in a given day of the Maintenance Department of Delhi Vidyut Board to attend to customer complaints. Based on analysis of customer complaints (pertaining to maintenance jobs), classification of work has been grouped into four categories.

1. *Classification of Work:*

Job Category	Hours Per Job
Related to meters	0.75
Related to installation	2.50
Related to maintenance	1.50
Related to emergency calls	1.10

2. *Forecast of jobs in a day for different years:*

Job Category	Year			
	2002	2003	2004	2005
Meters	15	13	11	8
Installation	85	95	110	125
Maintenance	27	35	41	45
Emergency	10	8	6	4

3. ***Converting forecast into man-hours required per day:***

Job Category	Year			
	2002	2003	2004	2005
Meters	11.25	9.75	8.25	6
Installation	212.5	237.5	275	312..5
Maintenance	40.5	52.5	61.5	67.5
Emergency	11	8.8	6.6	4.4
Total man-hours required per day	275.25	308.55	351.35	390.4

4. ***Converting man-hours into manpower requirement per day:*** This is done considering skill interchangeability of maintenance staff for the identified job categories with 20 per cent fatigue allowance and 20 per cent leave reserve. Therefore, in a given day of 8 man-hours per employee, net available time for attending customer complaints get reduced by 40 per cent per employee, i.e., only 4.8 man-hours per day, per employee is available to attend customer complaints. Thus manpower forecasting has to be done, considering 4.8 manpowers per employee, per day. Delhi Vidyut Board would therefore require maintenance staff per day for different years, as under:

No. of Maintenance Staff Required	Year			
	2002	2003	2004	2005
Employees	57	64	73	84

Note: Number of maintenance staff required has been rounded off to the nearest total as we cannot fractionate manpower requirement.

Time Series Analysis

Employment data over a time period (time series) are used under this method as the basis for manpower forecast. However, mere projecting the past into the future, without considering endogenous and exogenous changes, will increase the forecasting errors, which may be either under forecasting or over forecasting of manpower requirements. The relevance of such change factors has been discussed earlier.

When we record employment levels over a time period, we observe the following five distinct elements in it.

1. ***Trend:*** Fluctuations in level of employment over a time period.
2. ***Cyclical Effects:*** Change in employment in relation to some particular event, like economic liberalisation in India or WTO resolutions.
3. ***Seasonality:*** Seasonal fluctuations occur more than once in a given time period like, requirements of more maintenance staff in Delhi Vidyut Board during summer and rainy season while less in winter.
4. ***Step:*** This is a sudden change in employment level due to economic environment or increased market share or procurement of some new machines, etc.

5. ***Random Fluctuations:*** These are fluctuations in employment level which are random in nature, i.e., such fluctuations do not follow any obvious pattern. We can address this problem by following a moving average method.

Given below are some illustrations of manpower forecasts using time series analysis.

Moving Average Method

Under this method, average of the combined employment level data for the recent past is considered as the forecasted employment level for the next period. This technique is useful to guard against random fluctuations. However it requires careful selection of time periods, which may be a 6-period, 10-period, 12-period moving average. If time periods chosen are too few, we may get wide variability in our forecast. Therefore, considering more time periods, we get better results. Whatever time period we select for over forecast, it is necessary to continue the same number of periods for our computations. After each period elapses, the figure for the oldest period is dropped and the figure for the newest period is added for our subsequent computation of manpower requirements.

Example

Godrej has the following manpower data for their health care division for the past 6 years:

Year	Manpower Level/Data (in nos.)
1995	500
1996	600
1997	800
1998	1,000
1999	1,100
2000	1,300

You have been asked to forecast their manpower requirement in 2001 using a 6-period moving average.

Solution:

$$F_m = \frac{500+600+800+1000+1100+1300}{6}$$

$$= 5300/6 = 883 \text{ nos.}$$

If we are asked to use 4-period moving average to forecast manpower for 2001, then we require to drop the data of 1995 and 1996 and compute the forecasted manpower as under:

$$F_m = \frac{800+1000+1100+1300}{4} = 4200/4 = 1050 \text{ nos.}$$

From the above variation in results, we can well understand the danger of considering lesser time periods in manpower forecasting.

For achieving better results, weights may be assigned for different time periods at the discretion of the analyst. For example manpower levels of 1995, 1996 and 1997 may be less relevant, hence, for these years weights may be assigned as 1 each. For 1998, weight may be 2, for 1999 weight may be 3, while for 2000, weight may be 4. Now the forecasted manpower for the year 2001, would be as under:

$$F_m = \frac{1(500) + 1(600) + 1(800) + 2(1000) + 4(1300)}{\Sigma w, i.e., 12}$$

$$= \frac{500 + 600 + 800 + 2000 + 3300 + 5200}{12} = 12400/12 = 1033 \text{ nos.}$$

Exponential Smoothing

In moving average method, we need to carry forward a large volume of historical data. We can eliminate the need for such past records by adopting this method. This method smoothens random errors by giving exponentially decreasing weights to historical data.

Such weight factor is indicated by alpha (α), which is a smoothing constant, a non-linear decimal value which lies between 0 and 1. The formula for the exponential smoothing model is:

$$F_m = F_t - \alpha(A_{t-1} - F_{t-1})$$

Where,

F_m = Forecasted manpower

F_{t-1} = Forecasted demand for the previous period

α = Smoothing constant

A_{t-1} = Actual manpower required for the previous period

Example

Assume that the forecasted manpower requirement for an organisation was 500, while their actual requirement was 480. Considering an alpha value of 0.4 (which the company feels would produce the best results), compute the manpower requirement for the current period.

Solution:

500 + 0.4 (480 – 500) = 492 nos.

Double exponential smoothing can also be done to get further cushion in manpower forecasting.

Analysis of Productivity and Other Ratios

Productivity and performance analysis was discussed in the previous unit. We have seen, for short-range forecast, usually the normal budgetary process is followed.

Managerial Judgement

A manager has to make a judgement about the future employment levels. Such judgemental decision is based on his past experience, which he relates to past occurrences of some events and its effects on manpower plans. He has to use his judgement considering contingencies. Combining quantitative tools with judgement yield better results. There are, however, certain pitfalls in our assumed variables. In the following paragraphs, we have examined such pitfalls, which may lead to inaccurate manpower forecasts.

DIFFICULTIES IN MANPOWER FORECASTS USING QUANTITATIVE TOOLS

1. When productivity data is considered as available to decide about manpower requirement, it is important to understand that productivity rise cannot always be attributable to increased human effort. Thus increase of productivity due to changes in technology or the sum total of operational and managerial efficiency (total factor productivity approach) are the factors, which need to be integrated while doing manpower forecasts. But developing manpower planning models integrating the above two productivity variables is not so easy for obvious computational difficulty.

2. It is difficult to get units of output in the same form for all jobs. For example, maintenance jobs are difficult to quantify. Moreover, maintenance problem is time independent. Planning for maintenance staff is one of the difficult tasks for the manpower planner. Obviously for this reason, most of the organisations prefer to sub-contract their maintenance function. Even with Customer Relationship Management (CRM) solutions, quantification is difficult.

3. Relationship between output and manpower is not always straight forward. Increase in output may lead to economies of scale and resultant cost efficiency and rise in productivity, which may not be attributable to manpower productivity.

4. Effect of factors to improve productivity, i.e., new technology, incentive schemes, etc., may not be consistent over a time period. Therefore, projecting manpower requirement, considering effects of such factors may be inaccurate.

5. Effect of different factors may not always be linear. Interrelationship of different factors complicates forecasting of manpower. Although we have statistical techniques like multiple regression analysis, factor analysis, etc., their computational rigours often dissuade the manpower planners to use such tools.

6. Uncertainty about the future is again a major problem for the manpower planner. Thus extrapolating on past data may lead to a major inaccuracy in manpower estimation.

7. Data on past workload factors may not be available, creating difficulty in emulating the same.

8. Integration of manpower planning with corporate plans may not exist in an organisation, creating problems for enterprise-wide manpower plans.

9. Employees cannot always be related to output in a direct way.

10. Human Resource Information Systems (HRIS), may not exist in an organisation. Lack of such information support system leads to inaccurate estimation of manpower.

For obvious constraints, explained above, managerial judgement along with statistical tools, is often considered as the best option for manpower planning. Often it is said that planning for manpower within a given cost constraint, without bothering for past practices, leads to a better estimation.

USE OF QUALITATIVE MODELS FOR BETTER MANAGERIAL JUDGEMENT

Delphi Technique

The word 'Delphi' has come from Greek. In Athens of Greece during ancient times, it was a convention to consult an oracle representative of God Apollo who was believed to have contact with God. The advice of the oracle at that time could only be interpreted by the Priest.

In modern times this method is essentially a group process to achieve a consensus forecast. This method calls for selection of a panel of experts either from within or outside the organisation, whose comments are crystallised from a series of questionnaire responses and then used as the basis to forecast. A series of questionnaire are prepared from the responses received from a prior set of questions in a sequencing manner. At every stage, information obtained from the previous questionnaire is shared among the participating members, without, however, disclosing majority opinion, this otherwise may have peer-group influence on minority opinion.

The procedure of Delphi Technique may be enumerated as follows:

1. To start with, it requires selection of a coordinator and a panel of experts both within and outside the organisations.

2. The co-ordinator then circulates questions in writing to each such expert.

3. The experts then write their observations.

4. The co-ordinator then edits those observations and summarises, without, however, disclosing the majority opinion in his summary.

5. On the basis of his summary, the co-ordinator then develops a new set of questionnaire and circulates those among experts.

6. Experts then answer such new set of questions.

7. The co-ordinator repeats the process till such time he is able to synthesise from the opinion of the experts.

The success of the process again depends on the following factors:

1. Experts should be so chosen that they have the requisite knowledge and skills to give the best answers.
2. Questions should be relevant to the objective.
3. Criteria for evaluating responses should be consistent, unbiased and befitting with the objectives. Although there is no universal set of criteria for evaluating responses, it is often considered necessary to follow the undermentioned guidelines:
   (a) Consider the assessment made by the experts in terms of their knowledge in the area.
   (b) Consider the assessment in terms of feasibility, objectives, time and resource requirement.
   (c) Consider the assessment in terms of desirability.
   (d) Consider the assessment in terms of extraneous factors.

Nominal Group Method

Like Delphi method, nominal group method also involves a panel of experts. However, the major difference between the two is that while under Delphi technique, experts are not allowed to discuss among themselves, for assessing the questions, under nominal group method experts are given the opportunity to discuss among themselves. Under this method, the co-ordinator assumes the role of a facilitator, allowing the experts to sit together to discus their ideas and records of such discussions are made on a flip chart. After this, round table discussions on ideas, experts are asked to rank their ideas according to their perceived priority. The group consensus is then derived mathematically in terms of individual rankings. The process, therefore, affords creativity and facilitates scientific group consensus unlike consensus by qualification (as the coordinator ultimately decides the best course of action) under the Delphi technique.

ANALYSIS OF MANPOWER SUPPLY

Analysis of manpower supply at the enterprise level is also done using some quantitative techniques for accurate HRP. Some of the important techniques are discussed below:

Wastage Analysis

Manpower wastage is an element of labour turnover. Therefore, it is not labour turnover, per se. Wastage is severance from the organisation, which includes, voluntary retirement, normal retirement, resignations, deaths and dismissals. Marginal recruitment decisions, without wastage analysis may lead to inaccuracies in HRP. Tavistock Institute of Human Relations, U.K. suggested wastage analysis using the following curve.

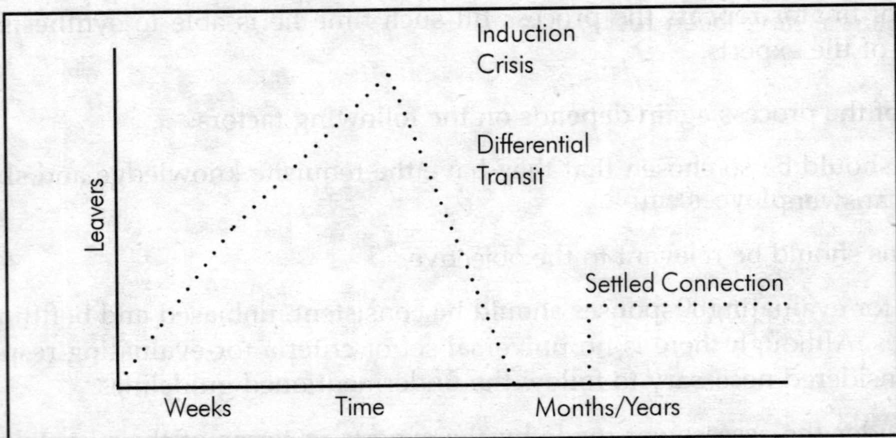

The above curve identifies three different phases. During induction phase, marginal employees leave. During differential transit period, an employee learns about the organisation and identifies his role in it. While during the period of settled connection, an employee settles down and decides to stay long. Wastage decreases with the increase of length of service. Wastage also decreases with the increased skill exercises and age of employees. Characteristically wastage of manpower is more in female than male employees. It varies with the level of employment and also exhibits seasonal variations. Working conditions and size of the firm are also important variables of manpower wastage.

DIFFERENT METHODS OF WASTAGE ANALYSIS

Labour Turnover Index

This index indicates the number of leavers as percentage to average number of employees. Average number of employees employed in a given time period is decided by adding the employees at the beginning and end and then dividing the same by two.

Example

At the beginning of a year, a firm has 250 employees, while at the end it has 230. Assume no recruitment has been made in between. Compute the labour turnover index.

Solution:

$$\text{Number of employees leaving} = 250 - 230 = 20$$

$$\text{Average number of employees employed} = \frac{250 + 230}{2} = 240$$

$$\text{Labour Turnover} = \frac{\text{Number of employees leaving}}{\text{Average number of employees employed}} \times 100$$

$$= \frac{20}{240} \times 100 = 8.33\%$$

Suppose 5 people have been recruited in between during the year, then labour turnover would be:

Number leaving $= (250 + 5 - 230) = 25$

Average number employees employed $= \frac{(255+230)}{2} = 243$

Labour turnover $= \frac{25}{243} \times 100 = 10\%$

Stability Index

This index indicates stable workforce percentage for a given period and can be computed as under:

$$\frac{\text{Number with more than 1 year service now}}{\text{Total Employed one year ago}} \times 100$$

Cohort Analysis

Cohort means homogeneous groups. Cohort analysis takes into account the length of service, which is an important variable of wastage analysis. This, therefore, eliminates the defect of labour turnover index. Cohort analysis is more accurate for a small homogenous group. However, changing social and economic conditions can invalidate this analysis. In the table below, we have illustrated a cohort analysis, assuming number of people engaged in the beginning of a year as 500 and number of leavers for different length of service as under:

1st Year	50
2nd Year	45
3rd Year	40
4th Year	35
5th Year	30

Length of Service (in years)	No. Leaving	Cumulative Leavers	Remaining	Survival as percentage of leaving
(1)	(2)	(3)	(4)	(5)
0	0	0	500	100.00
1	50	50	450	90.00
2	45	95	405	81.00
3	40	135	365	73.00
4	35	170	330	66.00
5	30	200	300	60.00

The percentage remaining in column 5 can be presented on a graph paper, which is known as the survival curve. This was obtained using the following formula:

$$\frac{\text{Number remaining at a given time}}{\text{Number engaged at the start}} \times 100$$

Census Analysis

One of the major deficiencies of cohort analysis is that it holds good for a small homogenous group. Census analysis can eliminate this problem, taking into account a cross section of the organisation, i.e., all the age-specific wastage rates at a given time and applying a smoothing algorithm to the resulting data to identify a general pattern.

Census analysis requires three sets of data as under:

1. The number of employees at the beginning of the census,
2. The number of employees at the end of the census, and
3. The number of levers during the census period.

Skills Inventories

For assessing effectively internal manpower supply, it is important for an organisation to maintain skills inventory containing various information about individuals and their suitability for different jobs. A typical skills inventories include the name of the employee and a listing (or "inventory") of job-related skills, training, and/or experience which could prove useful in a future assignment. The purpose of skills inventories is to quickly identify those candidates who possess the needed qualifications and other required attributes for a specific assignment. With the availability of standard HRIS packages, maintaining skills inventories in the organisation has now become much more easier.

MANPOWER PLANNING MODELS

Use of mathematical models for manpower planning dates back 1779, when John Rowe developed an actuarial model for planning careers in the Royal Marines (Jones, 1964). Manpower systems are described in terms of stocks and flows. Stocks are the number of staff in the system at a given point of time. Stocks are divided into categories like, sex, age, length of service, etc. Flows are recruitment, promotion, wastage, transfers, demotion, etc. Details of some of the conventional models have already been discussed in this chapter. Here we will be discussing some selected mathematical models which require fundamental knowledge of mathematics with greater details.

Markov Models-Hierarchical Systems

In hierarchical systems, routes for the employees, which is the promotion ladder, are well defined. It means every employee elevates himself in the organisation through a well defined career path. All employees start in an organisation at the bottom rung and climb up the ladder one at a time. Any wastage is falling off the ladder. Young and Almond (1961), devised a hierarchical manpower system, framing sub-groups on the basis of salary grade and length of service. They have used the theory of the Markov process to measure the long-term equilibrium distribution of staff among the sub-groups. The basic assumption of this model is that an employee in a particular grade or a status group has a fixed chance of promotion in a given year, independent of vacancy. Thus number receiving promotion depends on the number of eligible staff in the grade below, subject to fulfillment of eligibility criteria, which may be age, seniority, qualifications or experience. The central equation for this model is:

$$n(t + 1) = n(t) P + R(t+1)r$$

Where,

n(t) is the vector of stocks at a given time t, i.e. number of employees in each status group.

P is the matrix of transition probabilities between each of status groups.

r is the vector of probabilities of a recruit starting in particular status groups.

R(t) is the number of new recruits at time t.

If the number of employees n(t) in each status group at a particular time is known, the equation may be used to predict the value of n(t), i.e., number of employees in each status group at a later time t. This is, however, subject to the conditions that recruitment levels, i.e., R (t) during the period, i.e., t = 0 to t = T, are already known or specified. Alternatively, the total number of staff in the system, which is N (t) may be specified. The prediction equation, therefore, may be rewritten in the following form.

$$n (t + 1) = n (t) q + m (t + 1) r$$

This is the more usual form of the Markov chain model than the earlier one. Here, M (t +1) = N (t+1) and includes not only transition within the organisation but also the effects of wastage and recruitment to maintain the balance in the organisation. HRP using Markov Chain is considered mere probabilistic. Moreover, Markov models allow too much fluctuations of the sizes of the status group, while in practice sizes are tightly constrained. To avoid such problems the renewal theory of HRP was developed.

Renewal Models

This model is issued to predict the various flows in the organisation, when size of the stocks is fixed in advance. The equation for the renewal model can be presented as under:

$$L(T) = f(t) + (t) L(T - t) dt$$

where,

f(t) = frequency by length of service or leaving

L(T) = leaving rate at time T

It is assumed that the post is filled at time 0.

Example of Markov Chain Model

Consider an example where the manpower system is made up of four levels:

(i) Management Trainee (MT)

(ii) Assistant Manger (AM)

(iii) Manager (M)

(iv) Senior Manager (SM)

The progression from one level to another is straightforward and is up the hierarchy from (i) to (ii) to (iii). Obviously, not everyone moves up the ladder and the percentage of progression drops steadily as we go up the levels.

There are two entry points in the system, one at the MT level and the second at the Assistant Manager level. There is an employee turnover at every level, although the percentage of turnover drops at every level as we go up the hierarchy level.

The data for these employees are given below:

Particulars	MT	AM	M	SM
No. of employees	60	180	50	20
Emp. turnover rates	22%	30%	10%	4%
New recruitments as a % of total recruitments	95%	5%	–	–
Percentage promoted to next levels (per annum)	78%	5%	2%	–

There are two assumptions which underlie that, (i) the employee in any group (for example managers) has a fixed chance of promotion in any given year and, (ii) there is no requirement of vacancy to exist in the higher grade and, therefore, no delay in promotion to the next higher grade because of competition from other employees.

The central equation used in this type of model is written in the form:

$$n(t + 1) = n(t) P + R(t + 1)r$$

Where n(t) is the vector of employees at time t, P is the matrix of transition probabilities between each pair of employee groups, r is the vector of probabilities of a new recruit starting in each particular employee group, and R (t) is the number of new recruits at time t

In the above example the various figures would be as follows:

$$n(t) = \frac{\text{MT AM M SM}}{(60\ 180\ 50\ 20)}$$

$$P = \begin{array}{c} \text{MT} \\ \text{AM} \\ \text{M} \\ \text{SM} \end{array} \begin{pmatrix} 0 & 0.78 & 0 & 0 \\ 0 & 0.65 & 0.05 & 0 \\ 0 & 0 & 0.88 & 0.02 \\ 0 & 0 & 0 & 0.96 \end{pmatrix}$$

$$r = (0.95\ \ 0.05\ \ 0\ \ 0)$$

We have deliberately used the rotation in explaining so that we can be clear how these numbers come into being n(t) is the actual numbers of employees in each employees group, r is the number of new recruits (95% in MT & 5% in AM grade).

Let us try and understand the matrix P. We can see from the table that 78% of employees in MT are promoted to AM in the next year. So from MT on the left to AM we find a figure of 0.78. Just below that is the figure of AM who remain AM. This figure comes from deducting the employee turnover figure (30% in this case) and promoted to the next grade figure (5% in this case) from a total of 100% (100–30–5 = 65%) =(0.65).

From MT to MT, there is no figure as there is no MT which remains as MT after a year (either he is promoted or he leaves). Also note that there is no figure from MT to M or to SM as no jumps are possible.

Once we have data in place, we can use the equation to calculate the number of employees in each grade for any number of years that we so desire, provided our assumptions are fulfilled and number of new recruits each year are known to us. Let us calculate the number of managers for the next year.

= $n(t + 1) = n(t)\ P + R(t + 1)r$

= 0.05×180 (5% of last year AM's who were promoted)
$+ 0.88 \times 50$ (88% of current managers)

= $9 + 44 = 53$ managers.

If we assume that we are going to take 60 new recruits every year for the next two years, we can find out what is the number of employees in different grades.

It comes out to be,

n (1) = (57 168.23 53 20.2)

Which can be rounded off to:

n (1)	=	(57	168	53	20)
n (2)	=	(57	156.67	55.04	20.26)
	=	(57	157	55	20)

While the AM level employees are going down from the current 180 to 168 next year and to 157, two years from now, the number of managers are going up progressively.

The benefits of the model are obvious, it helps us to see the effect of our policies and plan for the future accordingly.

Cambridge Model

This model concentrates on steady-state age distribution, i.e., staff distribution by age, which remains unchanged year to year. Steady-state is a stable equilibrium. Thus if the system is affected, i.e., if it goes beyond equilibrium, it will tend to return to it. Everanuz (1975) developed the following models for steady-state age distribution:

(i) $A(j) = \dfrac{r(j)}{1+P}$

(ii) $B(j) = \dfrac{1-w(j)}{1+p}$

(iii) $H(_{jL}) = A(_{jL}) + B(j-1)$ for $j = j_L + 1, j_L + 2, \ldots\ldots\ldots j_H$

(iv) $c = 1\Big/\sum_{j=j_L}^{j=J_H} H_j$

(v) $g(j) = c_H(j)$ for $j_L \ldots\ldots j_H$

Here, g (j) = proportion of staff in the steady-state age distribution aged j

r (j) = proportion of recruits aged j, i.e., recruitment age distribution

w (j) = wastage rate for staff aged j

P = long-term expansion rate

(1+P) = Number of staff increases by a factor. If this is negative and it implies a contraction.

Simulation

To simulate is to initiate. In general terms, simulation involves developing a model of some real phenomenon and then performing experiments on the model evolved. It is a descriptive, and not an optimizing, technique. In simulation, a given system is copied and the variables and constants associated with it are manipulated in an artificial environment to examine the behaviour of the system. Using simulation, an analyst can introduce the constants and variables related to the problem, set up the possible courses of action and establish criteria, which act as measures of effectiveness. The benefit of simulation from the view point of the analyst stems from the fact that the results of taking a particular course of action can be estimated prior to its implementation in the real world. Instead of using hunches and intuition to determine what may happen, the analyst using simulation can test and evaluate various alternatives and select the one that gives the best results.

Broadly, there are four phases of the simulation process. They are:

a. Definition of the problem and statement of objectives.

b. Construction of an appropriate model.

c. Experimentation with the model constructed, and

d. Evaluation of the results of simulation.

Monte Carlo Simulation

It is also known as probabilistic simulation method. It can be described as a numerical technique that involves modeling with the objectives of predicting the system's behaviour. The chance element is a very significant feature of Monte Carlo simulation and this approach can be used when the given process has a random, or chance component.

Example 1

A hotel keeps a record of the number of staff requirement of various categories. Information relating to 200 days' requirement are as under:

	Demand								Total
No. of staff	5	6	7	8	9	10	11	12	
No. of days	4	10	16	50	62	38	12	8	200

Develop a simulation model to predict the demand of staff for a 10-day period.

Solution:

Firstly, derive the probability distribution of demand for the staff, expressing each of the frequencies in terms of proportions. This is done by dividing each of the values by 200, i.e. the total frequency. The resultant distribution would, therefore, be as follows:

No. of staff	5	6	7	8	9	10	11	12
Probability	.02	.05	.08	.25	.31	.19	.06	.04

Secondly, determine random numbers using any mechanism of random number generator. There are various ways in which random numbers can be generated. These could be result of some device like coin or die, published table of random numbers, etc. However, the most convenient method is to make use of the published table of random numbers, published by the Rand Corporation of USA.

An assignment has to be worked out so that the interval of random numbers correspond to the probability distribution. Since the probabilities have been calculated to two decimal places, which add upto 1.00, we need 100 numbers of two digits to represent each point of probability. Thus we take random numbers 00 through 99 to represent them. Now, as the probability of 5 staff is equal to .02, we assign two random numbers 00-01 to this demand level; the probability of 6 staff being equal to .05, the next five numbers, 02-06 would be assigned to this level. In a similar manner each of the demand levels would be assigned appropriate intervals as under:

Demand (No. of staff)	Probability	Cumulative probability	Random number interval
5	.02	.02	00-01
6	.05	.07	02-06
7	.08	.15	07-14
8	.25	.40	15-39
9	.31	.71	40-70
10	.19	.90	71-89
11	.06	.96	90-95
12	.04	1.00	96-99

The Cumulative probabilities column analyses the assigned numbers to correspond to the same probability range for each event.

Thirdly, once the random number intervals are determined, we select a tracking pattern for drawing random numbers from the random number table. We may start with any column and row of the table and read the values in any set manner – horizontally, vertically or diagonally. Using the pattern, we draw the random numbers and match them with the assigned events.

Let us assume for the purpose of this problem, we have decided to take every third value horizontally, starting with the fifth column and fourth row of the table of random numbers. The random numbers, according to this pattern are 61, 74, 24, 03, 59, 16, 84, 92, 52, 07........ etc. (for 10-day demand period). We draw as many random numbers as the number of days' demand required to be simulated.

The first number, i.e. 61, lies in the interval 40-70. Corresponding to the demand level of 9 staff. Thus, the simulated demand for the first day is 9 staff members. In a similar manner, we can obtain the demand for each of the day. For the 10-day period, we have the following demand:

Day	1	2	3	4	5	6	7	8	9	10
Number	61	74	24	03	59	16	84	92	52	07
Demand of staff	9	10	8	6	9	8	10	11	9	7

Example

A caterer keeps on reserve cooks during marriage season. Previous experience indicates the daily demand of cooks is as under:

Daily demand	0	10	20	30	40	50
Probability	.01	.20	.15	.50	.12	.02

Consider the following sequence of random numbers:

48, 78, 19, 51, 56, 77, 15, 14, 68, 09

Using this sequence, simulate the demand for the next 10 days. Find out the reserve situation if the owner of the caterer decides to maintain on payroll 30 cooks every day. Also estimate the daily average demand for the cooks on the basis of simulated data.

Solution:

Demand (No. of staff)	Probability	Cumulative probability	Random number interval
0	0.01	0.01	00
10	0.20	0.21	01-20
20	0.15	0.36	21-35
30	0.50	0.86	36-85
40	0.12	0.98	86-97
50	0.02	1.00	98-99

The simulated demand for the cooks for the next 10 days and the stock position for various days when the decision is to make available 30 cooks a day, would be as under:

Determination of Demand and Stock Levels

Day	Random number	Demand	Stock
1	48	30	–
2	78	30	–
3	19	10	20
4	51	30	20
5	56	30	20
6	77	30	20
7	15	10	40
8	14	10	60
9	68	30	60
10	09	10	80

Expected demand = 220/10 = 22 cooks per day.

Advantages and Disadvantages of Simulation

Advantage: The chief merit of the simulation technique is its capacity to lend itself to problems that are cumbersome, or impossible to handle mathematically using analytical methods. Not only this, the technique allows the analyst to experiment with the system behaviour without subjecting it to the risks that would be inherent in experimenting with the real system. It also compresses time to enable the manager to visualize the long-term effects in a quick manner. Besides, simulation is often used to test proposed analytic solutions as well.

Disadvantage: It does not represent a methodology for derivation of optimal solutions to the given problems. This approach is designed merely to provide characterisation of the behaviour of the system in question for a given set of inputs. Further, the simulation approach is not precise in the sense that it yields only estimates which are subject to sampling error. Of course, the sampling error can be reduced by increasing the sample size.

Another drawback is that it may not prove economical, as it requires lot of efforts to develop a suitable model.

It is a tool of solution evaluation and does not generate problem solution. Thus the analyst has to develop the proposed solution; then simulation can be used to test the relative desirability of those solutions.

Replacement Theory

A replacement is called for whenever new equipment offers more efficient or economical service than the old existing one. For example, the old equipment might fail and work no more, or is worn out and needs higher expenditure on its maintenance. The problem, in such situations, is to determine the best policy to be adopted with respect to replacement of the equipment. The replacement theory provides answer to this question in terms of optimal replacement period.

We consider the question of replacement in the following situations:

1. In respect of equipment/assets that deteriorate in performance over a time and may be restored in whole or in part by expanding maintenance costs. Thus, the existing assets might be good technically, yet on economic considerations, it may not be worthwhile continuing with them and hence replacement may be called for. Machinery, equipment, buildings fall in this category.

2. In respect of units that perform adequately until sudden complete failure. The length of their service until failure varies randomly over some predictable range. Car bulbs, tubes, some electronic components, etc,. are the items that are considered in this category.

3. In respect of replacement of staff of an organisation which diminishes gradually due to death, retirement, retrenchment and other reasons.

Staff Replacement

The staff of an organisation calls for replacement because people leave the organisation for several reasons. For planning a suitable recruitment policy, historical data are collected to estimate the likely stay of individuals with the organisation through time. Here also, the stay of an individual employee may be a random variable but the characteristics of the group of employees are likely to be fairly stable.

Example

Year	1	2	3	4	5	6	7	8	9	10	11	12
Percentage expected to leave by end of period	5	18	35	45	62	75	88	90	95	96	99	100

Using the above information, answer the following questions:

1. What recruitment level per annum would be necessary to maintain this strength?
2. If 15 of the sales persons are to be promoted to the next higher post, for which length of service in the organisation is the primary criterion and at what average length of service can a new entrant expect to be promoted?

Solution:

1. With an intake of 100 sales people every year, the distribution of the length of service of the sales force, when equilibrium has been reached shall be as follows:

Year	No. of people continuing
0	100
1	95
2	82
3	65
4	55
5	38
6	25
7	12
8	10
9	5
10	4
11	1
12	0
	Total = 492

Recruitment of 100 sales people every year would thus give a total strength of 492. To maintain strength of 80 sales people, we need to recruit then:

$$\frac{80 \times 100}{492} = 16.26, \text{say 16 persons}$$

2. With 80 persons in the sales team, the distribution of the completed length of service would be as follows:

Year	No. of Persons
0	16
1	15 (95%, of 16)
2	13 (82% of 16)
3	11 (65% of 16)
4	9 (55% of 16)
5	6 (38% of 16)
6	4 (25% of 16)
7	2 (12% of 16)
8	2 (10% of 16)
9	1 (5% of 16)
10	1 (4% of 16)
11	0
12	0

Since 15 sales people are to be promoted and the promotion would be on the basis of their length of service, the cumulation of the frequencies in this distribution reveals that a sales person can expect to be promoted after 5 year of service.

This is ascertained by counting backward, i.e., from the 12th year onwards. After the 5th year the total number of persons left is 16. Thus promotion after the 5th year is considered better, if 15 people are required to be promoted on length of service.

SUMMARY

Human Resource Planning process considers both macro- and micro-level issues. The problem of human resource planning is not unique for Indian organisations. It is now a global phenomena. Without proper human resource planning, organisations would continue to take manpower redundancy decisions on short-term operational results. The HRP process follows certain well-defined stages. At each such stage, it is necessary for the organisation to collect data (both macro and micro), analyse those and then plan for manpower. There are various tools for such analysis, some of these have been discussed, with examples, wherever necessary. However, quantitative tools and models may not be effective, when used in isolation. Combination of quantitative and qualitative techniques yield better results.

KEYWORDS

SWOT Analysis	Wastage Analysis
Timescale of Forecasts	Labour Turnover Index
Workload Factors	Cohort Analysis
Time Series Analysis	Census Analysis
Random Fluctuations	Markov Models
Moving Average Method	Monte Carlo Simulation
Managerial Judgement	Staff Replacement
Delphi Technique	

REVIEW QUESTIONS

1. Discuss the importance of Human Resource Planning process for Indian organisations.
2. What are the different stages of HRP process? Why it is important for us to consider the time-scale of HRP forecasts?
3. Discuss the process of HRP forecasts using workload analysis and time series analysis.
4. What are the difficulties encountered in manpower forecasts using quantitative tools? Do you think such difficulties can be removed by using qualitative tools?
5. What are the different methods of manpower wastage analysis? Do you think such methods are fool proof?
6. Discuss with examples different manpower planning models with a critical note about their limitations.
7. Write short notes on:

   (a) Workload Factors

   (b) Random Fluctuations

   (c) Delphi Technique

   (d) Wastage Analysis

   (e) Cohort Analysis

   (f) Markov Models

   (g) Monte Carlo Simulation Staff Replacement

Case Study 1

Processing Time to Assembly Line

A company is engaged in producing different types of equipment for use in a steel plant. The company has two different assembly lines to produce a particular equipment. The processing time for each of the assembly line is regarded as a random variable and is described by the following distributions:

Process time (minutes)	Assembly - 1	Assembly - 2
10	0.10	0.20
11	0.15	0.40
12	0.40	0.20
13	0.25	0.15
14	0.10	0.05

Using the following random numbers, generate data on the process time for 15 units of the item and compute the expected process time for the product. For the purpose, read the numbers vertically taking the first two digits for the process time on Assembly A1, and the last two digits for processing time on Assembly A2.

4134	8343	3602	7505	7428
7476	1183	9445	0089	3424
4943	1915	5415	0880	9309

Question

Consider there is skill interchangeability, i.e., same workers can be interchangeably used in both the assembly lines. If the company requires to produce 500 units in a day, what would be the manpower requirement in a 8 hour working day with 20 per cent fatigue allowance. Show your computation also in terms of man-hours and man-days basis.

CASE STUDY 2

HUMAN RESOURCE PLANNING OF A STEEL BAR MANUFACTURER

Human resources of an organisation are among the most challenging inputs to manage because people are much more complex than machines. Job design policies should recognise this human aspect and foster employee satisfaction. Work goals should be clear, moderately challenging, and accepted if they are to be useful.

A well-designed job should reflect both social (market) priorities and technical (organisational) capacities. Motivational techniques focus upon the following aspects:

- Variety (job enlargement and job rotation)
- Time (flexi time, 4-day workweeks and job sharing)
- Psychology (enrichment)

The Herzberg enrichment approach emphasises five motivational factors and the Hackman-Oldham model stresses meaningfulness and responsibility. Hackman and Oldham have also developed a job diagnostic survey which measures skill variety, task identity, task importance, autonomy and feedback.

Finally, the socio-technical approach is a view of production systems which incorporates much of this psychological knowledge into a working system that blends both social and technical components.

Work methods can often be improved by conducting a scientific study of present methods using well-developed questioning techniques and principles of motion economy. In office systems, significant productivity improvements can come from better information flow and better use of employee time.

Standards of performance should encourage the co-operation and participation of the workers to whom they will apply. Historical approaches, time studies, pre-determined time methods, and work samplings are also useful ways of developing standards. Both time study and work-sampling methods consist of sampling a worker's activities and subjectively rating the worker's performance level to determine a normal time. Allowances are then, taken into consideration and a standard time is determined. Work sampling is particularly suitable for analysing less structured activities and group operations.

Every operations manager has opportunities to foster a favourable work climate among the employees by providing safe working conditions, just wages and an environment that gives employees stake in what the organisation is doing. Many firms report favourable results from worker participation in problem solving teams, quality circles, and other involvement programmes.

Question

Assume that your organisation, a manufacturer of steel bars, has asked you to do manpower planning for its 10 lakh TPA plant. You are totally new to a steel-manufacturing organisation. Even various production processes are not very clear to you. Clearly write your steps with proper justification and tentatively draw a manpower plan at least at the shop floor level, assuming the unit makes use of conventional furnace and conventional machines.

UNIT 8

Recruitment, Selection and Induction

Learning Objectives

After completion of this unit, the students will be aware of the following topics:

- *Introduction*
- *Recruitment Function*
- *Defining Attitude*
- *HRD and Attitudinal Change*
- *Interview*
- *Induction*
- *Placement*
- *Importance of Induction and Placement*
- *Recruitment Metrics*

RECRUIT AND RETAIN – THE STRATEGIES OF RAVE TECHNOLOGIES

Most of the IT and software majors in India and abroad, recruit the technical and support staff in bulk. Such bulk recruitment is not always for their business expansion and diversification needs, but to replace the existing manpower who either become redundant or leave their jobs even before reaching their transition (less than one year) and settlement (after one year) phases.

Rave Technologies have very active presence in software development and other IT enabled services, including Business Process Outsourcing (BPO). Rave needs to recruit in bulk, new skill sets. Recruitment of technical and support executives in IT and business process outsourcing jobs, require a thorough understanding of the profile of candidates and also, their aptitude and skill-sets before finalising their selection. But for the in-bound and out-bound tele-calling jobs, frequent organising of recruitment camps are more important for on the spot selection based on their voice test and attitude towards the job. In both the cases, attrition rate is very high. Hence, along with recruitment, it is also important for the company to come out with innovative retention strategies.

Unlike other software companies, Rave first focused on attracting the talents sending campus recruitment notices to tier II and tier III institutes, knowing well that tier I institutes' students will not feel attracted for the job offers, though salary wise, Rave is competitive. Instead of recruiting in bulk from single campus, Rave visits multiple campuses to select the best. The interview process followed by Rave is rigorous and prospective candidates need to cross successive hurdles before coming into HR round. After the final selection, Rave offers the job with highly competitive salaries, even at times better than tier-I software companies. Selected candidates do not require to sign any bonds nor do they require to give any deposit for their employment continuation with the company; but they require to put their original certificates in Rave's custody for a period of three years. In the offer of employment, Rave undertakes that on completion of three years, they will give back the certificates with loyalty bonus of 10% of three years' salary. This recruitment process of Rave is not liked by all the selected candidates, but those who choose the option do this on the basis of informed decisions, and in the process, Rave gets the best and retains them.

INTRODUCTION

For staffing various positions in the organisation, we need to go for external hiring, as redeploying existing manpower through job restructuring may not be adequate. External hiring process succeeds Human Resource Planning. Through HRP we can understand the extent of external hiring after adjustment of internal manpower.

Recruitment, selection, induction and placement are important tools for procuring and effectively using human resources in an organisation. While recruitment involves employing suitably trained workforce, selection helps in choosing the right candidate for the right job. Induction and placement is putting the men to the right jobs. This unit focuses on these four important organisational activities.

The traditional approach to personnel management was to ensure routine human resources maintenance functions for the organisations. But recently, radical changes in human resource management, i.e. perceiving human resources like other important resources (physical and financial) of an organisation has developed new areas for personnel management. The human resources are the people who are part of the organisation. Broadly, they may be direct employees, the customers served, part-time persons, temporary employees or consultants or any person or persons with a variety of other relationships to the organisation. Within the human resources area, there are two major activities. The first is concerned with the recruitment, selection, placement, compensation and appraisal of the human resources (they are known as human resources utilisation functions or personnel functions). The other functions are directed to work with the existing human resources, improving their efficiency and effectiveness. These are known as Human Resources Development (HRD) functions which are designed to enable existing human resources to learn activities for their effective functioning in the present jobs, future identifiable jobs and so also for future undefined jobs.

For increasing importance of human resources, it is now imperative for all organisations to retain the manpower and at the same time to recruit and select best possible talents in the country. Most of the organisations are now facing technological changes, resulting the radical change in the recruitment process. Such a technological change, *inter alia*, calls for hiring manpower having higher skills and knowledge, which were not so far available. However, when we consider the recruitment of manpower for unskilled jobs, there seem to be no apparent problems for the organisation, as these people are abundantly available in our country due to the high rate of unemployment. For high technology employees, i.e. mostly those who are in managerial positions with professional skills, recruitment function is more complex and dynamic.

Recruitment Function

The term recruitment may be defined as the process to discover sources of manpower to meet the requirements or the staffing schedule and to employ effective measures for attracting that manpower in adequate number to facilitate the selection of an efficient working force.

The first important task of recruitment function is to frame a recruitment policy, which calls for review of manpower requirement, i.e. it should be adequately supported by effective manpower forecasting. Manpower planning and so also manpower forecasting of an organisation depends on many important factors like present nature of work, possible change in the future working of the organisation, the manpower records and information available in the organisation for the present strength, the diversification plans and programmes of the organisation, the environmental change and the change necessary in the organisation to respond to such environmental change, etc. Most of the organisations, in principle, believe in recruiting the best possible manpower from outside the organisation. However, the recruitment policy of some organisations considers recruiting the employees based on the recommendation of the present employees or recruiting employees from the wards of the existing employees.

For example, in Tata, there is a system to recruit employees for unskilled/low-skilled jobs, both technical and non-technical nature, from the wards of the existing employees. Such a policy of recruitment in Tata has been accepted in principle and Tata, in their manufacturing units, maintain separate employment exchange records to enlist the names and other details of the employees' wards to offer them employment as and when a vacancy arises. But such type of recruitment policy is not followed while hiring manpower for managerial jobs. In such cases, companies are looking for best available talents. Thus, they go either for advertising the vacancies in leading newspapers of the country, even in good professional journals or they may go in for recruitment of such managerial manpower by effecting campus interview, and also going for retaining the services of recruitment consultants. Such recruitment consultants, having maintained a separate data bank for the prospective job seekers, can make available a list of prospective managerial manpower to such companies. In addition to the framing of the recruitment policy, each organisation for making their recruitment a scientific process of selection, carries out regular forecasting of manpower recruitments.

Internal Recruitment

In some cases, organisations are also trying to internally man higher managerial vacancies from their existing employees. In those cases, organisations need to develop their existing manpower adopting suitable training and development functions. Training and development may not necessarily always ensure availability of the best talents internally. Organisations are then compelled to recruit from outside sources, mentioned above. Internal recruitment creates rippling effect in the organisational structure, cascading movement at different levels.

Recruitment Policy

A sound recruitment policy calls for adopting a scientific process of recruitment, i.e. those techniques, which are modern and scientific. Recruitment policy also requires one to consider the high cost of managerial turnover. Unless a company adopts a suitable recruitment policy, it may not be possible for the company to select the right candidate for the right job. A sound recruitment policy, therefore, needs to:

1. Identify, at the outset, the recruitment needs of the organisation,
2. Identify the preferred sources of recruitment,
3. Frame suitable criteria for selection and finally,
4. Consider the cost of recruitment.

Sources of Recruitment

As has already been discussed, a particular organisation may effect recruitment either from the internal sources, i.e. by promoting the existing employees for higher positions, or they may go for outside sources. Thus, internal and external sources of recruitment can either be resorted to by any organisation, subject to convenience and feasibility. Recruitment is an art of attracting applicants, from whom the most suitable ones may be selected in a particular job or jobs. Internal recruitment may often avoid unpleasantness, but it is not necessarily effective because it does not allow the organisation to get many alternatives to select the best available talent. External sources being available, it gives opportunity to an organisation to tap the best or suitable candidates from widely dispersed areas. The requisition for recruitment contains a brief description of the post, qualification and experience required, etc. Such requisitions are normally signed by the head of the human resource department. External sources of recruitment are taken recourse to keeping in view the type of personnel required. The workmen may be recruited at the gate itself or from the employment exchange. Management trainees are taken from the institutes and universities, effecting campus interviews. Senior executives are attracted through advertisements in leading newspapers and magazines. The major sources of recruitment for different types of personnel, therefore, are as follows:

1. Employment exchanges,
2. Consultants and private employment agencies,
3. Advertisements in periodicals and newspapers, radio and TV,
4. Deputation,
5. Universities and management institutes,
6. From the source of existing employees,
7. Trade unions,
8. Internet/job site, etc.

The employment exchanges maintain a register of candidates seeking various types of job. Under Compulsory Notification of Vacancies Act, 1955, the employers are required to notify certain types of vacancies to the nearest employment exchange and recruit candidates from among the applicants registered with them. The skilled and unskilled workers and the clerical staff are mostly recruited through employment exchanges. Private consultants and agencies assist organisations in locating technical and managerial staff. They charge prescribed fees for their services to the organisation.

Advertising in newspapers and magazines, radio and TVs, have now become most effective sources for attracting the prospective candidates. It also helps in building the image for the organisation because through such advertisements, the organisations make available certain information, like their products, their market share, their turn-over value, etc., to the public in general and target consumers in particular. Since written Press insertions or verbal advertisements through audio and audio-visual methods give first-hand information to the prospective job seekers, each organisation is required to give as much factual information as possible regarding the job-expectations from the candidates, their age group, qualifications and experience, salary and perks attached to the positions and important conditions of service, the time-limit and mode of applying, etc. There are some agencies who help organisations in drafting, publishing and broadcasting advertisements.

Deputationists are mainly appointed in public sector undertakings. The civil servants are often deputed for many senior and mid-level positions for a specified time.

Recruitment from universities and management institutes are effected through campus interviews. Almost all good private organisations select their management trainees through such method. Some organisations even sponsor the cost of prospective students during their learning to join them after completion of the course.

From the source of existing employees also, recruitment is done by many private organisations to ensure commitment and loyalty and at the same time to motivate the employees. Such type of recruitment, however, is restricted only to the clerical and unskilled jobs in most of the cases.

Trade unions also recommend candidates for clerical and unskilled jobs. This practice is not in vogue in many organisations. Only in technical training schemes, trade unions were found to influence the organisations to induct their recommended candidates as apprentices.

Recruitment through internet/job sites also have now become very popular for its wide reach to focussed job seekers, immediacy and cost-effectiveness. Because of its global reach, organisations also get the flexibility to attract the best talent. Many placement agents have now started this service to increase their business volume.

Selection of a Candidate

The next step in selection procedure is to personify such attributes in candidates, i.e. developing a specification of persons, to define the background education, training, personality and characteristics of the candidates to suit the vacancy position. This in reality is an exercise to pre-portray an ideal candidate for a job.

Preliminary Screening of Applicants

The number of applications normally received against any advertised vacancy are usually more. This creates the problem of selecting the right persons. Moreover, conducting tests and interviews for all the candidates may not be always feasible and cost-efficient. To obviate such problems, most of the organisations sort out unsuitable candidates before going ahead with the selection process. There are many different ways to do such preliminary screening. Some organisations conduct short tests for all the applications, while the best method may be the checking of 'application blank'. Each organisation before going for the selection process develops their own standards or potential attributes for the prospective candidates. This helps them also to define the rejection standards. For example, for the post of a stenographer, a particular organisation may define their rejection standards as below:

1. Those who are having shorthand speed below 100 words per minute and types speed below 40 words per minute.
2. Those who are not having any working experience,
3. Those who are above 35 years age.

By checking 'Application Blank' of the candidates, an organisation may reject a good number of applicants based on the above rejection parameters. All the above processes, therefore, enable the organisation to short list the candidates before going ahead with the subsequent stages of selection. The rejection standards, like the ones stated above, may also be mentioned in the advertisement itself so that the number of applicants is minimised.

Some organisations also adopt the 'successive-hurdles' technique as an effective screening process. This technique calls for arranging all selection factors in order of importance. For example, if for a particular post, aptitude test is considered most important, the first step should be to test the aptitude of the candidates, then the other successive tests, like qualification, job experience, personality, etc., may be conducted provided the candidates qualify these hurdles one by one.

Review of Application Blanks

The application blank form is designed to have detailed information about the applicants. Some organisations have their own printed application blank, while others ask the candidates to give their particulars in a standard format to elicit information like:

1. Personal data and biographical Information, i.e., name, address, telephone number, age, sex, martial status, children, nationality, education (school, college, university attended, degree/diploma passed, year of passing, subjects, grade or division obtained, etc.), professional qualification and membership of professional bodies, language known (ability to read, write and speak), etc.

2. Chronological employment history for all jobs (with joining and leaving dates in each case of employment change), employer's name, address and nature of business positions held and duties, reason for leaving (if any).

3. Personal circumstances, whether prepared to serve anywhere or not.

4. Medical history, brief details of any serious illness, remained absent for how many days during the last few years (in case the applicant served earlier somewhere) on medical grounds, record of hospitalisation (if any), disability, major operation, etc.

5. Interest, hobbies, sports and other activities.

6. Anything else which the applicant may like to add in support of his candidature.

Several other items may be included in the application blank on the specific requirements of the organisation and the job. Weighted application blanks are also prepared by some organisations to record personal history items associated with job success. For each item of the application blank, weight factors are pre-determined. Importance of weight factors for different jobs also vary. For example, for unskilled labourer's job, education may be given less weight, while for executive positions, education receives higher weightage. Application blank, therefore, helps in comparing the applications.

Reference Checking

Some organisations ask for references from the applicants in the application blank itself to get information on a candidate's character and antecedents. Such references are preferred from earlier employers and schools/colleges/universities who have some acquaintance with the candidates. Organisations try to verify candidates antecedents from the references either over phone, through correspondence or through personal visits. Most of the organisations send a brief questionnaire to such references along with a confidential note, requesting them to furnish such details.

Psychological Testing

Generally, psychological testing is used for purposes like, determining training needs and evaluation of training programmes, selection and placement, transfer and promotion, counselling. However, such testing is primarily used for selection and placement. Such tests are of different types like, group or individual tests, instrumental tests, aptitude or achievement tests, personality and interest tests, etc. Group tests are designed to test a group of candidates simultaneously. Individual tests are for individual candidates at a particular point of time. Instrumental tests can be group tests or individual tests. When it is an individual test, it makes use of different tools to study candidate's familiarity and skills. But in case of its application for a group, it involves a written test or paper-pencil test to study the written responses of the candidates. Aptitude tests are intended to assess the potentiality of the applicants to learn the job, while achievement tests enable us to assess how effectively an individual can perform his job. Conventionally, aptitude tests are administered on freshers, i.e. those who are not having any past job experience, while achievement tests are intended for experienced candidates. For marketing jobs and managerial and executive positions such tests have much relevance. However, psychological tests are mostly designed to measure the aptitude and skills of successful job performers. For selection and placement, most of the organisations retain the services of consultants and experts for psychological testing. This minimises the chance of error in selecting the wrong candidates for different job positions. Since psychological testing is a complex method and it has wide divergence, we have briefly introduced the concept of attitudinal measurement with simple examples and illustrations together with some conceptual details about different types of measurement and scales.

Defining Attitude

Attitude is a mental state of an individual who tends to act or respond or is ready to respond for or against objects, situations, etc., with which his/her vested feeling or affect, interest, liking, desire and so on, are directly or indirectly linked or associated. During the course of development the person acquires tendencies to respond to objects. These learned cognitive mechanisms are called attitudes. Changes in knowledge are followed by changes in attitudes. Attitudes are different from knowledge in a sense that attitudes are emotion-laden. Knowledge reinforces attitudes and reinforced attitudes in the long run reinforce individual and group behaviour. Hence, attitude is neither behaviour nor the cause of behaviour but it relates to an intervening pre-disposition or a frame of reference which influences the behaviour of an individual.

When the interest, feeling, etc., of an individual is not connected in any way with the object or situation, his/her responses (towards the said object or situation) will then not be attitude but opinion. Attitudes or psychic states cannot be observed because psychological variables are dormant or latent. Being covert, attitude measurement is difficult. Inference, prediction from behaviour data, interviews with structured questionnaires and scales are the usual tools for attitudinal measurement.

Attitude Survey

To recruit new incumbents and to evaluate the human relation in the factories, industries and different organisations, attitude survey is indispensable. The study of attitude is also important in designing a training programme, which is a core HRD function.

Attitude surveys focus on feelings and motives of the employees' opinions about their working environments. There are three basic purposes for conducting attitude surveys:

1. To compare results with other survey results,
2. To measure the effect of change that occurs and,
3. To determine the nature and extent of employee feelings regarding specific organisational issues and the organisation in general.

Usually attitude surveys are carried out by interviewing a person with a structured close ended questionnaire. The skill of the interviewer is all important here for correct measurement of attitude. While framing the questionnaire, the interviewer should be cautious, as simple opinion-laden questionnaire items will not depict the attitude of the interviewee. What is important is to put value-laden questionnaire items, use of behaviourally anchored statements, asking the respondents to rank any myth statements, etc. A sample list of such myth statements and value-laden questionnaire items are given below:

Myth Statements

1. Hard work ensures better result.
2. Liking to work with subordinates for prompt results.
3. Never say no to anyone; listen to everybody's problems.
4. One who is indispensable, is efficient.
5. Maintaining the hierarchical structure while taking decisions.

Sample Questionnaire Items for Attitude Measurement

1. Do you think the expenditure on training is wasteful? (Give your answer selecting any one from the given alternatives).

   (a) To a large extent

   (b) To some extent

   (c) To a very little extent

   (d) Not at all

2. Which, to your knowledge, are the major barriers to effective implementation of flexible working hours in India? (Please arrange the factors in order of your perceived preference).

(a) Lack of awareness

(b) Difficulty in implementation

(c) Supervisory problems

(d) Lack of support from workers

(e) Lack of support from unions

(f) Production problems

(g) Any other (please specify)

The first questionnaire item (which reflects the attitude of a person regarding training) can be evaluated by adding the weighted value of individual responses. How to give weight against questionnaire items has been explained in the scaling and attitude measurement part of this unit.

Example

Let the number of respondents be 15. Suppose they have given their responses as follows to the four alternatives.

Alternatives	No. of Respondents
(a) To a large extent	4
(b) To some extent	4
(c) To a very little extent	5
(d) Not at all	2
Total	15

Weighted Average Attitude

Alternatives	No. of Respondents	Weighted	Attitude
(a)	4	4	16
(b)	4	3	12
(c)	5	2	10
(d)	2	1	2

Alternative (a) 'To a large extent' is the group attitude.

The second questionnaire item allows the respondents to answer the question by selecting all alternatives in order of their perceived priority. This requires use of factorial method for quantification of all responses. Let us give an example to illustrate the matter.

Example

Let there be 15 respondents. Suppose they have responded by giving ranks to the alternative (a) as follows:

Respondent	1	2	3	4	5	6	7
Rank of (a)	1	3	5	7	1	4	3

Respondent	8	9	10	11	12	13	14	15
Rank of (a)	2	6	5	1	2	3	4	5

From the above, we get:

Priority/Rank	1	2	3	4	5	6	7
Number of Respondents (Tr)	3	2	3	2	3	1	1

(Total no. of respondents = 15, No. of priorities/ranks = 7, i.e., a to g)

Weighted Score Value (WSV) is calculated as follows:

Priority	1	2	3	4	5	6	7
Total Value	3	2	3	2	3	1	1
Weights (factorial)	7	6	5	4	3	2	1
WSV	21	12	15	8	9	2	1

In the same way, the total weighted score value for other alternatives can be calculated from the responses obtained against each. Suppose they are as follows:

Alternative	b	c	d	e	f	g
Total WSV	65	30	70	55	60	40

The total weighted score value of alternative (d) is highest. Therefore, alternative (d) i.e., "lack of support from workers" should be the attitude/opinion of the group of respondents.

Similarly, sample behaviourally anchored statements have also been discussed as a tool for performance appraisal in a separate unit.

For measurement of attitude, we can use various statistical tools. Since attitudes are psychological variables or qualitative variables, the first and foremost task for the rater is to assign numerals to objects, events or persons. Use of Likert type of scale, Thurstone Scale, etc., help the interviewer to assign numbers, either discrete or continuous. Analysis of variance, correlation, chi-square test, Kendal's co-efficient and concordance test are some useful statistical tools for attitude measurement.

HRD and Attitudinal Change

Changing attitudes, values and motivations are now the major issues before the organisations. Through appropriate HRD interventions, organisations can turn such change into advantages, ensuring quality of work life, keeping pace with the changing human expectations. The following area of attitudinal changes require HRD intervention.

1. Attitudes towards perceived threats to trade union legality and other large scale efforts to reduce trade union power or cohesion;
2. Attitudes towards methods of wage negotiations, whether by collective or local bargaining;
3. Attitudes towards working conditions and any administrative machinery for the discussion or regulation of such conditions;
4. Attitudes towards worker training or promotion and towards education in general as means of improving management and industrial skills.

As explained earlier, economic restructuring, market globalisation, international quality system standards, etc., have, *inter alia*, prompted the Indian organisations to go for radical organisational restructuring, which among others call for adoption of TQM principles in managing the human resources. TQM, inter alia, calls for Total Employee Involvement (TEI), employee empowerment, development of small group activities (quality circle forums), value engineering teams, etc. To translate the TQM requirements into corporate practices, therefore, requires lot of attitudinal changes at the top like developing flatter type of organisation, de-layering, delegation, and information, organisational culture, where every employee needs to be considered as a member of a well integrated family. To infuse attitudinal changes both at the top and down the level, it is necessary to adopt the following HRD strategy.

Employee Empowerment

Empowerment is to give everyone, instead of just people with certain positions or certain job titles, the legitimate right to make judgement, form conclusions, reach decisions and then act. Empowerment, therefore, calls for employee participation in day-to-day problem-solving and innovation. Traditional participative forums (works committees, joint consultative machinery, etc.) restrict employee participation in operational areas. But empowerment demands employee participation in each and every corporate functions, so much so as to accept that the employee is not a mere seller of his time and labour for a contracted sum of money. The empowered employee acquires necessary skill and authority to make decision concerning quality and productivity. They initiate changes on their own. Empowerment changes attitude of the employee as it develops employee ownership and commitment.

By Promoting Quality Circles and Developing the Culture of Total Participation

This strategy is used to infuse attitudinal changes and to facilitate personal involvement of employees.

Quality circles have been defined originally by JUSE (Japanese Union of Scientists and Engineers) as a small group of workers, voluntarily performing quality control activities within the workshop to which they belong. These small groups, with voluntary participation of each and every member of the organisation continuously engage themselves in promoting quality control activities, because of total participation of the members of the organisation, irrespective of their hierarchical levels. Quality circles in reality encompass the concepts of self-development and mutual development and at the same time, reinforce quality control techniques. Even though the concept of 'quality circles' eventually originated in Japan to survive under compelling circumstances, it has now been expanded far and wide, cutting across cultural and ideological barriers. It gained popularity gradually in most of the industrialized nations and among the developing nations of the world. India being one of the fast developing nations is no exception. Quality circles can be related to increased employee motivation and productivity and hence it is used as an important HRD tool in the organisation. Total knowledge, skill, creative abilities, talents and aptitudes together with values, attitudes and beliefs of the workers and/or individuals of the organisation represent the human resources in more aggressive terms. Quality circles ensure total involvement of employees through a number of small group forums. Experience shows that many organisations have succeeded to improve their productivity by quality circles activities. Increased productivity can be achieved by increased employee motivation, which quality circles can better ensure than any other methods like complex planning, rigorous execution, etc.

By Imparting Knowledge and Value-laden Attitudinal Changes in Training

Organisations need to focus on more training on human relations areas like leadership, communication, motivation, etc. Such knowledge inputs gradually reinforce the attitude of the employees.

By Focusing More on Team Spirit

To integrate employees with the organisation. This initiative is further strengthened when we simultaneously ensure a sense of belongingness among the employees.

Table 8.1: Types of Measurement

Type	Basic Empirical Operations	Typical Usage	Typical Statistics	
			Descriptive	Inferential
Nominal	Determination of equality	Classification of male-female, smoker, non-smoker, team-I,	Percentage mode	Chi-square, binomial
Ordinal	Determination of greater or less	Rankings: Pre-ference data, market position, attitude measurement, many others psychological measures, etc.	Median	Rank-order correlation
Interval	Determination of equality of intervals	Index numbers, attitude measurement	Mean, range, standard deviation	Product moment correlation T-test, factor analysis
Ratio	Determination of equality of ratios	Sales, units produced, number of customers, costs, age, etc.	Geometric mean	Co-efficient of variation

Accuracy, Reliability and Validity

Accuracy is the extent to which a measurement is free from systematic and variable errors. Freedom from variable errors is known as the validity of measurement. Reliability measure the yields same result in repeated applications to the same respondents or events. Validity measure is consistent as it is free from systematic errors and measures what it purports to measure.

Attitude Scales

Scale is an instrument with the help of which a concept is measured. It is used in all types of data collection techniques such as observation, interviews, projective techniques, etc. Broadly, there are two types of scales; rating scales and attitude scales.

Attitude scales measure one or more aspects of an individual's or group's attitude toward some object. An individual's responses to the various scales may be aggregated or summed to provide a single attitude for the individual. Similarly, group responses to the various scales may be aggregated or summed to provide a single attitude for the group.

These scales are of three types:

1. Likert's Summated Scales
2. Thurstone's Equal Appearing Intervals Scale and
3. Guttman's Cumulative Scale

Likert's Summated Rating Scale

A summated rating scale is a set of attitude statements of which all are considered or approximated a equal attitude value and to each of which, the subjects respond with a degree or agreement of disagreement (intensity) carrying different scores. These scores are summed and averaged to yield an individual's attitude score. Under this method each respondent's ranking is found out by totaling his scores on all the statements (usually 5). To illustrate this, let us take the following example:

S.No.	Statement	Agree	Disagree
1.	Advertising promotes sales	1	0
2.	HRD is exploitation of people	1	0
3.	Hard work increases productivity	1	0
4.	Effective time management reduces idle hours	1	0
5.	Money and other physical benefits are the only motivations	1	0

This procedure, however, suffers from the following drawbacks:

1. Ties in ranks occur quite frequently. There may be several respondents with total scores of 0, 1, 2, 3, 4, 5, who cannot be ordered in relation to one another.

2. It does not throw light on the different way in which given scores may be obtained. Different combinations of the score imply differences among individuals which are not revealed by this procedure.

3. It is not possible to determine whether the scale is uni-dimensional or multidimensional, i.e., whether the statements are measuring only one property or several properties of an attitude.

4. In this scale all statements are deemed to be of equal attitude value. There is no scale of statements as such. This method orders the individuals on the basis of their total scores and not statements.

Likert's Item Analysis

In this procedure, respondents are asked to respond to a certain number of statements (which is usually restricted to 15). Reply to each statement is given in terms of five degrees of agreement or disagreement, viz., 'Strongly agree', 'Agree', 'Undecided', 'Disagree', 'Strongly Disagree'. Each statement, thus, becomes a scale in itself having five points on it. At one end of this scale is strong approval and the other end is strong disapproval, between them there are many intermediate points. The respondent indicates with reference to each statement where he stands on this scale. The total of his scores on all statements is taken as the measurement of his attitude. Statement may be either favourable or unfavourable. For favourable statements, values given are 5, 4, 3, 2, 1, and for unfavourable statements values are 1, 2, 3, 4, 5.

The following examples will illustrate this:

Statement	SA	A	U	D	SD
Management is a science	5	4	3	2	1
Management is not a science	1	2	3	4	5

Thurstone's Equal Appearing Intervals Scale

This scale attempts to represent the attitudes of a group on a specified issue in the form of frequency distribution. The various opinions or items on a scale are allocated to different positions in accordance with the attitudes they express. Following steps are necessary to construct a Thurstone attitude scale.

1. Brief statements expressing attitudes about a particular issue are gathered from current literatures or are especially prepared for this purpose. The statements should cover different range of attitudes from extremely favourable to extremely unfavourable and also include neutral statements.

2. Statements are given an arbitrary number for identification and a group of judges are asked to sort those into several piles.

3. After sorting, a complete tabulation is made to determine the number of times each statement is included in the several piles.

4. The scale values for each statement are determined graphically in the form of an ogive or cumulative frequency curve.

5. The final scale is then made, selecting 15 to 20 statements (preferably those on which judges have had least disagreement).

6. Respondents then are asked to check only those statements with which they agree.

The construction of this scale being very cumbersome and time-consuming, it is usually avoided. Moreover, scale values assigned to statements are influenced by the attitudes, background and intelligence of judges who may see things as different from the actual respondents. This scale also does not allow subjects to express the intensity of the feelings of the respondents as they have only the choice to indicate their agreement with the finally selected statements.

Guttman's Cumulative Scale

This scale is made up of a relatively small number of statements which have been tested for their uni-dimensionality. A uni-dimensional scale measures one variable only. The scale is known as cumulative as respondents agreeing with the most favourable statements are theoretically presumed to agree with all other statements expressing 'lesser' degree of favourability. Use of this scale is also avoided for its complexity. Other scale to measure the attitude is Social Distance Technique of Bogardus, which is normally used to measure highly subjective attitudes.

INTERVIEW

In the literal sense of the word, an interview means a conversation with a purpose. Such purposes are classified under three categories, i.e., obtaining information from the candidates, giving information to the candidates and finally motivating the candidates. The first purpose is intended to get information from candidates regarding their background, experience, education, training and interests to evaluate their suitability as per the requirements of the organisation. The second purpose is to provide the candidates information regarding the organisation, its philosophy, personnel policies, etc. The third purpose is to establish a positive relationship to motivate the prospective candidates to join the organisation. However, all these purposes being successive stages of interview, the subsequent stages will be followed only when the interviewers are prima facie satisfied with the candidates in the first stage.

The human resource department of most of the organisations conduct preliminary interview for the candidates. However, for subsequent interview, a committee of executive is formed to select the right candidates. For managerial and executive positions, organisations prefer to retain the service of consultancy organisations with subject experts on the selection committee.

There are different types of interview as under:

1. ***The Patterned Interview:*** This is also known as structured or standardised interview. It is intended to assess the candidate's emotional strength and stability, industry, ability to

get along well with others, self-reliance, willingness to accept responsibility, motivation, etc.

2. ***Indirect or Non-indirective Interview:*** This type of interview is meant for helping the candidates to feel relaxed and free to talk. Interviewers become listeners and allow the candidates to reveal their personality, in-depth knowledge in a free and relaxed atmosphere.

3. ***Direct Planned Interview:*** It is a simple question-answer session to ascertain the suitability of the candidates.

4. ***Stress Interview:*** This interview assesses the candidates' emotional balance under a situation of tension and stress. Such tension is, therefore, deliberately created by interruptions, provocations, silence, criticism or even by firing questions. Interviewers in such a situation deliberately become more unfriendly and even, at times, hostile. For selection of executives, who are required to work under stress, such method is often adopted.

5. ***Group Interview:*** This method is intended to assess the leadership ability of the candidates. Generally, a topic is given to the candidates to discuss among themselves. The interviewers remain in the background to assess the best leaders, their initiative, poise, adaptability, awareness, interpersonal skills, etc.

6. ***Panel or Board Interview:*** Several interviewers collectively interview a candidate to rate his/her attributes. Generally, such a panel consists of several experts and each of them interview a candidate only in those areas on which they have the requisite expertise.

For conducting a successful interview, interviewers should be adequately competent and trained. Interview should be conducted in a suitable place. It should be well planned, job descriptions and information about the applicants should be adequately studied. Interviewers should be free from any conceivable prejudice. Interviewees should be allowed to feel relaxed, beginning and ending of an interview should be made in a best possible friendly manner, etc.

The limitations of traditional selection process like failure to select the right persons for the right jobs, too much emphasis on written tests and interview, resulted in the development of psychometric method. This method enables us to quantify the attributes, adding which we can select the candidates in order of their merit. Many organisations today are making use of this method to ensure proper selection of their employees.

INDUCTION

After selection of employees, the first step is to orient them to organisational life. Induction or orientation programme of an organisation is a process to guide and counsel the employees to familiarise them with the job and the organisation. This process helps an organisation to clarify the terms and conditions of employment, specific job requirements and also to inculcate confidence in the minds of the new entrants.

Objectives

General objectives of such a programme normally are:

1. To introduce new employees with the organisational environment, exposing them to the mission, history and traditions of the organisation, its achievements and future challenges, its personnel policy and expectations from the new employees.

2. To create a positive attitude in the minds of the new employees.

3. To create proper awareness in the new employees, enabling them to understand the business of the organisation.

4. To provide opportunity to interact with other fellow employees and also with other managerial employees of the organisation.

A good induction programme should contain the following areas which are conveniently distributed under organisation's point of view and employee's point of view.

Organisation's Point of View

1. History, mission, objectives and philosophy of the organisation.

2. Its product, production process, operations involved, state of technology.

3. Its past achievements, present status and future growth plan.

4. Structure of the organisation and the functions of different departments.

5. Delegation of authority and decision-making process.

6. Personnel policies, other miscellaneous policies, practices and regulations.

7. Job descriptions and responsibilities.

8. Expectations from new employees.

Employee's Point of View

1. Job responsibilities.

2. Office procedures.

3. Grievance handling procedures.

4. Salary and perks.

5. Service rules governing hours of work, overtime.

6. Rules covering probation, confirmation, promotion opportunities, transfer, etc.

7. Retirement and superannuation benefits.
8. Employee services and welfare activities.
9. Employee's participation in small group activities, question schemes.
10. Performance evaluation.

Steps in Induction Programme

An induction programme essentially involves the following steps:

1. *General Orientation:* It includes guided tours in different departments of an organisation, introduction with fellow employees, supervisors and executives, information about the organisations' mission, philosophy, achievements and future plans, etc. Some organisations have their printed manuals, which they give to their new employees to orient them with their induction training programmes for a week or so. The purpose of such general orientation programme is to build a sense of pride in the minds of the new employees and also to create an interest in them about the organisation.

2. *Specific Orientation:* This is intended to help new employees to get acclimatised with their new work environment. The supervisor or the departmental boss of the employee takes him to his place of work and imparts vocational guidance for his particular nature of work. He is also told about the technology, environment and other facilities available in the organisation, prevailing practices and customs and specific expectations from an employee. For executives and managerial employees, targets and key result areas for each of them are given to make them aware of what organisation expects from them.

3. *Follow-up Orientation:* This orientation is conducted sometime after the initial induction of an employee, i.e. preferably within a period of six months or so. The purpose of such orientation is to give guidance and counsel to the employees to ensure that they are reasonably satisfied and gradually settling in the organisation.

Employee Socialisation

Employee orientation and induction is also called employee socialisation process. Socialisation, however, is a continuous process, today's organisations being dynamic. For the new employees, Decenzo and Robins (1999) identified that socialisation process involves three distinct stages as under:

1. *Pre-arrival Stage:* At this stage individual employees come to an organisation with certain values, attitudes and expectations. This exercise being undertaken at the selection stage, to enable an employee to understand to what extent his perceived mapping gels with organisational culture and systems, it is the duty of the persons involved in the selection process to facilitate this. Now-a-days because of availability of information about organisations through different media, including websites and internet, an enthusiastic individual may also have some preconceived ideas about the organisation. Therefore, it

is better to first understand from the individual about what he understands about the organisation and then help him to synchronise this information with the reality. This helps the individual to take the right decision.

2. *Encounter Stage:* At this stage, perceptions earlier generated by an individual, are reaffirmed through a well planned induction programme. Any dichotomy between the employees perceptions and organisational perceptions, need to be properly identified and removed through increased socialisation process.

3. *Metamorphosis Stage:* At this final stage of socialisation, employees understand the organisations and identify them with the organisations. Employees develop a sense of belongingness and become a contributor to achieving organisational goals and objectives.

However, as explained earlier, socialisation is a continuous process, as organisations are now required to go for restructuring and re-engineering every now and then, keeping pace with the changing environment.

PLACEMENT

After the initial programme is over, an employee is put to a specific job, for which he has been selected. Most of the organisations put new employees on probation for a specified period after which they are confirmed or made permanent, provided they match the organisational requirements. The personnel department periodically reviews the progress of such employees getting feedbacks on their performance from their controlling authority. Some organisations have also a system to extend the probationary period, if the employees fail to match to the organisational expectations. Such placement is known as 'differential placement'.

Placement is defined as assigning employees jobs for which they have been identified as suitable based on the selection techniques. But such definition would be meaningless, if a particular employee is recruited against a particular vacancy. Generally, the question of placement arises when a group of trainees are recruited. Organisations, to identify the true potentiality of an employee, in such cases, make provision for short-term placement, during which phase, employees are allowed to work on different jobs, through a systematic job rotation programme. However, at a later stage, permanent placement is effected matching the employees' competence, knowledge, skill and job interest. Other forms of placement have been discussed in the unit on Transfer and Promotion.

IMPORTANCE OF INDUCTION AND PLACEMENT

Common use of higher technology, increased level of knowledge and skills of the new job entrants, production restructuring and flexibility coupled with perceptive change about human resource, which is now considered as most important resource of an organisation, have now transformed labour as an item for competitive sale and purchase. However, despite the problem of unemployment in India, there still exists dearth of knowledge and skilled workers and so also executives and managers. The recent economic liberalisation programme of the Government of India has now paved the way for entry of multinationals and foreign companies. Market globalisation has further intensified the competition. Development of total quality management philosophy, *inter alia*, is also demanding sea change in product and service-mix of an organisation. All these together have now increased the scope for job mobility for employees with knowledge and skills of appropriate type and degree.

Unfortunately, retaining employees after recruitment and selection is an utterly neglected area in Indian corporate sector. Many organisations spend several lakhs of rupees in terms of job advertisement, conducting tests and interviews, hiring the services of consultants and psychologists, etc., for selecting a managerial employee. A weak induction programme, without adequate emphasis on building confidence and sense of belongingness in the minds of the new employees, results in quick separation, so also wastage of colossal sum of money for the organisation. Such experience is quite common in public sector units. Very recently a leading Tata organisation has lost few hundreds of their young engineers and professionals, who left *en masse* to join elsewhere.

Some organisations, on the contrary, do not review the progress of the new employees, who become permanent automatically after completion of their probationary tenure, despite they being unproductive. Thus, a good induction and placement programme needs to ensure employees' retention by keeping their motivation high, while at the same time, getting rid of the unproductive employees within the organisations.

Recruitment Metrics

Efficient recruitment function benefits the organisation to gain sustainable competitive advantages through competent human resources. For measuring recruitment efficiency, organisations make use of several metrics as under:

1. Recruiting Cost ratio (This includes manpower hiring costs and the new employees' salaries for the period of induction. Also, it considers the cost of under-performance of new employees for the initial period of three to six months, depending on the nature of work assigned.) It is calculated using the following formula:

   RCR = (Total Hiring Costs/Total Compensation cost up to the period of induction + cost of underperformance during the initial period of three to six months) × 100

2. Recruiting efficiency (It is measured in terms of attracting more talented people for the vacancies. Talent attraction is understood considering the ratio of people finally selected after the interview.)
3. New hire performance (Measured in terms of performance results of newly recruited people even after the initial period of induction and training)
4. Recruitment manager's satisfaction (Understood in terms of degree of satisfaction on percentage of good performers among the new recruits, percentage of new recruits who are continuing more than a year, i.e., beyond transition phase, etc.)
5. Employee starts (Measured in terms of difference between date of offer and actual start date)

Likewise, organisations develop several recruitment metrics, depending on their requirements.

SUMMARY

Recruitment, selection, induction and placement are important tools for hiring manpower from external sources. HRP helps us to identify the manpower requirements, keeping pace with corporate objectives and strategies.

After assessment of manpower requirement, it is important to identify to what extent such requirements can be met from internal sources by restructuring and redeployment. After this exercise is over, additional manpower requirements, if any, have to be met through external hiring. While doing external hiring we need to follow several steps like recruitment, selection, induction and placement. At all these stages, certain norms are required to be followed to ensure proper selection and placement.

KEYWORDS

Recruitment	Successive Hurdles
Selection	Psychological Testing
Induction	Internal Hiring
Placement	Stress Interview
Recruitment through Internet	Attitude

REVIEW QUESTIONS

1. Define recruitment. What are the important recruitment functions? Why such functions are important for an organisation?
2. What is internal recruitment? Why is it important for an organisation? Do you think it is necessary to have a recruitment policy for an organisation?
3. What are the different recruitment processes? Briefly state their merits and demerits.
4. Briefly discuss the importance of selection process and mention the steps involved in such process.
5. You have been retained by an organisation to select few management trainees. What process you think you should consider and why?
6. What is the objective of an induction programme? What important areas need to be considered for an effective induction programme?
7. What are the different steps involved in an induction programme? In what way induction and placement have now become important for Indian organisations?
8. Define attitude. Why is the study of attitude necessary for HRD profession?
9. What are the different tools for attitudinal measurement? From an organisational point of view discuss in detail at, least two, measurement tools with due emphasis on their relative merits or demerits.

10. You have been retained by a company to study the attitude of 50 employees on the recently introduced pension scheme. Develop, at least, 5 structured close-ended questionnaire, using Likert's Item Analysis Scale and interview the employees. Analyse all the responses using factorial method and measure the attitude of the employees.

11. Write short notes on:

    (a) Differential Placement

    (b) Job Rotation

    (c) Probationary Period

    (d) Follow-up Orientation

    (e) Stress Interview

    (f) Application Blank

    (g) Deputation

    (h) Successive Hurdles

    (i) Equal Appearing Intervals Scale

    (j) Cumulative Scale

    (k) Summated Rating Scale

    (l) Employee Empowerment and Attitudinal Change

CASE STUDY

MENTAL BLOCK

Mr Vachani is a Quality Controller for four divisions in a family-owned manufacturing organisation in which functional heads enjoy a large measure of autonomy. Mr. Bose is the Production Superintendent of one of the four divisions of the company. By and large, both these senior executives, who report to the General Manager (Works) get along well as colleagues though they have their usual differences and disagreements over issues concerning quality.

One day Mr. Bose stormed into Mr. Vachani's office and shouted. "Your Senior Inspector, Mr. Sundaram, has misbehaved with me and I will not tolerate it. You must take immediate action against him." Mr. Vachani asked Mr. Bose to cool down and explain exactly what had happened. Narrating the incident, Mr. Bose said that in the morning he had observed one of his workmen carrying out a out-of-routine job. On being asked to explain why this was so, the workman said that he was working on the job as per the advice of Mr. Sundaram. On returning to his office, he called Mr. Sundaram, to make enquiries on the matter. The latter did not respond at first, but on being sent for once again, appeared before him. On being asked why he had assigned the out-of-routine job to a workman, Mr. Sundaram, did not give a satisfactory answer. He was told not to confuse his workmen. But Mr. Sundaram reacted by making rude remarks and misbehaving.

Mr Vachani listened patiently to Mr. Bose and advised him not to be agitated, adding that he (Mr. Vachani) would talk to Mr. Sundaram about the matter. On Mr. Bose's attempts to again tell Mr. Vachani as to what he wanted to be done, the latter said he would himself decide the best course of action, though of course, Mr. Bose was free to take any alternative action he felt necessary.

After some time Mr. Sundaram came to see Mr. Vachani in his office. The latter did not indicate that he was aware of the incident with Mr. Bose. After discussing various matters, Mr. Sundaram told Mr. Vachani. "Today, I had a fight with Bose" and proceeded to narrate the whole matter. His account of the meeting with Mr. Bose was "I went to Bose's office a little after I was called in." He asked me harshly to explain why I did not respond immediately on being sent for, I replied politely that I was busy in some work, and I did not want to disturb him. When Mr. Bose continued to press the issue I told him to discuss with Mr. Vachani whether I am required to respond immediately to his calls even if some work suffers in the process. About the out-of-routine job, I tried to explain that this became necessary in view of the important inspection on Monday (about which Mr. Bose was also aware) and that I had taken the initiative in the interest of work. Anyway, Mr. Bose told me rudely not to instruct his men directly and to get out. This infuriated me and I told Mr. Bose angrily that it was he who had called me. He then used some foul language and as a result hot words were exchanged, so much so that I felt like hitting him." Mr. Sundaram further added the he was nowhere at fault and that Mr. Bose's behaviour, specially in asking him to 'get out', really provoked him. He said though he always gave Mr. Bose due regard as a senior, the latter had no right to be as rude and insulting as he was.

It needs to be mentioned here that Mr. Sundaram has been working to the entire satisfaction of Mr. Vachani and at times carried out his own liaison with Mr. Bose and his department, whenever he was required to do so. After thinking over the incident for a few minutes, Mr. Vachani advised Mr. Sundaram to go to Mr. Bose sometime and talk to him reminding him (Mr. Bose) politely about the usage of strong words like 'get out', etc., and admitting that he had lost his temper. In this way he felt that Mr. Bose would not take offence to what Sundaram had said. After some persuasion, Sundaram agreed to do so and went back. About an hour later, Mr. Vachani received a call from Mr. Sundaram saying that he had information that Mr. Bose reported the matter to the Personnel Manager, and as such there was no need for him now to talk to Mr. Bose as suggested by Mr. Vachani and that he would rather let the matter be decided otherwise since he in any case was not at fault.

Questions

1. Was Mr. Vachani's suggestions to Mr. Sundaram to talk out the matter with Mr. Bose correct in the circumstances?

Contd...

2. Should he not have told Mr. Sundaram that his interpretation of the incident varied from that of Mr. Bose?
3. Was Mr. Bose justified in reporting the incident to the Personnel Manager soon after he had appraised Mr. Vachani of the same?
4. What action, if any, should the Personnel Manager take in this regard?
5. If Mr. Bose is found to be guilty of implicating Mr. Sundaram without any substantial reason, what remedy do you think the Personnel Manager should suggest to avoid recurrence of such incidents in future?

APPENDIX 1

APPLICATION BLANK FORMAT

Name of the Post ______________________________

Advertisement No. ______________________________

Personal Data

Full Name: Applicant's Photograph

Ms/Mr

Date of Birth, State, Marital Status

Nationality, Whether SC/ST

Height:........cm. Vision :

Weight:.......kgs. Normal/Corrected

Spectacle Lens Nos.

Address to which we should write: Permanent Address

Telephone No. Telephone No.

Father's/Husband's Name and Occupation:

If you have any relative employed in/or on the Board of our company, please give details.

Details of previous employment in this company or its sister concerns, with reasons for leaving.

Details of previous employment elsewhere, with reasons for leaving

Languages:	Speak	Read	Write
Mother Tongue			

Education

Examinations	School/ College/ University/ Institute	Year From	Attended To	Major Subjects	Class, %of Marks and Ranks
Scholastic					
Achievements					

Training

Name of the Firm/Institution	Period From	To	Details of Training	Stipend, if any

Work Experience

Employer	Period From	To	Position held and nature of work	Salary p.m. Basic Total

Extra Curricular Activities

Types of activities	At School	At College	Elsewhere

Contd...

Official Position held :

Sports

Participation

Positions held

- Captain, Secretary/Manager

Have you ever been convicted? It so, give full details

Have you had any major illness, operations or accidents?

Any other information that you would like to furnish:

Name and addresses of three persons other than relatives to whom we may write for references:

Name Address

Minimum Salary Expected:

We appreciate the time and effort you have spent in completing this application. Would you please check your application to ensure that you have completely and accurately answered each and every question?

I declare that the particulars given above, are to the best of my knowledge, correct and complete, and undertake to advise the company immediately of changes, if any, in respect of my particulars given above. I confirm that there is no legal bar in my applying for and accepting the above-mentioned employment.

Date Signature of the Applicant

I have verified the certificates and testimonials where necessary.

Date Officer-in-Charge

APPENDIX 2

FLEXIBLE RECRUITMENT THROUGH EMPLOYEE LEASING

Employee leasing is an arrangement under which an employer transfers all workers or groups to a leasing company which then assigns the same employees back to their original employer. Under the leasing arrangement employees get employed by employee leasing company, though they may be working with the same employer (who leased them), may do the same job, work under the same environment with the same pay packets. Under changed circumstances, however, employers do not necessarily transfer their paid employees to an employee leasing company to get them back subsequently under leasing arrangement, but do not retain any employees to the employee leasing companies from time to time, depending upon their production programme.

In the USA and other industrially developed countries in the world, all manufacturing and service organisations, to the extent possible, are trying to avoid retaining employees on permanent payroll and to the extent possible running their operations, which are highly flexible by hiring employees from employee leasing companies. Such manufacturing and service organisations, during the lean phase of production, send the leased employees back to the employee leasing company to gain relief from wage cost burden for the idle time and to achieve economic efficiency.

Employee Leasing in India

Employee leasing is not a much known concept in India. However, etymologically employee leasing is quite akin to an institutionalised approach like the contract labour system, which is prevalent in India and is legally sustainable.

The most formidable challenge before the Indian industries during the post liberalisation era is to withstand price competition both at home and from abroad. Wage cost and non-wage labour cost (NWLC) together form a considerable percentage of total cost for Indian industries, particularly those in the organised sector. The increased burden of NWLC made it inevitable for industries to restrict the number of workmen on permanent payroll. Moreover, since production plans and programmes are highly flexible for industries, industries from time to time are required to engage workers to share the increased workload. Simultaneously, industries are also required to pay for idle working hours and also required to bear the brunt of NWLC for such workers. Institutionalised contract labour system, i.e. employee leasing, therefore, offers economic benefits to industries, which, inter alia, enable them to sustain competition by cost minimisation.

This is a part of the technological revolution in Indian industries, gradually giving rise to the capitalistic mode of production in line with other developed countries in the world. This has made the skill factor in labour units more and more specific and transformed the labour as an item for sale and purchase in the competitive market. Moreover, because of technology, industrial occupations have rapidly changed from productive to supportive activities. This changed phenomenon is particularly evident from the 1981 census which shows swelling of professional, technical and related workers, clerical and related workers over the other occupations. This, therefore, indicates structural change in occupational pattern. Economic rationality and technical feasibility, therefore, sustain employee leasing in India.

However, in India we find contract labour system as an alternative to employees leasing practice going on since long. What is important here is to understand that there is a wide difference in the approach to employee leasing in India and in the developed countries, who have succeeded in institutionalising employee leasing. It is observed that many favourable infrastructural changes, both at government and at institution levels, have been initiated by these countries to effectuate employee leasing successfully. Adequate state supported social security measures, safety net, insurance and pension schemes etc. sustain employee leasing in these countries without much problem. Moreover, leased employees in these countries are getting higher paid wages than employees on permanent payroll, as organisations hiring leased employees can substantially gain from NWLC and overhead cost of personnel department, even after paying wages at higher rate to leased employees. Rights of leased employees also remain protected as their retirement benefits are taken care of by the leasing companies, subscribing to government sponsored schemes.

Contd...

In India, our experience shows contractors' labourers are getting less than the workers on permanent pay roll. Contractors' labourers and/or leased employees are engaged by organisations not only to save NWLC but even to gain substantially on paid wages costs (by paying less to them). Organisations engage them at substantially reduced wage rate than their permanent employees. A large number of placement agencies are extending such services to the organisation, in veil, making readily available various categories of manpower, details of whom they maintain in their data bank. In most of the cases such employees even do not know their employment status and continue as temporary employees for years together, which deprive them from all retrial benefits. Working as temporary employee on an organisation's payroll for certain period make them statutorily eligible to enjoy permanent employment status. To avoid such complication, organisations prefer to retain the services of such employees hiring them either from contractors or from placement agencies (who are in veil leasing companies).

Thus, it is evident that in India, employee leasing is a standing practice, which is continuing to flout all social and institutional norms. This practice is further gearing up under the New Industrial Policy of the Government of India which necessitates production restructuring through technological change. Technology upgradation, therefore, will affect the traditional employment relation, making it more contractual than institutional in the coming years.

Institutional theory empowers management to subordinate employees as they are in lower hierarchy of management, contractual theory advocates that the employer-employee relationship stems from the contract of employment.

BLOCK THREE

DEVELOPMENT

UNIT 9

Training and Development

Learning Objectives

After completion of this unit, the students will be aware of the following topics:

- *Introduction*
- *Definition and Purposes*
- *Need for Manpower Training*
- *Classification of Training Programmes*
- *Steps for Designing the Training Programme*
- *Training Policy*
- *General Information*
- *Training Methods*
- *Training Benchmarks Metrics*
- *Training Evaluation Models*
- *Training Strategy*

MICROSOFT – THE UNPARALLEL HRM PRACTICES THAT DEVELOP EMPLOYEES

Microsoft Corporation, one of the Fortune's 'Best Companies to Work For', is perhaps the best company that emphasises on work life balance, promoting strong organisational culture. The company respects diversity, allows flexible working hours, and offers best benefits to the employees, which encourage them to continue with the company. For Microsoft, training activities get the highest attention. Manpower development initiative gets boost with other employee socialisation activities like, fun events, team dinners, sport events, etc. Despite such people centric employment practices, Microsoft was affected by the global meltdown, and had to cut jobs, for cost optimization. But this could not deter Microsoft's employee centric HR practices. The company could quickly recover from the shackles of global meltdown and again, could enjoy the brand identify as the destination for new generation of knowledge workers. Every Microsoft employees feel the pride of identifying with the company. The opportunity to grow and learn, and the abundance of training activities, still attracts talents; and the company with their strategic HR activities ensures their retention.

INTRODUCTION

Training is an important HRD activity which reinforces HRM in an organisation. Apart from the need for internal staffing, training enhances job related skills and also facilitate acquiring of new skills required for averting skill obsolescence in an organisation.

HRD is a macro concept and it consists of a organised services of learning activities within a given time limit for achieving desired behavioral changes in the people. From the organisational point of view, HRD is a process and it helps employees to improve their functional capabilities for present and future roles. It also develops their general capabilities, harness their inner potentialities, and there by facilitates for self and organisational development.

Discussions on Training, remain incomplete without linking the same to Performance Appraisal. This is because Performance Appraisal is one single important tool, which helps in deciding about training requirements for an organisation and it reinforces training activities. There are lot of misconceptions about training, education and development functions vis-à-vis HRD, which we have clarified in introductory unit. Without precisely knowing the functions of training, education and development, as was pointed out earlier, it would further make it difficult for us to appreciate the objectives, roles and significance of training in an organisation.

DEFINITION AND PURPOSES

Training may be defined as systematised tailor made programme to suit the needs of a particular organisation for developing certain attitudes, actions, skills and abilities in employees irrespective of their functional levels. Training therefore serve following important purposes for an organisation.

- To increase the performance level of an employee and to develop him/her in such a manner that he/she can rise to the position of higher responsibility.
- To constantly develop manpower to meet the current as well as future needs of the organisation.
- To ensure effective utilisation of human resources.

- To integrate individual goals with the organisation goals creating a climate so that an individual employee can best achieve his goals by attending the goals of the organisation. To be more specific this is the stage of identifying employees with the organisation.

NEED FOR MANPOWER TRAINING

Most of the organisations prefer internal manning of position than external hiring for obvious motivational benefits and cost effectiveness. Even though training, prima-facie, emphasises on increasing the performance level of an employee, a continuous training function enables the organisation to develop employees for future responsible positions in the organisation itself.

The needs for manpower training in an organisation may be categorised as follows:

1. ***Updating Knowledge:*** Technological advancement, business environmental changes and new management philosophies have now made it imperative for the organisation to renew and update the knowledge and skills of the employees so that they do not become redundant for obvious functional incompetence. The first and foremost need for manpower training therefore, is to renew and update knowledge and skills of employees to sustain their effective performance and so also to develop them for future managerial positions.

2. ***Avoiding Obsolescence:*** Recent economic liberalisation programmes of Government of India are necessitating organisational restructuring, which *inter alia*, calls for training the employees, irrespective of their functional level, for their redeployment in restructured jobs. Therefore, the second important need for training is to avert functional obsolescence.

3. ***Improving Performance:*** Continuous training being required to renew and update knowledge and skills of employees, it makes them functionally effective. The third need is therefore, to make employees effective in their performance through continuous training.

4. ***Developing Human Skills:*** Apart from emphasizing on technical and conceptual skills, new training programmes also emphasise on developing human skills of employees. Such human skill is necessary for effective inter-personal relations and sustaining healthy work environment. This need for training therefore, also cannot be altogether ignored.

5. ***Imparting Trade Specific Skills:*** In industrial employment, the convention is to recruit workers and employees through compulsory apprenticeship training. Such apprenticeship training enables an organisation to impart industry and trade specific skills to workers. This also, therefore, is an important need for manpower training.

6. ***Stabilising Work Force:*** Throughout the world importance of training is now increasingly felt for stabilising the workforce to withstand the technological change and for making the organisation dynamic in this changed process. Management theorists now unanimously agree that it is the responsibility of the organisation to train and develop their manpower as a continuous process.

Classification of Training Programmes

Depending on the functional level and occupational categories of employees, an organisation can classify training programmes as under:

Level	Nos.	Types of Training
1. Workers	(i)	Introduction
	(ii)	Job Training
	(iii)	Craft Training
	(iv)	Special Purpose Training
2. Supervisors	(i)	Induction
	(ii)	Foremanship/Shopfloor Supervision
	(iii)	Manpower Management
3. Staff Members	(i)	Introduction
	(ii)	Professional
	(iii)	Technical
	(iv)	Human Relations
4. Managers and Executives	(i)	Induction
	(ii)	Executive Training
	(iii)	Training in Executive Development

Apart from the above routine training programmes for different levels, training on Total Quality Awareness and training encompassing all aspects of Total Quality Management have now become almost compulsory for all functional levels.

Induction and Orientation

These terms are interchangeably used to give a friendly welcome to the new employees as members of the organisation so also to introduce the new employees with the available installations (plant and machineries, systems), work norms, organisational objectives and the job positions of the employees. Some organisations make available programmed instruction materials to new employees to help them to get acquainted with the departmental rules and regulations, their entitlement for leave, pay, overtime, retirement benefits and other miscellaneous privileges, which affect their whole service. Tata Iron and Steel Co. circulate to all their new employees in addition a brief booklet under the name and style of 'Write your future in Steel' to illustrate their career prospects. However such documented materials cannot be made available by all organisations. They try to supplement it through a brief induction programme.

Supervisory Training Programme

Supervisors monitor the work of the workers and are arms of the management. They must have adequate skill, experience, ability and leadership. A Supervisor is required to do job in five broad areas, i.e., knowledge of the work, awareness of responsibilities, capacity to instruct, skill in improving methods and ability to work with people.

A tentative contents of a Supervisor Training Programme may be drawn after the charts of such contents prescribed by Earl Planty and William Mocorx as per chart given at the end of this unit.

Training for Top and Middle Management

Top and Middle Management Personnel are trained mainly on following eight areas to expose them to the managerial practice:

1. *Planning:* This covers the policy, general programme and plans of the organisation and also methods for effective action.

2. *Control:* To check current performance against predetermined standards (as mentioned in the plans) to ensure progress and also to record experience from the working of plans to serve as guide to possible future operations.

3. *Co-ordination:* To balance the team efforts ensuring proper allocation of activities among different members of the group.

4. *Motivation:* This covers employees morale and given by proper leadership. The art of self-motivation has to be included in the manager and executives.

5. *Inspiration*

6. *Communication*

7. *Decision*

8. *Integration*

Steps for Designing the Training Programme

Identification of Training Needs

Traditionally, training needs identification is left with HRD department. HRD department, to keep pace with organisational requirements used to identify series of training modules for different categories of employees and publish such training calendars to circulate among different departments to depute their employees for such training courses. Depending on the facilities available, some of these training courses are also offered utilising in-house training faculty, while for others (where expertise is not available) such training may either be offered by retaining professional trainers or by deputing employees to attend some outside training courses.

However, to ensure better utilisation of employees' acquired knowledge and skill, identification of training needs are now being left with the respective departmental heads, who because of their proximity with the employees concerned can better suggest the training and development needs. Hence, right at the beginning of the year, HRD department circulates the format for suggesting training requirements of different departments, which after necessary processing, they develop as training calendars. Head of the department through performance appraisal, job evaluation and keeping in mind future requirements (due to change of technology, etc.), may identify such training requirements and also study the cost-benefit aspect closely monitoring employees post-training performance.

Incidentally, it has now also become one important corporate practices in line with ISO Certification requirement.

Designing a Training Programme

The content of a Training Programme depends on whom we are involving and how much time we allocate for the same. But we always aim for a mix of approaches even if the training session is short. We must make sure that participants in a training programme are not just being talked at – that's a presentation not a training session. Training involves active participation. Irrespective of the training content, it is imperative to devote initial 10-15 minutes for introduction. Each session should not stretch beyond 1 hour in one go. Adequate ice-breaks, keeping in view the profile of the participants should be provided to put the participants at ease. Here we are detailing some of the Training Programme designs in various different formats. It is necessary for the readers to try on their own to design a training programme or two before achieving perfection.

Steps in Designing Training Programme

The following steps are involved in designing the training programme.

- *Selecting-Strategies:* The first step is to choose a strategy or strategies for training methods. Strategies prioritise training objectives and also help in selecting training areas which may be skill formation, developing conceptual understanding, etc.
- *Breaking Objectives:* The second step is to break the general training objectives into different parts like, knowledge, understanding and skills. Each constituent part of the training objective is matched with appropriate training events.
- *Choosing Methods:* The next step is to use specifications for different training methods to decide over time and the facilities required for the programme as a whole.
- *Deciding on Packages:* The fourth step is to decide different package in which programmes could be offered. An organisation at this stage considers different training packages, keeping in view the time and cost aspects.
- *Designing the Programme:* The final step is to design the training programme.

Sequence of a Training Programme

Any training programme should follow the order of sequence of action, as under, to make if effective.

- Designing the programme matching with the learning process.
- Matching the programme to the organisational expectations.
- Developing the Training group.
- Identifying the themes of training and development
- Achieving consistency in training.

Some Sample Training Programmes

We have already explained Training Programme designing requires practice and domain knowledge on the specific training areas. Keeping in view the specific requirements of organisations, some training programmes design on most topical areas are presented here as follows:

1. ***Three days Training Programme on Managerial Role in the new millennium:***

	ACTIVITY	PURPOSE (for participants)	PURPOSE (for organisation)
Day-1	Customer Relationship Management (CRM) – What it is and why it is important?	To help participant to know in details about CRM and how by developing CRM skills they can achieve excellence in their day to day function.	To develop CRM competencies and achieve increased business results by retention of customers. This will lead to increase the market share for the organization and leapfrog the pace of growth
	CRM practices and how it helps in turning around an organization?	To understand the CRM practices and how organizations world-wide benefit from adoption of CRM practices including cases of those who could turnaround practicing CRM.	To benchmark the CRM practices with other leading organizations world-wide and emulate their examples for better business results
	Personal Effectiveness – seven habits and how to develop and practice?	To understand the seven habits of Stephen Covey and how to develop and practice those for achieving excellence in dealing with people and feel individually enriched.	To get the advantage of excellent practices of employees which will reduce the customer response time and enhance customer satisfaction.
	Essentials of Quality Management with details of cost and quality relationship and how it enhances competitive strength of an organization.	To understand different quality management practices and save cost through quality enhancement.	To get the benefit of multi-skill and better results from employees to achieve business growth in globally competitive market.
	Quizzes and Case Studies to test the learned lessons.	To put learned lessons in action and achieve gradual perfection to deliver results.	To measure training effectiveness and consider for its continuance for developing all cross-section of employees.
Day-2	Creativity & Innovation in managing customers with exercises and quizzes.	To develop creative/lateral thinking and translate the same in action through innovation in dealing with customers and offering services to customers.	To get the benefit of increased result for creativity, translating the creative thinking into action. Creativity will enhance competitive strength for the organization.

Contd . . .

	Essentials of Team Management and Team Management Practices with exercises and quizzes.	To learn how team can be formed and managed and get the benefit of synergy through team building. Also how team formation can reduce the dissonance in day to day action and how customer can benefit from effective team.	To multiply gains for the benefit of synergy, which will enhance performance because of collective efforts and reduce customer response time and increase customer satisfaction.
	Managing Conflict with exercises and quizzes.	To manage conflict and translate conflict into better performance.	To reduce dysfunctional conflict and translate conflict into creativity for better organizational results.
	Understanding the change imperativeness. Why we need to change?	To understand the degree of change in individual way of doing day to day activities for their own survival and organizational stability and growth.	To reap the benefit of positive attitudinal change of employees and remain competitive with active support and cooperation from all cross-section of employees.
	Understanding model of Excellence	Integrating the organizational practice of Excellence with individual excellence.	To get the benefit of excellence by developing a pro-active employee role.
	Quizzes and Case Studies to test the learned lessons.	To put into practice learned lessons and measure their individual effectiveness.	To measure effectiveness in training and put into use the learned lessons.
Day-3	Introduction to HR with focus on motivation, leadership, compensation designing, competency mapping – 3 sessions till lunch break with usual tea break in between	To understand how HR can help an organization to get strategic advantage.	To derive benefit from pro-active HR Practices.
	Six Sigma and HR	To develop the Six culture and feel committed for the organization.	Develop an enabling organization culture to truly convert it into a good performing one. Also consider for future continuation of such training programmes for over-all growth of the organization.

2. ***Two days Training Programme on Pro-active Trade Unionism:***

	ACTIVITY	PURPOSE (for participants)	PURPOSE (for organisation)
Day-1	Understanding the change imperativeness. Why we need to change?	To understand the degree of change in individual way of doing day to day activities for their own survival and organizational stability and growth.	To reap the benefit of positive attitudinal change of employees and remain competitive with active support and cooperation from all cross-section of employees.
	WTO, EEC, Economic Reforms and its impact on Trade Unions	To appreciate how it influences trade union practices globally and nationally	To create the supportive role of trade unions.
	Change Situation in neighbouring countries like China	To understand how China could convert them to a most competitive nation	To benchmark the Chinese practices for better business results
	Collective bargaining scenario and its usages	To understand the changed senario globally and nationally	To get the advantage of excellent practices of trade unions and convert them to a partner in organizational growth.

Contd . . .

	Essentials of Quality Management with details of cost and quality relationship and how it enhances competitive strength of an organization.	To understand different quality management practices and save cost through quality enhancement.	To get the benefit of multi-skill and better results from employees to achieve business growth in globally competitive market.
	Quizzes and Case Studies to test the learned lessons.	To put learned lessons in action and achieve gradual perfection to deliver results.	To measure training effectiveness and consider for its continuance for developing all cross- section of employees.
Day-2	Creativity & Innovation in managing customers with exercises and quizzes.	To develop creative/lateral thinking and translate the same in action through innovation in dealing with customers and offering services to customers.	To get the benefit of increased result for creativity, translating the creative thinking into action. Creativity will enhance competitive strength for the organization.
	Essentials of Team Management and Team Management Practices with exercises and quizzes.	To learn how team can be formed and managed and get the benefit of synergy through team building. Also how team formation can reduce the dissonance in day to day action and how customer can benefit from effective team.	To multiply gains for the benefit of synergy, which will enhance performance because of collective efforts and reduce customer response time and increase customer satisfaction.
	Managing Conflict with exercises and quizzes.	To manage conflict and translate conflict into better performance.	To reduce dysfunctional conflict and translate conflict into creativity for better organizational results.
	Pro-active Trade Unionism under disinvestments scenario and labour reforms. .	To understand the degree of change in trade unions way of doing day to day activities for their own survival and organizational stability and growth.	To reap the benefit of positive attitudinal change of trade unions and remain competitive with active support and cooperation.
	Quizzes and Case Studies to test the learned lessons.	To put into practice learned lessons and measure their individual effectiveness.	To measure effectiveness in training and put into use the learned lessons.

3. ***Two-day Training Programme on Personal Style and Personality Development for Non-executive employees:***

Introduction

This Training Programme is intended to develop essential personality skill of non-executive employees. In a competitive market, retention of customers and aiming for repeat orders is considered as one of the top most priorities of the organisations. Customers' satisfaction is the index of organisational excellence and in fact it only determines the bottom-line in the long run. Like many world-class organisations, XYZ Co. also aspires to grow integrating its growth with customers. Achieving customers' satisfaction without quality and cost competitiveness is seemingly difficult. While systems, process, style, structure can play a great role in shaping the organisational competitiveness, behavioural issues cannot be neglected altogether. Behaviour of people is the function of personality. Hence developing positive personality and making it as another important enabler is imperative for XYZ Co. to excel in competition. From that perspective this programme is essential for non-executive employees as they are the major catalyst for achieving the organisational excellence.

Objectives

- To develop positive personality.
- To build confidence in successfully managing organisational requirements
- To nurture healthy personality for developing good interpersonal relations.
- To develop personal effectiveness and other important soft skills to become effective performer.

Programme Contents and Schedules

The Programme will cover following areas as per the schedule:

Day	Time	Programme Content
1st Day	9-30 A.M. to 9-45 A.M.	Introduction to the Programme
	9-45 A.M. to 10-45 A.M.	Understanding personal style – What it is and why it is important?
	10-45 to 11-00	Tea Break
	11-00 to 12-00	Personal style how it helps in turning around an organization? Case Study of Encyclopedia Britannica and other world class organizations.
	12-00 to 13-00	Personal Effectiveness – seven habits and how to develop and practice?
	13-00 to 13-45	Lunch Break
	13-45 to 15-30	Learning best habits from corporate practices.
	15-30 to 15-45	Tea Break
	15-45 to 17-30	Quizzes and Case Studies to test the learned lessons.
2nd Day	9-30 to 11-00	Personality measurement and gap identification. Developing personality through creativity and innovation with exercises and quizzes, Transaction Analysis, etc. The tests will include Personality type measurements and FIRO-B.
	11-00 to 11-15	Tea Break
	11-15 to 1-00	Continuation of earlier session
	1-00 to 1-30	Lunch Break
	1-30 to 2-30	Essentials of Team Management and Team Management Practices with exercises and quizzes.
	2-30 to 2-45	Tea Break
	2-45 to 3-30	Managing Conflict with exercises and quizzes.
	3-30 to 5-30	Understanding the change imperativeness. Why we need to change?

4. *Six Sigma as a Change Management Strategy:*

The Programme

To leapfrog ahead of competition in this world of uncertainty, corporate world is experimenting with one after another processes. From 'Conformance to Standards' to achieve total quality, the focus has now been shifted to add economic value and practical utility to both the organisation and the customer. Realising Value entitlement both by the customers and the organisations is now the determinant of business relationship. It is now a win-win situation for the both. For customers, it is their rightful expectation to buy quality products at competitive cost, while for organisations, it is to produce at highest possible profit. This synergy is what everybody tries to achieve in this corporate world. Rejection Allowance, Unavoidable Rejection (UR) are now the forbidden words. Six sigma as a business process is now allowing organisations to improve their bottom line by designing and monitoring business activities in a way that minimises wastes and resources without, however, compromising with customer satisfaction. Six Sigma process is broader than total quality management (TQM) programmes. While TQM focuses on detecting and correcting defects, six sigma re-creates the processes to ensure defects never arise right from the beginning. From organisations' point of view, it provides maximum value in the form of increased profits and from customers' point of view, it provides maximum value in terms of high quality products and services at competitive costs.

While six sigma, using rigorous analytical tools with the leadership from the top, develops a methodology for sustainable improvements. Six sigma is a more integrated approach with commitment to achieve success by way of quality improvement that increases profitability and customer satisfaction. It is a break through strategy that improves organisational values, infusing changes in the processes, which go into creating defect free product or service at minimum cost.

Every member of the organisation needs to be trained, following the system and then the players in the break through strategy need to be identified to play the role of catalysts in the change process. In the change process customer is the king. Customers define quality and set expectations and hence, they figure out at the top among change agents. Other change agents being internal to the company, they are graded through training process.

The Programme is intended to focus on the importance of six sigma practices, duly explaining its processes at the outset and then relating it to HR strategies for better results.

Methodology

The session will focus on following important issues:

- Concept and Process of Six Sigma
- Six Sigma Case Studies
- Six Sigma as a Change Management Strategy
- Selection of Projects and implementation of Six Sigma in Organisations
- Six Sigma through strategic HR intervention

It will be two-days programme with series of practical analysis from conceptualisation to institutionalisation.

Target Participants

This is intended for managers and executives from any functional area both from manufacturing and service organisations, including Universities and Institutes.

Pedagogy

All participants will be given essential reading materials. Twenty five sets of study materials along with pen, writing pad and folders will be provided. Traditional interactive class-room lecture methods will be followed with frequent practice materials to test the efficacy of learned training inputs. Lessons for getting measurable results both to understand individual progress and corporate benefit (if required) would be imparted.

Contd . . .

Requirements

- LCD Projector, P-4 P.C. with multi-media and Overhead Projector.
- Participants background (short) at least two-days before the programme.
- Provision for Tea/snacks and working lunch for participants.
- Color mike with PA System, if the hall is too large.
- Number of participants may be restricted to 25 only.

Trainer's Background

Dr. D.K. Bhattacharyya, Trainer is Professor and Head of the Department of Master of Human Resource Management Programme of Indian Institute of Social Welfare and Business Management, Kolkata. He was earlier with Centre for Management Education, All India Management Association, New Delhi as Director. He is also attached with XLRI, Jamshedpur as Visiting Faculty. He has rich experience in corporate training and consultancy, covering all important areas of HR, CRM, Quality Management (including Six Sigma), Innovation and Creativity. He is a regular trainer in organisations like; IFB Group, Indian Ordnance Factories, Hospitals of Government of West Bengal, Bharat Petroleum, Indian Oil, Electrical Manufacturers' Association, Bharat Chambers of Commerce, Hindustan Paper, NIPM, CESC, Calcutta Corporation, MCKV Group, ITM Group, NIT, Durgapur, Mitsubishi, Haldia, etc. He has so far written eight books on Management and contributed more than 50 articles in leading journals of national and international repute.

Note: The 4th programme design is for an organisation, which wants to market their training programme.

TRAINING POLICY

Liberalisation and globalisation, WTO agreement intensified global competition and for our organisation which resulted in sea change in our business processes and corporate practices. Organisations now require to renew their human resources continuously to keep pace with such changes. Among others, this require redefining of emerging job requirements, which influences skills, competencies, qualifications and trainings. For Indian organisations investment in training related activities is abysmally poor. But whatever resources our organisations earmark for such activity, we need back up of an effective policy.

Effective training policy establishes linkage with prevailing organisational HR systems like; performance management, career planning, succession planning, rewards and compensation, promotion, transfer, etc. Training policy also requires to specify various types of training requirements within the organisation, like for example, on the job training, induction training, training for upgradation of functional/managerial skills, training for specific assignments, etc. Every organisation rationalize their training requirements considering above issues. We have separately discussed issues concerning training needs assessment (TNI). But TNI only facilitates chalking out training requirements, while a Training Policy specifies all other issues concerning training, from developing a training calendar to training delivery.

An effective training policy serves following purposes for the organisation:

- Provides guidance for allocating department resources such as trainers, money, and time
- Gives a broad direction to training activities
- Outlines the authority given to the training department, as well as the limits to that authority
- Provides tools for evaluating the success of the department's efforts.

Need for a Training Policy

To ensure consistency in Training and Development Function, the HRM department of each organisation develops a suitable training policy, defining the scope, objective, philosophy and techniques. Such a Training Policy, *inter-alia*, serves the following purposes.

- It defines what the organisation intends to accomplish through training.
- It indicates the type of persons to be responsible for training functions.
- It identifies the formal and informal nature of training.
- It spells out the duration, time and place of training.
- It indicates the need for engaging outside institutions for training.
- It embraces and includes training in relation to labour policies of the organisation.

Structure of a Training Policy

Here we will illustrate a hypothetical training policy. But as mentioned above, such policy requirements may be specific to an organisation. A tentative Training Policy can be developed using the following format.

- Outline Mission statement
- Develop Objectives
- Outline of the training department's roles.

A tentative mission statement for training function of an organisation can be as follows:

Our mission is to provide training and development to all cross-section of employees of the organisation, ensuring measurable and demonstrable benefits keeping pace with organisational as well as individual needs.

Some of the tentative objectives of training functions can be as under:

- To provide product update training to all employees within the next 6 months.
- To support the company's objectives in reaching its goals.
- To develop and implement a management training program for all middle level managers within the next 12 months.
- To provide customer service skills training to all new help desk employees no more than two months after being hired.

Training Department's Role outlines the exact functions that the training department will fulfill. Some of the common guidelines for developing a training policy may be to relate to the company's goals, constantly asking whether the policies are in line with the stated mission and objectives. Policies must be clearly written and widely communicated. Finally a proper checklist should be developed to ensure effectiveness of such policy.

Checklist for an Effective Training Policy

- Evaluation of training programs
- Selection of employees
- Availability of training
- Location of training sessions
- Programs to be established
- Length of training day
- Training design standards
- Tuition-paid plans
- Outside services and programs
- Policy revision
- Link from training to performance appraisals

General Information

Here we are listing the general information of a Training Policy for an organisation. Now, it is recommended for readers to develop a Training Policy keeping in mind specific requirements of the organisation.

HR & ES Department provides training for a variety of computer applications, skill upgradation, management subjects, supervisory development, etc., for all staff members, supervisors, executives and managerial level employees. Minimum 6 man-days training is compulsory for all. All such training programmes are designed and delivered primarily using in-house faculty strength. But wherever necessary, the company may invite outside experts. In all training programmes, books and other instruction materials will be provided to the participants. In each training programme number of participants is limited to only 10 and Departmental Heads need to ensure registration of participants in advance. No training programme would be conducted if number of participants fall short of 10.

Training Methods

The following methods are mostly used for training of employees.

On-the-Job Training Method

Under this technique an employee is put on-the-job and is trained to perform the said job thereby helping the employee to acquire the skills for performing the said job in future. Most of the organisations utilise the services of senior workers to impart such training. Apprenticeship, creation of assistant to positions, job rotation and special assignments are different nature and forms of such training programmes.

1. ***Job Instruction Training:*** This is a training through step by step learning. Usually steps necessary for a job are identified in order of sequence and an employee is exposed to the different steps of a job by an experienced trainer.

2. *Vestibule Training:* This method duplicates on-the-job situation away from actual worksite with machinery and equipment similar to those used in actual production or operation and is used to help employees to acquire a new skill. Usually, training is given away from the production centre.

3. *Training Centre Training:* Such site trainings are given in the form of lectures, conferences, case-studies, role-playing and discussions.

4. *Simulation:* Simulation again duplicates the actual condition encountered on a job. The vestibule training method or the business-game method are the examples of business simulation.

5. *Apprenticeship:* Such training is given for a longer duration to help the employees to acquire skills in specific trade(s). A major part of this training is given on the job.

Off-the-job Methods

These methods consist of the following:

1. *Lectures:*Through lectures participants are motivated to learn. Lectures focus on understanding rather than enriching knowledge and skills through reading assignments and experience. However, empirical studies on the effectiveness of training through lecture methods indicate that this is not effective for obvious inability of participants to retain the information and failures of trainers to make such sessions more interesting relating to on-the job experience.

2. *The Conference Method:* It is a participative group centered method through which participants develop knowledge and understanding by small group discussions and active participation.

3. *Group Discussions:* This is also a very useful method of training and are usually based on papers prepared by trainees on a given subject. The trainees read their papers which are usually followed by critical discussions. It may, however be a follow-up discussion on some statement or on a paper presented by an expert.

4. *Case Study:* Case study method helps students to learn on their own by independent thinking. A set of data or some descriptive materials are given to the participants asking them to analyse, identify the problems and also to recommend solutions for the same.

5. *Role Playing:* This training method particularly helps in learning human relations skills thorough practice and imbibing and insight into one's own behaviour. Trainees of such programme are informed of a situation and asked to play their roles in such (imaginary) situation before the rest of the class. This therefore helps in the enriching of interactional skills of the employees.

6. *Programmed Instruction:* This method is pre-arranged desired course of proceeding to the learning or acquisition of specific skills or knowledge. Information in such programmes are conveniently broken into different units, to allow the trainees to learn at their convenient pace.

7. *T-Group Training:* T-group is sensitivity training, takes place under laboratory condition and are mostly instructed and informal kind of training. Trainer in such a training programme is catalyst. He helps the individual participants to understand how others perceive his behaviour, how he acts to others behaviour and how and when a group acts either in a negative or in a positive way.

8. *E-learning:* Training programmes delivered via intranet have now been thought of most cost effective route. It is not only cost effective but also caters to the real time information need of employees. However, it involves convergence of several technologies, like; hardware, software, web-designing and authoring, instructional design, multi-media design, telecommunications and finally internet intranet network management. Organisations can outsource e-learning training modules at relatively cheaper rate. Even though training through e-learning is globally increasing, we do not have adequate empirical evidence to justify this.

Training Benchmarks Metrics

There are several training benchmarks metrics. Such metrics help an organisation to measure the efficacy of their career development activities. These apart, there are several training evaluation models. Today many organisation insist on developing ROI measurement model for their training and development activities. We have discussed here only widely used models. However, organisations may develop their own measurement tool to understand the cost benefit of their training and development function. We have started here initially with benchmark metrices.

Total Career Path Ratio

$$\text{Total Career Path Ratio} = \frac{\text{Total Promotions}}{(\text{Total Promotions} + \text{Total Transfers})}$$

Definitions

1. ***Total Promotions:*** The total number of employees who were promoted to a higher-level position or one of greater responsibility during the survey period.

2. ***Total Transfers:*** The total number of employees who were transferred to a different department or different job category of an equal level of responsibility during the survey period.

Purpose

Total Career Path Ratio is promotions as a percentage of all employee movement (transfers and promotions) within the organisation. This metric is an indicator of career development opportunities existing within the organisation for all employees. Associated Human Capital Metrices are: Internal Accession Rate, Internal Add and Replacement Rate, Headcount Trained Percent, Voluntary Separation Rate, Unplanned Separation Rate, and Total Tenure. Associated Financial Metrices are: Cost per Hire, Time to Start, Time to Fill, Training Cost Factor, Training Headcount Investment Factor, etc.

Regular Employee Headcount Trained

$$\text{Regular Employees Headcount Trained Percent} = \frac{\text{Regular Employee Geadcount Trained}}{\text{Regular Headcount}}$$

Definitions

The total number of regular employees who participated in employer-paid or provided training during the survey period. This is a count of each employee trained per class.

Regular Headcount

The average number of regular employees, regardless of hours worked in the reporting unit for the survey period.

Purpose

Regular Employees Headcount Trained Percent is the number of employees taking training classes as a percentage of regular headcount. This includes all employees who attended any training program, each time they attended, thus, the result can be greater than 100%. This metric indicates how committed an organisation is to providing employees with training opportunities and whether employees are taking advantage of that training. ASSOCIATED HUMAN CAPITAL METRICS: Training Cost Percent, Voluntary Separation Rate, and Career Path Ratio. ASSOCIATED FINANCIAL METRICS: Training Cost Per Hour, Training Cost Factor, Training Headcount Investment Factor etc.

TRAINING EVALUATION MODELS

Evaluation is an integral part of Training. Evaluation tools help to determine the effectiveness of training interventions. Despite its importance, many organisations do not give adequate focus on training evaluation. Evaluation goals involve multiple purposes including evaluation of learning, evaluation of instructional materials, transfer of training, return on investment, and so on..

Six general approaches to training evaluation are as follows:

- Goal-based evaluation
- Goal-free evaluation
- Responsive evaluation
- Systems evaluation
- Professional review
- Quasi-legal

Goal-based and systems-based approaches are predominantly used in the evaluation of training (Philips, 1991). The most influential model or framework of training evaluation has come from Kirkpatrick (Carnevale & Schulz, 1990; Dixon, 1996; Gordon, 1991; Philips, 1991, 1997).

On the other hand, under the systems approach, the most influential models include: Context, Input, Process, Product (CIPP) Model (Worthen & Sanders, 1987); Training Validation System (TVS) Approach (Fitz-Enz, 1994); and Input, Process, Output, Outcome (IPO) Model (Bushnell, 1990).

Some of the widely used models are as under:

1. ***Kirkpatrick Four-level Approach for Training Impact Evaluation:*** This conceptual model helps in determining the types of data to collect and answer following four important questions.

Level	Questions
1. Reaction	Where the participants pleased with the Programme?
2. Learning	What did the participants learn in the Programme?
3. Behaviour	Did the participants change their behaviour based on what was learned?
4. Results	Did the change behaviour affect the organisation?

The model can be explained using following framework:

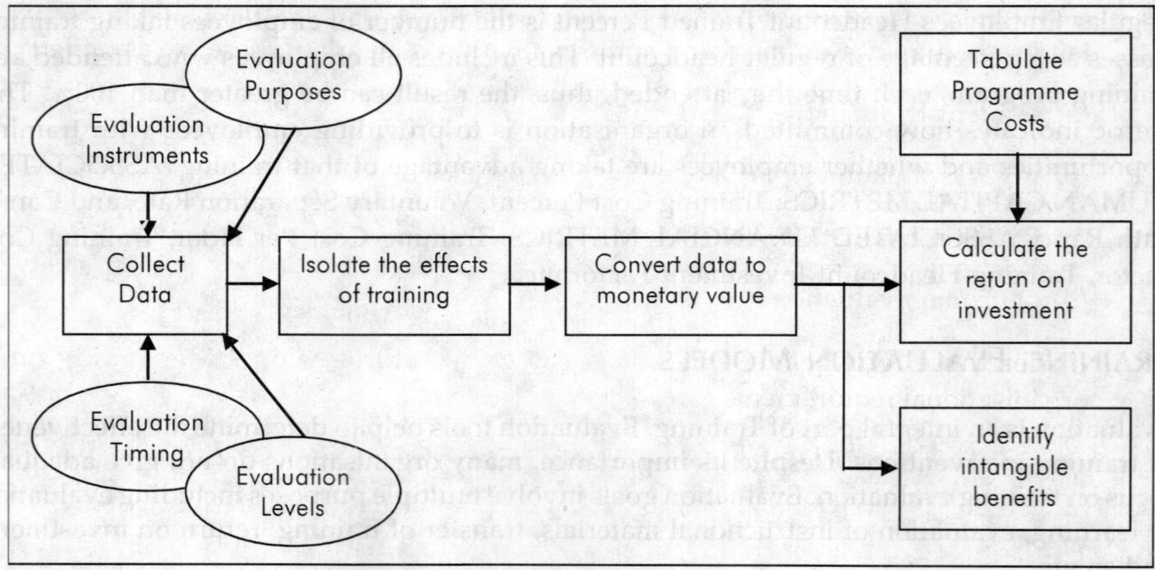

2. ***Hassett's Training Investment Analysis Approach:*** This model focus on following four important areas and then measures the training effectiveness.
   (a) Needs analysis
   (b) Information gathering
   (c) Analysis
   (d) Dissemination

3. ***CIPP Approach to Evaluation (Similar to CIRO) – Context, Input, Process, Product (CIPP) Model (Worthen & Sanders, 1987):*** Like earlier model this model also emphasize on four areas of training evaluation as under:
   (a) Context

(b) Input

(c) Process

(d) Product

4. ***Kaufman's Five Levels Evaluation of Training Impact:*** This model extends the scope of training impact evaluation beyond the organisation. It includes how training benefits the society and the surrounding environment in the organisation.

Level	Evaluation Areas
1.a. Enabling	Quality input availability like; human, financial and physical resources
1.b. Reaction	Methods, means and process acceptability and efficiency
2. Acquisition	Individual and small group mastery and competency
3. Application	Individual and small group utilization within the organisation
4. Organisational Output	Payoff to the organisation
5. Societal outcomes	Payoff to the society

5. ***CIRO Approach to assess Training Impact:*** The name of this approach is CIRO, as these letters are drawn from the name of the evaluation categories. These are as under:

(a) Content Evaluation

(b) Input Evaluation

(c) Reaction Evaluation

(d) Outcome Evaluation

Under these four heads, evaluation categories are developed depending on the organisational requirements.

6. ***Philip's Five Level ROI:*** This model extends Kirkpatrick's framework making the process of evaluation more specific.

Level	Brief Description
1. Reaction and Planned Action	Measures participants; reaction to the programme and outlines specific plans for implementation.
2. Learning	Measures skills, knowledge or attitude categories.
3. Job Applications	Measures change in behaviour on the job and specific application of the training material.
4. Business Results	Measures business impact of the programme.
5. Return on Investment	Measures the monetary value of the results and costs for the programe, usually expressed as a percentage.

These apart there are also some commonly used models like; Training Validation System (TVS) Approach (Fitz-Enz, 1994); and Input, Process, Output, Outcome (IPO) Model (Bushnell, 1990).

A comparison of several system-based models (CIPP, IPO, & TVS) with a goal-based model (Kirkpatrick's) is presented in Table below:

Kirkpatrick (1959)	CIPP Model (1987)	IPO Model (1990)	TVSModel (1994)
1. *Reaction:* to collect data on participants' reactions.	1. *Context:* to obtain information about the educational needs to establish programme objectives.	1. *Input:* to evaluate performance indicators like; trainee qualifications, availability of materials, appropriateness of training, etc.	1. *Situation:* to collect pre-training data on current performance levels and to define a desirable level of future performance.
2. *Learning:* to evaluate how far the learning objectives have been met.	2. *Input:* to identify training strategies to achieve the desired result.	2. *Process:* to plan, design, develop, and deliver the training programmes.	2. *Intervention:* to identify the reason for the gap between the present and desirable performance and assess how training can solve the problem.
3. *Behaviour:* to assess change in job performance as a result of training	3. *Process:* to assess the implementation of educational programme.	3. *Output:* to gather data from the training interventions.	3. *Impact:* to evaluate the difference between the pre- and post-training data
4. *Results:* to assess costs vs. benefits of training.	4. *Product:* to gather information on the results of the training intervention and interpret its worth and merit	4. *Outcomes:* to measure long-term results in profitability, competitiveness, etc.	4. *Value:* to measure differences in quality, productivity, service, or sales.

Various Utility Models

1. ***Financial Utility Model:*** Financial Utility model requires measurement of any given intervention or effect of training programme. This model was used by Godkewitsch (1987) to calculate the financial utility to a company for implementing a training programme. The model is described below:

$$F = N [(E \times M)] - C$$

Where,

F = financial utility

N = number of people in the training programme

E = effect or outcome of the training programme

M = financial value of the effect or outcome

C = financial cost per person of implementing the training programme

2. ***Net Present Value Method:*** Net Present Value (NPV) compares the value of money now with the value of money in the future, taking into account all the costs that are associated with that money. We can use the NPV to determine ROI in training. To illustrate income foregone during the training period, costs of courses, learning materials and other related expenses are to be considered as costs. Then we require quantifying the future benefits that are likely to accrue as a result of training. To assess the future benefits, we can

extrapolate the current performance changes (after training) using Learning Curve Formula.

To calculate the NPV we can use the following formula:

$$NPV = I_0 + I_1 / (1+r) = I_2 / (1+r)^2 + \ldots\ldots + I_n / (1+r)^n$$

(I = income amounts for each year, the subscripts are the year numbers, starting with 0. The discount rate is *r*. The number of years of the duration of the investment is *n*.).

Which Model is best?

Efficacy of training evaluation models may vary from organisation to organisation. What is best for one organisation may not suit another. However, in all these models one aspect is very clear that improvement in organisational performance is a common factor. Organisational improvement measurement areas also vary from organisation to organisation. However, common focus areas may be like cost savings, work output changes and quality changes. To achieve consistency in measuring effectiveness of training, it is recommended that organisation may make use of more than one model and then through the process of trial and error the best one may be selected.

TRAINING STRATEGY

Training strategy flows directly from a corporate strategy. Effective training strategy can ensure that organisation gets the right people in place with the right competencies, knowledge, experience or capabilities necessary for both current and future responsibilities. Depending upon the size and complexity of an organisation the training strategy may vary from organisation to organisation. Some of the training strategies for a hypothetical organisation can be enumerated as under:

1. Designing programmes of training and development that ensure people are available and have the necessary skills, knowledge and attitude to fill all jobs successfully.
2. Designing and providing training programmes to increase the competence of the workforce.
3. Recruiting and training a cadre of people sufficient in number to meet the organisation's short- and long-term resourcing needs.
4. Extend open-learning and self-development facilities to encourage and enable employees to enhance their training and education programmes.

Experiential Training

Experiential training recognises that people learn best from their own experiences and their own reviews. It subscribes to the notion that what people do is more important than what they know. Thus it renders behaviours and attitudes visible. Being built on the premise that it is not enough to explain to people what to do, they must be shown how to actually do it and then how to improve it, experiential training moves beyond knowledge by generating a learning experience. The more experience the greater the skill. Hence such training achieves change in behaviour and attitude much faster. It makes learning process enjoyable, motivating and rewarding.

The Experiential Training Process

In experiential training we make use of learning wheel, which is a cyclic process of setting goals, followed by thinking, planning, experimenting and decision-making. This is followed by action, observing, reflecting and reviewing. Experiential training utilises participants own experience and their own reflection about that experience, rather than lecture and theory as the means of generating understanding and transferring skills and knowledge.

SUMMARY

Training reinforces HRM in an organisation. In this era of technological change and global competitiveness, organisations are constantly required to renew and update skill of their people or else they are likely to encounter the problem of manpower obsolescence, which among others, will call for frequent downsizing or rightsizing. While Performance Appraisal updates organisations to take a stock on their skill inventories, training helps to address the skill-gap. In a separate unit we have also discussed about the need for skill and competency mapping to appreciate the contemporary trends in the corporate world.

KEYWORDS

Manpower Training	Induction and Orientation
Identification of Training Needs	Training Programme Design
Training Policy	Training Methods
Training Benchmark Metrics	Training Models
Training Strategies	

REVIEW QUESTIONS

1. Identify the need for manpower training in an organisation. What are the important purposes served by training?

2. List out training programmes for different levels of employees and elaborate at least two such types of training programmes for workers.

3. What are the steps involved in designing a training programme? What sequence of actions usually a training programme follows?

4. Do you think there is need for a training policy in an organisation? Briefly outline some of the areas which need to be focused in such a policy.

5. Develop at least three sample training modules for supervisors, duly pointing out their objectives, course contents, eligibility of participants, duration, etc.

6. What are the different training methods available for an organisation? Which are the methods you recommend for white collared and blue collared employees respectively?

7. Do you think recent economic liberalisation programme of the Government of India has made training function more important for an organisation? Elaborate your answer duly listing out important training areas in the context of changing environment.

8. Discuss briefly on various training evaluation models. In a consumer electronics manufacturing organisation, where competition is fierce, which models you think would be more effective for measuring effectiveness of sales training? Justify your answer.

9. What is Training Strategy? Why an organisation requires a Training Strategy? Frame a training strategy for a software development organisation.

10. Briefly discuss the steps necessary for creating a learning organisations.

11. Explain briefly why learning organisations work?

12. Define Knowledge Management. Explain why knowledge management should be a HR function?

13. Write short notes on:
    (a) T-Group Training
    (b) Role Playing
    (c) Vestibule Training
    (d) Simulation
    (e) Orientation Programme
    (f) Craft Training
    (g) Human Skills
    (h) Experiential Training
    (i) Financial Utility Models for Training Evaluation

CASE STUDY

TRAINING AND DEVELOPMENT – THE GODREJ WAY

Godrej Industries Ltd. (GIL), one of the oldest but young in innovation was started in 1897 by a lawyer-entrepreneur, Ardeshir Burjorji Godrej in Mumbai. The company started with the manufacturing of locks and gradually started manufacturing the safe in 1905. Godrej's pioneering efforts in locks and safes gradually made them most popular household name in security equipments. With Godrej lock, we still feel secured. From security equipments, the company gradually diversified into office equipments like, Almirah, Chairs, office tables, racks, etc. Further expansion of product lines into typewriters, etc., could strengthen the image of Godrej among Indians. Godrej's bond with Indian family further strengthened when the company started new product lines like, soaps, vegetable oils, etc., from 1928 onwards. Thereafter, from 1958 onwards, Godrej entered into home appliance products like, refrigerators in 1971; animal feed in 1982; electronic business in 1985; computer aided designing services, and thereafter one after another new verticals like, infrastructure, processed food, washing machines, air conditioners, software solutions, insecticides, etc.

With such a diversified business portfolio, Godrej today is an Indian conglomerate, meeting every household needs.

To sustain in competition and further grow, Godrej took over 26% stake of a training organisation, namely Personalitree Academy Ltd. The company is specialised in providing on-line and interactive training. This is the first initiative of Godrej to streamline the training and development activities. After the break-up of joint venture (for Godrej Soaps Ltd.) between Godrej and Proctor and Gamble (P&G), the company could realise without developing the human resources, they can sustain. Successful rebuilding of Godrej Soaps and repositioning its products in the markets could be possible because of developing Godrej's strong corporate culture of valuing human resources. The company trained large cross-sections of employees on Total Quality Management (TQM), Parivartan, a new initiative to train new and existing employees on business, along with the promotion of the culture of entrepreneurship, teamwork, mentoring and reverse mentoring, and encouraging employees to participate in strategic decision making could bring a performance driven work culture in Godrej. Godrej felt the need for developing the talents of existing employees and also developing the new recruits. For this purpose, the company introduced innovative training programme for management trainees known as GALLOP (Godrej Accelerated Learning Leadership and Orientation Programme). GALLOP develops the employees into professionals; takes every employee through the process of job rotation; develops their sense of belonging; and in the process, transforms them into leaders. Like GALLOP for management trainees, the company introduced Spark for managers to transform them as coaches. Further emphasis on training was given through E-Gyan, to facilitate self-learning by the employees.

In addition to strengthening the in-house infrastructure for the training and development, Godrej also emphasised on hiring the best professional services to train their employees. For example, the company hired Stern Stewart, a New York based management consultancy for training their managerial level employees on EVA (Economic Value Added), to help them understand and make the investment decisions and trading off between the income statement and the balance sheet.

REFERENCE NOTES

Knowledge Management and Learning Organisation

Today we come across two most commonly used terms like; Knowledge Management and Learning Organisation. These two terms are intertwined with Training and Development Function. Hence a brief discussion on these two terms will benefit the reader to update themselves with the changing need of HR professionals.

Knowledge is reinforced through learning. Learning is a process of acquiring new skills or knowledge, which results to a new behaviour. Learning can take place through multiple ways. But for organisations best way to promote learning is by exposure to new experiences. Knowledge is the ability and wisdom to use the learned experiences for achievement of individual and organisational objectives. Knowledge management, therefore, is the process of systematically and actively managing and leveraging the store of knowledge in an organisation. From organisation point of view, thus Knowledge Management is a concept in which an enterprise gathers, organizes, shares, and analyses its knowledge in terms of resources, documents, and periodically retires the old knowledge. Today, both knowledge and information are the main inputs of HR. This justifies that the Knowledge Management efforts should be lead by the HR department. It perhaps even prompted many organisations to rename their HR function as knowledge management function.

Learning organisation is defined as an organisation that learns and encourages learning among its people. It promotes exchange of information between employees hence creating a more knowledgeable workforce. This produces a very flexible organisation where people will accept and adapt to new ideas and changes through a shared vision. To create a learning organisation following steps are necessary:

Awareness

To start with organisations must appreciate that learning is necessary at all levels and not just limited to managerial level. This apart, need for change also has to be accepted first as the only way to survive. Such awareness at organisation level can only be created once organisation believe in emulating the examples of success stories of those who have leapfrogged their growth truly developing the learning organisation culture.

Environment

Creating a learning environment requires to share with all members of the organisation a comprehensive picture of the whole organisation and its goals by creating a flatter (organic) structure which encourages innovations. The flatter structure promotes transparency of information between members of organisation and thereby develops a more informed work force.

Leadership

Leaders are enabler for an organisation to gain competitive advantage. A leader sells the concept and encourages learning to help both the individual and organisation in learning. It is the leader's responsibility to help moulding the individual views of team members. It requires management to provide commitment for long-term learning with resource support.

Empowerment

Real testing tool for learning is the degree of empowerment. Empowerment requires involving workers in decision-making. Empowerment makes workers more responsible for their actions; without letting loose the managerial involvement. Managers still need to encourage, enthuse and co-ordinate the workers. Empowerment must be allowed at all levels so that members can learn from each other simultaneously.

Learning

Learning systems also need to replicate real-life situation through series of simulation games. This facilitates learning from mistakes to make the future learning more effective Learning environment need to be open, flexible and motivating. To facilitate continuous learning some organisations also make extensive use of electronic media like e-learning, duly providing a track to measure the learning progresses. But its acceptance largely depends on workers urge to learn. This can be ensured linking learning with various incentive packages and HR decisions.

Contd . . .

Implementation Strategies of Learning Organisation Philosophy

To implement a learning organisation philosophy in an organisation, we require an overall strategy with clear, well defined goals. Once goals and overall strategy are identified, specific action plans are required to implement the same. There are three generic strategies to develop a learning organisation. Peter Senge also focused on certain initiatives required at organisation level to implement learning organisation philosophy. Three strategies, however, are as under:

Accidental

For many organisations implementing learning organisation philosophy is more accidental than pre-conceived. In the process of achieving business goals quite often unknowingly they develop a framework, which fit the learning organisation philosophy. Therefore, even remaining unaware, organisations can emulate the learning philosophy to gain competitive advantage.

Subversive

Subversive strategy encapsulate the dissidence by exploiting ideas and techniques of people working in the organisation. It requires open endorsement of the learning organisation ideal, so that people can express their ideas.

Declared

The third option is the declared approach. It requires clear promotion of the principles of learning organisations, as part of the organisational ethos and are manifested openly in all organisational initiatives.

Why Learning Organisations Work

Development of people: A Learning Organisation facilitates learning which improves the personal skills and qualities of members of organisation. Members just not get benefited from their own but also from sharing of experience of others.

Greater motivation: Because of participation of people to improve their own skills, values and work, they become more matured about their role and feel motivated to contribute their best. Opportunities for innovation and creativity, free thinking develop their self and make them feel satisfied in their job roles.

Workforce become flexible: Learning organisation makes workers more flexible. Workers can move freely within the organisation in between jobs and thereby develop their capability to cope rapidly with a changing environment, to survive in competition.

Workers become more creative: People get more opportunities to be creative in a learning organisation. They can try out new ideas without bothering about mistakes. They get recognised about their creative contributions which makes room for new ideas to flourish.

Improvement in social interaction: Learning improves social interaction and develops interpersonal communication skills. This encourages team-work which as a result makes organisation to work better.

Teams and groups work better: Learning Organisation develops high performing teams. They learn, grow and develop and perform efficiently for the organisation to deliver better results.

Knowledge sharing: "Openness Creates Trust." In a learning environment, information and knowledge being flows around freely, intra and inter team sharing of knowledge also develops mutual trust and makes an high performing organisation.

Interdependency: A culture of interdependency in organisation increases awareness of its members and improves relations between them at a personal level. By knowing each other about their roles, needs and tasks, members can learn how to manage their time better and plan their work more efficiently. With the increased spate of learning, however, such dependency decreases and members can get on their own, plan their job better without relying on others.

These apart, a learning organisation can facilitate breaking down of traditional communication barriers, improves customer relations, develops the knowledge resources, fosters innovation and creativity, hedges against risk in decision-making, etc.

EXHIBIT 9.1

CONTENTS OF SUPERVISORY TRAINING PROGRAMME

Administrative Training	Orientation Training	Human Relations Training	Technical Training	Teacher Training
Duties and responsibilities of a Supervisor, Basic principles of industrial organisation. Discipline and Control.	The Company Size, structure of organisation, history, market share, achievements, objective and mission. Product Training. Shop Floor-rules and regulations. Personnel Policies. Union Contract. Company Services. Service Departments	Induction of new employees, Giving orders and directions, Communication. Developing Understanding. Correcting subordinates. Inculcating initiative and confidence. Placement and Supervision. Job evaluation, Performance measurement and incentives. Reducing absenteeism and labour turnover. Self improvement. Grievance Handling. TQM, Small Group activities. Employee Empowerment.	Basic science, mathematics and statistics. Special Technical Training. Trade Training. Training on Costing methods. Training on Time study and other industrial engineering techniques. Production Planning and control. Labour legislation. TQM and ISO 9000	Instructor Training. Conference Leadership

Exhibit 9.2

Feed-back Form

Training Programme on Strategic Human Resource Management

1. What was your expectation in joining the programme? (Indicate your choice in order of preference, if any).
   (a) To get some insights to the new concept
   (b) To understand the relevance of the content in present day business situation
   (c) To apply the learned skill in my present organisation
   (d) To have a break and no utilise time for a meaningful cause
   (e) All the above
   (f) None of the above
2. Do you think, your expectations have been fulfilled, (please tick your answer).
   (a) Very significantly
   (b) Significantly
   (c) Partially
   (d) Not at all
3. In columns 'b' and 'c' below, select a number that represents your opinion using the five-point scale (from low to high); also indicate your view on 'd' and 'e'.

a Topic	b Gained New Information	c Presentation	d Time allotted			e This was Difficult	
			More	Less	Right	Yes	No
Topic 1	1 2 3 4 5	1 2 3 4 5	☐	☐	☐		
Topic 2	1 2 3 4 5	1 2 3 4 5	☐	☐	☐		
Topic 3	1 2 3 4 5	1 2 3 4 5	☐	☐	☐		
Case Study	1 2 3 4 5	1 2 3 4 5	☐	☐	☐		
HR Games	1 2 3 4 5	1 2 3 4 5	☐	☐	☐		

4. Indicate three changes you would like to make to the Course.
5. Which aspects of the process helped you to learn?
6. Which aspects of the process were not liked by you?
7. How do you rate the over-all Course?
   (a) Excellent
   (b) Good
   (c) Moderate
   (d) Average
   (e) Poor
8. Any general suggestions?

Name : Signature with date:

UNIT 10

Performance Appraisal and Performance Management Systems

Learning Objectives

After completion of this unit, the students will be aware of the following topics:

- *Introduction*
- *Standards of Performance*
- *Building a Performance Management System*
- *Performance Management System (PMS) and Organisational Strategy*
- *Various Dimension of Performance*
- *Role of Appraisals in Performance Management*
- *Performance Mentoring*
- *Balanced Scorecard and Performance Management*
- *The HR Scorecard Approach*
- *HR Competencies*
- *Competency Mapping and Performance Management*
- *Performance Counselling*

McDonald's Performance Management System

McDonald's develop their performance objectives, after explaining the same to their employees. The process is done by the senior management people, clarifying to the people down the line, the overall objectives of the organisations for the coming year and then, making them understand how their contribution at the department and at individual level, would help the company in achieving the same. Such traceability of individual performance to the overall objectives of the organisation makes people feel responsible to deliver their best. The company essentially believes in team working. Hence, individual team members' understanding of their performance objectives and its cascading effect to team and the organisation as a whole, when further spelt out by the managers in measurable terms, automatically develops their self pride as they gain the sense of ownership. At this stage of performance goal setting, managers also emphasise on mutual agreement. The compelling culture of performance makes every member of the organisation to volunteer to achieve the results. Every employee of the McDonald's gets the opportunity to choose in which skill areas they need more inputs, and accordingly, they can choose their learning and also the option to renew their skills. Employees' development is also facilitated by systematic mentoring programme. Mentors help the mentees to acquire new skill sets on job and gradually, become a good performer. The primary focus of the mentoring programme of McDonald's is to make people gradually adapt to the culture of increased performance and a sense of responsibility and even, volunteer to develop their juniors. At McDonald's, people are enthusiastic about performance; learn new skills and are even eager to take up new responsibilities and more complex work.

Introduction

Performance Appraisal is one single important tool, which helps in deciding about training requirements for an organisation and it reinforces training activities co-ordination and balance the team efforts ensuring proper allocation of activities among different members of the group. Performance means the degree or extent with which an employee applies his skill, knowledge and efforts to a job, assigned to him and the result of that application. Performance Appraisal means analysis, review or evaluation of performance or behaviour analysis of an employee. It may be either formal or informal, oral or documented, open or confidential. However in organisations we find formal appraisal system in documented form. It is therefore a formal process to evaluate the performance of the employees in terms of achieving organisational objectives. Like any other function, Performance Appraisal is also an important management activity.

Performance management is the integrated process of objective setting, appraisal and pay determination which supports the achievement of the company's business strategies. At an individual level it will result in action plans related to performance improvement, career development and training. Thus Performance Management involves thinking through various facets of performance, identifying critical dimensions of performance, planning, reviewing and developing and enhancing performance and related competencies. It is an ongoing communication process that involves both the manager and the employee in:

- identifying and describing essential job functions and relating them to the vision and goals of the organisation
- developing realistic and appropriate performance standards
- giving and receiving feedback about performance
- writing and communicating constructive performance appraisals

- planning education and development opportunities to sustain, improve or build on employee work performance.

The evolution of the concept of *performance management* as a new Human Resource Management model reflects a change of emphasis in organisations away from command-and-control toward a facilitation model of leadership. This change has been accompanied by recognition of the importance to the employee and the institution of relating work performance to the strategic or long-term and overarching mission of the organisation as a whole. Employees' goals and objectives are derived from their departments, which in turn support the mission and goals of the organisation.

A Manager is involved in performance management when he:

- establishes specific job assignments
- writes job descriptions, assign responsibility for strategic initiatives develop and apply performance standards
- discusses job performance with the employee and provide feedback on strengths and improvements needed
- conducts an annual performance evaluation plan for improved performance and employee development goals.

Setting right objectives is critical for effective performance management. Such objectives as higher profits, shareholder value, customer satisfaction may be admirable, but they don't tell managers what to do. "They fail to specify priorities and focus. Such objectives don't map the journey ahead – the discovery of better value and solutions for the customer."

The objectives must be:

- be focused on a result, not an activity
- be consistent
- be specific
- be measurable
- be related to time
- be attainable

Smart Objectives

- Specific
- Measurable – that can quantify the results

- Achievable
- Relevant
- Time bounded – are governed by deadlines

Standards of Performance

Standards of performance are written statements describing *how well* a job should be performed. Performance standards are developed collaboratively with employees, whenever possible, and explained to new employees during the first month on the job.

The performance standard provides a benchmark against which to evaluate work performance. While the job description describes the essential functions and the tasks to be done, the performance standard defines *how well* each function or task must be performed in order to meet or exceed expectations.

Standards of performance are usually:

- developed in collaboration with the employees who do the tasks or functions.
- explained to new employees within the first month on the job.

When performance standards are in place, both the managers and employees will know what the expectations are for the performance of essential functions and related tasks. This common understanding provides the basis for ongoing feedback and performance counseling between appraisals as well as for the formal performance appraisal process.

Developing Standards Collaboratively

There are a number of approaches to developing written performance standards. One is the directive approach in which the manager writes the standards, in consultation with management and the Employee Relations representative for his or her department. Then the standards are shared with the employees affected for their information and to address any questions they may have.

Another is a collaborative approach in which employees work with you to develop the performance standards for their positions. While it is a legitimate option to develop the standards without employee input, the benefits of a collaborative approach are important. Both the manager and the employee bring valuable information to the process and the end result is more likely to be supported by everyone involved.

As a manager, however, one need to make the final decision about the appropriateness of the standards in consultation with management and the Employee Relations consultant for the department. Mutual *agreement* with the employee about standards is preferable, but not always possible.

In the collaborative process of developing standards for a task or function, it is necessary to include all those employees whose work will be evaluated according to those standards. If the task or function is unique to one position, then include the employee in that position in the development process. If more than one employee performs the task or function, involve all employees whose job description includes it. For the sake of fairness and consistency, consider collaborating with other units also if tasks or functions are the same.

Before the meeting, it is important to explain to everyone involved exactly what performance standards are, why they are important, and how they will be used. Ensure that the employees understand the process and if so required, solicit their comments and questions. We must give them a message that we would like to work together to develop standards for their positions and that their recommendations and concerns will be considered seriously. Also describe the process that would be followed. Also explain that the final determination about the appropriateness of the standards would be with the management.

Writing the Standards

Make sure that all participants in the standards writing process have access to the following documents:

- an up-to-date copy of their job description
- a copy of the department mission and goals, if available
- the form for the performance appraisal model

It is appropriate to define standards that apply to all essential function rather than writing a performance standard for every task in a job. Focus on those areas, which are most important to the position. Discuss and describe those behaviors and results, which would constitute the minimum acceptable performance for the task or function. Performance, which satisfies those standards, will receive the rating of *solid performance*. We may also describe the behaviours and results that would demonstrate performance, which would exceed expectations, and/or would fall below expectations. The same principles apply to the development of standards, regardless of the rating.

Standards should be written in clear language, describing the specific behaviours and actions required for work performance to meet, exceed or fail to meet expectations.

Use specific terms describing measurable or verifiable features of the performance. Thus principles of writing performance standards can be enumerated as under:

1. Describe performance expectations in terms of timeliness (deadlines, dates), cost (budget constraints, limits), quality (subjective and objective measures of satisfaction), quantity (how many), customer satisfaction, independent initiative demonstrated and any other relevant verifiable measure.

2. Specify the acceptable margin for error. It is very rare for perfection to be an appropriate standard, even for outstanding performance.

3. Refer to any specific conditions under which the performance is expected to be accomplished or performance assessed.

Performance standards may be written to different levels of complexity. The more general the applicability, the harder it is to be specific. Here we have illustrated a sample performance standards for four different levels of a Colour Television (CTV) manufacturing company.

Level	Description
Level-1	Simple description of general expectation. Example: Task Description: Assemble CTVs. Standard: Put different sub-assemblies CTVs in the Assembly line Example: Task Description: Write annual reports. Standard: Annual reports will be submitted by agreed upon date.
Level-2	Simple description of specific expectations. Example: Task Description: Assemble CTVs Standard: Complete assembly of 5 error free CTV per minute. Example: Task Description: Write annual reports. Standard: Prepare Annual reports and submit the same to the Business Heads 7 working days before March 31.
Level-3	Description of specific expectations and success indicators. Example: Task Description: Assemble CTVs Standard: Ensure simultaneous error free assembly of 5 CTVs per operator in 10 lines. Example: Task Description: Write annual reports. Standard: Produce Annual reports as per departmental format and submit to the Business Heads 5 working days before January 15.
Level-4	Description of specific expectations, success indicators, and conditions, if any. Example: Task Description: Assemble CTVs. Standard: Ensure 5 correct assembly of CTVs per minute per operator in 2 shop floors and also ensure that the necessary equipments are in working order. Example: Task Description: Write annual reports. Standard: Produce Annual reports as per departmental format and submit to the Business Heads 5 working days before January 15.

Guidelines for Performance Standards

Keep in mind the following guidelines when writing your performance standards:

- Performance standards should be related to the employee's assigned work and job requirements.
- Reporting systems should be adequate to measure and therefore should have more quantitative data.

- Quantifiable measures may not apply to all functions. Describe in clear and specific terms the characteristics of performance *quality* that are verifiable and that would meet or exceed expectations.
- Accomplishment of organisational objectives should be included where appropriate, such as cost-control, improved efficiency, productivity, project completion, process redesign, or public service.

Check List for Performance Standards

After writing the performance standards, to ensure its appropriateness, we can check them against the questions in the following list:

- Are the standards realistic? Standards should be attainable and consistent with what is necessary to get the job done. Standards for performance, which meets expectations, represent the minimum acceptable level of performance for all employees in that position.
- Are the standards specific? Standards should tell an employee exactly which specific actions and results he or she is expected to accomplish.
- Are the standards based on measurable data, observation, or verifiable information? Performance can be measured in terms of timeliness, cost, quality and quantity.
- Are the standards consistent with organisational goals? Standards link individual (and team) performance to organisational goals and should be consistent with these goals. The success of the University's and department's missions depends on this strategic connection.
- Are the standards challenging? Standards may describe performance that exceeds expectations. Recognizing performance that is above expectations or outstanding is crucial to motivating employees.
- Are the standards clear and understandable? The employees whose work is to be evaluated on the basis of the standards should understand them. Standards should use the language of the job.
- Are the standards dynamic? As organisational goals, technologies, operations or experiences change, standards should evolve.

What is a Performance Metric?

A performance metric is a standard measure to assess performance in a particular area. Metrics are at the heart of a good, customer-focused process, management system and any programme directed at continuous improvement. The focus on customers and performance standards show up in the form of metrics that assess individual's ability to meet the customers' needs and business objectives.

Uses of Performance Metrics

Most organisations use traditional performance measures, such as profit performance, return on investment or earnings per share, to determine success. These measures provide reasonable estimates of whether a company achieves its ultimate goals of making profits, but does not reveal how the business achieves this position. Was it by chance? A non-recurrent situation? Should they have done much better?

Many organisations have thus created a complete operating and process measures and ratios to track how well the business manage each process and their use of resources. Many CEOs (particularly those who have to make quarterly business forecast) have become interested to performance models which integrates the measures to predict future performance. The Balanced Score Card is one of the more popular conceptual modeling tools.

Effective Performance Modeling

An effective performance model is one, which allows management to be confident that the end results are not guesswork but a summation of all the different activities and process, given an attainable standard of performance. The requirements of such a model are:

- *Relevant relationships:* Process and activity metrics must form a chain of correlations leading to the ultimate end results of enhancing profits, brand equity and market valuation.
- *Measurability:* Data for the Metrics can be accurately collected in a timely manner without undue cost.
- *Comprehensible:* It must be easy to understood, impact on the effectiveness of other process and the end results.
- *Actionable:* It must be actionable. There is a set of corrective actions that may be taken.
- *Motivating:* It must be motivating: cause people to act positively, and not in a way contrary to the best interest of the business to simply "make their numbers."
- *Automation complaint:* Data collection and analysis should be automated so that employees do not have to be diverted from their main activity into data collection and analysis.

The Human Side of Performance Metrics

For a performance model to work, employee performance appraisal criteria must be aligned with the performance metrics, i.e., if an employee does his task well, this is directly linked to process performance and to ultimate department/division performance and the ultimate goals of the company.

Enthusiastic acceptance, not mere passive understanding is required from managers and employees at all levels of the organisation. Successful metrics must be capable of being cascaded down the line and to reinforce the desired behavior.

Customer Focused Metrics

For most businesses, the end objective of profits, brand equity and market valuation are dependent largely on how well the organisation meets and exceed customer expectations. Metrics must not therefore be developed to assist internal organisation meet external expectations.

The following process is important to develop a customer focused metrics:

- Identify your customers and the outputs they require and the processes through which we create the outputs. (Process Block Diagrams or Flowcharts may help at this point.)
- Determine your customer needs/requirements in terms of quality and service standards, determine the existing gaps in your delivery system.
- Determine the direct metrics that will help ensure that we meet customer expectations.
- Cascade these metrics horizontally and vertically through other processes that may impact their performance to develop a full suite of measures that would ensure we achieve customer satisfaction.
- Establish current performance level, short-term objective, long-term objective, and competitive benchmark that must be attained.

Designing Metrics

The development of a proper portfolio of organisational performance metrics has proven to be the most difficult aspect of the Balanced Scorecard approach. It requires deep and perhaps unprecedented re-examination of the vision, strategy, and mission of an organisation. The relationship between customers and the organisation's own survival needs will have to be considered.

One way to address the issue is this: if we could create any metrics we wish, what 'instruments' would senior executives like to see the most, to help them to make better strategic decisions? Ideally, these instruments would have the following features:

- ***Leading indicators*** - forecast future trends inside and outside the agency
- ***Objective and unbiased***
- ***Normalized*** - so they can be benchmarked against other agencies
- ***Statistically reliable*** - small margin of error
- ***Unobtrusive*** - not disruptive of work or trust
- ***Inexpensive to collect*** - small sample sizes adequate
- ***Balanced*** - qualitative/quantitative, multiple perspectives
- ***Appropriate*** - measurements of the right things
- ***Quantifiable*** - for ease of aggregation, calculation and comparison

- *Efficient* - can draw many conclusions out of data set
- *Comprehensive* - show all the significant features of agency's status
- *Discriminating* - small changes are meaningful.

This is a tall order. However, it seems undebatable that these are desirable features of the portfolio of metrics. By listing these desired features in advance, it may help us to identify how to design the metrics to meet at least some of these requirements.

A tentative performance metrices covering some of the critical areas can be illustrated as under:

Quality

- Rework
- Discrepancies found
- Availability
- Mean (or average) Time Between Failures
- Failures per hour/day/week/month
- Customer Returns

Customer Complaints

- Mean Time to Repair
- Mean Time to Respond
- Requirement Change Rate
- Customer Satisfaction
- Number of Complaints
- Customer Returns
- Customer Survey
- Referrals

Employee Satisfaction

- Participation Rates in Company Sponsored Events
- Employee Turnover Rates
- Employee Exit Interviews/Surveys
- Number of Employee Suggestions
- Productivity Metrics

- Incidents of Violence
- Revenue (or sales) per Employee

Financial

- ROI
- CPI
- SPI
- RONA
- ETC/EAC

BUILDING A PERFORMANCE MANAGEMENT SYSTEM

Performance Management System (PMS) is set of techniques and procedures for improving organisational performance. To sustain competitive advantage, organisation not only require to recruit the best people but also focus on their continuous development through an effective PMS. While development of people is possible through ongoing training and development and skill and knowledge renewal, it must precede PMS, as PMS, inter alia, establishes the basis for identifying training and development needs.

In line with Bevan and Thompson (1992), main features of PMS can be outlined as follows:

1. ***Focus on objective setting:*** Objectives are the targets which an organisation set for its employees. It is in the form of an action statement and it starts with a verb. At the strategic or corporate level, overall organisational objectives are decided. PMS helps to percolate the organisation objectives to employees translating organisational objectives to individual targets.

2. ***Develops systems for ongoing review of objectives:*** Through the process of periodic performance review, PMS helps to keep a track on achievement of objectives. Such review system largely depends on type of PMS techniques used by an organisation. It may be an age old MBO systems or a 360 Degree PMS (multi dimensional) or a more recent performance tracking technique like a balanced score card. Review of objectives helps in performance control and initiate steps to correct deviation in performance or to revise the targets.

3. ***Develop personal improvement plans:*** Since PMS helps in individual performance monitoring, it ensures developing of personal improvement plans for the employees. A particular employee may lack in performance or he/she may exceed the targets given. In both the cases, it is important to design the personal improvement plan. While in the first case, it may be importance to provide performance counseling and training and development reinforcement, in the second case, the employee may be motivated further through proper reward system. Thus PMS helps in developing personal improvement plans in both the cases.

4. ***PMS aligns with training and development:*** Since focus of PMS is to manage and develop employee performances, to sustain competitive advantage of an organisation through proper alignment, PMS helps in identifying training and development needs. This helps in developing need based training and also in measuring the Return On Investment (ROI).

5. ***Ensures formal appraisal with feed back:*** By introducing a formal appraisal system, PMS helps in giving performance feedback to employees. Both negative and positive feedback sensitise employees and help them to objectively analyse their shortfalls and positive aspects. While shortfalls can be met by learning reinforcement and setting the right direction, positive aspects can be leveraged by the employee concerned to further develop himself setting higher targets and accordingly grow.

6. ***Helps in pay review:*** Performance based pay is the modern concept. PMS helps in objective designing of compensation package for employees, thus rewarding the performance and reducing the variable pay (performance linked) of non-performers. This way organisation can remain competitive optimizing the cost of compensation.

7. ***Develops competence based organisational capability:*** Competence based organisational capability helps in appropriate organisational change, keeping pace with competition. It also helps in human resource planning. PMS through qualitative and quantitative appraisal can assess the prevailing competency level of employees and thus helps in organisational capability review.

Performance Management System (PMS) and Organisational Strategy

Strategy is the direction and scope of an organisation over long term, matching its resources to its changing environment and in particular its markets, customers or clients, so as to meet stakeholders' expectations.

Strategic Human Resource Management (SHRM) is a competency-based approach for management. There are many definitions on SHRM, including:

A human resource system that is tailored to the demands of the business strategy.

– Miles and Snow 1984

The pattern of planned human resource activities intended to enable an organisation to achieve its goals.

–Wright and McMahan 1992

Reviewing such definitions we can relate SHRM as a 'reactive' management field, where human resource management is a tool with which to implement strategy, to a more proactive function in which HR activities can actually create and shape the business strategy (Sanz-Valle *et al.*, 1998) of HR. It focuses on developing HR for sustainable competitive advantage.

Strategic human resource management requires formulation of HR objectives, strategies and policies. These enable the provision of the skills and abilities needed to meet the requirements of an organisation's overall objectives. In other words, they provide the framework, which ensures that an organisation's people needs are met.

PMS is one of the most important HR strategy factors. HR strategy factors are largely encompass six areas like; recruitment and selection, career development, performance appraisal, training and development, compensation designing and human resource planning. Career development and performance appraisal have direct linkage with PMS. While career development considers career mapping, succession planning and management development, integrating career development with OD initiatives; performance appraisal designs appropriate tools and aligns such appraisal with training needs, promotion, transfer and relocation.

PMS involves thinking through various facets of performance, identifying critical dimensions of performance, planning, reviewing and developing and enhancing performance and related competencies.

How PMS can be aligned to organisational strategy would be more clear from the following tabular details, which hypothetically captures the performance goals for the organisation and also details the various measures.

Goals: Business Unit, work group or key process	Individual goals and/or tasks	Measures and Targets
Contribute to the company's bio chemical research program	Manage staff in execution of assigned research projects	• Completion, on time • Professional standards, met • Interim and final reports, complete and on time
	Complete own assigned projects and present reports	• Completion, on time • Professional standards, met • Interim and final reports, complete and on time
Achieve effective and efficient technical effectiveness	Contribution to the project team on laboratory systems improvement	• Meeting attendance, all • Contribution, full • Team report, complete and on time
Operational Effectiveness	Carry out administrative roles and tasks	• Timeliness, accuracy and service, meet agreed standards

Various Dimensions of Performance

Performance has many dimensions.

- Output or result dimension;
- Input dimension;
- Time dimensions;
- Focus dimension;

- Quality dimensions; and
- Cost dimension.

Performance is what is expected to be delivered by an individual or a set of individuals within a time frame. What is expected to be delivered could be stated in terms of results or effort, tasks and quality, with specification of conditions under which it is to be delivered.

Results and Output

The most acceptable and visible as well as measurable dimension of performance is result or the output. It describes the consequence of inputs in a summary form or a final or semi-final product form or service form. It describes the standard. It is easily measurable. For example 95 percent is the result. Salary figures, customer numbers, financial targets, production targets, completion of tasks to meet some deadlines etc. are all stated in result form/output form. Sometimes these are also called key result areas.

Input Dimension

The input dimension deals with the activities or tasks to be accomplished by the individual. The nature of activities to be undertaken by the individual, the time frame, the quality of inputs to be given, etc. constitute the input dimension. Performance can be managed better if the nature of inputs required to be put in can be envisaged without mistake, planned properly and implemented.

Time Dimension

Another dimension of performance is time. Performance can be defined for a task, for a day, for a week, for a month, year or for life. The time period for performance is important. Time for information technology organisations is limited to a quarter or a three-month period. They may also be defined by tasks or project and not time. Time may become the target.

Focus Dimension

Performance also has a focus dimension. The focus can be on anything. In defining the focus of a sales executive, the focus of performance can be on market share, profits, or new areas covered, or some of these or most of these. The focus of performance can be on many other dimensions. It could be on quality or on cost or financial dimensions.

Who Manages Performance?

The answer is obvious. The performer or the candidate whose performance is being planned, analyzed, assessed, developed, etc. It is he who manages his performance. It is a mistaken notion to think that the primary responsibility for managing the performance of a person lies with his boss. The boss is an important instrument in managing performance. He has the responsibility to ensure that is defined, planned, analyzed, measured, reviewed and developed.

He is a partner in this. It is the performer who has to manage his performance. The roles of the performer and the boss etc. are also highlighted in various chapters.

ROLE OF APPRAISALS IN PERFORMANCE MANAGEMENT

Performance management is a continuous process. Appraisals are periodic activities. Management is a dynamic process while appraisals are static. Appraisals are a part of performance management. If the management involves improvements, the moment you assess where we stand there is an appraisal taking place. Therefore without some form of appraisal management becomes difficult. Appraisals do not mean reducing the performance of individuals and dyads or teams to a five-point scale or a number. It is the reduction of annual performance into a number and equating one number with another that has created havoc in managing performance of in appraisals. Numbers generated from the appraisal process are not comparable across functions, levels, departments and organisations.... This is because the scales are not calibrated and equated. Some use liberal scales, some use conservative scales, and some use no scales but merely feelings. It is this lack of calibration and treating the incomparable as comparable that has created havoc.

Performance management with performance appraisal should lead to increased performance. However, in most organisations, performance appraisals have lead to decreased performance. This happens particularly when appraisals are linked to rewards and when fewer people are rewarded than those expecting them. Those who are not rewarded get demotivated. If those who expect to be rewarded exceeds the number of those who actually get rewards, the net outcome of performance appraisal may be negative. If people continue to perform in spite of appraisals and they do not have a positive attitude to appraisals, then the organisation is spending more psychological energy.

The effort should be to make the performance management process more effective and productive using appraisal systems. Appraisal systems help managers manage their performance. They should be seen by line managers as aids for performance management. Managers should not be overwhelmed with appraisals and appraisal outcomes and ignore the most important aspects of performance management – performance improvements and competency building. This happens when the concerns get focused on appraisals rather than improvements or on ratings and rewards rather than performance enhancement and development. Managers need to learn to enjoy the performance management process itself as it occurs round the year and is not blocked by appraisals as they occur once in a while.

Performance management systems with an appraisal component built into them should mean improved performance, more motivated people and more competent people.

Types and Methods of Performance Appraisal

Different methods of performance appraisal are followed in different organisations to achieve the above objectives. Since some methods of performance appraisal are complicated and calls for adequate knowledge in quantitative techniques, many organisations follow traditional methods of appraisal while others consider modern methods as the basis for evaluating job performance of their employees.

Traditional Methods

Traditional methods of performance appraisal may be categorised broadly under the following heads:

1. *Straight Ranking Method:* This is the oldest and simplest method of Performance Appraisal by which employees are tested in order or merit giving some numerical rank and placed in a simple grouping. Such grouping separates employees under each level of efficiency, which may vary from most efficient to least efficient. Since, it is a blunt quantification of performance, it does not account for behavioural parameters and only considers an individual employee's level of efficiency relation to others. For such obvious deficiency, this system does not provide scientific basis for performance appraisal of employees.

2. *Paired Comparison Techniques:* This is a somewhat better method of Performance Appraisal as each employee is compared with others in pairs at a time. For each Performance trait, an individual employee's performance is tallied with others in pairs and then rank order is decided. This system is also not suitable in those cases where number of employees are usually high. For better comprehension, a sample table of comparison on trait reliability is presented below :

For Trait Reliability of Person Rated

AS COMPARED TO	A	B	C	D	E
A	X	-	-	-	-
B	X	+	-	+	-
C	+	-	X	_	-
D	+	-	+	X	-
E	+	+	-	+	X

3. *Man-to-Man Comparison:* Under this method certain factors are selected for analysis, like; leadership, initiative, inter-personal relationship, etc. and a scale is designed by a rater for each such factor. After rating such factors individually and accordingly, the aggregate performance of an individual employee is decided and such aggregative performance is also given a scale. Likewise an individual employee is considered with others. This method is somewhat like factor comparison method and widely used in job evaluation. Since developing uniform rating scale is a complicated task, this factor is not much in use in practice for Performance Appraisal of employees by organisation.

4. *Grading Method:* Under this method certain features, worth understanding the performance of an employee are identified. Such features may be leadership, communication power, analytic ability, job knowledge, etc. The raters mark/rate such features here also according to a scale and match and employees performance compared to his own developed grade definition. For example A, B, C, D, E types of grade definitions for each feature may be developed by a rater to indicate, A= very significant, B= Significant, C = Moderate, D= Average, E= Poor, Such types of grading are of much use for selection of an employee or grading them in written examinations.

5. ***Graphic or Linear Rating Scale:*** Such a rating scale is normally a continuous scale which enables a rater to mark somewhere along a continuum. Usually a printed form is given to a rater alongwith the factors to be rated, giving a continuous scale against each such factors. This method therefore enables quantification of performance scores and to analyse its significance using statistical techniques. Since making a rating cluster is difficult for obvious difference in individual characteristics of each job, this system may not always ensure objective appraisal.

6. ***Forced Choice Description Method:*** It is a combination of objective and subjective judgement on an individual employee's performance against each rating element. Positive and negative phrases are given asking the rater to indicate applicability of such phrases as objectives in describing the employee whose performance is rated. For its obvious complexity this system is not much used.

7. ***Forced Distribution Method:*** It is a method to evaluate employees performance according to a pre-determined distribution scale. For example under such a method the rater is asked to distribute 5% of the total employees on top of the scale, indicating their superior performance and promotability, 10% may be put immediately under this level, indicating their good performance and future promotability. This system is easy to understand and can be applied to organisations without much hassles.

8. ***Checklist Method:*** It is a mere process of reporting employees' performance, compiling yes/no responses. Final rating is done by the Personnel vis-à-vis HRD Department based on such reports. Since this is not an objective method of appraisal, it is not free from bias.

9. ***Free Essay Method:*** It is open ended qualitative appraisal of employees performance, giving an opportunity to the rater to put down his impression in subjective form on important job factors. Since it is descriptive and essay type, it is likely to be biased and judgemental errors may crop in.

10. ***Critical Incident Method:*** This method measures employees' performance in terms of certain 'events' or 'critical incidents' instrumental for success or failure on the job. Such critical incidents are identified by the rater after in depth study of the employees' working. As negative incidents get more focused and recording for incidents demand for utmost care, it is not free from defects.

11. ***Group Appraisal Method:*** It is an evaluation of an employee by multiple judges. The immediate supervisor of the employee and a few other discuss the performance standards and then evaluate the performance of the employee. The greatest advantage of this method is that it is relatively free from bias even though it is time consuming.

12. ***Field Review Method:*** This type of review is conducted by the HR Department by interviewing the supervisor of an employee to understand the subordinate employees' performance. Normally for such type of appraisal, the appraiser, i.e., the representative of the Human Resource department gets equipped with certain questions and more in the form of informal interview, asks those questions about the employees, whose performances are to be reviewed, to their respective supervisors. Since this process of

appraisal is an indirect method of appraising the performance, it may not always reflect the true performance level of the subordinate employees. Such an interview is always having a sensitising effect on the interview, whose responses may be some opinionated generalisation. Moreover, this method keeps the key managerial personnel always busy for appraisal. Despite such defect, the process being simple and being possible to administer, centralising the task of performance appraisal function, most of the organisations prefer to have this type of appraisal for lower level employees.

Modern Methods

The traditional methods of performance appraisal, discussed above, suffer from major limitation for their obvious emphasis on assessing individual performance or task, considering it as an isolated factor. To eliminate such narrow and partial approach, the newer techniques of performance appraisal have been developed and are widely practiced by the organisations, particularly for managerial and supervisory employees. Some of the modern techniques are discussed below:

1. ***Appraisal by Results for Management by Objectives:*** Management by Objective (MBO)_ is a comprehensive management approach which is adopted for performance appraisal and so also for organisational development. When MBO is used for performance appraisal only, its primary focus is on developing objective criteria for evaluating the performance of the individuals. Identification of common goals is jointly done by the superior and subordinate managers of an organisation. After such identification, each individuals's major area of responsibilities are defined. Such defined responsibility becomes the basis for evaluating the performance of the individual employee.

   Most of the organisations emphasise on developing KRA's through MBO exercise, as this approach necessitates joint meeting of the supervisor and the employee to define, establish and set goals or objectives, which the individual employees would achieve, within a prescribed time limit (mostly it is the form of early targets). Such an exercise also establishes ways and methods to measure performance. Goals are mostly work related and career oriented and are integrated with over all organisational objectives. Periodic evaluation of employees' performances are done in terms of goals and if required, goals may be revised. MBO also calls for superior subordinate interaction and supportive role of the supervisor (which as well includes counseling/coaching).

   However, MBO system lays more stress on tangible goals and hence intangible goals like morale, good inter-personal relations, commitment to the job etc, are often ignored. Moreover MBO exercise is too much time and money consuming.

2. ***Assessment Centre Method:*** This method is to test candidates in a social situation by a number of assessors, using a variety of criteria (which may be a paper pencil test, interviews, in-basket exercise, business game, role playing incident or a leaderless discussion). The assessors or evaluators are drawn from experienced executives, working at different levels of management. Under this method performance of employees are evaluated both individually and collectively. This method is useful in measuring inter-personal skills, organising and planning ability, creativity, resistance to stress,work motivation, decision making power, etc.

3. ***Human Asset Accounting Method:*** This method attaches money estimates in the value of manpower of an organisation. The process is somewhat like estimating the goodwill value and can be appraised by developing a procedure to undertake periodic measurement of certain variables. Such variables are either categorised as key variables or Intervening variables. Key variables are policies and decisions of an organisation, its leadership strategies, skills and behaviour of an employee, etc. Intervening variables are loyalties, attitudes, motivations, interpersonal relations, communication and decision making. Measuring such variables over several years, quantification of human assets are difficult for the obvious problem in developing the accounting procedure. It is not a very popular method of Performance Appraisal. However, this system is more appropriately used for evaluating the collective performance of an organisation, rather than individual appraisal of an employee. This method is useful for organisational development, as it helps in identifying the changed areas more scientifically than any other method. We have discussed this method in a separate unit.

4. ***Behaviourally Anchored Rating Scales (BARS):*** This method helps in measuring and improving job performance more accurately. For each performance area, some standard statements are provided. These are then put on the scales in BARS. While developing such BARS, group discussions are conducted to identify significant job dimensions that need to be evaluated. BARS may be of different types for different job dimensions. Normally BARS are presented vertically with scale points ranging from five to nine. Because of its behavioural orientation, it is considered as the most useful techniques of performance appraisal. Moreover, this system provides opportunity to both appraisee and appraiser to interact and participate in developing standards for each performance area. This system being time-consuming and painstaking, despite its advantages, organisations try to avoid this.

5. ***360 Degree Appraisals:*** This appraisal method is now largely in use throughout the world. It requires performance feedback from all important stakeholders of the organisation, like; the ratee himself, his superiors, peers, other team members, customers and suppliers. Apart from its effectiveness in reporting performance, this method also ensures Total Employee Involvement (TEI) and employee empowerment. This method also reduces subjective evaluation system in an organisation.

6. ***360-degree Feedback:***

N.K. Sahay, General Manager (Operations) in a BPO outfit knew he was a demanding boss. During a 360-degree feedback from his subordinates, he was in for a shock. The subordinates did not stop at saying he was a hard taskmaster; they also called him a "cold and uncaring individual". Sahay was dumb founded when he could realize that not appreciating people and not tempering his criticism were having a rundown effect on his subordinates. Today, he says, "When people are doing well, I take care to tell them about it. I am more open in my discussions. The results have been amazing: Team work is up and lead times are down."

Chitra, Head of Human Resources at a call-centre, was surprised to know that colleagues thought she had no sense of humour. She'd been one of the first people to laugh at herself in college. Her rueful reaction to this feedback was, "I do have a sense of humour but, evidently, I've become very good at hiding it. I guess that needs to change."

These two are examples of people who have been affected by 360-degree feedback. Also known as multi-rater feedback, full-circle appraisal and group performance review, this feedback system has today become a very popular tool for employee appraisal worldwide. It involves collecting feedback on an individual's behaviour and the impact of that behaviour from his boss, colleagues, fellow members of project teams, internal and external consultants/ customers, and direct reports.

However 360-degree can be considered in an organisation only when following are true for an organisation:

- Organisation is not able to meet challenges that come its way because of increased competition or global expansion.
- People in the organisation feel the need to change their behaviour to combat increasing competition and to progress in their careers but are unsure about what and how to change.
- There is no formal system in place through which people receive information on what others think about their behaviour.

360-degree feedback is not a package, which can be delivered by a given date; it is a process that needs to be implemented in steps. Before implementation of 369-degree feedback, it should be designed to support a corporate strategy or goal.

- Every employee should understand what it is and how it works.
- Employee development should be high on your company's agenda, and employees should believe that the organisation and manager would support feedback processes.
- Sufficient resources should be available to ensure that the integrity level of the process is high.
- The staff should be trained in the process.
- Employees must trust that the information would be used for developmental purposes and should be willing to receive and give feedback.

Most companies implement 360-degree feedback in stages. It is a good idea to start with small groups, using them as tools to gain maximum value from the total experience.

360-degree Feedback is used as follows:

1. ***Performance Appraisal:*** Even though 360-degree feed back is primarily used for performance appraisal, it is not desirable to make use of such feedback as the basis for appraisals at least for the first few cycles. Linking the 360-degree feedback to appraisal is a complex process, and employees are likely to be less honest in the beginning if they feel that the money they get is going to be affected by this process. An atmosphere of trust develops after one or two rounds and employees would not resist it being used for appraisal.

2. ***Cultural Change:*** Many organisations bring in this process to effect cultural change and develop a more open atmosphere in the organisation. 360-degree feedback does add to openness in the atmosphere and also increases employee empowerment provided a top down approach is taken while implementing it.

3. ***Organisational Development:*** Aggregating 360-degree feedback can realistically help assess the training needs for the organisation as a whole. It can also help identify skill gaps in the organisation and provide direction vis-a-vis competition.

PERFORMANCE MENTORING

The term mentor has come from Greek mythology. It was first institutionalised by Kram (1985). Since then, globally, organisations are emphasising on mentoring of their employees for continuous performance improvement. Mentoring is defined as those activities conducted by a mentor for the mentee, primarily to help the mentee to perform a job more effectively, and gradually rise through the career ladder. Through systematic coaching, training, counseling, or even by simple discussion, mentor conducts the mentoring exercises. Thus, mentor plays the role of counsellor or a teacher and through some patterned behavioural processes guides the mentee.

Mentoring as an essential component of training and development process, and its importance in Performance Management Systems has been highlighted by Burke and McKeen (1989), Hunt and Michael (1983), Zey (1988), and Scandura (1992). Operationally, mentoring is done through relationship development process to expose the mentees, i.e., the employees under the mentoring programme, to gain practical insights to the nitty-gritty of the jobs. With practical knowledge, guidance, support and feedback, mentees get matured and with upgrade skills can perform better. Apart from development and consequential performance improvement, mentoring also helps in orienting employees to the culture of the organisation. Many organisations emphasise on getting distinct competitive advantage, building culture of their own. We have seen this in the case of McDonald (opening case-let). Aligning mentees with the corporate culture make them more compatible with the organisational requirements and they can effectively deliver the performance results for long-term sustainability of the organisation. Yet, in another way, mentoring benefits the organisation, i.e., multi-skilling of employees. Mentoring process through the balanced development of cognitive, inter-personal, and technical skills, and through the situational or experiential learning, matures the mentees and they can develop their problem solving ability even in cross-functional areas.

Therefore mentoring broadly provides two types of benefits; vocational and psycho-social. Vocational benefits are skill acquisition, while psycho-social benefits are employees' ability to socialize; interpersonal abilities; collaborative and critical thinking; planning; decision making; collegiality, etc.

Mentoring process goes through four different phases of relationship like, Initiation, Cultivation, Separation, and Termination (Kram, 1983). Effective mentoring programme first develops the positive mentoring relationship and then, focuses on guiding the desired behavioural changes. Mentoring process can be both formal and informal.

The terms mentoring and coaching are often used interchangeably. But, contextually these are different. Mentoring is a more holistic approach as it is often considered as the transfer of wisdom. Coaching is the process of creating a supportive environment of learning to develop critical thinking skills, ideas and behaviours. It is, therefore, less facilitation and development of personal qualities of mentees than mentoring. In another way, we can also consider coaching as the sub-set of mentoring.

Thus, mentoring is an effective performance improvement tool. Many Indian and global organisations systematically take their employees through structured mentoring programmes to transform them to achievers for the overall benefits of the individual employees and the organisations. For organisations, mentoring programme may be either an on-going process or based on the performance gap analysis of the employees. Those employees, who lag in performance, are taken through the mentoring programmes to transform them to good performers.

Balanced Scorecard and Performance Management

A new approach to strategic management was developed in the early 1990's by Drs. Robert Kaplan (Harvard Business School) and David Norton. They named this system the 'balanced scorecard'. The balanced scorecard approach provides a clear prescription as to what companies should measure in order to 'balance' the financial perspective.

The balanced scorecard is a ***management system*** (not only a measurement system) that enables organisations to clarify their vision and strategy and translate them into action. It provides feedback around both the internal business processes and external outcomes in order to continuously improve strategic performance and results. When fully deployed, the balanced scorecard transforms strategic planning from an academic exercise into the nerve center of an enterprise.

Kaplan and Norton describe the innovation of the balanced scorecard as follows:

"The balanced scorecard retains traditional financial measures. But financial measures tell the story of past events, an adequate story for industrial age companies for which investments in long-term capabilities and customer relationships were not critical for success. These financial measures are inadequate, however, for guiding and evaluating the journey that information age companies must make to create future value through investment in customers, suppliers, employees, processes, technology, and innovation."

The balanced scorecard suggests that we view the organisation from four perspectives, and to develop metrics, collect data and analyze it relative to each of these perspectives:

- The Learning and Growth Perspective
- The Business Process Perspective
- The Customer Perspective
- The Financial Perspective

The Learning and Growth Perspective

This perspective includes employee training and corporate cultural attitudes related to both individual and corporate self-improvement. In a knowledge-worker organisation, *people* — the only repository of knowledge — are the main resource. In the current climate of rapid technological change, it is becoming necessary for knowledge workers to be in a continuous learning mode. Government agencies often find themselves unable to hire new technical workers, and at the same time there is a decline in training of existing employees. This is a leading indicator of 'brain drain' that must be reversed. Metrics can be put into place to guide managers in focusing training funds where they can help the most. In any case, *learning and growth constitute the essential foundation for success of any knowledge-worker organisation.*

Kaplan and Norton emphasize that 'learning' is more than 'training'; it also includes things like mentors and tutors within the organisation, as well as that ease of communication among workers that allows them to readily get help on a problem when it is needed. It also includes technological tools; what the Baldrige criteria call "high performance work systems." One of these, the Intranet, will be examined in detail later in this document.

The Business Process Perspective

This perspective refers to internal business processes. Metrics based on this perspective allow the managers to know how well their business is running, and whether its products and services conform to customer requirements (the mission). These metrics have to be carefully designed by those who know these processes most intimately; with our unique missions these are not something that can be developed by outside consultants.

In addition to the strategic management process, two kinds of business processes may be identified: (a) mission-oriented processes, and (b) support processes. Mission-oriented processes are the special functions of government offices, and many unique problems are encountered in these processes. The support processes are more repetitive in nature, and hence easier to measure and benchmark using generic metrics.

The Customer Perspective

Recent management philosophy has shown an increasing realization of the importance of customer focus and customer satisfaction in any business. These are leading indicators: if customers are not satisfied, they will eventually find other suppliers that will meet their needs. Poor performance from this perspective is thus a leading indicator of future decline, even though the current financial picture may look good.

In developing metrics for satisfaction, customers should be analyzed in terms of kinds of customers and the kinds of processes for which we are providing a product or service to those customer groups.

The Financial Perspective

Kaplan and Norton do not disregard the traditional need for financial data. Timely and accurate funding data will always be a priority, and managers will do whatever necessary to provide it. In fact, often there is more than enough handling and processing of financial data. With the implementation of a corporate database, it is hoped that more of the processing can be centralized and automated. But the point is that the current emphasis on financials leads to the "unbalanced" situation with regard to other perspectives. There is perhaps a need to include additional financial-related data, such as risk assessment and cost-benefit data, in this category.

Balanced Scorecard (BSC) is a concept helping you translate strategy into action. BSC starts from the company vision and strategies, from here critical success factors are defined. Measures are constructed that aid target-setting and performance measurement in areas critical to the strategies. Hence, Balanced Scorecard is a performance measurement system, derived from vision and strategy, and reflecting the most important aspects of the business. The Balanced Scorecard (BSC) concept supports strategic planning and implementation by federating the actions of all parts of an organisation around a common understanding of its goals, and by facilitating the assessment and upgrade of strategy.

Traditional performance measurement, focusing on external accounting data, was quickly becoming obsolete and something more was needed to provide the information age enterprises with efficient planning tools. A typical balanced score card model is illustrated as under:

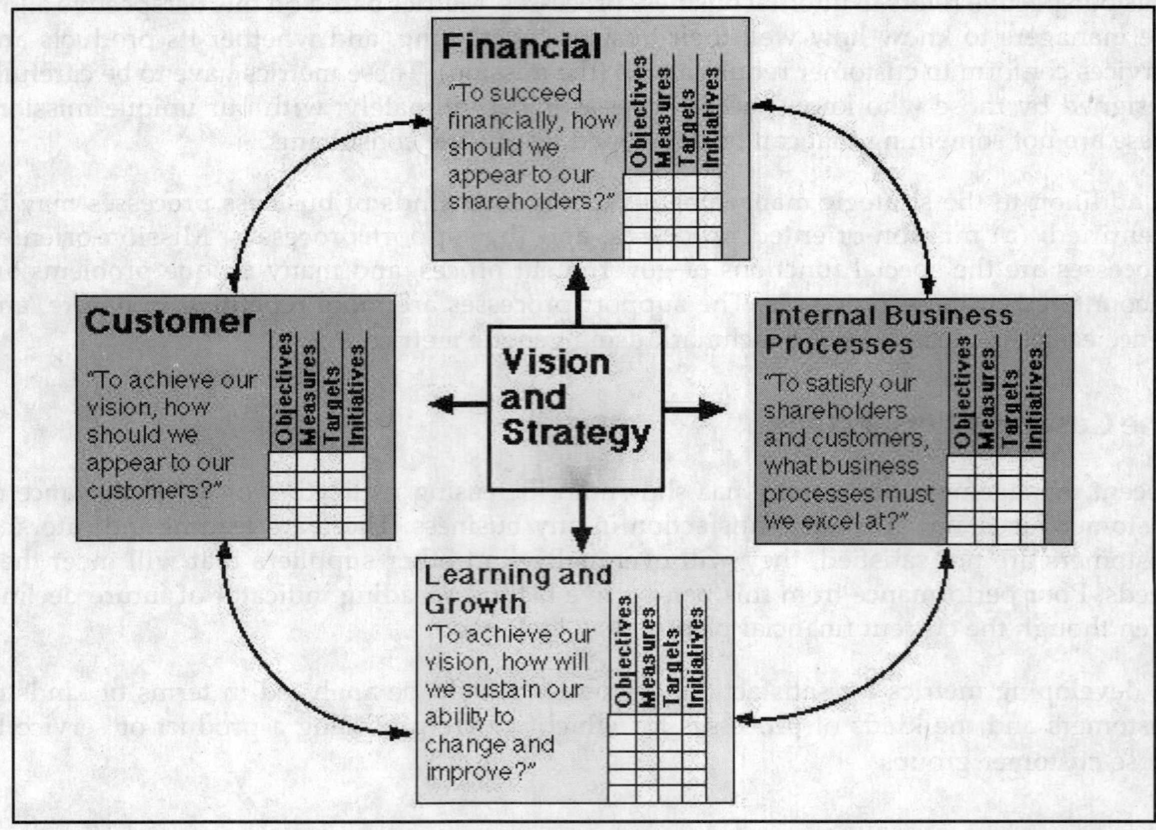

Figure 10.1: Balanced Scorecard Model

Benefits

The benefits of applying Balanced Scorecard can be summarized as follows:

- Balanced scorecard helps align key performance measures with strategy at all levels of an organisation.
- Balanced scorecard provides management with a comprehensive picture of business operations.
- The methodology facilitates communication and understanding of business goals and strategies at all levels of an organisation.
- The balanced scorecard concept provides strategic feedback and learning.
- Balanced scorecard helps reduce the vast amount of information the company's IT systems process into essentials.

The HR Scorecard Approach

Once integrated, the HR Scorecard aligns support functions with the business strategy illustrating:

- The strategic impact of HR services and projects and enables HR to demonstrate its value through
- More than short-term financial outcomes. Adopting the HR Scorecard as a strategic management
- System ensures that HR views all of its activities in terms of their contribution to the organisation's
- Goals. By developing a strategic program for measuring and managing Human Capital, HR executives have the opportunity to spearhead the development of better strategic management.

How to develop HR Scorecard?

If structured properly, adopting the HR Scorecard would allow the HR organisation to take the initiative, instead of being reactive to the demands of the enterprise. A comprehensive approach that creates strategic alignment between HR and the enterprise at all levels including strategy, resource allocation, budgeting, reporting is absolutely essential.

Developing the HR Scorecard as a new management process provides the foundation to make HR a true strategic partner and enable the enterprise to realize the full value of its human capital.

The first step in establishing HR as a strategy focused organisation requires the development of a HR Scorecard that can be linked to enterprise strategy and achieve perfect organisational alignment. Successful project execution requires a HR Scorecard, which is a management system project that demonstrates a high level of user friendliness. All scorecard users should be able to manage scorecards unaided by IT specialists or power users. Training must be straightforward to accelerate adoption, and information must be accessible without a tedious navigation process.

The HR Scorecard development process will entail the completion of several processes using the following methodology:

1. ***Development of a Solid Strategy:*** Development of a solid strategy that is aligned with the enterprise strategy is a keystone to success. Without a solid strategy, success is unobtainable. However, without execution, a solid strategy is meaningless.

2. ***Strategy Mapping:*** Development of a strategy map, including selection of performance measures, establish targets, establish objectives, identify initiatives and identify ownership to deliver the strategy.

3. ***Establish Measures for each Objective:*** After translating strategy into objectives, managers and employees must know if and when objectives are being achieved. Therefore, each objective is given at least one measurement that is included in the Key Performance Indicators.

4. ***Cascading of Scorecard:*** Keeping in mind operational, management and front line employees do the actual work that makes strategies happen. Organisations must develop Scorecards at every level so that each person can see how his or her specific responsibilities align and contribute to the higher level goals.

5. ***Scorecard Implementation:*** Finalize Scorecard designs and develop an implementation plan.

6. ***Post Implementation:*** After the Scorecards are deployed, managers need to periodically re-examine their existing core processes to ensure they are linked to the corporate strategy.

HR Scorecard Key Benefits

- Formulate HR strategy that is aligned with the overall corporate strategy
- Clarify the vision/mission of the organisation
- Create a consensus and ownership of the strategy in the management team
- Improve communication of the strategy across the enterprise
- Prioritize HR initiatives by linking activities to business goals
- Helps support functions identify and communicate their unique strategies

- Create a framework for initiative prioritization and budgeting
- Align measurement with business goal achievement
- Measure HR's strategic contribution in concrete and clearly understood terms
- Provide real time graphical display of Key Performance Indicators

Successful Execution

Research conducted by the Harvard Business School demonstrates that overall only one out of every ten companies that formulate strategy can effectively implement it. Many factors make it difficult to implement strategy today. The pace of change continues to accelerate, technology changes frequently and the workforce is more diverse and mobile than ever before. While the business world continues to evolve, management systems have not kept up. The majority of measurement and management systems were designed to meet the needs of a stable, incrementally changing world not the needs of today's dynamic economy. Statistics confirm that a Balanced Scorecard approach has emerged as the most effective way of managing and executing enterprise strategy.

HR Competencies

1. ***Business Partner – competencies include:***

   ❖ Knows mission

   ❖ Understands business process and how to change to improve efficiency and effectiveness

   ❖ Understands clients and organisational culture

   ❖ Understands public service environment

   ❖ Understands team behavior

   ❖ Communicates well

   ❖ Possesses the ability to be innovative and create a risk taking environment

   ❖ Applies organisational development principles

   ❖ Knows business system thinking

   ❖ Possesses good analytical skills including the ability to think strategically and creatively

   ❖ Possesses the ability to build trust relationships

   ❖ Links HR to the organisation's mission and service outcome

2. *Change Agent – competencies include:*

- ❖ Understands business process and how to change to improve efficiency and effectiveness
- ❖ Understands clients and organisational culture
- ❖ Understands public service environment
- ❖ Understands team behavior
- ❖ Communicates well
- ❖ Assesses and balances competing values
- ❖ Knows business system thinking
- ❖ Applies information technology to human resource management
- ❖ Possesses good analytical skills including the ability to think strategically and creatively
- ❖ Designs and implements change process
- ❖ Uses consultation and negotiation skills including dispute resolution
- ❖ Possesses the ability to build trust relationships
- ❖ Possesses marketing and representational skills
- ❖ Uses consensus and coalition building skills
- ❖ Demonstrates customer service orientation

3. *Leadership – competencies include:*

- ❖ Understands team behavior
- ❖ Communicates well
- ❖ Assesses and balances competing values
- ❖ Possesses good analytical skills including the ability to think strategically and creatively
- ❖ Uses consultation and negotiation skills including dispute resolution
- ❖ Uses consensus and coalition building skills
- ❖ Understands, values and promotes diversity
- ❖ Practices and promotes integrity and ethical behavior

COMPETENCY MAPPING AND PERFORMANCE MANAGEMENT

Hay-Mcber company founder David McClelland, a Harvard University psychologist in the late 1960's, pioneered competency-based methodology. McClelland set out to define competency variables that could be used in predicting job performance and that were not biased by race, gender, or socioeconomic factors. His research helped identify performance aspects not attributable to a worker's intelligence or degree of knowledge and skill. McClelland's article, appearing in American Psychologist in 1973, entitled "Testing for Competence Rather Than For Intelligence," was a key point of development of the competency movement as an alternative to the intelligence testing movement.

What is Competency?

There is difference between the words 'competence' and 'competency'.

'Competence' means a skill and the standard of performance reached while 'competency' refers to the behaviour by which it is achieved. In other words, one describes what people can do while the other focuses on how they do it. Competencies refer to the range of skills, which are satisfactorily performed, while competencies refer to the behavior adopted in competent performance.

There are various definitions of competency but most of them refer to competence. Hogg B (1989) defined 'competencies are the characteristics of a manager that lead to the demonstration of skills and abilities, which result in effective performance within an occupational area. Competency also embodies the capacity to transfer skills and abilities from one area to another.'

A more detailed definition synthesized from the suggestions of several hundred experts in HRD is a 'cluster of related knowledge, skills and attitudes that affects a major part of one's job (a role or responsibility), that correlates with performance on the job, that can be measured against well-accepted standards and that can be improved via training and development' (Parry, 1996).

There are five types of competency characteristics:

1. *Motives:* The things a person consistently thinks about or wants and that which causes action. Motives 'drive, direct, or select' behavior towards certain actions or goals and away from others.

2. *Traits:* Physical characteristics and consistent responses to situation or information.

3. *Self-concept:* A person's attitudes, values or self-image.

4. *Knowledge:* Information a person has in specific content areas.

5. *Skill:* The ability to perform a certain physical or mental task.

As illustrated, knowledge and skill competencies tend to be visible and relatively 'on the surface' characteristics of people. Self-concept, trait and motive competencies are more hidden, 'deeper' and central to personality.

Surface knowledge and skill competencies are relatively easy to develop; training is the most effective way to secure these employee abilities. Core motive and trait competencies are more difficult to assess and develop; it is most cost effective to select these characteristics.

Developing Competency Models

The key to gaining a competitive advantages are the ability of the workforce of an organisation to maximize the advantages of state-of-the-art technology, superior products, and steady source of capital to enter into the marketplace. A company's technological tools are only as useful as its employer's ability to employ them; they are perceived in terms of how effectively the benefits are communicated (McLagan, 1989).

Determining whether the workforce possesses the abilities critical for its success is indeed difficult. Behaviours necessary for effective performance vary from business to business and roles to roles. Many organisations have thus developed competency models to help them identify the essential knowledge, skills and attributes needed for successful performance in a job aligned with the strategy and integrating it to the HR strategy.

A competency model describes the combination of knowledge; skills and characteristics needed to effectively perform a role in an organisation and is used as a human resource tool for selection, training and development, appraisal and succession planning.

Attributes or characteristics of the person are most complex and most difficult to measure. Aptitude, reasons and inclination suggest a potential to acquire a particular skill or knowledge. Traits such as extroversion, self-sufficiency and tenacity may indicate a disposition for dealing with certain types of situations or performing certain roles.

A competency model includes both innate and acquired aspects. It is essentially a pyramid built on the foundation of inherent talents, incorporating the types of skills and knowledge that can be acquired through learning effort and experience. At the top of the pyramid is a specific set of behaviors that are manifestation of all innate and acquired abilities.

Formation of a Competency Framework

Competency models are position models, which are at the heart of every competency-based HR application. A competency model is a GIGO (garbage in-garbage out) test factory. In spite of timely administration intricacies and sophistication, if the models are not accurate and do not represent the relative position, the purpose of the model is doomed. The basis of generating competency models is processes. If the flow charts of the job processes are laid, determining of competencies is easier. If the competencies are not related to the specific process step then the model is not valid.

Sources of Competency Information

The best way to get started is to follow a top-down approach from general to specific.

By assumption: Certain assumptions are assumed to be present in every employee

By law: Government and its associated regulatory agencies create requirements that apply to all workers.

By industry: Individual industries have their own professional competency models and assessment approaches.

By Organisation: The vision and mission statement of the organisation reflect the overall philosophy of the organisation: Where it is headed, what it does and how it should act.

By Work Group: Departments in many organisations have their own resources of vision and mission statements.

By Background Information: A special category of competency input has to do with background knowledge of the company and industry in general.

This information is generated from:

Position documentation: Industry Research, Vendor Information, Customer feedback, Regulations, Certification Programmes, Quality Programmes.

Process Documentation: Procedure Manuals and Flowcharts, Time Logs, Job Task Analysis.

Existing Documentation: Job Descriptions, Union Contracts, Departmental Planning Documents, Performance Plans, Appraisal Forms.

Personal Development Process: The training and development department is an excellent source of information on competencies.

Interviews: Hard information can be attained from data process, procedures, manuals, etc.

Behavioral Event Interview: Behavioral Event Interview (BEI) is an interview technique based on the premise that the best predictor of future behavior is past behavior.

Behavioral Description Interview: BDI is a version of BEI, but differ from it in the scope and length of the example or 'events' that interviewees are asked to describe, and in the trigger questions the interviewer to elicit these examples uses that.

Benchmarking: Whether interviews or feedback, the important parameter in the development of the models is creating a benchmark of those employees who exceed and fall below performance standards.

Established Model

Other than starting from scratch and developing a model, another resource is to adapt a completed model from an outside source.

Competency Mapping and Assessment Centers

Identification of competencies and the development of a competency model, both generic and specific, are finally achieved through a rigorous process. Linked with the HR systems the competency model is applied in the various HR functions. Competency is to be mapped, along with other techniques, on the supply side with the developed competency framework model to the job requisition. Competencies-namely, knowledge, skills, traits, motives-have to be integrated with the HR system. An assessment center is an alternative to validate the competencies with the help of various tools. The assessment center is the most important step in mapping the competencies once they have been identified.

How Competencies help in Organisational Renewal?

Organisations are human systems and their system structure includes the worldview, beliefs, and mental models of their leaders and members. Changing organisational behavior requires changing the belief system of its personnel. This process of changing beliefs is called learning. Effective learning requires clear, open communications throughout the organisation. Organisational performance ultimately rests on human behavior and improving performance requires changing behavior. Therefore organisational restructuring should have as a fundamental goal the facilitation of clear, open communication that can enable organisational learning and clarify accountability of results.

The need to link the intellectual capital of the firm to the strategic objective is the order of the day. Firms have realized that unless they align themselves accordingly they will not be able to gain a competitive advantage. Thus, a competency-based approach is today being used by a lot many organisations in achieving their strategic objectives.

Organisations are using competencies in virtually each human resource domain. They provide criteria, which can be applied to each of the human resource practices shown below:

Competency Mapping therefore has now become essential for every organisation to achieve excellence, gain competitive advantage and renew them through proper restructuring. Only focus on skill and continuous skill development is not the answer for gaining competitive advantage for today's organisation. It is essential to leverage the human potential in respect of competency mapping to understand both the existing set of competencies and the gap if any.

Competency Map for a Trainer

Job title	Trainer
Department	
Reporting to	Vice President - HR
Job purpose	Design and deliver practical learning solutions to client groups and individuals in order to meet clients' needs and benefit ourselves/organisation.

Key result areas		% of time spent
1. Design, planning and development	In partnership with the client and sales consultant/account manager design learning solutions to meet their needs Creatively, using specialist knowledge, design and develop innovative learning (if appropriate) solutions/identify possible areas for product development Design learning programmes for inclusion in proposals and tenders	10%
2. Deliver and evaluate	Deliver learning in a way that most effectively facilitates learning to meet clients' needs Delivery to standards of quantity and quality expected by the organisation and client Evaluate effectiveness and validate learning (if appropriate for the client)	60%
3. Development of client relationships	Monitor, anticipate and respond to customer requirements Build and maintain mutually beneficial relationships Respond to enquiries for new business with flexibility and initiative	10%
4. Management of people and resources	Build, maintain and sustain effective internal relationships with administrator and support staff throughout the team. Ensure clear communication with sales team prior to and throughout contract Effective use of IT for the benefit of the client, management of the contract and organisation Financial – together with sales/account manager ensure contracts are financially viable and correct expenses are charged Responsible for controlling and efficient administration of chargeable and non-chargeable expenses.	5%
5. Campaigning and influencing	Appreciate and act on the organisations campaigns and values Seek to translate campaigning messages and values where appropriate into practical solutions for benefit of the client	5%
6. Intellecutal capital	Continually develop own learning in specialist areas to enable leading edge delivery Apply own knowledge and learning to development of new products and methods according to clients' and organisation's needs Contribute to continuous learning for self, colleagues and the organisation. Feedback into 'future focus' and 'policy' work knowledge and understanding of issues and practice gained through client relationships.	10%

Potential Appraisal

Potential appraisal is a holistic approach for studying wholesome qualities of an employee with a given intellect, personality and character. Industry practices apply two widely used approach for potential appraisal, i.e., Helicopter and Whole Person Qualities. Helicopter method tries to measure the potentiality of a person on large as well as on specific issues. Whole person qualities method measures the wholesome qualities/potentialities of a person with a given set of variables, mentioned above, which are already determined for the person. Potential appraisal data is extremely useful for career planning, as the latent abilities of an individual can be captured and matched with the future role and responsibilities. However, in India, we do not have documented practices on potential appraisal in the corporate world.

Basic purpose of potential appraisal is to identify the hidden talents and skills of employees, which may not even be known to the employee himself/herself. It is a future-oriented approach and organisations consider its integration with the performance evaluation process. Among others, potential appraisal serves the following purposes:

- To make employees aware about their career development and future prospects
- To help the organisation to draw effective succession plans
- To focus on further development of employees' competencies
- To effectively identify the training needs.

All the techniques used in performance appraisal can be used in potential appraisal. However, more emphasis is given on psychological and psychometric tests, management games, role playing, and team building and leadership exercises.

Steps to Performance Appraisal

Irrespective of the methods applied for performance appraisal, its steps follow more or less a set pattern, which are listed as below :

- Establishment of performance standards. This is done mostly while developing job description.
- Communication of standards to the employees.
- Measurement of performance
- Comparison of performance with the job standards.
- Discussing the appraisal results with the employees
- Initiating the corrective action, where necessary.

PERFORMANCE COUNSELLING

It is a process of advising an employee, listening to his problems and enabling him to find a satisfactory solution on his own. Performance Counseling is a process to help subordinates to analyse their performance objectively. It helps in identifying training and development needs and also ensures improvement in future performance of an employee.

Primarily, performance counselling attempts to help an employee in the following ways.

- It helps an employee to understand his own strengths and weaknesses. More effective counseling sessions even enable employees to make their independent SWOT analysis, i.e., opportunities and threats in achieving the performance can also be made clear to such employees for their independent performance.

- Since good performance counseling believes in giving feedback information about the employees' behaviour, so also their performance, it helps in improving professional and interpersonal competence of employees.
- It helps in setting goals, formulating action plan for further improvement of employees.
- It helps the employees to identify different alternatives for dealing with problems.
- A good performance counselling session being supportive and being empathetic, employees feel encouraged to openly discuss their aspirations, conflicts and problems.

Conditions for Effective Performance Counselling

Conditions for effective Performance Counselling may be listed as follows:

1. A climate of mutual trust, confidence and openness need to be ensured at the outset.
2. Climate should be such that it can ensure subordinates' free participation in the review process and also in their giving the correct feedback. This is important as counseling is not a one way process of communication, but a two-way traffic.
3. The focus of performance counseling is on employee development. Employee development should not be considered isolated from other issues of performance appraisal, i.e. remuneration and rewards, promotion, motivation, etc.

Different Phases of Performance Counselling

There are different phases of Performance Counselling Processing. They are mentioned below:

1. *Rapport Building:* The first phase of performance counselling is rapport building, i.e., establishing a climate of acceptance, support, openness, etc. Subordinates should be assured in this phase that their superiors are keenly interested in their development. A successful rapport building phase, therefore, generates confidence in the employees, which facilitate sharing openly their perceptions, problems, conscience, feeling, etc.
2. *Exploration:* In this phase, apart from visiting the employees and creating a climate of openness, the counselors help the employees to understand their strengths, weaknesses, opportunities and threats. The success of this phase lies in making the employees discover all these on their own and at the same time initiate remedial measures independently.
3. *Action Planning:* Specific plans and actions for the development of employees are identified at this phase of performance counselling. The counselor helps the employees to implement such action plans for effective results. For making such action plans acceptable, some counselors prefer to develop the action plans exposing employees to a series of brainstorming sessions. This process enables the employees to develop the action plans independently.

Performance Counseling Process

The counselor in performance counseling sessions should be an excellent listener. He should pay attention to the ideas, feelings and sentiments of the person being counseled. This enables the counselor to understand and analyse the subordinate's concern. The effectiveness of performance counseling session, therefore, depends on efficiency in asking questions. The questions should be framed in such a way that they should try to seek constructive suggestions from the subordinate, should be open-ended and empathetic. The questions should not be critical or should not appear as if the intention of the counselor is to test or evaluate the subordinate person.

Secondly, performance counseling process should ensure communication of feedback to the subordinates in such a manner so as to evoke constructive response from them. Since, giving negative feedback is embarrassing, feedback should always be descriptive and non-evaluative. It should be focused on the behavioural attributes rather than on the subordinate himself. Feedback should be made more data based and suggestive. It should be continuous and verifiable.

Counselling Interview

Before beginning the counseling session, the counselor needs to study subordinate's job responsibilities, his education, training and experience, job performance and his past jobs. He should make adequate planning of the discussion, the issues involved and determine the development need for discussion with the employee.

The interview should be sincere, informal and friendly. The counselor should explain the purpose of the discussion to the interviewee and also emphasise on the issue that the interview is essentially a two-way communication. The subordinates should be encouraged to discuss their own appraisals about themselves. The counselor should focus on the strong points and encourage the subordinates to suggest their own developments. It is essential for the counselor to reach agreement on development plans and also to summarise the points discussed in the session at the end of the interview. He should make record on plans mutually agreed to in the interview.

SUMMARY

Performance Appraisal reinforces HRM in an organisation. In this era of technological change and global competitiveness, organisations are constantly required to renew and update skill of their people or else they are likely to encounter the problem of manpower obsolescence, which among others, will call for frequent downsizing or rightsizing. While Performance Appraisal updates organisations to take a stock on their skill inventories, training helps to address the skill-gap. Today world-wide it is acknowledged that effective performance management systems is an essential pre-requisite for an organisation to achieve and even to sustain competitive advantage. More contemporary tools like Balanced Scorecard and Competency Mapping now make performance management systems more measurable and scientific.

KEYWORDS

Performance Appraisal	Standards of performance
Performance metrics	Performance Management Systems
Methods of Performance Appraisal	Balanced Scorecard
HR Scorecard	Competency Mapping
Potential Appraisal	Performance Counseling
Performance Mentoring	

REVIEW QUESTIONS

1. Define Performance Appraisal. Briefly state its importance and objectives. What are the steps you would like to follow for appraising the performance of a managerial employee?

2. What are the different performance appraisal systems followed in an organisation? Select at least five methods and briefly discuss their strengths and weaknesses.

3. Traditional Performance Appraisal System emphasises on assessing the individual performance as an isolated factor. Briefly discuss the newer techniques of performance appraisal, critically reviewing the shortcomings of traditional system.

4. Discuss the effectiveness of MBO and BARS in performance appraisal. Develop KRAs for a HR Manager of an organisation and identify five important performance criteria for assessing the performance on a six point Behaviourally Anchored Rating Scales.

5. Critically review the performance appraisal system in India. Elaborate your answer visiting at least two organisations.

6. Develop a standard performance appraisal form for supervisors in an organisation, selecting at least ten factors for review. Recommend your proposed development plans for such supervisors based on your review.

7. Briefly state the importance and objectives of performance counseling. What are the conditions for effectiveness of performance counseling?

8. What is a balanced score card? What are its different perspectives? Explain how a BSC is related to the vision and mission of an organisation?

9. Explain the term HR competencies and detail areas of such competencies.

10. Explain HR scorecard. How can it be developed? What are the key benefits?

11. Explain how HR can be a strategically important function.

12. Explain the concept of competency. How competency development helps in organisational renewal?

13. Develop a competency map for a Marketing Manager of a new generation software company, clearly showing the weight distribution to different competency areas.

14. What are the important sources of competency information? How do you relate such sources for competency development?

15. Write short notes on:

    (a) Counselling Interview

    (b) Assessment Centre Method

    (c) Field Review

    (d) Critical Incident Method

    (e) Key Performance Areas

CASE STUDY

SOFTTECH'S PERFORMANCE MANAGEMENT SYSTEMS

The 360 Degree Appraisal System is a performance management tool used today by 90% of fortune 1000 companies. SoftTech, a new generation software company, catering mostly to clients from Europe and Scandinavian countries, had to opt for this because of their clients' requirements. Clients' feedback and immediate response mechanism require SoftTech to review performance of their employees almost on daily basis, integrating their performance management systems with IT-enabled Balanced Score Card. The system can track quickly any performance disorder, sending a warning signal to the controlling unit. Controlling Unit is supposed to initiate corrective action within four hours and report back in the system itself, to facilitate tracking of the results by the immediate senior level. Likewise, performance disorder issues can reach to the CEO level within 8 hours time schedule. SoftTech's jobs are highly protocol bound and any deviation simply makes the clients' eligible to impose penalty to recover their business loss.

Of-late, SoftTech started observing their automatic performance tracking system fail to track the finer interpersonal relational issues, causing performance drop of employees. Customers' dissatisfaction, to some extent also depends on employees' dissatisfaction. An unsatisfied employee cascades his/her dissatisfaction to customer service, resulting in drop in business revenue. SoftTech's jobs may be protocol bound but people are not machines that deliver same standards of performance all the time.

A critical evaluation of SoftTech's performance management system indicated that it leans heavily on customer feedback, rather than the internal dynamics. Many employees made a system of mutual appreciation in peer review, depriving the management to understand their real feel and the subordinates who do not give fair feedback, fearing that they get identified and their superiors take them to task. Superiors' review system is also not foolproof. SoftTech could observe several elements of bias. To check this some absurd rating (like too high and too low), certain performance parameters have been disallowed by the system. For example, in attendance regularity, nobody could get 5 out of 5 or 1 out of 5. Both are extreme cases. For SoftTech, employees with 5 out of 5 in attendance in the long run become junk. They are not taking pleasure trips with families and friends for which the company allows Leave Travel Concessions every year to the extent of one month pay. Employees, however, are free to use this amount for excursion or otherwise.

SoftTech realized that their existing performance management system is not a reliable management evaluation/assessment tool. It failed to achieve the objectives of good performance management systems like, correct identification of training and development needs, better team development, and understanding of correct HR intervention methods to ease the organisational dysfunction.

Question

Suggest possible ways to improve the performance management systems based on the above observations. Recommend your courses of action.

Exhibit 10.1

Managerial Appraisal Review Form

APPRAISAL PERIOD: FROM TO:

I. PERSONAL DATA

Name	Designation	Grade
Personal No.	Department	Division
Date of Birth		

Academic Qualifications	Years of Experience
Professional Qualifications	In Present Organisation
Professional Membership	Outside Present Organisation
Date of Retirement	Date of Last Promotion

II. APPRAISAL

II.A. IMPORTANT POINTS

1. Assess the employee on his performance in his present position only.
2. Try not to allow personal prejudices to influence your appraisal. The rating should be as objective as possible.
3. Assess the ratee on his performance during the whole year. Do not allow isolated incidents or recent instances to bias your assessment.
4. Assess each factor independently, uninfluenced by the rating on the other factors.
5. Assess the ratee on all factors.
6. The rater and reviewer must initial in ink in the box against the most appropriate rating in each case.
7. All entries in this form should be handwritten in legible condition.

II.B. GENERAL PERFORMANCE FACTORS

Please initial in the box against the appropriate rating.

Factors	Rater	Reviewer		Degree
1. KNOWLEDGE OF THE JOB All round knowledge of the job including concepts and techniques required and their application; know-how of the latest trends, developments and innovations in the field of work.			Excellent	Exceptional mastery of all phases of work. Has up to date knowledge of his field.
			Good	Thorough knowledge of job
			Satisfactory	Adequate knowledge of job for the position he is occupying.
			Unsatisfactory	Poor knowledge of his job.

Contd...

2. PLANNING OF WORK Scheduling of one's assignments in order to meet deadlines; setting of well defined targets; concentration on task priorities; ability to anticipate problems and take corrective action.			Excellent	Highly effective in setting of goals and their prioritisation. Anticipates problems and takes corrective action.
			Good	Effective in meeting tough deadlines most of the time
			Satisfactory	Usually effective in meeting routine schedules
			Un-satisfactory	Is indifferent to planning and cannot meet deadlines
3. ABILITIES TO ACHIEVE RESULTS Utilisation and productivity of subordinates and resources; target achievement; follow-up system and co-ordination with departments; coping with sustained work pressures; quick response to special jobs without letting routine matters suffer; keeping superiors and subordinates informed about relevant jobs, problems and results			Excellent	Highly effective in organising resources and getting extra ordinary results
			Good	Achieves superior results and is able to withstand work pressures and crises
			Satisfactory	Achieves normal results expected of him through good organisation and follow-up
			Unsatisfactory	Does not use available resources; does not achieve expected results.
4. SENSE OR RESPONSIBILITY Ability to handle given assignments independently or with minimum supervision; degree of chasing or control required from superiors; setting of self targets and their completion; seeking information on problems; willingness to take a decision or do a job without passing the buck.			Excellence	Very high sense of responsibility; can handle assignments independently; displays rate initiative and drive.
			Good	Is willing to shoulder greater responsibility than the job demands; displays considerable initiative.
			Satisfactory	Takes on responsibilities of his job and copes with routine problems. Takes routine decisions.
			Unsatisfactory	Does assigned tasks reluctantly; requires constant direction and supervision

Contd...

5. MAINTAINING DISCIPLINE Sense of organisational discipline and ability to maintain it in the work force; punctuality; on the job presence; setting of personal example to subordinates; firmness in dealings with subordinates; standards of cleanness, safety and housekeeping in the work place; willingness to accept the consequence of unpleasant decisions made by superiors			Excellent	Maintains high standards or organisational discipline and sets personal example to his men.
			Good	Achieves above average standards of discipline, safety and housekeeping; is committed to decisions of superiors.
			Satisfactory	Meets and maintains expected standards of discipline and punctuality
			Unsatisfactory	Is not punctual and is noted for unscheduled absences; talks loosely about superiors.
6. GETTING ALONG WITH PEOPLE Clarity and effectiveness in communicating with superiors, peers and subordinates; handling of conflicts, levels of maturity in dealing with bosses and peers, ability to take feedback and correct one self; skill in influencing others without arousing antagonism. Caring attitude towards colleges and subordinates.			Excellent	Has a marked ability for fruitful interaction with people
			Good	Is highly effective in understanding, relating and communicating with people
			Satisfactory	Has the ability to communication with people and influence them for good performance
			Unsatisfactory	Finds it difficult to relate with bosses, peers or subordinates
7. TEAMWORK AND CO-OPERATION Ability to work with colleagues, peers and other departments; kind of participation in meetings; degree of involvement in team project; willingness to share one's resources with others in the department if needed; seeking and offering peer assistance; degree of sensitivity to group feelings and response			Excellent	Highly productive and successful in working with colleagues and peers
			Good	Positive participation and integration with team.
			Satisfactory	Adequate commitment and contribute to team efforts. Notable peer collaboration.
			Unsatisfactory	Does not function as a team member. Goes all out for himself. Tends to disrupt rather than contribute to team efforts.

Contd...

8. IDENTIFICATION WITH THE COMPANY Sense of identification with the company's values and interests; concern for satisfaction of clients/customers' needs: pursuit of excellence in performance; concern for cost reduction through optimum utilisation of men, materials or equipment; concern for preservation of company's property			Excellent	Thoroughly identifies himself with company's values and interests and transmits them to peers and subordinates.
			Good	Is involved with and loyal to company's interests. Has a high sense of belongingness to the company.
			Satisfactory	Shows necessary concern for company's values and interests.
			Unsatisfactory	Low commitment to company's interests. Talks loosely about the company and has no belongingness to it.
9. DEVELOPMENT OF SUBORDINATES Ability to guide subordinates in their work assignments; delegation of work; steps taken for training and development of subordinates; ability to get them to accept the challenge of higher responsibilities or targets.			Excellent	Gives very high priority to development of subordinates.
			Good	Takes positive steps for subordinate development like training and job enrichment/ enlargement.
			Satisfactory	Shows concern for development of subordinates; is able to motivate them.
			Unsatisfactory	Has no interest in the development of his subordinates.
10. APPROACH TO PROBLEM SOLVING Ability to seek alternative ways to solve a problem or meet a deadline within the rules of the company; flexible and practical approach; ability to cope with unusual problems and situations; generation of original ideas and enduring solutions to problems			Excellent	Is extremely resourceful and has practical and original skill to solve problems.
			Good	Is flexible in approach and successful in finding solutions to many unusual problems.
			Satisfactory	Able to find solutions to routine problems; is receptive to new ideas.
			Unsatisfactory	Is upset when problems come. Fails to solve them.

Contd...

III.A. TRAINING PLANS

Please tick below selectively, the type of training courses which you think will help to improve the ratee's performance.

1. Technical (please specify the area)
2. Functional (please specify the area)
3. Computers
4. Management Training
   (a) General Management Programmes
   (b) Total Quality Management
   (c) Problem Solving Skills
   (d) Communications Skills
   (e) Leadership Skills
   (f) Inter-personal/Behavioural Skills
   (g) Value Engineering
5. Any other (please specify)

III.B. DEVELOPMENT PLANS

What are your plans to develop the ratee? (e.g. special assignments, increased responsibility, etc.)

I have seen my performance appraisal for the year...... and it has been discussed with me with respect to my performance and development plans.

Date.........   Signature of the Ratee

IV. CHECKLIST OF OBSERVABLE BEHAVIOUR

Please go through each of the items listed below. Whenever the item description distinctly tallies with the observable behaviour in the ratee, tick in the column marked. YES. If it is not so, please tick in the column marked NO. This checklist is not an assessment of performance. It is be used for developmental purposes.

Contd...

S.No.	Description	Yes	No
1.	Pay attention to documentation. Is systematic in record keeping for future references.		
2.	Is clear and concise in written communication.		
3.	Has the capacity for self-analysis and correction of his weaknesses.		
4.	Has the aptitude for systematic and methodical work. Is patient with minute details		
5.	Makes positive attempts to update himself in his professional field and learn new things		
6.	Does not accept sub-standard work.		
7.	Does not lose heart in spite of failures or setbacks.		
8.	Has a sense of humor.		
9	Promotes healthy industrial relations in his department or work place.		
10.	Is skilled in organising complex activities.		
11.	Is trustworthy. Does not let down colleagues for personal gain.		
12.	Has the courage of his convictions. Express dissent where he is convinced of a different approach to the task or problems.		
13.	Respectful of elders and superiors. Polite. Does not hurt colleagues or subordinates		
14.	Finds it very easy to get to know people and get along with them.		
15.	Clear in his verbal communication. Is seldom misunderstood. Can convey his thoughts precisely and clearly.		

Contd...

V. CONFIDENTIAL RATING OF OVERALL PERFORMANCE

Please initial in any one of the following	
The individual has achieved an exceptionally high standard of performance. In significant areas of responsibility, he has exceeded expected standards. Performance is consistently excellent.	Outstanding
The standard of performance has been consistently above aggregate; and in several areas, responsibilities were discharged so as to merit favourable comment rather than mere satisfaction.	Superior
The individual has performed well by and large and to the satisfaction of his superior,	Satisfactory
Not upto the minimum requirements of the position	Unsatisfactory

This employee has worked under my supervision

From ___________

to ___________

Signature of the Rater Date: ________

Designation

Department

Signature of the Reviewing Authority Date: ________

Designation

Department

EXHIBIT 10.2

STRENGTHS AND WEAKNESSES OF DIFFERENT PERFORMANCE APPRAISAL METHODS

Methods	Strengths	Weakness
1. Appraisal by Objectives (MBO etc.)	1. It provides a quantitative measurement of performance, which is verifiable. Quantification of performance being objective, subjectivity in analyses can be avoided.	1. Appraisal being result oriented, it is not suitable for determining the potential.
	2. Weak performance area can be quickly identified, thus it provides a meaningful basis for improving the performance.	2. Individual performance area being different, it does not facilitate peer comparison.
2. Graphic Rating	1. It is a simple and popular method.	1. Highly subjective and unreliable.
	2. It facilitates peer comparison, therefore it provides an objective basis for decision on remuneration, rewards and promotion.	2. Being subjective, weighting of factors may be necessary for improving the quality of analysis.
	3. Certain common criteria may be provided for improving the quality of comparison.	3. It does not provide facility for feedback and employee development.
3. Essay Type	1. Its proper use can provide quality information which can help in taking meaningful decisions for placement, promotion and development.	1. It requires good writing ability.
		2. Appraisers should have the power to take mature judgement.
		3. Being subjective, inter-employee comparison is difficult.
4. Critical incidents Method	1. Being highly objective, it provides factual data on employee's performance and behaviour.	1. Since performance is analysed on incidents, it tends to be fragmentary.
	2. Usually helps in improving the communication and development of employees.	2. It can't be an independent method of evaluation.
	3. It is useful as a supportive evaluation.	3. It does not provide any basis for comparison.
5. Forced Distribution	1. It is free from any bias and is uniform in standards.	1. It can't also be an independent method of appraisal. It is better used as a control instrument.
		2. Not suitable for communication and employee development.
6. Straight Ranking Method	1. It is simple and helps in taking decisions on salary progression and promotion	1. It does not provide feedback and also it cannot be used for large groups and interdepartmental comparison.

EXHIBIT 10.3

BEHAVIOURALLY ANCHORED RATING SCALE GUIDE TO PERFORMANCE APPRAISAL

Criteria \ Assessment	A	B	C	D	E
1. Quality	Leaps tall building single bound	Must take running start to leap over tall building	Can only leap over a building with no spire	Needs some improvements	Can not recognise building at all, must less jump
2. Timeliness	Is faster than a speeding bullet	Is as fast as a speeding bullet	Not as fast as speeding bullet	Would you believe a slow bullet?	Wounds self with bullet
3. Initiative	Is stronger than a loco motive	Is stronger than a bull elephant	Is stronger than a bull	Shoots the bull	Smells like a bull
4. Adaptability	Walks on water consistently	Walks on water in emergencies	Washes with water	Drinks water	Passes water in emergencies
5. Communication	Talks with God	Talks with the Angel	Talks with himself	Argues with himself	Loses the arguments

UNIT 11

Career Planning and Development

Learning Objectives

After completion of this unit, the students will be aware of the following topics:

- *Introduction*
- *Career: Definition and Elements*
- *Overview of Career Development*
- *Different Stages or Cycles of Career Development Process*
- *Career Anchors*
- *Career Development and Employee Empowerment*
- *Career Planning and Career Development Process*
- *Future of Career Planning and Development in India*
- *Succession Planning*
- *Management Development*
- *HRM and Organisational Culture*
- *Organisational Development*

CAREER PLANNING AND GROWTH AT NTPC

'People before PLF (Plant Load Factor)' is what the country's largest power company, NTPC believes. With 26,000 people in their payroll, NTPC currently generates 33,194 MW of power and poised to become a 75,000 MW power generation company by 2017. Unlike other public sector company, NTPC successfully leverages its human resources, and makes them enablers in achieving excellence through sustained development and growth programmes for all cross-sections of employees. NTPC started its journey in 1975 and since then, consistently growing, making its vibrant presence in the complete value chain of power business.

NTPC today attracts the country's best pool of resources. Every new recruit of NTPC gets the promise of a challenging career. The talent management system of NTPC carefully crafts the career plans so that employees, both as an employee and as an individual, can get the opportunity to grow exponentially. The career plans are integrated with NTPC's performance management systems. Each employee is assessed against a KPA (Key Performance Areas). The standardised system tracks functional, managerial, and potential competence in objective and transparent manner. NTPC's career plans are so designed that employees' career growth contributes to accomplishing vision and mission; and the business goals. NTPC reinforces the career plans through 'promotion from within', succession plans, job rotation, systematic training and development, and through lateral movement between different job families. Incubating leadership competence in every employee, as a philosophy, prompts NTPC to strictly enforce the career plans. With the slogan of 'Grow your own timber', NTPC gives the message to employees' the need for rising through the career ladders and effectively partnering with the organisation.

INTRODUCTION

Effective HRM encompasses career planning, career development and succession planning. Even though in this era of rapid technological changes, organisations are besieged with the problem of manpower redundancy, organisations are equally concerned with the problem of retention of manpower. While one way to increase retention is by extrinsic motivational reinforcers, the other way obviously is to address to the need of employees, which centres around individual career planning and career development. From an organisation's point of view also, these initiatives reinforce their strategic plans and make their goals and objectives achievable. An organisation without career planning and career development initiatives is likely to encounter the highest rate of attrition, causing much harm to their plans and programmes. Similarly without succession planning, manning of vacancies, particularly at higher levels, become difficult. There are examples of many organisations, who had to suffer for not being able to find a right successor for their key positions. With the increase scope for job mobility and corporate race for global headhunting of good performers, it is now a well-established fact that normal employment span for key performers remains awfully short. At times it is even shorter than three years. This again strengthens the need for effective career planning, career development and succession planning.

The terms career planning and career development are used interchangeably in most of the organisations. It is also correct that but for their subtle difference in the definitional context, their process remains the same. For the purpose of this book also, we have considered both the concepts more holistically, except for some discussions on their meaning.

Similarly, any discussion on succession planning remains incomplete without relating the same to management development and organisational development as succession planning immediately succeeds it. Moreover, success of one is dependent on the other.

CAREER: DEFINITION AND ELEMENTS

Career is a sequence of attitudes and behaviours associated with the series of job and work-related activities over a person's lifetime. Yet in another way, it may be defined as a succession of related jobs, arranged in hierarchical order, through which a person moves in an organisation. As the literal definition of career focuses on an individually perceived sequence, to be more accurate, career may be either individual-centered or organisation-centered. Therefore, career is often defined separately as external career and internal career. External career refers to the objective categories used by society and organisations to describe the progression of steps through a given occupation, while internal career refers to the set of steps or stages which make up the individual's own concept of career progression within an occupation. For such two different approaches, in organisational context, career can be identified as an integrated pace of vertical and lateral movement in an occupation of an individual over his employment span. Such integrated approach is intended to minimise diversity of hopes and expectations of employees matching individually perceived career with organisation-centered career.

Important Elements of Career

Analysing the definitional context, it is therefore, clear that career has the following important elements:

1. It is a proper sequence of job-related activities. Such job-related activities vis-à-vis experience include role experiences at different hierarchical levels of an individual, which lead to an increasing level of responsibilities, status, power, achievements and rewards.

2. It may be individual-centered or organisation-centered. Individual-centered (internal) career is an individually perceived sequence of career progression within an occupation. For example, in medical profession, we have clearly defined stages of education, internship, residency, hospital affiliation, or private practice. Similarly, in college teaching, we have stages like lecturership, readership and professorship. In industrial occupation those who get entry in Indian Administrative and Allied Services also have such clearly defined stages of career. For example, in Indian Ordnance Factories, Class-I officers start at Assistant Works Manager level and gradually rise to the level of Works Manager, Deputy General Manager, Additional General Manger, General Manager and so on. These being clearly defined stages of career, an individual before joining such services can very well perceive his sequence of career progression. But such clearly defined stages of career progression are not made available for all occupation or job titles both in public and private sectors. In such cases, individuals nurture their own perceived stages of career progression.

3. It is better defined as an integrated pace of lateral movement in an occupation of an individual over his employment span. Individual-centered career being not an objective or at times even realistic description of career steps in a given occupation, often goes against the hopes and expectations of employees as organisations may have a different perceived career plan for the employees. Integrated approach, therefore, minimises such dissonance and ensures a mutually acceptable and satisfying career progression.

Overview of Career Development

Career development essentially means the process of increasing an employee's potential for advancement and career change. In other words, it is a process of planning the series of possible jobs which an individual may hold in the organisation over time and developing strategies designed to provide necessary job skills as the opportunity arises. Therefore, career development relates to the readiness for progression through a series of positions during an individual's working life. Career development may be differentiated from career planning and career management. Career development is a systematic process of guiding the movement of human resources of an enterprise through different hierarchical positions, whereas career planning is a process of establishing career objectives for an employee (or by the person himself) and developing planned strategies to achieve them including activities which help in making choices with respect to occupations, organisation's job assignments and self-development measures. Career management, on the other hand, relates to specific human resource management activities, such as recruitment, selection, placement, and appraisal to facilitate career development.

Every organisation needs to provide career development opportunities to its employees. The Indian corporate sector at present is facing major restructuring to keep pace with the economic restructuring programme of the country. Market globalisation, technology upgradation, import liberalisation, de-licensing, increased competition together have now prompted Indian companies to restructure their production vis-à-vis organisation. Redeploying the manpower, through proper training, in restructured jobs is one of the important priorities for the organisations, particularly for those who are down the level. But employees with matching skill and knowledge now find them successful in better bargaining position due to increased job mobility. Most of the foreign and multinational companies are now winning away the employees with matching skill and knowledge from Indian organisations with better offer of pay and career. Therefore, poor career development programme may affect an organisation at least in two ways:

1. High employee turnover, particularly those in their beginning of the career.

2. Decreasing employment involvement, i.e., commitment to work.

Recruitment expenses, training expenses and reduced performance during orientation (loss of output, increased wastages, etc.) together add to the cost of employee turnover.

Decreased employee involvement also affects functional efficiency and productivity of the employees. Other important reasons for career development can be listed as follows:

1. Changing environment is now making jobs more complex. A suitable career development programme enables employees to be better prepared for future positions in the organisation. It also gives the opportunity to identify prospective managers from within. Manning vacancies from within is cost-efficient and at the same time the system motivates employees.

2. A suitable career development programme enables the organisation to receive maximum contribution from employees. Since this helps employees to enhance their skills for higher positions, both under utlisation of employee's potential work energy and their underemployment can be avoided.
3. Career development makes employees more adaptable to changing requirements of the organisations. The requirements may either change due to new technology [Computer Numerically Controlled Technology (CNC), Numerically Controlled Technology (NC), Direct Numerically Controlled Technology (DNC) and Flexible Manufacturing System (FMS)], or new management philosophy and style (like, just-in-time manufacturing, total quality management, etc.).
4. It provides an objective basis to describe the steps of progression in a given organisation, and therefore, minimises unfair promotion practices of employees reducing the change of 'promotion by discretion'. Thus a suitable career development programme avoids employees' resentment on promotion issues, which has now become a major casual factor of industrial disputes in India.
5. Most of the organisations are now also manned by women and other minority classes of employees. A career development programme ensures equitable opportunity for career progression of these classes of employees also. Thus it meets the requirements of equal employment opportunities for all.
6. A career development programme gives opportunities to employees to acquire more skills, obtain desired jobs, share increased responsibility, enjoy scope of job mobility and derive increased job satisfaction.

Significance and Advantages of Career Development

The significance and advantages of career development both from organisations and employees' point of view can be summed up as follows:

1. It reduces employee turnover by providing increased promotional avenues.
2. It improves employee morale and motivation.
3. It enables organisations to man promotional vacancies internally, thereby, providing opportunities to reduce the cost of managerial recruitment.
4. It ensures better utilisation of employees' skills and provides increased work satisfaction to employee.
5. It makes employees adaptable to the changing requirement of the organisation.
6. It reduces industrial disputes related to promotional matters and thereby provides opportunity to the organisation to sustain harmonious industrial relations.

7. Employees' loyalty and commitment to the organisation can be substantially increased and thereby organisations can enjoy the privilege of increased employee productivity.
8. Career development programmes being an objective description of career progression, ensure equitable promotional decisions even for women and minorities in an organisation.

Objectives of Career Development

The objectives of a career development programme, therefore, can be listed as given below:

1. To attract and retain effective persons in an organisation.
2. To utilise human resources optimally.
3. To improve morale and motivation level of employees.
4. To reduce employee turnover.
5. To practice a balanced 'promotion from within' policy.
6. To make employees adaptable to changes.
7. To increase employees' loyalty and commitment to the organisations.
8. To maintain harmonious industrial relations.
9. To inculcate equitable employment practices providing equal career progression opportunities to women and minorities.

Types of Career Development Programmes

In an organisation, there are different types of development programmes to enrich different skills of human resources. These include organisation development, employee development, and management development and career development. Organisational development programmes are planned and managed from the top to bring about planned organisational changes for increasing the organisational effectiveness. Management development is concerned with upgrading the manager's skills, knowledge and ability of the employees to enable them to accomplish the additional process of guiding the movement of human resources through different hierarchical levels. Whatever may be the differences, career development is interrelated with other human resource development functions.

Inter-relation with Other HRD Functions

Difference with Career Planning

Career Planning process evaluates one's abilities and interests, considering alternative career opportunities, establishing career goals and planning practical development activities. Thus from an individual's point of view, it helps in making choices with respect to occupation, organisation, job assignment and self-development measures. However, organisational career planning is different from individual career planning, as organisational career plan is a map of sequence of jobs for an employee within the organisation itself, whereas, individual career planning is a map of sequence of jobs of the individual concerned without regard to the organisation. Career development process on the other hand, aims to increase an employee's potential for advancement and career change by providing necessary job skills.

Career pathing, personnel skills inventories, career information systems and career counselling are different career planning activities in an organisation. Thus information of jobs to decide the skills needed through an effective system of job analysis and job descriptions is required. Suitable performance appraisal system to monitor performance, clear career goals of employees, effective human resource planning system and designated career paths and job families enable the career planning process to move logically and scientifically. In addition, the career planning process being concerned with the individual employees, an effective information system is necessary to make all these data available to the employees concerned from time to time. Career development process, on the other hand, calls for assisting employees in assessing their own internal career needs, developing and publishing available career opportunities in the organisation and finally aligning employee needs and abilities with career opportunities.

However, there cannot be an effective career development without career planning in the organisation. Therefore, the career development is an integral part of career planning process as career planning provides the opportunity for assessing occupational and career choices of an employee, his performance appraisal and devising a suitable development programme for him. Conventionally in any given organisation, the career planning process primarily deals with employees at a lower level, whereas career development entails objective description of career progression path for all levels of employees.

Difference with Manpower Planning

Manpower planning, among other things, provides higher management with the data on the inventory of skills and potential available in the organisation, based on which, expansion, technology upgradation, etc., are undertaken by the organisation. Inventory of manpower resources, manpower needs in terms of number, types, skills, levels and time, possible changes in functions and activities with the passage of time, desired behavioural or attitudinal changes required to meet the manpower needs, training opportunities, resources and training time, etc., is the basic information required for manpower planning. However, manpower planning also encompasses career development process as the latter provide the basis of manpower planning by planning the series of possible jobs which an employee may hold in the organisation over time.

Difference with Succession Planning

Succession planning involves identification of likely vacancies for higher level executives and locating likely successors to man such vacancies. Career development on the other hand covers employees at all levels including executives in an organisation. Succession planning in reality, therefore, is management development for the executives. A career development programme normally considers likely career progression in a given occupation, while succession planning chart is a 'runner up chart' for higher generalist positions like General Manager, Managing Director, etc., who may be groomed up for different specialist positions like marketing, production, personnel, finance, etc.

Different Stages or Cycles of Career Development Process

In order to design a suitable career development programme it is necessary to understand the different career stages or development cycles of an individual employee. Actual stages differ from individual to individual due to obvious differences in perceived internal career. However, career development cycle or stages, keeping in view the general requirements of people at different hierarchical stages, may be grouped under the following four categories:

1. *Exploratory Stage:* This stage starts when a new employee joins the organisation. An employee who with his qualification and knowledge joins an organisation and finds himself in an apparent mismatch condition which cannot be set right with the induction programme of the organisation. It takes quite some time for him after thorough training to adapt to the organisation and more particularly to his job assignment.

   Therefore, it is essential for the organisation to sustain the behavioural as well as operational deficiencies to help him to develop in the course of time. The best solution at this stage is to allow the new entrant to perform some specific job and to confer freedom in functioning. This will help the new entrant to gradually develop according to the requirements of the organisation. Some companies even allow the new entrant to undergo a compulsory job rotation for reasonable time period. The purpose of such job rotation is to allow the employee to select his preferred job from a wide range of available jobs in the organisation. However, due to obvious functional specialities and different educational requirements, such a scheme is not quite successful in Indian organisations.

2. *Establishment Stage:* After a new entrant chooses his career from different given alternatives (where such options are available), he needs to be provided with regular feedback on his performance. Such performance feedback enables the new employee to understand the effectiveness of his performance and at the same time he can also initiate required corrective action to overcome his functional deficiencies. Performance appraisal and its feedback have also motivational values as the new employee enjoys a sense of accomplishment when he gets feedback on his assignment from management and specifically when he understands that his promotional decision has been taken based on his performance. A successful career development process at establishment stage, therefore, is important to retain employees in the organisation and at the same time to develop a sense of loyalty and commitment to the organisation.

3. *Maintenance Stage:* This is a mid-career stage for employees, who strive hard to retain their established name and fame. Therefore, at this stage employees need to put their continuous efforts for self-development. For an organisation, career development process at this stage, therefore, calls for renewing and updating the skills of employees particularly in the context of the changing environment to help employees to overcome their mid-career crisis. In many organisations, absence of career development programmes makes employees in this stage of their career to opt for a job switch. Therefore, this stage is crucial and unless the organisation adopts suitable career development programmes, it may face high employee turnover.

4. *Stage of Decline:* Employees at this stage being prepared for retirement, get scared from the possible threat of reduced role or responsibilities in the organisation. Such complexity is behaviourally associated with old age of the employees which, unless set right through a suitable career development programme, may even render such employees inefficient or mis-fits for the organisation. Career development process at this stage, therefore, should aim at helping the employees to get mentally prepared for retirement rituals, particularly to prepare them to accept a reduced role and responsibilities, so that, they can accommodate with their family and the society in the later part of their life.

Issues in Career Development Process

Edgar H. Schein suggested the following issues to be considered at different stages or cycles of career development process.

Exploratory Stage

At this stage an organisation should:

1. Ensure the availability of accurate information about the organisation and the various occupations existing in the organisation to the new employee.
2. Create opportunities to enable new employees to get acquainted with the organisational careers through job rotation, internship, visit to different units, seminars, etc.
3. Sponsor educational and training programmes for ensuring supply of potential talent in future.

Establishment Stage

At this stage an organisation should ensure:

1. Identification of the best possible talent for the organisation.
2. Communicating the correct and positive image of the organisation to the employee.
3. Maximum learning and favourable attitudes of the employees towards the organisation.
4. Assigning challenging jobs to employees to enable them to test their abilities and skills.
5. Providing adequate feedback on performance to the employees to enable them to assess their strengths and weaknesses.
6. Designing of development plan, identification of development needs, deciding next career steps, etc.

Maintenance Stage

This being a mid-career stage, the organisation should provide:

1. A continuing process of performance appraisals, feedback, career counselling, long-range career planning to ensure proper deployment of the employees and also to enable them to feel challenged, motivated and committed to the organisation.

2. Strategies to motivate plateaued employees, so that they can be productively utilised even without promotion.

3. Adequate opportunities for transition from specialist cadres to generalist positions at higher echelons of the organisation.

4. Adequate career paths to enable employees to accommodate their personal and family needs, especially during critical phases in their life or family cycle.

5. Help employees to adjust to their changing role as their career shifts from active (operational) positions to advisory positions.

6. Help employees to prepare for retirement.

Decline Stage

This being a stage of separation, the organisation should try to:

1. Manage retirement without destroying the employee's sense of self-worth.

2. Invent new and creative part-time roles for retired employees which can use their knowledge, experience and wisdom.

At every stage of the career, employees also make an effort to develop their own information sources. They analyse the feedback on their performance, seek opportunities for development, study the career paths available to them and provide the organisation with details of their perceived needs, goals and ambitions. Thus career is as much the responsibility of the individual employee as it is the responsibility of the organisation.

CAREER ANCHORS

Career anchor is a syndrome of talents, motives and values which gives stability and direction to a person's career. Such talents, motives and values give shape to certain attributes, which an individual derives from his early experiences and which help him to conceptualise his own perceived career. This perceived career anchor, therefore, often goes against organisational career plans and thus, employees develop a sense of dissonance or incongruity about their career plans. Many organisations, therefore, try to identify perceived career anchors for their employees to develop matching career development programmes. Many empirical studies have so far been carried out to identify the perceived career-anchor of different type of employees. Edgar H. Schein, summing up the findings of an empirical study on management graduates, identified five such career anchors for employees.

Managerial Competence

This competence is a fundamental characteristic for those who prefer to rise to the top. Such employees were found to have the following three areas of competence:

1. *Interpersonal Competence:* They have the ability and desire to handle a variety of interpersonal and group situations. They can give leadership, resolve group conflicts and also feel at ease while tackling unfavourable situations to their advantage.

2. *Analytic Competence:* This competence help such employees to identify problems, analyse the same and to develop situations to resolve the problems. Analytical skill being an important prerequisite for success of managers, such competence naturally makes such employees befitting for managerial positions.

3. *Emotional Competence:* Employees bestowed with such competence can bear high levels of responsibility and even can afford to remain cool in difficult situations which make them competent to exert leadership powers without much of a problem. Such competence develops empathetic skills in employees leading to a matured decision-making power even in a situation of crisis.

All these competencies together develop matured employees who are suitable for managerial positions in an organisation.

Technical/Functional Competence

Persons with such competence prefer to remain in technically satisfying jobs than rising to the higher managerial level. Such technically satisfying jobs may be either engineering, systems analysis or even different functional areas of management like, finance, personnel, marketing, etc. In manufacturing units some executives always prefer to remain on the shop-floor as they derive satisfaction from such jobs rather than general managerial jobs at the higher echelon of management. Such people are committed to the profession and consider their work important rather than the benefits and/or future prospect.

Security and Stability

Employees who are anchored in this competence will always get motivated for a career which ensures job security and/or long range stability in the form of good retirement programmes. Such people get motivated only when they are ensured a stable career situation which may not even at times be fitting to their level of knowledge and skills and they may subordinate some personal needs (for example, acceptance of less pay and amenities) to satisfy their perceived security. Effecting transfer and promotion for this type of employees is quite difficult. Most of the employees under this category may be identified in government and public sector undertakings.

Creativity and Challenge

People with such syndrome are very few in number. They become entrepreneurs more for the sake of creating something new and to have their own identity than for making money.

Such people when employed in an organisation always want to be functionally autonomous to exercise their own special talents. They crave for independence. Such type of employees being anchored for creativity and developing something new, they be always given challenging work assignments and scope for their identification through innovative product designs.

Freedom and Autonomy

There are some people in the organisation who always like to work at their own pace. Organisational constraints like fixed working hours, lack of variety of work, defined working conditions, etc., prevent them from becoming functionally autonomous and independent. Such people, due to absence of freedom or independence in their organisation, often leave the job to start their own consultancy and freelancing. Teachers, professors, advertising professionals like artists and copywriters, management consultants, etc., fall under this category.

Other Anchors

The complexity of behavioural parameters, has of late identified some other career anchors which we find are very much related to different occupations. A separate class of people may have a strong craving for identity. Those who are in military organisations get such identity as their occupational title, which they use as a prefix to their names, like Major, Colonel, Brigadier, etc. Such identification is so visible that they get special uniforms matching their levels in the organisation. Affiliate needs and interpersonal talents to work for a cause is yet another anchor which we find in some persons. The search for power, influence, control and job variety are examples of other career anchors which people try to achieve in their occupational roles. Knowledge of these career anchors are essential for any organisation in order to plan for career development. Each employee who nurtures specific career anchors (internal motives and values), should make it explicit to the organisation so as to find matching occupational roles without much of behavioural dissonance. Such a matching process, therefore, is the principal task of planning for career development.

Career Development and Employee Empowerment

Employee empowerment etymologically means an extension of employee participation vis-à-vis involvement. This definition of empowerment is more explicit when we review the contribution of Judith Bardwick (1991), who states, empowerment means giving everyone, instead of just people with certain positions or certain job titles, the legitimate right to make judgements, form conclusions, reach decisions and then act.

A career development process ensures promotion of employees from one career path to another. It gradually makes them independent functionaries at later career stages. Such a system, therefore, often makes managers uneasy to open up the organisational planning process to individual employees. On the contrary, it will also develop a sense of misgiving as they may not really believe that the organisation is truly opening up its planning process to them.

Issues Involved

The following issues need to be considered to empower employees through a successful career development process:

1. Commitment of the top management to ensure that the organisational career planning process will adequately consider individual career planning (which is internally perceived by the employees).
2. People need to be infused with a sense of confidence to enable them to work to their true potential.
3. Basic information like mission of the organisation, its objectives and plans, career opportunities, etc., need to be communicated to the people.
4. Available career planning resources in the organisation should also to be communicated to the employees from time to time.
5. The organisation should help employees to make them competent to sort out data, formulate goals and overcome obstacles to realise the goals.
6. Employees also need to be communicated about the status of their present position, organisational expectations and their level of performance.
7. Individual managers should support their employees in career planning.
8. The organisation should be responsible for the individual career plans adopting an integrated career development process, which accommodates both individual and organisational needs.

It is, therefore, amply clear that the career development process can be successfully utilised as an empowerment tool by any organisation if the above issues are duly taken care of.

Indian Scenario

In India, most of the organisations seriously lack in a scientific career development scheme for employees working at various levels. Due to the absence of such objective schemes, career development as promotional decisions often suffer from managerial discretion causing employee unrest and unfavourable industrial relations. In some organisations career development for employees at higher echelons exist, making such occupational groups entitled for career development on a regular basis. Such organisations do not have effective career development schemes for employees down the level where such decisions, as mentioned above, are exerted by managerial discretion. This difference in career development approach, therefore, demotivates employees and even at times stands against successful empowerment from which an organisation can otherwise reap motivational benefits and increased functional effectiveness and productivity.

Career Planning and Career Development Process

The dynamics and complexities of career development process have been made amply clear through earlier discussions. It is clear that the career development process cannot be undertaken in isolation. Some issues have to be taken care of by the organisation itself, while some others concern the individual employees. Thus an improved career planning process is the joint responsibility of both the organisation and the employee. Internal career needs (of individual employee), therefore, need to be integrated with the external career opportunities (of the organisations). Unfortunately, organisations do not interact with the employees to understand their perceived career needs, instead they depend on guess work to assume the needs, motives and anchors and move them around on discretion. Such practices, therefore, lead to employees' dissonance. Thus for having good and improved career development process it is necessary both for the organisation and the employees to understand each other's needs and opportunities.

Integration of Career Development Process with Family Issues

Since career development process is a continuous one and encompasses the entire employment so also the lifespan of an individual, it should also examine how the work, reward system, etc., can be integrated with the personal and family issues of the employees at different career stages. Most of the organisations experience mobility or job switch of executives at their maintenance or mid-career stage. This is because most employees at this stage experience structural changes or life plateauing due to the absence of adequate career paths, which can accommodate their personal and family needs.

At this career stage, promotion and outstation transfers of employees often invite problems, unless such decisions of the organisation are favourable to the employee's family. Moreover, at this career stage, employees prefer to have an advisory role. All these aspects, therefore, deserve adequate attention of the organisation, while it works out career development plans for employees who are at their mid-career.

Developing Career Paths Compatible to Changing Needs

The career development process should be made compatible to the changing needs of the employees in their life cycle. This calls for creating flexible opportunity structures and career paths to enable employees to identify them with such role positions at different stages of their life cycle. New employees should have adequate opportunities to gain on-the-job knowledge and experience, and undergo training and education programmes for enriching job skills. The organisation, therefore, needs to identify suitable role positions for such employees, who are at their beginning of career stage. Similarly, organisations should have adequate provision for renewals and updation of knowledge and skills for old employees, particularly in the context of the changing environment, so that they should not lose their self-worth. For such employees, this is also to be followed by active pre-retirement planning and counselling to enable them to accommodate nicely with their family and society.

Improved career development process should also appreciate changing social values with respect to work, life and leisure. Work, per se, is differently perceived by different people. For some, it is a source of self-fulfillment, creative pursuit, future growth and development, rising to the higher corporate ladder, etc. Different employees are at different places in the Maslow's hierarchical needs ladder. Hence, different yardsticks should be employed for each employee depending upon his/her perception of values.

Education and occupational mis-match need not always be for reasons of non-availability of matching jobs but due to the perceived values of the individual. Many educated persons may opt for low profile artistic or craftsmanship jobs purely to derive creative satisfaction. Similarly, there are people who give more priority to such work which do not demand much of their time and effort. These people give more importance to their leisure time activities (hobbies, drama, music, etc.) to seek self-satisfaction. The career development process, therefore, should consider these aspects, or otherwise, the whole exercise will suffer from the problem of employee dissonance.

Steps in the Career Planning Process

The career planning process involves the following different activities or steps in an organisation:

Preparing Personnel Skills Inventories

The first step is to prepare personnel skills inventories, which contains data on employees skills and career goals. In addition, there are required data banks, which provide the following information.

1. The organisation structure and the persons manning different positions in the organisation, their age, education, experience, training and career goals, status, duties and responsibilities.
2. The performance record and ratings, interpersonal abilities of the employees.
3. Their preferred location, desires and constraints.
4. Whether the present strength is short or surplus to the requirements, if it is short, the extent of shortage at different levels and the organisational resources available to make good such shortages in future. If it is surplus, the measures available to redeploy them through proper restructuring.
5. Future requirement of manpower for expansion or diversification of the company or for natural wastages like death, disability, retirement, discharge and dismissal, resignation, etc.

In most of the organisations, such information is computerised and periodically reviewed and updated. After preparation of personnel skill inventories and additional data, it is necessary to develop career paths for employees.

Developing Career Paths

Career paths are logical mapping out of jobs, which represent a potential progression tract that an employee may follow over time. Such mapping of job progressions are done in the form of career by ladders clubbing together similar lines of occupations in job families. Job families are groups of homogenous jobs, i.e., jobs with similar characteristics. An illustrative model of career paths for marketing jobs is presented in Figure 11.1, which shows a simple job ladder.

General Manager (Sales)
Sales Manager
Domestic Sales
Sales Manager
Institutional Sales
Officer
Domestic Sales
Officer
Institutional Sales
Executive
Domestic Sales
or
Institutional Sales

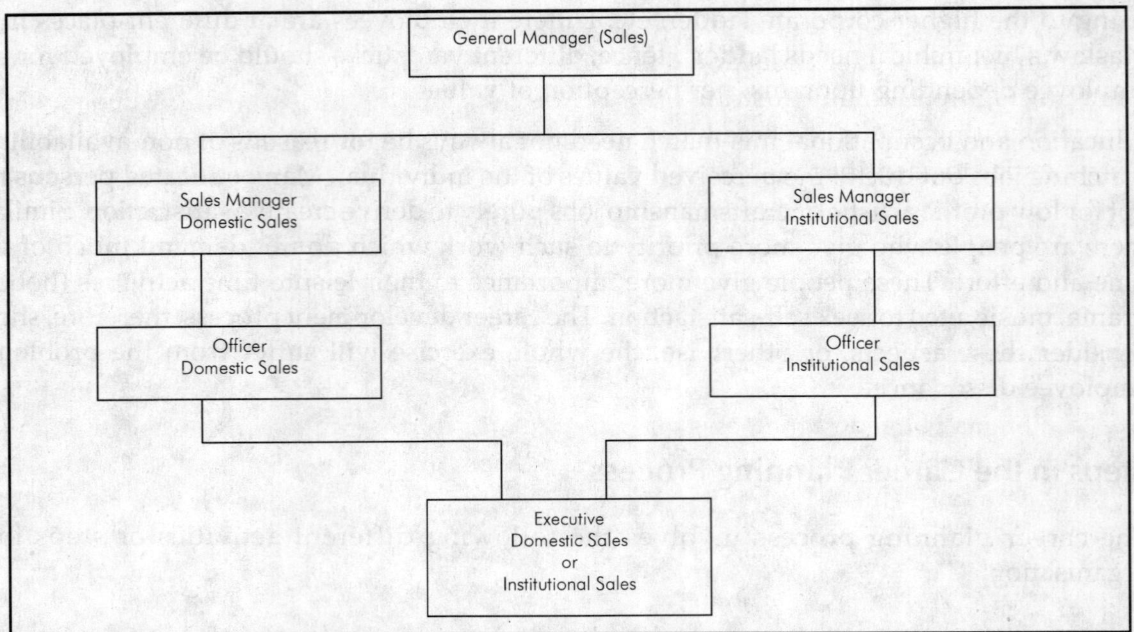

Figure 11.1: Career Paths for Marketing Jobs

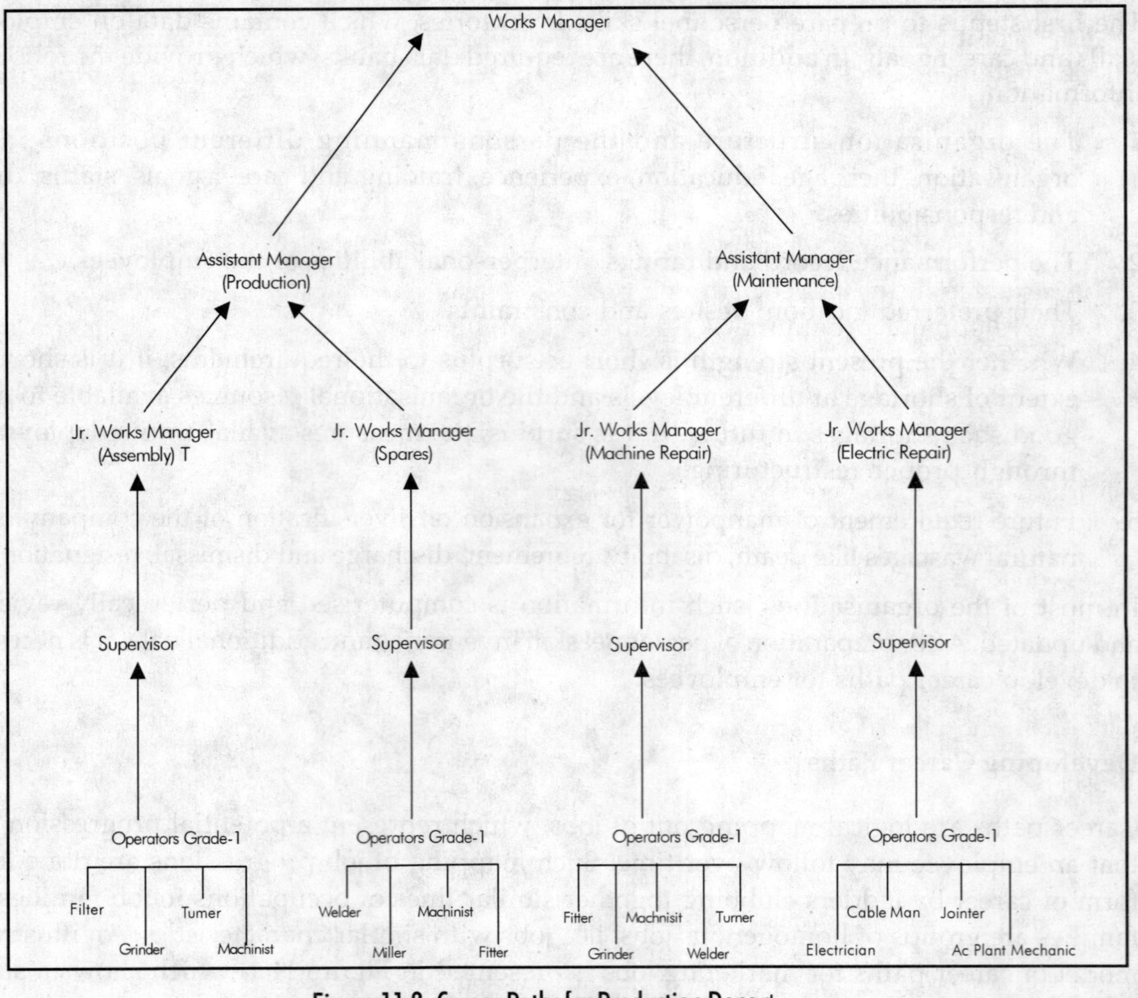

Works Manager
Assistant Manager
(Production)
Assistant Manager
(Maintenance)
Jr. Works Manager
(Assembly) T
Jr. Works Manager
(Spares)
Jr. Works Manager
(Machine Repair)
Jr. Works Manager
(Electric Repair)
Supervisor
Supervisor
Supervisor
Supervisor
Operators Grade-1
Operators Grade-1
Operators Grade-1
Operators Grade-1
Filter
Turner
Grinder
Machinist
Welder
Machinist
Miller
Fitter
Fitter
Machnisit
Turner
Grinder
Welder
Cable Man
Jointer
Electrician
Ac Plant Mechanic

Figure 11.2: Career Paths for Production Depart

However, in all cases, career paths are not so simple. For example in manufacturing jobs having multiple feeder posts down the level, career paths are more complex than the earlier one. In Figure 11.2, an illustrative model of career paths for production department of a manufacturing unit is presented. For successful mapping out of career paths, at the outset, it is essential to identify the job families. After such identification, requisite skills for all the positions along these paths need to be determined. This helps in developing such skills in employees where these are deficient and selecting the person with such skills for different positions in the organisation. However, the most distinguishing feature of career paths is that it need not always be linear or straight. Similarly, it also does not always indicate upward movement in the organisation's hierarchy. Some organisations often redesignate employees down the level only to prepare them for future promotion. For example, highly skilled workmen may be redesignated as master craftsmen in a manufacturing organisation without any effect on their pay packets only to elevate them gradually to supervisory positions later. Thus lateral movement within the levels is also a distinguishing feature of the career paths.

Put the Right Man at the Right Place

The third step in the career planning process is to identify suitable employees who have the ability, potential and willingness to take up higher responsibilities and rise up the organisational ladder. For this, most of the organisations have performance appraisal and merit rating system. This system enables organisations to compare the performance measures of different individuals in terms of job requirements and helps in identifying training requirements, selecting for promotions, providing financial rewards, etc.

Impart Training

The next step in the career planning process is formulation and implementation of training and development programmes. Such programmes should be designed, in such a manner that they can improve technical and conceptual skills of employees, particularly in those areas, which have been identified as deficient through the performance appraisal system. For continuous change in environment, it is also necessary to constantly renew and update the knowledge and skills of the employees to make them adapt to the changing requirements. Most of the Indian organisations today impart training to their employees on quality circles (small group activities), value engineering technique, total quality management principles, ISO:9000, etc.

Review and Counselling

In addition to the above, career planning process is also concerned with developing suitable promotion and transfer policies, periodic review of career development plans and career counselling. Career counselling provides guidance to the employees on occupational training, education and career goals.

Future of Career Planning and Development in India

In India, we do not have any empirical studies worth the name on career planning and development. New challenges like, competition, market globalisation, deregulation and total quality management have now made it imperative for organisations to restructure their career planning and development programmes to retain best talents. Companies like Bajaj Auto, Arvind Mills, Gujarat Ambuja, Essar Gujarat, Reliance Industries, Bombay Dyeing, Hindustan Lever, Crompton Greaves. Tatas, etc., have now brought in many perceptive changes which can be listed as below:

1. Most of the companies now consider employees as their important assets. The concept of total quality management considers every employee as customers (internal) to the organisation. Making employees entrepreneurs for the organisation and empowering them, is now compelling the organisation to re-design career progression tracks to attract and retain the best employees. Making people psychologically prepared for ownership, some organisations are also experimenting with flatter organisation structure with adequate decentralisation.

2. For manning senior executive positions, organisations are now giving more importance to knowledge than functional skills. This, perhaps, is the only reason for selecting people even in their early thirties for senior managerial posts.

3. Organisations are now more keen to get rid of those employees who are now redundant due to changing requirements, by offering golden handshake, rather than developing these persons for better redeployment.

4. Merit is now getting overriding priority than seniority. This, therefore, renders career progression paths less important. Many, however, feel that even with greater priority of merit over seniority, career progression paths do not become completely meaningless, since for even promotion by merit, the lines of progression paths are relevant. For any succession planning or promotion planning this is still important.

In addition, organisational restructuring programmes are now rendering many employees surplus and it has become a major problem for the organisations to redeploy employees in restructured jobs. Career panic has now become a global issue. Most of the organisations, fearing employee turnover, are now working on designing jobs which can offer employees recognition, creativity (by lateral transfers, etc.), challenges and empowerment.

Succession Planning

Growth and survival of the organisation are the responsibilities of the top management. To fulfil such responsibilities each organisation needs to plan management succession. Succession planning is done in different time frames to ensure the availability of right managerial personnel at the right time in right positions for continuing organisational vitality and strength. Most of the organisations plan for immediate requirements matching with their budgets and business plans. This short sightedness leads them to an alarming situation, when they find shortage of managerial manpower to man different positions in the organisation, resulting in organisational collapse. To avoid this, good organisations try to make succession planning in three different time frames, i.e., immediate (within 1 year), intermediate (1 to 5 years) and long range (beyond 5 years). Prevailing managerial attitude, i.e., a potential threat from successor, which may not sustain the desire of the managers to cling to their chairs, also stands against the success of the succession planning.

Steps of Succession Planning

- The first step is to prepare and develop a management staffing plan for all anticipated needs in different time frames. For important positions at the top managerial level, such planning should be done even for shorter duration, keeping in view the potential threat from eventual natural wastages (death, disability, premature retirement, etc.) and so also from job switch and change (which has now increased many times due to the obviously enhanced scope of job mobility). Other effects of external factors like economic factors, overall manpower factors should also be considered while making such plan. Each organisation has to review their business plans. Effects of such plans on managerial needs also need to be studied.

- The second step is staffing and development. Staffing is concerned with recruitment, selection and placement. Selection and placement may be either done from outside or from within the organisation through promotion and transfer. Development of managerial personnel is done through training, job rotation, creating 'Assistant-to' positions, projects and boards assignments, performance appraisal, counselling and guidance. In many organisations, management adopts what they call a grooming process for filling up important managerial positions. A manager is 'groomed' by giving temporary assignments, attaching him/her with the higher officer or sometimes designating the potential promotee as "officer on special duty".

- The third step is to ensure congenial organisational environment to retain the desired managerial personnel. Unless this is done, the whole exercise of developing a successor may have to be repeated.

- The fourth step is to develop a good performance appraisal system to get feedback on managerial performance and to review their progress and shortfalls.

- Preparation of the management resource inventory is the final step in the succession planning. Such inventory contains details of personal data, performance records, skills, potential, career goals and career paths of managerial personnel.

MANAGEMENT DEVELOPMENT

Any succession planning initiative becomes ineffective without management development, which is a scientific training process for managers and executives to enrich their knowledge and skills, so as to make them competent to manage their organisations effectively. Unlike general purpose training, management development programmes aim at developing conceptual and human skills of managers and executives through organised and systematic procedures. In India, many professional institutes like Administrative Staff College of India, Management Development Institute, Indian Institutes of Management, Quality Management International, National Institute of Training in Industrial Engineering, All India Management Association, Indian Society for Training and Development, National Institute of Personnel Management, etc., conduct different management development programmes to sensitise managers and executives to different emerging problems of the corporate world. Most of the programmes being on general purpose issues, some corporate houses have also designed their own management development programmes for their managers and executives. In the private sector, Tata Management Development Centre (TMDC) at Jamshedpur conducts such programmes for Tata executives. In the public sector, the Steel Authority of India Ltd. (SAIL) has its full-fledged management development centre at Ranchi. Kirloskar Group, Reliance Group and Lakshmi Group (Madras) have developed their own management development centres to train their executives on general and organisation specific issues. In addition, in-house training divisions of the business houses are also developing requisite infrastructure to train their executives, in an attempt to reduce their dependence on outside agencies.

Characteristics of Management Development

To understand the concept of management development better, it is important to list out its characteristics.

1. ***A continuous process:*** Management Development is a continuous process. It should encompass the entire professional career of managers and executives. In India, so long management development used to be considered as a sporadic activity, resulting in its failure to meet the organisational requirements. In Japan, Zen philosophic base facilitates in considering management development as a systematic and continuous activity of any organisation.

2. ***A knowledge updating activity:*** The imperative need for management development should be appreciated as there always exists a gap between actual and potential performance. This, therefore, provides scope for continuous improvement in all functional areas. Management development programmes always attempt to bridge this gap enriching the functional capacity of executives and managers, continuously updating their knowledge and skill. The gap between potential and actual capacity is always high for managers and executives across the world as knowledge and skill can never get plateaued.

3. ***A vehicle for attitudinal change:*** Human behaviour is dynamic. Its complexity can only be appreciated once management development programmes are attempted to understand the behavioural and attitudinal aspects through simulating sessions. Better inter-personal skill is an important prerequisite for managerial success, which can be ensured through such properly designed management development programmes.

4. ***A stimulant to higher competence:*** Unless managers and executives are stimulated to the intricacies of managerial stress and strain through different management development

programmes, their full potential cannot be exerted for the benefit of the organisation. Management development programmes can be designed considering such issues like employees' motivation, habits, age-mix, pattern of conflict and chaos, and this can enable elevation of managerial functions of the executives during the post-training phase.

5. ***A deficiency improver:*** Management development programmes are catered to the individual requirements to improve the functional deficiencies of the individual managers, thus enabling the organisation to derive immediate benefits from such programmes.

6. ***A self-development process:*** Management development facilitates self-development of managers, as they learn many things through action learning methods, sharing the experiences of each other in a simulated classroom atmosphere.

Components of Management Development Programmes (MDP)

Analysing the characteristics, therefore, we can identify three important components of MDP, i.e., selection, intellectual conditioning and supervised training.

1. Selection process enables us to understand the innate potentiality of the executives and the degree and extent of their managerial abilities.
2. Intellectual conditioning is the process of educating managers and executives on different managerial tools and techniques.
3. Supervised training, on the other hand, is the process of guiding managers and executives while they apply and use their knowledge in day-to-day work.

Steps of Management Development Programme (MDP)

Steps of a good MDP may be listed as follows:

- To look at the organisation's objectives;
- To ascertain the development needs;
- To appraise the present performance of managerial staff;
- To prepare manpower inventory;
- To plan for individual development programmes;
- To establish training and development programmes;
- To evaluate different programmes as above.

Objectives of Management Development Programmes

Objectives of management development programmes can be better understood in the context of changing requirements of the environment which constantly interact with the business. Many Indian organisations have now been exposed to the problem of major restructuring to respond to the economic liberalisation programmes of the government. Such programmes of the government are now compelling the Indian managers to face the challenge of competition, survive under economic uncertainty, take decisions, move quickly, shoulder the risk, improve the quality of work-life, making their organisation more socially responsive and transparent, etc. Market globalisation is also compelling Indian Organisations to update their technology. Management philosophies also are constantly changing, particularly in the context of development of the concept of total quality management (TQM), which inter alia calls for employee empowerment, total participation, small group activities like quality circles, attitudinal change of the managers cutting across structural barriers, etc. Change in public policies, increased consumer awareness, increased social and institutional requirements (pollution control, etc.), labour relations, etc., are also compelling the organisations to introduce management development programmes for their managers and executives for renewing their knowledge and skills. The primary objective of management development programme, therefore, is to make the executives and managers vis-à-vis the organisations socially responsive and managerially competent to survive in an atmosphere of uncertainty.

In addition, management development programmes also aim at achieving the following objectives:

- To make available managers and executives with requisite knowledge and skill to meet the present and anticipated future needs of the organisations.
- To encourage managers to develop their full potentiality for handling greater responsibility.
- To improve the functional competence of the managers, making them more transparent and responsive to the changing needs of the organisation.
- To sustain good performance of the managers throughout their career by, not allowing them to develop managerial obsolescence.
- To develop managers for higher assignments, duly replacing the elderly executives.

However, such objectives of MDP vary for various levels of management. Their commonality for all levels is to infuse:

- Attitudinal change
- Behavioural change
- Change in knowledge and skills
- Change in performance
- Change in desired operational results.

Personal characteristics, level of intelligence and learning efforts of people at different managerial levels being different for each level, there exist different sets of objectives, which an organisation should strive to achieve.

MDP Objectives for Top Management

For top management, such objectives are mostly general, primarily intended to develop their understanding and decision-making power. Such objectives can be listed as below:

- To improve the thought process and analytical ability so as to enable the top level managers to understand the problems and take managerial decisions in the best interest of the organisations in particular and the country in general;
- To broaden the outlook in regard to their role, position and responsibilities in the organisation and outside;
- To think through the problems that confront an organisation at present or might crop up in the future;
- To understand economic, technical and institutional forces to solve business problems; and
- To acquire knowledge about the problems of human relations.

MDP for Middle-level Management

For middle-level management, MDPs are intended to develop their intellectual faculty and at the same time to improve their decision-making power with some knowledge of specialised fields. However, such objectives can be listed as follows:

- To establish a clear picture of executive functions and responsibilities.
- To bring an awareness of the broad aspects of management problems, and an acquaintance with, and appreciation of interdepartmental relations;
- To develop the ability to analyse problems and to take appropriate action;
- To develop familiarity with the managerial uses of financial accounting, psychology, business law and business statistics;
- To inculcate knowledge of human motivation and human relationships; and
- To develop responsible leadership.

MDP for Functional Executives and Specialists

- To increase functional knowledge in specific fields in which the executive works, like marketing, production, finance, personnel, etc.;
- To increase proficiency in different management techniques like work study, inventory control, operations research, quality control, etc.;
- To stimulate creative thinking for improving methods and procedures;

- To understand different functions in a company,
- To understand human relations problems; and
- To develop the ability to analyse problems in one's area or function.

However, without favourable climate in the organisation, MDP cannot attain the desired objective. Every organisation should have well-defined policy for the development of managers.

Techniques of Management Development

Planning MDP deserves utmost attention and importance. These objectives of the programmes need to be defined at the outset. Objectives may be either to impart knowledge and skills for more effective functioning of the managers in their present positions or may be to equip them for holding higher positions in future. Most of the organisations through adequate career planning, work out promotion paths for the managers. Unlike career planning programmes for non-managerial employees, which shows such career progression path in similar or allied job families, MDP may even chalk out career planning for managers and executives in different functional areas cutting across departmental barriers. Good MDPs are carefully planned so as to give responsibility to each executive to prepare a replacement for him in successive grades.

Job Rotation

Another technique of MDP is to plan a systematic movement and deliberate re-assignment of managerial personnel, carefully selected by a top management committee into a series of positions. This device makes it possible to diversify the experience of the executives in a variety of activities. This method attempts directly to broaden the vision of administrators, developing the perspective on the total organisation. The period of their movement from job to job depends on their individual need and future prospectus. They learn mostly by observation and practice which come through substituting for vacationing managers.

There are different types of job rotation, which may be for specified observation, assignment, managerial training positions or for unspecified managerial positions.

The system is criticized mainly for its high cost and 'jack-of-all trade' type development. It deters specialisation and also lowers job efficiency at each new post.

Assistant-to-Positions

'Assistant-to-positions' at executive level is a variation of the job rotation system. This helps to broaden experience of the executives by exposing them to many areas of managerial practice. The success of such arrangements, however, depends upon the ability and willingness of the superiors to pass on the qualities to the successors, its adequacy, superiority', extent of up-to-date knowledge and talents and finally on the efforts of the subordinate officers to learn with utmost sincerity.

Projects and Boards

Another practical method of management development is to put management personnel on special projects or committees to provide them opportunities to analyse and solve actual problems facing top management. Since the executives encounter different sets of problems in dealing with such project and boards, it broadens their perspective and inculcates confidence and a sense of responsibility in them. However, unless the executives are allowed to take time necessary to become experts, its purpose may get defeated. Other techniques of MDP have been discussed earlier.

Auditing the MDP

John M. Elliott, Vice President of Dale, Elliott & Company, Inc., New York identified 15 aspects, more in the form of questions, to determine the functioning and effectiveness of MDP. These are as follows:

1. Identification of an organisation's different job levels for establishing promotional channels for managers and at the same time determining the likely job vacancies at each level.

2. Determining whether enough promotable manpower is available at each level to fill all managerial openings, the possibility of filling such vacancies through the organisation's own (internal) manpower, the extent of hiring from outside or to determine the queuing problem for promotable executives.

3. Whether career planning at all levels adequately meets financial and other long range growth plans.

4. Whether an organisation is able to get a flow of management trainees through the annual campus interview.

5. Whether proper utilisation of employee's knowledge and skills is ensured.

6. Identification of specific job assignments, which will contribute most to prepare outstanding men for key jobs in the company.

7. Whether an organisation can afford to retain potential executives on a particular job assignment for a long time to allow him to prove his ability to handle it competently.

8. Whether scheduling of the job assignments have been designed to round out experiences and training to enable the executives to mature ultimately to head a division or a department.

9. Whether a sufficient number of intermediate level jobs have been reserved as training spots for effecting job rotation or committee/board assignment.

10. Whether adequate recruitment facility exists to ensure that best talents are available for managerial vacancies including the positions of management training.

11. Whether best available tools and procedures including psychological tests and interview guides have been developed to identify the potentiality of the executives.

12. Whether the organisation is taking full advantage of outside training facilities such as seminars and courses available through universities and professional bodies, so also whether in-house training facilities have been well equipped to train the executives to enable them to develop their potential knowledge and skill.

13. Whether every potential managerial personnel now work under a superior, who is able to give guidance, counsel and so also to instill confidence and a sense of responsibility.

14. Whether adequate feedback system exists to review and update MDP from time to time depending on changing requirements.

15. Whether a comprehensive guidebook has been developed for the use of all senior managers for the success of MDP. Such a guidebook comprises the following sections:

    (a) The objectives of the programme

    (b) Characteristics needed in a managerial trainee

    (c) Job scheduling procedure

    (d) Performance appraisal techniques and procedures

    (e) Training counselling, etc.

Answers to the above checklist of MDP enable us to understand the effectiveness or otherwise of MDP.

Why MDPs Fail?

Most of the business organisations fail to provide an environment which can encourage, nurture and promote the growth of management development, i.e., a climate which can support it rather than oppose it. Following reasons may be listed for failure of management development programmes.

1. Purposes of the management development efforts in most of the organisations are often characterised by insincerity. They conduct it as a matter of ritual rather than a systematic one. Some organisations also arrange MDP for their executives only to enable them to enjoy a paid vacation.

2. Some organisations are too much concerned to get the immediate benefits of MDPs. They always concern themselves with the immediate pay-out and select MDPs which are designed only to impart business like knowledge rather than giving philosophic ideas or conceptual insights.

3. Organisations retain the services of consultants and professional trainers to conduct MDPs for their executives. Such an arrangement often suffers from difficulties, happenings in the organisations, as such professional trainers and the consultants do not get adequate information about the functioning of the organisation for whom the programmes are designed. Due to absence of interaction with such outside agencies, MDPs suffer from major limitations like impracticability in introduction, irrelevance, etc.

4. In some cases, lessons imparted in MDPs are in direct conflict with the philosophy of the organisation. Such incongruence, therefore, becomes a source of immediate frustration for the executives as they confront different situations in the respective organisations.

5. There is no system to evaluate the effectiveness of the MDPs by such outside agencies. Post-training evaluation system, in the form of scientific feedback mechanism, therefore, is considered essential for success of such programmes.

HRM AND ORGANISATIONAL CULTURE

An organisation does not operate in isolation. In fact every organisation continuously interacts with its environment. This, therefore, requires an organisation to balance between the internal features and the characteristics of the external environment, which is part of the contingency theory in organisation science. The theory suggests that an organisation has to understand the dynamics of its environment in order to be able to adapt to the changing demands of the outside and inside (inside the organisation) world. There are many different ways of scanning the organisational environment. After scanning the organisational environment, it is imperative to go for Organisational Development (OD).

The concept of 'organisation culture' has become popular since the early 1980s. There is no consensus about its definition but most authors agree that it is something holistic, historically determined, related to anthropology, socially constructed, soft and difficult to change. It is something an organisation has or in a different way it can also be seen as something an organisation is.

Organisation cultures are different from national cultures. Organisation cultures manifest in symbols, heroes, rituals and values. National cultures differ mostly on the values level. Organisation cultures together labeled as 'practices'.

Prof. Geert Hofstede studying differences in national cultures over fifty countries, have identified five independent dimensions of values: power distance; individualism versus collectivism; masculinity versus femininity; uncertainty avoidance; and long-term versus short-term orientation. National culture differences are reflected in solutions to organisation problems in different countries. Different national cultures have different preferred ways of structuring organisations and different patterns of employee motivation. For example, they limit the options for performance appraisal, management by objectives, strategic management, humanization of work and even HRP.

To illustrate we can site the example of Hewlett-Packard (HP). They are successful to create a conscious corporate culture, which they call 'The HP Way'. HP's corporate culture is based on (1) respect for others, (2) a sense of community, and (3) plain hard work (Fortune Magazine, May 15, 1995). This conscious culture they have developed and they are sustaining through extensive training of managers and all cross-section of employees. Today HP's growth and success may be traced to their conscious corporate culture. We can have a quick review of HP's Corporate culture as under:

HP's culture is commitment to diversity, inclusion and non-discrimination. Since its formation HP has demonstrated ongoing commitment to people and to fair employment practices. As HP has grown and expanded throughout the world, its work force has become more diverse. HP believes that this diverse work force helps the company realize its full potential. Recognizing and developing the talents of each individual brings new ideas to HP. The company benefits from the creativity and innovation that results when HP people who have different experiences, perspectives and cultures work together. This is what drives invention and high performance at HP. HP believes a well managed, diverse work force expands HP's base of knowledge, skills and cross-cultural understanding, which in turn, enables to understand, relate and respond to diverse and changing customers throughout the world, connecting them to the power of technology. HP's overall commitment is reflected in their diversity and inclusion philosophy, which we can list as under:

- A diverse, high-achieving workforce is the sustainable competitive advantage that differentiates HP. It is essential to win in the marketplaces, workplaces and communities around the world.
- An inclusive, flexible work environment that values differences motivates employees to contribute their best.
- To better serve customers, HP attracts, develops, promotes and retains a diverse workforce.
- Trust, mutual respect and dignity are fundamental beliefs that are reflected in HP's behaviour and actions.
- Accountability for diversity and inclusion goals drives HP's success.

Similarly, Jack Welch, CEO, General Electric, created a new corporate culture. Key elements of GE's corporate culture are as under:

- Redesigning the role of the leader in the new economy: creating followers through communicating a vision, and establishing open, caring relations with every employee
- Creating an open, collaborative workplace where everyone's opinion is welcome
- Empowering senior executives to run far-flung businesses in entrepreneurial fashion

- Liberating the workforce; making everybody a participant through improving vertical communication and employee empowerment.

Thus impact of prevailing organisational culture on HRM theoretically as well as from corporate practices is widely evident.

Lean Production, Shingo Prize Model and HRM

Lean production as management techniques are becoming more popular. The Shingo Prize for Excellence in Manufacturing is primarily advocating the principles of lean production. The lean business philosophy "is expanding and growing mightily." It was first practiced by Toyota. The philosophy emphasises on improvements in productivity, cycle times, on-time delivery (leading to customer satisfaction) and inventory turns. The practicing organisations can reduce the waste in their value streams. The Model is illustrated below:

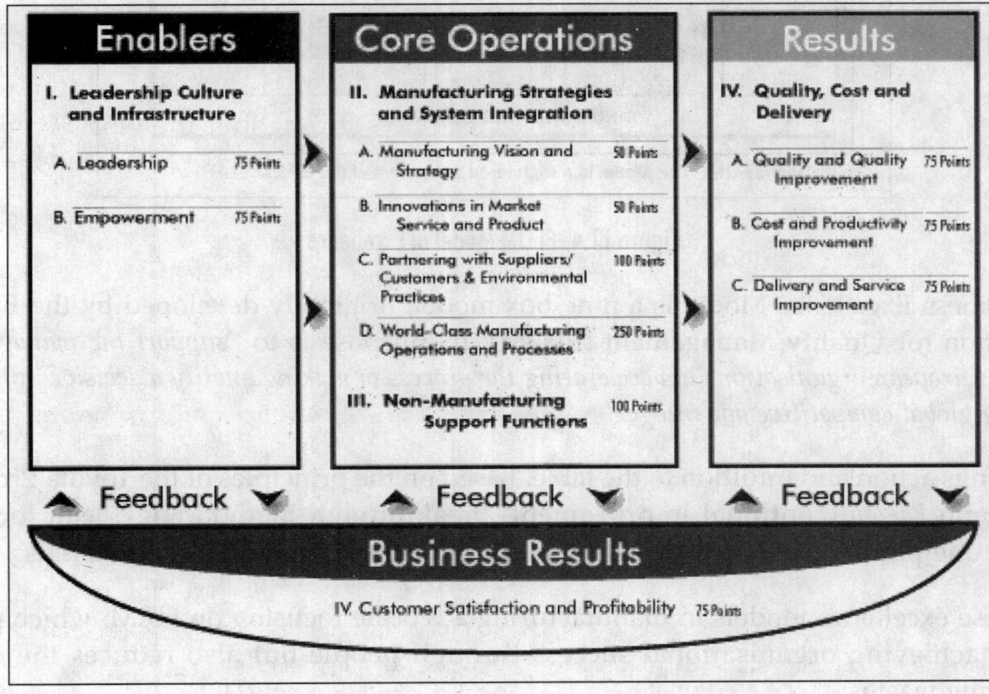

Figure 11.3: Shingo Prize Model

It includes 11 key elements of world-class manufacturing. These elements are grouped into five categories, signifying that it is necessary to integrate them into a complete system to achieve world-class results. The Shingo Prize criteria do not prescribe specific methods, techniques, practices or processes. Rather, for each element the criteria lists practices and techniques that might be incorporated to achieve world-class level quality, cost, delivery and business results. The model is named after the Japanese industrial engineer Dr. Shigeo Shingo had created and evolved many aspects of the revolutionary manufacturing practices of Toyota Production System.

The Prize was established in 1988 to promote awareness of Lean manufacturing concepts and recognize companies in the United States, Canada, and Mexico that achieve world-class manufacturing status. The Shingo Prize philosophy is that world-class business performance may be achieved through focused improvements in core manufacturing and business processes.

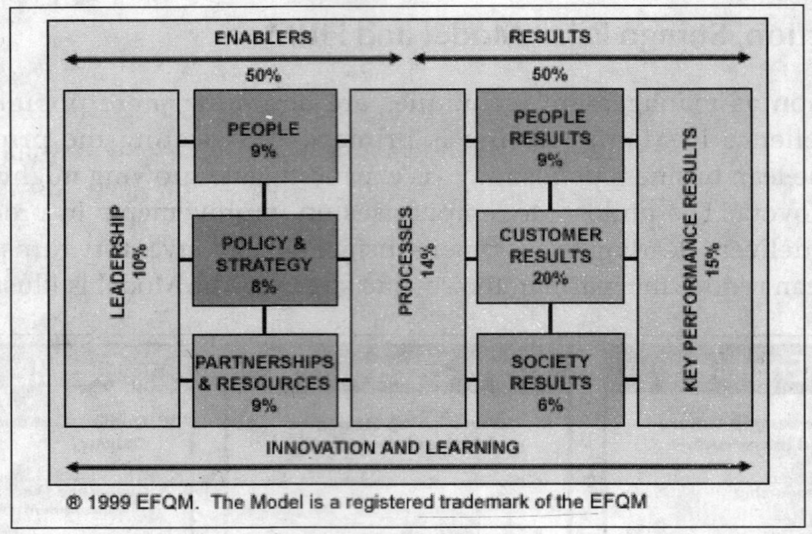

Figure 11.4: EFQM Model of Excellence

The Business Excellence Model is a nine-box model, originally developed by the European Foundation for Quality Management (EFQM). Its purpose is to *"support the management of Western European organisations in accelerating the process of making quality a decisive influence for achieving global competitive advantage."*

Lean brings action and intuition to the table. Based on the principles of the Toyota Production System and *kaizen* (continual improvement) breakthrough methodology, lean focuses on creating one-piece flow with just-in-time management of inventory and materials.

Both these excellence models in manufacturing advocate focusing on HRM, which not only ensures achieving organisational success through people but also reduces the costs by eliminating wastes.

ORGANISATIONAL DEVELOPMENT

Organisation development is a strategy or an effort, which is planned and managed from the top, to bring about planned organisational changes for increasing organisational effectiveness through planned interventions based on social philosophy.

The following statement amply clarifies the need for OD in an organisation.

> *Circumstances of an ever-changing market and an ever-changing product are capable of breaking any business organisation which is unprepared for change and has not provided procedures for anticipating change.*

The Characteristics of OD are:

1. ***Planned Organisation Change:*** It involves identification of the problem, diagnoses the organisation, develops strategies for improvement. The variables considered by organisation development programmes are: values, attitudes, organisation culture and team development.

2. ***Planned Intervention:*** It is a planned intervention in the existing organisation that helps it to become more viable. It, therefore, examines present working norms, values and possible areas of conflict of the organisation and develops alternatives for better health. The interventionist needs to diagnose different sub-systems of the organisation and develop alternatives for its better health. The important areas of intervention are planning and decision making processes, goal setting, team development, organisation structure, values and culture and upgrading employees' skills and abilities.

3. ***Top Management Commitment to OD:*** Top management should feel interested in the programme and its outcome and effectively support efforts in this direction. Unless mutual trust and collaborative relationships are developed between the change agents (who in most of the cases are consultants or professionals) and the management of the enterprise, organisation development efforts may not succeed.

4. ***Social Philosophy as a Norm of Change:*** Bureaucratic model of organisation ignores basic human factors and thereby reduces organisation effectiveness. The intervent therefore, requires to use the behavioural science knowledge and develop a syste is more humane and democratic.

Organisation Development, however, should not be confused with managemer Management development is virtually development of managers and is, the with upgrading of managers' skills and abilities, whereas organisation d includes management development, is primarily concerned with impr within the organisation.

Goals of Organisation Development

The important goals of OD are as follows:

1. To emphasise the need for changing from the clos various changes in the organisation. Such cha of concepts of social philosophy in the organi more responsible and transparent.

2. To supplement authority and hierar more congenial work environmen

3. To build mutual trust and co reducing conflict.

4. To change structure and roles in

5. To encourage a sense of ownership and pride in the organisation.
6. To decentralise decision-making close to the source of activity.
7. To emphasise on feedback, self-control and self-direction.
8. To develop the spirit of cooperation, mutual trust and confidence.
9. To develop a reward system based on achievement of goals and development of people.

It is apparent from the above discussion that the goal of OD is basically to change the attitudes of people in the organisation so as to enable them to identify the change areas and implement the desired organisation changes on their own.

Steps in Organisation Development

Robert Black and Jane S. Mouton (1963) suggested a six-phase approach to Organisational Development as under:

1. Investigating by each member of the organisation of his own managerial styles,
2. Examination of boss-subordinate relationship,
3. Analysis of work team action,
4. Exploration of co-ordination issues of interrelated terms,
5. Identifying and defining major organisational problem areas, and
6. Planning for executing agreed upon solutions that result in changes in the organisation.

However, the OD effort progresses through a series of well-defined stages, which can be enumerated as follows:

Identification and Diagnosis of the Problem: Required changes in relation to various units in the organisation should be identified and diagnosed duly examining the feedback from employees. Effective identification and diagnosis of the problem should be preceded by an employee survey.

eveloping of Strategy: While developing appropriate strategy, it is necessary to study ople, sub-systems and organisation as a total system. Strategy is the direction and pe of an organisation in the long run, matching resources and changing environment.

menting the Programme: OD programme should be implemented in a phased er, i.e. it should be tried at the outset only in a small part of the organisation and on positive results only it should gradually be implemented in the total organisation. al organisational change precedes attitudinal change, change in values and beliefs ople, the initial thrust should be given to training of employees, improvement ll, developing self-awareness, improving interpersonal relationships, reducing

4. ***Reviewing the Progress of the Programme:*** Review of OD programme should be preferably done by a qualified person who was not involved in designing and developing the OD programme, for getting an unbiased opinion.

SUMMARY

Career planning and development is a holistic approach for objective description of the career progression path for all levels of employees in an organisation. Even though the two concepts are used with different connotation in some organisations, like career planning for non-executive level and career development for executive and managerial levels, for our purpose, we have considered both the terms more in the general, rather than specific sense. Since, availability of internal manpower for manning present and future vacancies, is extremely important for an organisation to address to either planned strategic moves or uncertainties, without career planning and development, HRP becomes meaningless and short-sighted – limited to focus on current operational issues.

Retention of the key performers is an important strategic issue for organisations. Retention is best ensured for those organisations who have a well transparent career planning and development initiative. Similarly for internal manning of managerial vacancies, organisations should also have appropriate succession planning, or else this may jeopardize organisational plans. Succession planning succeeds management and organisational development. Thus suitable management and organisational development initiatives also reinforce HRP, particularly for employees at higher levels.

KEYWORDS

Career Planning	Career Cycle
Career Development	Career Anchors
Succession Planning	Employees Empowerment
Management Development	Career Paths
Organisational Development	Career Plateauing

REVIEW QUESTIONS

1. What is career development? Why is it important for an organisation? Does it differ from career planning?
2. Do you think career planning should be individual centered or organisation-centered? Briefly discuss the career planning programme of an organisation you know.
3. What are the factors you consider important for successful career planning?
4. Discuss the important steps in the career planning process.
5. What is the future of career planning and career development in India? Do you think recent economic restructuring has any bearing with such process? Elaborate your answer.

6. Define succession planning. Enumerate the steps involved in succession planning.
7. What is management development? Outline the characteristics of management development.
8. What are the objectives and purposes of a management development programme? Do you think such objectives are different for different level of employees?
9. What important steps you consider necessary for designing a management development programme? What are the techniques you recommend for management development?
10. What are the important aspects to be considered while auditing the management development programme?
11. What are the reasons for failure of management development programmes in India? What are your suggestions for making a management development programme effective?
12. What is organisation development? What are its important characteristics? How does it differ from management development?
13. Write short notes on:
    (a) Career Plateauing
    (b) Career Ladders
    (c) Job Families
    (d) Skill Inventories
    (e) OD Intervention
    (f) Succession Plans
    (g) Culture-specific Management

CASE STUDY

INFOSYS – THE CULTURE THAT PROMOTES ACHIEVING EXCELLENCE THROUGH GROUP EFFORTS

Mr. N R Narayana Murthy started his journey in 1981 with ₹ 10,000. His partners were six other co-founders with the objective to providing cost-effective IT services to the companies in the developed world. With this goal in mind, he engaged talented Indian engineers in his firm. The only aspiration of the company was "to become the most respected company in the world." Extending IT services to global clients from India was initially not possible. However, after deregulation, with the massive investment in telecommunications, communication links between India and rest of the world could be made possible, which enabled the company to connect the mainframes in the USA from the terminals in India. Such possibilities completely changed the landscape of company's business. With its own Global Delivery Model (GDM) to company could send software every now and then to any destinations on real-time basis. With GDM, the company could also provide all remote services, including ongoing maintenance and user support.

To successfully meet the expectations of international clients, the biggest challenge that the company faced is to recruit, enable, empower and retain the best talents. Mr. Murthy realised the need to transcend the compelling value proposition from customers to employees, to make them the best performers. The emphasis on new recruits is not only the strong technology skills, but also the zeal to continue learning. The zeal for ongoing learning is possible only when people are humble, i.e., open to learning. It is necessary for Infosys' employees to continuously acquire new skills in order to keep pace with the rapidly changing technology. Also from employees' point, it is important to quickly rise through the positions, as the growth rate of the company is quite high. "Powered by Intellect, Driven by Values" – these are the slogans of the company, which reflect on company's commitment on employees' development through continuous learning. Some of the values that the company advocates are:

- Openness to new ideas;
- Subordination of individual egos;
- Meritocracy;
- Emphasis on logical discussions, i.e., powered by data and facts;
- Speed;
- Imagination;
- Excellence in execution.

Managers in Infosys need to know the employees' needs. Understanding such needs and putting endeavour to achieve the results only can help them to gain the productivity and loyalty from the employees. Infosys believes that employees' motivation can make a difference in achieving their business goals. The company believes in 'C-LIFE', i.e., the values that ensure customer delight and pursuing the leadership, by example. Customer delight is achieved in terms of commitment to customers, even surpassing their expectations. Practice of leadership by example, requires commitment to set standards in business that the company will emulate. In C-LIFE concept, integrity, transparency, fairness and the pursuit of excellence are also embedded. Integrity and transparency values require employees to be ethical, diligent and open in dealings. Fairness values transpire from employees' commitment to objectivity that elicits trust and respect from others. Pursuit of excellence transpires from employees' relentless commitment for self and the development of team members which transcends to products and services, quality-wise which are second to none.

Mr. N R Narayana Murthy, chairman of the board and former Chief Executive of Infosys says, "The first responsibility of a leader is to create mental energy among people so that they enthusiastically embrace the transformation." He invites his high-performing team members to present before large audiences drawn from across the country to showcase how the company values the high performers. An ardent believer of self-renewal, Murthy himself chose his job title as the Chief Mentor of the company. This was his positive attempt to reinvent himself, setting aside his formal managerial authority. Such self sacrifice of Murthy not only set an example before his employees, but also encouraged his successor to become more and more successful in the job.

CASE STUDY 18

INFOSYS—THE CULTURE THAT PROMOTES ACHIEVING EXCELLENCE THROUGH CORE VALUES

[illegible]

[illegible]

- [illegible]
- [illegible]
- [illegible]
- [illegible]
- [illegible]
- [illegible]
- [illegible]

[illegible]

[illegible]

UNIT 12

Skills and Multi-skilling

Learning Objectives

After completion of this unit, the students will be aware of the following topics:

- *Introduction*
- *Definition and Concepts*
- *Multi-skilling*
- *Competencies*
- *Business Planning*
- *Organisational Flexibility*
- *Human Capital Return-on-Investment*
- *Managing Manpower Redundancy*

MULTI-SKILLING OF MURUGAPPA

Murugappa Group is one of India's prestigious business conglomerates with successful existence for over 100 years. The group's business turnover exceeds US$1 billion with presence in 12 states in India with 42 manufacturing units. The group is respected for its high ethical standards, environment friendly practices and transparency in business. An ardent believer in Indian social values, the group always subscribe to a win-win business deals.

EID Parry, one of the constituent units of the Group was established in 1788 and was attached with Murugappa in 1981. Parry is perhaps the oldest surviving company in India. Parry's business encompasses sugar (sugar alcohol, co-generation), bio-products and nutraceuticals. As a standalone group under Murugappa, Parry has huge maintenance and engineering division which continuously requires technology upgradation. Recent technological changes required Parry to install new equipments with vendor supported built-in test capability. This called for huge reduction of skilled manpower. Even with skeletal recruitment for years together, Parry could not stop such manpower redundancy, for obvious business requirements as technology vendors insisted for in-built maintenance contract along with the supply of new equipments. Moreover, existing maintenance and operations team members' skill mismatch complicated the issue of immediate redeployment of available skilled manpower. All these culminated to huge reduction of available manpower.

It was at this stage, EID parry decided to multi-skilling of their existing manpower, for cross-functional usage of their employees, ensuring skill interchangeability. The first thing that the company did was development of Master Jobs Matrix and comparing the same with the available competency matrix to identify 'cross-over' tasks for the redundant manpower, outside their conventional discipline. With inter-disciplinary cross-training, the company could successfully reduce the competency gap, realigning the knowledge and skills of the existing manpower and gradually, could arrange for their successful redeployment, including in new maintenance jobs. Such strategic multi-skilling efforts could result in increasing in-house maintenance engineers to the extent of 30% both for the routine and specialist tasks.

INTRODUCTION

Skills of the human resources have now become an important factor to address global competitiveness both at the organisational and national level. Obviously imparting skills through training and development is yet not recognised as an important initiative at the organisational level for problem of quantification of benefits. Return-on-investment worksheet of Edward E. Gordon (2000) which suggests 9 steps to analyse monetary returns, now eased the problem to a great extent. Even then its acceptance at the corporate level is yet to gain ground. Gordon's concepts of performance index and planning maps simplified the process of decision-making on investment on human capital. We have discussed these issues at the end. To begin with, concepts and definitions of skills and multi-skilling have been discussed, relating its importance in the corporate world and its significance to manage manpower redundancy and Human Resource Planning and Human Resource Management.

DEFINITION AND CONCEPTS

Skill is defined as a co-ordinated series of actions that serve to attain some goal or accomplish a particular task. Operationally, skills are defined widely as overt responses and controlled stimulation. Overt responses may be verbal, motor or perceptual. Verbal response typically stresses on speaking (which requires memorisation of words); motor responses stress on movements of limbs and body while perceptual responses stress on understanding of sensory response. Controlled stimulation on the other hand is energy inputs to the workers, which we express in units of frequency, length, time and weight. Technological change and skill requirements have been made a subject of investigation in many studies across the world. There is a general consensus that technological change alters the job but the observations differ in its nature and form. The neo-classical economic theory advocated technological changes, requiring broader variety of skills and higher average skills from the workers. New forms of skill and responsibility alongwith technological change have been studied in continuous process industry and chemical manufacturing units, petroleum refining, metal working industries, banking operations and in many other industries, which used advanced mechanisation.

Another school of thought advocates that technology is instrumental in fractionating and de-skilling of jobs. Redesigning of jobs subsequent to technological change separates the planning and the concept of job in its totality from the execution aspect of work. De-skilling and skill downgrading also occurs due to differential growth of higher versus low skill occupations and industries. The focal point of this hypothesis, is technology induces differential point of growth for sectors of the economy and produces skill polarisation by eventual occupational shift to skilled jobs in some industries and un-skilled jobs in many others. These phenomena are especially evident in India. From the 1981 census reports onward we find a major occupational shift of workers from primary to secondary and from secondary to tertiary sector. Simultaneous structural change in occupational pattern is also evident, as the number of blue-collar workers has been drastically reduced while the number of white-collar workers has significantly increased. Another school of thought argues de-skilling is a secondary consequence of de-industrialisation, which again is prompted by the technological change. The other approach, i.e., the mixed change or conditional position, is more a characterisation of the empirical evidence than a well-developed theory.

Transformations in skill due to technological change occur along two tracks; (i) compositional shift, i.e., structural change in occupational pattern due to creation or elimination of jobs of a given skill level and the distribution of persons to job in a sectoral economy and, (ii) changes in work content (the technical nature of work and the role relations surrounding work performance).

Internationally, the careers of the future will require greater education (more in the form of institutionalised knowledge) at the job entry level and will also demand continuing education to keep pace with technological dynamism. Greater level of technological literacy even for lower skill and low paying occupations will be in demand in future.

Tracing back history, we find that the Indian social system had definite orientation towards developing and maintaining different social groups in terms of certain crafts. The quality elements in a particular craft and the necessary skill were the deciding factors for the purpose of ranking that craft along with others in order of importance.

There was a time when carpenters, goldsmiths and weavers were the craftsmen-groups in India who enjoyed the highest status. However, it is pertinent to mention that Indian psycho-philosophy attaches more importance to values than formal occupational skills. It is, therefore, the value-laden skills, to which actually Indian psycho-philosophy gives importance than skills, per se.

From the above perspective, we can therefore, categorise skill either as generic of technical; entry level or advanced. Conventionally skills can be defined as those knowledge or attributes, which are deemed vital to organisational success. There are four general types of skills:

Technical skills – which relate to specific concepts, methods and tools specific to an organisation.

Supervisory skills – which enable one to effectively supervise others.

Interpersonal skills – which enable people to communicate and interact effectively.

General business skills – lines of business and support infrastructure.

Technical skills are observable, demonstrable and testable. The other skill types are softer, more subjective and difficult to quantify.

Any organisation going for skill renewal or skill-change exercise, needs to undertake the following tasks:

1. Profile the skills required by jobs,
2. Assess the skill levels acquired by individuals, and
3. Conduct a gap analysis between required and acquired skill.

Training should ideally occur before the skill is needed so that daily work can reinforce training.

MULTI-SKILLING

Multi-skilling is defined as the process to train employees in specific skills that cross the traditional trade-specific or craft-specific skill sets. Thus to develop multi-skills, employees require additional training to enable them to perform more jobs within the same job family or to do the entire jobs from a holistic point of view. Multi-skilling is often misconstrued to succeed downsizing. But downsizing occurs due to skill obsolescence, among other reasons, while multi-skilling is for holistic development of human potentialities to effectively address to the requirements of changing production process (more flexible and customised) organisational systems (decentralised control) and state-of-art technology (numeric control, computer numeric control, direct numeric control, etc.). Multi-skilling facilitates intra-occupational and inter-occupational job mobility and thereby reinforces HRP.

Multi-skilling is an institutionalised practice in Japanese organisations. In Japan, bottom-up decision-making approach is followed. Workers down the line, take vital decisions, concerning management of the organisations. Such empowerment in Japan is possible for institutionalized multi-skilling. Moreover, multi-skilling is essential in Japanese organisations for their focus on continuous process improvement to achieve excellence in quality and effectiveness in products and services; and frequent introduction of new products. Strategic multi-skilling in Japanese organisations not only helps them to achieve high performance results; but also helps in containing the employee attrition rate which is abysmally low and perhaps, the lowest in the world.

Japanese organisations believe in horizontal information structure which facilities decision making power even at the workers' level. Multi-skilling in Japan is essentially ensured through on-the-job training and job rotation. Because of lower attrition rate, Japanese organisations are able to individualise the human capital accumulation. To ensure perpetual utilisation of human resources, multi-skilling is observed in Japanese organisations as a regular practice. Moreover, as an essential HRM practice, Japanese organisations encourage their workers to continuously improve the work methods. Every worker needs to be innovative and be in some activity to bring new changes in their work processes.

COMPETENCIES

Competencies are set of behaviours, which encompass skills, knowledge, abilities and attributes. Competencies need to be assessed at the organisation and individual level. Individual competencies together reinforce organisational competencies. However, there always exists a possibility of major incongruence between individual competencies and organisational competencies. Manpower planning exercise helps us to analyse such gaps and develop a competency model. A competency model is a map to display a set of competencies. It is future-oriented and it helps to describe an ideal workforce. A competency model when developed and documented helps in managerial decision-making, as it is well aligned with vision, mission, objectives, goals and strategies of an organisation. It also helps employees of an organisation to understand the functional requirements and self-initiate the enrichment of their skills, knowledge, abilities and attributes. This would be independent of an organisation-wide competency enrichment exercise.

How Competency Mapping is Done?

Competency mapping is always done in the defined job context following a set of approaches:

1. Workforce Skills Analysis
2. Job Analysis
3. Supply and Demand Analysis
4. Gap Analysis
5. Situation Analysis

Skill analysis helps to describe skills required to carry out a function. However, this is a dynamic approach, as it also considers nature of work changes in an organisation.

Job analysis focuses an tasks, responsibilities, knowledge and skill requirements, which are required for successful job performance.

Both the workforce skills analysis and job analysis are done from inputs collected from survey (through questionnaire responses), interviews with managers and employees and benchmarking information with successful organisations. For technology intensive and machine-enabled jobs, skill set requirements and cycle-time for jobs (as printed in the literatures) also contribute as critical input information for such jobs.

Supply analysis is done considering workforce demographic (in terms of occupations, grades, structure, race, origin, gender, age, service experience, education, training, health status, retirement time and similar other information), trends and present workforce competencies. This, therefore helps to understand the existing workforce status.

Demand analysis on the other hand helps to identify workforce of the future in line with the vision, mission, objectives, goals and strategies of an organisation. Critical inputs from demand analysis contribute to development of competency model for workforce of the future.

With the above input reinforcers, organisation undertakes gap analysis to understand the differences between the workforce of today and the workforce of the future. After such identification of differences, organisation need to plan to address those.

Addressing such gaps is done through solution analysis, taking into account both ongoing and planned changes in the workforce. Solution analysis also weighs different options to get the work done, either considering institutional or contractual employment. New recruitment, restructuring, training and retraining, redeployment and rightsizing, all are done, in the light of the new competency model, in this phase.

After suitable competency mapping, next course of action for an organisation, however, is to decide whether to downsize/rightsize or to go for training, re-training and redeployment.

Indian Scenario

Inadequate competency mapping is the root cause of large-scale manpower redundancies in Indian organisations. Of late this has become a nightmare for HR professionals and instead of addressing this issue from a long-term or strategic perspective they are now forced to adopt a firefighting approach with a short-term or operational view.

Compulsion for continuous technological upgradation, to gain edge over quality and price, over the domestic and global players, gradually made the trade or occupation specific skill redundant. The problem is further aggravated for obvious incapability of the organisation for renewal of skill of existing manpower, presumably due to overage (at least macro-level data indicate this).

We do not have much data to speak on the success of manpower rightsizing in Indian organisations. At least the report of National Renewal Fund (NRF) supports. NRF was especially constituted to make available money on soft interest terms to take care of skill renewal for rightsizing manpower in Indian organisations, particularly during post-reform days. Most of the Indian organisations, whosoever have availed such money from NRF, utilized the same for giving effect to Voluntary Retirement Scheme (VRS) or golden handshake for permanent separation rather than redeployment with skill renewal.

One such study, with which, the author was directly associated and which was published in details in the proceeding of an international seminar with the theme "Economic Transition with a Human Face" (1995) establishes the fact that lack of formal education and problem of overage cannot dissuade success of skill-development and skill change programmes. The captioned study was carried out in one of the ordnance factories in India for a period of 15 months on more than 7,000 workmen with average age-group of 50+, with trade-specific skills and formal education upto mid-school level. This exercise helped the factory to ensure management of surplus labour, duly averting the problems of manpower obsolescence.

Unfortunately, similar exercises have not been done in most of the privately controlled and Government controlled units and even in other departmental undertakings. The HR strategy for rightsizing manpower in Indian organisations mostly centre around the following path:

1. Identification of employees who are redundant.
2. Asking them to relocate, if the organisation has multiple units.
3. Redeploy them if they are agreeable.
4. Ask them to leave, if it is otherwise.

However, it is important to mention that the redundancy issue in Indian organisations is not always due to skill obsolescence. It is often for imminent organisational restructuring, relocating, and downsizing, which may be due to change in business strategy. Whatever may be the reasons, most of the organisations are apprehensive about skill renewal through re-training. They fear this re-training and re-deployment will not be cost-effective, rather offering them VRS or replacing the existing manpower with new incumbents will be more strategically important decisions in terms of cost efficiency and immediate usability.

Whether such strategic move is correct or not can only be understood in terms of cost-benefit analysis. Unfortunately, we do not have any data to support or authenticate this. One particular issue is very much relevant for the service sector-that technology can supplement the existing job process but cannot do away with basic job-related skill, i.e. the business skill, which is also the core skill-set, associated with the job performance. To illustrate, commercial banking organisations may go for replacement of their existing manpower with more tech-savvy new manpower but they cannot obviously buy the business skill, i.e., the core banking knowledge from the new recruit. Hence any decision about manpower rightsizing needs to be weighed in terms of relative merits and demerits, instead of opting for the most popular VRS route.

Where the Malady Lies?

Alan Fowler's (1999) macro-level study on HR practices reveal that most of the organisations are facing the problem of manpower redundancy due to the following reasons:

1. Inadequate business planning
2. Inadequate human resource planning
3. Absence of policies on redundancy
4. Inflexibility of job description, which restricts lateral job movement
5. Inflexible conditions of employment
6. Absence of retraining and redeployment programmes

Indian organisations are not adequately tuned to respond to the threats and opportunities of the fast-moving external environment. Technological change, global competition, emergence of new markets and new economy, demographic and political changes, etc., continuously call for frequent changes in the customers and other stakeholders. Largely they lack a perspective plan envisioning the above aspects. Therefore, inadequate business planning inevitably give rise to the problem in Indian organisations.

Similarly, recruitment strategy in Indian organisations also needs to be reconsidered in the context of changing environment. While it is difficult to alter the employment conditions for the existing employees, for the new incumbent, such conditions like appointment on tenure-track, assignment basis, fixed-term contract (subject to renewal on mutually acceptable terms), outsourcing of manpower from agencies are some of the strategies which need to be considered to avert the problem of redundancy. Inflexibility in job descriptions and conditions of employment similarly inhibit cross lateral movement or transfer or employees during implementation of organisational restructuring, to relocate them in restructured position, which ultimately gives rise to the problem of manpower redundancy. Absence of continuous training and skill renewal efforts from organisations also stands against successful management of manpower redundancy programme.

Business Planning

Aspects of business planning that have particular relevance to the assessment of the possibility of redundancies are:

1. What is planned regarding the size of the business? Is it expected to expand, contract or remain relatively stable in size?
2. The expansion is planned on what basis? Is this to be a general growth across all business activities, or is to be concentrated on one or more particular aspects?
3. Are changes planned in the nature of the business, such as increased specialisation, or the launch of new products or services?
4. Do any of the plans involve changes to business or unit locations?
5. Are there any plans to change qualitative or cultural aspects of the business, such as going up-market with products, or placing greater emphasis on customer service, or introducing a total quality management programme?
6. What external trends are expected – economic, technological, statutory that will necessitate change in the scope of the business or how it operates?

Human Resource Planning

HRP basically includes statistical analysis, but it has several other important additional features:

1. It is built into the business planning process, rather than being treated as a separate and specialist function. As a result, human resource issues and projections may influence

the business plan – instead of business decisions being made first and their personnel implications being left to the personnel manager to deal with later.

2. It is concerned as much with the design, implementation and monitoring of action plans as with statistical forecasting and analysis.

3. Qualitative factors are given as much attention as quantitative data (example customer care).

In relation to redundancy avoidance, it is for the human function to explain why this is important and to evolve the practical measures that need to be taken. Three types of information and analysis are involved:

1. The business planning data about such issues as technological and market trends and the options under consideration for the development of the organisation in the light of these trends.

2. External influences on the organisation's human resourcing capability, particularly;

   (a) demographic change

   (b) the availability of competition for the skills of the organisation

   (c) employment related legislation.

3. The characteristics and constitution of the current workforce, with particular reference to:

   (a) age and gender profiles

   (b) stability and turnover levels and trends

   (c) the stock of skills and competencies

   (d) organisation structures and the design of jobs

   (e) the extent of other than conventional full-time employment, i.e., part-timers, temporary staff, contractors, etc.

Organisational Flexibility

If organisations are structured along functional or specialist lines, there exists a rigidity which inhibits change, other than marginal change. It may also reinforce a sense of identity with, and loyalty to the particular profession or occupation rather than to the organisation as a whole. This can work against the long-term interests of the organisation by limiting its ability to adapt to change, and against the job security interests of employees by restricting their knowledge and skills within relatively narrow boundaries. Attitudinally displaced employees from one specialist section may be reluctant to move to other sections which they perceive as alien or lower in status in professional or occupational terms.

Job Flexibility

Organisational flexibility is primarily about how jobs are grouped. Job flexibility is concerned with the design or content of individual jobs. These two issues tend to be linked, as it is often a feature of a rigid organisational structure that individual jobs within it are narrowly defined, each employee is concerned with just one small element in a broader work process, and is unable to complete a whole transaction.

Flexibility in Human Resourcing

This issue centres on core and periphery organisation. In order to enforce flexibility in resourcing, following three forms can be considered:

1. A relatively small central core of highly skilled employees on direct, permanent contracts, with the size of this workforce set at close to the minimum expected level of requirement.

2. A larger group of secondary employees, on terms such as fixed-term and temporary contracts which make it possible to change their number relatively quickly and without incurring redundancy costs.

3. An outer ring of workers of various kinds (not employees) such as agency staff, self-employed freelance workers, contractors and consultants. Their use can be changed even more rapidly than that of the secondary employees.

Flexible Conditions of Employment

From the viewpoint of a redundancy avoidance policy, there are several key elements of the employment package where flexibility is of the most significance. Following issues need to be addressed:

- Contractual duties
- Working times
- Relocation schemes
- Retirement and pensions

For effective redundancy management, it is necessary to involve trade unions and adopt a redundancy policy and collective agreements. The main elements in a redundancy agreement are normally:

- A commitment by the organisation to take all reasonable steps to avoid redundancy, or if it becomes necessary, to minimise its impact.
- A commitment by the organisation to effective consultation in the event of the possibility of redundancy and how such consultation would be effected.

- A commitment by the trade union to co-operate in action to avoid or minimise redundancy.
- Agreed selection criteria for redundancy and the procedure for notifying the trade union and the employees involved.
- Details of redundancy compensation
- Details of any other assistance the organisation would provide to redundant employees.

Operational Approach

Short-term operational measures that can be taken to avoid or reduce such action, in particular are as under:

- Natural wastage and recruitment restrictions
- Stopping or reducing overtime
- Terminating the employment of non-permanent workers (temporary, casual, fixed-term contract, self-employed, agency employees)
- Retraining and redeployment
- Retirement measures
- Volunteers for redundancy

Capability Maturity Model (CMM)

In November, 1986, the Software Engineering Institute (SEI) of Carnegie Mellon University of Pittsburg with assistance from the MITRE Corporation, began developing a process maturity framework to help organisations to improve their software process. After four years of experience with the software process maturity framework and the 1987 maturity questionnaire, SEI evolved the maturity framework into the capability maturity model for software. The CMM is based on the actual practices, reflects the best of the state of the practice and reflects the needs of the individuals performing software process improvement and software process appraisals. It is a documented process.

A process is a sequence of steps performed for a given purpose. The process integrates people, tools and procedures. Process is what people do, using procedures, methods, tools and equipments, to transform raw material (inputs) into a product (output) that is of value to the customers. The CMM focuses on process as a way to empower the people doing the work. An effective process ties together people, tools and methods into an integrated whole. Process capability describes the range of expected results that can be achieved by following a process. Thus process performance focuses on the results achieved while process capability focuses on results expected. Process maturity is the extent to which a specific process is explicitly defined, managed, measured, controlled and effected. Maturity implies a potential for growth in capability and indicates both the richness of an organisation's software process and the consistency with which it is applied in projects throughout the organisation. Process maturity implies that process capability must have grown. Improvement requires strong management support and a consistent long-term focus. As an organisation matures, it needs an infrastructure and culture to support its methods, practices and procedures so that they endure after those who originally defined them have gone. Organisational culture can be summed up as the way things are done. It is seen in people's expectations for how they are to work together. One of the determinants of organisational culture is its infrastructure, which is the underlying framework of an organisation or system, including organisational structures, policies, standards, training, facilities and tools that support its ongoing performance.

Institutionalism is the building of infrastructure and culture to support the methods, practices, and procedures so that they are the ongoing way of doing business. The result of institutionalisation is the deployment of processes that are effective, usable and consistently applied across the organisation.

People Capability Maturity Model (P-CMM)

P-CMM adapts the maturity framework of the Capability Maturity Model for software to managing and developing an organisation's workforce. To attract, develop, motivate, organise and retain talent to continuously improve capability of an organisation, P-CMM is now widely used in organisations across the world. This is designed to integrate manpower improvement with process improvement programmes. Based on the best current practices in the fields such as human resources and organisational development, the P-CMM provides organisations with guidance on how to gain control of their processes for managing and developing their human resource. P-CMM helps organisations to characterise the maturity of their human resource practices, guide a programme of continuous manpower development, set priorities for immediate actions, integrate manpower development with process improvement, and establish a culture of software engineering excellence. It describes an evolutionary improvement path from ad hoc, inconsistently performed practices, to a mature, disciplined development of the knowledge, skills and motivation of the human resources.

The P-CMM consists of five maturity levels that lay successive foundations for continuously improving talent, developing effective teams, and successfully managing the people assets of the organisation. Each maturity level is a well-defined evolutionary plateau that institutionalises a level of capability for developing the talent within the organisation.

Except for level 1, each maturity level is developed into several key process areas that an organisation should focus on to improve its human resources capability. Each key process area is described in terms of the key practices that contribute to satisfying its goals. The key practices describe the infrastructure and activities that contribute most to the effective implementation and institutionalisation of the key process area.

The five maturity levels of the P-CMM are:

1. ***Initial:*** Workforce practices applied without analysis.
2. ***Repeatable:*** The key process areas at level 2 focus on instilling basic discipline into workforce activities. They are:
   (a) Work environment
   (b) Communication
   (c) Staffing
   (d) Performance management
   (e) Training
   (f) Compensation
3. ***Defined:*** The key process areas at level 3 address issues surrounding the identification of the organisation's primary competencies and aligning its people management activities with them. They are:
   (a) Knowledge and skill analysis
   (b) Workforce planning
   (c) Competency development
   (d) Career development
   (e) Competency-based practices
   (f) Participatory culture
4. ***Managed:*** The key process areas at level 4 focus on quantitatively managing organisational growth in people management capabilities and in establishing competency-based teams. They are:
   (a) Mentoring
   (b) Team building
   (c) Team-based practices
   (d) Organisational competency management
   (e) Organisational performance management

5. *Optimising:* The key process areas at level 5 cover the issues that address continuous improvement of methods for developing competency, at both the organisational and the individual level. They are:

   (a) Personal competency development

   (b) Coaching

   (c) Continuous workforce innovation

Process Areas

Key Process Areas refer to the particular tasks and activities, which must be completed in order for an organisation to gain maturity and progress towards optimizing their training initiatives. The following matrix identifies the appropriate Key Process Areas necessary to address each of the four themes of the P-CMM, and allow the organisation to mature.

Maturity Levels	Process Categories			
	THEME 1: Developing Capabilities	THEME 2: Building Teams and Culture	THEME 3: Motivating and managing performance	THEME 4: Shaping the workforce
MATURITY LEVEL 5: Optimizing	Coaching Personal Competency Development	Continuous Workforce Innovation		
MATURITY LEVEL 4: Managed	Mentoring	Team Building	Organizational Performance Alignment Team-Based Practices	Organizational Competency Management
MATURITY LEVEL 3: Defined	Competency Development Knowledge and Skills Analysis	Participatory Culture	Competency-Based Practices Career Development	Workforce Planning
MATURITY LEVEL 2: Repeatable	Training Communication	Communication	Compensation Performance Management Work Environment	Staffing
MATURITY LEVEL 1: Initial				

Version 2 of the People CMM has been designed to correct known issues in Version 1, which was released in 1995; to add enhancements learned from five years of implementation experience; and to integrate the model better with CMMI® and its IPPD extensions. The primary motivation for updating the People CMM was the error in Version 1 of placing team-building activities at Maturity Level 4. Version 2 of the People CMM is being produced only in a staged representation. After lengthy review of the literature and experience gathered from implementors on programs to improve workforce practices, the authors determined that these programs often fail when workforce practices are not introduced as a system of practices or in reinforcing bundles, but rather are deployed in isolation. For instance, efforts to install empowered teams are likely to fail if compensation practices continue to reward individual performance without recognizing contribution to team performance and team success.

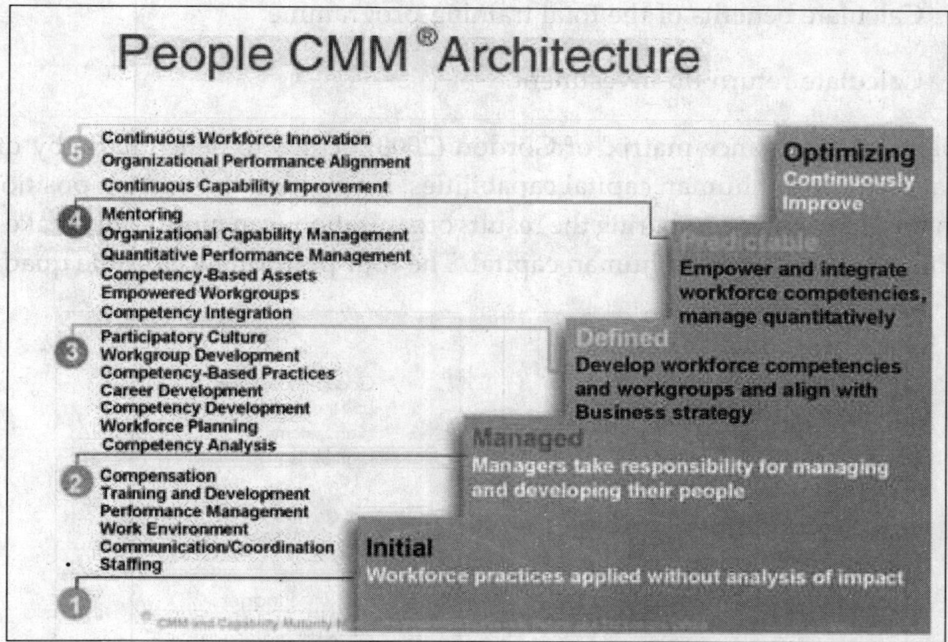

MM guides an organisation through a series of increasingly sophisticated practices and techniques for developing its overall work-force. These practices have been chosen from experience as those that have significant impact on individual team, and, organisational performance.

Human Capital Return-on-Investment

Two ROI systems widely in use are utility analysis and performance value. Nine-step human capital ROI worksheet of Gordon (2000) allows us to accurately estimate the monetary returns both before and after most training programmes.

Step 1 : Calculate all direct costs associated with the training programme.

Step 2 : Calculate lost productivity while trainers are in the programme.

Step 3 : Calculate the total cost of the programme.

Step 4 : Estimate expected hourly, weekly or monthly productivity benefits per trainee. Methods may range from establishing control groups to using a standard linear regression formula.

Step 5 : Estimate the actual quality benefit from the training.

Step 6 : Using a standard discount rate formula, estimate the time length of the training's effect.

Step 7 : Calculate profit per trainee.

Step 8 : Calculate benefits of the total training programme.

Step 9 : Calculate return on investment.

Then 'Managed performance matrix' of Gordon (2000) begins to benchmark, by quadrants, an organisation's current human capital capabilities. By plotting the current position of their business on this matrix and comparing the results organisations can more easily make decisions regarding how to invest in their human capital. The four performance profile quadrants are:

Master	Apprentice
- High Performance - High Innovation - High Systems - High Skills	- Good Performance - Low Innovation - High Systems - High Skills
Now 5% / Future 20%	Now 20% / Future 30%
Novice	**Plugger**
- Fair Performance - Low Innovation - Low Systems - High Skills	- Low Performance - Low Innovation - Low Systems - Low Skills
Now 50% / Future 40%	Now 25% / Future 10%

This matrix builds an information bank on human capital that can be used in preparing a reliable business plan and business strategy. To use this matrix successfully, a business will measure all people on four core competency areas: performance, innovation, systems and skills:

High Performance

- Meets or exceeds personal work goals and objectives, while leading others to high personal work standards.
- Is not afraid to learn something new and try it out.

High Innovator

- Good at solving problems, prioritising solutions, and abstract reasoning/combinational logic, generates new ideas for service or product and gets the job done right.

High Systems

- Understands how to motivate, coach, and lead people
- Understands the uses and integration of information and other appropriate technologies.

High Skills

- Communication skills; oral, written and text comprehension exceed the 13th grade level.
- Mathematical skills' computation and conceptual application.

The 'Human capital development map' offers a specific method of assessing how well personal employee development is aligned with business objectives. It not only identifies the benefit in the form of a business objective, it also pinpoints the specific development applications needed to achieve the desired business objectives. Each division of an organisation can use this Human Capital Development Map as a method to relate different business plans/strategies to the specific applications and benefits required of its training programmes.

The 'knowledge profit model' of Gordon (2000) offers a useful management tool as under:

Policy – a workforce education triad of skills, training and education.

Practice – a community of learning from many sources.

Profit – the measurement of business results by using a credible human capital return-on-investment worksheet.

Workforce Education Triad

Any person who needs skills training and/or education to help achieve the business plan will receive the requisite workforce education components. Technology and globalisation ensure that employees will need higher skill levels that increase their overall personal comprehension and application abilities. Writing, maths, reading, foreign language and English as a second language are important examples of these skill.

MANAGING MANPOWER REDUNDANCY

In today's volatile world of work, the survival and success of organisations depend on their ability to adopt a strategic move for continual adaptation, keeping pace with the threats and opportunities of the fast changing external environment. Technological developments, global competition, the emergence of a new economy and markets, demographic and political changes are some of the factors which influence organisations to go for frequent adjustments in existing structure, systems and processes and redefine their relationships with customers and other stakeholders.

The effective planning and implementation of these developments are highly influenced by people management issues, particularly when changes are required to rightsize or downsize workforce and more specifically managing manpower redundancy. Any organisation which wishes to manage redundancy has to consider what it can do to prevent redundancy. Or else, if at all it occurs, to minimise its impact. The ideal objective is to manage the organisation's human resource requirements in such a way that need for rightsizing, downsizing or redundancy never arises. These are two aspects to redundancy avoidance – long-term or strategic and short-term or strategic action can be put in place as a preventive measure, i.e., before anything approaching a redundancy situation occurs, whereas short-term or operational action is taken to avoid or minimise actual or imminent redundancies. The key feature of long-term or strategic measures is planning. Alan Fowler (1999) in his famous work on 'Managing Redundancy' identified several characteristics of an organisation facing the risk of manpower redundancies.

Characteristics of Organisations facing the Risk of Manpower Redundancies

1. Organisations have made no assessments of the likely trends affecting the viability of the business. While facing the problem of rightsizing, such organisations' decisions will eventually be reactive, i.e., adopting of crisis management measures, which includes making of sudden changes in the constitution and size of the work force.

2. Such organisations would not have any clear business objectives, values or standards. Due to the absence of this vision it will not be able to take long-term action to ensure matching training and development of its people to meet future business needs. When changes become necessary in the type and mix of employees' skills, these organisations will consequently tend to make employees with old skills redundant and acquire the necessary new skills as replacement of the old ones through recruitment.

3. Such organisations would not have analysed the age and service profiles of its workforce, or maintained statistics on the trends of employee turnover. Faced with the need to change the nature or size of its workforce, it will find difficulty in forecasting the effect of natural wastage, and it may suddenly discover an imbalance in the age distribution of its staff. Such a situation will make measures like voluntary retirement scheme relatively ineffective.

4. Such organisation would probably have a complex organisational hierarchy and rigid and centralised management systems. The risk of managerial redundancies would be relatively greater and the centralised nature of its management system will inhibit rapid operational adjustments.

5. Jobs in such organisations will be very closely defined, with a multiplicity of work demarcations. This will inhibit the transfer of employee from job to job to cope with changing operational pressures. Also in such organisations employees will be unwilling to accept cross-lateral job transfers.

6. Almost the entire workforce of such organisations would be permanent, full-time employees, with little or no use being made of part-timers, temporary and fixed-term contracts, or external contractors. There will consequently be very limited scope for

varying the size of workforce to reflect fluctuations in the level of organisation's activities– other than by redundancy or recruitment.

7. Such organisations would operate a complicated and very detailed set of conditions of employment, in which changes in working time or in job duties are difficult to introduce. Although changes in employment conditions do not directly cause redundancy, inflexibility in matters like overtime, shift patterns and payment systems will restrict the organisation's ability to reorganise and therefore will have an indirect effect on its ability to avoid redundancies.

8. Such organisations would not have concluded any redundancy agreements with its trade unions, with the result that when redundancies occur, there is immediate disagreement as to how these should be handled.

SUMMARY

Skills, multi-skilling and competency are the major issues concerning HRP. The Problem of skill obsolescence is now a global phenomena. At the organisation level, skill renewal initiative is seriously lacking, as they are more comfortable opting for downsizing or rightsizing through redundancies. In India also, despite creation of the National Renewal Fund (NRF), organisations prefer to spend NRF money (which is available on soft interest terms) more on VRS than skill renewal and redeployment of existing workers. There exist a gross misconception that skills the Indian workers cannot be renewed for their obvious trade-specific and industry-specific bent. Moreover, existing workmen are by and large in the older age bracket. This misconception further accentuated due to the problem of quantification of benefits of skill development, change or renewal training. However, we have now more developed tools for such quantification and at least some empirical evidence to counter such apprehensions. A well structured competency mapping with systematic HRD intervention can successfully renew the skill and contribute to competitive advantage. Skill renewal, among others, can avert manpower redundancies. It has a strategic dimension for long-term profitability and growth of an organisation.

KEYWORDS

Human Capital Return-on-Investment	Competency Mapping
Performance Index	Capability Maturity
Controlled Stimulation	Model
Generic Skills	Knowledge Profit Model
Multi-skilling	Workforce Education Triad

REVIEW QUESTIONS

1. Discuss the need for skill-renewal in Indian organisations.

2. Can we use the terms skills, multi-skilling and competency interchangeably? What are their differences, if any?

3. How can we do competency mapping? In what way does it contribute to HRP?
4. Why it is important for us to study P-CMM? Does its compliance helps an organisation in any way?
5. For redundancy avoidance, which strategic move is important?
6. Write short notes on:
   (a) P-CMM
   (b) ROI in Human Capital
   (c) Multi-skilling
   (d) Occupational pattern
   (e) Knowledge Profit Model
   (f) Performance Index

CASE STUDY 1

RAYMOND – THE RIGHT FIT RECRUITMENT AND RETENTION

Raymond Textile, the flagship company in Indian textile industry primarily recruits textile engineers and MBAs through systematic campus recruitment process. Raymond, while recruiting, emphasises on those who fit into their value systems. With multi-level screening, including psychometric testing, Raymond analyses the compatibility of the prospective candidates. Such compatibility is more important for Raymond particularly for hiring at the mid and senior level. Along with the domain knowledge, Raymond's compatibility analysis of candidates' profile with their value systems reduces the recruitment errors, which Raymond validates through subsequent performance and retention data.

Raymond faces talent crunch in textile designs and so also in textile engineering. Many textile engineers dislike the shop floor level jobs. Textile designing is yet to become an institutionalised job in India due to lack of formal training in collegial environment. Very few textile engineers can become textile designers as among others, this profession also requires innovation and creativity. Raymond, therefore, emphasises on recruiting the entry level talents to subsequently groom them to specialists in all other branches of textile manufacturing, design and research & development. The typical character of the textile industry restricts the scope of inter-industry job mobility. Hence, retaining the talent is more important as trained and skilled manpower can always move to competitors, creating typical talent crunch for the company.

In functional areas like Finance and HR, Raymond can attract the talents from other industries. Textile industries' pay band is considerably less than other industries, but Raymond makes their compensation package more attractive to attract the talent from other industries. Raymond's emphasis on attracting talents from the other industries is primarily due to the fact that such people can always come out with new ideas to Raymond's business. Although to make them compatible with the Raymond's requirements, the company needs to give them more orientation and training. Orienting new hires in entry or middle level requires giving them the exposure to the textile manufacturing process. Every new recruit learns the operations through systematic orientation in Raymond's plants.

Raymond's experience in recruitment says that talents look for brand identification than the compensation packages. Raymond however, pays very competitive compensation to their employees. Craze for more compensation is more evident at the mid level. Senior level employees are, however, more interested in the management control, job description, and reporting structure.

With less attrition, Raymond's HRD is able to retain talents creating a culture of personal touch and inculcating a sense of belonging.

CASE STUDY 2

SKILL REDUNDANCY

A recently released survey report of 1,600 recruiters across the globe by the Wall Street Journal ranked almost 27 attributes that recruiters look for in B-School graduates. Among the soft-skills, recruiters give more emphasis on interpersonal skills, team-work abilities, analytic problem solving skills, ability to derive results from the beginning, etc. Recruiters also give priorities to other aspects while selecting a prospective B-School graduate, like; willingness to relocate, fit with corporate culture and retention probability. Anderson and Knowledge Systems and Research in yet another survey (2001), rank most vital skills in the job market in the ascending order of technical skills, communication skills, job experience, networking/relationship building experience, management skills, industry expertise and sales/marketing skills. Most layoff prone industries, identified by Anderson are manufacturing, technology, retail, telecommunications, hospitality and financial services.

99,225 employees of the public sector banks in India recently opted for voluntary retirement, fearing their redundancy, primarily for skill obsolescence, costing the exchequer to the tune of ₹ 10,073 crores A certain percentage of them might be for obvious personal reasons or for certain anti-employee organisational practices (like; transfer, relocation, increased accountability, etc.) but largely they have opted for VRS on their perceived skill redundancy. In this respect we have evidential congruence between management and employees. This is an example of a well-planned organisational initiative to address to the problems of manpower redundancy with a long-term perspective. We will not debate how good or how bad it is. But we get surprised when organisations, on their annual operational results, decide on downsizing (we don't use the term rightsizing deliberately), be it Compaq or Lucent today, ABN Ambro and American Express tomorrow! Typical Indian organisations are also not lagging behind, NIIT, BILT, BALCO, IBP, SAIL, TISCO and many more are in the fray.

Question

Discuss the need for skill renewal and multi-skilling initiatives in Indian organisations with macro-and micro-perspectives and finally suggest a perspective model for reducing the perennial problem of manpower redundancy.

BLOCK FOUR

EMPLOYEE COMPENSATION

UNIT 13

Wages and Salary Administration

Learning Objectives

After completion of this unit, the students will be aware of the following topics:

- *Introduction*
- *Wage Policy*
- *Wage Determination*
- *Dearness Allowance (DA)*
- *Overtime Wages*
- *Incentive Schemes*
- *Performance-based Pay*
- *Fringe Benefits*
- *Executive Compensation*

ITC's Distinctive Compensation Design

'We nurture excellence and keep alive the spirit of healthy competition by providing each of our employees' equal opportunities to grow as well as numerous performance incentives.' This is what ITC believes. ITC ensures employees to enjoy the work environment, devising multiple reward systems and incentives. ITC's reward and recognition framework is aligned with their performance management systems. Their competitive compensation system compares with the best in the industry and it provides for fair and equitable compensation opportunities for individual contribution to the organisational success. A dynamic year-round performance management system of ITC involves, setting of objectives, managing performance, assessing performance as well the means employed, evaluating individual effectiveness as well as the contribution to the corporate objectives and recognition systems. This system ensures attraction, retention and honing of the best talent available in the market; and also enables the company to propel employees towards a promising future. Instantaneous award, excellence/value award and best of best achievement award are some of the unique compensation features which require tracking of employees' achievement, even beyond formal performance management systems, making ITC distinctive in compensation management practices.

Introduction

In constructing a wage structure in a given case, industrial adjudication does take into account to some extent considerations of right and wrong, propriety and impropriety, fairness and unfairness. As the social conscience of the general community becomes more alive and active, as the welfare policy of the state takes a more dynamic form, as the national economy progresses from stage to stage, as under the growing strength of the trade union movement collective bargaining enters the field, wage structure ceases to be a purely mathematical problem. Considerations of the financial position of the employer and state of national economy have their say and the requirements of a workman living in a civilized and progressive society also come to be recognised, it is in the sense and no doubt to a limited extent, that the social philosophy of the age supplies the background for the decision of industrial disputes as to wage structure.

It is against this background that the framers of the constitution incorporated in Article 43 of the Constitution as part of the Directive Principles of State Policy that, "The State shall endeavour to secure, by suitable legislation or economic organisation or in any other way, to all workers – agriculture, industrial or otherwise – work, a living wage, conditions of work ensuring a decent standard of life and full employment of leisure and social and cultural opportunities." By this declaration the state not only bound itself to the importance of the State's role in directly promoting welfare, it recognised the inadequacy of the market forces to determine a wage level which is consistent with any welfare standards of a living wage. The declaration, in effect, gave assurance to labour that where they were not able to secure for themselves a living wage, the government through legislation or other means will come to their aid. Two aspects of the State's role vis-à-vis the workers can be seen here, one, use of the State's authority to prevent employers from taking undue advantage of the workers' weak bargaining strength and two, direct participation of the State on the economic life of the nation through planning and expansion of the public sector. The former was meant to give the worker a fair share in the kitty and the latter to enlarge the kitty itself.

WAGE POLICY

The recommendations of the Committee on fair wages, 1948, provided the basic approach for tribunals, Wage Board and others to fix wages of workers, a large part of which has been accepted by the Supreme Court in the case of *Express Newspapers (Pvt.) Limited and others vs. The Union of India*, 1938. Broadly speaking, wages have been classified into: (1) Minimum Wages, (2) Wages and (3) Living Wages.

There is under any set of economic circumstances a minimum that a worker must have. This minimum is 'need based' and represents a level of wages which are just adequate to satisfy the minimum human needs of a worker and his family. The notion of 'minimum wage' implies that irrespective of any other consideration a worker must receive this wage. If any industry is not in a position to pay even this level of wages then, it is clear that non-labour resources are being utilised inefficiently and should better be utilised in a different channel.

Accordingly, the resolutions adopted at the 15th Indian Labour Conference, 1957, with regard to minimum wage are as under:

1. In calculating the minimum wage, the standard working cost per family should be taken to consist of three consumption units for one earner. The earnings of women and children and adolescents should be disregarded.
2. Minimum food requirement should be calculated on the basis of a net intake of 2700 calories as recommended by Dr. Aykroyd (Dr. Aykrod's Health Bulletin No. 23) for the average Indian adult doing moderate activity.
3. Clothing requirement should be estimated at per capita consumption of 18 yards per annum which would give for the average workers' family of four, a total of 72 yards.
4. In respect of housing, the norms should be minimum rent charged by the government in any area for house provided under the subsidised scheme for low income groups.
5. Fuel, lighting and other miscellaneous items of expenditure should constitute 20 per cent of the total minimum wages.

Even these needs just as any other set of needs cannot be described as the 'minimum' for all the different groups and categories, for they are flexible and relative in respect to time, place, class, etc. Realising the difficulty in applying them to real life situations, no tribunal or wage board has made any attempt to quantitatively define the minimum needs precisely while fixing workers' wages although, every tribunal wage board has made a passing reference to those recommendations.

The concept of fair wages involves a rate sufficiently high to enable the worker to provide a standard family with food, shelter, clothing, medical care and education of children appropriate to his status in life but not at a rate exceeding the wage earning capacity of the class of establishment concerned. A fair wage, thus, is related to a fair work load and the earning capacity.

The Fair Wages Committee set up by the government in 1948 recognised that "no wage policy can be regarded as just or even economically sound unless it encourages increase in the national income and secures to the wage earners a legitimate share of the increase."

The living wage concept is one or more steps higher than fair wage. According to Mr Justice Higgins, the living wage must provide not merely for absolute essentials such as food, shelter and clothing, but for condition of frugal comfort estimated by current human standards including provisions for evil days, etc., with due regard for the special skill of the workman. Fair wage lies between the concept of minimum wage and the concept of living wage.

While the lower limit of the fair wage must obviously be the minimum wage, the upper limit is equally set by what may broadly be called the capacity of industry to pay. This will depend not only on the present economic position of the industry but on its future prospects also. Between these two limits the actual wages will depend on the productivity of labour, the prevailing rates of wages in the same or similar occupations in the same or neighbouring localities, the level of the national income and its distribution, the place of the industry in the economy of the country.

Confining within the boundaries of the fair wage concept, every industry must also strive to ensure fair growth in the remuneration to its workmen. First of all the current purchasing power of workers should be maintained against price rise by providing for adequate neutralisation in respect of the rise in the cost of living so that there is no erosion in their total emoluments in terms of their purchasing power. The workers resist any attempts in direct and visible cut in their wages. But in case of indirect cuts in their wages in the form of erosion, they suffer in silence and misery. This despair on the part of workers leads to low morale, etc., which in turn results in low efficiency and productivity.

Secondly, a reasonable growth in the real earnings of workers should be aimed at improving their living standards, commensurate with their level of productivity, firms' profitability and other factors.

In Table 13.1 per capita daily earnings by industries during the years 1996 and 1997 have been presented. Even though at all industry level the per capita daily earnings showed an increase from ₹ 42.15 in 1996 to ₹ 44.84 in 1997, in many industries, per capita daily earnings have dropped over the year. Incidentally these are the latest data available from Indian Labour Year book.

Table 13.1: Per Capita Daily Earnings by Industries during the years 1996 and 1997 (P)

Code No.	Industry	Per Capita Daily Earnings ₹	
		1996	1997
1	2	3	4
00-06	Agriculture, Hunting, Forestry and Fishing	37.04	36.55
20-21	Manufacture of Food Product	34.61	31.51
22	Manufacture of Beverages, Tobacco and Tobacco Product	40.69	55.39
23	Manufacture of Cotton Textiles	41.85	57.22

Contd...

24	Manufacture of Wool, Silk & man-made Fibre Textiles (except cotton)	58.55	55.74
25	Manufacture of Jute, and other vegetable Fibre textiles (except cotton)	58.18	52.21
26	Manufacture of Textile Products (including Wearing Apparel other than Footwear)	48.16	42.18
27	Manufacture of Wood and Wood Products, Furniture and Fixtures	37.86	50.39
28	Manufacture of Paper & Papers Products & Printing, Publishing and Allied Industries	51.96	48.99
29	Manufacture of Leather & Products of Leather	47.12	41.53
30	Manufacture of Basic Chemicals and Chemical Products (except Products of Petroleum and Coal)	38.14	45.13
31	Manufacture of Rubber Plastic, Petroleum and Coal Products and Processing of Nuclear Fuels	45.34	43.7
32	Manufacture of Non-Metallic Mineral Products	37.07	45.17
33	Basic Metal and Alloys Industries	53.38	46.82
34	Manufacture of Metal Products & Parts except Machinery and Transport Equipment	47.41	55.46
35-36	Manufacturing of Electric/Electronic Machinery, Apparatus, Appliances & Supply and Parts	48.42	50.21
37	Manufacture of Transport Equipment and Parts	49.23	51.80
38	Other Manufacturing Industries	55.91	53.83
39	Repair of Capital Goods	58.78	53.95
40	Electricity Generation, Transmission and Distribution	37.60	49.42
41	Gas and Steam Generation and Distribution through Pipes	46.72	45.78
42	Water Works and Supply	35.42	40.52
50	Construction	35.77	48.49
51	Activities Allied to Construction	53.00	
60	Wholesale Trade in Food, Textile, Live Animals, Beverages and Intoxicants	41.60	60.14
61	Wholesale Trade in Wood, Paper, Skin, Leather and Fur, Fuel, Petroleum, Chemicals Perfumery, Ceramics, Glass and Ores and Metals	32.51	43.01
62	Wholesale Trade in all types of Machinery, Equipment including Transport Equipment	39.07	63.11
63	Wholesale Trade not Elsewhere Classified	25.16	–
64	Commission Agents	38.33	43.30
65	Retail Trade in Food & Food Articles Beverage, Tobacco & Intoxicants	39.74	–
67	Retail Trade in Fuel and other Household Utilities and Durables	35.33	38.60
68	Retail Trade not Elsewhere Classified	42.67	45.01
69	Restaurants and Hotels	37.52	39.25
70	Land Transport	27.32	41.61
71	Water Transport	–	–
72	Air Transport	45.29	
73	Services Incidental to Transport	–	–
74	Storage and Ware Housing Services	39.20	57.10
82	Real Estate and Business Services	39.84	36.43
89	Business Services not elsewhere classified	35.76	55.15

Contd...

90	Public Administration and Defence Services	–	–
91	Sanitary Services	39.84	–
92	Education, Scientific and Research Services	45.46	–
93	Health and Medical Services	51.41	59.36
94	Community Services	–	–
95	Recreational & Cultural Services	48.01	47.74
96	Personal Services	39.43	37.56
97	Repair Services	39.80	51.36
98	International & other Extra Territorial Bodies Services	52.81	–
99	Services not Elsewhere Classified	45.85	30.22
XI	Activities not Adequately Classified	–	25.51
	All Industries	42.15	44.84

Source: Indian Labour Year Book, 1998

Objectives of a Sound Wage Policy

The following are the objectives of an ideal wage and salary policy:

1. To establish good labour relations.
2. To decide on appropriate wages.
3. To decide wages based on individual's capability.
4. To develop a pre-determined scheme for payment of wages.
5. To establish linkages of wage payment with performances.
6. To maintain parity of wages with other organisations.
7. To provide for incentive payment.
8. To guarantee minimum wages.
9. To provide for neutralisation of price rise.
10. To develop a wage structure which can attract talent.

WAGE DETERMINATION

Wage determination involves job evaluation, job design, job assessment, job analysis and job description.

Job Evaluation

Job evaluation has been discussed in detail in a separate unit on Job Analysis and Job Designing. This method was originated in the United States in 1971. Since then the method is in extensive use in industries for wage and salary administration. For practising job evaluation, we must understand the basic process, discussed earlier.

Job Design

Like job evaluation this has also been discussed in the unit on Job Analysis and Job Design. Suitable designing of job facilitate in proper job pricing and compensation management.

Job Assessment

At this stage information about each job is made available to the assessors to facilitate job pricing. This was also discussed earlier.

Job Analysis

This process helps to examine the facts about some specific job and determine the essential job factors. Therefore, the exercise helps to identify the qualities like skill, training experience, etc., required of the worker to perform his jobs satisfactorily. The analysis is primarily based on Job Description Sheet. However, to supplement the analysis further details may be obtained from personal observation and discussion. We have also discussed the process in detail earlier.

Job Description

This process helps to give a title to a job, considering the conditions, tasks and responsibilities involved and qualities required for a job. Even though, the terms 'job description' and 'job specification' are used interchangeably, there is a distinction, like job description process defines the job content, i.e., the conditions, tasks and responsibilities, while job specification denotes the job requirements, i.e. the qualities that are necessary in a worker, to satisfy the demands of the job. Qualities may be either physical or mental attributes or the both.

1. Purpose of the tasks, i.e. the end-result,
2. Frequency of recurrence of the tasks,
3. Accuracy limit,
4. Environment and conditions under which the job has to be done,
5. The tools and equipment that are required to perform the job,
6. Co-ordination and contacts with others required to perform the job,
7. Nature and amount of supervision and instructions required for the job,
8. Type and nature of specialised skills and knowledge required to perform the job,
9. Responsibilities involved in the job,
10. Origin of the job and its end-use, etc.

After recording the above details and its analysis, job-titles are given to designate various occupations. While designating occupations, it may be required to consider a specific job, like the job of a carpenter or the job as a whole like a Systems Executive. Some jobs may be classified or described under some common job-families, where instead of giving any specific title to a job, it is the usual practice to define various grades, like highly-skilled, skilled, semi-skilled or unskilled. Combining jobs in common job-families is done considering the job proximity, like job of a book keeper, accounts assistant, cashier, may be grouped under one common job-family, i.e. clerk.

In the determination of wage differentials and wage structure, job evaluation as a tool has to be thought of with adequate caution. Other techniques, discussed above also to a great extent influence the wage determination process. Additional inputs about job description can be obtained from earlier discussions.

Wage Boards

Wage Boards consist of an impartial Chairman, two other independent members and two or three representatives of workers and employers each. The recommendations of the board are first submitted to the government for its acceptance. After acceptance, the government requests the parties to implement them.

The board is required to take the following points in determining the wage structure:

1. Need-based minimum wage,
2. Industry's capacity to pay,
3. Productivity of labour,
4. Prevailing rates of wages,
5. Level of national income and its distribution,
6. Place of industry in the economy of the country;
7. Need of its development,
8. Requirements of social justice,
9. Adjustment of wage differentials in such a manner as to provide incentives for skill formation.

Collective bargaining is also another important method of wage determination and is very successful in industries. We have discussed this technique in details in a separate unit.

Time Study

Time study technique is also used for wage determination. We have briefly introduced the concept here and then illustrated the method suitably designing a problem.

ILO defined time study as "a technique for determining as accurately as possible from a limited number of observations the time necessary to carry out a given activity at a defined standard of performance". For carrying out a time study, equipments like stopwatch, study board, pencils, slide-rule, etc., are required. The stopwatches are of different types like:

1. Stopwatch which records one minute per revolution by intervals 1/5th of a second with a small hand record 30 minutes;
2. Stopwatch which records one minute per revolution, calibrated in 1/100th of a minute with a small hand record 30 minutes;
3. Decimal-hour stopwatch record 1/100th of an hour per revolution graduated in 1/100th of an hour and a small hand records up to one hour in 1,000 divisions.

Steps in Time Study

Following steps are necessary for carrying out a time study for measurement of work:

1. To collect and complete all available information about the job, which should also include surrounding conditions and so also the attributes of the operators, which are likely to affect the work.
2. To record the details of the method and also to break down different operations into elements.
3. To record the time taken by the operators to perform the operation (element-wise) measuring preferably with a timing device like stopwatch.
4. To assess the working speed of the operators comparing the same with a predetermined normal speed.
5. To convert the observed time to normal time.
6. To decide the rate of allowances which may be given over and above the normal time of the operation.
7. To determine the allowed time for operation.

Problems on Time Study

Time study is a work measurement technique, which is wisely undertaken in industry to decide the standard time and then to compare the time taken by the workmen. Though, it basically helps in pricing a job, it is also used for other purpose like deciding on training requirements, payment of incentives and rewards, etc. Let us try the problem below to understand its computational details.

Example

You have been asked to set the standard time for manufacturing ball point pens based on the following activity details. You have observed the ongoing job for 100 hours and have seen that within this period 1000 ball point pens have been manufactured. Assume that during work, the workmen get personal time allowance @ 10 per cent. Compute standard time for manufacturing a single ball point pen.

Activity	Rate (per cent)	No. of Times Jobs Observed
A	120	200
B	90	300
C	80	500
D	70	100
	Idle Time	200
	Total Observed Time	1300

Solution:

To solve this problem at the outset, it is necessary to compute average cycle time, dividing observed period by number of ball point pens produced, i.e. 100 hours/1000 ball point pens – 1/10 an hour, i.e., 6 minutes.

Thus, 6 minutes on an average is taken for manufacturing a ball point pen.

Now we have to compute activity-wise distribution of time using this formula:

Average cycle time × (observed time/total time) × rating

Average cycle time has already been computed, which is 6 minutes.

Observed time is the activity-specific time, already shown in the problem.

Total time is total observed time. Rating is the perceived rate of efficiency of the rater given in the problem.

(i) Time taken for Activity 'A'

$6 \times (200/1300) \times (120/100) = 1.1$

(ii) Time taken for Activity 'B'

$6 \times (300/1300) \times (90/100) = 1.2$

(iii) Time taken for Activity 'C'

$6 \times (500/1300) \times (80/100) = 1.8$

(iv) Time taken for Activity 'D'

$6 \times (100/1300) \times (70/100) = 0.3$

Total normal time = 4.4

Now, we have to compute standard time using this formula:

(Total activity-wise time or normal Time/(1 – personal fraction time) i.e. $4.4/(1 - 0.1) = 4.4/0.9$ = 4.8 minutes.

DEARNESS ALLOWANCE (DA)

To give effect to price neutralisation, DA is paid over and above the basic wages to ensure that real income of the workers is not falling short. There are several methods of computation of DA, which can be enumerated as follows:

1. ***DA not linked to Consumer Price Index:***

   (a) Flat DA

   (b) Graduated Scale of DA

2. ***DA linked to Consumer Price Index:***

   (a) DA computed according to changes in C.P.I.

   (b) DA linked to pay scales and to C.P.I.

Supreme Court of India has laid down certain criteria for regulating payment of DA as under:

1. Capacity to pay
2. Rates prevailing in comparable concerns in the region
3. Extent of neutralisation of price rise

The views of the National Labour Commission are:

1. The basic wages in all cases should be adjusted to a common base year.
2. DA should be adjusted every time when there is a 5 point change in the C.P.I.
3. Neutralisation should be allowed at the rate of 95 per cent in the non-scheduled employment.
4. Capacity to pay is irrelevant for payment of DA at the minimum level.

OVERTIME WAGES

Overtime wages are calculated on the basis of the working hours prescribed to the several types of workmen. If 36 hours a week are prescribed as working hours, the company should pay extra wages to workmen if they are required to work beyond 36 hours. Usually the rate of wages for a period beyond 36 hours should be at the ordinary rate, while the rate should be double if the workers are required to work more than 48 hours a week for the period beyond 48 hours. However, where wages are paid on a piece-rate basis, the State Government in consultation with the employer concerned and the representatives of the workers, shall fix the time-rate as nearly as possible, considering average rate of earnings of those workers and the rates so fixed shall be deemed to be the ordinary rate of wages of the workers and hence, overtime rate should be decided following the above principles.

Incentive Schemes

Incentives are paid to the workmen over and above the normal wages to regard their good performance. In places, where piece-rate system of wages is existing, payment of incentives is relatively simple as for manufacturing additional units than the standard one, workers can be paid extra wages, which they are supposed to get for each additional unit.

This incentive scheme is known as Straight Piece-Rate Scheme. In time-rate system, however, such incentives are computed following Standard Hour Systems. To illustrate, let us assume a given volume of job is given to a worker for standard 8 hours' work. If the worker is able to complete the job within 6 hours, then for hours saved, i.e. 2 hours, he should be given the incentives duly upgrading his hourly wage rate apportioning his 8 hours rate for 6 hours. Let us assume 8 hours are needed as standard time for completing a job and the rate per hour is ₹ 1. If the worker finishes the work in 6 hours, he will also get ₹ 8, which upgrades his hourly wage rate then from ₹ 1 to ₹ 1.33.

There are several other incentive schemes too, which can be briefly stated as follows:

1. ***Barth System:*** Under this system, there is no minimum guaranteed wage. The formula (considering hourly wage rate of ₹ 1) is as follows:

   Wage = Standard time (8 hours) × time taken (6 hrs) × hourly rate ₹ 1= ₹ 7 (approx.)

2. ***Bedaux System:*** This system is also called 'units' or 'point' system. It has a guaranteed basic rate like the Halsey and Rowan Systems. Under this system each minute or standard time is expressed in terms of units or points after a detailed time study. The guaranteed basic wage is paid up to 60 points per hour scored by the worker. Points earned above 60 are paid at 75 to 100 per cent of the basic wage rate (the standard daily rate for the job which is always higher than the minimum guaranteed wage).

3. ***Taylorian System:*** In this scheme there are two piece-rates one lower and one higher plus a bonus paid as a percentage of the time rate. Obviously such a system would automatically discourage low production and would be installed where the average performance is well below expectations.

4. ***Merrick Differential Piece Rate System:*** Under this system there are three piece rates:

   (a) Up to, say, 83 per cent of standard output – piece-rate + 10 per cent of time rate as bonus.

   (b) Above 83 per cent and upto 100 per cent of standard output – same piece rate + 20 per cent of time rate.

   (c) Above 100 per cent of standard output – same piece rate but no bonus.

5. ***Gantt Task System:*** This has three stages of payment:

   (a) Below the standard performance, only the minimum guaranteed wage is to be paid.

   (b) At the standard performance, this wage + 20 per cent of the time rate will be paid as bonus.

(c) When the standard is exceeded, higher piece-rate is paid but there is no bonus.

The main objective of this scheme is to raise the performance up to the standard level which is the task set before the workers.

6. ***The Emerson Empiric System:*** Under this system, standard time is established for each job. The efficiency of the worker is determined by dividing the time taken into the standard time. Up to 67 per cent efficiency, the worker is paid at this time rate and from this point to 100 per cent a bonus of 1 per cent is paid for every additional 1 per cent output. At 100 per cent efficiency, a bonus of 20 per cent is paid.

7. ***Accelerating Premium System:*** This provides for a guaranteed minimum wage for output below the standard. For low and average increase in output above the standard small increments in earnings are allowed. Increasingly large earnings are conceded for the above average output, the increment being different for each 1 per cent increase in output.

8. ***Scanlon Plan:*** The Scanlon Plan was designed to involve the workers in making suggestions for reducing the cost of operation and improving the working methods and sharing in the gains of increased productivity. The Rucker Plan is similar to the Scanlon Plan, the only difference being that in the latter the incentive earnings are calculated on the basis of the 'value added' by the manufacturing process. The Kaiser Plan is also like these – a gain-sharing scheme. While the Rucker Plan excludes all the supply and material costs, the Kaiser Plan excludes all costs over which the workers have no control.

9. ***Halsey Premium Plan:*** It guarantees a fixed time wage to slow workers and, at the same time, offers extra pay to efficient workers. Extra pay in the form of bonus is given based on the amount of time saved by the worker, which is calculated @ 33½ per cent of the time saved. Thus, the cost of labour is reduced because of the percentage premium system.

10. ***Rowan Premium Plan:*** Under this plan, the time saved is expressed as a percentage of the time allowed and the hourly rate of pay is increased by that percentage so that total earnings of the worker are the total number of hours multiplied by the increased hourly wages.

11. ***Employee Stock Option Plans (ESOP):*** It is a recent introduction which provide opportunities to employees to participate in profit sharing, buying shares of the companies under preferential quota at a preferential price (less than the market value). ESOP strengthens the loyalty of the employees and also increase their motivation level.

Computation of Incentives

Appropriate incentive determination using different incentive methods has a direct relation with manpower requirement analysis. Some of the incentive schemes when applied in a group work environment act as wonder. While on the contrary some individual incentive schemes may be effective in cases where individual performance receive more weightage. Here we have detailed some of the incentive methods.

Straight Piece Rate Methods

This method considers a fixed rate per piece, which remains constant for different output level. Under this system workers get paid strictly as per their output. Most of the organisations follow this method as a substitute for time rate. The major difficulty in this system is that workers do not get any guaranteed payment for their work, excepting some basic hourly rate, which again depends on achieving some fixed level of output. We can illustrate this using following formula:

Work Piece Rate = Adjusted hourly rate/Average production per hour

Using this formula, let us consider the day's earning of a particular worker in the following case:

Example

A company pays a worker for a given job as under:

Basic hourly rate	:	₹ 6
Increase on rate	:	25%
Standard hourly output level for the job	:	800 Units

The worker in a particular day of 8 hour work produced 7000 units. Compute the day's earning for the worker.

Solution:

Basic hourly rate	:	₹ 6
Increase on rate	:	25%
Adjusted hourly rate	:	1.25 × 6 = ₹ 7.50
Average output per hour	:	800 Units
Therefore, hourly workpiece rate	=	Adjusted hourly rate/Average output per hour
	=	7.50/800
	=	7.50×8^{-3}

Hence for producing 7000 units in a 8 hour work day, the worker will receive as under:

Day	Day's Production	Work Piece Rate	Day's earnings
1	7000	7.50×8^{-3}	₹ 65.63

Differential Piece Rate Methods

Taylor's Method

There is no guaranteed minimum wage. Workers are required to produce at 100% level of efficiency as specified by established standard time. There are two piece rates specified for each job. A lower piece rate is applicable for performance below the standard level and a higher piece rate is applicable for performance higher than the standard level.

Example

A company using time study fixed the standard output level per hour for a given job as 125 units. Hourly labour rate is ₹ 7. The company applies two differential rates for determining earnings of a worker. Workers get 80% of the standard piece rate for below standard level of performance and 120% of the standard piece rate for above standard level of performance.

Calculate the earnings of a worker in two following cases for two different days:

1. In a 8 hours work day when the worker produces 900 units
2. In a 8 hours work day when the worker produces 1200 units

Solution:

Standard output per hour	=	125 units
Labour rate per hour	=	₹ 7
Standard piece rate	=	7/125 = 0.056
Lower piece rate	=	0.056 × 0.8 = 0.045
Higher piece rate	=	0.056 × 1.20 = 0.067
Earning of the worker in day 1	=	900 × 0.045 = ₹ 40.5
Earning of the worker in day 2	=	1200 × 0.067 = ₹ 80.4

Notice here day 1 the worker produced less than the standard level. With 125 unit per hour, the standard output level for 8 hour work in a day should have been 1000 units.

Merrick Differential Piece Rate

Here also there is no guaranteed minimum wage. A standard time is established for each job and workers are paid accordingly.

Example

In a particular week, a worker has produced one item as under:

Day	Quantity Produced
1	170
2	185
3	210
4	195
5	220
6	198

Standard output per day of 8 hours work is 190 units and hourly rate is ₹ 5. Calculate the earnings of the worker for different days of the week using Merrick's **Differential Piece Rate Method.**

Solution:

Standard output per day of 8 hours work = 190 Units

Labour hourly rate = ₹ 5

Rate differentials:

- For output upto 83% = Basic Piece Rate
- For output above 83% and up to 100% = Basic Piece Rate + 10% of hourly rate as bonus
- For output above 100% = Basic Piece Rate + 20% of hourly rate as bonus

Standard output per hour = 190/8 = 24 units

Basic Rate per piece = 5/24 = ₹ 0.21

We can now tabulate the earnings of the worker for the entire week as under:

Day	Standard Output	Actual Output	Output Performance	Rate applicable	Day's earnings (quantity x rate) - in Rupees
1	190	170	89%	Basic Rate (BR) + 20%	170x1.10x0.21 = 39.27
2	190	185	97%	- do -	185x1.10x0.21 = 42.74
3	190	210	111%	BR + 20%	210x1.20x0.21 = 52.92
4	190	195	103%	- do -	195x1.20x0.21 = 49.14
5	190	220	116%	- do -	220x1.20x0.21 = 55.44
6	190	198	104%	- do -	198x1.20x0.21 = 49.90

Gantt Task System

The only difference between this system and earlier systems is that it provides minimum guaranteed wage even if the performance is below the standard level.

Example

The hourly wage rate for an worker is fixed at ₹ 5. The standard time set for the job is 10 minutes per unit. High rate for the job (above the standard level) is ₹ 1.70 per unit. Assume the worker has produced output for the entire week as per the figure given in the 'Actual output column' in the table. Compute day-wise earnings of the worker for the week.

Solution:

Standard output per day = Standard time per unit × 8 hours (assuming 8 hours work per day)

Standard time per unit	=	12 minutes
Standard output per hour	=	60/12 = 5 Units
Standard output per day	=	5 × 8 = 40 Units

DAY-WISE EARNINGS OF THE WORKER

Day	Actual Output	Actual output as percentage of standard	Payment Rate	Day's earnings (in rupees)		
1	36	90	Day wages	5 x 8	=	40
2	44	110	High piece rate	44 x 1.70	=	75
3	56	140	- do -	56 x 1.70	=	95
4	50	125	- do -	50 x 1.70	=	85
5	40	100	Day wages + 20% Bonus	1.20 x 5 x 8	=	48
6	50	125	High Piece rate	50 x 1.70	=	85

Emerson's Efficiency Plan

Under this plan efficient workers are rewarded at an increasing rate with the increase of their performance, measured in terms of saving of time. Main features of the plan are as under:

1. Guaranteed day wages are paid irrespective of performance.
2. Standard output is determined based on past performance, which is taken at 100% efficiency.
3. Performance of the workers is measured in terms of the efficiency achieved, comparing actual output with the standard output, using following formula:

   Efficiency per-centage = (Actual Output/Standard Output) × 100
4. Incentive bonus is paid if workers efficiency exceed two thirds (66.67%) of the standard performance (taken as 100%). Incentive rates vary with the increase of performance beyond two thirds (66.77%) at an increasing rate.

Efficiency Rate	Remuneration
Below 66.67%	No incentive bonus only time wages
Over 66.67% but up to 100%	Time wages + proportionate Bonus for Incremental output percentages, rising up to 20% at 100% level of efficiency
Over 100%	Time wages + 20% bonus + 1% Bonus for each 1% increase in efficiency beyond 100%.

The worker is assigned different jobs in a day and for each job unit the company has fixed a standard time. Based on the tabulated information, compute the total earnings for the day.

Job code	Quantity Produced	Standard time set per unit (in hours)	Time taken (in hours)
A-1	2	½	1.25
B-3	4	½	1.75
C-1	20	1/3	5.00

So, bonus for each job has to be computed separately. The calculation can be tabulated as under:

Job Code	Standard time for the job (in hours) – Qty. x Standard time per unit	Time taken (in hours)	Bonus earned, if any (@50% of time saved) in ₹
A-1	2 x ½ = 1 hour	1.25	Nil
B-3	4 x ½ = 2 hour	1.75	0.625
C-1	20 x 1/3 = 6.67 hour	5.00	4.175
		Total	Rs. 4.8

Total earnings for the day = (8 x 5) + 4.8 = ₹ 44.8

Rowan Premium Plan

Rowan Premium Plan is different from Halsey Premium Plan in respect of computation of incentive bonus payable to worker. Incentive bonus here is not calculated at a fixed percentage of time saved. It is the ratio of the actual time taken to the standard time of the job. Therefore, incentive bonus is computed using following formula:

$$\frac{T}{S}(S-T)\times R$$

Where; T = Actual time taken by the worker

S = Standard time set for the job

(S-T) = Difference between standard and actual time

R = Hourly rate of wages

Example

In a factory, standard time set for a job is 8 hours and the basic wage rate is ₹ 3 per hour. The workers receive normal wage for their actual work and incentive bonus at a fixed proportion of the time saved. Compute incentive bonus payable to workers for different level of actual time, as mentioned in the 'actual time' column.

Actual time Taken (T)	Standard time (S)	Time Saved (S – T)	Incentive earned $\frac{T}{S}(S-T)\times R$
8	8	0	0
7	8	1	2.625
6	8	2	4,5
5	8	3	5.625
4	8	4	6.0
3	8	5	5.625
2	8	6	4.5
1	8	7	2.625

It is evident from the table that when time saved is beyond 50% of the standard time, workers get bonus at a diminishing rate. This is the major defect of the scheme as it discourages workers to save time more than 50% of the standard time.

The Scanlon Plan

It is a popular group incentive scheme, which relates labour cost ration to the total sales value to measure labour effectiveness. Incentive bonus is paid to the workers based on the percentage reduction in the labour to sales ratio, comparing between base period and assessment period. The formula for computing percentage reduction in labour index is as under:

$$\frac{\dfrac{L_b - L_a}{R_b - R_a}}{\dfrac{L_b}{R_b}} \times 100$$

Where; L_b = Total labour cost for the base month

R_b = Total sales value for the base month

L_a = Total labour cost for the assessment month

R_a = Total sales value for the assessment month

$\frac{L_b}{R_b}$ = Standard labour to sales ratio for the base month

$\frac{L_a}{R_a}$ = Actual labour to sales ratio for the assessment month.

Example

A company employs 150 workers. Sales during the base month was ₹ 15 lakhs. For the same period, labour cost was ₹ 2.5 lakhs. Compute the group incentives payable, if any, to the workers in following two situations:

(a) Sales value is ₹ 16 lakhs against labour cost of ₹ 2.25 lakhs.

(b) Sales value is ₹ 16 lakhs against labour cost of ₹ 2.8 lakhs.

Solution:

(a) Labour cost during the base month (L_b) = ₹ 2.5 lakhs

Sales value during the base month (R_b) = ₹ 15 lakhs

Standard Labour to Sales ratio $\frac{L_b}{R_b} = \frac{L_b}{R_b} \times 100$

$= \frac{2.5}{15} \times 100 = 16.67\%$

Labour cost for the assessment month (L_a) = ₹ 2.25 lakhs

Sales value for the assessment month (R_a) = ₹ 16 lakhs

Actual labour to sales ratio during the assessment month

$$= \frac{L_a}{R_a} \times 100$$

$$= \frac{2.5}{16} \times 100$$

$$= 14.06\%$$

Here the actual labour to sales ratio is lower than the standard labour to sales ratio. Therefore, employees would be entitled to receive incentive bonus as under:

$$\frac{\frac{L_b}{R_b} - \frac{L_a}{R_a}}{\frac{L_b}{R_b}} \times 100$$

$$= 16.57 - 14.06 / 16.67 \times 100$$

$$= 2.61 / 16.67 \times 100 = 15.66\% \text{ (approximately).}$$

(b) In situation (b), this would be as under:

L_a = ₹ 2.8 lakhs

R_a = ₹ 16 lakhs

$\frac{L_a}{R_a} \times 100$ = ₹ 17.5%

In this case since actual labour to sales ratio is higher than the standard labour to sales ratio, workers would not be entitled to receive any incentive bonus. Hence their wages would be restricted to fixed rate.

The Bedeaux Point Plan

Under this plan minute is considered as time unit. For each job standard time in minutes are determined. Unit of measurement under Bedeaux point is named as ***B***. Therefore, if standard time for a job is 6 hours, it is expressed as 360 ***Bs***. If the workers fail to complete a job within the standard time or just finish the same within the standard time are paid just the normal time rate. If, however, they can complete their work earlier, they receive incentive bonus equal to the wages for the time saved, measured in terms of excess of ***B*** points over the actual time taken. Incentive bonus is paid to the workers normally @ 75% of the time saved. Rest 25% goes to the supervisors.

Let us explain the plan using following illustration:

Hourly rate for workers (R) = ₹ 6

Standard time for the job (S) = 360 Bs (6 hours)

Actual time taken by the workers for the job (T)

= 300 Bs (5 hours)

Value of time saved = 360 – 300/60 × 6 = ₹ 6

Total wages payable = S × R + 75% of the value of time saved

= 6 × 6 + (75/100 × 6)

= 36 + (0.75 × 6)

= 36 + 4.5 = ₹ 40.5

Priestman Production Plan

This is also a popular group incentive plan, where employees are paid a guaranteed time wage and incentive bonus for increase in productivity in proportion to the increase in per-capita output. Under the scheme, a standard output level is determined on mutual agreement between the employer and the employees. Then actual output is compared with the standard output to decide about incentive bonus. Percentage of productivity bonus payable to each employee is determined as per following formula:

$$\frac{\frac{P_a}{W_a} - \frac{P_b}{W_b}}{P_a} \times 100$$

Where, P_a = Actual production during the assessment month

W_a = Number of workers in employment during the assessment month

P_b = Standard production in the base month

W_b = Number of workers in the employment during the base month

$\frac{P_a}{W_a}$ = Actual production per worker during the assessment month

$\frac{P_b}{W_b}$ = Standard production per workers during the base month

Example

A steel plant employs 500 workers. Standard output of steel is fixed at 1000 tonne per month. As per the agreement, each worker is entitled to get productivity bonus for percentage increase in production over the standard output level. Compute bonus, payable, if any, to workers is following two situations:

(a) Output has increased to 1200 tonnes but number of workers engaged during the corresponding period increased 550.

(b) Output is 1100 tonnes workers engaged is 520.

Solution:

Standard output in the base month (P_b) 1000 Tonne

Standard output per employee $\frac{P_b}{W_b} = \frac{1000}{500} = 2$ Tonne

(a) Output during the assessment month (P_a) = 1200 Tonne

Number of employees during the assessment month (W_a) = 550

Output per employee during the assessment month $\left(\frac{P_a}{W_a}\right) = \frac{1200}{550} = 2.182$ Tonne

Percentage increase in production per Employee $\dfrac{\frac{P_a}{W_a} - \frac{P_b}{W_b}}{\frac{P_a}{W_a}} \times 100$

$$= \frac{2.182 - 2}{2.182} \times 100$$

$$= 8.34\%$$

Hence in this case all workers would receive a productivity linked bonus of 8.34% over their basic pay.

(b) Output per employee during the assessment month $\frac{P_a}{W_a}$ is $\frac{1100}{520} = 2.12$

Percentage increase in production per employee $= \frac{2.12 - 2}{2.12} \times 100 = 5.66\%$

Incentives and its correlation with HRP is obviously for incremental changes in productivity percentage due to motivation of employees for increased earnings.

PERFORMANCE-BASED PAY

Designing performance based pay involves rewarding employees as per their performance or results achieved or contribution to organisation's overall performance either as an individual employee or as part of the group. It shifts focus from compensation models based on job worth and employee skills. It cannot be tailor made as it depends on variety of factors like;

nature of business, nature of technology, attitude of unions and HR strategies of the organisation. It has the potentiality to reduce labour costs while sustaining motivation of employees and competitiveness of the organisation. Before introducing performance related pay it is important to study the likely impact on employees motivation and create performance oriented culture in the organisation. It involves developing a proactive attitude through dissemination of proper information, consultation, communication and training and development of employees.

There are different types of performance linked reward schemes. These can be classified into following categories:

1. Schemes that are based on individual performance, like; piece rates, merit pay and commission.
2. Schemes which are based on small group performance, when such group is engaged in homogenous nature of activity and their performance is traceable in terms of increased quality of output.
3. Schemes based on contribution to productivity and profitability, where such achievement is measured in terms of a pre-determined formula.
4. Schemes that relate pay to profits based on a pre-determined formula.
5. Schemes based on productivity bargaining.
6. Employee stock options plan (ESOP).
7. Competency based pay.

We have discussed these methods while explaining various incentive schemes in the chapter. However, competency based pay is the recent addition in performance linked reward systems. Competencies are critical determinant of performance. Competencies are attributes, which encompass skills, knowledge, values, attitude and behavioural characteristics and influence performance in present and future jobs. Therefore, rewarding employees for acquiring competencies is thought of a better way of designing compensation in professional organisations. This is now widely practised in knowledge intensive organisations. However, as explained at the outset, no particular system may hold good for an organisation. It has to be tailor made based on variety of factors indicated earlier and ultimately aligned to HR strategies. While designing a performance-based reward system, it is important to follow certain steps in order to ensure its appropriateness and efficiency. Such steps require at the outset to customise/tailor-made the schemes based on typical characteristics of an organisation. While customising the schemes, it is important to understand the objectives. Objectives guide the selection of performance measures and the basis. Once these are established, designing the system becomes much easier. While designing the system it is also important to consider likely impact of such schemes on future changes in production process, product-mix and prices of inputs and outputs. Such changes being prompted by exogenous factors, we can categorises these as external influencers. This apart, rule for distribution among employees should be developed in simple and unambiguous manner, so that computation become much easier and the systems do not lead to significant variation in pay. It has to be also based on principles of equity and it should not substitute wage increases. While designing the system it is also important to involve unions. This ensures transparency and support, which are important prerequisite for its success. Finally the systems also require periodic review for time to time modifications.

FRINGE BENEFITS

The fringe benefits have often been described as 'welfare expenses', 'wage supplements', 'perquisites other than wages', 'sub-wages' and 'social charges'. ILO has defined fringe benefits as under:

Wages are often augmented by special cash benefits, by the provision of medical and other services or by payments in kind that form part of the wage for expenditure or other goods and services. In addition, workers commonly receive such benefits as holidays with pay, low-cost meals, low rent housing, etc. Such additions to the wage proper are sometimes referred to as 'fringe benefits' . However, it is important to note that 'benefits' which have no relation to employment or wages should not be regarded as 'fringe benefits', despite the fact that it may constitute a significant part of workers total income. Fringe benefits account for the services rendered to workers and their families by an industrial enterprise for the purpose of raising their moral, material, social and cultural levels and to prepare them for a better life.

From the above discussion, therefore, we can list following important features of fringe benefits:

- Fringe benefits are supplementary forms of compensation.
- Such benefits are paid not as incentives but based on membership of the employees with the organisation.
- Benefits are not linked to performance, these are extended as a condition of employment.
- Such benefits raise the standards of living of employees, therefore, contributes to enrichment of quality of work life (QWL).
- Some of the benefits may be statutory while others may be voluntary.

Payment of fringe benefits in India are primarily made for reasons like; employee demands, trade union pressure, employers' preference to motivate employees, as social security measures and finally to create a motivating environment.

From organisation's point of view, administration of fringe benefits is done considering the following important aspects:

1. ***Objectives of Benefits:*** Primarily fringe benefits accomplish certain objectives like; external competitiveness, cost effectiveness, satisfaction of employees' needs and complying with statutory requirements. Therefore, while establishing objectives, organisations need to consider several factors and design the benefits package to meet those objectives.
2. ***Assessment of Environmental Factors:*** Internal and external environmental factors need to be assessed to understand their influence on benefits. While internal factors are

influenced by trade unions, external factors are dependent on Government polices and regulations, covering wage regulations, tax policies and different other laws related to employee benefits and welfare. Trade unions as an internal agent bargain for improving employee benefits and services.

3. ***Assessing Competitiveness:*** To benchmark benefits, organisations often cull the competitors' information on benefits package. Such information can be obtained from the published data or by instituting a focussed survey, retaining the services of consultants. However, organisations may not always try to match their benefits package with the competitors. They may even surpass the competitors' package to attract and retain the talent.

4. ***Communicating the Benefits:*** In this phase, organisation communicates to employees the indirect benefits programmes and give it wide publicity through house journals, with clear indication about its benefits to the employees. Since fringe benefits are indirect remuneration, which are not printed in pay slips, employees should know their usefulness. Such knowledge enhances their motivation level and contributes to increased productivity. In terms of high employee benefits, TISCO and Bata are two ranked organisations in India. While TISCO is successful in its communication with employees and derives motivational benefits out of it, Bata is not, as largely their employees are ignorant about it. This was observed by the author while doing a research study. Incidentally Bata is more strike prone despite such high cost of indirect remuneration.

5. Finally, the usefulness of fringe benefits need to be ascertained through evaluation and control. Such review facilitates re-designing of benefits package, matching organisational objectives and strategies. Evaluation is done using following parameters:

   - To what extent employee earnings have improved?
   - To what extent benefits package are able to attract and retain talent?
   - Does the employee feel motivated?
   - Does it contribute to any improvement in Industrial Relations?
   - To what extent it could reduce employees' turnover?
   - Is their any improvement in employees' productivity?
   - To what extent employees' morale has increased?

Answers to the above questions, therefore, facilitate realistic assessment of benefits package and help in redefining the objectives again.

Cost control on fringe benefit is also important from an organisational point of view. To a great extent an organisation can reduce the cost burden by outsourcing. We have discussed these issues in unit on Human Resource Costs.

Since some of the fringe benefits are given in the form of deferred benefits, they are categorised under non-wage-labour cost (NWLC) group. Organisations often find it beneficial to give such benefits integrating the same to paid wage cost to attract and retain young people, who are in their exploratory age group.

Fringe benefits can broadly be classified under six main heads as under:

1. Extra payment for time worked (over time, weekend holidays shift premiums, etc.)
2. Payment for time not worked (lunch period and rest time, medical care time, sick leave, maternity leave, death in family leave, grievance handling, voting time, paid holidays and vacations, severance pay and lay-off, etc.).
3. Monetary prizes for special activities and performance anniversary award, quality bonus, waste reduction, safety awards, attendance bonus, suggestion plan award, etc.
4. Bonus payment.
5. Payment for personal security and financial protection – medical care, old-age pension, unemployment insurance, family allowance, compensation for disability and death, housing, room and board allowance, etc.
6. Payment for the welfare facilities like maintaining dining room, cultural and recreational facilities, etc.

Employee Services

These services are those which are provided by the organisations, in addition to the usual fringe benefits, either at no cost to the employee or at highly subsidised rate. Such services include eating facilities, transportation facilities, child care facilities, educational services, flexible working hours, etc.

EXECUTIVE COMPENSATION

Executive compensation issue directly relates to organisational performance. On the one hand, high burden of executive compensation reduces organisational competitiveness; on the other hand, less competitive executive compensation gives rise to higher rate of attrition level of executives and consequential business loss for the organisation. Hence, effective executive compensation design is what we look for in today's organisation.

Executive compensation has various dimensions. Gomez-Mejia (1994) conducted the most thought provoking research and focused on such dimensions as the size of the organisation, performance of the organisation and the individual characteristics of executives. Likewise, executive compensation design issues may also have the consequences of pay level and pay risk, depending on the employment practices of the organisation.

Effective executive compensation design motivates executives and makes them the perfect enablers to achieve the business results. Executives contribute to critical performance areas and thereby, enable the organisations to achieve the business results. While designing executive compensation, it is not only important to understand the base salary, but also various short- and long-term incentives (STIs and LTIs). STIs and LTIs need not be always in cash, it may include the stock options and other innovative deferrals like, loyalty bonus (tagged with the vesting period), golden parachute schemes, etc. While loyalty bonus becomes payable to executives after they complete certain years of service with the organisation, golden parachute scheme enables executives to enjoy the privilege of pay protection in the event of merger or acquisition of the company. Particularly, when an organisation is acquired by another company, executives become the first casualty as they face the threat of job cut and the cut in compensation level. With the availability of golden parachute scheme, these aspects are protected. Hence, availability of this scheme motivates executives.

While designing executive compensation, it is important for the organisation, right at the outset to help the executives to achieve their financial goals. Payment of increased executive compensation package no doubt motivates executives and increases their retention, but it may also adversely affect the profitability of the organisation. Hence, organisations always need to design executive compensation, adopting various innovative approaches to ensure its optimisation.

One of the most important components of executive compensation is performance aligned variable pay in the form of bonuses, commissions, profit sharing, etc. For executives, base pay considers the fixed salary and prerequisites. Along with the base pay, executives enjoy the employment status.

We can design the tentative list of executive compensation as under:

- Base Salary
- Annual Incentives
- Long-term Capital Accumulation
- Deferred Compensation Arrangements
- Supplemental Benefits and Perquisites
- Special Severance and Retirement Arrangements
- Employment and Change of Control Agreements

Based on the above discussions, we can list some of the theoretical issues pertaining to executive compensation as under:

- *Agency Theory:* The basic premise of this theory lies in the assumption that shareholders are the agents of the company and they delegate control to executives to represent their ownership interest. While doing so, executive compensation is designed, keeping in view the mutual interest of both the executives and the organisations.
- *Tournament Theory:* According to this theory, executive compensation is the prize in a series of tournaments or contests. Winners of the tournament at one level enter the next tournament. In other words, an executive's promotion to a higher rank signifies a win and more lucrative compensation represents the prize.
- *Social Comparison Theory:* This theory suggests designing of compensation by comparing with similar individuals.

- *Balance Sheet Approach:* This approach provides expatriates the standard of living, they normally enjoy in their own country. Indian Software companies or other companies when depute their executives and employees abroad allow their current salary to accumulate and provide separate salary/compensation to accommodate their cost of living in countries where they are posted.

- *Headquarters based pay:* Compensation to all, according to the rate used at the headquarters.

- *Golden handcuffs:* Compensation components earned over a period of time that assist in retaining an employee. Many organisations practice this approach to avoid attrition. Some organisations deliberately provide a designation and salary to newly recruited or relatively less experienced employees, disproportionate to their deserving level. Say, an MBA with 2 years experience, is given a designation of Vice President with a compensation package much higher than the market benchmark. This dissuades the young executives to leave the job as they know it well, they will not get a befitting salary and status in other organisations. In India, such practices are evident in many new generation companies. Another example of golden handcuffs may be giving loyalty bonus points or phantom stock for every year of completed service with a cap (qualifying services) of 5 or 10 years service. This means that to get the benefit, employees should remain with the company.

- *Competency based pay:* Pay related directly to the kinds and levels of competencies required in the performance of the work/job.

- *Golden parachutes:* Provide pay and benefits to executives after their termination resulting from a change in ownership or corporate takeover. This is particularly for very senior level executives, who may dictate this condition in their terms of employment to protect their interests in the event of take over. However, in India, some recent judgments of Supreme Court questioned the sanctity of such practices, leaving it to the discretion of the acquiring organisation to alter or not to alter the service conditions of employees of the organisation which is being acquired. A Hay Group study in 2006 shows the French executives' golden parachutes are the highest, as they receive double of their salary and bonus in their golden parachute.

  An alternative to golden parachutes is the golden handshake plan. With the provision of golden handshake in the terms of appointment of executives, they become eligible for significant severance package, when they get fired or retired or even required to quit due to organisational restructuring.

- *Cafeteria plan:* For executives, options for different nature of benefits is commonly termed as cafeteria plan. For example, health insurance, group-term life insurance and flexible spending accounts, all represent medical benefits. Executives may select either of the alternatives as compensation benefit. Cafeteria plan is also evident in some Indian organisations which give the employees the flexibility to choose between the contributory provident fund and pension.

- ***Profit sharing plan:*** It provides direct or indirect payments based on organisation's profitability, apart from regular compensation. Although employee stock options fit here as a good example, more applicable fit is Tata Group's EVA plan.

SUMMARY

Wages and salary administration is one of the major HR functions today. While compliance with procedures and regulations is one aspect, cost to the organisation and employees' motivation are other aspects between which HR managers need to trade-off. In percentage terms, salary and wages and bonus taken together are still major causal factors of industrial disputes in India. Hence determining wages based on certain defined methodologies should receive priority. Linking wages to performance is again a major issue. Suitable incentive schemes need to be identified to reward good performers. Fringe benefits again another major instrument for employee motivation. Organisations can be innovative in designing employee compensation considering various aspects.

KEYWORDS

Minimum Wages	Job Evaluation
Fair Wages	Job Design
Living Wages	Job Assessment
ESOP	Job Analysis
Time Study	Job Description
Dearness Allowance	Incentive Schemes
Quality of Work Life (QWL)	Employee Services
	Flexible Working Hours (FWH)

REVIEW QUESTIONS

1. What are the important objectives of a wage policy? Distinguish between fair wages and living wages.

2. Describe some important techniques of wage determination.

3. To what extent job evaluation technique is useful for wage determination? What are the different types of job evaluation? Which type you consider better and why?

4. Describe the role of time study in wage determination.

5. Describe various incentive schemes. Which type you consider better and why?

6. What way fringe benefits help in employee motivation?

7. What are the components of executive compensation? Which components do you feel are more important for retention of executives?

8. Examine different theories of executive compensation. Which theories do you consider more applicable for a labour intensive manufacturing organisation?

9. Write short notes on:

   (a) Tournament Theory

   (b) Agency Theory

   (c) Golden Handcuffs

   (d) LTIs

   (e) Scanlon Plan

CASE STUDY 1

THE FAILED JOB CHANGE

Nikhil has joined as Director of an organisation during early March, 2001 in New Delhi, shifting from Calcutta. During the selection process, the committee duly considered his earlier pay package and has given him a proportionate rise in pay adding also the tax savings which he will accrue due to splitting of 50 per cent of his pay as reimbursement. He was happy for such compensation design, as his savings will be more in his new position. Within two weeks of his joining, government has issued a notification, declaring ceiling on all perquisites and bringing all reimbursements given as perquisites within the ambit of tax net. Nikhil raised this issue and asked for reprieve with upward revision of his compensation package. The company pleaded its helplessness as government orders are beyond their control and any revision at this stage will set a bad precedence to other employees of the organisation. He was told to continue and wait for the next revision after a year, when these issues will be taken care of.

Salary information in the company is not confidential. It is so transparent that even the lowest rung of the organisation knows what others get. Internally employees feel de-motivated when they find their pay raise is disproportionate to the pay raise of their bosses. The company has a system to give Diwali gifts to all in cash and kind. This is kept strictly confidential and nobody knows what others are getting. The Board approves the total amount for this purpose and distributes among employees, keeping in view their performance and hierarchy. Performance feedbacks are obtained from the structured performance appraisal system.

Nikhil was tipped off that he will be able to reduce his loss through the Diwali gift and hence he should not feel de-motivated at this stage. During early November, 2001, Nikhil received a sealed packet with a gift cheque of ₹ 10,000 and gift vouchers worth ₹ 20,000. Next morning he received a phone call from the Chairman, who asked him to indicate his feelings when he met him in person during the afternoon. In between, Nikhil did a detailed computation in consultation with his Chartered Accountant and found that he cannot get him absolved from tax burden from this gift amount as he has to show this in 'other income category' and pay about 33 per cent towards tax. A visibly perturbed Nikhil decides to quit. He loses all hopes for re-negotiation and sends his 3 months' notice to the Chairman.

Questions

1. Do you think Nikhil is right in his stand?
2. What could be the alternatives for the organisation to reduce the pay gap?
3. Should the Chairman initiate any action to retain Nikhil considering his outstanding contributions?

CASE STUDY 2

GEOMAC'S CATCH-22 IN COMPENSATION DESIGN

Compensation discrimination is a serious flaw in compensation design in organisations. Many organisations often ignore the diversity issues and discriminate compensation becoming gender biased. GeoMac is a computer hardware assembler in Chandigarh. Computer hardware semis are procured by the company from Southeast Asian countries and assembled in a plant in a suburb of Chandigarh where representation of male and female employees is 60:40. Computer hardware assembling jobs are very mechanical and hardly require any skill inputs. Hence, job evaluation and compensation designing perspective is literally redundant in this case. GeoMac recruited SSLC passed candidates with high marks in science and mathematics paper, who can understand the basic circuit designs and soldering jobs. All the newly recruited employees are required to undergo one week training and then, are given placement, which is segmented in various stages. The final stage of the job, i.e., stage 4, is allocated to diploma engineers who are highly skilled to test the functionality and who can also make good the bad workmanships in earlier stages, if any. Obviously from this level, the company follows scientific compensation designs based on job evaluation and several performance criteria.

At the workers' level, the company negotiates the wages individually and based on the negotiated figure, decide the compensation package. Female employees alleged that they are being paid less by the company. The management has never considered compensation disparity as an issue. However, with the increased awareness about the workers' rights and privileges, female employees formed their independent union to persuade the company to enforce pay equity with their male counterparts. Based on their complaint, a prima facie charge of disparity has been framed against the company by the labour department of the ministry and they have been asked to clarify the charges, before issue of any stricture by the government for such discriminatory compensation designs.

Question

You have been given the following wage data by the company and then, asked to analyse, whether there exists any such discrimination, traceable to gender biased employment practices by the company.

No.	Employee ID	Gender	Salary per year (in rupee terms)	
1	1-23-46	Female	22,100	
2	1-23-17	Male	22,200	
3	1-23-19	Male	22,300	
4	1-23-27	Male	22,400	
5	1-23-44	Female	22,500	
6	1-23-47	Female	22,600	
7	1-23-48	Female	22,700	**Median Value**
8	1-22-12	Female	22,800	
9	1-22-15	Female	22,900	
10	1-22-18	Female	23,000	
11	1-23-55	Male	23,200	
12	1-23-68	Male	23,500	
13	1-22-25	Male	23,600	
14	1-23-72	Male	24,000	

Statistically determine, whether there exists any significant differences between the wages of male and female employees and can we really attribute this to gender bias in compensation designing?

(*Hints:* Compare between the expected (the median value) and actual salaries of female employees and then find out statistically the degree of differences. We recommend here the Chi-square test).

REFERENCE NOTES

Flexible Working Hours

Flexible Working Houses (FWH) was introduced in a German aerospace company, Messrs. Schmidt-Bolkov-Gmbh (M.B.B.), at Ottoburn in 1967. This system was developed from the practical needs of the company and was not preceded by any experimental support. The company was then suffering from a chronic problem of late attendance of the workers caused by the rush-hour crowding of the company's narrow access and congestion around its parking facilities. In addition, only one-fourth of the total working force used public transportation and company's subsidised transport facilities and the rest had their own cars that resulted in traffic congestion near the access to the plant which ultimately affected the productivity seriously and morale of the employees as well. This historic and unique innovation was complimented by "The Economist" (London) as 'this is one of the most humanising innovations in the world of work.' Flextime has heightened the interest in the concept of improving the quality of working-life and has added a new dimension to employer-employees and union-management relationships.

The concept of FWH is relatively simple and the scheme is, undoubtedly, qualitatively superior to the concept of fixed working hours. This technologically enriched scheme facilitates flexibility in starting and finishing working hours. Unconventionally, it is left to the employees' own choice to start and finish their work at any time. In fact, the FWH system is allowed only within the limits set by the management. The scheme divides a day typically into two, viz., flexible hours and core time. During the core time, it is mandatory for every employee to be present at their work, usually fixed in the mid-day. Secondly, the FWH is fixed in the morning and the afternoon so that an employee can start and finish his job to suit his own personal lifestyle provided he completes the contractual working hours per settlement period.

As for the lunch break, it is totally up to the discretion of the organisation concerned. It may introduce flexible lunch period or not. Sometimes, again each employee is permitted to create debit and credit times over the total number of working hours. Interestingly, the credit and debit times are carried forward to the next settlement period. Above all, the employees have the opportunity to utilize the credited time as flexi-leave with due permission.

The success of the FWH system depends substantially upon the time recording system. It is necessary not only to calculate the credit and debit balances but also to know whether the employees have been working according to contracted working hours per settlement period.

The FWH system was first introduced in the year 1967 in MBB. The management of the company extended FWH system to cover 4500 employees. Just after 2 years of its implementation, a survey of MBB's employees revealed that 65.5 per cent felt that their working life had improved, 27.3 per cent stated to be same as before and the rest was not in favour of the same.

A pilot survey in 1969 for introducing it at Lufthansa German Airline indicated that the employees were in favour of the system and by 1971 more than 6,000 employees were covered. An opinion survey showed that 98 per cent liked the system.

By 1972, 30 per cent of Swiss labour force was covered by the FWH system. Omega Watch introduced this unique system to include 90 per cent of their employees. Another Swiss firm 'Sulzer Freres' implemented it successfully for their foundry operations.

Some multinational companies, viz., Sandoz, Wander, Burmah Shell, Bosch, etc., exported their experiences to other countries.

The Personnel Manager of California State Auto Association, also has introduced it in his company. According to him around 1000 employees have already been covered.

Japan is also following the flexi-time schedule in their over-crowded cities.

The first American firm to adopt is Nestle Company for its employees in White Plains, New York.

Contd...

Hewlett-Packard is an another American company which is operating the FWH system starting with its Boston unit since 1972. In 1973, it extended the system to their West Coast Divisions and has ultimately covered approximately 15,000 employees throughout the world.

Industrial National Bank of Providence, Rhodes Island, has introduced it with an intention to provide the employees more freedom of action.

In India, although we do not have many companies which have implemented this system, staggering duty hours are largely followed in most of the organisations for few employees in order to facilitate timely opening of shop floor, switching on electrical installation, maintaining water supply and for doing morning cleaning. Similarly, some employees are kept for closing duties to facilitate safe closing of the shop floor, switching off electrical installations and to perform such duties which are important from the point of security and safety. Such groups of employees are, therefore, allowed to make their working hours flexible, compulsorily, however, making them available during the core hours.

Some organisations arrange for such staggering duties by rotations, while others give the opportunity to the intended employees to meet their own exigencies. Usually, departmental heads are empowered to retain employees on such duties.

Such system largely prevails in manufacturing organisations along with the shifting working hours. For companies having expensive installations and more than one shift of operation, this system is compulsorily followed to reap the benefits of maximum utilisations in mind. Workers can opt for evening shift or so in consultation with their departmental heads.

Service organisations in India, however, are following some form of FWH system in order to improve the quality of work life for their workers. This apart it has now become essential to render efficient customer services. Very recently Bangalore-based software development company, M/s VeriFone, has reported increased in productivity and employee motivation by introducing the FWH system.

BLOCK FIVE

EMPLOYEE MOBILITY

UNIT 14

Promotion and Transfer

Learning Objectives

After completion of this unit, the students will be aware of the following topics:

- *Introduction*
- *What is Transfer*
- *Transfer Policy*
- *Promotion*
- *Forms of Promotion*
- *Promotion Policy*
- *Basis of Promotion*
- *Job Rotation*

OPTIMISING THE COST OF RELOCATION – INFOSYS EXAMPLE

Transfer and relocation often complicates the problems in the organisations. Such problems apart from resistance from the employees often become less cost effective, rendering the company to suffer from the increased cost burden. Even then organisations, especially those who are located in different places, do system transfer with relocation, both for the benefit of internal restructuring and employee development. At times, however, transfer is used as a tool for disciplining the employees.

Infosys, the IT giant of India, successfully implemented a Global Delivery Model (GDM) to reduce the cost of relocation of employees in clients' sites. For business imperatives, Infosys executes various projects at customer sites. However, GDM could make these requirements which significantly could reduce the cost of travel and at the same time, optimise the vast talent pool of India (as many talented engineers decline to relocate to abroad). GDM links data between the United States and India, which makes it possible to send software code back and forth through electronic media. This could provide real time customer services, even working in India for US clients. Also, GDM ensures parallel working of programmers in the U.S.A. and in India.

INTRODUCTION

HRM at the enterprise level is integrated with transfer, promotion and job rotation. For internal staffing of vacancies, suitable policies on the above areas must exist, or else, the organisation would be constrained to frequently go for redundancy, leaving its fate only to external hiring. For managerial and executive levels, this is addressed by succession planning. For non-executive positions, suitable policies on promotion and transfer and also job rotation, facilitate restructuring of manpower and their redeployment to meet the requirements of HRP. In this unit, we have discussed the basic concepts and pointed out their importance for HRM.

Organisational environment is dynamic. Besides environmental changes there are changes in the job, their specifications, the technology used to execute them and the employees carrying out various organisational functions. The changes in the employees can be in the form of their movement within and outside the organisation. The movement of employees within the organisation can be in the form of transfer, promotion or job rotation. Transfer is movement of employees from one unit to another, the responsibilities and functions remaining the same. Promotion relates to vertical movement of employees in the hierarchy involving better status and increased responsibility. Job rotation is movement of the employees from one job to another to break the job monotony and to enable the employees to understand the total organisational system.

WHAT IS TRANSFER?

Transfer is the lateral movement of employees from one position, division, department or unit to another. Such movement of employees from one job to another may be either due to promotion, demotion, organisational restructuring or may be for routine administrative reasons (some organisations do not allow employees to remain in the same job for a longer duration, which are sensitive in nature). Generally transfer does not involve any significant change in compensation, duties, responsibilities or even status.

Objectives of Transfer

The objectives of transfer are to:

1. Increase organisational effectiveness.
2. Add to the versatility and competence of key personnel.
3. Cope with the fluctuations in work requirements.
4. Rectify erroneous placement.
5. Relieve boredom and monotony.
6. Set right incompatibilities in employees relations.
7. Look after the interests of the employees (their health or age-group, family problems, etc.)
8. Provide creative opportunities
9. Train employees for their future advancement or promotion.

Different Types of Transfers

1. ***Production Transfers:*** Such transfers are done for stabilising employment. In an organisation, there may be several independent plants for different product-mixes or shopfloors to produce sub-assemblies or components. Production in any of such plants or shopfloors may get discontinued, either for dropping of the product or for other miscellaneous reasons. Such a situation necessitates production transfer.

2. ***Replacement Transfers:*** Such transfers are effected during lay-off, when senior employees may be transferred or relocated to protect their interest against employees with short service.

3. ***Versatility Transfers:*** To prevent employees to develop proprietary interest in the job, materials and equipment used on the job and workloads, such transfers are effected, both for the benefits of the organisation and the employees (employees gain varied job experience).

4. ***Personal or Remedial Transfers:*** Such transfers are usually made in the interest of the employees, as they often may request for transfer on grounds of health, age or family issues. To correct erroneous placement also such transfers are made.

5. ***Shift Transfers:*** Such transfers are effected within the shift itself (without any change in job, etc.), where the shift system of work is prevalent. Shift system is a regularised rotation of employees from one shift to another.

TRANSFER POLICY

In order to be impartial and objective, transfer policy and procedures must be established and made known to all employees.

A good transfer policy must answer the following questions:

1. What type of transfers are to be used? When?
2. What is the area over which transfers will be effected?
3. What is the basis used for effecting transfers?
4. Who is responsible for initiating and approving transfers?
5. Should transfers be permanent or temporary?
6. What is the rate of pay and other facilities the transferred employee should receive on his new job?
7. Is training necessary to effect a transfer?

However, in India, most of the organisations do not have a well formulated transfer policy, resulting in its gross misuse (often as an instrument to victimise the employees). Public sector enterprises and departmental undertakings (government departments) often use this instrument without any regard to the cost aspect. Recently, Ordinance Factories Board had been adversely criticised for effecting meaningless transfers of officers and staff members, which involved crores of rupees of expenditure from the public exchequer. For such irrational use, transfer related issues have now become important causal factors of industrial disputes in India.

Limitations of Transfer

The right of transferring abroad is not implied. However, in the absence of a provision in a contract of service to the contrary, a firm of Chartered Accountants with accounts in foreign countries may order an employee to go into a foreign state to work on a client's accounts. Many organisations, however, make it a point to include a paragraph in the terms and conditions of the letter of appointment of their would be employee before its issue in a language or similar there to "you would be liable to transfer from your present place of posting to anywhere in India or abroad." This often saves the organisation from future confusion or embarrassment.

When an employee is hired by a firm with no branches, there is no implied contract which permits his transfer to a branch thereafter established. Although transfer, per se is not punishment in the eye of law, transfers are limited by the standard of reasonableness. For example, although a bank can transfer its employees, it cannot harass them by doing so repeatedly. An order of transfer cannot be made which will result in a material change for the worse in the employee's contractual rights, such as reduction in his amenities like free quarters, medical assistance, fuel, electricity and cheap rations. Similarly, a radical change in the employee's duties may invalidate a transfer. And, in any event, an employee is entitled to reasonable time upon transfer to wind up his affairs.

At the end of this unit, we have discussed the lateral transfer and horizontal transfer as promotion alternatives.

PROMOTION

Promotion basically is a reward for efficiency. It is conferment of additional benefits, usually in the form of higher pay, for an increase in responsibility or skill which is formalised by an increase in status or rank. Yet, in another way, promotion can be defined as advancement of an employee in an organisation to another job, which commands better pay/wages, better status/prestige and higher opportunities/challenges and responsibilities, a better working environment, hours of work and facilities, etc. Thus, it has been observed that promotion is usually associated with the assignment of an individual to a position of more responsibility or to one which requires the application of his particular education or experience in a better way.

'Promotion from within' as a system in an organisation outlines the policies and procedures for internal promotion of personnel. The basic difference between 'promotion' and 'promotion from within' lies in the fact that promotion policy in an organisation, as such, may incorporate provisions for recruitment from the outside to man promotional vacancies but 'promotion from within' policy in an organisation strictly provides for internal recruitment only to man such vacancies.

From the legal standpoint, however, no distinction, as such, is made between 'promotion' and 'promotion from within' and these two terms are interchangeably used.

FORMS OF PROMOTION

Informal and Formal

The two major forms of promotion are:

1. Informal promotion, and
2. Formal promotion.

The informal form of promotion or the promotion at the discretion of the employer is the oldest form of promotion, which enables the employer(s) concerned to promote those employees who have the requisite ability and merit.

The real problem of the informal form of promotion is that the senior managers may recommend for promotion only those individuals with whom they have already worked, or who, for one reason or the other, have impressed them by their activities or presence. This may sometimes result in promotion on the basis of prejudices of the employer and specialised knowledge and the abilities of the employees (which should form the basis of promotion) may be overlooked.

The formal form of promotion, contrarily, ensures objective evaluation of the responsibilities and duties vis-à-vis different levels of an organisation. The significance of all the positions in the organisation structure is considered with a view to facilitate the objective appraisal of the capabilities of the individuals in the context of promotion. The formal form of promotion is also known as the standardised or systematic form. Seniority and length of service serve as the criteria to qualify for promotion under this form.

This form of promotion is strictly followed in the organisations having the 'promotion from within' policy.

Open and Close

Promotion may also be classified in a different manner,

1. Open form, and
2. Close form

In case of the open form of promotion, organisations do not restrict themselves to the existing employees only for the purpose of filling promotional vacancies. They announce such vacancies in order to harvest from the nation's 'personnel-crop' and to attract the best talents to the maximum extent possible. But the closed form of 'promotion from within' policy, restricts the candidacy for filling promotional vacancies to the existing employees only of the organisation concerned.

Other Forms

Promotion can be grouped according to the following four forms:

1. Movement to an authoritative position;
2. Movement to a highly-skilled and highly-evaluated job;
3. In-grade progression (upgradation) and
4. Widening of duties and responsibilities associated with the existing job with some increase in payment.

Elements of Promotion

We can deduce the following elements of promotion from the definition contents of promotion and 'promotion from within':

1. ***Upward Advancement:*** Whatever may be the form of promotion, it necessarily implies upward advancement, i.e. movement of employees to higher positions in the organisational hierarchy. Although there are some promotions which, in reality, indicate upgradation or in-grade progression (i.e. promotion-in-situ), e.g. promotion of a clerk form Grade II to Grade I, strictly speaking, such promotions also imply upward advancement because the promoted employees now occupy positions higher than juniors in the organisation structure.
2. ***Enhanced Responsibilities, Status and Prestige:*** Since change of job(s), consequent upon promotion, is quite common, the promoted employees are normally expected to assume higher responsibilities on being promoted. However, where promotion is somewhat in the nature of upgradation, the nature of the job being unchanged, responsibilities of the promoted employees mostly remain the same. In all other cases, enhanced responsibilities, status and prestige together constitute an element of promotion.

3. ***Better Pay and Wages:*** It is the next important element of promotion. But, promotion may not always entitle the promoted employees to higher emoluments, even though their responsibilities, status and prestige may be enhanced. In order to encourage creative behaviour in his functional area, an employee, whose contentment has almost reached a plateau, may be entrusted with a qualitatively different job which demands increased responsibilities and which enhances his status and prestige but not his emoluments.

4. ***Other Elements:*** Better working environment, functional autonomy, scope for application of specialised knowledge, skill(s) and work experience, etc., are certain other important elements of promotion.

Objectives of Promotion

Promotion serves one important purpose of the employer, i.e., it enables him to adjust his workforce to the changing requirements. Moreover, from an employer's point of view, promotion is an important motivational tool as it can reduce employees' discontent and unrest.

Promotion can, therefore, improve the effectiveness of an organisation's structure in order to meet the targets and, at the same time, can considerably increase the effectiveness of its employees through assignment of suitable positions.

According to an expert in this field, the main purpose of promotion is to staff a vacancy that, in general, is worth more to the organisation than to the incumbent's present position.

In a more comprehensive manner, the purposes of promotion can be stated as follows:

1. To put an employee in a position where he will be of greater use to the organisation and where he is expected to derive increased personal satisfaction and have an increase in his emoluments;

2. To recognise an individual's performance and reward him for his work so that he may have an incentive to forge ahead;

3. To boost morale and encourage loyalty and help develop a sense of belongingness so far as an employee is concerned;

4. To promote job satisfaction and to motivate an employee to continue in the organisation;

5. To attract suitable and competent employees to the organisation and finally;

6. To provide opportunities to an employee (who has not succeeded in gaining promotion) to enhance his skills and abilities required for superior performance.

It is important to note here that all the above-mentioned purposes are equally served by the 'promotion from within' policy as well. That apart, the 'promotion from within' policy serves the following important purposes:

1. It reduces employee-turnover and consequently reduces replacement cost;

2. It maintains high employee morale and productivity, and finally;

3. It maximise utilisation of human resources.

Promotion Policy

Promotional disputes in the recent years have become an important causal factor vis-à-vis industrial disputes in India (as these form an important part of the personnel related disputes and the disputes arising out of indiscipline and violence). Therefore, in order to avoid any possible complications in future and its consequential adverse effects on industrial relations, union-participation, as far as possible and should be encouraged by management while formulating promotion policies.

Some of the important requirements of an effective promotion policy are presented below:

1. Preparing a statement showing ratios of internal promotions to direct recruitments at each level, mentioning the method(s) of selection (e.g., trade test and interview) and indicating the qualifications desired.
2. Identifying the network of the related jobs and the promotional channels for each job, taking into account the job relatedness, the opportunities for interacting with the executive placed in the higher levels with a view of fostering job learning and the qualifications (both academic and professional) and the work experience required.
3. Developing the procedural norms for determining employees' seniority and deciding whether it should be considered in a plant-wise or unit-wise or an occupation-wise manner.
4. Developing the relationship between disciplinary action and promotions.

The Indian Institute of Personnel Management (now renamed as the National Institute of Personnel Management) has suggested that the following statements, etc., should be included in any standard promotion policy:

1. A statement regarding promotion from within the organisation with a view to filling vacancies in higher posts;
2. A statement regarding the promotional bases like ability and seniority;
3. A well-drawn organisation chart in order to help all concerned understand the ladder of promotion; as well as the structural relationship of the employees working in the different positions among various professions/functions and within their own profession/function;
4. A statement clearly mentioning the officials who may initiate and handle cases of promotion in order to help all concerned; and
5. A statement regarding provision for reversion in case a promotee's performance is not satisfactory.

Basis of Promotion

After formulation and acceptance by management of a sound promotion policy the next question that an organisation faces is "What should be the basis for such promotions?"

A decision in this regard is of utmost importance. In promotional decisions, the most important base is seniority. The Japanese concepts of Nenko Seido (i.e. promotion on the basis of age and length of service) and Shike Seido (i.e. status ranking), reflect nothing but seniority considerations in promotional decisions. In the USA and in the UK, seniority is an important factor of promotion. In India, seniority consideration in promotional decisions has not received much cognizance from organisations until recently. But, due to pressure from unions and subsequent changes in the government policies regarding promotional matters, seniority is fast emerging as an important consideration in the public sector. Different basis of promotion, however, are discussed as follows:

Seniority

Seniority refers to the relative length of service of employees. It may also be determined in relation to the age, occupation, department or organisation, of an employee. Basically, seniority implies skill formation through experiential learning. Seniority being quantifiable, provides an objective means of identifying the personnel eligible for promotion. Since biased managerial decisions on promotion can be averted to the fullest extent, seniority-criterion is widely accepted by employees. As promotion is predictable under the seniority system, it greatly reduces employee-turnover.

However, the seniority system has many disadvantages as well. Since merit or ability is altogether ignored, it does not guarantee quality staffing of promotional vacancies. Even though it is believed that, through experiential learning an individual develops his knowledge that aids in 'skill formation', during his long tenure of service, due to 'trained incapacity', he may be incapable of undertaking new assignments.

Moreover, what should be the basis of such seniority? Is it the total number of years of experience of the employee in the organisation plus the experience already gained in his past employments with other organisations or the experience (length of service) in the present organisation only? Would the experiences unrelated to the promotional vacant post be taken into account?

Mere consideration of seniority in the context of promotion, in reality discourages creativity and innovation. Despite, the above demerits, the seniority-based promotion system is widely prevalent.

Merit Rating

The weaknesses of the seniority-based promotion system have resulted in developing the merit-based promotion system because that encourages excellence in an organisation. Merit is defined as efficiency and capacity of an individual judged in the light of his past performance. The obvious advantages of the merit-based promotion system are that it enhances organisation efficiency and maximises utlisation of talent (as only the deserving employees are promoted after thorough assessment of their abilities and performance). However, integrity of managerial personnel vis-à-vis determination of merit-criteria objectively is suspect from the employees' side in general. And, that defers most of the organisations from using merit as the sole criterion in promotional decisions.

Even though the seniority-based promotion system is largely followed in the public sector organisations in India, the merit-cum-seniority approach plays a major role in promotional decisions in the private-sector organisations.

Quota System

This system of promotion is mainly practised in government departments and public sector undertakings. The Government of India has framed rules/regulations regarding promotion of SC/ST employees who enjoy fixed quota. The organisations have to prepare and maintain rosters for this purpose and whenever the turn comes, the existing SC/ST candidates have to be promoted without consideration of either seniority or merit.

Trade Tests

For staffing certain vacancies through promotion, specific trade tests are conducted in order to rate the candidates' trade-specific knowledge and skills. The ultimate promotional decisions are taken only after the candidates qualify in the specific trade test(s). For certain posts like fitter, turner, welder, etc., (technical) and stenographer, typist, etc. (non-technical), specific knowledge and skills are important prerequisites. Thus, effecting promotion to these posts is subject to the candidates' ability to acquire such knowledge and skills. While some organisations stipulate minimum qualifying service vis-à-vis one's eligibility to appear for such trade tests, most of the organisations usually allow their employees, irrespective of their length of services, to compete for such posts. In a strict sense, selection of an existing employee (after qualifying the stipulated trade test(s)) is not considered as promotion and can better be termed as re-appointment (without break of service).

Promotion by Examinations

Examinations also play a major role in promotional decisions. Examinations, to a large extent, supplement the merit-rating system and provide opportunities to the talented employees for getting promoted to the higher posts without waiting for a long time. In some organisations, a minimum qualifying-service is stipulated vis-à-vis one's eligibility to appear for such examinations. In other organisations, qualifying in such examinations helps employees become eligible for promotion to certain posts. The Subordinate Accounts Services (SAS) Examination and Limited Departmental Section Officers' Examination for certain categories to the Central Government employees, the CAIIB Examination for the bank employees, the Associateship Examination (conducted by the Institute of Actuaries) for the employees in the insurance companies, etc., are some examples of these types of examinations. However, the scope for promotion based on examinations is very limited because only a few departments of the Central Government and a handful of private organisations practise this.

Age-group Preference

In many organisations, a particular age-group is preferred to other age-groups for staffing vacancies. The idea of preference for a particular age-group is based on following considerations:

1. Expected number of years of services;
2. Professional source of supply of required manpower in future; and
3. Personality, dynamism, initiative, challenging attitude, etc.

Age is used as an index of stamina and flexibility and for determining the possible length of service before retirement. Although, no empirical support, as such, is available to relate promotion to preference for age-group, many organisations, as a matter of policy, follow some norms regarding age groups vis-à-vis staffing of certain vacancies from within. In some cases, where the existing employees also contest with the outsiders for a particular vacancy, some relaxation in age is given to them. Thus, for the reasons stated earlier, preference for age group also influences promotional decisions.

Personal Attributes

Personal attributes like intelligence, health, energy, stamina, inherent attitudes, interest and preferences, taken together, also form an important basis for promotional decisions. Since these attributes are not quantifiable in the strict sense, rating by the superior is usually considered as an yardstick. More job experience, acquired knowledge and strong educational background may not make one competent or eligible for promotion. For example, certain jobs demand aptitude for figure work, which can only be found among those employees who have an inherent interest in doing figure work. Similarly, poor health, lack of energy and stamina, etc., makes one unsuitable for sales jobs, supervisory jobs; requiring dealings with the public and leadership quality. Inherent attitudes, interests and preferences also, at the same time, act, in one way or the other, as important prerequisites for certain jobs. In many organisations, the system of writing annual confidential reports about employees exists. Certain columns in this report pertain to personal attributes. This report which is usually written by the superior concerned, thus, serves an important purpose of the management, i.e., considering the personal attributes of an employee for the purpose of taking promotional decisions.

Performance Appraisal

Performance appraisal, in reality, is an important variable in promotional decisions. However, the term merit-rating is quite a narrow one and limited in approach. Performance appraisal has wider applicability in the context of evaluation of employees vis-à-vis their characteristics, qualifications, traits, capacities, proficiencies and abilities for the purpose of inter alia taking promotional decisions. Performances appraisal is basically a formal exercise in an organisation with a view to evaluating the employees performance in a documented form at periodic intervals. A leading management theorist has identified the following three basic purposes of formal performance appraisal:

1. To provide systematic judgements on salary increases, promotions, transfer, etc;
2. To make an employee know 'where he stands' with respect to his boss; and
3. To provide a basis for coaching and counselling of an employee by his superior.

Although there are various methods of performance appraisal, the most widely used method is ranking. Under this method, ranking of an employee is done on the basis of comparison with others. An employee, who gets the highest numerical value to his credit (as compared to other employees), is considered most suitable for promotion.

Because of its simplicity and objective, the performance appraisal system is widely used throughout the world. An Indian study, covering 60 organisations, has indicated that companies, both in the public and private sectors, give considerable weightage (58 per cent) to performance appraisal for effecting promotional decisions.

Promotion Alternatives

'Promotion from within' as a regular process, apart from resulting in in-breeding, lack of dynamism and innovativeness etc., has an inevitable danger of overstaffing of an organisation. Japanese organisations, which follow this system compulsorily even without 'objective assessment of employees' performance, have introduced an excellent promotion alternative, known as "status ranking system", in order to obviate the problems of over-staffing. Under this system, a worker, who is otherwise eligible for promotion but cannot be promoted because of the problems of overstaffing is awarded a status rank with increased allowances so as to make his pay almost at par with that of the promotable post. Thus, without actually promoting the eligible employees, this system ensures increased status for them in order to maintain their motivation levels and ensure their loyalty towards the organisation.

Inability to promote the eligible employees, for one reason or the other (e.g. the problem of overstaffing), is a problem of structural nature (because most of the employees have reached a plateau) before the management in any organisation. While job enrichment, job enlargement, lateral transfer, horizontal transfer, etc., which focus primarily on the change of work content, can in one way or the other, fulfil the intrinsic needs of the employees, these, in reality, reduce only the stresses resulting form content-plateauing. The problem of structure-plateauing remains unless suitable restructuring of the organisation, with due emphasis on reducing the importance of promotion and increasing the value of challenge, is attempted.

Since, temporary measures, job enrichment, job enlargement, lateral transfers and horizontal transfers can successfully reduce the stress of the employees, who are otherwise promotable, but are not promoted for the obvious inability of the organisations, these are considered as promotion alternatives. Ensuring timely promotion of employees is a major problem even for well organised and professionally-managed organisations in India. Government organisations, for the low-paid white-collar employees, relate their promotional decisions to the availability of vacancies, while, for the direct recruits in the officers' cadre, they have a system of promotion based on time-scale. This clearly indicates poor career planning, which results in serious motivational problems in the government organisations. Stagnation in different cadres for years together is a result of such ill-framed policy. Commercial banking organisations have made some progress in this matter, i.e., in the case of senior employees, the probability of getting promotion after completion of a certain number of years of service is quite high. But such types of measures are not at all adequate. However, job enrichment, job enlargement, lateral transfer and horizontal transfers can, to a large extent, alleviate the motivational problems of employees, in such cases, at least, for the time being. Thus, an organisation gets an opportunity to restructure itself and can take some provisions for promotion during the intervening period.

Lateral Horizontal Transfer

Two other promotion alternatives are lateral and horizontal transfer. In the strict sense, transfer is the moving of an employee from one job to another. Such movement may either be horizontal or lateral. For internal mobility of the manpower, periodic transfers of employees are effected by an organisation either for the interests of the organisation or for the interests of the employees or for both. Although need for transfer may arise for one reason or the other (e.g. fluctuations in work requirements, increasing versatility and competence of key employees, correcting erroneous placement, relieving employees from monotony, protecting the interests of employees vis-à-vis their health or age and providing creative opportunities for employees), Indian organisations mostly relate transfer decisions to promotions, excepting cases where transfers of senior employees are affected for the maintenance of a tenure system. Since transfers, in most of the cases, involve change of place(s) and even, in some cases, result in reduction in material gains, transfer-decisions of an organisation, quite often, are resented by the affected employees. This is particularly evident in the government and commercial banking organisations. Problems of housing, education of children, inadequacy of compensation, disruption of family life and social life, etc., are some of the common grounds for which even promotional transfers are not accepted by many employees. In order to obviate such problems relating to implementation of transfer either for routine administrative reasons or for promotional reasons, transfer liability is usually made a pre-condition to employment. Most of the organisations have well drawn transfer policies in this regard. While, in other organisations, transfer is still a prerogative of the management.

Lateral transfer is the vertical movement of employees and denotes significant change in the work content. Cross-functional or cross-lateral transfers, throughout the career of an employee, keep him fresh and receptive to new ideas and make him more creative and productive.

Horizontal transfer, on the other hand, is the movement within the same job-family. While job enrichment and job enlargement exercises do not involve, in reality, any movement from one job to another, lateral and horizontal transfer indicate physical movement from one job to another and, thus, have some potential to motivate employees intrinsically.

Both lateral and horizontal transfer can be effectively used for structure and content-plateaued employees as temporary promotion alternatives. In some organisations, such transfers are made to equip the employees for assuming higher responsibilities, consequent upon promotion.

JOB ROTATION

Job Mobility

Repetitive tasks develop boredom and jobs become increasingly dehumanised and dissatisfying to the employees. Some companies try to reduce this boredom through job rotation, which is a systematic movement of workers from one job to another. Such movement or rotation in different functions increases the skills and functional efficiency of the employees as they are exposed to different business situations. Some companies even encourage such movement from one unit to another to enable employees to understand the organisation as a total system. For manning higher positions in the organisation, such knowledge of employees is an important prerequisite. A staff executive, who is posted in an office, may be encouraged to move to the factory (which may not be attached to an office) to get exposed to the intricacies of functioning, only to promote him later to a more senior position. Job rotation, for employees at lower level also, helps in multi-skill development whereby the organisation can get the advantage of their services at the time of exigency. However, frequent job rotations do not allow employees to get specialised knowledge and skill and reduce them to an unskilled functionary or at least 'a jack of all trades and master of none'. For such obvious disadvantage of job rotation, other forms of job mobility like; job enlargement and job enrichment are considered as better alternatives. These two forms have been discussed below.

Job Enrichment

Job enrichment is basically the restructuring of a job to make it more interesting and stimulating. This concept has been developed by Herzberg. Job enrichment seeks to improve task efficiency and human satisfaction and to provide greater scope for personal achievement and recognition, challenging assignments and opportunities for individual advancement and growth. Enough experimental supports, like the American Telephone and Telegraph Company experiment and the ICI experiment, have indicated that job enrichment has tremendous motivational potential and, if implemented properly, can significantly increase job satisfaction and productivity.

Job Enlargement

Job enlargement is the horizontal regrouping of tasks and implies mere addition of more functions and increase in the task variety. By enlarging job content, de-humanisation of work, as a result of excessive functional specialisation, can be reduced and the creative needs of employees can be satisfied to a large extent.

Even though job enrichment is a better alternative to job enlargement, as the former one is restructuring of a job in order to make it more interesting and stimulating and the latter is mere additions to a present job, both of these are considered important vis-à-vis satisfaction of intrinsic needs of the employees and fulfillment of their creative urges.

SUMMARY

Transfer, promotion and job rotation are three different types of employees movement, which facilitate adjustment of manpower both within and outside the organisations. Today's organisations are required to frequently restructure the jobs, to keep pace with the changing technology, systems and practices. This necessitates restructuring of manpower. Without suitable policies on promotion, transfer and job rotation it is difficult for an organisation to enforce them. Again policies need to be periodically reviewed to ensure their relevance. For HRP, all these three instruments provide adequate flexibility.

KEYWORDS

Transfer	Job Enrichment
Promotion	Job Enlargement
Promotion from Within	Job Mobility
Promotion Policy	Standardised Stroke
Promotion Alternatives Trade Tests	Grading System

REVIEW QUESTIONS

1. Define transfer. Why is transfer necessary for an organisation? What are the different types of transfer?
2. Is it necessary for an organisation to have a transfer policy? Justify your answer duly pointing out important components of a transfer policy. Do you think transfer is absolutely a management prerogative?
3. What is promotion? In what way does it differ from 'promotion from within'? What are the different forms of promotion?
4. Briefly state the elements and purposes of promotion.
5. You have been asked by an organisation to draft a promotion policy for their employees. What are the areas, you think you should consider, while drafting such a policy?
6. Briefly state the different basis of promotion. Identify at least three factors, which you think are important while taking a promotion decision.
7. Is it possible to ensure increased status for employees without actually promoting them? Select at least three promotion alternatives, which can confer increased status and job satisfaction to plateaued employees.
8. Explain how internal job mobility reinforces HRP in an organisation.
9. Write short notes on:

   (a) Career Plateauing

   (b) Standard Stroke Grade System

   (c) Lateral Transfer

   (d) Job Enlargement

   (e) Job Enrichment

   (f) Trade Tests

   (g) Replacement Transfer

   (h) Merit Rating

CASE STUDY

RELOCATE OR PERISH

Rajeev was recently selected by an MNC to head their Marketing function. This MNC has their units in multi locations in India and in some other parts of the world. Rajeev has a track record of good performance in his past jobs and about 15 years experience as SBU head with exposure to Marketing, Operations, Corporate Planning and HR. He is an engineer from IIT and MBA from IIM with marketing as major and systems as minor specialisation. He is in his mid forties and very dynamic and pro-active with consistent track of achievement. For any organisation, Rajeev is a prized possession. This MNC has to pay a whooping sum of three months pay to a head hunter to whisk away Rajeev from his past organisation. Rajeev has got 50 per cent more than his past salary in the MNC with other competitive perquisites befitting with the status. During the first quarter itself Rajeev has showed outstanding performance, achieving 50 per cent more than the budgeted target.

To reposition them in the world market, this MNC, which is a world leader in FMCG products, decided to restructure their business. Their consultant suggested to relocate the corporate headquarter from New Delhi to Hong Kong. New Delhi office would be converted to a country office to overview the India operation. The Board decided to relocate Rajeev in Hong Kong. Hong Kong by Indian standards is much more costly and accommodation itself cost almost 50% of one's salary. The company decided all the key employees (like Rajeev) at Hong Kong Headquarter would be given a bachelor type single room accommodation and other support staff would be put up in dormitories. All will receive a substantial relocation allowance per month to compensate the increased cost of living at Hong Kong and would receive 15 days leave along with return air fare to their place of residence. Only two Directors of the company would be given family type accommodation, considering their age and long association with the organisation. The company is all set to shift and identified the personnel (along with Rajeev) for relocation to Hong Kong. A meeting was called to discuss this issue with all those set to relocate at Hong Kong. The Chairman of the company asked for the personnel details to HR Chief, who from well maintained HRIS given the information in the format below:

S. No.	Designation/Level	No. of Years with the Company	Age Group	Marital Status
1.	Director-operation	20	55	Married with two children above 15 years.
2.	Director-Marketing (Rajeev Saxena)	1	44	Divorced with one child below 5 years and mother as dependent
3.	Director-HR	15	52	Bachelor
4.	Director-Finance	16	51	Divorced and free from any encumbrances
5.	Director-Systems	5	47	Married with no issue
6.	Support Executives (Total-20) Male-15 Female-5	5-10 years	25-40	Two female bachelor and three are married with no issue. Ten male bachelor and one divorced, rest four are married with one issue each.

With the personnel data, Chairman foresees no problem, per se, in relocating to Hong Kong, excepting for support staff as some of them may ask for separation. As per the standing norms, if employees ask for separation themselves, they get only their normal entitlements, while in the reverse case, the company pays to such employees in addition a lump sum of ₹ 5 lakh each for support executives and staff members and ₹ 8 lakh to senior executives up to the level of Directors. The Chairman also believes attrition of directors would not threaten the company from any competency gap, as such requirements can be met from local (Hong Kong) hiring on contractual terms. In Hong Kong labour laws are much more relaxed and employment is contractual. The Chairman convened the meeting and announced the names of those who are required to relocate to Hong Kong within a month. For such decision, it is not the practice of the company to reach to any consensus. If any one dissents, he or she is free to leave.

Contd...

Within next 10 days the company received following documents in connection with the relocation:

I. Consent from all the Directors, excepting Rajeev.

II. A letter of resignation from Rajeev with a claim of compensation of ₹ 10 lakh, alleging this decision is in contravention with his terms of employment.

III. A court order for 5 support executives stalling their relocation to Hong Kong.

IV. Letters of resignation, requesting for VRS benefits from 15 support executives.

Questions

1. What went wrong in this plan?
2. What could have be done to make this plan successful?
3. Assuming you are the Chairman of the company, how will you now manage the situation.

Appendix 1

Sample Promotion Policy in Commercial Banks

A commercial bank considers the following common factors in order to effectuate promotional decisions for the existing employees:

1. Seniority and/or length of service,
2. Professional qualifications,
3. Knowledge of practical banking,
4. Performance on the job, and
5. Potential for development and growth

However, weights assigned to each of the above factors vary from one bank to another and also depend on the levels of promotion. For each such factor, a maximum weight is assigned (stipulating certain conditions). The total score of each employee (applying for a higher post) is computed and the highest scorer is given the promotion. For example, for effecting promotion from the Junior Management Scale I post to the Middle Management (Lower) Scale II post, a maximum weightage for each one of the above factors is fixed as follows:

1. Seniority and/or length of service – maximum weightage is 20 per cent (special weightage is given to those who are posted in the rural areas);
2. Professional qualifications – maximum weightage is 15 per cent;
3. Knowledge of practical banking (evaluated through a process of written examination) – maximum weightage is 20 per cent;
4. Performance on the job (assessed on the basis of evaluation of the performance of officers) – weightage varies from 10 per cent to 50 per cent depending on the ranks; and
5. Potential for development and growth (assessed through a process of interview) – weightage varies from 15 per cent to 20 per cent.

Guidelines like these are followed in the case of effecting promotion from within for officers in the general stream. However, for officers in the specialists' stream like law officer, engineers, economists, personnel officers, etc., the policy of direct recruitment is followed.

For effecting promotion from the clerical cadre to the officers' cadre (Junior Management, Scale I), factors like service-seniority, educational attainments and performance in the written test are given weightage.

For such promotion, commercial banks have introduced the following quotas for all the declared vacancies:

1. 20 per cent of the declared vacancies are to be filled by direct recruitment through the Banking Service Recruitment Board;
2. 50 per cent of the declared vacancies are to be filled on the basis of merit-cum-seniority from amongst the members of the clerical staff;
3. 30 per cent of the declared vacancies are to be filled on the basis of seniority from amongst the senior clerical staff (including the employees holding the special allowance posts).

Usually, the maximum age limit for promotion of the departmental candidates is fixed at 56 years both for promotion from the Junior Management Scale I post, to the Middle Management (Lower) Scale II post and promotion from the clerical cadre to the officers cadre (Junior Management, Scale I).

However, the above promotion policy of commercial banks, is likely to get altered and changed. The Narsimhan Committee Report of 1992 *inter alia* suggested that individual banks should be free to make their own requirement, instead of the present common recruitment system. The committee suggests that there is no need for setting up a Banking Service Commission for centralised recruitment of officers. This will provide scope for the banks to scout for talent and impart new skills to their personnel. The committee, however, predicts this recommendation on the assumption that the banks will set up objective, fair and impartial recruitment procedures and, wherever appropriate, they could voluntarily come together to have a joint recruitment system. As regards clerical grades, the present system of recruitment through Banking Service Recruitment Boards may continue but we could urge that the appointment of the Chairman of these boards should be totally left to the co-ordinating banks.

APPENDIX 2

PROMOTION POLICY OF STEEL AUTHORITY OF INDIA (SAIL) EXECUTIVES

Policy Objectives

1. To man executive posts in the company with competent personnel having growth potential and to utilise their capability in the working environment to the maximum through opportunities available for advancement.
2. To provide for a system which is conducive to equity, fairness and objectivity in matters concerning promotion of executives.
3. To ensure uniformity and consistency, to the extent possible in the promotion of executives of all units of the company.
4. To motivate executives of the organisation for better performance, by rewarding their contribution to the growth of the organisation, in deciding promotions on the basis of overall merit.

Scope

The policy shall cover all promotions made in executive posts (other than promotions from non-executive posts to executive posts) and shall apply to all units of Steel Authority of India Limited. For the purpose of promotion and career planning, all executives of SAIL will be classified as under:

Cadres	Grade Code
Jr. Managerial	E-0 to E-3 (B)
Managerial	E-4, E-5
Sr. Managerial	E-6(A), E-6(B) and E-7
Top Managerial	E-8

The executives will have to pass through all the standard scales without skipping any grade in accordance with this policy.

Minimum qualifications and eligibility criteria are different for different levels.

Promotion System

Vacancy Promotion System

This will apply in all grades except from E-1 to E-2. Subject to minimum requirements of promotion and fulfillments of criteria of promotion, the executives will be promoted to the next higher grade on availability of vacancies. Eligibility will be two years from (E-3(A) to E-3(B), E-6(A) to E-6(B), E-6(B) to E-7 and E-7 to E-8 will be through interview. Out of the candidates found suitable, promotion will be effected in order of seniority.

Standardised Strokes Grade System

Promotion from E-1 to E-2 would be on the basis of appraisal reports and qualifications as prescribed irrespective of vacancy. The eligibility for professionally qualified executives and management trainees (both technical and administrative) would be 4½ years including the period of training of management trainees. For others, eligibility would be after completion of minimum 5½ years service in E-1 grade. This selection will be subject to personal review/interview by the competent authority from amongst those who have the prescribed appraisal rating. The prescribed appraisal rating will be three consecutive confidential reports being minimum C+ both under performance rating and potentiality rating.

Promotion from E-3(A) to E-3(B) would be on the basis of appraisal reports and qualifications only as prescribed, subject to completion of two years service in E-3(A). Individuals will get the monetary benefits, but not the designation which will be against the vacancy only.

Contd...

Executives in E-6(A) will be eligible for promotion to E-6(B) provided they have put in two years service in the grade of E-6(A) on the basis of appraisal reports and qualifications only as prescribed. Individuals will get the monetary benefits but not the designation till a vacancy arises.

Criteria for Promotion

Following criteria for promotion would be followed:

- Appraisal reports, as prescribed,
- Qualification, as prescribed,
- Interviews, as prescribed,
- Eligibility, as prescribed,
- Discipline, viz., clearance for vigilance and disciplinary angle.

Minimum Educational Qualifications Required for Promotion within Executive Posts

Category of Posts	Minimum Qualifications	Level
1. Technical	(i) Matriculation with pre-selection training. (ii) B.Sc. or Diploma in Engineering (iii) Degree in Engg. or equivalent	E-0 to E-2 (up to and including) E-3(B) (upto) For E-4 and above
2. Non-technical	(i) Bachelor's degree (ii) Bachelor's degree with professional qualification	Up to E-3 (B) E-4 and above
3. Mining	(i) Qualification required under statute (ii) Matric with pre-selection training (iii) Degree in Geology/Mining	Statutory posts Up to and including the level of E-2 Posts in E-3 (B) and above
4. Finance and Accounts	(i) Graduation with a pass in the departmental examination for accounts or SAS Accountants Examination of the government (ii) Professional Qualifications like CA/ICWA	Up to and including the level of E-3 (B) Posts in E-4 and above
5. Research and Development	(i) Degree in Engg. or M.Sc. in related discipline (ii) Degree in Engineering preferably a Master's Degree or Doctoral Degree or Ph.D. in Pure Science	Up to and including the level of E-3 (B) Posts in E-4 and above

Contd...

Schematic Representation of Promotion Systems

	System-A (Vacancy)	System-B (Standardised Stroke Grade)	System-C (Service Linked Promotion)
1. Interview	Interview at job change level E-2 to E-3(A), E-3 (B) to E-4, E-4 to E-5, E-5 to E-6 (A), E-6 (B) to E-7 and E-7 to E-8	Review/Interview	No Interview
2. Appraisal	Last three appraisals with minimum 'C' and promotability rating	Appraisals with minimum 'C' and promotability rating.	Last three appraisals with minimum 'C' and performance rating
3. Qualification	As stated	As stated	As stated
4. Eligibility	Three years from E-2 to E-3(A), E-3(B) to E-4, E-4 to E-5, E-5 to E-6 (A), E-6(B) to E-7 and E-7 to E-8	I. E-1 to E-2: 5½ years or 4½ years. II. E-4(A) to E-3 (B): 2 years as E-3 (A). III. E-6(A) to E-6(B):2 years as E-6(A)	10 years
5. Discipline	Clear from vigilance and discipline angle	Clear from vigilance and disciplinary angle	Clear from vigilance and disciplinary angle

BLOCK SIX

EMPLOYEE RETENTION

Unit 15 Employee Motivation

UNIT 15

Employee Motivation

Learning Objectives

After completion of this unit, the students will be aware of the following topics:

- *Introduction*
- *What is Motivation?*
- *Mechanism of Motivation*
- *Major Theories of Motivation*
- *Theory X and Theory Y*
- *Cognitive or Process Theories of Motivation*
- *Miscellaneous Theories on Motivation*
- *Motivation and Morale*
- *Participative Management*
- *Total Quality Management*
- *Empowerment*
- *Quality of Work Life (QWL)*

MOTIVATION THROUGH STRESS MANAGEMENT

Workplace stress often becomes an important source of de-motivation for employees. To manage stress at work, a leading Japanese collaborated unit, engaged in producing industrial chemicals, adopted a policy delineating the responsibilities of the managers, individual employees and the organisation. The main thrust of the policy is to adopt proactive approach in matters of stress management, rather than waiting for the problem to arise. The policy document spells out that management of stress in the work place is inseparable from the duties and the job roles of managers and supervisors. Being in the business of hazardous chemicals, stress in the workplace of the company also occurs due to occupational health hazards, in addition to the work related stress. To guide the managers and supervisions, the policy document categorised the possible reasons for stress as under:

- Culture
- Demands
- Control
- Relationships
- Change
- Role
- Support

After categorisation of possible stress issues that are likely to occur or have occurred, through brainstorming, managers and supervisors decide the possible courses of action and recommend the same to the top management, who after review, recommend its implementation within a day or two. Reviewing the initial pilot testing report on the suggestive approach to stress management, managers and supervisors, streamlined it as policy documents. To help the workers to self-manage the workplace stress, a detailed FAQ (frequently asked question) has been hosted by the company, and prominently displayed in canteens, shop floors, etc.

This approach to stress management helped the company to reduce the workplace stress, significantly. Backup support of counseling also helped the company to reduce stress exogenous to the organisation like, family matters, relationship problems, etc.

INTRODUCTION

After employees are hired and trained, it is important to motivate them to get the desired efforts from them to achieve organisational objectives. While designing their compensation package, at the outset, we try to meet their expectations suitably identifying their extrinsic and intrinsic needs, within the given policies and procedures of the organisation. However, this is restricted only to those cases, where, we can afford to become flexible, to attract and retain talents in key positions, without contributing to general dissatisfaction of other employees. But major problems on employee motivation become evident, when employees of an organisation started perceiving that there is wide mismatch between their expectations and organisational commitments. At times such perceived expectations of employees far exceed the organisational commitments, resulting in a significant drop in their perception.

Motivation is a dynamic HR process and there cannot be any greatest organisation-specific motivation tool. The subject of motivation, perhaps received attention from management thinkers worldwide. Even then we find we are not able to address the problem, as employee demotivation is a perennial issue from the days of industrial revolution. Before industrial revolution, such a problem was non-existent, as owners of labour services and owners of means of capital had the same identity and motivation for work was spontaneous in a home-centered production system.

In this chapter, we have first discussed different theories of motivation, mentioned briefly about different empirical studies on motivation in India and abroad, before we culled the other issues like concepts, objectives, process and benefits. Such a journey is necessary as we find this is one of the much discussed and much debated subject of HRM.

WHAT IS MOTIVATION?

Motivational perceptions of all type of employees throughout the world are fast changing in response to a number of key variables. The conventional motivational reinforcers, either extrinsic or intrinsic are gradually loosing importance. What exactly can motivate again varies with time and space. In India also, it is not at all possible to identify and indicate one single motivational tool commonly applicable to various cross sections of employees. But we can try to appreciate the relative importance of one or the other tool for a particular segment of employees belonging to some homogenous organisations.

Here we have discussed motivational elements in detail, supported by various leading theoretical and empirical works.

By now it has been established that motivational factors are perceived needs of the employees, satisfaction of which contribute to employees' performance and productivity. But motivation, per se, can be better defined as a process governing choices. This process may be 'internal or external' to the individual, that arouses enthusiasm, and persistence to pursue a certain course of action. Motivation process starts with a physiological or psychological deficiency or need that activates behaviour or a drive that is aimed at a goal or incentive. All the definitions, therefore, authenticate that motivation is a behavioural syndrome, which develops when there is a perceived incongruence in employees needs and expectations. With the widening of such perceived gap, employees feel demotivated and reduce their level of performance and productivity. Contrarily, if the gap gets reduced employees feel motivated and contribute their best for achieving organisational objectives. From the organisational point of view, motivation process follows certain defined steps, which as a continuum, need to be periodically reviewed and strategised to ensure its proper renewal. This helps to maintain the motivation of employees, which is evident from their behavioural congruence, matching organisational objectives.

In the first stage, it is important to identify the need deficiency of employees, if any. Need deficiency centres around extrinsic and intrinsic needs. Extrinsic needs are those which are related to material and tangible gains. Increased pay, incentives, bonus, better medical facilities, better retirement benefits, better canteen facilities are some examples of extrinsic needs. Intrinsic needs on the other hand are those which are related to mental satisfaction and are abstract in nature. Increased status, challenge, sense of belonging, scope for growth and creativity, recognition, sense of achievement, etc., are examples of such needs. Identification of need deficiency is possible through direct observation of employees behaviour and through a survey using structured questionnaire response. But employees, by and large, feel sensitised about giving responses to a survey questionnaire, obviously fearing they will get identified for giving any response that criticises organisational policy. Confidentiality in survey responses can be ensured through a secret opinion poll, where questionnaire does not require any employees' identity. However, for better results, it is always desirable to integrate survey findings with personal interview, which can be in the form of a open discussion with employees by their respective seniors. Some organisations try to document such information from 3600 performance appraisal, incorporating certain items in the appraisal form itself. Existence in need deficiency can also be understood from the trend of employees performance, developing a performance or productivity index.

In the second phase of the motivational process, organisations try to identify appropriate strategy to close the perceived need gap of employees. There are many innovative ways to close such need gaps without much impairing the budget. For example, need for increase in pay can be ensured by reducing deferred benefits (NWLC) and including such reduced amount to the current pay of the employees. This is particularly important for those organisations who employ mostly young people in the exploratory age group (less than 35 years). Similarly making pay performance linked also facilitates developing of proper compensation structure to reward and so also to motivate good performers. Similarly gap of intrinsic needs can be reduced, by adopting an enabling organisation structure, which among others foster creativity and growth.

Table 15.1

Cause Group	YEARS							
	1994		1995		1997		1998	
	No. of disputes	Percentage to total	No. of disputes	Percentage to total	No. of disputes	Percentage to total	No. of disputes	Percentage to total
Wages and Allowances	354	29.4	320	30	305	23.4	233	21.2
Personnel	194	16.2	195	18.3	261	20.0	175	16.0
Retrenchment	19	1.6	10	0.9	7	0.5	8	0.7
Lay-off	3	0.2	4	0.4	7	0.5	6	0.6
Indiscipline	185	15.2	145	13.6	246	18.9	225	18.9
Violence	20	1.7	14	1.3	13	1.0	7	0.6
Leave and Hours of Work/Shift working	17	1.4	21	2.0	31	2.4	14	1.3
Bonus	92	7.8	79	7.4	112	86	123	11.2
Gherao	1	0.1	1	0.1	–	–	–	–
Non-implementation of agreements, Awards, etc.	37	3.1	43	4.0	43	3.3	32	2.9
Charter of Demands	55	4.6	61	5.7	68	5.2	97	8.8
Workload	10	0.8	10	0.9	9	0.7	6	0.6
Surplus Labour	1	0.1	–	–	1	0.1	–	–
Betterment of Amenities	16	1.3	18	1.7	34	2.6	12	1.1
Suspension/Change of Manufacturing Process	1	0.1	–	–	–	–	1	0.1
Standing Orders/Rules/Service/Conditions/Safety Measures	50	4.2	52	4.9	34	2.6	13	1.2
Others	118	9.8	57	5.4	85	6.5	89	8.1
Not Known	21	1.7	29	2.7	37	2.8	49	4.5
Total	201	100	1066	100	1305	100	109	100

To understand the importance of extrinsic and intrinsic needs, we have illustrated the industrial disputes scenario in India at macro-level. Table 15.1 shows, in terms of percentage share, intrinsic factors are also very significant. However, severity of extrinsic and intrinsic factors in terms of 'man-days loss' can not be measured for inherent problem in data collection of Labour Bureau, Shimla. Identification of appropriate strategy to close need gaps helps an organisation to develop goal directed behaviour among employees to achieve organisational objectives. Thus in the third phase of the motivational process, organisations enforce goal directed behaviour. Goal directed behaviour enhances performance and productivity of employees, which further influence compensation strategy and other motivational reinforcers.

Likewise, the cycle continues as an ongoing process in an organisation, as at the end of the continuum, needs are again re-evaluated to understand emerging need deficiency, if any. In Figure 15.1 we have illustrated the model as a continuum.

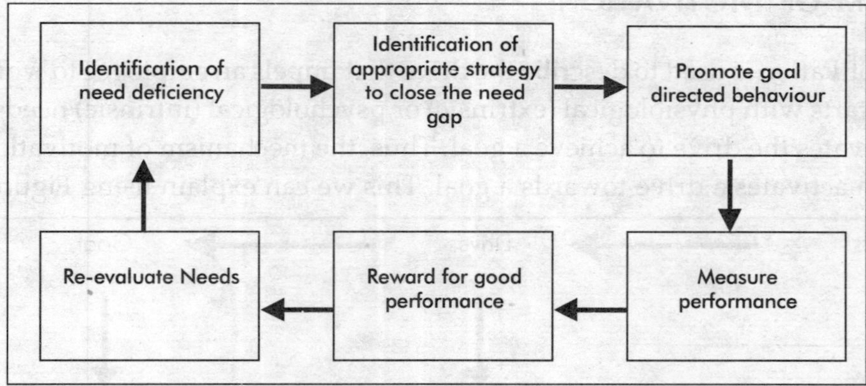

Figure 15.1: Motivation Model

Important Objectives of Motivation

Motivation enhances performance and improves productivity. Therefore, motivation fulfils following important objectives of an organisation:

1. Ensures productive use of resource – Physical, financial and human resources are the important resource constructs for an organisation. Proper utlisation of such resources is only possible when people in the organisation feel motivated. Motivation leads to goal directed behaviour, which in turn facilitates productive utilisation of all such resources. Important measures for productive use of resources are 'total factor productivity indices' and labour productivity indices, which we have discussed separately.

2. The second important objective of motivation is increased efficiency of people. Efficiency of motivated people increases, as it augments their willingness to work. Increased efficiency also contributes to cost reduction.

3. Thirdly, a motivated employee also becomes quality conscious, as behaviourally he identifies himself with the organisation and always tries to take extra care for his jobs. Motivation, therefore also strengthens quality objectives of an organisation.

4. Fourthly, by promoting goal directed behaviour, motivated employees also help to realise organisational objectives and strategies.

5. Motivation also promotes friendly work culture, increased morale, increased sense of responsibility, sense of belonging, integration of individual identity with organisational identity, teamwork, participative decision-making, etc. All these together create an environment for creativity and growth and truly transforms an organisation into an enabling one.

6. Finally, motivation ensures organisational stability by reducing employee turnover and absenteeism.

MECHANISM OF MOTIVATION

The word motivation is used to describe the drive that impels an employee to work. Therefore, the process starts with physiological (extrinsic) or psychological (intrinsic) needs, satisfaction of which activates the drive to achieve a goal. Thus, the mechanism of motivation starts with a need which activates a drive towards a goal. This we can explain using Figure 15.2.

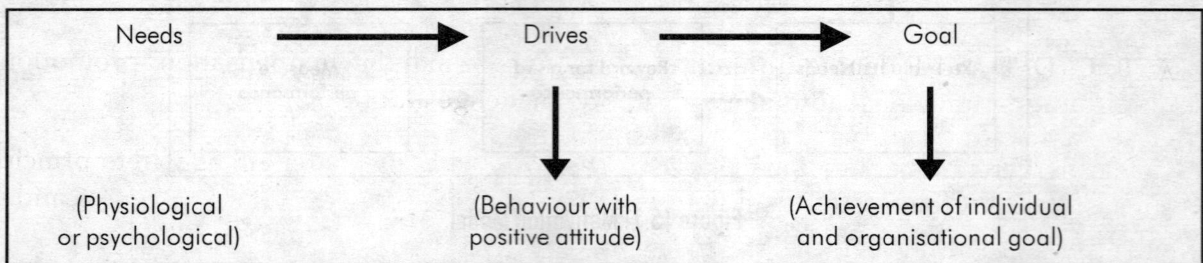

Figure 15.2: Mechanism of Motivation

At this stage it is important to understand the basic differences between motive, motivation and motivating. Motive is the inner state that activates and directs the behaviour of individuals towards certain goals. Inner state of an individual is created out of perceived need imbalance. Degree of imbalance decides a strong motive or a weak motive and accordingly an individual propels himself into action. Thus motives create drives that energize people into action. While motive energizes action, motivation is the actual action or a work behaviour. The degree of work behaviour decides the level of motivation. If an employee performs well, putting his best efforts, we consider his motivation as high while in the reverse case, we consider it as low. Motivating implies inducements to energise work behaviour. This is a managerial role, as it satisfies both individual and organisational needs. Mangers always try to sustain the motivating environment to get the work done in an effective and efficient manner. For this purpose managers need to understand the degree of motive strength of employees. We have already explained the process of identification of need deficiency. Since needs or motives are the reasons for a work behaviour, for effective decision, managers need to plot the motives with the degree of importance, which can be done in the following manner:

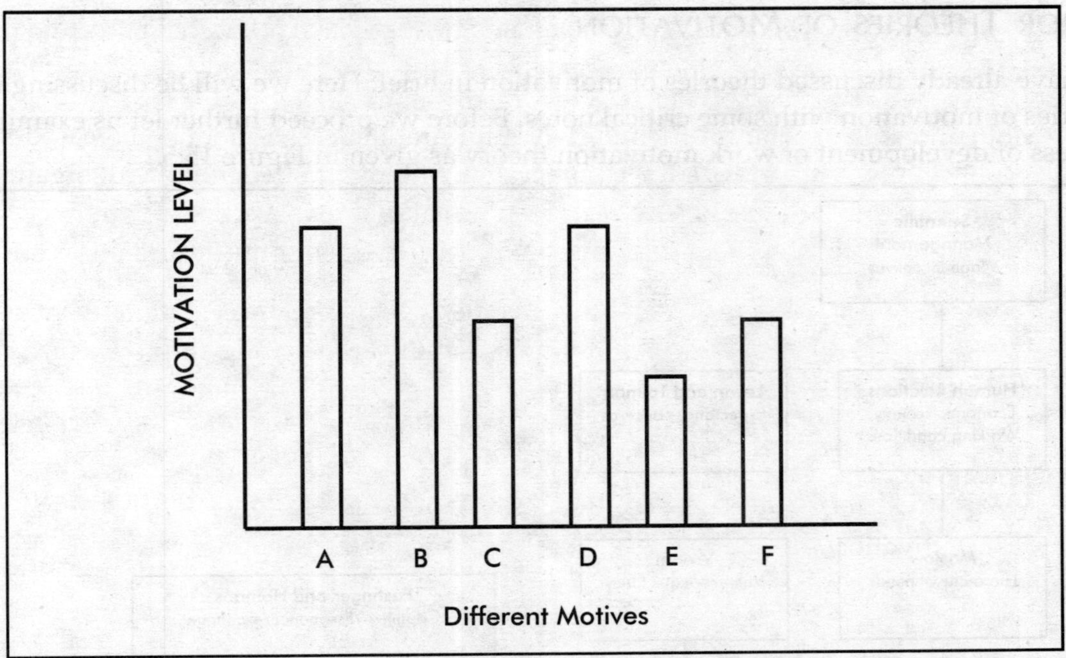

Figure 15.3: Motives with Degree of Importance

A, B, C, D, E and F denote different motives, which may be compensation, promotional opportunities, functional autonomy, creativity, challenge and flexibility in policies.

Using the Pareto diagram, a manager can optimise the motive strength as Pareto principle suggests every problem (for us it is the motive strength) is the result of few causes and all causes are not equally important, 'a vital few: trivial many'. This means by taking care of 10-15 per cent of motive strengths, managers can reduce the need gaps in 70-80 per cent areas. This is because of interdependence and inter-relationship in motive strengths. A typical Pareto diagram looks as under:

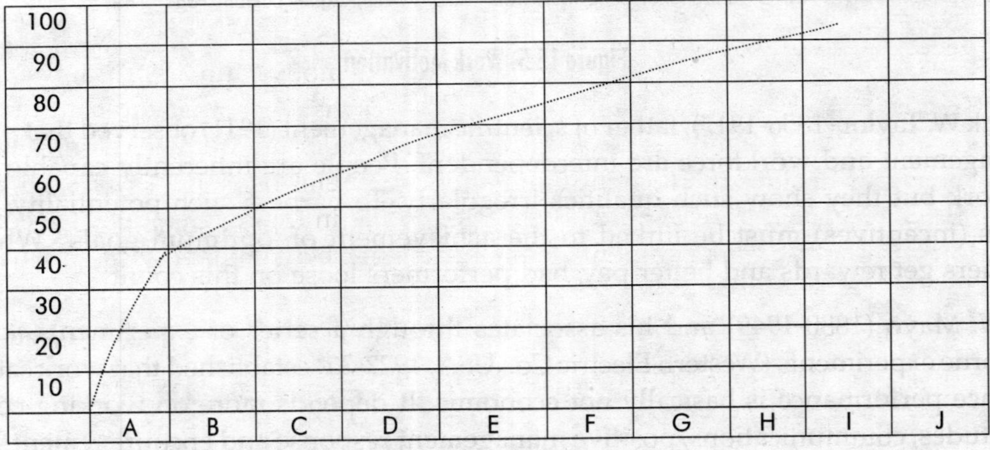

Figure 15.4: Pareto Graph

MAJOR THEORIES OF MOTIVATION

We have already discussed theories of motivation in brief. Here we will be discussing major theories of motivation with some critical notes. Before we proceed further let us examine the process of development of work motivation theory as given in Figure 15.5.

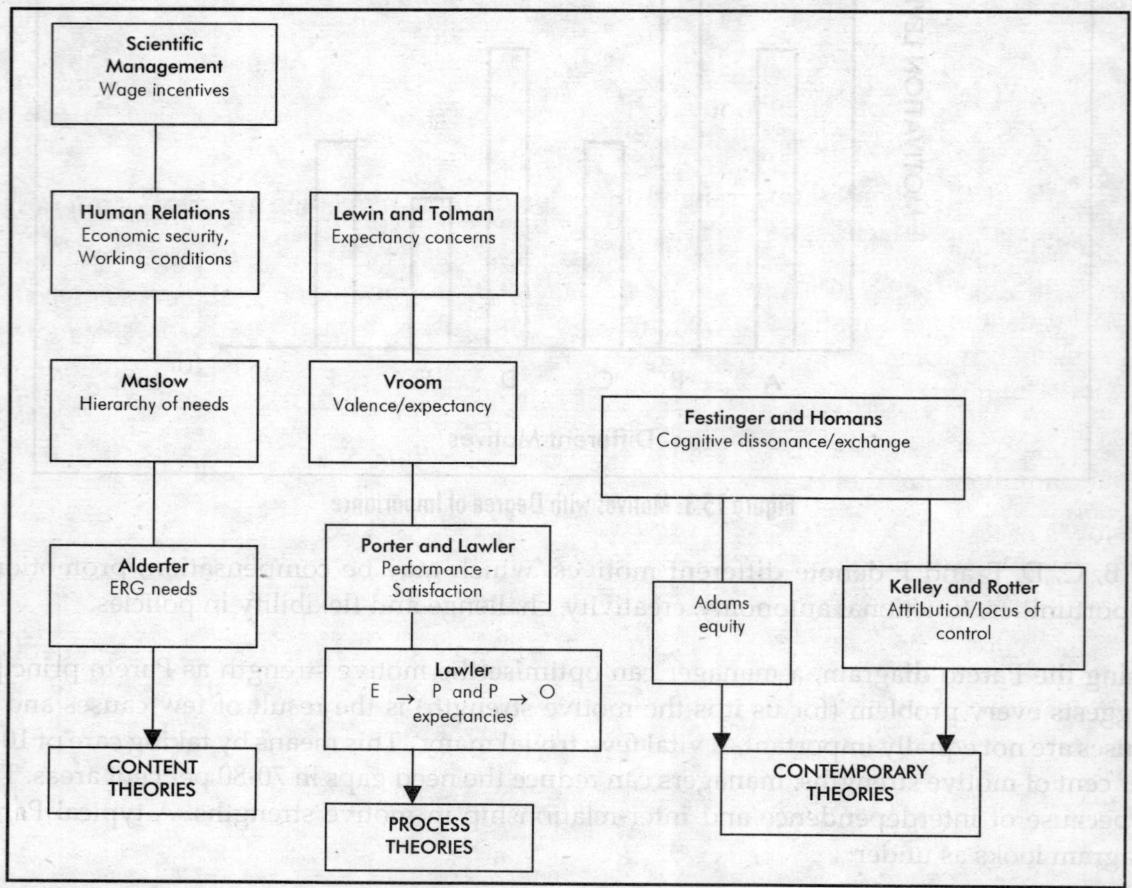

Source: Fred Luthans (1998), *Organisational Behaviour*, Irwin McGraw-Hill, Eighth Edition, Page: 169.

Figure 15.5: Work Motivation

Frederick W. Taylor (1856-1917), father of scientific management (1911) observed that prosperity of management and workforce are interdependent. People are inherently capable of doing hard work but they show such qualities irregularly. To harness such potentiality, pay and rewards (incentives) must be linked to the achievement of 'optimum goals'. While good performers get rewards and better pay, bad performers loose on this count.

Elton W. Mayo (1880-1949) and his associates through a series of experiments, known as Hawthorne experiments (Western Electric Co., USA, 1927-32) established that work satisfaction and hence performance is basically not economic. It depends more on working conditions and attitudes, communications, positive management response and encouragement, working environment, etc.

Maslow's Need Hierarchy Theory

Abraham Maslow (1908-1970) through his need hierarchy theory established that motivation of people arises from levels-a hierarchy of needs. We have briefly introduced this earlier. Here we will elaborate his concepts first examining essence of his theory and then critically examine his theory. The essence of his theory can be summarised as follows:

1. Wants and desires of human beings influence their behaviour. Already satisfied wants and desires do not act as motivators. People show their motive or behaviour to fulfil their unsatisfied wants and desires.

2. Needs of the people are arranged in order of their perceived priority or hierarchy. Perceived need factors of people vary.

3. People can advance from one level of need hierarchy to another, only when their preceding need factors are satisfied. For example, without satisfaction of lower order needs, like physiological and safety, people cannot advance to satisfaction of need for belongingness or social needs.

4. The more people advance to higher order needs, the more they display their satisfaction and motivation to work.

Maslow's need hierarchy theory divides human needs into five distinct category as under:

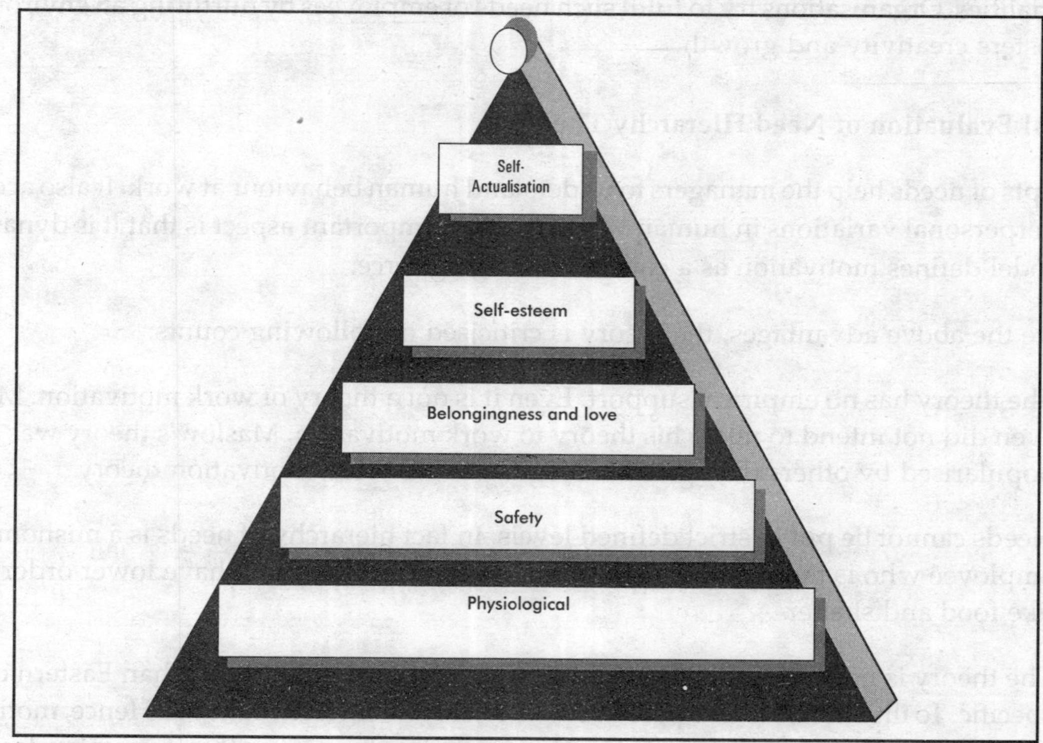

Figure 15. 6: Maslow's Hierarchy of Needs

Physiological needs are the basic needs of human beings which are essential to sustain or survive. Such needs include, food, water, air, clothing, shelter, etc. From the organisational point of view such needs are met through salary and basic working conditions.

Safety needs ensure protection from economic and physical environment. People expect some reasonableness in their perceived environment, which minimises the degree of uncertainty. Job security, degree of continuity, order, structure and predictability are such needs. Organisations fulfil such needs of the employees by ensuring a protective work environment. Need for belongingness and love arises after satisfaction of earlier two lower order needs. This is also known as social needs. People in this need level develop a strong sense of affiliation and get concerned with love, affection, belongingness, acceptance and friendship. Organisations meet such needs by providing appropriate work culture to help employees to identify themselves with the organisation.

At self-esteem need level, employees look for satisfaction of their esteem or egoistic needs. Esteem needs pertain to self-respect and respect or esteem from others. Self respect is ensured by achieving competence, confidence, personal strength, adequacy, achievement, independence and freedom, while respect from others come from prestige, recognition, acceptance, attention, status, reputation and appreciation. Organisations to fulfil such needs of employees provide challenging work assignments, performance feedback, performance recognition, participative work culture, empowerment, participation in decision-making, etc.

At the self-actualisation need stage, employees desire to become what they are capable of becoming. They want to create something of their own using their talent, capacities and potentialities. Organisations try to fulfil such needs of employees by nurturing an environment that fosters creativity and growth.

Critical Evaluation of Need Hierarchy Theory

Concepts of needs help the managers to understand human behaviour at work. It also accounts for interpersonal variations in human work. Another important aspect is that it is dynamic as the model defines motivation as a constant changing force.

Despite the above advantages, the theory is criticised on following counts:

1. The theory has no empirical support. Even it is not a theory of work motivation. Maslow even did not intend to relate his theory to work motivation. Maslow's theory was in fact popularised by others (Douglas McGregor, etc.) as work motivation theory.

2. Needs cannot be put in strict defined levels. In fact hierarchy of needs is a misnomer. An employee who is motivated by self-actualisation need may still have lower order needs like food and shelter.

3. The theory is not culturally aligned. It is more Western value laden than Eastern culture specific. To illustrate, work is perceived differently in different cultures. Hence, motivation to work is different in different countries and also it varies within a country, from one individual work group to another. Therefore, the theory cannot hold good for heterogeneous work groups.

4. Maslow's existential philosophy is questioned as people may like to remain content plateaued with the satisfaction of their lower order needs. They may like to move further up in the hierarchy.

5. Diagnosing need deficiency for employees, following Maslow's approach is time consuming. Even after such diagnosis, it may not help an organisation to develop a tailor-made model for employee motivation.

Herzberg's Two-factor Theory or Motivation-Hygiene Theory

Frederick Herzberg (1959), extending the work of Maslow, developed the content theory of motivation. His study is based on responses of 200 accountants and engineers, drawn from eleven industries in Pittsburgh area. Using critical incident methods, he had asked the samples to respond on two aspects as follows:

1. When did they feel particularly good about their job.
2. When did they feel exceptionally bad about their job.

Herzberg found that the samples described different types of conditions for good and bad feelings. Factors responsible for job satisfaction are quite different from the factors they perceive as contributors to job dissatisfaction. Their reported good feelings were found to be associated with job experiences and job content. While, their reported bad feelings were found to be associated with the peripheral aspects of job, i.e., job context. Since his study was based on a two-factor hypothesis, we call his theory two-factor theory. As his study established that opposite of satisfaction is not dissatisfaction and removing dissatisfying elements from a job does not necessarily make the job satisfying, he has classified the factors into two categories:

1. Motivation factors
2. Hygiene or maintenance factors

Herzbeg mentioned six motivation factors as follow:

1. Recognition
2. Advancement
3. Responsibility
4. Achievement
5. Possibility of growth
6. Job content or work itself

Presence of these factors in the job creates a motivating environment but its absence does not cause dissatisfaction.

Similarly, Herzberg mentioned ten hygiene or maintenance factors as given under:

1. Company policy and administration
2. Technical supervision

3. Interpersonal relations with subordinates
4. Salary
5. Job security
6. Personal life
7. Working conditions
8. Status
9. Interpersonal relations with supervisors
10. Interpersonal relations with peers

These factors are context factors. Their existence just creates an environment for doing work. But factors by itself cannot motivate people to work. In Herzberg's words, their absence can dissatisfy people but their presence per se cannot satisfy people.

The crux of the two-factor theory of motivation, therefore is that managers should cater for both satisfiers and dissatisfiers. Mere improvement of hygienic factors cannot guarantee a motivating environment. In Figure 15.7, we have presented the essence of Herzberg theory, using a diagram.

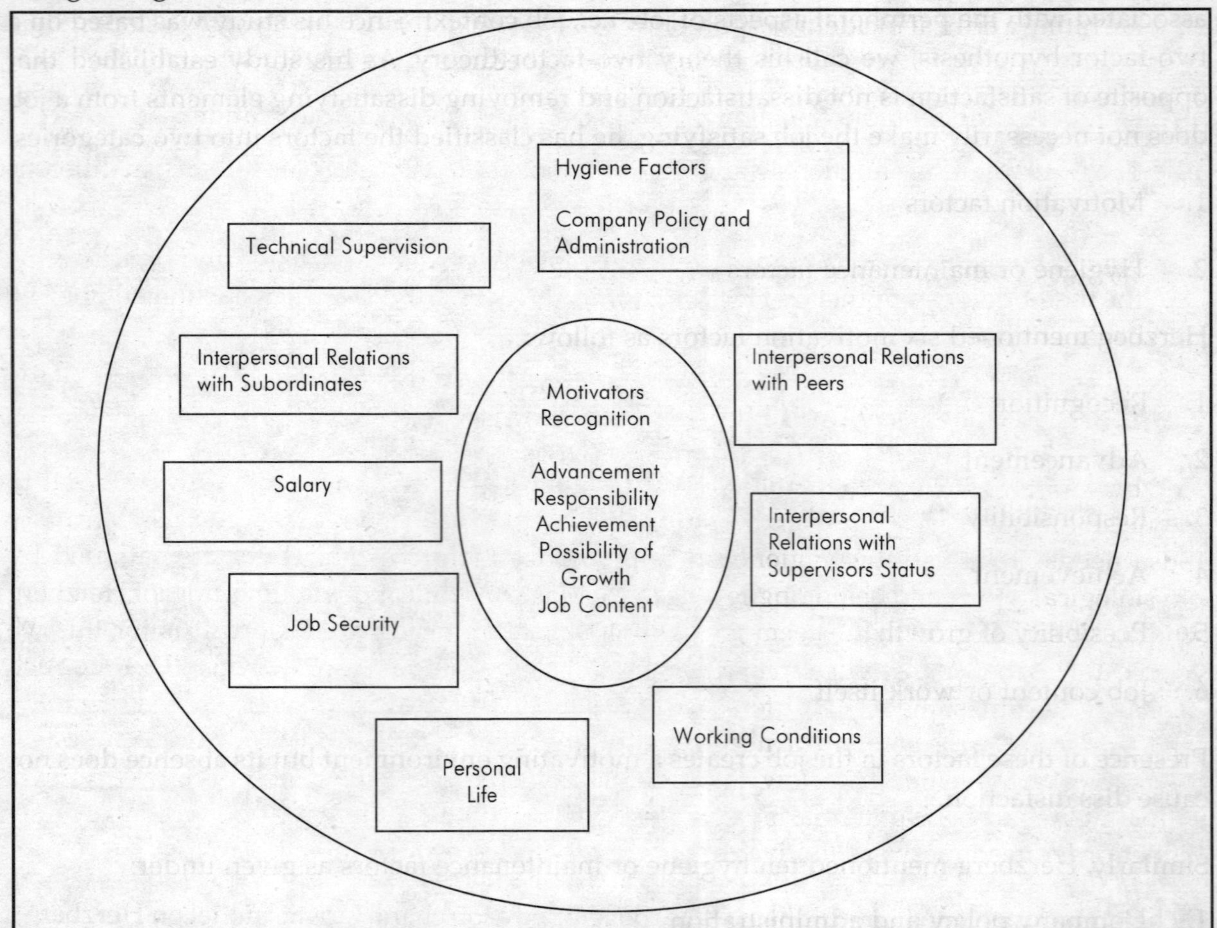

Figure 15.7: Hygiene Factors and Motivators

Critical Evaluation of Herzberg's Theory

Herzberg's theory is the first of its kind based on field research. While Maslow's work was based on clinical observations (laboratory-based findings), Herzberg did his study to understand motivation in work environment. Secondly, Herzberg's study recommends actions for managers to improve motivation in work environment. His emphasis on content factors, shift our focus from traditional money motivators concept, which were earlier viewed as the most potent factors for work motivation. Thirdly, Herzberg also has contributed to the alternative approach to motivation by job enrichment. Finally, Herzberg had double dimensionalised the needs, instead of its absolute categorisation into five distinct levels, as was done by Maslow.

Despite all the above listed merits, Herzberg's theory has also been subjected to the following criticism:

1. It is limited by its methodology, when things go well people tend to take credit for themselves. Contrarily they attribute failures to the external environment.
2. Herzberg's theory is also method bound. Using other methods, we can not get similar results. Critical incidents method by nature may cause people only to recall the recent incidents or experiences. But experiences are always subject to change. Moreover, while narrating a critical incident, respondents get wide flexibility to give vent to their opinions rather than the realities. Thus survey findings became more opinion-laden.
3. Herzberg's model more talk about job satisfaction than on job motivation.
4. The theory ignores situational variables as it is not backed by adequate research in different work environments.
5. Even though the theory assumes a relationship between job satisfaction and productivity, the methodology applied by Herzberg limits its focus only on job satisfaction and not on productivity.

Comparison of Maslow and Herzberg's Models

Herzberg's framework is compatible with Maslow's hierarchy of needs. Maslow referred to the needs or motives, while Herzberg dealt with goals or incentives which tend to satisfy those needs. To illustrate, hygiene or maintenance factors of Herzberg are satisfied by physiological, safety and belongingness needs of Maslow, while motivation factors of Herzberg tend to be satisfied by self-esteem and self-actualisation needs of Maslow. It is for this we often call Herzberg's theory as an extension of Maslow's need hierarchy theory. Despite such similarity, we find some major differences between the two theories. Maslow's need hierarchy is a sequential arrangement of needs, while Herzberg's model does not have any such hierarchical arrangement. Maslow believed that any unsatisfied need, irrespective of its level of hierarchy can be a potential motivation. On the contrary, Herzberg believed that only higher order needs serve as motivators.

Richard Hackman and Greg Oldham (1975) developed a job characteristic model on Herzberg's two-factor theory, showing how a good job design can lead to internal motivation of the employees and contribute to better job performance. The theory postulates that five job characteristics lead to three psychological states, which affect the motivation and satisfaction of the employees. The five job characteristics are skill variety, task identity, task significance, autonomy and feedback.

Skill variety is the extent or range of skills, abilities and talents of employees. The more they are able to utilise their skills in the job, the greater their level of satisfaction. Hence, jobs are to be designed in a way that ensures utilisation of wide skill variety of individuals. Task identity signifies the extent of involvement of employees in the total job. This enables an individual to identify himself in the total creation, which gives him a sense of pride and satisfaction. Task significance on the other hand denotes significance of a job on the life of others – both within and outside the organisation. A positive significance of a job gives psychological satisfaction to the person who does it. Autonomy is the extent of freedom given for a job. The degree of autonomy depends on the extent of independence given to an employee in deciding about job scheduling, formulating the procedures, decision-making without interference of others. The more the job autonomy, the greater the job satisfaction and so also motivation. Feedback provides the opportunity to assess the right or wrong for doing a job.

The three psychological states, which an individual experiences are as follows:

1. Skill variety, task identity and task significance provide 'experienced meaningfulness', Autonomy provides 'experienced responsibility'. While feedback ensures 'experienced knowledge of results'.

2. Once an employee experiences arousal of these three psychological states, they feel intrinsically rewarded, which results in intrinsic motivation.

3. Hackman and Oldham developed a motivating potential score (MPS), based on their study, which measures the propensity of a job to become motivating. The formula is presented below:

$$\text{MPs} = \left[\frac{\text{Skills Variety} + \text{Task Identity} + \text{Task Significance}}{3}\right] \times (\text{Autonomy}) \times (\text{Feedback})$$

ERG Theory

Clayton Alderfer (1972) of Yale University developed the ERG theory based on empirical research. He modified Maslow's five levels of needs to three levels and labelled them as needs for existence, relatedness and growth. The name ERG has been derived from the first letters of each such need. ERG theory differs from Maslow's need hierarchy theory in following ways:

1. Instead of five need hierarchies, ERG theory considers only three need hierarchies.

2. Need hierarchy theory postulates rigid progression from one need level to another, while ERG theory assumes that more than one need may be operative simultaneously. This means an employee working on growth need, may even remain unsatisfied in relatedness and existence needs.

3. Basic postulates of ERG theory is that it works on the frustration – regression model. If for any reason, employees continually become frustrated in satisfying their needs at one level, they intensify their desire to satisfy lower level needs. It is like a failure to get recognition is compensated by the desire to make more money. Contrarily, Maslow suggests people will stay at a certain need level, till they are able to satisfy the same.

Critical Evaluation of ERG Theory

ERG theory is pragmatic in its approach, as it considers individual differences among people. Individual differences in terms of education, family background and culture can alter the motive strength vis-à-vis perceived need factors. The theory is more appealing, intuitive and logical than Maslow's need hierarchy theory. Despite such advantages, the theory does not offer any clear-cut guidelines. It just indicates people will be motivated to behave in a particular way to satisfy one of the three sets of needs, i.e., need for existence, need for relatedness and need for growth. Moreover, the theory is yet to be backed by adequate research.

McClelland's Three Needs Theory (nAch, nAff, nPow or Achievement Motivation Theory

David C. McClelland (1976) through his twenty-year study at Harvard University documented differences in needs of the people in three important areas as under:

1. *Achievement Need (nAch):* People in this need category drive to excel, to achieve in relation to a set of standards. They like challenge and they like to succeed in a competitive environment. They work hard willingly and volunteer for work which stretches their ability fully. This category of people do not get motivated by money. They feel more motivated with a sense of accomplishment and achievement.
2. *Affiliation Need (nAff):* This need emerges from the desire for friendly and close interpersonal relationships. Obviously people try to fulfil such needs with satisfying relationships with the organisation, peer groups, work teams, etc. Since this need group people try to identify themselves with the organisation, they always prefer to foster a friendly work culture and try to meet their needs through friendly relations.
3. *Power Need (nPow):* People in this need group always try to get satisfaction by controlling others. This need emerges from the drive for superiority and obviously people in this need category look for leadership positions in the organisation.

Evaluation of the Theory

McClelland highlighted the importance of matching individual and the job. People with high achievement need always prefer challenging job assignments while people with low achievement need, prefer a job situation that ensures stability, security and predictability. Organisations by manipulating the achievement need can get complex jobs accomplished by high achievers. However, McClelland's work is criticised on many important counts like;

how a sense of achievement or other associated motive can be inculcated in an adult employee. McClelland contends this can be taught and thus motives related to achievement, etc., can be developed in an adult. This contention is not tenable in psychological literature. Secondly, McClelland contends needs can be changed through education and training. But psychologists contend needs are permanently acquired.

Third, thematic appreciation test (TAT) used for the study by McClelland is also subject to criticism as interpretation of responses using TAT is subject to the researcher's bias.

THEORY X AND THEORY Y

Douglas McGregor (1990) of MIT defined organisations as psychological entities and, therefore, can be characterised by their assumptions about what motivates people. The basic hypothesis is that managerial decisions and actions are based on certain assumptions about human nature and behaviour. McGregor proposed two distinct views and assumptions about human behaviour. Negative behaviour group people was categorised by him under theory 'X' and positive behaviour group people was categorised under theory 'Y'. Theory 'X' labeled employees dislike work, are lazy, dislike responsibility and they need to be coerced to get the work done. Theory 'Y' labelled employees like work, creativity, responsibility and they can exercise self-direction. Motivational implications of McGregor's analysis, therefore, can be best analysed in the context of Maslow's need hierarchy theory. Theory 'X' labelled people can be motivated by satisfaction of lower order needs while theory 'Y' labeled people can be motivated by satisfaction of higher order needs.

Different attributes of theory 'X' and theory 'Y' labeled people as observed by Maslow is presented in the Table given below.

Therefore, to motivate, process theory suggests that organisations must understand how an individual takes decisions and what efforts he puts in the job. Expectancy theory, equity theory and performance satisfaction model are the important approaches to understand the cognitive or process theories of motivation.

Theory-X Attributes	Theory-Y Attributes
1. The average human being inherently dislikes work and will always try to avoid work.	1. People of this group exercise self-direction and self-control in achieving objectives to which they have committed.
2. For such inherent human characteristics, people must be coerced, controlled, directed and threatened with punishment to get work from them.	2. Commitment to objective is a function of reward associated with their achievement.
3. The average human being prefers to be directed, avoids responsibility, is less ambitious and likes security above all.	3. The average human being learns (under proper conditions) not only to accept but to seek responsibility.
4. For motivating this group of people, organisation has to enforce strict control with a stick and restrict the motivational reinforcements only to those areas, that fulfil their lower order needs.	4. They have the capacity of imagination, intensity and creativity in the solution of organisational problems.
	5. Organisations are able to only partially utilise their potential. 6. People with these attributes need to be developed so that they can release their potential towards common objects. These people by and large can be motivated with the satisfaction of their higher order needs.

Cognitive or Process Theories of Motivation

Content theories of motivation emphasised on the importance of inner needs in motivation. On the contrary cognitive models or process theories of motivation emphasise on the idea that people take conscious decisions about their job behaviour. Therefore, to motivate, process theory suggests that organisations must understand how an individual takes decisions and what efforts he puts in the job. Expectancy theory, equity theory and performance satisfaction model are the important approaches to understand the cognitive or process theories of motivation.

Expectancy Theory

This theory essentially emphasises that people feel increasingly motivated if they perceive that:

1. Their effort will result in successful performance, and
2. Successful performance will ensure desired results.

It has different names like instrumentality theory, path-goal theory and valence-instrumentality-expectancy (VIE) theory. It has its roots in the cognitive concepts of Kurt Lewin and Edward Tolman and in the choice behaviour and utility concepts from classical economic theory. However, it was Victor H. Vroom (1964), who formulated an expectancy theory, as an alternative to content models, for work motivation. The theory identified relationships among variables, which affect individual behaviour in a dynamic environment. It was an attempt to capture how people determine their extent of effort for a job and how such effort gets influenced by their perceived expectation. Strength of a tendency to act in a certain way depends on the strength of an expectation of outcome, which is likely to accrue upon accomplishment of the job. So motivation is the product of strength of one's desire (valence) and perceived probability of getting something good (expectancy). We can show such relationship as under:

$$\begin{pmatrix}\text{Valence –}\\ \text{Strength of one's}\\ \text{desire for something}\end{pmatrix} \times \begin{pmatrix}\text{Expectancy –}\\ \text{probability of getting}\\ \text{it with a certain action}\end{pmatrix} = \begin{pmatrix}\text{Motivation –}\\ \text{Strength of drive}\\ \text{towards an action}\end{pmatrix}$$

$$V \times E = M$$

Valance is the degree of desirability of certain outcomes. It is, therefore, the strength of an individual's preference for a particular outcome, which may be a promotion, pay rise, recognition, etc., after he successfully accomplishes the job. Since people may have positive or negative preference for an outcome, valence may be negative or positive. Hence valance may vary from – 1 to + 1.

Expectancy is the perceived possibility of a particular outcome, that would follow after an action. It is, therefore, the strength of belief that an act will be followed by particular outcomes. The strength of expectations is based on past experience. People expect what will happen in the future on what has occurred in the past. As expectancy is an action-outcome association it may range from zero to one. If employees perceive no possibility of an outcome from certain acts, their expectancy would be zero, while on the contrary value of expectancy would be one, when they feel (from their experience of action-outcome relationship) that they are likely to achieve something with certainty.

Vroom has used one more term in between expectancy and valence, which is usefulness or instrumentality. Instrumentality is the belief that the first level outcome would lead to the second level outcome.

For example, one may be motivated for superior level performance for his desire to get promoted. Here first level outcome (superior level performance) is seen as being instrumental for second level outcome (promotion).

Therefore, the strength of motivation to perform a certain act will depend on the sum of the products of the valences (including instrumentality) and the expectancies, which can be represented as under:

Motivation strength = $\sum V \times I \times E$

Evaluation of the Theory

It is believed that content theories oversimplified the complex process of work motivation. While on the contrary Vroom's model highlights the importance of organisation behaviour, clarifying relationships between the employees and the organisations. His model has generated research interests among the corporate and academic circles. The theory also has a cognitive dimension, as individuals are viewed as thinking and reasoning beings and they just do not simply act for the satisfaction of their unfulfilled needs.

Despite such unique features in Vroom's approach, his theory was also criticised in following aspects:

1. It needs to be adequately tested in different work environments.
2. Employees may always not take a conscious decision. It was observed they are also prone to take unthoughtful decisions and later try to rationalise the action with their own logic.
3. Linkages between efforts performance and performance-rewards may not be linear. Organisational policies may further complicate the process. For example promotion may be on seniority, educational background, etc.
4. The theory is complex. In real-life situation managers may have time and resource constraints to implement it.

Equity Theory

This theory owes its origin to several contributors like Festinger, Heider, Homans, Jacques, Patchen, Weick, etc. However, James Stacy Adams's (1965) contribution is much discussed in the literature on motivation. The theory proposes that in the work environment, motivation is influenced by one's perception of how equitably he or she is treated compared to others. The theory is also known as 'social comparison theory' or 'inequity theory'. Perceptively employees try to reduce their inequity through such comparison or by establishing a hypothetical exchange relationship. An individual accounts for the amount of work he puts in and corresponding rewards he gets for the same and then he compares the efforts and rewards of a similarly placed person in the organisation. If equity exists, the individual feels o.k. In case of inequity it propels him into action to create a condition of equity. Since inequity propels action, it is the motivator. The greater the perceived inequity, the greater the motivation to reduce it. While doing so, individuals can make any of the following choices:

1. Change or alter inputs
2. Change or alter outcomes
3. Distort inputs and outcomes
4. Distort inputs and outcomes of others (with whom they compare themselves)
5. Select a different referent (to compare)
6. Withdraw from the field

Evaluation of the Theory

It is a promising theory of work motivation as well as job satisfaction. For this reason it has generated extensive research. Since the basic theory works on perception in a social comparison process, it is by default dynamic as inequity in perceived perception motivates employees to restore equity.

However, the theory is criticised on following counts:

1. It is complex and difficult in application.
2. Perceptions are difficult to measure or assess.
3. Choosing a 'comparison other' may not be always correct.
4. A given factor may be an input as well as an outcome.
5. The study is based on laboratory experiments rather than in real-life situations in organisations.

Performance Satisfaction Theory

Layman W. Porter and Edward W. Lawler (1968), based on Vroom's expectancy model, observed that performance leads to satisfaction contrary to our belief that satisfaction leads to performance. Other interesting observations made by them are that motivation (efforts), performance (accomplishment) and satisfaction are separate variables. This is again in contrast to our belief that motivation leads to performance, which in turn leads to satisfaction. Efforts (force or motivation) do not directly lead to a performance. It is mediated by abilities, traits and role perceptions. After performance, rewards that follow and the way they are perceived, determine the satisfaction. The theory is illustrated in Figure 15.8.

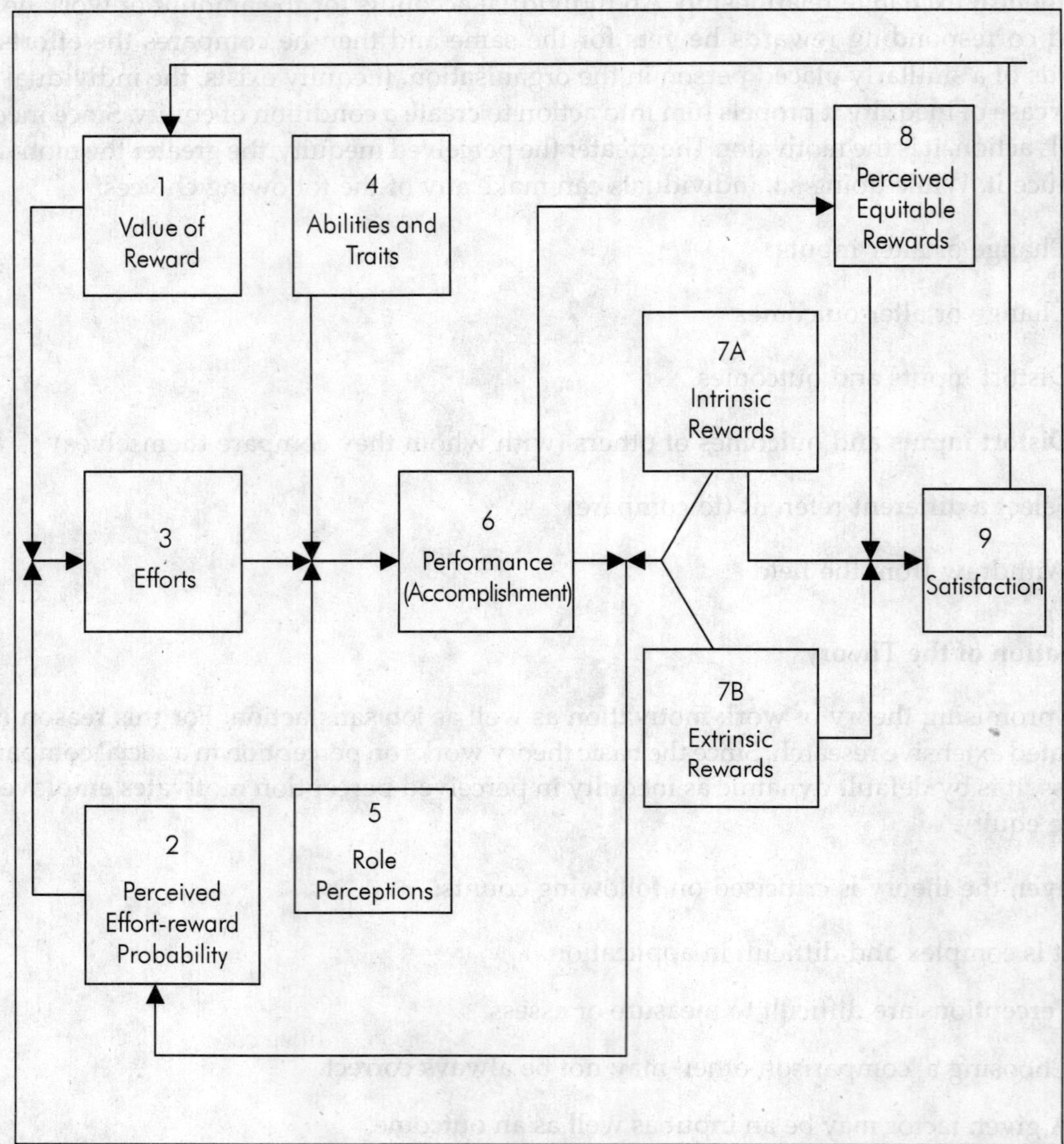

Figure 15.8: Performance Satisfaction Theory

Whether an individual will make an effort depends on interaction between the value of reward (Box 1) and perceived effort-reward probability (Box 2). Effort (Box 3) is the motivation. Performance (accomplishment) (Box 6) is not the direct consequence of effort. It is the product of effort (Box 3), abilities and traits (Box 4) and role perceptions (Box 5). Performance leads to certain outcomes in the form of intrinsic rewards (Box 7A) and extrinsic rewards (Box 7B). Both intrinsic and extrinsic rewards provide satisfaction (Box 9). However, such reward-satisfaction relationship is moderated by the perceived equitability of rewards (Box 8).

Attribution Theory and Locus of Control

Harold Kelley advocated this theory which is mainly concerned with the cognitive process by which an individual interprets behaviour attributing to certain parts of the relevant environment. Such casual relationships or attributes are interpreted by an individual for his own behaviour or for others' behaviour. Fritz Heider contended that both perceived internal forces (ability, efforts and fatigue) and external forces (others' supervision, machines, methods, climate, rules and procedures) together determine the behaviour of an individual. Since the perceived causes are the determinants of work behaviour and the perception differs, people behave differently in a given situation. The concept of locus of control is different from the concept of attribution. While attribution theory is concerned with identifying the causes of one's own as well as others' behaviour, 'locus of control' theory is applicable to oneself only. Employees may perceive that their own behaviour is internally or externally controlled. Since external control factors (which influenced their own behaviour) are beyond their own control, employees believe that their rewards and punishments are dependent on factors like fate, luck or chance. For internal control factors, they feel they can influence their outcomes through their own ability, skills or effort. Julian Rotter (1966) developed a 23-item scale for measurement of locus of control called as Internal-External (1 - E) scale.

Goal Setting Theory

Edwin Locke (1968) considered two cognitive determinants of behaviour; values and intentions (goals). Emotions and desires represent the form of values and value judgements. Intentions are goals to satisfy desires or emotions (values). This results in consequences, feedback and reinforcement. The study suggests that individuals are willing to work hard when they know what is required from them. Setting specific attainable goals is related to high level performance.

MISCELLANEOUS THEORIES ON MOTIVATION

Apart from the theories of motivation listed above, there certain other theories, which, however, revolve around the core content or process theories. Those can be briefly discussed as under:

H.A. Murray (1938) discussed about manifest needs theory, which is basically a multivariate approach to the structure of needs. The basic difference between Murray's formulation and Maslow's and Alderfer's formulations is that Murray does not suggest a hierarchical order of various types of needs. Based on several years of clinical observations at the Harvard psychological clinic, Murray argues that intensities of various personality-related needs, taken together, represent a central motivating force.

R.W. White's (1959) competence motive theory (some what similar to the power motive theory of Adler) relates motivation to the desire of employees for mastery over physical and social environs (Cornell Study).

S. Schachter's affiliation motivation theory (1959) relates motivation to the strong need for affiliation.

C. Argyris's maturity-immaturity theory (1957) relates motivation to an environment which serves both the needs of the organisation and the needs of the members of the organisation (Yale study).

W. F. Whyte's money motivation theory (1955) suggests that people are motivated primarily by the desire to make money. However, Whyte contends that monetary incentives should not be considered in isolation from other non-monetary incentives.

R. Likert and D. Katz's Michigan studies (1948) have emphasised the vital point that a productivity motivated work-team is really a function of a particular type of supervisory style. Since productivity has its root in employee-motivation, it can be harnessed by carefully designing an organisation in which the individual develops a feeling that he has some importance in the organisation.

Megginson, for the sake of our convenience, has classified the leading theories of motivation into three groups (stated below).

1. *Perspective Theories:* Taylor's scientific management approach, various human relations theories, mcgregor's theory y, etc., which, in reality, tell management to motivate people.

2. *Content Theories:* Maslow's hierarchy of needs theory, herzberg's two-factor theory, McClelland's achievement need theory, etc., which try to identify the causes of behaviour.

3. *Process Theories:* Various behaviouristic theories which believe in stimulus-response relationship vis-à-vis motivation (e.g. Skinner's behaviour modification theory) and cognitive theories (e.g., Vroom's expectancy theory and Porter-Lawler's future-oriented expectancy theory) which deal with the genesis of behaviour.

The brief discussions above regarding different motivation theories, studies and experiments, taken together, reflect our basic understanding of the concept of motivation and related aspects in a systematic manner.

Our next phase of discussion has mainly focussed on the relevant Indian studies in this field in order to understand the underlying motive forces determining the behaviour and performance of the Indian employees.

In India, not many empirical studies on motivation and its related aspects have been carried out. There are some studies on industrial workers and some on technical personnel, supervisors and managers. Most of the studies in India have attempted to find out the job-satisfaction variables, which have been construed as the motivational variables.

The first such study in India, is by Bose (1947) on industrial workers and that has paved the way for other researchers to investigate into the perceived importance of job-factors to workers.

Most of the studies relating to the industrial workers, during the period 1951-1971, have rated adequate earnings, job security, boss and personal life as the main factors which determine their behaviour.

Ganguli's study (1964) on first-line supervisors (N = 44), has ranked incentive, adequate income, promotional opportunities, job security and sympathetic treatment from superiors as the important job-factors vis-à-vis motivation.

Lahiri and Srivastava's study (1967), on middle-management personnel (N = 93), has ranked good organisational policies and administration, better scope for promotion, good salary, good superior-subordinate relationship and opportunity for growth as the major determinants of satisfaction.

Sawalapurkar and others' study (1968), on middle-level managers (N = 30), has ranked nine job-factors in the following order of importance; job content, opportunity for advancement, job security, boss, company, working conditions, facilities, working hours, and grievance redressal.

Padaki and Dolke's study (1970), on job-attitudes of supervisors (N = 15) (based on Herzberg's two-factor theory), has found lack of recognition, unfavourable superior-subordinate relationship, lack of technically-competent supervision, unfavourable organisational policies and administration and inadequate salary as the major dissatisfiers. Another study conducted by them has also found more or less the same as perceived dissatisfiers.

Rao's study (1970), on bank managers (N = 60), with a view to testing the Herzberg's two-factor theory, has found promotion, company policies and salary on the dissatisfaction scale.

Narain's study (1971), on public-sector managers (N = 1213), has ranked eight factors in the following order or importance; feeling of worthwhile accomplishments, recognition, decision-making authority, opportunity for personnel growth and development, promotional opportunity, prestige of the organisation in the community, pay and fringe benefits, and job security. So far as the need-deficiencies are concerned, he has found that promotion, recognition and personal growth and development respectively show very high degrees of dissatisfaction in that order.

Bhattacharyya's study (1972), on managers (N = 210), has shown lack of participation in goal-setting, inadequacy of pay, inadequate job-authority and 'lack of opportunity given to help people' on the dissatisfaction scale.

Pestonjee and Basu's study (1972), on executives (N = 80), has shown promotion and growth, recognition, prestige, organisational policies and administration, and autonomy as the major determinants of satisfaction.

Singhal and Upadhyay's Study (1972), on supervisors (N = 22), has also found opportunities for promotion, job security, working conditions, work group, opportunities for training, competent and sympathetic supervisors, adequate income and other facilitates, etc., as major motivational factors.

Agarwal (1976) has sharply criticised the Indian studies on work motivation, alleging that such researches suffer from a number of inconsistencies mainly because those have been carried out practically as a part of the job done for the employees with a view to helping them reduce production costs. Thus, the measures, suggested by such researchers, have always proved to be short-term remedies and much-spoken-about theories on motivation have come more like fads or fashions than something substantial and lasting. Thinking in line with Pareek (1974), he has developed a stratification model of work motivation with variables like; social system, self-status and role. Pareek (1974) has assumed that societal system is a very important variable in the field of motivation that causes or determines that behaviour of an individual in an organisation.

Sharma's study (1981), on administrators in Delhi (N = 67), has found power-motive as the main guiding force for motivation.

Sharma's study (1982), on supervisors (N = 3378) – drawing samples from 50 manufacturing organisations both in the public sector and the private-sector, has obtained score values for different factors that influence motivation (presented below):

Superintendent-management relations	63.21%
Monetary benefits	60.30%
Objectivity and rationality	56.00%
Recognition and appreciation	51.32%
Welfare facilities	48.39%
Scope for advancement	47.32%
Grievance handling	45.83%
Training and education	43.46%
Participative management	39.68%

The study has been carried out on a 3-point scale – low, medium and high frequencies.

Neelamegham and Vaid's study (1986), on motivation of the sales-force (N = 116), has found highest need-deficiencies with respect to prospects of promotion and recognition for good work.

It is important to note that the major Indian studies are on supervisory and managerial personnel. Another important feature of the Indian studies is that most of the studies have been carried out with a small sample, using only conventional methods like ranking, percentage calculation, etc. Some studies have been carried out simply to authenticate Herzberg's two-factor theory, while some others are highly opinionated studies without much adherence to the norms of sampling and survey methods. Even, in most of the cases, suitable structured close-ended questionnaire was not administered. Those are simple inferences after informal discussions with the samples mostly drawn without following proper sampling procedure. Another feature is that most of the studies are based on experiences of single industrial units. Representative results are difficult to obtain from a survey based on a small sample drawn from a single unit.

The author (1993) himself carried out a study on bank employees (N = 390) to understand the importance of promotion as a motivational reinforcer. Since it was a structured study, as a part of doctoral thesis, it would not be out of place to mention the outcome of such a study to understand the perceived motivational factors of bank employees. The study indicates that the bank employees, in general, are de-motivated to a significant extent mainly due to major deficiencies vis-à-vis fulfillment of their needs. Absence of job assignments that are satisfying and challenging enough because of traditional banking functions, which are basically routine in nature and job-specialisation at the macro-level, a poor grievance-handling system, very limited scope for upward mobility, increasing lack of job security, threat of transfer, improper job distribution and non-recognition of commendable performance of employees by management are some of the key examples of highly de-motivating factors vis-à-vis effectiveness of the bank employees. Their de-motivation increases further because, practically speaking, there is a definite lack of harmonious management-employees relations and that is undeniably reflected from the responses of the sample-employees (i.e., a majority of them have ranked 'indiscipline' and 'disobedience' as the two most common grievances of management against them).

Inadequate scope for advancement, inter alia, happens to be the most significant de-motivator. However, the sample-employees, as such, are not seriously discontented with the existing promotion policies in their organisations. In fact, the commercial banks, as a matter of routine, periodically review and restructure their promotion policies in consultation with their respective unions. Thus, the bank employees do participate (through their unions) in the process of formulation of promotion policies (mainly in line with the authorities' thinking for obvious reasons). But due to paucity of declared vacancies, only a few vacancies are actually made available (at periodic intervals) to be manned by promotion. Therefore, only a few employees, who fulfil the eligibility-criteria, ultimately qualify in the selection tests for promotion, leaving a good number of employees aspiring for promotion to wait till the next chance. And, the number of such employees aspiring for promotion is multiplying every year. In this context, we offer some suggestions below, which require serious consideration on the part of the authorities of the commercial banks in India.

1. The commercial banks should seriously try to enlarge their existing service-packages by careful inclusion of some new functions. Although some progress to this effect has already been made, many commercial banks still prefer to remain within their traditional functional ambit. Merchant banking, venture capital, mutual fund operations, leasing, hire purchase, factoring services, housing finance, credit card facilities, etc., are some of the emerging financial-services which the commercial banks can very well include in their service packages. These will, inter alia, certainly facilitate increase in job opportunities at various organisational levels. A good number of employees who are otherwise eligible for promotion, after undergoing adequate training in these comparatively new service-areas, can be promoted and placed in the newly-created positions. In this way, promotional vacancies can be increased considerably.

2. Varieties of functions enable many organisations to offer promotion-alternatives to their employees. But, for the banking organisations, due to similarity of functions, cross-lateral transfers are often misconstrued by unions as arbitrary decisions of management. Thus, job rotation, which can relieve many content-plateaued employees from functional drudgery to a significant extent and can encourage creative behaviour on their part, faces undue resistance from the employees' side. In order to set this right, employees should be trained properly, keeping the need for their attitudinal changes in mind, with a view to helping them develop a rational view on transfers either within or outside the station. Outstation transfers, at times, result in substantial reduction in material benefits for employees. This problem has to be seriously looked into by management.

3. Many commercial banks are now retaining the services of outside agencies to avail of computer facilities. Apparently, this approach may be a costefficient one (if we consider only the direct costs involved). But, if we can account for (even indirectly) the costs of employees de-motivation (in the form of loss of man-days, etc.), the undeniable conclusion will be that the banks are losing significantly on this count. A substantial number of Scale-II officers can be promoted (after adequate formal training in the relevant subjects) to various newly created positions at different organisational levels, when such banks install their in-house computer systems.

4. For staffing specialist-positions, the banks should reduce their dependence on recruitment from outside to the extent possible and should encourage internal promotions more and more. This is because still a good number of bank employees, in spite of possessing requisite academic and/or professional qualifications, do not have much promotional opportunities vis-à-vis specialist positions.

5. The commercial banks in India should restructure their cadres through a systematic process of cadre-review from time to time and identify new functional positions which are to be manned by promotion. At present, the posts equivalent to the 'special assistant' posts are very limited. Since very few direct promotions are there from the clerical cadre to the officers' cadre (Junior Management Scale-I) and many clerical employees are stagnating in their present positions for years together, an increase in the number of 'Special Assistant' posts (even though, strictly speaking, such posts are upgraded clerical posts only) can, at least, partly take care of the promotional needs at the lower levels.

6. Conversion of the specialist-positions to the general ones at the higher levels should be stopped forthwith. All the specialist-positions should have their own promotional-tiers up to the board level. This will certainly lessen the queuing problems in the context of promotion. Promotional opportunities will also increase at the higher levels vis-à-vis both the specialist-positions and the general positions.

Since, non-fulfillment of needs inevitably de-motivates the employees in any organisation (which, consequently, affects their performance and productivity), the banking organisations can, in no way, afford to ignore the significance of effective 'promotion from within' policies for their employees. Structurally, the present generation of white-collar employees (which consists of a very large number of employees working in banks and allied organisations) have a different type of expectations of their organisations. This is mainly because, by and large, they posses high educational qualifications and technical skills which they have to acquire in order to become eligible for going through the selection process in the job market. Such different types of expectations on their part would further be strengthened due to the steady development of occupational labour makers as a result of massive technological changes. Labour has become a competitive item for sale and purchase in the occupational labour markets. Job mobility for swelling wage-earners has increased significantly because industry-specific and/or trade-specific skills are getting diluted due to commonness of technology and growth of occupational labour markets. This trend is going to continue unabated and the coming years will have a new generation whose expectations of organisations will be entirely different. Therefore, the problem of retention of efficient man-power is going to throw a serious challenge to the existing organisations, unless they can effectively develop suitable motivation-packages for their employees. As promotion has been identified as a major unfulfilled need of the bank employees in general, effective planning for their promotion and career progression becomes imperative for the bank authorities. In fact, 'promotion from within' can very well serve as a positive motivational reinforcer for the white-collar employees in the commercial banking organisations in India and that has been adequately substantiated by the findings of our empirical survey.

MOTIVATION AND MORALE

Edwin Flippo (1961) defined, "Morale is a mental condition or attitude of individual and groups which determines their willingness to cooperate." Yoder Dale (1972) on the other hand explained morale as "the overall tone, climate or atmosphere of work perhaps regularly sensed by the members. If workers appear to feel enthusiastic and optimistic about group activities, if they have a sense of mission about their job, if they are friendly with each other, they are described as having a good or high morale. If they seem to be dissatisfied, irritated, cranky, critical, restless and pessimistic, they are described as having poor or low morale." Elton Mayo defined it as "the maintenance of co-operative living", which means a sense of belongingness. On the other hand many authors defined morale as a 'pursuit of a common purpose', attitude, individual and group job satisfaction, participative attitudes, team spirit, etc. Whatever may be the way of defining, it is evident, morale is a cognitive concept, encompassing feelings, attitudes and sentiments, which together contribute to a general feeling of satisfaction in the workplace.

Like morale, motivation is also a cognitive concept but it is different from morale on certain important aspects. Motivation stimulates individuals into action to achieve desired goals. It is, therefore, a function of needs and drives. It mobilises energy, which enhances the potential for morale. Morale on the other hand is the individual or group attitude towards a particular subject. It contributes to a general feeling of satisfaction at the workplace. It, therefore, is the function of freedom or restraint towards some goal. It mobilises sentiments, which form an important part of organisational climate. Attitudes and sentiments, i.e., morale, per se, affect productivity. High morale is an index of good human relations, which, inter alia, reduces labour turnover, absenteeism, indiscipline, grievances, etc.

Factors which affect morale are primarily attitude and job satisfaction level of individual employees. We have discussed the attitude and its measurement, in the unit on 'Recruitment, Selection and Induction'. From the organisational point of view, such factors can be delineated into organisational goals, leadership style, co-workers attitude, nature of work, work environment and the employee himself.

High morale is conventionally considered as a contributor to high productivity, but such correlation may not be always true. This is because high productivity may be the outcome of many other organisational initiatives, which may be independent of employee morale. Hence even with low employee morale, high productivity is achievable. This can be illustrated using the model of Prof. Keith Davis, which goes as under:

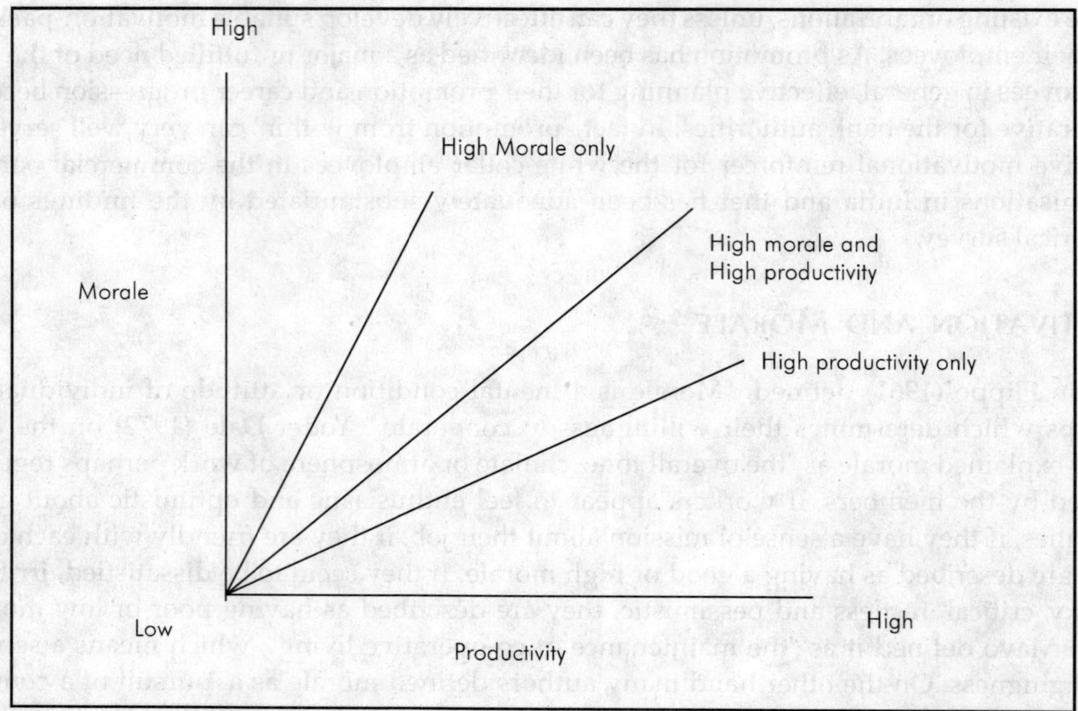

Figure 15.9: Employee's High Morale

Participative Management

Men should live in mutual love and amity. This saying of Yajurveda dates back to 4000 BC-100 BC and amply recognises the importance of group cohesiveness for happiness. In India during the era of kings also there are enough records of participative culture. Periodic meetings of the rajas with prajas were nothing but crude participative forums for grievance handling. Lessons from such participative forums later served as important guidelines to the administration.

However, more organised and institutionalised approach to workers participation in management dates back to 1920, when Gandhiji advocated the principles of trusteeship in Industry. The idea has further been concretised during the Plan era and through enactment of various legislations and policy decisions.

Though benefits of participative management have since long been drawn by many countries in the world, in India it came a bit late to institutionalise the approach. The statutory support has now made it obligatory for Indian industries to introduce the culture. Participation in some form or the other has now almost become unavoidable for many organisations.

However, in the new age economy, we require total participation than statutory participation through works committees, departmental councils and other representative forums. One such possible way to enforce total participation is by way of formation of quality circles or small group forums.

Quality Circle (QC) can be related to increased employee motivation and productivity and hence it is used as an important HRD tool in the organisation. Total knowledge, skill, creative abilities, talents and aptitudes together with values, attitudes and beliefs of the workers and/or individuals of the organisation represent the human resources in more aggressive terms.

QCs ensure total involvement of employees through a number of small group forums. Experience shows that many organisations have succeeded in improving their productivity by QC activities. Increased productivity can be achieved by increased employee motivation, which QCs can better ensure than any other methods like complex planning, rigorous execution, etc.

For successful implementation of QCs in the organisation, most of the organisations in India have now started training their workers and employees on QC concepts and following up the setting up of QC forums by each and every worker, forming homogeneous groups of 8-12 employees, who systematically meet once in a week, at least, for an hour to deliberate on work related problems and to identify possible solutions to those problems. Many organisations started gaining benefits like cost minimisation, changing the method of production, work simplification, etc. To operationalise QCs in an enterprise the following structure of QCs could be used.

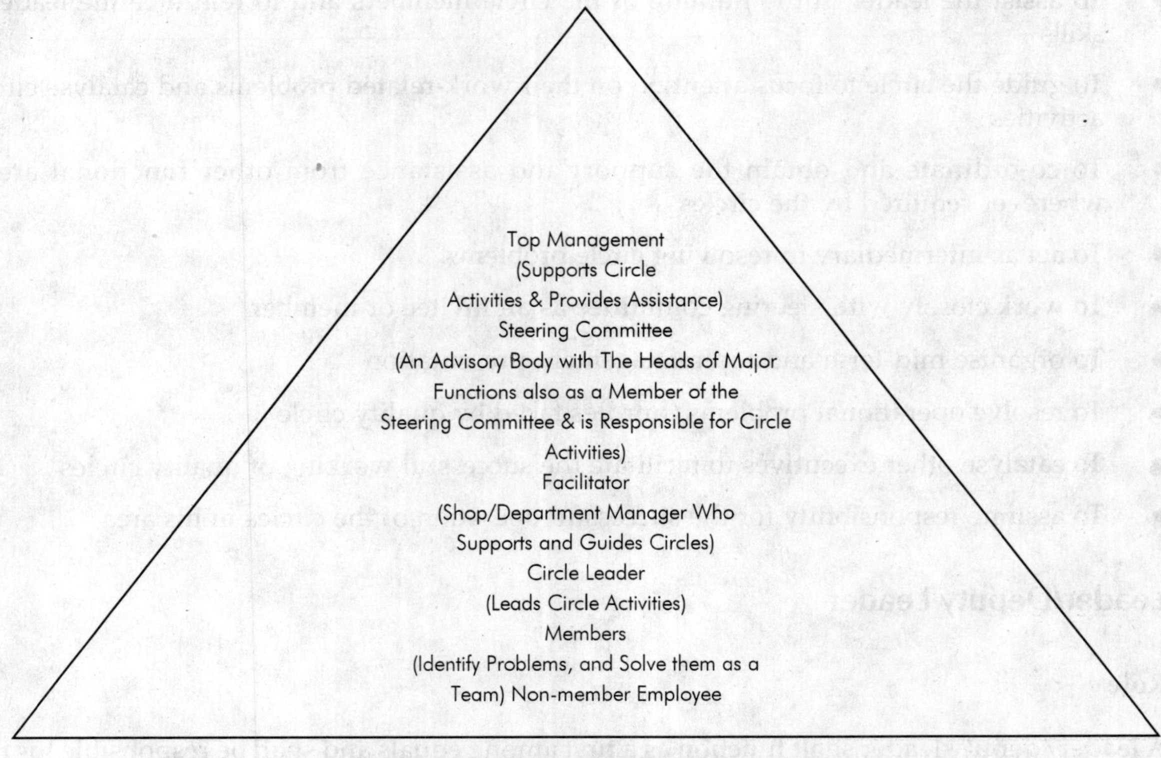

Figure 15.10: Structure of Quality Circle

Steering Committee

- To take an overview of the operation of the quality circles
- To establish the programme objectives and resources
- To provide policy guidance and direction
- To promote quality circles in the organisation
- To obtain feedback from facilitators and review circle activities
- To attend "management presentation" by circles
- To include circles activities as part of the organisation goal
- To provide a budget for quality circle activities

Facilitator

- To demonstrate support of the management
- To attend QC meeting at least for brief periods
- To assist the leader in the training of the circle members and to reinforce the leader's skills
- To guide the circle to focus attention on their work-related problems and catalyse circle activities
- To co-ordinate and obtain the support and assistance from other functional areas wherever required by the circles
- To act as intermediary in resolving circle problems
- To work closely with steering committee as an invitee or member
- To organise mid-term and top management presentation
- To resolve operational problems/hurdles faced by quality circle
- To catalyse other executives to facilitate the successful working of quality circles
- To assume responsibility for the successful operation of the circles in his area

Leader/Deputy Leader

Role

A leader/deputy leader shall function as a first among equals and shall be responsible for the effective performance of his circle.

Functions

- To train the members with the assistance of the facilitator/co-ordinator
- To maintain a high degree of cohesiveness of his team with a sense of identity

- To bring about a consensus approach in problem-solving
- To chalk out action plans and assign roles to members
- To maintain process record/minutes of circle meetings
- To interact with other functional areas in problem-solving
- To review progress vis-à-vis goals/objectives set for themselves
- To arrange for mid-team and top management presentation
- To catalyse non-members to join existing circles or start new ones
- To involve every member in circle meetings/activities

Members

Role

- To contribute actively to the effective functioning of their quality circle, aiming at better performance of their work area in every way on an ongoing basis.

Functions

- To participate actively in the circle meetings
- To contribute ideas for problem solving
- To assist the leader in data gathering, record-keeping, interacting with other areas, etc.
- To catalyse generation of cohesive team working in the work area
- To strive for the highest standards of performance of the circle
- To be involved in the improvement of the total performance of the organisation
- To take part in the mid-team/top management presentations.

Quality circles for their total involvement undoubtedly enhance productivity as the basic philosophy of quality circles is an attempt to involve all the employees vis-à-vis workers in an organisation. Different studies carried out both in India and abroad indicate that successful implementation of quality circles is directly related to following areas of improvement like; productivity, quality, house-keeping, cost minimisation and safety in an organisation. For effective productivity improvement through QCs the first pre-condition is to involve trade unions, ensure total participation, institute rewards and recognition system and focus on continuous training.

CHEVRON Corporation is a leader in petroleum industry, practising 'direct participation', as an efficient process of designing and implementing change. This has helped the company to develop a response capability for the workforce (using their 'collective wisdom') to outmaneuver competitors. The system works like this:

- Organise large-scale conferences (two-three days) involving variety of stakeholders.
- Discuss on issues that require change.

- Bring multiple perspectives for action.
- Select the line of action.
- Communicate the same throughout the organisation.
- Implement identified changes.

TOTAL QUALITY MANAGEMENT

TQM is a focussed corporate culture to satisfy present customers with low cost and high quality, developing new procedures and controls.

The definition of TQM is better understood in relation to the term 'total quality'. Total quality is the quality of work of all people at all levels in all functional areas. Management in relation to total quality, therefore, denotes an organisational improvement strategy. The definition of TQM can further be simplified as under:

Any organisation aspiring for total quality should ensure quality of work, i.e., the quality of goods and services, at the first instance. Quality of work can be ensured by strict inspection/ quality control as well without taking into cognizance other areas. But that does not serve the purpose of TQM philosophy. TQM philosophy emphasises on achieving quality of work by enriching quality of all people directly or indirectly related to that work irrespective of their hierarchical levels and functional areas. Thus, broadly speaking, TQM is an organisational improvement strategy.

Yet in another way we can define TQM as value addition activities, which focus on four key performance areas in an organisation, viz.: (i) quality, (ii) process (iii) equipment, (iv) people.

Tracing history, we find that the Japanese concept to total quality control has actually been renamed as total quality management. Definition of TQM given above is actually derived from ISO specification series, commonly known as ISO:9000. However, TQM per se is not a standard. It is based on total quality principles.

So far, whatever has been written on TQM, is based on the works of W. Edwards Deming, Joseph Juran and Karou Ishilkawa. Their works suggest the core values and a distinctive set of interventions to promote such values. Such core values emphasise the need for customer satisfaction, creating of supplier partnerships, use of cross-functional teams to identify and solve quality problems, use of scientific methods to monitor performance and use of process management techniques to enhance team effectiveness.

Drawing lessons from organisations who successfully practised TQM, it is evident that the most commonly used TQM technique is the formation of short-term problem-solving group for simplifying and streamlining work practices. The second most commonly used technique is training. The third common practice is to have a top down approach (quality is ultimately the responsibility of top management). The other two practices call for developing relationship with the suppliers and obtaining data about customers. The first three techniques of TQM are, in fact, the part of HRD activities in an organisation. HRD efforts in the organisation are now emphasizing on the need for formation of quality circles (small group activities) and value engineering teams, who work as effective problem solving teams and which, *inter alia*, leads to increased motivation (through intrinsic need satisfaction and productivity).

EMPOWERMENT

Empowerment means giving every one instead of just people with certain positions or certain job titles, the legitimate right to make judgements, form conclusions, reach decisions and then act. Empowerment, therefore, calls for employee participation in a operational area. But empowerment demands employee participation in each and every corporate function, so as to accept the employee as a total man. Therefore, an empowered employee is not a mere seller of his time and labour for a contracted sum of money. The empowered employee acquires necessary skill and authority to own. Employee empowerment, involvement and participative management as important corporate practices have been experimented in other multinational organisations like Miracle Food Mart, Linclon National Insurance Company, Nissan (USA), etc. In all such cases, it was identified that the employee ownership and commitment (which is possible through employee empowerment) are the two ingredients to achieve efficiency and productivity. Some organisations are even empowering their employees at the strategic level rather than confining their involvement only to limited operational activity.

QUALITY OF WORK LIFE (QWL)

QWL is most conventionally defined as those perceived important personal needs, which an individual tries to satisfy by working in an organisation. Its conceptual foundations, though laid by behavioural scientists, were advocated by Chris Argyris (1975) in his famous work on Personality and Organisation. The socio-technical systems theory, pioneered by Tavistock Institute of Human Relations, London during 1960s is considered as an important QWL construct. Basic conceptual criteria for QWL, *inter alia*, incorporate growth and security as important personal needs of an individual. The possibility of furthering one's career within the organisation, has, therefore, been identified as one of the important criteria for QWL. Although common QWL strategists emphasise more on job re-design, formation of autonomous work groups and worker participation in management, there exist wide differences among the pioneers in this areas as to what should be construed as QWL factors. Riched Walton (1979) explained the process of QWL with the help of the following criteria:

1. Adequate and fair compensation
2. Safe and healthy working conditions
3. Immediate opportunity to use and develop human capacities
4. Future opportunity for continued growth and security
5. Social integration in the work organisation
6. Work and total life space
7. The social relevance of working life

Summing up the studies carried out both in India and abroad, it is evident that the essence of QWL is the opportunity for employees, at all levels, to have substantial influence over their work environs by participating in the decision-making process relating to their work and thereby, enhancing their self-esteem and overall satisfaction from their work. Hence QWL calls for an open style of management, i.e., sharing of information and genuinely encouraging the efforts relating to the improvement of the organisation. This, therefore, amply makes it clear that QWL in fact is an important HRD activity and proper HRD intervention can enrich the QWL for employees of an organisation. Even though quality circles, TQM and QWL have been separately discussed and related to HRD activity, in fact QWL programmes and so also activities related to quality circles and value engineering teams can be integrated to TQM programmes at the corporate level. TQM, therefore, encompasses QC and QWL and success of TQM programmes, per se, largely depends on the appropriate HRD interventions like; emphasis on continuous training and development activity, encouraging participation in management through small group forums, increasing employees' motivation, looking after the career development of the employees, employee empowerment, infusing attitudinal changes at the top (like accepting a flatter organisation structure, following an egalitarian approach, becoming receptive to changes on a continuous basis, supporting group performance, etc.).

Repetitive tasks develop boredom and jobs become increasingly dehumanised and dissatisfying to the employees. Some companies try to reduce this boredom through job rotation. Job rotation is a systematic movement of workers from one job to another. Such movement or rotation in different functions increases the skills and functional efficiency of the employees as they are exposed to different business situations. Some companies even encourage such movement from one unit to another to enable employees to understand the organisation as a total system. For manning higher positions in the organisation, such knowledge of employees is an important prerequisite. A staff executive, who is posted in an office, may be encouraged to move to the factory (which may not be attached to an office) to get exposed to the intricacies of life functioning, only to promote him later to a more senior position, job rotation, for employees at lower level also, helps in multi-skill development whereby the organisation can get the advantage of their services at the time of exigency. However, frequent job rotations do not allow employees to get specialised knowledge and skill and reduce them to an unskilled functionary or at least 'a jack of all trades and master of none'. For such obvious disadvantage of job rotation, other forms of job mobility like, job enlargement and job enrichment are considered as better alternatives.

SUMMARY

Motivation is a dynamic HR process and there cannot be any organisation specific motivational tool. The content and process theories on motivation suggested various methods of enhancing employee motivation. Many empirical studies, carried out in India and abroad, validated such tools, either partially or in its entirety. Motivation, either through intrinsic or extrinsic reinforcers, contributes to employee satisfaction and thus enhances performance and productivity.

KEYWORDS

Extrinsic Motivation	Attribution Theory
Intrinsic Motivation	Locus of Control
Morale	Goal Setting Theory
Hierarchy of Needs	Competence Motive Theory
ERG theory	Expectancy Theory
Motive Strength	Affiliation Motive
Pareto Diagram	Maturity-Immaturity Theory
Content Theories	Motivation and Morale
Process Theories	Morale and Productivity
Motivation-Hygiene Theory	Job Characteristic Model
Motivating Potential Score (MPS)	Achievement Need
Thematic Apperception Test (TAT)	Theory 'Y'
Equity Theory	Performance Satisfaction Theory

REVIEW QUESTIONS

1. Define the term motivation. Why it is so important for HR managers?
2. What motivational tool you may like to use for knowledge workers? Would your approach be different for operators in a shop floor?
3. Critically review the contribution of Maslow and Herzberg in theories of motivation. Do you think they have any relevance for new generation workers?
4. How do you distinguish process theories and content theories of motivation?
5. Distinguish between motivation and morale. Discuss how morale can influence productivity?
6. Can motivation be defined as perception? What are the circumstances, when perception can influence motive strength of a worker?
7. Write short notes on:

   (a) Job Enrichment

   (b) Job Enlargement

   (c) Quality of Worklife (QWL)

   (d) Total Quality Management (TQM)

   (e) Employee Empowerment

   (f) Quality Circles

   (g) Job Satisfaction

   (h) Performance Satisfaction Theory

CASE STUDY

MOTIVATING THROUGH OWNERSHIP

Sharing ownership through an Employee Stock Ownership Plan (ESOP) is one of the necessary ingredients to establish a successful ownership culture. However, employee ownership by itself will not increase employee motivation and performance. Combination of employee ownership and employee participation yields substantial improvement in organisational performance. It is genuine employee partnership which can make employees responsible.

A High performance workplace provides employees with "incentives, information, skills, and responsibility to make decisions essential for innovation, quality improvement, and rapid response to change." Such an environment exist in companies which integrate their business, human resources, and technology strategies and have following common characteristics:

- Give workers a stake in the performance through employee ownership and gain sharing;
- Create employment security strategies that recognise the value of workers to long-term economic safety;
- Push responsibility down to frontline employees by organising work into self-managing teams;
- Provide workers with necessary information to exercise a high level of autonomy and discretion;
- Build employee relations on trust, mutual interest, and co-operation;
- Focus on customers' satisfaction, both internal and external by improving quality by building organisations that adapt easily to market change;
- Encourage employees to learn new skills through skill-based pay and pay-for-performance compensation systems;
- Invest in training and retraining to develop employees as critical business assets, rather than treating them as costs to be minimised; and
- Provide employees with safe and supportive work environments.

Therefore, it is; ownership + participation + information + training, which contributes to high performance.

Employee ownership, coupled with participation, education and information, leads to higher financial performance. An equally important observation is that companies which reward employees with stock ownership, outperform those which only reward participation with profit sharing.

The transformation of employees into owners requires cultivating a genuine sense of ownership where the employees take the responsibility of ownership seriously and their actions contribute to the company's success. This process obviously does not occur immediately. Developing an ownership culture among employees means: equity, a 'say in how things get done', information and training. Employees need to understand the company's financial reports and develop their decision-making, communication and problem-solving skills.

Equity makes a big difference. The difference is like 'renting and owning a home'. Unlike a person who rents, the home owner has equity in his or her investment and therefore will have an incentive to increase the value of that investment. How many renters paint the outside of their residence? Just like a home owner, an employee-owner has a greater incentive to drive the value of stock in his or her company. This could result in reducing scrap, generating creative ideas on how to improve a process, and producing better quality products. This ownership could be in the form of stock options, a cooperative or an Employee Stock Ownership Plan (ESOP). Although rewards like profit sharing and bonuses are great supplementary incentives, they do not provide employees with an ownership stake.

When employees have an ownership interest in their company and are valued for their input, their jobs become more meaningful. Satisfied employees as well as satisfied customers stay with the company longer! Ownership is just the first step in creating a successful ownership culture. The remaining ingredients are participation, training and information.

Contd...

Motivated employee owners need the opportunity to express their ideas for improving the business to management. Effective communication requires that managers listen, appreciate dissent and tolerate opposition. Likewise, supervisors need to lead rather than order, assist rather than discipline, and teach rather than threaten. It is the responsibility of employees to make suggestions without confrontation, learn basic business concepts, and work cooperatively with others. Open channels for input should be maintained throughout the company. To initiate increased levels of participation, one might consider creating problem solving teams or shop floor committees.

Whether a company is employee-owned or not, the goal of participation is to maximise employee involvement in all areas of company decision-making, from the shop floor to the boardroom. It is through participation on decision making bodies that employees can truly accept greater responsibility.

An owner needs access to financial and other strategic information to make sound business decisions, responsible employees also need access to company information like financial reports, scrap rates, customer satisfaction indicators, and on-time delivery records. Of course, information is only useful if it is communicated effectively. This information can be in the form of regularly published newsletters, annual or quarterly meetings to review business issues, and company financial statements. Of course, employees need to understand the information presented. This requires a long-term commitment to education and training.

The American Society for Training and Development confirmed that two-thirds of corporate training monies go into training for those who already have college degrees. If one wants to create a successful ownership culture in an organisation, just informing employees is not enough. They also need to understand the information they receive in order to be informed and become involved owners. Opening books to employees is meaningless unless employees understand how to read financial reports. Meetings to improve quality lead nowhere if the participants lack effective meeting skills.

Education is a process of learning, and coordinating an effective training programme requires a long-term commitment. Training non-managerial employees in problem-solving and group process techniques helps make employee participation programmes work successfully.

It is relatively inexpensive and highly cost-effective to undertake some combination of employee participation, training, open-book management, and financial incentives to increase company competitiveness. These foster an environment that allows employees to think and act like owners.

Question

What are the important lessons of motivation, you have learned from the passage. List out those in order of your perceived priorities.

BLOCK SEVEN

SYSTEM AND HR

UNIT 16

Human Resource Control Systems

Learning Objectives

After completion of this unit, the students will be aware of the following topics:

- *Introduction*
- *Modern HRM Concepts*
- *Human Resource Control Systems*
- *Human Resource Control Systems for MNCs*
- *Model of HR Control*
- *Measurement Tools used in Human Resource Controlling*

Self Regulating Control at De La Rue

De La Rue is the world's largest commercial security printer and papermaker, producing over 150 national currencies and a wide range of security documents such as passports, fiscal stamps, travellers' cheques and authentication labels. In business since 1813, De La Rue is a member of the FTSE 250 and employs over 6,000 people across 31 countries.

Lead by CEO, Leo Quinn, De La Rue is currently driving forward a programme of operational improvement, aimed at increasing efficiency and improving shareholder value. In December 2004, the executive team announced the results of a Strategic Review: the review highlighted a number of Group Actions and focused on the need to improve efficiency through clearer definition of accountability for business units, greater emphasis on controls over working capital and capital expenditure, and increased productivity. As part of the drive to improve productivity, De La Rue introduced "My Contribution", to empower all individuals to drive improvements. My Contribution enables individuals, from any De La Rue had, at this time, also decided to implement HR.net, a powerful web-enabled HR system, developed by Vizual Business Tools plc. Through the installation of HR.net, the company intended to automate a range of HR processes as well as to consolidate information held in disparate, pre-existing HR systems, on to one central database, housed at the company's Head Office Using the latest .Net technology, HR.net allows any manual HR process to be replicated in electronic form and enables a wide variety of tasks to be carried out by employees on a self-service basis. In addition, HR.net has a highly flexible, customisable workflow engine which makes suggestions aimed at increasing efficiency. All ideas are evaluated, with those likely to generate greater operational efficiency or cost saving, translated into projects. The project has already led to some 1,500 ideas being put forward by employees, with 250 being resourced as projects. Following the inception of "My Contribution", and in order to achieve the full benefits from the programme, it became clear that a reporting system was required that would allow suggestions to be received from employees around the globe and then tracked through to review, investment, implementation and recording of benefit which enables organisations not only to automate standard HR procedures but digitize a range of other (non-HR specific) business processes. As any business process can be defined and re-created within HR.net, organisations have the opportunity to streamline not only the HR function but refine processes and create cost-efficiencies in other areas. De La Rue managers soon realised that HR.net could be used to facilitate "My Contribution": HR.net's powerful workflow and project tracking technology could be exploited to support the programme and as the company had already invested in the HR.net system, no further capital expenditure was required.

INTRODUCTION

Market volatility and risk has now made it imperative for organisations to rigorously implement HR control systems, as it directly relates to organisational performance. Human resource control systems are composed of various HR practices that lead the organisation to the accomplishment of its established objectives. HR control systems are characterised as output, input or behavioural and are based on different control theories such as organisational theory (Ouchi, 1979), agency theory (Jensen & Meckling, 1976), or transaction cost analysis (Williamson, 1981). Studies have shown that organisations tend to use elements of behavioural, input and output control, simultaneously. (Darmon, 1998; Jaeger & Baliga, 1985; Oliver & Anderson 1995; Ouchi, 1979; Ouchi & Maguire, 1975; Snell, 1992) Again, HR control systems can be differentiated between formal, organisation-initiated controls such as staffing, performance appraisal, training and rewards; and informal controls based on personal influence. Input control is basically enforced through selection and socialisation.

Operationally, at the organisational level, HR control is primarily enforced by regulating the performance. It involves three types of control, i.e., behaviour, output and input (Snell, 1992). Behavioural control is enforced through surveillance of subordinates' behaviour. Output control is measured in terms of results. Input control is measured in terms of the opportunity for training and development. Through HR control, organisations can programme how actions lead to outcomes and behavioural control (Govindarajan and Fisher, 1990).

For organisations, HR control is the application of HR practices for performance assessment and incentives designs. Such HR practices are commonly known as best practices or high commitment practices (Becker and Huselid, 1998; Huselid, 1995; Delery and Doty, 1996). Anderson and Oliver (1987) defined the two forms of managerial control; archetypical forms of control and behaviour-based or outcome-based control that form the basis of the HR control. According to them, managers can adopt two behaviour-based controls as managers are involved in the monitoring, directing, evaluating and rewarding of their people. On the other hand, outcome-based control supposes greater interest in the consequences of behaviours than in the behaviours themselves. Subsequent researches, however, suggested that HR control systems may adopt different orientations along a continuum whose extremes are the two proposed systems, i.e., archetypical and behavioural (Krafft, 1999; Baldauf et al., 2001, 2005).

As a process; HR control helps in aligning the actions of individuals with the interests of their organisations (Tannenbaum, 1968). Typically, organisations use a cybernetic system (Boulding, 1956) to model the control process, including (1) superiors' intentions; (2) an influence mechanism; and (3) evaluation and feedback. Some researchers (Ouchi, 1977) have focused primarily on the evaluation component of control systems; others have presented control in its expanded form, including superiors' intentions and influence as well as evaluation and feedback. (Cheng & McKinley, 1983; Hofstede, 1978; Kerr, 1985; Michael, 1973; Reeves & Woodward, 1970; Tannenbaum, 1968; Turcotte, 1974)

As a system, HR control systems are certain accepted principles, which are commonly applicable in organisations. HR managers cannot adopt a reactionary approach in a globally competitive economy. They need to be pro-active in addressing to the organisational problems, shunning their age-old propensities to adopt incremental strategies (short-term) to fix some events. We call HR control as systems as it needs to follow certain pattern of events in a cycle. Each pattern of event indicates some specific phases and at each phase, behaviour of the organisation changes. Any system, by nature, interpretes patterns and events in the organisations, balances the organisational environment and finally, ensures circular relationship between the system and its parts. According to the concept of Viable Systems Model (VSM) of Beer (1979), a system is viable when it can adapt effectively to environmental changes, even if such change cues are unforeseen. Likewise, HR control systems in the organisation need to be developed not only to ensure effective management of human resources, but also to ensure that people autonomously control themselves to survive in the era of uncertainty.

Broad categorisation of human resource control systems indicates that we have a variety of typologies to differentiate control systems (Ouchi, 1977, 1980; Reeves & Woodward, 1970; Tannenbaum, 1968). More prominent among them is the bureaucratic mechanisms (Govindarajan & Fisher, 1990; Jaeger & Baliga, 1985; Ouchi, 1979, 1980). This approach focuses more on formal human resource management practices such as staffing, training, performance appraisal and rewards. Obviously, exerting control through informal modes of personal influence cannot be considered within the ambit of this model. In relatively smaller organisations, human resource control is primarily an informal process. Schuler and Jackson

(1989) observed that the human resource management controls used at lower levels of firms tend to vary from those used at higher levels.

It is for this reason that human resource control systems as a generic method need to emphasise on three areas, i.e., behavioural control, output control and input control (Thompson, 1967).

Only with strategic capabilities, organisations can effectively enforce control over its product, resources and people. Human resources play the important role in increasing the organisational strategic capabilities. Enforcing control over human resources truly helps the organisations, as people deliver the results and aggregation of such individual level achievement ultimately leads to the achievement of business results. HR control systems can not only help in meeting the current business challenges but also solidly build the future of the organisation through development of new competencies, new visions, strategies, structures, systems and processes. The transformation of HR functions, after considering it from the control percepts will add value to the organisation. Ulrich (1997) suggested the improvement of organisational capabilities through human resources. There are, however, other contributing factors to organisational capabilities like, organisation structure, responsibility, the practices, functions, etc. Re-engineering HR with more critical emphasis on visions, strategies, structures, systems and processes, particularly to respond to change make HR control systems more significant. With HR control, organisations can gain values. With HR control systems, HR practices change, which cascades to the change in the HR architecture. Particularly for MNCs, HR control functions assume importance, as in a borderless business environment, MNCs need to integrate and co-ordinate across national boundaries and also, require to adopt sensitivity and responsiveness to national differences. (Barlett and Ghoshal, 2002; Barlett, Ghoshal, and Birkinshaw, 2003) Accordingly in the international human resource (IHR) strategies, organisations embed the HR control systems balancing the global integration and local responsiveness. (Caligiuri and Stroh, 1995; Schuler et al., 1993; Taylor et al., 1996)

Modern HRM Concepts

Modern Human Resource Management practices leverage people to increase the competitiveness of the organisation at the global scale (Best, 1990). The Japanese success in the international market in automobile and electronic products in 1970s and 1980s is attributed to people factor (Ouchi, 1982). Ouchi's studies showed that Japanese employers embraced those HR practices which could enhance the labour productivity and at the same time, could achieve success in process innovation. These, perhaps, led to the success of large Japanese corporations like, Toyota and Matsushita. Some of the characteristics of Japanese HRM practices are:

- Rigorous selection and recruitment
- High level of training, particularly, induction training and on the job training
- Team working
- Multi-skilling
- Transparency in management-worker communications

- Extensive use of quality circles to emphasise on quality, right at the first level and to promote total employee involvement
- Promotion of employee suggestions and innovation
- Lessening of hierarchical barriers with single status symbols such as common canteens and corporate uniforms
- Institutional employment practices to ensure permanent employment bond
- Shared vision setting common business goals and cascading it even at the team and individual level
- Making people feel responsible for delivering the results
- Balancing the seniority and merit in promotional decision
- Enforcing strict discipline.

All these human resource management practices in Japan created the organisational culture which could allow workers to identify their own success with that of the company. Such experience of Japanese organisations could make organisational culture, an important variable in understanding the competitive success of the organisations and it was a major theme of understanding organisational excellence in the early 1980s (Peters and Waterman, 1982). However, such new human resource management practices with a distinctive corporate culture are in sharp contrast to the regulatory perspectives of personnel management of the mid 20th century. The new human resource management practices made line managers of the organisations as the key responsible persons, transforming the role of human resource department to facilitate the process (Guest, 2002). This was the beginning of the modern human resource management, i.e., the creation of a culture to harnesses the commitment of individuals to the organisation (Guest, 1987). Walton (1985) institutionalised the idea of employees' commitment to the organisations. Walton's model explains how organisations moved from the control based human resource management practices to employees' commitment. The model is explained below:

Table 16.1: Walton's Model

Management Practice	Control	Commitment
Job Design	Focussed on the Individual	Focussed on the Team
Performance Management	Measured standards for minimum performance	Higher "stretch" objectives
Management Structure	Top down and hierarchical. Emphasis on management symbols	Flat organisation structure. Minimum status differentials
Compensation	Individual pay linked to job evaluation	Pay linked to skills and mastery
Employment	Employees viewed as variable cost	Assurances that participation will not result in job losses
Employee Voice	Employee input allowed on a narrow agenda	Employee participation enacted on a wide range of issues
Labour Management Relations	Adversarial labour relations	Mutuality with joint planning and problem solving

Source: Adapted from Walton (1985)

This clearly explains how modern HRM practices have emerged shifting from control to commitment and developed the concepts of team working, flat organisation structures, and pay linked to skills and employee involvement. Walton's findings further extended by David Guest (1987) suggest a normative model of human resource management. Guest defined four outcomes of human resource management – strategic integration, commitment, flexibility and quality. According to Guest, these outcomes would lead to higher levels of job performance, higher levels of innovation and change, reduced rate of employee turnover, absence and employee grievance rates. Guest's normative model is explained below:

Table 16.2: Guest's Normative Model

Human Resource Management Policies	Human Resource Management Outcomes	Organisational Outcomes
Organisation and job design. Management of change	Strategic integration	High job performance
Recruitment, selection and socialisation	Commitment	High problem solving, change and innovation
Appraisal, training and development	Flexibility/adaptability High	Cost-effectiveness
Reward systems Communication	Quality	Low turnover, absence and grievances

Source: Adapted from Guest (1987)

Guest's model, therefore, speaks of human resource management that certainly embraces the old regulatory norms, but at the same time emphasises on other key levers of organisational success that encompasses the management of change, job design, socialisation and appraisal. Modern human resource management, therefore, tries to integrate with the business strategy of the organisations, focussing on employee commitment, flexibility and quality, where employees' commitment still remains the major determinant of human resource management. The concept would be further clear in the light of Storey's (1995) definition on modern human resource management, which goes as under:

"Human resource management is a distinctive approach to employment management which seeks to achieve competitive advantage through the strategic deployment of a highly committed and capable workforce using an array of cultural, structural and personnel techniques."

Storey (2001) further expanded the modern HRM concepts with the following inputs, which he considered are distributed into certain essential domain areas.

1. ***Beliefs and assumptions:***

   (a) It is the human resource that gives competitive advantage.

   (b) The aim should not be mere compliance with rules but employee commitment.

   (c) Therefore, employees should, for example, be very carefully selected and developed.

2. ***Strategic qualities:***

   (a) Because of the above factors, HR decisions are of strategic importance.

   (b) Top management involvement is necessary.

   (c) HR policies should be integrated into the business strategy – stemming from it and even contributing to it.

3. ***Critical role of managers:***

   (a) Because HR practice is critical to the core activities of the business, it is too important to be left to personnel specialists, alone.

   (b) Line managers are (or need to be) closely involved as both deliverers and drivers of the HR policies.

   (c) Much greater attention is paid to the management of managers themselves.

4. ***Key levers:***

   (a) Managing culture is more important than managing procedures and systems.

   (b) Integrated action on selection, communication, training, rewards and development

   (c) Restructuring and job re-design to allow devolved responsibility and empowerment.

Summing up the above discussions, we can understand that modern HRM concept focuses more on such practices, which minimises the role of traditional human resource control functions. Some of the salient points of departure from the traditional personnel management function can be like, the HR role of line managers, embedding of HR with the business strategy, shaping of organisational culture, making people committed to work, etc.

Such perceptive changes in HRM practices, however, are not free from criticism. Many scholars still maintain the previous paradigm of personnel management, as they feel the modern approach dilutes the role of employee relations in unionised work environment, where managers need to negotiate with the unions to run the organisations, addressing the critical HR issues. In a non-unionised work environment, such perceptive changes in HRM practices may be possible.

Let us now move to Porter's (1985) three basic strategic choices for organisations:

1. ***Cost leadership:*** Leading by grabbing the opportunity of lowest costs in the industry, for instance, Videocon's acquisition of Thompson's picture tube manufacturing facilities is intended to enjoy cost leadership for their Colour Television (CTV) manufacturing facilities. Videocon's CTV is market leader in India and some adjoining countries for obvious price effectiveness, quality being for all competitors same.

2. ***Differentiation:*** Leading by superior product quality or innovation, viz. introducing low-priced 'Nano' car, TATA could augment their sales position in the automobile market. Nano's range of cars is now within the purchasing power of many Indians, who earlier did not even dare to dream a four wheeler.

3. ***Focus:*** Leading by change in business focus, viz., with the increased number of low-cost competitors in the Desktop market, IBM had to change the business focus to IT enabled services (ITeS).

Various studies by Schuler and Jackson (1987) and Schuler (1989, 1996) relate human resource management practices to the Porter's prescriptions of competitive strategy. Under Schuler's model, organisations need to work out the required employee behaviours for implementing a particular competitive strategy and then, devise supportive human resource management policies to enable these behaviours to be encouraged in the workforce.

Hence, considering human resource management as a control function, yet appreciating its competitive advantage, which requires commitment of people, do not conflict our approach, as effective HRM control empowers people to self develop and understand their importance more and truly make them better performers in future to sustain the competition.

HUMAN RESOURCE CONTROL SYSTEMS

Control aligns the actions of people with the organisation (Snell, 1992). In human resource management, the concept of formal control is embedded with the 'agency' function. Agency theory empowers managers to acquire and deploy resources (including human resources), keeping pace with the regulatory mandates for the best interest of the organisations (Rousseau and Arthur, 1999). HR managers, therefore, function as a control agent and focus on reducing the variance in behaviour and outcomes. Different scholars have suggested different ways of reducing such variances. For controlling behaviour or reducing the variation in behaviour, Child (1973) suggested structuring of activities and centralisation. Ouchi (1977), on the other hand, made the distinction between behavioural and output control within formal control systems. As per Ouchi, behavioural control (say through standard operating procedures) is needed when the output is deviating from the expected results. In other words, when output becomes ambiguous, we reduce the variation enforcing behavioural control. On the other hand, output control (say performance goals) is possible when the output is measurable. Control of behaviour and output can be enforced in organisations both through formal and informal mechanisms, or in other words, formalisation and socialisation.

It is now clear to us that human resource control is a critical element to manage today's organisations. Although the primary onus to enforce human resource control lies with HR department, it is, at times, necessary to enforce control through other departments, also. Standard Operating Procedures (SOP) for marketing department, certainly developed with the inputs from the marketing functions and enforced by the marketing person over viewing the functions of marketing department. According to Quintanilla (2002), any control and co-ordination mechanism influences the human resource management practices in organisation. Formal co-ordination and control mechanisms emphasise on centralisation, standardisation, planning, formalised behavioural and output controls. On the other hand, informal co-ordination and control mechanisms emphasise on participative management, team working, employee participation, decision making, etc. Therefore, informal control and co-ordination mechanisms are essentially embedded in the culture of organisation, shared vision, values and norms, and the socialisation of employees (Jaeger, 1983; Martinez and Jarillo, 1991). We can further distinguish between formal and informal control mechanisms, stating while the formal control is tangible, informal control is intangible. Today's organisations are increasingly shifting to informal control, as it facilitates innovation and creativity. Innovative organisations, even with HR control systems, ensure autonomy to people, to make them performers even in changing work environment. Thus, the new type of HR control tends to be more informal than formal. Even within formal HR control mechanisms, informal HR control can also co-exist. For example, quality control norms may be formal, but process re-engineering to improve the quality may be possible through informal control. Again, one specific control mechanism may not be fool-proof in all situations. Organisations need to select the appropriate control-mix or even can adopt a mid-way approach (with the blend of both formal and informal controls), keeping pace with the exogenous and endogenous variables (that may affect the functioning of the organisations).

Types of HR Control

We have three types of HR control systems: (1) behaviour, (2) output, and (3) input controls. Context of organisations determine which HR control systems need to be emphasised at what point of time. Organisational contexts also vary with respect to Organisational Life Cycle (OLC). Various types of HR controls are:

Behaviour Control

Behaviour control is enforced through those HR practices which influence on-the-Job activities of the people. Primarily, Performance Management System, including the measurement, focuses on behavioural control as it mandates documented behavioural norms for the people to follow (Ouchi and Maguire, 1975). Also, Performance Management Systems emphasise on improvement over time (Thompson, 1967). Performance feedback is provided frequently in order to correct deviations as soon as they occur (March and Simon, 1958). Two specific behaviour controls are enforced through performance management systems: (1) use of behavioural performance appraisals, and (2) evaluations based upon historical trends/ improvement. Through cause-effect analysis and standards of desirability, managers can enforce control. Both of these require extensive knowledge and competence of managers, as control process require regulating of specific on-the-job actions. Operationally, behaviour control includes the use of standardised operating procedures, close monitoring by superiors, behavioural performance evaluation and immediate feedback. The advantage of a behaviour control is that it is direct and straightforward. The disadvantage of behaviour control is its inflexibility (Child, 1973).

Aditya Birla Group of India

Under Mr. Kumar Mangalam Birla, the Aditya Birla Group of India has transformed itself into a modern multi-cultural transnational with more than 72,000 people drawn from 20 different countries. To transform the organisation, the group also embraced the need for cultural diversity. Departing from the traditional percepts of Indian business houses, the group for the first time, believed in heterogeneous mix of people, while going through the process of change. Through heterogeneity, the group could improve the quality of constructive dissent, improvement in the quality of decision making and both of these could effectively play in bringing the positive changes in the organisation. Also, it was the experience of the group that engaging people from different cultures, in fact, provides better opportunity to leverage the varied skill sets. Similarly, for its business expansion plans beyond the national boundaries, the group could also benefit from the practice of cultural diversity. To make people value gender and cultural diversity in workplace, the group adopted the inclusion strategy as stated above and also made it essential behavioural requirements, through strict control and monitoring with empowered diversity councils, with representation in every work groups. Making it mandatory to value diversity in workplace and demanding the desired diversity-neutral behaviour from the people, the group could institutionalize the diversity management practices in all its establishments.

Output Control

In organisations, mangers are often not capable to enforce behaviour control, for obvious absence of knowledge in establishing cause-effect relationships and setting of appropriate performance standards. In such cases, use of output control to regulate performance is recommended. Output control differs from behaviour control in that performance appraisals focus on the accomplishment of end results (Ouchi and Maguire, 1975). Performance targets are set consultatively between managers and subordinates instead of being imposed top-down (Hrebiniak, 1978) and are left tentative, flexible, and adjustable (Cheng and McKinley, 1983). Rather than evaluating subordinates in terms of improvement over time, managers instead make relative comparisons using some referent other (Thompson, 1967). Most importantly, rewards are linked to results as a substitute for surveillance (Kerr, 1985). Three output controls were examined in this study: (1) results appraisals; (2) evaluations based upon referent comparisons; and (3) performance-reward linkage. Output control in HRM regulates the effects of employee work-the results achieved. Operationally, this includes joint manager-subordinate goal-setting, results oriented appraisals and rewards which are tied to preset targets (cf., Kerr, 1985). The advantage of output control is that it provides discretion over the means of performance while still providing incentives to pursue ends that benefit the firm (Michael, 1973). The disadvantage of output control is the relative absence of a mechanism to prevent mistakes until they occur.

Walmart

Walmart always endeavours to make their work place a great place to work. Every Friday, Walmartians discuss the issue of workloads for the coming week. The meeting room contains a large board to detail the initiatives that every store requires to implement. Review of the previous week's progress is indicated by Red, yellow and green lights. Stores are not assigned additional responsibilities unless the board shows enough green lights which indicate achievement of previous week's assigned tasks. Walmart's review process autonomously enforces output control, as laggard stores step up their activities to get more green lights in coming weeks.

Input Control

Finally, when managers do not have access to a crystallised index of desired performance (i.e., ambiguous standards); they can neither control behaviours nor outcomes with certainty (Ouchi and Maguire, 1975). In these cases, managers may resort to input control (Mintzberg, 1979). Input control is comprised of HRM practices designed to standardise or enhance the knowledge, skills, abilities and motives of subordinates. Examples include rigorous staffing requirements, training and development programs, socialisation activities, etc. Two specific input controls were examined in this study: (1) staffing requirements and (2) emphasis on training. Input control in HRM has been acknowledged only briefly in previous research (cf., Jaeger & Baliga, 1985; Ouchi, 1977; 1978). Essentially, input control is a formalised equivalent of clan control (Ouchi, 277, 1980). Operationally, this includes the use of staffing, training, development and socialisation programs to regulate the knowledge, skills, abilities and motives of employees. The advantage of input control is that it pre-empts performance problems before they occur (Flamholtz, (1979). The disadvantage of input control is that it only manages potential, rather than actual, performance. Proposed but untested in previous research (e.g., Ouchi, 1977) is the proposition that input control is most appropriate when both cause-effect knowledge is incomplete and standards of desirability are ambiguous. Under these circumstances, input control constitutes a ritualistic "fall-back" strategy for managers in the absence of either behaviour or output control.

TATA

TATA group recruits through TATA Administrative Services (TAS), candidates at the entry-level executive position in general category, without emphasising on specialisation areas of the candidates. The company believes that learning is different from areas of interest in jobs. All new recruits go through systematic job rotation and monitored to understand their areas of interest. Individual employees are also asked to indicate their choice. When both the identified areas of interest match, candidates are placed in the job. Through such recruitment practices, TATA ensures input control. Managers and executives recruited through TAS mostly have track record of long services with expected level of performances.

Thus, the overall pattern of HRM practices can be conceived as a control system-the characteristics of which vary across firms. The underlying premise of control is that idiosyncratic actions of individuals must be moulded to achieve the purpose(s) of the firm (cf., Tannenbaum, 1968). HRM practices constitute an important set of options available to accomplish this task and different HRM practices control employees in different ways. Theory about control has been developed in the economic and organisational literatures (Jaeger & Baliga, 1985). Typically, Thompson's (1967) framework has been adapted for recent work on bureaucratic control (Govindarajan and Fisher, 1990; Goold and Quinn, 1990). This framework outlines different types of control as well as the conditions where each is appropriate. Behaviour control in HRM regulates the actions of subordinates on the job.

Human Resource Control and Organisational Life Cycle

In organisations, different strategies require different behaviours and different HRM practices to elicit and reinforce those behaviours. A control perspective is consistent with behavioural perspective (Liao, 2005; Snell, 1992). Similarly, organisations also change with respect to different Organisational Life Cycle (OLC).

Organisational Life Cycle (OLC) research shows the evidence that firms change over time (Miller & Friesen, 1984; Quinn & Cameron, 1983). Quinn and Cameron (1983) classified OLC into four stages: entrepreneurial, collectivity, formalisation and control, and elaboration of structure. Kazanjian (1988) suggested a four-stage model of growth in technology-driven ventures. The first stage, conception and development stage, involves the invention and development of a product or technology. Structure and formal procedures are virtually non-existent and all activities are decided by the entrepreneur. The second stage, commercialisation stage, must create structures and task systems beyond product development. The third stage, growth stage, is characterised by high growth in both sales and number of employees. A hierarchy and functional specialisation develops. The fourth stage, stability stage, concentrates on developing next-generation products, establishing a market position and seeking other growth opportunities. Each stage would manifest integral complementarities among variables of environment, strategy, structure and decision making methods. Organisational growth and increasing environmental complexity would cause each stage to exhibit certain significant differences form all other stages along these four classes of variables.

Every organisation is a metaphor of living beings and possesses common characteristics like, environmental conditioning, recycling needs, homeostasis, evolution, survival of the fittest, fluctuating health conditions, etc. Organisational life cycle, like living beings, crosses through the distinct phases like, birth, growth, maturity, aging and eventually death. Analysis of organisational life cycle helps in understanding the problems at every stage of the life cycle. Such analysis, therefore, helps in adopting the suitable control measures to help the organisation to stabilize and grow. For example, in a growth stage, firms are characterised by a rapid sales growth and an expansion of activities and products (Miller and Friesen, 1984).

HR control systems need to focus on recruiting the best talent, developing the talent through training and development initiatives, adoption of performance management systems, etc. In a maturity stage, the sales of the firm level off, more formal and bureaucratic organisation structures are established and innovation declines. HR control systems at this stage, need to focus on adoption of those HR practices which can delayer the organisation structure with the formation of more autonomous work groups, establish strategic or independent business units, develop the learning organisation culture and promote innovation. The control should gradually shift from formal to informal, and people should be developed to feel accountable for the results. In the revival stage, organisations gradually shift to divisionalised structures to cope with more complex and heterogeneous markets (Miller and Friesen, 1984). These life cycle stages of the firm are described in organisational life cycle theories according to which the internal characteristics of firms and the external contexts in which the firms operate differ across firms depending on the stage of development (Greiner, 1972; Miller and Friesen, 1983, 1984; Merchant, 1997).

Organisational life cycle stage is a contingency to which organisational responses have to be matched (e.g. Miller and Friesen, 1983, 1984). This implies that the use of HR control systems that differs across the stages of organisational life cycle as different systems, are needed in different stages.

General Discussion on Human Resource Control Systems

Human resource control systems are composed of various HR practices that lead the organisation to the accomplishment of its established objectives. We understand control system as a process, if it aims to align the actions of individuals with the interests of their firm (Tannenbaum, 1968) and that individual actions have a basic influence on organisational performance. Keeping in view all these perspectives, the study of HR control systems assumes primary importance.

The human resource control system can be defined as the execution of the monitoring, directing, evaluating and rewarding activities with the aim that the firm's human resources carry out their functions and responsibilities (Anderson and Oliver, 1987). Several works, both theoretical and empirical, subscribe to that definition (Cravens et al., 1993; Oliver and Anderson, 1994; Baldauf et al., 2001). Challagalla and Shervani (1996) state that the purpose of a human resource control system is to guarantee that the organisation achieves its objectives while also ensuring that its members behave in the appropriate way. To be specific, we can say that control systems consist of the applications of the HR practices of performance assessment and incentives. These practices are commonly referred to as best practices or high commitment practices (Becker and Huselid, 1998; Huselid, 1995; Delery and Doty, 1996) and, although there is a proven positive relationship with firm performance, it has not been analysed in such detail as this study. In the area of sales personnel management, Anderson and Oliver (1987) defined the two forms of managerial control that form the bases of the vast majority of theoretical and empirical works on the sales force. According to their proposal, managers can adopt two archetypical forms of control: behaviour-based or outcome-based. Behaviour-based control means that the managers are, to a great extent, involved in the monitoring, directing, evaluating and rewarding of their salespeople. On the other hand, outcome-based control supposes greater interest in the consequences of behaviours than in the behaviours themselves. Despite this definition, those authors and later researches have reflected that control systems may adopt different orientations along a continuum whose extremes are the two proposed systems (Krafft, 1999; Baldauf et al., 2001; 2005).

Behavioural control systems, within the bureaucratic framework, ensure formal behaviour control to regulate the actions of subordinates on the job. More generally, it structures the transformation process of work (Ouchi, 1977). Based on the assumption of a centralised hierarchy, behaviour control is initiated top-down in the form of articulated operating procedures (Cheng & McKinley, 1984; Hitt, Hoskisson & Ireland, 1990). To ensure that subordinates adhere to procedure, superiors closely monitor and evaluate subordinates' actions over time (Ouchi, 1977; Ouchi & Maguire, 1975; Thompson, 1967). These appraisals tend to be subjective because they are based on the idiosyncrasies of the information that reaches superiors (Turcotte, 1974). In this case, feedback is used principally as a remedial tool to correct deviations as soon as they occur.

The advantage of behaviour control is that it is direct. At the extreme, superiors' engineer performance protocols that subordinates follow unquestioningly; in effect, control becomes a task design problem. Of course, one disadvantage of behaviour control is the substantial cost of personal surveillance (Eisenhardt, 1985), which may, for example, limit span of control.

If monitoring costs exceed the marginal gains from control, behaviour control may be an inefficient way to regulate performance. In addition, to the extent, behaviour control standardises work processes, it reduces the discretion afforded to subordinates and may lead to rigid and cautious behaviour (Child, 1973; Hitt et al., 1990; Inkson, Pugh & Hickson, 1970).

Thompson (1967: 85) argued that behaviour control assumes managerial knowledge of cause/ effect relations or the link between the actions subordinates take and the results they achieve. Eisenhardt (1985) referred to this connection as task programmability and Ouchi (1977) called it knowledge of the transformation process. When cause-effect knowledge is incomplete and managers do not fully comprehend the transformation process, it is difficult for them to translate their intentions into specific actions (Cheng & McKinley, 1983; Ouchi & Maguire, 1975; Turcotte, 1974). Consequently, they cannot standardise actions a priori (Argote, 1982; Brass, 1985; Cheng & McKinley, 1983). Similarly, they have no basis upon which to evaluate the appropriateness of subordinates' behaviour vis-a-vis their intentions (Ouchi, 1977). From this standpoint, Ouchi and Maguire (1975) showed that cause-effect knowledge can be viewed as a prerequisite to the use of behaviour control in human resource management.

Output control systems are an alternative to use behaviour control. Managers can control outputs (Ouchi, 1977). Output control differs from behaviour control in that superiors do not translate intentions into standardised operating procedures but instead set targets, such as financial results, for subordinates to pursue (Hill & Hoskisson, 1987). This form of control provides subordinates discretion in the means they use to achieve desired ends, thus decentralizing control. It does not allow them to choose goals, only the methods used to pursue established targets. Agency theory suggests that in the absence of close supervision, output control might lead to asymmetric information or information that is withheld from superiors, resulting in control loss (Williamson, 1975). In order to avoid this problem and induce performance that fulfils superiors' intentions, elaborate information systems are used that explicitly attach appraisal (Ouchi, 1977) and rewards (Kerr, 1985) to results achieved. A prevalent example of output control is "management by objectives" (Lawler & Rhode, 1976).

One advantage of output control is that it allows for some subordinate discretion; yet, provides both the incentive and responsibility for results that benefit the employing firm. Subordinates can adapt their behaviour to capitalise on opportunities and avoid threats that arise unexpectedly (Michael, 1973). In addition, in the absence of cause-effect knowledge, an output control like Return on Investment provides an objective criterion for performance evaluation (Hoskisson & Hitt, 1988). However, output control is reactive, providing what Flamholtz (1979) referred to as ex-post control. There is no mechanism for preventing mistakes until after they occur. In addition, output control can elicit myopic behaviour wherein subordinates pursue specified targets to the exclusion of other important, though untargeted, goals. Several authors (Hill & Hoskisson, 1987; Rappaport, 1978) have argued that overemphasis on short-term financial results may deter executives from making the kind of investments – like R&D investments – needed for long-term firm effectiveness. Since subordinates bear more risk under output control, they are likely to be risk-averse and to pursue relatively safer courses of action.

Viewed with logic, parallel to that involving cause-effect knowledge and behaviour control, output control depends on managers having crystallized "standards of desirable performance"

(Thompson, 1967: 84). Crystallized standards require reliable and valid criteria that represent performance benefiting firm. Other authors have called this requirement "outcome observability" (Eisenhardt, 1985) and "availability of output measures" (Ouchi, 1977). On the front end of the control cycle, crystallized standards operationally define managerial intentions, and on the back end, they constitute the basis upon which performance is evaluated. When standards shift from crystallized to "ambiguous" (Thompson, 1967), managers cannot establish concrete targets for subordinates to pursue.

Input control is used when employee behaviour cannot be standardised nor has a measurable outcome. The various terms associated with input controls are "clan control" (Ouchi, 1979), clan socialization (Govindarajan & Fisher, 1990) and selection and training (Snell, 1992). In its broadest definition, socialisation can be defined as the process by which an individual assimilates the values, attitudes, behaviours and knowledge essential for participating as an organisational member (Bauer, Morrison, & Callister, 1998; Louis, 1980; Van Maanen & Schein, 1979). Socialisation can encompass formal training, mentoring, reward and punishment systems, as well as informal and disjunctive tactics that require the organisational member to "figure it out as they go" (Harrison & Carrol, 1991). Researchers suggest that socialisation tactics range on a continuum from those tactics that are highly institutionalised to those that are highly individualised. Institutionalised socialisation tactics tend to be formal, collective, sequential, fixed and serial in nature. Examples of institutionalised socialisation tactics include, classroom training, clearly defined reward systems, career paths and mentoring programmes. Individualised socialisation tactics reflect an absence of structure and tend to be informal and random. On-the-job training is an example of informal socialization tactic. Institutionalised socialisation tactics create and reinforce standardised responses throughout the organisation while individualised socialisation tactics encourage innovation and cause individuals to question the status quo (Ashforth & Sacks, 1996; McMillan & Lopez, 2001).

Selection is a form of input control that attempts to prevent performance problems by ensuring that new employees have the requisite knowledge, skills, and abilities (KSAs) to perform well in the job (Snell, 1992). Effective selection focuses on creating a good fit between the organisation and the newcomer and may serve to reduce the need for intense socialisation (Harrison & Carrol, 1991). For example, Chatman's (1991) research involving accounting firms and new hires found that recruits whose values match the organisations' adjust more quickly, feel most satisfied and actually remain with the organisation longer. Therefore, as Chatman (1991) concluded, selection and socialisation may be seen as complementary processes, i.e., time spent on one activity (selection) will reduce the amount of time needed in the other activity (socialisation).

Improving quality and productivity, cutting costs and enhancing the spate of control as short-term strategies are all along being practiced by the organisations. Economic uncertainty has further increased such practices. However, such practices, without considering the human side of control, cannot lead to long-terms results and sustenance. It is for such reasons that organisations need to embrace the appropriate HR control systems with due cognizance to the human dimension so that control cannot transpire to be ultimately a bureaucratic disciplinary approach.

Human resources controlling, therefore, is a method of improving organisational effectiveness. All the measurement techniques applicable for human resource management can form the basis of tracking the trends; however, effective HR control systems require mutual tracking of such trends to help the employees to enforce self control. It does not demean the human values, rather allows employees to understand, where they need to guard against. It, in reality, helps the organisation to grow, making people to feel more responsible to deliver the results.

HR Control Systems Characteristics

Key drivers of HR control systems are: behaviour control, input control and output control. Hence, controlling these three aspects, among others, can also enforce HR control, provided organisations embrace those HR practices which ensure productive utilisation of resources. At the organisation level, firms' pursuit mainly focuses on cost efficiency, basically to counter competitive pressures. However, in such pursuit, firms often neglect the human dimension, resulting conflict and significant drop in productivity. Characteristically, HR control systems differ, for obvious variation in the strategic characteristics and strengths of the organisations. Each organisation varies with the standards, needs and demands (Brewster, Sparrow, and Harris, 2005; Hiltrop, 2002). One of the consumer electronics majors in India, which has acquired some erstwhile Phillips units and at the international level, acquired the colour picture tube manufacturing facilities of Thompson, even on date name their HR as liability centre. Although it sounds a bit off-the-cup, the firm's strategy is very clear – with a strong customer centric lens, compete and grow in the market, raging a price war! The company achieves the monthly production target and even overshoots it, much ahead of schedule which substantially reduces their cost of operation. Following extensive Work Break Down Structure (WBS), the firm is able to fragment the job, resulting in effective utilisation of the low skilled people to perform the structured micro constituent of a job. Also, it has made it possible for the company to interchangeably use people in different operation level jobs. Almost eighty percent of the operation level people are in the payroll of the outsourcing vendor, which makes the people available on daily basis, based on the company's demand. The Indian company, based on its business plan, first estimates the workload and then, decides the manpower requirement and requisition them from the outsourcing vendor. Temporary work suspension for lay-off then, substantially benefits the company by way of saving the wage cost, and so also other overheads. Strategically, the company produces independent of market demand and stock pile their finished inventories to rage the price-war to peg the demand of customers. Saving wage costs through lay-offs, in fact, helps the company to benefit the customers, as proportionate savings adjusted the price of finished inventories. Obviously, managing HR as a liability centre is a strategic move to achieve price efficiency. The company focuses more on marketing, brand building, research and development, to reach through the customers. With two Korean giants of consumer electronics in India, the company is able to sustain and grow in the market. Some of the common denominators for HR control Systems are the organisational history, its decision-making systems, power dynamics and its administrative heritage. All these could be the strength and so also the barrier for effective implementation of HR control systems.

Again characteristically, HR control systems are defined with respect to the cultural constructs of different countries. For example, the Japanese companies believe in the personal centralised control relating to decision-making at the centre of the top level of the companies and followed by direct personal surveillance of their execution. Bureaucratic formalised control, by contrast, is impersonal. Written manuals attempt to standardise the behaviour of employees by clearly prescribing courses of action to be followed.

Again, HR control systems cannot work in isolation, such systems have to interact (Martinez and Jarillo, 1989). Output control, as the key driver of HR control systems, resembles market approaches to co-ordination, focusing on outputs rather than on behaviour. The output is evaluated and controlled. Control by socialisation and networks mean all other control mechanisms that are not hierarchical, bureaucratic, and formal or output oriented. The other two drivers, i.e., the behavioural input and other inputs are characterised by environmental stability, a low level of technological development and transparent transformation processes or there may be an emphasis on personal centralised control in a smaller company and bureaucratic, formalised control in larger companies. On the contrary, a combination of output and social/network controls is better suited to situations with high environmental instability, complex technology and limited knowledge of transformation process (Legewie, 2002).

All the above characteristics of HR control systems are more formal and depend on co-ordination, centralization, standardization, planning, formalized behaviour, etc. However, effective HR control is also possible through informal mechanisms of participation in committees and teams as well as decision-making. So, HR control is possible autonomously when it forms the part of organisation culture of shared norms and values and the socialisation of its employees to these values (Gomez and Sanchez, 2005).

Control and Commitment Continuum of Human Resource Systems

Robert Simons's (1995) levers of control framework are a formal information-based routine or procedure which can be used by the management to maintain or alter patterns in organisational behaviour balancing the tension between (value) creation and control (managing and measuring value). Simons's levers of control though not exclusively earmarked for HR practices, help us in basing our discussions on commitment-control continuum of HR. Components of levers of control suggested by Simons are as under:

1. ***Internal Controls:*** The customary safeguards that a company establishes to protect company assets and ensure reliable record-keeping. Internal controls are structural, staff and systemic checks and balances that guard against duplication, inaccuracy, mischief and inadequate documentation.

   Belief Systems are those that an organisation must put in place so that it can control commitment to the organisation's vision, core values, mission statements, vision statements, credos and statements of purpose.

   Boundary Systems which an organisation must have so that it can stake out the territory for each participant: codes of conduct, predefined strategic planning methods, asset acquisition regulations and operational guidelines.

2. *Diagnostic Control Systems:* These must be put in place by a company so that it can optimize outcomes and get the work done: output measurement, valuation standards, incentive systems and compensation systems.

3. *Interactive Control Systems:* Smart organisations use these for tracking new ideas, for triggering new learning and for properly positioning the organisation for the future: incorporating process data into management interaction, face-to-face meetings with employees, challenging data, assumptions and action plans of subordinates.

A distinction is made between those HRM practices that focus upon enhancing employee commitment and those practices that increase control of the owner-manager over employees and the production process. These two aspects of HRM practices are considered the extremes on a continuum, where HRM practices tend to be either more commitment- or more control-oriented. The distinction between commitment and control is not new and can be traced back to McGregor's (1960) Theory X and Y, referring to the tension between the instrumental rationality of bureaucratic systems and the affective needs of employees or the need to achieve both control and consent of employees to maintain or improve performance (Legge, 1995). Other classic organisational classifications, resembling the control-commitment dichotomy and varying in scope (organisation structure versus management style), include autocratic versus democratic decision making (Lewin and Lippitt, 1938); mechanistic versus organic organisations (Burns and Stalker, 1961); task versus interpersonal oriented styles (Bales, 1950; Blake and Mouton, 1964); Likert's (1967) systems 1 to 4; transactional versus transformational leadership (Bass et al., 1996); direct control versus responsible autonomy (Friedman, 1977) and Tannenbaum and Smith's 1958) continuum (tell-sell-consult-join). These management modes either emphasise maintenance of tasks through direct forms of control or nurturing of interpersonal relationships through indirect or self-control of employees (Van Engen, 2001).

Based on the dimensions of the traditional versus high-commitment work system as proposed in Beer et al. (1984), Walton (1985) explicitly proposes the distinction between commitment and control strategies within the organisation. This distinction is further elaborated in the context of HRM by other authors (Guest, 1987; Arthur, 1992, 1994; Legge, 1995; Godard, 1998). Commitment and control are two distinct ways in which employee behaviours and attitudes can be influenced (Arthur, 1994). Given the assumption that HRM consists of a series of internally consistent HRM practices, which combine into a specific HRM system, it can be argued that HRM systems are either control- or commitment-oriented.

Control of HRM systems are characterised by a division of work into small, fixed jobs for which individuals can be held accountable and direct control with managers supervising rather than facilitating employees (Walton, 1985). This type of HRM system aims at reducing direct labour costs or improving efficiency, by enforcing employee compliance with specified rules and procedures (Walton, 1985; Eisenhardt, 1985; Arthur, 1994). In contrast, commitment HRM systems are characterised by managers who facilitate rather than supervise. This type of HRM system emphasises employee development and trust, establishing (psychological) links between organisational and personal goals. Commitment here is seen as an individual's bond with an organisation, referred to as attitudinal (affective) commitment (Allen and Meyer, 1990).

Arthur (1992) tried to develop the classification of organisations based on control-commitment continuum of human resource system characteristics. He could classify the organisations into two types; (i) cost reducers (those who believe in HR control) and (ii) commitment maximisers (those who believe in HR commitment). Arthur's study indicated that HR control and HR commitment represent two distinct approaches to shaping employee behaviours and attitudes at work. The goal of control human resource systems is to reduce direct labour costs or improve efficiency, by enforcing employee compliance with specified rules and procedures and basing employee rewards on some measurable output criteria (Eisenhardt, 1985; Walton, 1985). In contrast, commitment human resource systems shape desired employee behaviours and attitudes by forging psychological links between organisational and employee goals. In other words, the focus is on developing committed employees who can be trusted to use their discretion to carry out job tasks in ways that are consistent with organisational goals (Organ, 1988). In general, commitment human resource systems were characterised by higher levels of employee involvement in managerial decisions, formal participation programmes, training in group problem solving and socialising activities and by higher percentages of maintenance or skilled employees and average wage rates. The existence of the control and commitment variations in organisations is generally thought to be associated with certain organisational conditions. Most human resource strategy researchers have taken a behavioural perspective (cf. Snell, 1992). Research using this perspective rests on the often implicit assumption that the successful implementation of a business strategy requires a unique set of employee behaviours and attitudes and that a unique set of human resource policies and practices will elicit those behaviours and attitudes (Cappelli & Singh, 1992). Alternatively, control theory researchers (Eisenhardt, 1985; Ouchi, 1979; Snell, 1992) have noted that the use of a control system depends on managers.

HR Control Systems in Organisations

HR control systems in organisations need to be aligned, linked and integrated with the business objectives. We can appreciate such need in line with Stephen Covey's rocks of HR impact, which encompasses financial management, general management, HR impact, change management and systems integration. These five rocks form an integrated business system, designed to achieve above-average returns through sustainable means, the definition of Shareholder Value Assurance (SVA). The financial management system creates the SVA context, which serves as the framework for the general management system. Together, these two systems create a value-added framework for the HR Impact Toolkit. Change management technologies and systems integration skills are then, applied to these three interdependent systems to deliver SVA. This business system is the anatomy of the healthy organisation.

Human Resource Control Systems for MNCs

HR control systems for MNCs assume importance as MNCs have their presence in different countries. In MNCs, headquarters delegate work and responsibilities to overseas subsidiaries. To align a subsidiary's action with the headquarters' goals, an MNC may choose cultural control from various control strategies through shared values and norms or by employing expatriate parent country nationals (Gong, 2003). US companies are good examples of cultural implication with the image of pioneering spirit and a sense of limitless opportunity, the cultural forces that influenced management of US companies are completely different from the

European influenced derived from the concentration of wealth and power in a small socio-economic class. The US cultural forces created an environment that was less tolerant of the elitism and paternalism found in large, family-dominated companies that had developed in Europe. The US fostered the development of professional managers, to whom owners delegated the authority of running the business. Thus, a corporate norm was carried down through the organisation.

Such delegation could succeed only if top management retained access to information as a means of control. This model helped develop the classic American management processes built around divisionalised structures, which were transferred worldwide as US companies expanded abroad. This combination of delegation of responsibility to professional management and co-ordination and control through sophisticated management systems proved immensely powerful (Bartlett, Ghoshal, and Birkinshaw, 2003).

Culture constructs of Hofstede (1980) assume more importance, as it describes the attitudes of people across the nations. In MNCs, stereotypes reflect the societal or cultural norms (Gerhart and Fang, 2005). According to Hofstede, four organisation-relevant value dimensions of culture differentiate nations with respect to Power Distance; Uncertainty Avoidance; Individualism – Collectivism; and Masculinity - Femininity (Ueno and Sekaran, 1992).

Power distance reflects the extent to which a society accepts the unequal distribution of power in institutions and organisations. Uncertainty avoidance refers to a society's discomfort with uncertainty, preferring predictability and stability. Individualism/collectivism indicates the extent to which people refer to take care of themselves and their immediate families, remaining emotionally independent from groups, organisations and other collectivities. And the masculinity/femininity dimension reveals the bias towards either "masculine" values of assertiveness, competitiveness, and materialism, or towards "feminine" values of nurturing, and the quality of life and relationships (Bartlett, Ghoshal, and Birkinshaw, 2003).

High and low power distances differentiate the organisational practices. With high power distance, decision-making is centralised, organisations are structured on hierarchical lines and the people down the line, hardly interact with the top bosses. With low power distance, people take decisions in a decentralised manner; they co-ordinate their activities and work in a team. They enjoy autonomy in work. Countries which believe in high power distance mostly belong to old agrarian societies. Bypassing a superior is considered insubordinate, and can even merit disciplinary actions. This is, however, not believed in countries with low power distance.

In individualist cultures, individual uniqueness is given importance and hence, people are expected to perform their jobs with self-determination. In collectivist cultures, people work in groups. They believe in loyalty and compliance. Although both these types of culture have good or bad implications, a good way of explaining the differences is the experience of many international researches, particularly those who are required to generate information through cross-country survey. A market research organisation, while conducting a cross-country survey, noticed that the response to mailed questionnaires from the countries with individualistic culture is more, compared to countries which believe in collectivistic culture. This is primarily for the reasons that in collectivist culture, responsibility to send the questionnaire responses was given to all, while in individualist culture, such responsibility was assigned to a single official.

Based on the Hofstede's (1980) survey results, in the individualism dimension, U.S. is more individualistic and Japan is more collectivistic. In the uncertainty avoidance dimension, Japan had a much higher need to avoid uncertainty than the U.S. While there are differences between the two countries in two other dimensions, the contrast is most striking in Individualism/ collectivism (Ueno and Sekaran, 1992). The survey also revealed that with high power distance, a company will tend to have more formalisation evident, in greater amount of written rules and procedures. With high power distance, there are indications of more centralised decision-making, more layers and narrow span of control in organisation. In countries with a high collectivist orientation, group decision making and consensus and co-operation would be more valued than individual initiative and effort, rewards are based on loyalty and tenure. In countries ranked high on masculinity, task accomplishment and bottom line profits will come first instead of focusing on employee well-being as in a high feminine culture organisation.

Based on the study conducted by OJ Stevens in 1991 (Barlett, Ghoshal, and Birkinshaw, 2003) on British, French and German organisations, it was concluded that the German organisations where power and hierarchy is played down is formalized but not centralized; management intervention is limited to exceptional cases because the rules resolve problems, as they were more likely to be decentralized, specialized and formalized. German organisations tended to be flatter and have a broader span of control and participation in decision-making. In the Japanese firms, with both collectivism and hierarchal orientation, decision proposals are circulated, requiring individuals to "sign on" which means that if the decision is taken, the person agrees to support it. It is a way to preserve group harmony and relationships. In US organisations, participation is to preserve everyone's right to decide for integrating individual perspectives. As indicated in an article entitled "Culture and Organisation" (Bartlett, Ghoshal and Birkinshaw, 2003), the Confucian tradition of patriarchal authority is extraordinarily persistent in Chinese organisations. Control is exerted through authority. In this study, it is perceived that the culture factor is very important to this study not only because it plays a role as a factor which shapes HR practices (Andolsek and Stebe, 2005); but also because the interaction and movement of people across national boundaries are involved in international business. It is essential in the appreciation of cultural differences and when these differences are important (Gerhart and Fang, 2005). Furthermore, to cope with the transformation era, there is a need to recognise cultural divergence and this is critical for HR professionals, especially for those who play a culture change agent role in organisations.

With respect to the cultural variations, organisational systems and HR practices also vary, which exerts impact on HR control systems. Among others, culture influences the administrative and economic systems and our individual and collective behaviour is influenced by the interface of these two systems, along with the interface of three other systems, i.e., technological, wealth and education systems. Thus, while designing the HR control systems, it is necessary to consider these constructs so that the value dimensions in the process of enforcing control do not get lost.

Distributed Human Resource Control System

A distributed human resource control system is essential for MNCs to survive in global market. However, this requires standardisation of HR practices and documents those for the subsidiaries to follow. Most of the MNCs require recruitment validation for recruitment of executives and managers in their subsidiaries. The power to recruit people below executive level only lies with the subsidiaries. Mitsubishi Chemicals, a Japanese organisation, however, follows different approach in recruiting people in their Indian subsidiary even at the non-executive level. All recruitment requires vetting from the representatives of the Head Quarter. MNCs therefore differ in their approaches to human resource control systems.

MODEL OF HR CONTROL

Snell (1992) developed a model of HR control based on the idea that HR practices represent the principal means used by the organisation to control the performance. His model, based on the previous work by Ouchi (1979) and Thompson (1967), lists various HR practices and suggests that the selection of a control type should be based on the availability of two types of administrative information: "cause/effect knowledge" and "standards of desirable performance."

Table 16.3: Snell's Model of Administrative Information and HR Control
Knowledge of Cause/Effect Relations

Complete	Incomplete
Crystallized Standards of Desirable Performance Ambiguous Behavioural Control, Output Control or Both	Output control Decentralization Results criteria Performance-rewards link
Behavioural Control Centralization Articulated procedures Close supervision Behaviour appraisal	Input Control Rigorous staffing Training and Development Socialization

This figure is from Snell (1992), Control Theory in Strategic Human Resource Management, The Mediating Effect of Administrative Information, Academy of Management Journal, 41(2) 292-327, Adapted from Thompson (1967) and Ouchi (1977, 1978)

Knowledge of cause/effect relations indicates that the manager understands the transformation process and the specific actions subordinates must take to achieve the desired results. "Task programmability" (Eisenhardt, 1985) and "knowledge of the transformation process" (Ouchi, 1977) are similar terms used in control literature that refer to the ability to define explicitly appropriate behaviours. Where knowledge of cause/effect relations is high, behavioural controls are appropriate. As knowledge decreases, effective behaviours cannot be clearly specified and behavioural controls lose their effectiveness (Cheng & McKinley, 1983; Eisenhart, 1985; Govindarajan and Fisher, 1990; Snell, 1992).

Standards of desirable performance refer to the degree to which the criteria for judging performance are reliable and valid. If the standards lack either attribute, then output controls are not appropriate (Ouchi, 1979) because managers are unable to give subordinates defined targets (Snell, 1992). Eisenhardt (1985) referred to the reliability and validity of standards as "output measurability"; while Ouchi (1977) used the term "availability of output measures."

According to A. Sikorski, some of the important goals of human resource controlling are:

- To ensure co-operation between the HR department and the organisation as a whole, facilitating execution of departmental tasks.
- To achieve clarity in understanding the rationale behind increase of organisation's HR costs.
- To measure the influence of HR policies in terms of achieving organisational goal.
- To understand the results connected to human resource management in relation to other areas of the organisation.

Thus, human resource control fulfils the objective of creative co-ordination of mutually defined goals of the people and organisation, support human resource process and prepare for activity, focussing on corrective and preventive measures. It is for this, A. Pocztowski considered that HR control fulfils two important functions, i.e., information function and controlling function. Information function collects, designs and generates information to facilitate the decision-making process. The controlling function standardises plans and programmes, the recruitment for on-going verification. HR control, therefore, considers the needs that may arise within the organisation, in introducing change in the areas connected to human resource management.

Again, human resource controlling can be both strategic and operational. Strategic human resource control observes and analyses to forecast future process of human resource management. Its main focus is to leverage human capital to gain market leadership in a competitive environment. Operational control, on the other hand, ensures short-term direction to the organisation to achieve a specific human resource objective within the short time.

MEASUREMENT TOOLS USED IN HUMAN RESOURCE CONTROLLING

To enforce control in HR functions, organisations still use relatively less analytical tools. However, scholars like, John Sullivan and others have enriched this area, providing new insights to HR metrics. HR control is possible through generating data based on employee satisfaction surveys, periodic HR audits and through various statistical analyses of employee responses and data. The real problem starts after such data collection, as HR managers need to collate it with their vital HR decisions to enforce control in the organisations. Sullivan's HR metrics provide some quick fix solutions to such problems of interpretation, but in true sense, we cannot draw a borderline on HR metrics, as organisations' approaches to management of resources widely varies. For example, strategically, one organisation may like to recruit people with mono-skill and make these people redundant, once the job process changes. But in other cases, organisations may be interested to recruit multi-skilled people to ensure time to time skill renewability, to keep pace with the changing business process.

Some of the core HR metrics like, cost of turnover, cost of recruitment process, training costs, productivity costs, percentage improvement in workforce productivity, degree of employee engagement data, average performance appraisal score, percentage of diversity hires, employee retention data, compensation and benefits data, etc., are vital to enforce HR control. Using such metrics, HR managers enforce control. HR tools like HR scorecard, etc., can also supplement the HR control process in the organisations. In fact, when employees are taken through the HR scorecard and are facilitated to understand its application and interpretation, they themselves can enforce self-control, to keep them aligned with the organisations.

Again, a distinction is made between those HRM practices that focus upon enhancing employee commitment and those practices that increase control of the owner-manager over employees and the production process. These two aspects of HRM practices are considered as the two extremes on a continuum, where HRM practices tend to be either more commitment or more control-oriented. This debate, however, is not new, as it is evident from McGregor's (1960) Theory X and Y, which suggests the need to achieve both control and consent of employees to maintain or improve performance (Legge, 1995). Also, the debate on control-commitment dichotomy extends to various other dimensions of the organisations like, organisation structure versus management style, autocratic versus democratic decision-making, mechanistic versus organic organisations, tasks versus interpersonal oriented styles, transactional versus transformational leadership, direct control versus responsible autonomy (Friedman, 1977) and Tannenbaum and Smith's (1958) continuum (tell-sell-consult-join). These management styles and practices either emphasise maintenance of tasks through direct forms of control or nurturing of interpersonal relationships through indirect or self-control of employees (Van Engen, 2001).

Human resource control systems, therefore, are composed of various HR practices that lead the organisation to the accomplishment of its established objectives. Based on the dimensions of the traditional versus high-commitment work system as proposed in Beer et al. (1984), Walton (1985) explicitly proposes the distinction between commitment and control strategies within the organisation. Given the assumption that HRM consists of a series of internally consistent HRM practices which combine into a specific HRM system, it can be argued that HRM systems are either control or commitment-oriented. HR control systems are characterised by a division of work into small, fixed jobs for which individuals can be held accountable and direct control with managers supervising rather than facilitating employees (Walton, 1985). This type of HRM system aims at reducing direct labour costs or improves efficiency, by enforcing employee compliance with specified rules and procedures (Walton, 1985; Eisenhardt, 1985; Arthur, 1994). In contrast, commitment HRM systems are characterised by managers who facilitate rather than supervise. This type of HRM system emphasises employee development and trust, establishing (psychological) links between organisational and personal goals. Commitment here is seen as an individual's bond with an organisation, referred to as attitudinal (affective) commitment (see Allen and Meyer, 1990).

Human resource control systems, which we are debating in this book, have two dimensions: (1) organisation-wide control, and (2) self regulating autonomous control by the employees.

Summary

HR control is primarily enforced by regulating the performance. It involves three types of control, i.e., behaviour, output and input (Snell, 1992). Behavioural control is enforced through surveillance of subordinates' behaviour. Output control is measured in terms of results. Input control is measured in terms of the opportunity for training and development. Through HR control, organisations can programme how actions lead to outcomes and behavioural control. For organisations, HR control is the application of HR practices for performance assessment and incentives designs.

Reviewing the concept of modern HRM concepts and its extension to HR control, the chapter distinguishes the control and commitment with respect to the HR management practices and argues, how HR control systems work, even after keeping people commitment for the performance. Taking cues from Porter's three basic strategic choices for organisations, the chapter argues that HR control systems need to look beyond traditional percepts of behavioural, output and input control. Drawing lessons from the global organisations, it is now possible for us to understand the terms of references for HR control systems which differ from organisations to organisations.

KEYWORDS

Human Resource Commitment	Organisational Life Cycle
Human Resource Control	Control-commitment Continuum

REVIEW QUESTIONS

1. Define the concept of HR control. Explain how HR control concepts fit with the modern HR management practices.
2. Explain how HR control concepts differ from the concepts of HR commitment. How does control-commitment dichotomy influence various HRM practices in organisation?
3. What are the different types of human resource control? How does human resource control relate to organisational life cycle?
4. Explain the characteristics of human resource control.
5. Why are human resource control systems more important for MNCs?
6. What are the different models and measurement tools to enforce human resource control?
7. Write short notes on:
   (a) Control-commitment continuum
   (b) Behaviour Control
   (c) Organisational Life Cycle
   (d) Cost Leadership

CASE STUDY

ENFORCING HUMAN RESOURCE CONTROL THROUGH KRAs

You are working as the Corporate Human Resources Director of a large automobile manufacturer. You have been given the following KRAs, which forms the basis of your functional domain.

Corporate Human Resources Director – KRA

Results/Weights	Goals
• HR policies and interpretations (25%) • Exception decisions • Drafts of notices to employees	• No more than 3 to 5 requests for exceptions to the policy granted within first year. • Managers and employees: ❖ Are able to follow the policy without having to ask questions. ❖ Give positive comments about the policy which outweigh the negative comments. • VP HR says the policy: ❖ Considers the needs of both the company and the employees ❖ Satisfactorily addresses issues raised by employees and managers in opinion surveys and focus groups ❖ Is concisely written and can't have any language removed without changing the meaning ❖ Has a cost which is justified by the value it contributes to the company or the employees ❖ Is based on sufficient input or feedback from employees ❖ Legal staff approves the policy.
• Completed projects (20%) • Work-at-home recommendations • Casual day policy recommendations	VP HR and executive management say that the recommendations: • Are supported by data from other companies • Fit the unique situation at the company • Contain summaries of both the benefits and drawbacks • Take a position • Contain all the information needed to make a go/no-go decision • Completed by 2nd Quarter
Motivated and productive subordinates (20%)	The VP HR is satisfied that: • All employees have written performance standards. • All employees know how they are doing as compared to their standards. • All employees receive at least one informal interim review per year. • All employees receive an annual written performance appraisal. • All employees are meeting their performance standards or there is a performance improvement plan in place. • A reward and recognition system exists and there is an evidence of using the system. • Salary increases are differentiated based on performance. Surveyed subordinates say that: • They understand the company's direction, department's goals and their role in achieving these goals. • They understand specifically what their supervisor expects of them. • They understand how well they are performing and where they need to improve. • They have the necessary authority to perform their job. • Their performance appraisal accurately reflects their performance. • They have the skills and knowledge they need to do their jobs or there is a plan to obtain them.

Contd...

	• Their good performances are acknowledged and appreciated. • Their decisions are not reversed without reason or explanation and their suggestions are taken seriously.
Guidance and direction on HR policy development (15%)	VP HR is satisfied that the guidance and direction provided: • Produced practical solutions which fit real-life situations at the company • Solved the original problem • Produced an easily defensible policy • Looked for all the weaknesses and negative consequences in the recommendation • Produced a policy which is consistent with existing policies • Looked beyond the facts of a particular situation
Consistent application of HR policies (shared with line management) (10%)	• VP HR is satisfied with the number of formal complaints brought against the company. • VP HR is satisfied with the number of complaints from employees for inconsistent application of policies. • No second complaints are made on the same issue. • No decisions are reversed by a higher level of management when the Corporate HR Director was the first point of contact.
Solutions to "people" problems (10%)	Parties involved say that: • The solution resolved the problem. • The advice is consistent with the intent of company policies. • Their viewpoints were understood and addressed. • They understand the philosophy behind the solution. • No second complaints are made on the same issue. • No decisions are reversed by a higher level of management when the Corporate HR Director was the first point of contact.

Your company has been worst affected by the global recession, resulting in absolute slow-down in production. As a temporary measure, your company has to lay-off workers and even declares temporary closure. During this period, at the top level, a decision has been taken to adopt the human resource control approach, without, however compromising with the traditional value precepts about people. Being technology driven manufacturing process, the company need to engage highly skilled workers who are in great demand in the automobile and so also in other comparable verticals.

Identify the changes in the aforesaid KRA, assuming you have been designated as the Human Resource Controller.

UNIT 17

Human Resource Information Systems (HRIS)

Learning Objectives

After completion of this unit, the students will be aware of the following topics:

- *Introduction*
- *Definition and Concepts*
- *HRIS – Stages of Development*
- *Human Resource Development and Human Resource Information Systems*
- *Steps in Implementing HRIS*
- *HRIS Modules*
- *HRIS Products*
- *Illustration of an HRIS Module*

HRIS OF NILKOMAL

With the availability of HUMAN RESOURCE MANAGEMENT SYSTEM (HRMS) technology, Human Resource Information Systems (HRIS) are becoming more effective for organisations. Nilkomal, automated furniture manufacturer makes customised furniture for their customers using CNC machines (Computer Numeric Control). Nilkomal is now capable to produce doors and windows from wooden logs within few minutes. All these are possible for Nilkomal for obvious availability of trained and talented manpower. For Nilkomal, HRIS plays very crucial role not only in managing human resources, but also in taking effective strategic decisions leveraging their human resources. However, effectiveness of HRIS for Nilkomal is largely attributable to their degree of quantification of the human resource metrics. With such developed metrics, Nilkomal is plotting those in HRIS. Common human resource metrics for Nilkomal are: compensation cost per employee; revenue-to-employee or productivity-to-employee metrics; employee turnover rate; employee assessment or satisfaction; recruitment lead time and the cost of recruitment; employee performance index; etc. With the HRIS, such metrics are compared by Nilkomal over a time period both across the organisation and even across the industry. Nilkomal also aligned their HRIS with the organisational strategy and accordingly, customised the same, keeping pace with their requirements. HRIS vendors supplied to Nilkomal the standard systems and then, depending on their specific needs, customised the same. In Nilkomal's retail outlets, they are more interested to understand the sales trend per employee on daily footprints; while for institutional sales, they are more interested to evaluate the capabilities of credit sales in terms of sales realisation. For getting better results, Nilkomal expects their HR department to link the strategic objectives with the employees' performance. Also optimising HR costs, increasing employee retention, continuous improvement of performance, etc. are some other strategic objectives which they try to address through HRIS.

INTRODUCTION

Human Resource Systems have been acknowledged as important inputs to corporate decisions making process. Financial, operational and strategic business objectives are now not being considered in isolation of human resource objectives. Hence, Human Resource Systems are now enterprise-wide Decision Support Systems. Broderick & Boudreau (1992) defined Human Resources Information Systems (HRIS) as "the composite of data bases, computer applications, and hardware and software that are used to collect/record, store manage, deliver, present and manipulate data for human resources". Traditionally, HRIS is considered as automated record keeping of employees and computerisation of their payroll. However, it is now well established that HR managers with information systems can now play a greater role beyond their administrative role and in fact they are now being able to play even strategic support role. Today's organisations are besieged with mounting cost burden. With increased competition, they are not able to transfer this cost burden to the end users or customers. To maintain stable price of their end products or even to reduce it further for better market share, the only option is to look within, i.e., cost minimisation. Cost minimisation without technology support is difficult. Technology (in our case computers, more broadly Information Systems) not only substitutes manpower, it also substantially contributes to efficiency, automating repetitive operations. Dealing with Human Resource Information manually hardly allows any flexibility to HR professionals to address to managerial issues of HRM. Such managerial issues not only limited to optimal utilisation of manpower, but its effective planning, development and management.

For effective Human Resource Management, an HR professional requires accurate and timely data on recruitment, selection, training and development, career planning, compensation, productivity, skills inventory, motivation level, attrition rate, etc. Basing planning decisions on such input information, if not eliminate at least minimise the risk or uncertainty.

Even though, we have restricted our discussion on HRIS, limiting its importance as a strategic decision support systems, in the succeeding paragraphs, we have examined its holistic role both from organisations and HR professionals point of view. At the end we have illustrated a real-life incident, showing how an organisation suffered for not considering HRIS, before going for technological change.

Definition and Concepts

HRIS is the systems to acquire, store, manipulate, analyse, interpret and disseminate relevant information on Human Resources. It is not mere computer hardware or some customised or standard HR Software. It broadly includes people, policies, procedures (both endogenous and exogenous) and data. It need not limit its focus on automation of manual HR jobs like; record keeping or payroll preparation. It is a service in the form of information. Nature of information depends of users' requirements. Users' may not be limited to HR Department, it may be even an MD of an organisation. To illustrate, a Finance Manager, to prepare his annual budget may like to have data on aggregate compensation cost to the organisation. Mere extrapolating on head-counts may give an inaccurate figure. But simulating this with other factors like; attrition rate, likely DA increase/decrease, absenteeism, mandays loss, due to IR related problems, increments, incentive, promotion, redundancy etc., will certainly ensure a better projection. Similarly at the corporate level, for competency mapping of manpower, to decide about technological change, nature of information may be data on biographical details (which we commonly call manpower inventory) skill sets, training and development programmes, etc. Even for HR people, such information need may be different for different purposes. To evaluate the impact of some HR related policies, it may concentrate on data of grievances, work stoppages, litigation, strikes and lock-outs, mandays loss, productivity rate, attrition rate, etc. Earlier we have examined the nature of information, required for Human Resource Planning (HRP). Thus depending on the nature and level (strategic or corporate, tactical or business, operational), information requirement varies.

An HRIS is a systematic procedure for collecting, storing, maintaining, retrieving and validating data needed by an organisation about its resources. The HRIS is usually a part of the organisation's larger management information system (MIS). The HRIS need not be complex or even computerized. But computerization has its own advantage of providing more accurate and timely data for decision making. Thus Human Resource Information Systems (HRIS) are defined as the range of computerized technology that is used to store, record, link, analyse and present data about the human element within the business. Connections to the external environment through the Internet are significant in this definition, as are Intranets, which allow organisations the potential to communicate from within more rapidly and effectively. HRIS will assist in the provision of high-level customer focus and lowering an organisation's operational costs. Although HRIS includes hardware and software, it also includes people, form, policies, procedures and data. The areas of application of HRIS are many. Some of them include training management, risk management, turnover analysis, succession planning, flexible benefits, compliance with government and legal requirements, attendance with governments and legal requirements, attendance reporting and analysis, HRP, accident reporting and prevention, strategic planning, financial planning and other related areas.

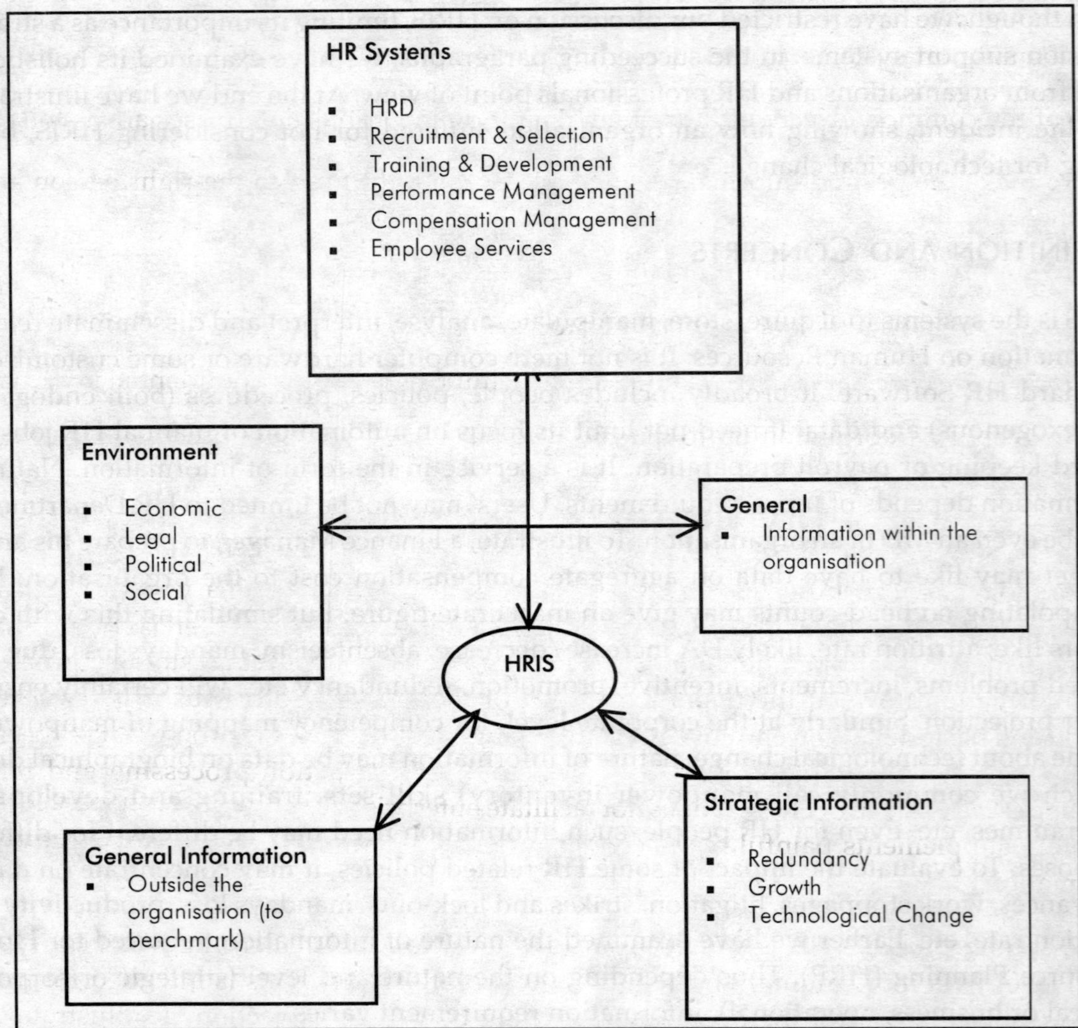

Figure 17.1: HRIS Model

Objectives of HRIS

Objectives of HRIS can be listed as follows:

1. *Effective Planning and Policy Formulation:* HRIS provides support for future planning and also for policy formulations, both at macro and micro levels. At enterprise or micro level, HRIS forms the basis for HRM and more particularly HRP.

2. *Monitoring and Evaluation:* HRIS facilitates monitoring of Human Resources demand and Supply imbalances and evaluation of the policy on development and utilisation of human resource.

3. *Provide Inputs to Strategic Decision:* HRIS provides required inputs to enterprise-wide strategic decisions, like redundancy, rightsizing, competency profiling, change of technology, etc. Other routine objectives of HRIS is to automate employee related information, cost minimisation, faster response to employee related services, faster HR

related decisions (like, promotion, transfer, payroll administration, compensation planning, manpower planning, etc.)

Some of the common objectives of HRIS in operation in various enterprises are as follows:

1. To make the desired information available in the right form to the right person and at the right time.
2. To supply the required information at the reasonable cost.
3. To use the most efficient methods of processing data
4. To provide necessary security and secrecy for important and/or confidential information.
5. To keep the information up-to-date.

HRIS – Stages of Development

Nature and types of HRIS depend on the level and ease of use. At the primary level, organisation may be interested to automate processing of routine information. It is an exercise of automating routine paperwork at operational level. Therefore, its focus is on data, storage, processing and information flows at the operational level of the organisation. Thus it is restricted to payroll and basic details on employees. In HRIS language we call it Electronic Data Processing (EDP) stage, which facilitates data and files storage, Transaction processing and reports summary. At this stage of HRIS, it does not facilitate enterprise-wide decision support systems. It merely supplements painful manual preparation of payrolls and basic employee related information.

In the second phase, focus is shifted from EDP level to Management Information Systems (MIS) level with more inquiry and report generation flexibility. This is intended for middle level manages to control the operation, matching budget or projection. To illustrate, over suiting of expenses on overtime, its extent and magnitude, can be analysed to enforce control on the same. Similarly, compilation of different statutory reports, for filing before statutory authorities can be done with MIS. Thus MIS facilitates information retrieval, analysis, inquiry and report generation to support middle level managers to enforce operational control and at the same time to address to statutory requirements (like filing of reports on accident, mandays loss, retrenchment, employee turnover, strikes, lockouts, layoffs, etc.).

The third type of HRIS is enterprise-wide Decision Support Systems (DSS) to facilitate decisions at the higher level in the organisation. At this stage HRIS is more interactive and capable of developing decision models on many strategic issues. For HRP, competency mapping of existing manpower, their future utilisation under changed technology, downsizing on rightsizing, training and development initiatives, etc., are the crucial issues for internal manning in tune with corporate goals and objectives.

Even for internal benchmarking, restructuring, designing suitable compensation packages, retention and motivation of good performers, etc., DSS is important. To illustrate, an organisation can design compensation packages for different age-group of employees differently without deviating from core compensation policy. Let us assume Non-Wage Labour

Cost (NWLC) component, which is more in the form of deferred benefits, payable to the employees and the personnel overheads, is forty per cent of the paid wages for an organisation. Now a static system of compensation for all age-groups may lead to loosing of young talents in an organisation. Particularly, this group is in their exploratory phase of career and they can be easily enticed by other organisation with minor wage increase. But such groups can be easily retained with more paid wages, reducing proportionate deferred benefits, without sacrificing the overall compensation plan. Knowledge intensive organisations are particularly besieged with this problem. DSS, therefore, is more interactive phase of HRIS to facilitate developing of decision models, duly examining the decision alternatives, to support corporate level for important strategic decision.

It is important to mention that all these types of HRIS is equally important for an organisation. Without EDP, i.e., the basic data storage of employees information and payrolls, MIS cannot be developed. Because at MIS stage, middle level managers, duly retrieving information, try to enforce control at operation level. Similarly, without EDP and MIS, DSS cannot develop decision models, examining decision alternatives, as at corporate level, inputs from EDP and MIS reinforce DSS with enhanced interactively.

Human Resource Development and Human Resource Information Systems

Human Resource Development (HRD) represents an integrated approach to the learning of employees, which enhances the capacity of the organisation to survive and advance.

Linking HRD with Business Objectives

It involves convincing management of the value of HRD, and questioning and reevaluating the notions of organisational effectiveness, to the end of its alignment and with business objectives. The process of analysing what behaviour or skills are likely to determine the organisation's survival and advancement is critical in this regard, involving a review of existing skills and competencies and selecting appropriate learning activities for future action. Technology can play an important role in each of these stages. Use of Intranet or 'Groupware' technology allows key management to confer more readily about the characteristics that are seen as necessary for moving the organisation forward. HR databases can provide customised reports about existing employees, on any aspect of their characteristics, providing that information is held in the first place. Such is the case with knowledge-based systems, which seek to replicate the problem solving and decision-making approaches of 'experts'- i.e. those who are likely to possess or have access to knowledge about a particular problem or issue. They have the potential to create a knowledge infrastructure, which is unique to a particular organisation. Training delivery and evaluation can then also be facilitated via these systems, building an electronically held knowledge resource for the organisation. Thus HRIS supports effective HRD, essential for achieving organisational strategy.

According to Broderick and Boudreau (1992) there are three types of Information and Communication Technology (ICT) application in HRM:

1. ***Transactions processing/reporting/tracking applications*** covering operational activities for e.g. payroll, record keeping and performance monitoring.

2. ***Expert systems*** to improve decision-making based on an analysis of decisions concerning such issues as sources of new recruits, salaries and training needs.

3. ***Decision support systems*** to improve decision-making through the use of scenario modeling in areas where there are no clear answers, for example, team formation and management development programs.

There are widespread use of HRIS for transaction applications in operational areas such as employee records, payroll and absence control. There are, however, less use in expert systems and decision support applications, which represent more advanced uses of HRIS. The use of HRIS for expert systems and decision support applications that reduce people to numbers might, however be resisted by many HR practitioners as representing too much of a clash with people oriented values (Kinnie & Arthurs, 1996). Therefore, it is argued a 'half-way position' has been adopted that emphasises the value of a limited use of HRIS but adds to cost effectiveness when combined with the professional performance of HR tasks that cannot be performed by IT.

Achieving Integration between HRD Processes and Other HR Initiatives

HRIS, when part of a performance management system can contain and record criteria and performance to achieve 'fit' between HR processes and can become a centralised point where each HR function is articulated and integrated (Hill, 1998). Context is vital here. Performance management systems operate most effectively in a good communicative environment and when they appear consistent across the organisation. HRIS can play an important role in communicating the vision articulated by top management because they allow for the rapid transfer of information.

Creating an Environment within which Individuals can take Responsibility for their Own Learning

Using HRIS ensures huge potential for individuals to play an active role in their own development. Employee self-service and widespread access to HRIS for training and development purposes are most significant. The benefits of this type of technology are the timely and accurate noting of competency and skill development changes in the organisation. Similarly, work station-based training can be inter-active and can test new skills, and can allow people to work at their own pace. Used in conjunction with traditional training delivery methods, technology based training delivery is a useful method by which HRD can reach individuals organisation wide.

Gaining the Support and Commitment of Line Managers in the Learning Process

HRIS have a great potential to allow line managers to become involved in the HRD process: they can bring together the developmental experiences of their subordinates and make informed decisions about how to make the best use of their team. Access to related HR data, such as working patterns, absenteeism and rewards, places the line manager in a stronger position in terms of understanding those issues that may impact positively or negatively on the HRD process.

Characteristics of HRIS

HRIS is mainly used for data administration and management rather than manipulation. A crucial element in any HRIS is how information is used, especially in decisions concerning how people are employed at work.

1. An HRIS may provide an objective view of an organisation in which the information used is comprehensive and accurate, allowing the best decisions to be made.

2. The design of an HRIS, including the categories and classifications that should be collected, plays a vital role in constructing the reality of organisation. Of vital importance here is the purpose of one category of data compared with another.

3. The way in which people relate to the information provided will depend on the 'maps' they hold concerning the organisation, that is, the store of existing knowledge held by each person to make sense of what happens. Information will be used in making sense of what is going on and what needs to be done, and such information may be accepted or rejected on the basis of how far it accords with a person's map. It is thus quite possible, since each person has a different view of life at work (a different 'map'), that the same information will be interpreted in different ways, leading to different decisions.

Steps in Implementing HRIS

Proper planning is an absolute necessity for successfully developing and implementing an HRIS. Following steps are important in implementing HRIS:

Step 1 (Inception of Idea): The idea for having an HRIS must originate somewhere. The originator of the idea should prepare a preliminary report showing the need for an HRIS and what it can do for the organisation.

Step 2 (Feasibility study): It evaluates the present system and the benefits of an HRIS. It evaluates the cost and benefits of an HRIS.

Step 3 (Selecting a Project Team): Once the feasibility study has been accepted and the resources allocated, a project team should be selected. The project should consist an HR representative who is knowledgeable about the organisation itself and the representatives from both management information systems payroll. As the project progress additional clerical people from the HR department need to be added.

Step 4 (Defining the Requirements): A statement of requirements specifies in default exactly what the HRIS will do. A large part of the statement of requirements normally deals with details of the reports that will be produced naturally; the statement also describes other specific requirements. This typically includes written descriptions of how users collect and prepare data, obtain approvals, complete forms, retrieve data and perform other non technical tasks associated with HRIS use. The key here is to make sure that the mission of the HRIS truly matches management's needs for an HRIS.

Step 5 (Vendor Analysis): This step determines what hardware and software are available that will best meet the organisational needs for the lowest price. This is a difficult task. The best approach is usually not the organisation's requirements but how it will meet those requirements. The result of this analysis will determine whether to purchase an off-the-shelf package or develop the system internally.

Step 6 (Package on Tract Negotiations): After a vendor has been selected, the contract must be negotiated. The contract stipulates the vendor's responsibilities with regard to software installation service maintenance, training and documentations.

Step 7 (Training): Training usually begins as soon as possible. After the contract has been signed. First the members of the project team are trained to use the HRIS towards the need of the implementation. The HR representative will then train managers from other departments on how to submit information to the HRIS and how to acquire information from it.

Step 8 (Tailoring the System): This step involves making changes to the system to best fit the needs of the organisation. A general rule of thumb is not to modify the vendor's package, because modifications frequently cause problems. An alternative is to develop programmes that augment the vendors' programme rather than alternating it.

Step 9 (Collecting the Data): Prior to start up of the system, data must be collected and entered into the system.

Step 10 (Testing the System): Once the system has been tailored to the organisation's needs and the data entered, verify the output of the HRIS and make sure it is doing what is supposed to do. All reports should be critically analysed for accuracy.

Step 11 (Starting Up): Start up begins when all the current actions are put into the system and reports are produced. It is wise to attempt to start up during a full period so that maximum possible time can be devoted to HRIS. Even though the system has been tested, some additional errors often surface during the start up.

Step 12 (Running is Parallel): Even after the new HRIS has been tested, it is desirable to run the new system in parallel with the old system for the period of time. This allows for the comparison of outputs of both the system and examination of any inaccuracies.

Step 13 (Maintenance): It normally takes several weeks or even months for the HR people to feel comfortable with the new system. During the stabilisation period any remaining errors and adjustments should be handled.

Step 14 (Evaluation): After the HRIS has been in place for the reasonable length of time, the system should be evaluated. Is the HRIS right for the organisation and is it being properly used?

HRIS MODULES

Modular approach to HRIS facilitates a user to look for his data of interest restricting his focus to some elements of the data. It is directed to some specific function of HRM. For HRP in an organisation, there may be specific requirement of a module, while for Training and Development, there may be another. To decide about specific requirement of HRIS modules, it is always essential to do a Need Analysis. Needs are specific to an organisation. Therefore, needs of one organisation may not match with another, unless these are generic in nature and intended to address only some technical requirements like; security, user interface and navigation, standards, data integrity, validation, etc. To ensure proper HRIS in an organisation vis-à-vis appropriate selection of HRIS modules, it is important to integrate needs with the technology strategy of an organisation. For example, if in near future, your organisation decides to change the technology platform, then to decide about HRIS modules, you have to ensure its compatibility with changed platform, or else, you will soon identify obsolescence of your HRIS. Similarly, to perform need analysis for HRIS, it is also essential to integrate it with your corporate strategy. If your corporate strategy limits its focus only on automation of payroll in HRIS, you may only look for best of those modules, which address to payroll automation requirement. But if your corporate strategy is to go for enterprise wide applications then look for those HRIS modules that support enterprise wide applications. Most of the organisations today are re-engineering their Business Processes, which calls for holistic HRIS approach, than specific payroll or employee information. Going for enterprise wide systems is always a better choice for important strategic decisions about HR.

HRIS need analysis is also integrated with critical success factors within an organisation. This is ensured by duly taking into cognizance critical inputs from different cross functional teams. Such cross functional teams will include HR, Finance, line managers and IT Professionals. Such critical inputs facilitate documentation of various expectations and relate such expectations to the HRIS requirements.

Once needs analysis is performed, it is better to go for a final sign-off of the requirements by participating cross-functional team members. This ensures documented concordance and commitment from the end-users, during subsequent implementation and operation of HRIS.

A final documentation is done for subsequent selection of HRIS vendors.

HRIS PRODUCTS

Some of the HRIS products are listed below:

1. CSS Horizon™
2. elabour.Com™
3. Genesys™
4. Lawson™
5. Oracle

6. PeopleSoft
7. ProAct
8. SAP@
9. SmartStream@
10. UltiPro@
11. Goodwoodhr.com
12. VIP Manager

There are many other vendors with standard HRIS packages and each of them disseminates the nature of information that could be made available by their packages in different HR areas. In addition there are HRIS Consultants who can customise HRIS package of an organisation duly addressing to their specific needs.

HRIS Product Contents and Features

Most of the HRIS vendors have defined their product contents and features, which can be downloaded from Internet. Here we have given a general outline for better appreciation, without, however, mentioning a specific product.

Products on Recruitment Management

Recruitment Management is one of the core HRIS modules, which is in the product profile of all HRIS vendors. To hire and deploy the best people of minimum cost and within a time bound schedule, HRIS modules on Recruitment Management, generally cover following areas:

1. Applicant/vacancy Details
2. Short-listing
3. Job/Person specifications
4. Skills Matching
5. Mail Merge facility
6. Standard Reports
7. Cost Analysis
8. Internal Job Posting
9. Interview Scheduling
10. Internet Job Posting, etc.

Products on Training and Development

Planning, implementing and costing of training are again essential part of HRIS for any organisation. Control and monitoring of training events, maintenance of training records of employees are also the critical inputs for this HR function. A standard HRIS module on training and development incorporates following areas:

1. Course Specification
2. Course Scheduling
3. Evaluations
4. Mail Merge Facility
5. Cost Analysis
6. In-house faculty database
7. External faculty database, etc.

Products on Attendance

This module provides HRIS data on unplanned absence, list of late arrivals, report on attendance incentives, leave record, work patterns, break profiles, overtime profiles, shift patterns, etc. Tracking of information on attendance also provides critical inputs to HR function. HRIS module on Attendance may have following features :

1. Automatic exception reporting
2. Accurate attendance roll
3. Integration with payroll
4. Reports on unplanned absence and late arrivals
5. Working hours regulation
6. Overtime hours calculation
7. Integration with personal records, etc.
8. Mail merge facility

There are various other HRIS modules on important areas, like; payroll, contact labour management, etc. Some vendors also provide generic HRIS modules like, Enterprise Project, Personnel Management, Human Resource, etc.

It is important to mention that any particular product may not be specific to any specific organisation. Hence, customisation of HRIS products may be necessary matching with specific organisational needs. For HRP, inputs from HRIS are very important, which can be further analysed using other statistical tools to develop appropriate models and to optimise Human Resource requirements. Some organisations also use some standard Statistical Packages for more accurate and timely planning of human resources. There are, however, specific HRP modules which provide information to estimate future manpower supply and demand. Such modules analyse current staffing levels, skill sets, turnover rate, promotions and transfer, succession plans, etc. Since HRP is a part of strategic plan, such modules also have interfaces with enterprise-wide databases.

Templates of a standard HRIS products, known as VIP Manager are given as annexure to this unit.

Illustration of an HRIS Module

HRMIS provide efficient and fully integrated human resource management tools that enables a organisation to effectively manage resources. With complete integration throughout all components, it can offer a package that not only assists business processes, but proves to be a critical tools in the management of organisation's most valuable assets – its people.

Establishment Management

Establishment Management enables organisations to be defined within a hierarchical structure containing an unlimited number of business units. The organisational data held within records details of the organisation structures, reporting relationships, titles of levels, positions and staff levels within the structure. An online interface to "OrgPlus" enables the automatic generation of graphical organisation charts. Establishment Management caters for:

- Occupancy
- FTE Management
- Job Evaluations
- Establishment Reporting, including Organisation Charts.
- Employee Details

Employee Details provide a solid foundation for the entire Human Resources system. It enables the effective management of employees through an immediate and integrated solution. Employee Details includes:

- Biographical Details
- Professional Data
- EEO
- Employee Reporting

Training & Competency Management

Training & Competency Management provides the mechanism to assist in the identification, scheduling and updating of training details for employees. Allowing seamless integration with Establishment Management and Employee Details via a skills matching process, and with the Organisational Development via course nominations and Development Plans. The key areas of Training & Competency Management includes:

- Competency Management
- Program Creation and Maintenance
- Resource Booking
- Update of Employee Training Data
- Identification of Potential Nominees
- Course Appraisals/Evaluations
- Statistical Reports

Recruitment & Selection

Concept Consisto Recruitment and Selection enables recruitment action to be managed and tracked through the life of the recruitment cycle. Each step of the recruitment process is designed to reflect current business practices. It is also possible to mandate events and sequences in the recruitment process in line with organisation business processes. Recruitment & Selection allows organisation to monitor:

- Vacancy Management
- Applicants Tracking
- "What If" Processing
- Letter Generation
- Recruitment & Selection Reporting

Salary Packaging

Salary Packaging provides benefits administration and modeling function for the creation of salary packages within an organisation. Key components include:

- Benefits Administration
- Benefits Proposal
- Letter Generation
- Workplace Health & Safety: These functions cover the spectrum of processes, including incident and accident management, claims processing and proactive employee health and safety management. The numerous user-defined description tables allow configuration in accordance with Standards. Standard functions of Workplace Health & Safety include:
    - ❖ Incident & Accident Management
    - ❖ Claims Processing
    - ❖ Rehabilitation
    - ❖ Employee Health & Safety Reports

SUMMARY

HRIS is now an important input to corporate decision-making process. It not only helps in HRP and other HR functions, but also provide decision support for formulating operational, business and corporate strategies. HRIS vendors provide different standard modules on HRIS, but for meeting specific requirements of an organisation, HRIS may be customised. For selecting an appropriate HRIS module, it is always better to perform needs analysis.

KEYWORDS

EDP	Benchmarking
MIS	Restructuring
DSS	NWLC
HRIS	Critical Success Factors
BPR	

WHY HRIS ?

Incident

A departmental undertaking employing about 7000 persons is engaged in production of small arms for country's armed forces. It had the captive market privilege as its production had ready buyers, i.e., army. To ensure quality and cost efficiency, Government had suddenly decided to procure small arms from best available global manufacturers. Suddenly the Departmental Undertaking had to be competitive and more quality conscious. It had to go for major technological changes, from conventional and special purpose machines to CNC, NC and DNC. The decision on technological changes was taken by a high powered committee at Ministry level and it involved a total cost of ₹ 250 crore during 1993-1994. Since, the employment practices of Departmental undertaking was not to hire and fire, more institutional than contractual, initial effort was to utilise existing manpower by suitable skill-change training. Technology vendors in their literatures printed that it required 7 days in-house training for successful operation and production run. They had a clause that a team of people from the undertaking would be trained at their cost and at their premises for 15 days. The core team of ten people was formed and sent to the vendor's premises, which was outside the country. On their return, the core team monitored the installation and certified the production-run. The core team then started in-house training of identified workers for new technology. The idea was to train a batch of 100 workmen per week and put them on trail production run. After one month of such exercise, it was observed, trained workmen are not successful in operation of new technology and in fact miserably failed in trial production run. The situation likewise continued over a year and the undertaking failed to address to this perennial learning problem.

On getting serious criticism from the Ministry, the Departmental Undertaking had to form a high powered committee with one core consultant from outside to review the situation. The committee after six months could identify the real problem lies in present skill-set and knowledge-base of the workers.

By the time the Departmental undertaking could start commercial production run, it was delayed by more than 2 years, resulting huge loss of interest cost on investment. HRIS in this situation could have averted the problem, providing inputs on employee details.

Notes

1. Benchmarking is an important tool for strategic management. It supports and enhances strategies by providing information of competitors. For compensation designing, framing of reward and incentive

Contd...

policy and even for HRP, benchmarking helps. Some HRIS modules also cater to benchmarking to facilitate in decision-making.

2. Re-engineering or Business Process re-engineering (BPR) helps to identify key processes and make the organisation as lean and efficient as possible. BPR has become synonym for redundancy, downsizing or right-sizing, which, however, is incorrect.
3. Non-Wage Labour Cost (NWLC) is an important component of Compensation package, which is a load on paid wage cost, in terms of deferred payment to employees. While computing NWLC, apart from deferred benefits, personnel overhead is also added. NWLC in U.K. are equivalent to 40% of paid wage costs, in the U.S.A, it's 38%, in Germany it is 82% while in France it is as high as 93%. In India NWLC is 20% to 25% of the paid wage costs. The author, however, could trace NWLC in one of the Indian organisations as high as 57% of paid wage cost.
4. Strategy is the long term direction and scope of an organisation. It emphasises on matching of organisational resources, keeping pace with the changing environment, to meet the expectations of different stakeholders. HRIS strategy is the long term plan for acquiring and storing information of HR function.
5. Competency Mapping is done, suitably identifying competencies needed in the future. Competencies are set of behaviours, which encompass skills, knowledge, abilities and attributes. Competencies are assessed both at organisation level and at individual level. Suitable Workforce Analysis, Job Analysis, Supply and Demand Analysis, Gap Analysis and Situation Analysis do competency mapping in the defined job context.
6. Exploratory Career Phase is the initial Career Stage of a person with relatively young age. At this stage people always look for better option, even sacrificing their deferred benefits. For compensation planning, a flexible approach for this group is essential, or else organisation may experience highest rate of attrition.

Review Questions

1. How would you computerise the Human Resource Information System in your organisation or any other hypothetical organisation? Give your answer with examples.
2. Explain the purpose and objectives of HRIS is an organisation.
3. Explain how HRIS can reinforce Strategic decision in an organisation?
4. You have been asked to identify one HRIS Vendor and select modules for your organisation. Explain the way you want to proceed and select the vendor.
5. Design a payroll for an organisation, keeping in view all possible entries.
6. Write short notes on:
   (a) Critical Success Factors
   (b) Mail Merge
   (c) Payroll
   (d) Decision Support Systems
   (e) EDP

CASE STUDY

THE SUCCESSION CRISIS OF AXIS BANK

Axis Bank is the third largest private sector bank in India. Under the dispensation of the Chairman-cum-Managing Director, Mr. Nayak, the Bank could substantially grow its business. However, Mr. Nayak could not groom the right successor of the Bank, after his departure. Mr. Nayak's failure to identify and groom the successor in-house, prompted the Bank to requisition the services of a global sourcing agency to identify the new Chairman-cum-Managing Director and finally, the bank could zero their search for Sikha Sharma, The CEO of ICICI Prudential Life Insurance Company Ltd., as the new CEO and MD of Axis Bank. However, Mr. Nayak opposed the move, as he preferred some in-house talents to succeed him. Mr. Nayak's contention was that Ms. Sharma's exposure to banking is not befitting to assume the office of CEO of Axis Bank. The Axis Bank's Board, however, did not accept the contention of Mr. Nayak, as in-house talents are experts in the banking business but they do not possess the experience of all verticals of the bank's business portfolio. The Board attributed this to the failure of Mr. Nayak, as developing the successor within the Bank was the responsibility of Mr. Nayak. Board's such decision was vehemently opposed by Mr. Nayak, and he made his departure before the normal end of his tenure. Excepting Mr. Nayak, all other top brass of the management of Axis Bank voted for Ms. Sharma with the contention that Mr. Nayak did never listen to them to groom talents from within. Had this been done on time, the results could have been better. At this critical juncture, Ms. Sharma's appointment is justifiable.

For the new incumbent for CEO's position, Ms. Sharma; it has now become the great challenge to spur the growth of the bank. For Ms. Sharma, it is again a great challenge, as culturally Axis Bank and ICICI are different.

Question

From the above case, discuss whether such crisis of Axis Bank could have been avoided with proper HRIS.

ANNEXURE 1

HRIS Product of VIP Manager, a especially designed software for HR management

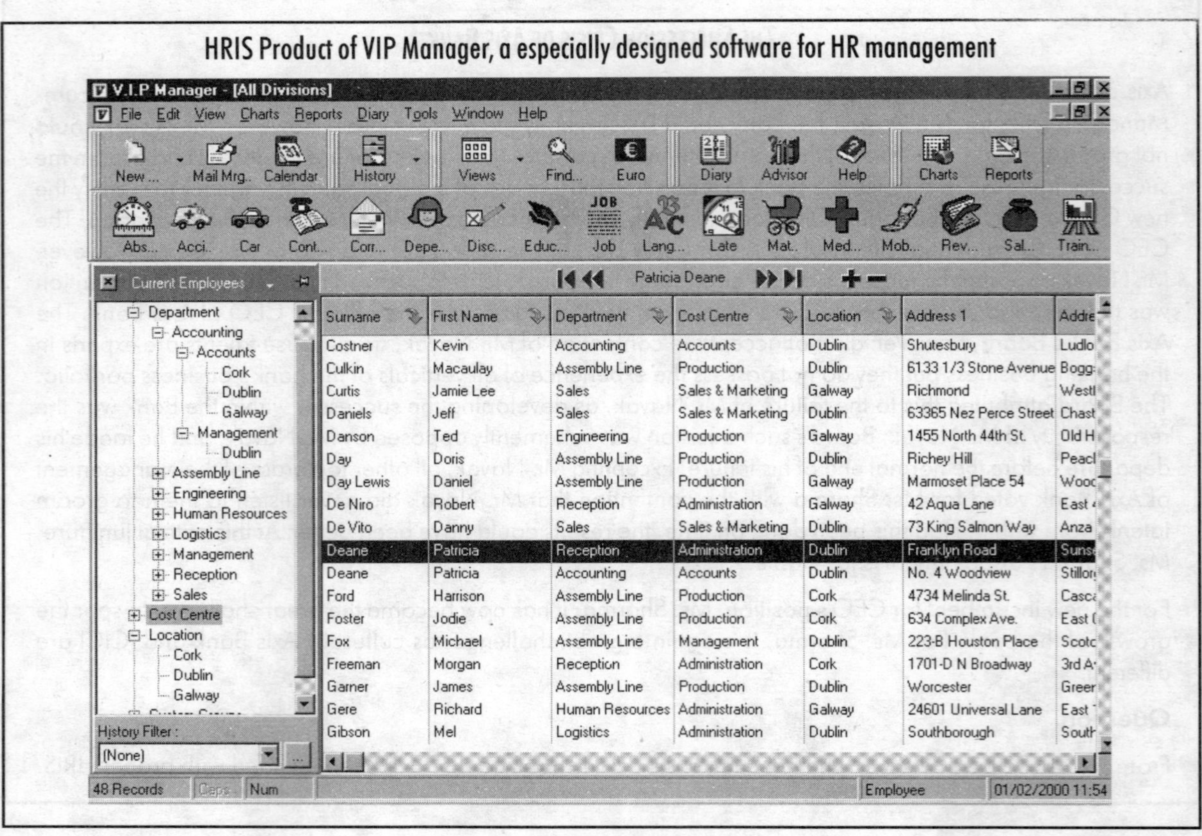

ANNEXURE 2

HRIS Product of VIP Manager, a especially designed software for HR management

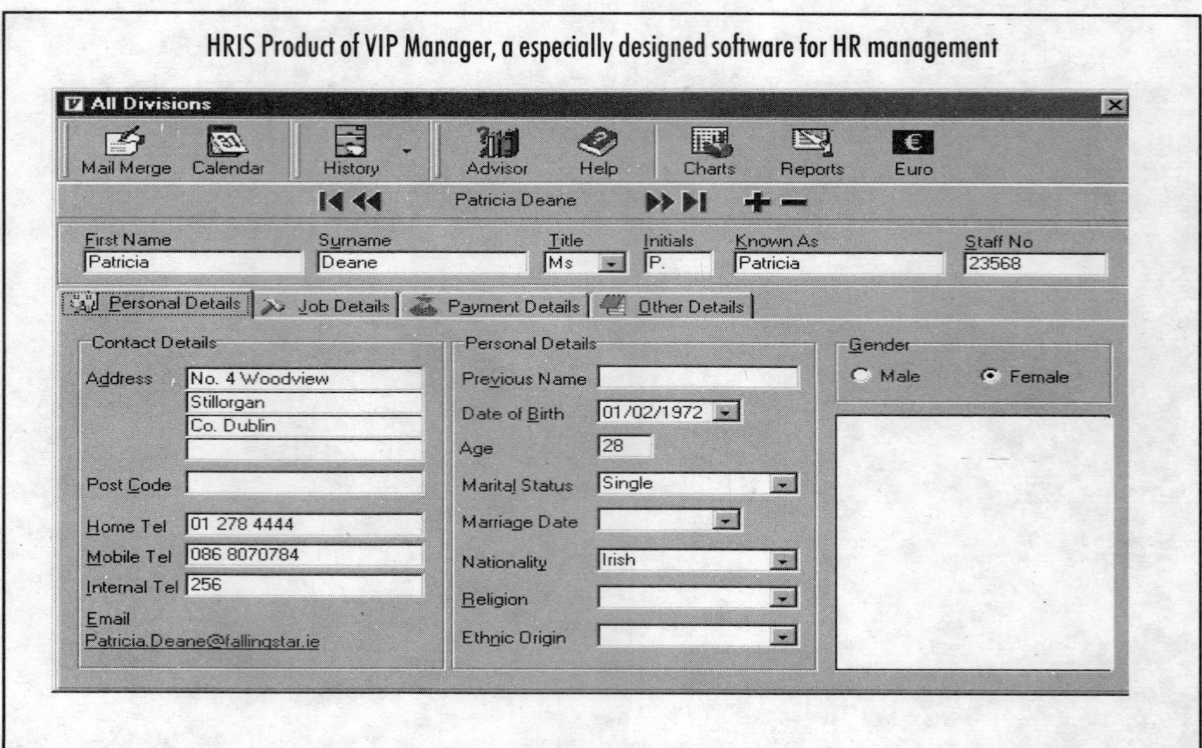

EXHIBIT 17.1

Some of the HR related forms which have been designed by various organisations to develop their HIRS can be illustrated as under:

ABC & Co.

Module	HRM	Form	Employee Registration	Details
Description	This form is used to Manage Employee details			

Loading Page Information...

Enter Employee Detail

Employee Code	
First Name	
Second Name	
Parent Name	
Spouse Name	
Nominee	
Location	Head Office
Code	
Department	
Designation	MANAGING DIRECTOR
Grade	CON
SEX	(•) Male ( ) Female
DOB	11
MARITAL STATUS	SINGLE
Bank Name	
P. ADDRESS	
PHONE	
L. ADDRESS	
PHONE	

Contd...

E-MAIL	
DOJ ABC & Co.	11
Appointment	New
PF No	
ESI No	
Salary	
DA	
Increment Date	11
Last Exp	
Appointment Code	
Application Code	
Date Of Confirmation	11
Category	Officer (Head Office)
Group	General Shift
STATUS	Active
Account No	
Blood Group	A+
Pan No	
Service Weightage	
GGS No	
GGS ID	
Education Details	

EXHIBIT 17.2

A SAMPLE PAY SLIP USING HRIS MODULE OF KURL-ON LIMITED

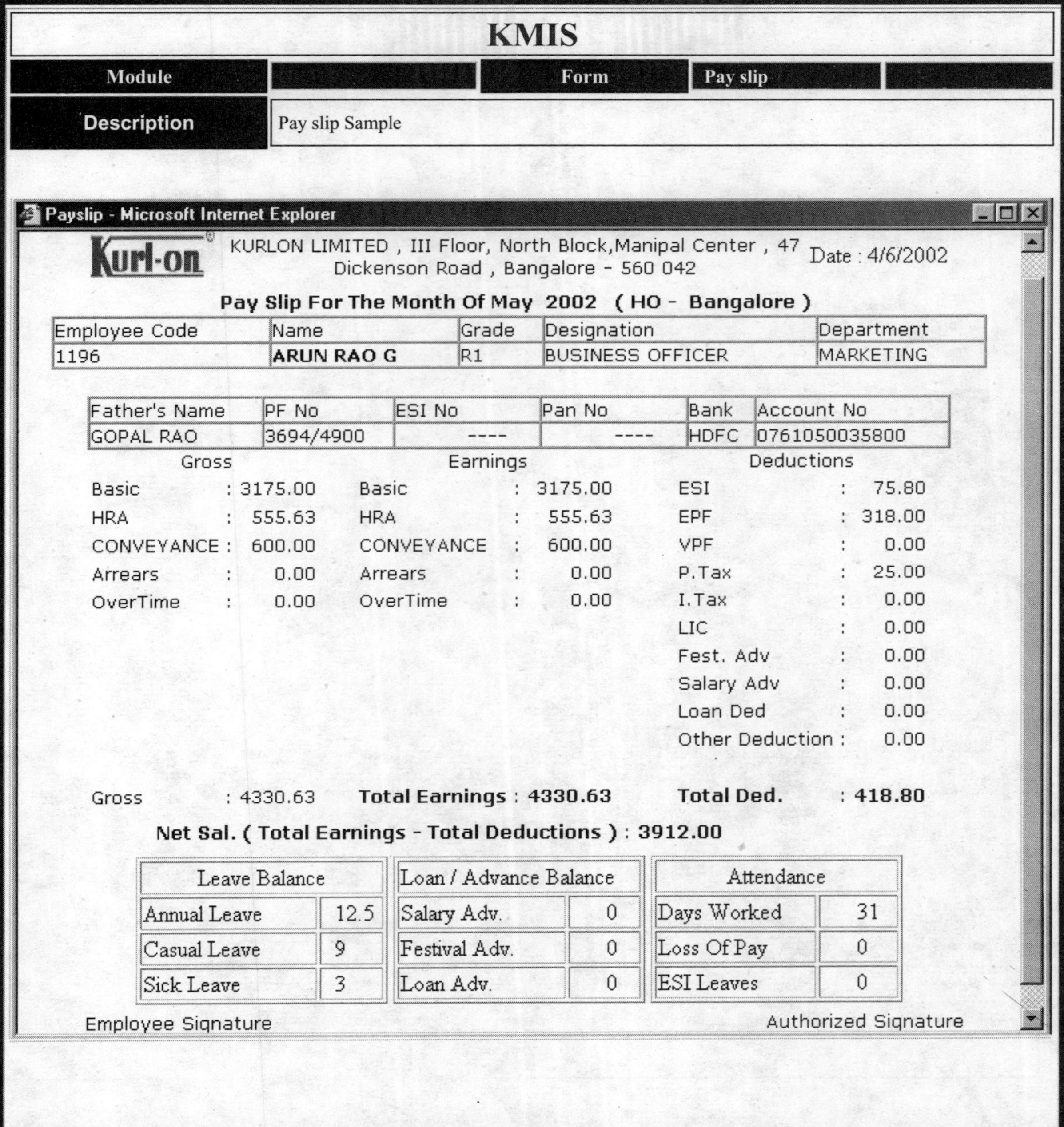

KMIS

Module		Form	Pay slip	
Description	Pay slip Sample			

Payslip - Microsoft Internet Explorer

Kurl-on KURLON LIMITED , III Floor, North Block,Manipal Center , 47 Dickenson Road , Bangalore - 560 042 Date : 4/6/2002

Pay Slip For The Month Of May 2002 (HO - Bangalore)

Employee Code	Name	Grade	Designation	Department
1196	**ARUN RAO G**	R1	BUSINESS OFFICER	MARKETING

Father's Name	PF No	ESI No	Pan No	Bank	Account No
GOPAL RAO	3694/4900	----	----	HDFC	0761050035800

Gross		Earnings		Deductions	
Basic	: 3175.00	Basic	: 3175.00	ESI	: 75.80
HRA	: 555.63	HRA	: 555.63	EPF	: 318.00
CONVEYANCE	: 600.00	CONVEYANCE	: 600.00	VPF	: 0.00
Arrears	: 0.00	Arrears	: 0.00	P.Tax	: 25.00
OverTime	: 0.00	OverTime	: 0.00	I.Tax	: 0.00
				LIC	: 0.00
				Fest. Adv	: 0.00
				Salary Adv	: 0.00
				Loan Ded	: 0.00
				Other Deduction	: 0.00
Gross	: 4330.63	**Total Earnings**	**: 4330.63**	**Total Ded.**	**: 418.80**

Net Sal. (Total Earnings - Total Deductions) : 3912.00

Leave Balance		Loan / Advance Balance		Attendance	
Annual Leave	12.5	Salary Adv.	0	Days Worked	31
Casual Leave	9	Festival Adv.	0	Loss Of Pay	0
Sick Leave	3	Loan Adv.	0	ESI Leaves	0

Employee Signature Authorized Signature

UNIT 18

Human Resource Management Research

Learning Objectives

After completion of this unit, the students will be aware of the following topics:

- *Introduction*
- *Different Approaches to Management Research*
- *HR Research*
- *Questionnaire and Survey*
- *Using Statistical Test in HR Research*
- *Computer Aided Research in HR*
- *Presenting HR Reports*

INTRODUCTION

Research is a scientific endeavour. Research explores unknown facts, unknown applications of theory, from which we build knowledge and theory and decide about its practical applications. Through the process of identification, critical examination, generalisation and dissemination of useful practical experiences, management research helps us to develop relevant approaches for successful management of organisations. Management research, like any other research, therefore, is a rigorous scientific activity. It is systematic development and acquisition of knowledge and is tailored to specific management needs to answer specific questions within a given timeframe. It is now a subject of study: to understand how organisations are structured and function; the practices of decision-making; the factors that affect organisational operations, the strategies that contribute to enhancement of strategic advantage of an organisation, etc. Management research reveals causal connections between variables, i.e., to demonstrate that one variable is a cause of another variable. When such causal relationship is established, we can control the "effect" (caused) variable to achieve our intended goals and objectives. Such control may be to change the causal variable, e.g., eliminate it or to strengthen it. This apart, management research is sometimes carried out for descriptive purposes also. However, the results of descriptive research are rarely of great interest. For example, a manager may wonder why costs of some operations are higher in one unit than other and may collect data relevant to that question. If this can be determined, then the manager may be able to intervene to reduce the excess costs, bringing desirable changes in the operation.

DIFFERENT APPROACHES TO MANAGEMENT RESEARCH

While the process of management follow a typical structure, approaches may be different and vary from situation to situation. It may be purely academic or theoretical or action oriented. But what approach is appropriate for a given situation largely depends on specific need of a researcher. Commonly we find five types of management research. Those are:

1. ***Pure basic research:*** This research intends to develop a basic discipline by resolving, illuminating and exemplifying a theoretical issue. Therefore, its basic purpose is to enhance knowledge and understanding. The results of such research become the source of knowledge for the practicing managers. Most of the core management concepts developed from pure basic research.

2. ***Objective research:*** This research focus on how to overcome a general problem in application of an established knowledge. It is, however, not intended to solve a specific management problem. For doing such research, the researcher frames certain clear objectives and hypotheses and then tests the validity of established knowledge in a given situation.

3. ***Evaluative research:*** This research, in contrast assesses some aspects of the organisational function by analysing the effectiveness of a given problem, like; effects of performance linked pay over fixed pay on workers' motivation, effects on change in organisational culture in post-merger situation over pre-merger, etc. This type of research is most

common in organisations as it helps practising managers to develop 'scientific neutrality' to look into some issues and develops a framework for future management.

4. *Applied research:* This type of research is more specific to solve a particular problem within an organisation by application of appropriate knowledge. To illustrate, we may apply our existing knowledge on leadership to identify most appropriate style for knowledge workers, suitably changing our existing style in organisation. Since it is more specific to solve a given organisational problem, we often allege such research do not add to our existing knowledge. However, others may emulate experience of one organisation, as 'best practice management' concepts now require every organisation to benchmark with others.

5. *Action research:* In this research action (i.e., solution of a problem) is both an outcome and a part of the research process. Its main purpose is to improve the stock of knowledge by tackling a problem, which has relevance to theory. However, the researcher in such a case bring changes to the research. During the process, the outcome, it is often alleged, cannot be replicated, which put a constraint to test the validity of research in another situation. Thus, it may prevent development of general knowledge.

Concept Mapping for Management Research

For doing effective management research, it is necessary to explore knowledge and to gather and share information. This is done using a concept map. Concept map is a special form of diagram and used as a formative assessment tool and as a research tool. Thus concept mapping is a technique for visualising the relations between concepts. Its purpose is to form or assess a person's cognitive map, using a diagram and showing the relationships between concepts. Concept mapping significantly improve the level of meaningful learning and communication of the research concept. Concept maps are also used to stimulate and organise idea generation. For effective management research, concept mapping helps in following ways:

- Developing an understanding of a body of knowledge.
- Exploring new information and relationships.
- Accessing prior knowledge.
- Gathering new knowledge and information.
- Sharing knowledge and information generated.
- Designing structures or processes.
- Problem solving.

Literature Review in Management Research

A literature review is a summary of previous research on a topic. Literature reviews can be either a part of a larger report of a research project, a thesis or a bibliographic essay that is published separately in a scholarly journal. We do literature review to understand our research problem better. We also try to find any knowledge gap, degree of agreement on the topic, past debate on the topic, problems identified in the past on the topic, current status of research on the topic, etc. If the literature review is part of a Ph.D. dissertation, this review will be comprehensive covering all possible research on the topic. This, however, does not mean that as researcher one should identify all research on the subject. The purpose of a literature review is to convey what knowledge and ideas have been established on a topic and what are their strengths and weaknesses. It allows us to remain up to date regarding the state of research in the field and familiarises us with any contrasting perspectives and viewpoints on the topic, if any. A literature review before starting a research is always desirable for following reasons:

- To see what has and has not been investigated.
- To develop general explanation for observed variations in a behaviour or phenomenon.
- To identify potential relationships between concepts and to identify researchable hypotheses.
- To learn how others have defined and measured key concepts.
- To identify data sources that other researches have used.
- To develop alternative research projects.
- To discover how a research project is related to the work of others.

To do literature review, it is desirable for a researcher to first outline his research problem and then do the concept mapping. While doing so, he may refer to several management indices like; Harvard Business Index, published by Harvard Business School, Social Science Index, Guide to Indian Periodical Literature, published by Indian Scientific Documentation Centre, various management abstracts, including abstracts on HR areas, etc. These indices, compiles all possible publication in several research areas. These apart, the researcher now can get access to various electronic journal repositories. Harvard Business School also publishes subject specific reports. Scanning all these, a researcher can successfully outline his requirements. However, it is recommended that the search can extend up to five years or so to trace all possible background information. If the research pertains to some fundamental theoretical issues, it may even extend to some more years to do justice to the research. Now-a-days due to internet access it is possible to get wide access to the research information globally.

Model Building in Management Research

In management research, it is important to build models to represent cause, effect and other relationships. Model basically refers to a dynamic framework or scheme to portray the key concepts, propositions, etc. of a theory. It is a representation of a process or a system and it shows the most important variables in the system in such a way that analysis of the same leads to insights into the system. However, it must be understood that a model is not an explanation; it is only the structure or functions of some aspect of a system or the system as a whole. It may be highly conceptual or theoretical (theory itself being a model), developed at the start of a research and then tested through the process of data gathering, analysis and reasoning. A model can also be the end result of a research (in cases where we may have a week conceptual framework at the beginning of a research). Model building is a sophisticated process. A researcher has to leverage his research findings to develop a model. Description, explication and simulation are the three major functions of modelling. Quite often computers and advanced statistical tools are used to develop the model.

There are various types of model used in management research:

- ***Verbal/written/descriptive/physical Models:*** These models are categorised under one group because of their commonality to explain the situation by scaling down to a manageable limit. Verbal/written/descriptive models explain a situation in words (e.g. behaviour of elements in a system), while physical models explain a situation by a physical replica duly scaling down a machine or a structure. Physical models are also known as iconic models.

- ***Explicative Models:*** These models extend the application of well-developed theories or improve our understanding of key concepts.

- ***Schematic Models:*** These models are shown by charts, graphics, maps of routings, network diagrams, etc.

- ***Mathematical Models:*** These models show functional relationships among different variables using mathematical symbols and equations. In management, most commonly used mathematical models are:

  - Optimisation Models, which help to analyse problems and suggest solution, and;

  - Heuristics Models, which are some established decision-making procedures to solve a problem.

HR Research

Human Resources being the ultimate source of competitive advantage for an organisations and have the strategic relevance, systematic HR research at corporate level has now become very significant. Even HR research is gaining importance for academic and professional interest. While methodological issues for HR research are not very different from other management research, yet it is important for a scholar to understand the basics, keeping in view the specific requirements of HR area. At corporate level, many HR decisions may be taken based on HR research outcome. Similarly, many models, theories, findings on HR research at macro level may be emulated by the organisations to base their decisions. Hence it is important to develop a separate knowledge depository for HR research. Here, however, our intention is to spell out only some general issues.

A recently concluded survey by HR.COM identifies 'Top Ten Areas of Interest in HR Research.' This survey was conducted at the international level. Here we are presenting the outcome of survey with their respective weights. HR.Com based on a global survey has compiled this. HR researchers can pick up their research ideas from the areas, which have their significance internationally.

HR's Top Ten Areas of Interest

1.	Performance Management	65%
2.	Leadership Development	63%
3.	Career and Succession Planning	59%
4.	Change Management	59%
5.	Talent Retention	55%
6.	Assessment and Measurement	52%
7.	Indicators and Metrics	48%
8.	Culture Assessment	45%
9.	Talent Management Systems	31%

Other Hot Topics on HR Research

1. **Compensation and Benefits**	
Health Care Cost Containment	38%
Executive Compensation	34%
Job Analysis, Evaluation and Grading	25%
Employee Benefits	23%
Benefits Outsourcing	17%
Retirement and Pensions	15%
2. **Employment Selection/Staffing**	
Pre-Employment & Employee Testing	28%
Job Boards, Online Media, Print-Media	20%
Background Investigations	18%
3. **HRIS**	
Workforce Analytics	20%
Employee Self Service	15%
Benefit Administration & Communication Tools	13%
4. **Organisational Planning and Development**	
Employee Surveys	35%
Mergers and Acquisitions	20%
5. **Training and Development**	
Assessment	38%
Mentoring	31%
e-Learning	24%
Diversity	24%
Distance Learning	18%
Learning Management Systems	15%
6. **Other**	
Research and Best Practices	38%
HR Management	30%
International and Global HR	14%
Labour Relations	14%

Concept Mapping in HR Research

Aligning people with the business strategy of an organisation is an important priority area for HR managers. To identify whether people are properly aligned or not, it is important to check whether people can visualise them with the vision and mission of the organisations. Many organisations develop their vision and mission statements and then direct people to relate them with the same to get a common direction. However, the best approach could be to develop a participative vision and mission statements, i.e., getting inputs from all cross-section of people working in the organisation. To do this, however, it is important to involve them in identifying their critical success factors (in doing their jobs successfully). Then identify common critical success factors, which may be most important inputs for developing a participative vision and mission statements for an organisation, which can help people to relate them with the business strategy. This is a very simplistic approach and tried by the author in number of organisations with success.

Critical Success Factor (CSF) analysis is a method developed at MIT's Sloan school by John Rockart to guide businesses in creating and measuring success. It is a top-down methodology that is especially suitable for designing systems. CSF is a reductionist method for going from an abstract vision to concrete requirements. Therefore, CSF is a key area where satisfactory performance is required for the organisation to achieve its goals. It is a means of identifying the tasks and requirements needed for success, a means to prioritise requirements.

Research on Employer Branding

Let us take another example like; employer branding. This is again another important emerging area for HR research. Employer branding is defined as 'the development and communication of an organisation's culture as an employer in the marketplace.' It affects the experience of being employed by a particular firm. The underlying idea is that all employees are discriminating consumers, to be engaged, won over and retained by employers. To ensure that employee attrition rate is within a manageable limit, organisations endeavour to go for branding to differentiate itself from the competition. Suppose one wish to do research on employer branding. As HR person it is first essential to understand the concept and then develop ideas for implementation of employer branding strategy. Some of the steps involved could be; to develop measurable and attainable business objectives, retain the services of a recruitment advertising agency, launch an information gathering process, create a branding strategy, execute the branding strategy and periodically monitor the progress of branding strategy.

Sampling for HR Research

A sample is a subset of a population from which data are collected and then used to estimate parameters of the total population. In other words, a sample is that part of a population which is actually observed. In normal scientific practice, while drawing a sample, we must ensure to avoid presenting a biased view of the population. If we want to draw statistical inference we must then assign known probabilities of selection to each sample. If the probabilities of different samples are all equal, we call this method simple random sampling. Random means the occurrence of things by chance alone in such a way the overall pattern of occurrences conforms to certain laws of mathematical probability.

For doing research on HR areas basic sampling ideas need to be clear to the researcher, so as to ensure that scientific norms are followed to make the sample observations representative for the whole population. For example to do an employee attitude survey for a very large organisation, employing more that 10,000 workmen, it may not be possible to follow the census method, i.e., covering all workmen. Moreover outcome of the survey may be very important to take some HR related decisions like; designing an incentive system or introducing a shift work system, etc. In such cases obviously sampling helps. Two to three hundred workmen may be drawn as sample, and observations on them may be hold good for the population (10,000 workmen).

In statistics, we call it random or probability sampling. However, in all HR research we may not be able to following random sampling approach. For some quick HR decisions or to study some possible implications of some HR decision, quite often we may do non-probability sampling. In this case selection of population elements is based on arbitrary quotas, volunteers, the judgment of the researcher or any other technique in which sample elements do not have a known probability of being selected. We also call it convenience sampling, snowball sampling, judgemental sampling or purposive sampling.

However, for more detailed discussions, it is recommended to refer the Book on `Research Methodology' by the same author.

Questionnaire and Survey

No HR research can achieve success without a survey and no survey can achieve success without a well-designed questionnaire. The design of a questionnaire depends on the nature of information that the researcher may wish to collect, which may be exploratory information (i.e. qualitative information) or quantitative information. Unfortunately, questionnaire design has no theoretical base. It is more of an art than a science.

Exploratory questionnaire: For collection of qualitative information, which need not require to be statistically evaluated, we may not require any formal questionnaire. For example, in interviewing the workers to find out how decisions pertaining to children education are made within the family, a formal questionnaire may restrict the discussion and prevent a full exploration of the views and processes. In such cases, open-ended questionnaire may be more suitable, rather than closed-ended structured questionnaire.

Formal standardised questionnaire: For testing, quantifying and statistical testing of hypotheses, researcher is required to make use of formal standardised questionnaire We have made available two such questionnaire samples in the book.

A questionnaire may be developed for individual interview of workmen or focus group interviews. Focus group interviews are a survey research instrument, which is used to obtain information from groups of people. The groups of individuals (e.g. non-performers in different sections) are invited to attend an informal discussion. Usually between 6 and 8 participants are involved and the discussion would last between 1 and 2 hours. Small groups tend to lose the mutual stimulation among participants, whilst large groups can be difficult to manage and may prevent some participants having the opportunity to get fully involved in the discussion.

The researcher raises issues for discussion, following a 'guide list of topics' rather than a structured questionnaire. The participants are encouraged to discuss the issues amongst themselves and with the researcher in an informal and relaxed environment. The researcher records comments made by the participants (usually utilising a tape or video recorder).

The participants within a focus group are selected in such a way that they exhibit a high degree of homogeneity with respect to background, behaviour or both. Group discussions are also useful as a cost-effective means of generating background information and hypotheses on a particular subject prior to the launch of a quantitative survey. In this respect group interviews can have advantages over personal interviews. To deal with non-performers, absenteeism, troublemakers, in an organisation focussed group research may be an excellent alternative. Some of the successful areas of focused group research can be listed as under:

Applications of Focus Groups

- New product development
- Positioning studies
- Usage studies
- Assessment of packaging
- Attitude and language studies
- Advertising/copy evaluations
- Promotion evaluations
- Idea generation
- Concept tests....

USING STATISTICAL TEST IN HR RESEARCH

For doing HR research, quite often we may require to choose the right statistical test. Selection of right statistical test depends on following factors:

- Nature of the data
- Sample characteristics
- Inferences to be made

A consideration of the nature of data includes: Number of variables not for entire study, but for the specific question at hand.

Type of Data

Data may be of following types:

- Numerical, continuous
- Dichotomous, categorical information
- Rank-order or ordinal

Sample Characteristics

A consideration of the sample characteristics includes:

- Number of groups
- Sample type
- Normal distribution (parametric) or not (non-parametric)
- Independent or dependent

Statistical Inferences for HR Decisions

A consideration of the inferences to be made includes:

- Data represent the population
- The group means are different
- There is a relationship between variables

Statistical Tests

Before choosing a statistical test, ask:

- How many variables?
- How many groups?
- Is the distribution of data normal?
- Are the samples (groups) independent?
- What is your hypothesis or research question?
- Is the data continuous, ordinal, or categorical?

Statistical analysis offers a systematic way of describing results and determining their reliability. Descriptive statistics are used to summarize the results using means, standard deviations, frequencies and other methods, which describe the central tendency and variability of the data. Significance tests state the probability that the results are due to chance. Statistical tests such as t-test, F-ratio, and chi-square ultimately lead to a p-value, which is used to make a statement about the statistical significance of the results.

COMPUTER-AIDED RESEARCH IN HR

For effective research and more accurate inference, data analysis and decision-making, we have many user-friendly time saving software. While some of these software are commonly used and now are being available widely in research institutions, others are not so user-friendly and are used in a very limited way for scientific research. Some of these commonly used software packages, which help in HR research, are as under:

SPSS

SPSS is the world's leading provider of predictive analytics software and solutions. The company's predictive analytics technology improves business processes by giving organisations consistent control over decisions made every day. By incorporating predictive analytics into their daily operations, organisations become Predictive Enterprises-able to direct and automate decisions to meet business goals and achieve measurable competitive advantage. Founded in 1968, SPSS is headquartered in Chicago, Illinois.

SPSS 13.0 provides better reporting capabilities through improvements to the presentation graphics system (added in SPSS 12.0). Most commonly used SPSS module for organisational research is Dimension. With Dimensions, a firm can centralise not only the creation and fielding of surveys in any mode and in any language, but also data analysis and reporting. This means one can manage complex, global, multilingual projects smoothly and efficiently.

More importantly, Dimensions is a platform on which one can create customised tools and branded applications, including those using innovative data collection methods such as virtual environments and text or instant messaging. By centralising survey data and streamlining or automating routine tasks and processes, Dimensions can conduct more sophisticated analyses.

Some of the benefits that an organisation can get using Dimensions may be as under:

- Streamline processes and eliminate costly "bottlenecks"
- Deliver results in easy-to-use formats quickly and automatically
- Develop unique, customized offerings more rapidly
- Optimise staff skills
- Leverage your IT infrastructure investments
- Deliver the high-quality results clients demand

WINKS

The WINKS is one of the most well known statistical package, which helps in analysing research data. WINKS have two versions, WINKS BASIC and WINKS Professional. Winks is designed for researchers who need to get statistical answers quickly. Plenty of examples are available in WINKS. Descriptive statistics include: mean, standard deviation, variance, median, minimum, maximum, standard error of the mean, percentile calculations, Tukey 5 number summary, confidence intervals, detailed Cp and Cpk calculations, and more. Descriptive graphics include a histogram with a normal curve fit, a box-and whiskers plot, cumulative normal and cumulative distribution graph, etc., are all available in WINKS. Graphs include: Histogram with bell curve fit, comparison charts including box-and-whiskers plot, mean chart, median chart, and standard error chart. Also available are a multiple group (XY) scatterplot, multiple correlation scatterplot, survival analysis plot, and more. First Impression charts give a wide range of graph display options including 3D, tape, area, pie and more. T-tests and Analysis of Variance (ANOVA) features include independent group t-tests and analysis of variance (up to 20 groups), paired t-tests and repeated measures analysis of variance, single sample analysis of variance and Dunnett's test. We can perform most of these analyses from raw data or from summary information.

Non-parametric analyses include Mann-Whitney, and Kruskal-Wallis analyses for independent groups. Wilcoxon's Signed Rank Test and Friedman's test is provided for paired or repeated measures analysis. Cochran's Q test is provided for dichotomous data analysis.

Frequency and Cross tabulation includes Goodness of fit test, Frequency distribution, McNemar's test, Chi-square, Fisher exact test (one and two-tailed), Yate's Chi-square, Phi and Cramer's V, Relative Risk, Odds Ratio and comparison of proportions.

Regression and Correlation features include simple linear and multiple regression, point-biserial correlation, correlation matrix, R-square and Adjusted R-square, Pearson's and Spearman's coefficient tests for significance, data plots and residual plots, point biserial correlation, and regression through the origin.

Survival Analysis includes actuarial and Kaplan-Meier life tables and comparison of survival curves. Simulations and Demonstrations include a coin flip simulation, a confidence interval simulation and a central limit theorem demonstration.

WINKS uses industry standard dBASE files. Easily import from Excel or from other programs such as MSAccess and 123. Also imports ASCII files from other programs, which makes getting your data into WINKS quick and easy.

Professional Winks provide some advanced features like two factor analysis of variance (balanced or unbalanced), paired and repeated measures analysis, three-factor ANOVA, and Analysis of Covariance. Analysis of Variance output includes a summary listing of the input data, ANOVA Table, multiple comparisons (Newman-Keuls, Tukey HSD, or Scheffé), graphical summary of multiple comparisons and interaction plots. ANCOVA (Analysis of Covariance) output includes significance tests and graphical output showing line comparisons.

STATISTICA 7

STATISTICA Enterprise-wide Data Analysis System (SEDAS). SEDAS is an integrated multi-user software system designed for general-purpose data analysis and business intelligence applications in research, marketing, finance, and other industries. SEDAS can optionally offer the statistical functionality available in any or all of the STATISTICA products. In addition, it features:

- Integration with data warehouses
- Intuitive query and filtering tools
- Easy-to use administration tools
- Automatic report distribution
- Alarm notification and much, much more...

AMOS

Amos implements the general approach to data analysis known as structural equation modelling, analysis of covariance structures, or causal modelling. This approach includes as special cases many well-known conventional techniques, including the general linear model and common factor analysis. Structural equation modelling is sometimes thought of as an obscure method that is difficult to learn and use. This is a complete mistake. Indeed, much of the importance of structural equation modelling lies in the case with which it allows non-statisticians to solve estimation and hypothesis testing problems that once would have required the services of a specialist.

In other words, structural equation modelling is a multivariate analysis technique that encompasses and extends standard methods, including regression, factor analysis, simultaneous equations, and analysis of variance.

Many researchers are now going beyond traditional techniques such as Exploratory Factor Analysis and regression to explore complex relationships, adding more terms in their models. Amos software makes structural equation modelling easy.

Amos comes with two interfaces—Amos Graphics and Amos Basic:

With Amos Graphics, the path diagram is the model. All modelling can be performed within the diagrams. No programming is needed. Amos's intuitive, drag-and-drop drawing tools provide for rapid model specification in presentation-quality path diagrams.

Amos Basic provides a contemporary, object-oriented application programming interface to structural equation modelling. Power users will enjoy coding specialized macros and applications in Visual Basic or C++.

SYSTAT

SYSTAT® is a high value, integrated desktop statistics and graphics software package for engineers, and statisticians that provides a vast selection of reliable statistics and high quality, scientific and technical graphing options, enabling users to analyse their data, make meaningful discoveries, and present their results more efficiently than most other statistics or graphics tool.

Systat is a comprehensive statistics and graphics package. We can use it to manipulate data, display graphic summaries, calculate numeric summaries, and test the validity of hypotheses about the data. Though intended for professional use, it is reasonably easy to learn.

LISREL

Lisrel is statistical software for estimating the coefficients in a set of structural equations. Prelis is a pre-processor for Lisrel. Prelis does a fair amount of data screening before processing (including tests of univariate and multivariate normality) it with Lisrel. It is also used to compute a specified matrix for reading into a Lisrel session. A fairly high level of statistical sophistication is required to use Lisrel/Prelis effectively.

Some of the capabilities of Lisrel include:

- Measurement models and confirmatory factor analysis
- Causal models for directly observed variables
- Structural equation models for latent variables
- Analysis of ordinal and other non-normal variables
- Multi-sample analysis
- Linear and non-linear constraints
- Fit measures
- Path diagrams
- Bootstrap estimates with Prelis
- Multivariate multinomial goodness regressions with Prelis

Even though it is very reliable, this software is not at all user friendly and that is why excepting in scientific research, its use is very limited.

All these software can facilitate HR research duly interpreting data. However, it is important to have functional knowledge and a proper research design to make effective use of this software.

Presenting HR Reports

There is no prescribed right style for a research report, but there are some basic principles for writing a research report. Writing is the last step in the research report preparation process. Before writing the results it must be fully understood and thoughts must be applied to elicit as to what would be the content of a research report. It involves basically three steps, i.e., understanding, organising and writing. The general guidelines that should be followed for any report or research paper are as follows:

Consider the audience: The report should not be too technical and laden with jargons. Quite often for reporting the results of statistical analysis, we forget the grasp of the target audience. Target audience may not understand complicated statistical concepts. Hence, it is important to translate such terms into their perceived level like; standard deviation, significance level, confidence interval etc. This may not be an easy task. Similarly qualitative research also presents difficulties. Target audience may not understand the behavioural sciences vocabulary, like; cognitive dissonance, perception, self-actualisation, situational leader, competency gap, etc. This also may develop misunderstandings. Thus the researcher should always be cautious for reporting the quantitative and qualitative results of his research findings as target audience may be in hiatus.

Be concise, but precise: A research report should be complete, i.e., it stands by itself and no additional clarification should be required. However, some researchers may elude the preciseness, as they may like to convey everything in the report, which they might have collected in the process of doing the research. The report must be concise and must focus on the critical elements and exclude unimportant issues. What is important for a researcher is to realise that no body is interested to measure the elegance or effort involved in the research methodology but only the critical elements that deduce from the research.

Understand the results and drawing conclusions: Most important part of a management research is the interpretive conclusions. Thus the researcher must understand the results and be able to interpret these. Simply reiterating facts is not enough. The report must focus on the implications of the findings. This is ensured by constant questioning on findings, like; 'so what?' Answer to 'so what' will illustrate the findings more correctly.

The following outline is the suggested format for writing the research report:

- Title page
- Summary of findings
- Table of contents
- List of tables
- List of figures

Introduction

- Background to the research problem
- Objectives
- Hypotheses

Methodology-Data Collection

- Sample and sampling method
- Statistical or qualitative methods used for data analysis
- Sample description

Findings

- Results, interpretation and conclusions.

A Sample HR Research Report

Inter-organisational Career Movement – A Study on Young Executives of Commercial Banks in India

Introduction

Effective human performance at all levels in an organisation is instrumental for its growth. Self development and career development through work is now being viewed more important, more particularly, for the new generation of workers. There always exist gross incongruence between individual's own concept of career progression and organisation's own career progression path, barring few those who always integrate individual's goal with the organisational goal by creating an enabling organisation.

Human Resource Planning encompasses Career Planning, Career Development and Succession Planning. Even though in this era of rapid technological changes, organisations are besieged with the problem of manpower redundancy, organisations are equally concerned with the problem of retention of manpower. While one way to increase retention is by extrinsic motivational reinforcers, the other way obviously is to address to the need of employees, which centres around individual Career Planning and Career Development. From organisation's point of view also, these initiatives reinforce their strategic plans and make their goals and objectives achievable. An organisation without career planning and career development initiatives is likely to encounter highest rate of attrition, causing much harm to their plans and programmes. Similarly without succession planning, manning of vacancies, particularly at higher levels, become difficult. There are examples of many organisations, who had to suffer for not being able to find right successors for their key positions. With the increased scope for job mobility and corporate race for global headhunting of good performers, it is now a well-established fact that normal employment span for key performers remains awfully short. At times it is even shorter than three years. This again strengthens the need for effective Career Planning, Career Development and Succession Planning.

The terms Career Planning and Career Development are used interchangeably in most of the organisations. It is also correct that but for their shuttle difference in definitional context, their process remains the same.

Economic slowdown or impelling needs for organisational restructuring now require organisations to go for manpower redundancy every now and then. This process, inter alia, has affected the perceived individual career plans of professionally qualified employees, particularly those who are in their mid thirties. The problem is more acute for organisations, as they are now unable to retain young talent and map their competency for strategic HRM (SHRM).

In simplistic terms, HR strategy is the pattern of decisions concerning policies and practices associated with the HR System. SHRM is a competency-based approach for management of HR. It develops HR for sustainable competitive advantage. However, there exist general disagreement about the role of HR strategy or SHRM, per se, among the researchers. Behavioural role theory pioneered by Katz and Khan (1978) and Jackson and Schuler (1995) considers employee behaviour as key to strategy implementation. Similarly, Resource-based theory of Barney (1991) and Prahalad and Halem (1990) considers HR has sustainable competitive advantage for the organisation, for its obvious unique 'inimitable and non-substitutable' character. Human capital theory (Becker, 1964; Flamholtz, 1981), Transaction cost theory (Williamson, 1981), Agency theory (Eisenhardt, 1989) also justifies alignment of HR with organisation-wide strategy. All these theories are grouped under Rational Choice Theories of HR.

On the contrary, Institutional (Meyer & Rowen, 1977; Powell & DiMaggio, 1991) and Dependency (Pfeffer & Salancik, 1977) theories on HR strategy, however, focus on constituency based interest. This is because strategic approach to HR is not empirically proved as contributor to organisational performance. Institutional theory argues strategic approach to HR should emanate from legitimacy and acceptance from stakeholders. Dependency theory argues, this will unduly enhance the level of influence over the organisations (from HR) and thereby will defeat the purpose. Prima facie, environmental, organisational, institutional and technological factors are potential influencers in strategy. Relative importance of each such factor will depend on organisational characteristics.

Contd....

Whatever may be the general disagreement, corporate practices focus on HR strategy factors like; Recruitment and Selection, Career Development, Performance Appraisal, Training and Development, Compensation Designing and Human Resource Planning. Such strategy formulation, however, is not possible, or it becomes meaningless, per se, unless it is aligned with organisation-wide strategies.

The Study

This study intends to investigate into typical attitudinal responses of randomly selected executive level (Scale-1 and Scale-2) bank employees falling below the age-group of 35 years, i.e., those who are in exploratory and establishment stages of their career cycle to accept inter-organisational career movement opportunities.

Banking organisations, per se, are now facing lot of challenges, particularly after economic reforms programme of the Government of India and different policy changes favouring liberal financial markets. For increasing the service-mix and for introduction of technology, this sector is also experiencing occupational shift, job restructuring, which necessitates continuous renewal and updating of knowledge and skill of the employees to enable them to keep pace with the changing requirements. The increased spate of competition (for entry of private banking organisations), in one way influencing commercial banks to achieve competitive efficiency by reformulating their strategies, while on the other increased the scope of job mobility for existing employees. For the present, such job mobility is restricted to commercial bank executives, who in large number, even after reaching maintenance or mid-career stage, leaving their jobs to join private banks, foreign banks or financial services companies. However, at this pace, it is expected that commercial banks will be their potential source of manpower (for all categories) in future, creating a problem of employee retention at commercial banks. Further for achieving operational efficiency by cost minimisation, commercial banks recently reduced their manpower by 30% offering VRS. Some of the banks have to reject VRS applications, fearing further loss of manpower of certain categories.

Methodology

As indicated earlier, while introducing the study, it is intended to investigate into the attitudinal responses of randomly selected executive level bank employees, who are below the age-group of 35 years, i.e., those who are in exploratory and establishment stages of their career, regarding their perceived factors of willingness to accept inter-organisational career movement opportunities.

Altogether employees numbering 155 (N = 155) have been selected at random from 65 branches, who are falling within age bracket of 35 years or less and working in executive categories. All such sample employees were then interviewed in person with a structured questionnaire to identify factors influencing their willingness to accept inter-organisational career movement.

Numerous studies carried out earlier (Hill and Miller, 1981; Moore, Miller and Fossum, 1974; Vardi, 1980) indicated that when employees move into the later career stages they lower their expectations for promotion and career advancement. While on the other hand employees who are in their exploratory career stage (initial career stage) or establishment stage are more interested for inter-organisational career movement both for exploring different types of jobs and evaluating personal competence in different skills areas (Solcum and Cron, 1985) and for perceiving promotions and career development (which includes also lateral movement) as indicators of success.

Keeping in view the above, following attitudinal factors were measured using 5-point Likert type scale:

(i) **High salary and benefits as criterion to prefer inter-organisational career movement.**

Money Motivation theory of W.F. Whyte (1955) suggests that people are motivated primarily by the desire to make money. He himself, however, contended that monetary incentives should not be considered in isolation from other non-monetary incentives. Herzberg (1968) again contended monetary incentives as Hygiene factor, satisfaction of which may not motivate but dissatisfaction may have negative motivational impact. Emoluments vis-à-vis employees motivation have not been studied in India. However, number of motivational studies carried out in India identified emoluments, inter alia, as an important factor of employee motivation. Studies by Ganguli (1964), Lahiri and Srivastava (1967), Sawalapurkar (1968),

Contd....

Padaki and Polke (1970), Rao (1970), Narian (1971), Bhattacharyya (1972), Singhal and Upadhayaya (1975), Agarwal (1976), Sharma (1987; 1982) have identified emoluments also as an important factor of employee motivation in India. Emolument difference, therefore, can be a perceived factor of inter-organisational career movement. However, it is important to mention that taxable income, per se, can't be an important factor for inter-organisational career movement for bank employees. Most of the private banks and financial services organisations ensure substantial savings to their employees by making available the option open to employees to accept a sizable portion of their emoluments in cash, showing it as reimbursement of miscellaneous expenses. In a separate study by the author this was amply evident for those bank employees who are in their mid-career stage and in large numbers opting for voluntary retirement to have employment in private commercial banks. The position also does not vary widely for relatively young employees, who are in the age group of 35 years or less, i.e., those who are in exploratory or establishment stage of career, as they perceive this factor as instrumental to move from one career to another.

(ii) **Increased scope for career advancement as criterion for inter-organisational career movement.**

Increased scope of career advancement or promotional opportunities, as an important factor for taking inter-organisational career movement decisions by bank employees, have been extensively studied by the author himself while doing his doctoral thesis. Many Empirical studies carried out in India and abroad can also be evidently related to author's observation. However, here also a cursory view of the relevant literatures would be taken to appreciate how increased promotional opportunities can influence the inter-organisational career movement.

Screening available literatures, it is evident that promotion ensures; upward advancement, enhanced responsibilities, status and prestige, better pay and wages, and finally better working environment, functional authority, scope for application of specialised knowledge, skill(s) and work experience. Thus prima facie, increased promotional opportunities by itself should have been the single dominant factor to influence the inter-organisational career movement decision. But, promotions, in practice, may not satisfy all the elements mentioned above. While for some organisations it may really ensure increased status and prestige but not necessarily better pay and wages, better working environment, functional autonomy, etc.

Screening the theories on motivation, it is evident Vroom's Expectancy theory (1964), Porter-Lawler's Future-oriented Expectancy theory (1968), White's Competence Motive theory (1959), Schachter's Affiliation Motivation theory (1959), Argyris's Maturity Immaturity theory (1957), McClelland's Achievement Need theory (1962), Herzberg's Two-Factor theory (1968), Mayo's Series of experiments (1945) and Likert and Katz's Michigan Studies (1948), are in fact suggest, inter alia, promotion as an important identified factor for employees motivation. Indian studies, indicated earlier, equally equivocal on promotional needs. Neelamegham and Vaid's study (1986) identified promotion as highest need deficient factor for employees' motivation.

Characteristically Indian workers are attitudinally different from Japanese workers, as a typical Japanese worker perceives his job as a stage in his career. He prefers to defer immediate gain, keeping future prospects/pay-off in mind. This is quite unlikely for workers in India and other countries. This is particularly evident in India, as many PSU executives, despite attaining mid-career stage, do not hesitate shift to other organisations with better offer, forgetting their loyalty and commitment to the organisation. A very recently released study of Hudson Institute (2000), however, rates Japan (26th) lower than many other countries, in the world, including India (10th) in terms of employee loyalty. However basis of measurement is yet to be made available for its validation.

(iii) **Employee Friendly HR Policies reduces inter-organisational career movement**

Unhealthy personnel practices is understood from taking cursory view to employees' grievance pattern, their chosen grievance redressal option, etc. For bank employees high degree of dependence on unions, tribunal and other legal machinery for redressal of their grievances indicate that in general they have

Contd....

lost their confidence in the departmental machinery available for amicable settlement of their service-related disputes. Similarly, bank employees' perceived nature of grievances further indicate that improper job distribution, bias of the management, unhealthy work environment, flow of command from different superiors, non-recognition of commendable performance of the employees by the management, etc., are more responsible (reflecting unhealthy personnel practices) than salary, bonus, leave and hours of work, transfer, promotional matters and job security.

(iv) Functional Independence

Functional independence being intrinsically satisfies employees, it is considered as an important factor of job satisfaction vis-à-vis employees' retention. Bank employees enjoy functional independence due to the fact that the contents of their jobs in most of the cases are well defined and routine and repetitive in nature. Armed with this observation, it is, therefore wrong to assume that functional independence can, per se, influence the decision of Bank employees to accept inter-organisational career movement.

(v) Scope for Skill Enhancement

New forms of skill and responsibility alongwith technological change have also been studied extensively in Banking Operations among others. A global study of Andersen and Knowledge Systems and Research (2001) ranks technical communication, job-experience, net-working/relationship building experience, management skills, industry expertise and sales and marketing skills in order of priority in changing job market. The study also identifies banking and financial services as most lay-off prone industry, among others. Banking industry are likely to be besieged with general skill obsolescence and consequent problem of manpower redundancy. Such perceived threat of employees can be validated from their overwhelming response to opt for recent VRS (30%). While, transfer, relocation, increased accountability, among others can be their other perceived reasons for opting for VRS, but largely they have opted for VRS fearing skill redundancy. Banking industry in India never had taken any initiative for multi-skilling and competency mapping beyond induction training excepting skill training to enhance computer literacy. This approach limited their focus to map individual competencies during recruitment only and non-integration of such competencies with changing organisational competencies. Scope for skill enhancement, therefore, per se, can be an important perceived factor for bank employees to opt for inter-organisational career movement.

For selecting sample employees from 65 branches, we have considered only those which are public sector banks. Field for the study was in and around Kolkata of West Bengal. Sample size (N=155) is unusually low widely dispersed across 65 branches obviously for our selected age-group, i.e., less than 35 years in executive category. This again is obviously for reasons that recruitment in public sector banks are almost negligible for last one decade. The study was carried out during January, 1999 to February 2001, as a part of longitudinal analysis of author's own Ph.D. work in 1993.

I such randomly selected executive employees from sample 65 branches, were personally interviewed with the structured questionnaire to understand their perceived factors to accept inter-organisational career movement.

Results

Basic details of the sample employees have been presented in Table-1. This table shows, number of sample employees are more in age bracket of 25-30 year, followed by 30-35 year and 'less than 25 year'. Results of statistical test on basic biographical details of sample employees indicate that sample employees are not widely dispersed obviously because of their concentration in a specific age group, i.e., 20-35 years. Minimum 20 year was considered as some of the sample employees were found in this age group though small in numbers. Willingness of sample employees to accept inter-organisational career opportunities when measured in percentages, 90% of them surprisingly show interest while 2% would like to give more thought before they take such decision. Even these 2% can not be categorised under unwilling group, they are for the present undecided. Such trend was, however, not measured with the incidence of their biographical characteristics.

Contd....

Table 1: Basic Details of Sample Employees

Age-Group	20-25 year	25-30 years	30-35 years	Mean	Standard Deviation	S.E. of Sample Mean
	35 (23)	75 (48)	45 (29)	27	4.03	0.32
Service Experience	Below 5 year16(10)	5-10 year 31 (20)	10-15 year 105 (70)	10.5	3.87	0.31
Salary and benefits (in ₹ 000)	6 – 8 14 (9)	8 – 10 111 (72)	10 – 12 30 (19)	9.2	1.04	0.08
Qualifications	Graduates 72 (46)	Post Graduates 55 (36)	Professionally Qualified 28 (18)	-	-	-
Hierarchical Level	Scale-I 109 (70)	Scale-II 46 (30)	-	-	-	-

Source: Field Survey

Note:

i. *Sixty*-five branches selected from 15 nationalised/PSU banks, i.e., State Bank of India, United Commercial Bank, United Bank of India, Allahabad Bank, Bank of India, Bank of Baroda, Union Bank of India, Central bank of India, Indian Bank, Canara Bank, Punjab National Bank, Bank of Maharashtra, Dena Bank, Indian Overseas Bank and Syndicate Bank.

ii. *Figures* in parenthesis indicate percentages.

iii. *Scale-I* is the minimum executive level, entry to which is restricted through probationary officers' Examination.

iv. *Scale-II* is a promoted post from Scale-I. Some direct recruitment to Scale-II is, however, made for specialist cadre. We, however, have no such executive as direct recruitee to Scale-II in sample.

Variation in the response pattern when measured with respect to bio-graphical characteristics, however shows, sample employees with age group of 25-30 years, with service experience of 10-15 years, with education level of graduation and finally with salary and benefits level of ₹ 8000-10000, per month are more inclined to accept such career movement opportunities than the other. Responses of sample employees have been further analysed based on their perceived priority in ranking the factors. Such responses have been analysed using simple factor score method, commonly used for attitudinal measurement. Each sample employee ranked all the 5 factors including those 3 (2%) who are for the present undecided but if they decide they will perceive their factors of choice. Therefore, 155 sample employees ranked such factors in five different ways based on their own perception. Results indicate employees show general concordance on 'higher salary and benefits factor' as their perceived reasons to accept inter-organisational career movement. Scope for skill enhancement and training, employee friendly HR Policies, increased scope for career advancement and functional independence are their perceived order of ranking of other factors to accept inter-organisational career movement.

Table 2: Willingness to accept Inter-organisational Career Movement

Perceived Factors	Total Score (in percentage)	Rank
Higher Salary and benefits.	28	1
Increased scope for career advancement	19	4
Employee friendly HR Policies	23	3
Functional independence	16	5
Scope for Skill enhancement	24	2

Source: Field Survey

Note:

(i) Simple factor score was determined by analysing the perceived ranking order of all the five factors by sample employees. For example, factor-1, i.e., 'higher salary and benefits' as a perceived factor for inter-organisational career movement

Contd....

opportunities was ranked by each sample employee in 5 different ways. Number of sample employees were multiplied by each order of ranking for each factor and then aggregated to understand the factor score. On 5-point scale, number of sample employees who had given first priority to higher salary and benefits was multiplied by 5. Similarly number of samples who gave second priority was multiplied by 4 and so on. Each priority level results then added to compute the aggregate score value. For all these 5 factor we have computed the score value and presented in percentage terms.

In Table-2, we have presented the results. Finally, the Kendall coefficient of concordance (W) have been worked out based on the responses of the sample employees. This measure helped us to understand the extent of association among ranking of sample employees (K sets of judges) of different, perceived factors ('N' sets of objects). 155 sample employees represent 'K' set of judges, who rank 'N' sets of objects or entities, i.e., perceived factors. The computed 'W' value in such tests vary between 0 to 1 and it can not be negative. A strong or weak association is understood in terms of 'W' value, significance of which is further measured using Chi-square (c2) test, in case 'N' is larger than 7. However, in our case 'N' being 5, we have not tested the significance of 'W' using c2. Computed 'W' value obtained from the results is. 06, which indicates relatively weak association or concordance in sample employees while they rank the identified factors for inter-organisational career movement. Such weak association, however, does not constraint our simple factor store presented in Table-2. Reasons for weak association may be for our sample characteristics. In Table-3 we have presented the results.

Table 3: Ranking of Factors by Sample Employees for Computing Kendall's Coefficient of Concordance (W)

Factors (N) / Sample Employee (k)	Salary and benefits (1)	Scope for Skill enhancement and Training (2)	HR Policies (3)	Scope for Career Advancement (4)	Functional Independence	∴N=5
1	1	3	2	4	5	
2	2	1	3	4	5	
3	2	3	1	5	4	
4	1	3	2	4	5	
5	1	2	3	4	5	
6	1	2	4	4	3	
:	:	:	:	:	:	
:	:	:	:	:	:	
155			:		:	
Sum of Ranks (R_j)	314	330	353	403	456	ΣR_j
$(R_j - \bar{R}_j)^2$	3249	1681	324	1042	7225	∴s=13503

Note:

(I) $\bar{R}_j = \frac{\Sigma R_j}{N} = \frac{1856}{5} = 371$

(i) S = 13503

(ii) Formula used':

$$W = \frac{S}{\frac{1}{12}K^2(N^3 - N)}$$

Contd....

$$=\frac{13503}{\frac{1}{12}155^2(125-5)}$$

$$=\frac{13503}{240250}=.06$$

Discussion

Preference for increased salary and benefits, therefore, would be the single factor for non-executive employees of public sector commercial banks to opt for inter-organisational career movement. This, therefore, requires public sector commercial banks to relook into their compensation strategy to retain young talents, who can be a potential banker in years to come. Interestingly, such preference is more for the 25-30 years age group of employees, who have gained couple of years of experience in baking industry. Most of the private banks and non-banking finance companies (including mutual funds and retail financing companies) prefer this age-group of people with couple of years of experience in executive categories to meet their 'ready-to-use' manpower requirement . Banking knowledge and skill being earned more through practice (either at managerial or operational level), these organisations get the benefit of such experience by recruiting such people, rather than recruiting a college/university or even a B-school fresher.

On way to check such inter-organisational career movement can be designing of a flexible compensation plan by reducing NWLC component and also by outsourcing personnel services. NWLC in India is as high as 40% of the paid wage cost. It is the wage load for deferred benefits. Employees in their exploratory and establishment age-groups do not visualise long time career goal and prefer job movement merely on increased pay. Most of the IT companies, adopted this strategy to attract new talent. Even pharmaceutical, FMCG and IT-enabled industries are now following this strategy. One has to appreciate that the new generation of knowledge workers are immuned from the lure of employment security. They do not get excited for institutional employment rather they prefer to earn quick bucks in short or contractual employment span. This perceptual shift has been further accentuated for increased scope of job mobility.

Similarly public sector commercial banks also emphasise on training and development. During interview, it was observed that none of the sample employees had any opportunity for training beyond what they had during induction, accepting limited training on computer operation.

The third important aspect which public sector commercial banks need to look into is re-designing their HR Policies in order to make it more employee friendly. Transfer with relocation, punishment even for judgmental error, inefficient grievance handling are some of their complaints against HR systems, which even persuade them, though in lower magnitude, to opt for career movement.

Increased scope for career advancement as a perceived factor, received lower priority, obviously for reasons that public sector commercial banks within their defined promotion policy can hardly give superseding opportunity for promotion on merit count. One has to wait for his turn to become eligible for selection test and interview for promotion. Another counter effect of career advancement plan of public sector commercial banks is that usually any promotion succeeds transfer even with relocation. Sample employees therefore give less priority to this factor for their continuance with employment. Functional independence, per se, is also not a major determinant for accepting inter-organisational career movement. This is primarily for the nature of the banking jobs, mentioned earlier.

Therefore, executive employees of public sector commercial banks who are in their exploratory and establishment age-groups do not perceive the existing scope for career advancement in public sector commercial banks as important motivator to remain in employment. Their perceived priority to 'salary and benefits' factor, call for redesigning the compensation strategy. Deviation from the structured compensation plan is only possible by increasing the paid wage cost with proportionate reduction in NWLC or deferred salary and benefits for this category of employees.

Contd....

Limitations of the Study

The study, however, suffers from following limitations :

(i) It is limited to a small field, i.e., in and around Kolkata.

(ii) Sample size is low, though well representative within the field limitation.

(iii) Testing measures limited to uni-dimensional perceptual analysis, rather than studying the inter-correlation of identified variables or analysing the responses with a better statistical tool like ANOVA or Factor Analysis.

(iv) We have no knowledge about the previous use of Kendall's Co-efficient of Concordance in similar cases, excepting in author's own Ph.D. work in 1993, which was vetted by an onymous reviewer of Belgium.

(v) Questionnaire design was made close-ended, limiting the respondents, choice to answer in their own way.

(vi) Sample employees are likely to be influenced in their response pattern for policy of public sector commercial banks on VRS.

Future Research Directions

Despite the limitations listed above, the study provides future research direction on identifying perceived factors for employees' motivation, particularly those who are in their exploratory and establishment age-group. For banking industry, retaining the young talent is very important particularly during post-VRS days. The study sets the trend for a longitudinal national level research for inputs for effective manpower planning in public sector commercial banks.

Reference Notes:

(i) Exploratory age-group

(ii) Establishment age-group

(iii) NWLC

REFERENCES

1. Bhattacharyya, D.K. (1988), Impact of Technology on Human Resource Management; Personnel Today, January-March.
2. Bhattacharyya, D.K. (1993), Promotion from Within – A Positive Motivational Reinforcer for White Collar Employeers, A Study on Commercial Banking Organisations in India, Ph.D. Thesis, University of Calcutta.
3. Bhattacharyya, D.K., (1994),Employees Leasing and Labour Market Flexibility – An Empirical Study of its Problems in Selected Manufacturing Units; Indian Journal of Labour Economics, Vol. 37, No.4, , 549-555.
4. Bhattacharyya, D.K., (1995) Employees Empowerment – A Study of Selected Banking Organisation in India, in HRD Repositioning; National HRD Network, Conference Volume, pp. 33-48
5. Bhattacharyya, D.K.,(1995), Corporate Body Builder – The Emerging Role of HRD Professionals - A Prescriptive Model for Success; Indian Journal for Training and Development, New Delhi, April-June.
6. Bhattacharyya, D.K.,(1995), Manpower Obsolescence – A study in Indian Ordnance Factories, International Congress on Economic Transition with Human Face; Indian Industrial Relations Association, New Delhi, September 3-6..
7. Bhattacharyya, D.K. (1995), Career Planning & Development; IIMS, Calcutta.

Contd....

8. Bhattacharyya, D.K. (2000) Competency Mapping and Manpower Redundancy – A Macro Level Study of Indian organisations; Management and Accounting Research, October-December, Volume 4, Issue-2, PP. 97-105.

9. Ball, Kirstie, (2000), Interface Value; People Management, January 6, pp 40-42

10. Bhattacharyya, D.K.,(2001), Impact of Labour Earnings on Productivity; Management and Change, New Delhi, January-July.

11. Bhattacharyya, D.K., (2001), Managing Manpower Redundancy – A Strategic Human Resource Manager Approach for rightsizing employees, In: Contemporary Trends on Human Resource Management; SAS Consultants, Calcutta, PP. 5 -1 3.

12. Carl, C. Hoffmann, Kathleen, P., Hoffmann and Emily, D., Eason (1992), Complexities of the "Simple" Report Request; HR Magazine, November issues, PP. 49-57.

13. Carnegie Mellon University, Software Engineering Institute (1995), The capabiiity Maturity Model; Addison Wesley Longman, Inc.,

14. Dreyfuss, J., (1988), Catching the Computer Wave; Fortune, Sept. 26, pp. 77-82.

15. Drucker, P.F., (1989), The New Realities; Harper & Row., New York, p. 175.

16. Eric, G. Flamholtz (1974), Human Resource Accounting: Dicken Son Publications Co., Inc., California

17. Ellen, Enst, Kossek, Willard Young, Debra C., Gash, and Victor, Nichol, (1994), Waiting for Innovation in the Human Resource Department – Godot Implements a Human Resource Information System; Human Resource Management, Vol. 33, No.1 pp. 135-159.

18. Fombrum, C., Noel, M.T., and Marry, A.D.(1984) – Strategic Human Resource Management; John Willey, New York.

19. Falicia Nathan (1987), Analysing Employers' Costs for Wages, Salaries and Benefits; Monthly Labour Review, October, PP. 3 - 10.

20. Hal, Glatzer (1995), HR Systems get reengineering; HR Magazine, July issue, PP. 44-47.

21. John Edwards, Chris Leck, Ray Loveridge, Roger Lumley, John Morgan and Mick Silver (1983), Manpower Planning; John Wiley & Sons, New York.

22. John, Bramham (1994), Human Resource Planning; University Press (India) Limited, Hyderabad.

23. Martin, Godfrey (1997, edited), Skill Development for International Competitiveness; Edward Elgar Publishing Company, Cheltenham, U.K.

24. Michael, J., Kavanagh, Hal, G.. and Scott, I, Tannenbaum (1990), Human Resource Information Systems; Development and Application, PWS-Kent Publishing Company, Boston, Massachusetts.

25. Paul, Miller (1992), Integrating Strategy and Human Resource Management in Brian Towers edited. The Handbook of Human Resource Management, Blackwell Publishers, Cambridge.

26. Robert, E., Sibson (1992), Strategic Planning for Human Resources Management, American Management Association, New York.

27. Steven, A., Larson (1993), Selecting a new payroll/HRIS, Management Accountant, October issue, PP. 28-31.

28. Walker A.J., (1980), A Brief History of the Computer in Personnel; Personnel Journal Vol. 16, pp. 33-36.

29. William P. Antony, et al., (1991), Strategic Human Resource Management, Dryden Press.

30. William, E., Berry (1994), The Human Resource Information System, Management Accountant, January Issue, PP. 56-57

SUMMARY

Like any other management research, HR research also follows basic process of social science research. From macro level academic pursuit, HR research has now become a necessity in organisations for both programmed (routine) and non-programmed (strategic) HR related decisions. It also facilitates organisation to frame strategies based on inferences drawn from HR research. For doing effective HR research, it is necessary to make use of appropriate statistical tools. Making use of computer software, now a day such statistical analysis can be done quickly at high level of precision.

KEYWORDS

HR Research	Computer aided HR research
Concept mapping for HR research	Model Building in management research

REVIEW QUESTIONS

1. Define management research and explain its different approaches.
2. With examples develop a concept map for HR research issues.
3. Explain the importance of literature review in HR research.
4. What is model building in HR research? Develop an optimisation model in any of the HR areas.
5. Draw a research plan on performance management system in an organisation.
6. Design a questionnaire for doing a survey research on employees' attitude in an organisation.
7. Write short notes on:
   (a) Employer Branding
   (b) Critical Success Factor
   (c) Exploratory Questionnaire
   (d) Focus Group Research
   (e) SPSS
   (f) AMOS

CASE STUDY

CIZIKO – TESTING TIME FOR MARKET INTELLIGENCE CONTROL

Enforcing control through direct supervision was all along considered as the strategic approach to achieve the business goals for Delhi based family owned construction chemical organisation, Ciziko. Ciziko is a known brand for North Indian market, where real estate business has witnessed the unprecedented pace of growth over the decades. Professional real estate companies always prefer Ciziko for its quality and lifelong guarantee. Ciziko's products range from roof treatment chemicals, anti-termite and anti-insect chemicals, quick fix chemicals for cement mix to earthquake resistant chemicals. Ciziko's nature of business demands strict quality control in production and continuous building of customers' confidence through direct visit to sites and guidance to construction people through a 24 x 7 tool free help line. Sales people are essentially chemical engineers from country's premier engineering colleges, who after recruitment undergo compulsory on-site induction and training for three months. During this phase, Ciziko requests its prestigious customers to allow the new recruits to learn on-the-job application and usages of their chemicals. Each trainee also requires performing masonry jobs and during the evening as helper to the masons. This process helps in not only understanding the process of use of the chemicals, but also develops the confidence of the sales people to interact well with the customers in future. Moreover, Ciziko has become the preferred choice among the masons, as they feel, allowing the engineers to work with them during induction, tantamounts to recognition of their importance and showing respect to their profession.

Ciziko enforces control on their sales force with a two-tier approach. In the first tier, Ciziko makes sure that every individual sales people are achieving their sales target and in the second tier, Ciziko ensures that every sales person delivers to the satisfaction level of the customers. Buying Ciziko should inculcate a sense of pride to every customer. No customer should buy Ciziko with suspicion. It is more like buying an insurance policy, i.e., customer solicits and do not buy for sales people's manipulative buying pressure. 'Buy it because you need it' – this marketing strategy of Ciziko is often viewed critically by the marketing people, as it often stand against achieving their sales target. Ciziko, however, is very particular about it, as the company's value systems endorse this philosophy. Ciziko believes that customers will gradually feel the compelling pressure to buy Ciziko's products, when they realise its utility value and using Ciziko's product ultimately becomes one of the USPs of the Real Estate business. Being proprietary items, Ciziko's profit margin is considerably higher as customers buy Ciziko's products considering it more as an investment than expenses.

After closing of every sales deal, Ciziko's outsourced Red Force screens the sales process to understand the degree of violation of company norms, if any. Degree of violation is quantified by in-built sales systems, and individual sales people are immediately tracked and informed. With more than 0.5% cases of violation, sales people looses their incentives and sales commissions, and when it exceeds 1%, they are dropped from the market and sent for retraining. With successive failure, sales people even risk their jobs. Ciziko helps their sales people to understand on their own, where they stand vis-à-vis Ciziko's value systems on marketing. Such self tracking control system gradually makes sales people conscious about the self control.

Initial market success in Northern India, prompted Ciziko to consolidate their market position at all India level with ambitious expansion programme. Ciziko's philosophy at this time is put into real test. With sales people scattered in every nook and corner of the country, Ciziko now considers this task difficult as Red Force's market intelligence is not sustainable to local market conditions in Southern, Western and Eastern part of the country. Customer care Centre of Ciziko, based at New Delhi failed to track the market pulse, and ultimately Ciziko lost its market reputation like any other construction chemical companies.

Question

You are required to help Ciziko to develop foolproof control systems. Suggest your line of action.

UNIT 19

Human Resource Costs

Learning Objectives

After completion of this unit, the students will be aware of the following topics:

- *Introduction*
- *Developing an HR Costs Checklist*

AVIVA CUTS HR COSTS WITH SELF-SERVICE HR CONTROL SYSTEMS

Cutting HR costs through effective HR control systems is not new in the corporate world. This was earlier practiced by CISCO with great success. Now, it is the Insurance Company Aviva, which could cut HR costs through an online self-service HR search engine. Aviva believes that this has, in fact, reduced the burden of HR department and also enabled the employees to get real-time help in most cost effective manner. The manner is simple and user friendly. Based on the company's experience, 23 categories of HR information have been standardised and based on the same Frequently Asked Questions (FAQs) have been prepared. Aviva receives 12,000 calls in a month from its 23,500 staff members. With 10 helpline staff, Aviva runs the HR search engine. When the staff queries do not match with the FAQs, employees can send e-mails which are attended by the HR department on day-to-day basis. Company's experience shows 23 per cent of the HR calls in this process could be answered by the HR Systems itself, requiring less face to face interaction. However, over the years, Aviva expects, this percentage will increase, requiring less interaction and saving of precious HR time. All these are cost saving and at the same time, more employee friendly for obvious on-time information sharing.

INTRODUCTION

HR cost analysis is the study of behaviour of cost in relation to one or more HR criteria. Controlling manpower costs has now become important for organisations, particularly when we are required to look within for cost savings to sustain organisational growth and profitability. To enforce control on HR costs, it is essential to develop a checklist at the outset. This requires grouping of activities under different cost heads and then Identifying the individual cost elements under each head. By developing an HR costs spreadsheet, we can understand the magnitude of HR costs in an organisation. Element-wise cost trend over the years facilitates regular monitoring and operational control. At the macro-level, net value added per employee is an indicator of cost efficiency. At the end of this unit, we have given an example of such computation for a public sector undertaking over a six-year period, from the published data of Comptroller and Auditor General (CAG), 1999.

DEVELOPING AN HR COSTS CHECKLIST

Bramham (1998) developed an indicative checklist for HR costs. However, this checklist varies from organisation to organisation due to obvious differences in their practices. Here we have mentioned about those cost elements which are common.

Remuneration

Remuneration costs include basic pay, dearness allowance, city compensatory allowance, house rent allowance, conveyance allowance, etc. However, these are paid remuneration costs. Organisations are also required to cater for deferred benefits to employees, which we have referred as NWLC earlier. Certain statutory payments to employees are also accounted under this head, like, contribution to provident fund, pension fund, medical benefits, payment for holiday, sickness, bonus, etc. To retain and attract talent, organisations may also give various fringe benefits to their employees. Even the latest practice to provide stock options to employees involves certain opportunity cost to the organisation. The best practice is to delineate such cost elements and arrange the same in the form of a spread sheet. Element-wise cost trends then can be studied over the years and also can be benchmarked with other comparable organisations to understand the nature of variance and to enforce control, wherever necessary. Some organisations prefer to increase the paid wage cost by reducing the NWLC burden. Such strategy is very effective in cases, where employees are mostly in their exploratory age group (less than 35). This in one way helps the organisation to reduce their cost burden and at the same time to retain young and talented employees. Cost savings on certain statutory payments is also possible by participating in Group Gratuity Scheme, Group Medical Insurance Scheme, Group Pension Scheme, etc., of public finance institutions, like, Life Insurance Corporation, etc.

Recruitment

Recruitment cost is also another major cost head for HR. Right from developing job specifications to describing job requirements, it includes costs of recruitment promotion (through advertising), head hunting, evaluation, interviewing, induction and orientation. A well defined job specification minimises the search for the right fit and consequent costs. If recruitment plans are to meet short-term requirements, it may be better to outsource than go in for direct recruitment. There are many specialised manpower agencies, who make people with required skill sets available on contractual terms. Similarly, internal hiring also needs to be explored vis-a-vis external hiring. Internal hiring involves restructuring and relocation costs, a clear policy on 'promotion from within' (wherever recruitment is made for the higher posts), etc. A detailed study on cost of hiring is necessary to explore an alternative recruitment process.

Training Costs

Gordon's (2000) 9-step analysis of ROI on Human Capital has already been discussed in earlier unit on 'Skills and multi-skilling'. In fact this 9-step model considers all aspects of training cost and its benefits. To be more specific, training costs include, cost for induction period, cost of remuneration for the trainee and trainer, cost of travel for the trainee and the trainer, if any, cost of training materials, imputed cost of machines and equipments, used during the training, cost for development of training modules, cost of training evaluation, cost of material wastage during training, if any, cost of production loss for the trainee and the trainer (if he is within the organisation, for in-house training), etc. To accurately ascertain cost of training, it is necessary to develop a checklist or a worksheet, delineating all direct and indirect costs of training. There are various methods of training delivery, which we have discussed in unit on 'Training and Development'. Relative benefits and costs of each such method also need to be weighed to understand the most cost-efficient system. Any training on skill renewal needs to be weighed in terms of expanded skill cycle of the trainees. If the trainees are in the higher age bracket or due to retire within a short span, then offering them voluntary retirement (VR) may be more cost-effective than putting them on training for skill renewal and skill change. A model for cost-benefit analysis is illustrated in Figure 19.1:

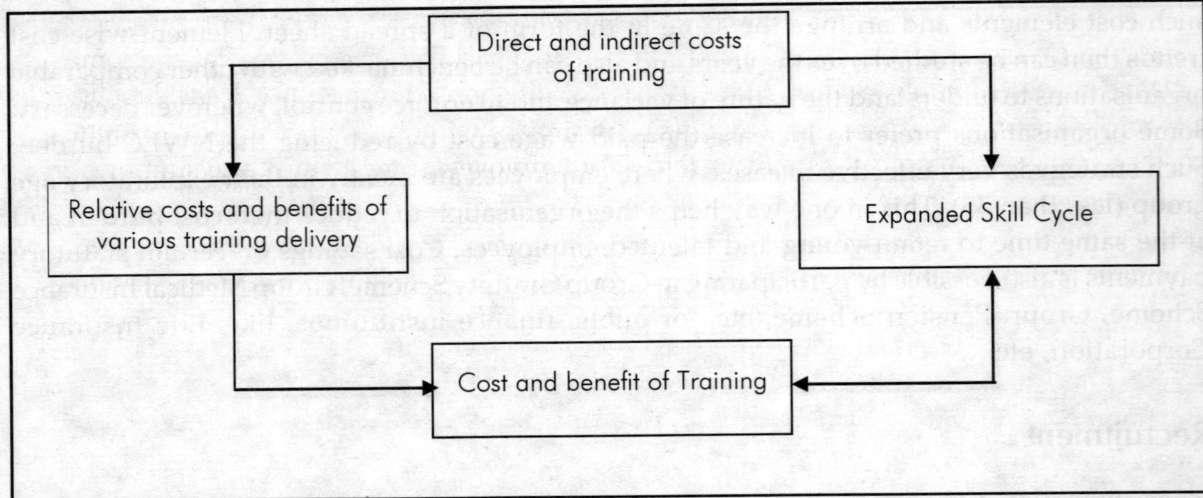

Figure 19.1: Cost-Benefit Analysis of Training

Relocation Costs

Many organisations have their policy on periodic relocation of employees, as part of their restructuring exercise. This is more appropriate for those who have their units in multiple locations. Such decisions from organisational point of view, involve costs related to disturbance allowance, costs of possible litigation, cost of housing, cost of travel, etc. Many departmental undertakings and public sector units thoughtlessly relocate their employees adding cost to the exchequer. For example, in one of the published reports, it was evident that Indian Ordinance Factories have spent in one year ₹ 40 crore for relocation of their employees. Hence, the relocation decision must be cost-effective or else this will defeat the purpose, straining organisational viability.

Separation Costs

Relocation also induces separation. There may be other reasons for separation, which may be either for organisational initiative or for individual employees' reasons. Since, separation requires replacement, immediate cost-effect is on loss of production. Other costs of separation are redundancy benefits (if separation is organisation induced), ex-gratia payments (if any), etc. Since separation follows immediate liquidation of fringe benefits, savings of the organisation on this count, also need to be considered to compute the actual costs. Indian organisations have now replicated global practices, to go for large-scale redundancy. Offering VRS in PSU banks to 99,425 employed at a cost of ₹ 10,073 crore is the latest example. While this may prove to be effective for obvious reasons of savings on manpower (redundant) cost, it may also have the ill effect of skill mismatch (particularly business skills) with new recruits, which will further add to the cost of separation.

Support Costs

Some of the employee support services are statutory, while others are offered voluntarily by the organisations. For computing support costs, therefore, it is necessary to distribute these under two different heads and then study their impact. Medical welfare, canteens, safety, security, insurance (medi-claim, etc.) death benefits, parking space costs, etc., are some of the statutory costs for employee support services. While house journal, club membership, music at workplace, long service awards, suggestion schemes, library services, holiday homes, etc., are examples of voluntary support services for employees. Since, employee support services have direct effect on employee motivation, cost curtailment decisions must have reference to this aspect.

Personnel Overhead Costs

Personnel overhead costs spread over personnel record keeping, costs for maintaining Human Resources Information Systems (HRIS), cost of personnel decisions and overall costs for maintaining personnel department (salary of the people working in this department). Outsourcing personnel services to a great extent can reduce such cost burden. However, its relative merits and demerits need to be studied.

SUMMARY

To enforce control over human resource costs, it is necessary to develop worksheets on each cost element, duly grouping these under different cost heads. Decisions on cost control need to be weighed in terms of lost opportunity for employee motivation and consequent loss of productivity. To understand the trend of HR costs, ratio analysis can be done from the data collected from the spreadsheet.

KEYWORDS

NWLC	Stock Options
Relocation Costs	Expanded Skill Cycle
Personal Overhead Costs	

REVIEW QUESTIONS

1. What are your suggestions for controlling HR Costs?
2. Since HR costs control may require curtailment of benefits, do you think this strategy is de-motivating for employees?
3. How can you ensure a win-win compensation designing without adding to the HR Costs?
4. Write short notes on:
   (a) Checklists for HR Costs
   (b) Relocation Costs
   (c) Employee Stock Options
   (d) Intrinsic Benefits

CASE STUDY 1

COMPENSATION GAME

A multinational call centre retains your services to design their compensation structure without overshooting their present wage costs. This company mostly employs young boys and girls within the 20-25 age group. While you have data on the company's HR cost details, you have no such information about competitors to benchmark the compensation practices. The company's documented policy shows the present break-up of employers costs for compensation as under:

Wages and Salaries	73.2%
Other benefits	0.1%
Supplemental pay	2.4%
Pensions	3.6%
Insurance	5.4%
Paid leave	6.9%
Legally required benefits	8.4%

To rationalise this break-up you have tried to benchmark this with macro-level data for private sector organisations in India. From the available data of 1994 and 1995, you could obtain 'wage and salaries' alone responsible for major percentage of industrial disputes in India (30.9%) and 29.1 per cent respectively. In fact the trend is equally significant for public sector (25.6% and 32.1% respectively). However, classification of disputes with the incidence of other casual factors, shows most of the disputes (when accounted together) are related to deficiency in man management systems.

You have also collected certain data from the company, which indicate, the company during the past financial year lost about 50% of their employees, who have mostly joined the rival organisations. Absenteeism rate is much higher in the company (40% against national average of 24.9%). You are aware that there are many intrinsic aspects to correct the situation. But the company restricts your services only to compensation designing, without adding to the overall HR cost.

Question

Design your perceived structure of break-up with some logic.

Case Study 2

Pay Less through Job Outsourcing – Smriti's Approach to Labour Cost Optimisation

In a labour surplus economy like India, the contract workers who are mostly not unionised do not get access to the mandated benefits, which are provided by the legal provisions. Contract labourers consent to accept less wages, accept long working hours, poor work environment, etc. Minimum Wages Act, 1948 is also applicable for contract workers.

Smriti Agro foods, is a Rajasthan based food processing company. Smriti employs up to 1000 employees during the season lasting for four months' period in a year, when agricultural raw materials are available in abundance for processing. Smriti markets their products round the year, but their production unit remains operational only for a period of four month in a year. Obviously, Smriti's production is not based on market demand. This type of industry always survives when they can sustain in price competition. In different states of India, Smriti pickles sells well. Smriti sells their produces in different parts of the country at different price bands. Smriti's practices, at times, compel them to sell at less than the cost of production only to dispose their finished stocks. Normally, the entire produces sells and the new production cycle starts. This is very typical for any agro-based food processing unit.

At the plant level, Smriti maintains a lean manpower of 20 people, mostly production supervisors, marketing, finance and HR people. During the beginning of a production cycle, Smriti hires ihe labour contractors, who on paper guarantee payment of minimum wages and other statutory benefits; but in reality, pay less than half of the minimum wages, not to talk about other statutory benefits. Smriti also pays less to the labour contractors. Smriti never pays to the contractors on head counts, but pays on the volume of production achieved. This gives flexibility to the contractors to maximise production with minimum workers. For many contractors, workers are bonded labourers and they come from remote village areas of Rajasthan and other adjoining states.

Question

Critically evaluate whether Smriti's actions will optimize HR costs in the long run.

Appendix 1

Table 1: Employees' Cost and Value Addition of PPL

	1992-93	1993-94	1994-95	1995-96	1996-97	1997-98
1. Sales including subsidy and trading activities.	50992	38241	87207	77107	76852	116803
2. Increase/decrease(-) in the stock of finished and intermediate goods	3462	575	10950	11304	(18594)	8499
3. Value of Mfg./Trading activities (1+2)	54454	38816	98157	88411	58258	125302
4. Other income including writing off interest, prior period and other adjustments (credit)	4765	15082	1183	311	278	332
Total	**59219**	**53898**	**99340**	**88722**	**58536**	**125634**
5. less: Value of raw materials and other materials, stores & spares, power & fuel consumed and purchase of finished goods	50886	31793	76069	72136	48619	111 023
6. Net value added	8333	22105	23271	16586	9917	14611
7. Expenditure contribution to net value added:						
(a) Salary (including Bonus, Gratuity, contribution to PF, FPS etc.)	632	712	1059	1021	1028	1277
(b) Workmen & staff welfare expenses	100	165	177	210	197	245
(c) Depreciation	3260	2714	2623	2635	2692	2623
(d) Interest	5648	5205	1161	1673	2539	5794
(e) Other expenses and charges after prior period adjustments (debit)	6784	8573	15483	10825	9525	15225
8. Total expenditure	16424	17369	20503	16364	15981	25164
9. Profit/loss after prior period adjustment	(8091)	4736	2768	222	(6064)	(10553)
10. Net value added	8333	22105	23271	16586	9917	14611
11. No. of employees	1008	1072	1064	1065	1031	1068
12. Percentage of value added to the total expenditure contributing to net value added	50.74	127.27	113.50	101.36	62.05	58.06
13. Employees' cost per employee (including staff welfare expenses) (₹ in lakh)	0.73	0.82	1.16	1.16	1.19	1.43
14. Employees' cost as a percentage of total cost of production	4.46	5.05	6.03	7.52	7.67	6.05
15. Net value added per employee (₹ in lakh)	8.27	20.62	21.87	15.57	9.62	13.68

Source: CAG, 1999

Contd....

Table 2: Actual Manpower of the Company against Sanctioned Strength

Category	Sanctioned Strength	Actual Strength			
	1993-94	1994-95	1995-96	1996-97	1997-98
Executive	400	408	400	371	399
Non-Executive	672	656	665	660	669
Total	1072	1064	1065	1031	1068

Source: CAG, 1999

Table 3: Expenditure Incurred for Contact Labour

Year	Amount (Rs. in crore)
1993-94	1.78
1994-95	3.11
1995-96	3.28
1996-97	3.67
1997 -98	5.88

Source: CAG, 1999

Table 4: Overtime Payment in the Company

Year	Employees Remuneration (₹ in lakh)	Overtime (₹ in lakh)	Percentage of Over Time to Employees Remuneration
1993-94	712	35.38	4.97
1994-95	1059	84.71	8.94
1995-96	1021	115.43	11.31
1996-97	1028	95.82	9.32
1997-98	1277	192.65	15.09

Source: CAG, 1999

UNIT 20

Human Resource Accounting and Audit

Learning Objectives

After completion of this unit, the students will be aware of the following topics:

- *Introduction*
- *Concepts and Theories*
- *Various Methods for Valuation of Human Resources*
- *HRD Audit*
- *HR Research*
- *HRD and National Planning*

HUMAN RESOURCE ACCOUNTING AT MANGALIK

Human Resource Accounting is used as a scaling tool used by many organisations to quantitatively measure effectiveness of human resources in terms of performance and productivity. To map the future value adding potentiality of human resources and accordingly price their efforts on quantitative terms, organisations make use of various models. Today like all other resources, value of human resources is also reflected in the balance sheets. MANGALIK is engaged in high knowledge intensive activities and for them, systematic development of human resources and enhancement of their capabilities to rise through the changing situation is extremely important. The engineering major today is highly diversified and literally, could make its presence in almost every branches of engineering, essentially leveraging their talent pool. For MANGALIK, human resource accounting information makes their stakeholders aware about the energy of their employees and the extent of their value for the organisation. Stakeholders can understand the productivity on the investment on people and accordingly, can make informed decisions about the strength of the organisation in terms of future potentiality for incremental changes in the profitability.

Also, MANGALIK gets the advantage to enforce internal control on human resources, when through scaled information, they could understand the depletion in their human resource values. MANGALIK value diversity and hence, equally emphasise on the development of their employees with absolute gender neutrality. However, the value of human resources, particularly for the female employees, relatively shows a declining trend than male employees. Although the company attributes this to the relatively shorter employment life-cycle for female employees, as many of them leave job in their mid-age groups for family compulsion or ill health, Neha, an NGO working for gender neutrality, attributes this to the typical management approach towards female employees.

INTRODUCTION

A resource is defined as an object which can provide expected future services. Hence, objects which do not have expected future service potential, cannot by definition, be resources. People being capable rendering future services, such potential services constitute a form of capital.

Human Resource Accounting (HRA) is the process of identifying, measuring and communicating data about human resources. Flamhoitz (1974) defined HRA as:

Accounting for people as an organisational resource. It involves measuring the costs incurred by business firms and other organisations to recruit, select, hire, train and develop human assets. It also involves measuring the economic value of people to the organisation.

HRA, therefore, shows how the organisation makes investment in its people and how the value of the people changes over time. Value of the employees increases by training (the core HRD activity) and experience over a time period. Such information on human resources facilitates effective management within an organisation.

Certain information on the human capital can be reported by an organisation in their annual reports. In the process of developing such information, organisations can address the requirements of HRP integrating their HRIS. Information pertaining to employees can be listed under the following broad heads:

Basic information about human resource:

- Number of employees
- Categories

- Grades
- Total value of human resources
- Value per employee

HR Acquisition:

- Number of employees acquired during the year
- Cost of acquisition
- Levels for which they were acquired
- HR development
- All information pertaining to HRD activities of the organisation
- HR maintenance
- Cost related to HR maintenance
- HR Separation
- Cost related to HR separation, attrition rate
- Details of benefits provided to the employees

However, the extent of disclosure of such information depends on the respective organisational practices. For example, Engineers India Ltd. (EIL) widely disclosed information on its human capital on all the areas mentioned above and reported the human valuation during 1998-99 as under:

Table 20.1: Employee Details of EIL

Category	No. of Employees as on March 31, 1999
Senior Manager and above Executives up to the manager level	613
Technical	2097
Non-technical	295
Supporting staff	719
Total	3724

Table 20.2: Human Valuation of EIL

Category	Human Valuation during 1998-99 (Rupees in lakhs)	
	Category-wise Total HR Value	Value Per Employee
Senior Manager and above executives up to the manager level	24151	39.39
Technical	65007	31.00
Non-technical	9145	–
Supporting staff	16264	22.62

CONCEPTS AND THEORIES

Knowledge and information today drive the organisations. Physical capital still continues to enjoy the highest priority, however, in new economies, human capital also gains almost equal importance. That is why, today's organisations focus on continuous development of human and intellectual capital through training and development, to improve the performance. Human capital accumulation of any organisation can best be understood through Human Resource Accounting (HRA). HRA is also used as a managerial tool to gain the valuable information by measuring the costs of recruiting, hiring, compensating and training employees. HRA also helps us to evaluate employee training programmes. For example, we can evaluate the effectiveness of training programmes on Customer Relationship Management (CRM) through HRA system, in terms of incremental changes in number of increase in customers' recall (repeat purchases), reduction in customers' complaints, etc. Similarly, through HRA, we can assess the extent of increase in productivity, improvement in the quality managerial decision-making, particularly in areas like, promotions, transfers, layoffs, replacement and turnover.

Contrary to conventional accounting system which only considers the costs as expenses, HRA considers accounting of expenses on human resources, considering human resources as assets. Rather more specifically, HRA concepts believe that expenses on human resources add value to people, making them more competent and bringing incremental changes in their performance, which ultimately positively changes the company's profitability and growth. Hence, HRA system considers people as the capital or resources as it has the potentiality to generate future value. As expenses on human resources need to be considered in investing or building future capital, the accounting approach to asset measurement is different in nature.

It was Rensis Likert (1961, 1967), who had pioneered the concept. Subsequently the idea was more concretized by Brummet, Flamholtz & Pyle (1968). Flamholtz's (1969) Ph.D. dissertation dealt in details- the HRA, which ultimately developed the process of measuring the human value through HRA. Also, his study elaborated the process of using HRA as a tool to enhance managerial effectiveness in all areas of human resource management like, acquisition, development, allocation, maintenance, and utilization. More recent studies on HRA, acknowledged its crucial role in managerial decision-making and positive changes in the long-term profitability of the organisation (Bullen, 2007). When we consider human resources as capital assets for our organisations, we subscribe to the concept of long-term investments on our employees. Subsequent studies of Flamholtz (1979) describe HRA in terms of the "psycho-technical systems" (PTS) of organisational measurement. PTS approach believes in two functions of measurements, i.e., (1) process functions and the (2) numerical functions. Process functions emphasise on the process of measurement, while the numerical functions help in generating information on human resources.

From the foregoing discussion, therefore, it is clear that HRA can be done in terms of human resource costs and so also in terms of human resource value. Human resource costs can be explained in terms of the two major categories of acquisition costs and learning costs. Acquisition costs include the direct costs of recruitment, selection, hiring and placement; and the indirect costs of promotion or hiring from within the firm. Learning costs include the direct costs of formal training and orientation and on-the-job training. In a human resource accounting system, these costs are reported in asset accounts with future economic benefits rather than as expenses. Flamholtz (1999) noted that the concept of human resource value is derived from general economic value theory and like all resources; people possess value because they are capable of rendering future service. Thus, as Flamholtz notes, an individual's value to an organisation can be defined as the present value of the future services that the individual is expected to provide for the period of time the individual is expected to remain in the organisation. The Stochastic Rewards Valuation Model, originally developed by Flamholtz (1971) for human resource valuation is a five step process that begins with defining the various service states or organisational positions that an individual may occupy in the organisation. The next step is to determine the value of each state to the organisation, the service state values, which can be calculated either by using a number of methods such as the price-quantity method or the income method. Then, the person's expected tenure or service life in the organisation is calculated and the person's mobility probability or the probability that a person will occupy each possible state at specified future times is derived from archival data.

Next, the expected future cash flows that the person generates are discounted in order to determine their present value. According to Flamholtz (1999), there is a dual aspect to an individual's value. First, the person's "expected conditional value," is the amount that the organisation could potentially realise from his or her services if the person maintains organisational membership during the period of his or her productive service life. Second, the person's "expected realisable value." is the amount actually expected to be derived, taking into account the person's likelihood of turnover. Using the Flamholtz model, Flamholtz, Bullen & Hua (2003) showed a practical method for calculating ROI on management development, and showed the incremental cash flows that an organisation will receive due to investment in management development.

Similar to the Flamholtz model, another earliest model of human resource value measures human capital by calculating the present value of a person's future earnings (Lev & Schwartz, (1971). Dobija (1998) proposes an alternate model for capitalisation, where the rate of capitalization is determined through the natural and the social conditions of the environment. Utilising a compound interest approach, this method takes into account the three factors for valuing the human capital embodied in a person. These include the capitalised value of cost of living, the capitalised value of the cost of professional education, and the value gained through experience. Alternately, Turner (1996) refers to the framework issued by the International Accounting Standards Committee and recommends the use of the present value of the value added by enterprise, and measures assets by the four methods of historical cost, current cost, realizable value and present value. Cascio (1998) proposed a method for measuring human capital based on indicators of human capital of innovation, employee attitudes and the inventory of knowledgeable employees. According to this method, innovation commands a premium and therefore, needs to be measured, for example, by comparing gross profit margins from new products to the profit margins from old products. Employee attitudes predicting customer satisfaction and retention are an important indicator of human capital and therefore, need to be measured, as well as measures of tenure, turnover, experience and learning.

Interest in HRA related reporting has grown in a number of countries across continents. In discussing "HR metrics," Hansen (2007) notes that two thirds of the 250 largest companies in the world now issue sustainability reports along with their financial reports in order to capture the full value of the organisation. Global standards for sustainability reporting require the disclosure of workforce data that reflects the potential for future performance and profitability. Sustainability reporting has been formalised under guidelines by the Global Reporting Initiative, an international network of business, labour investors and accountants. Schwartz and Murphy (2008) also comment on human capital metrics, suggesting that a class on the subject would benefit all undergraduate management majors. They suggest that primary among those benefits is a change in mind set towards using data and metrics to design and evaluate management policy rather than relying on experience, fad or hype; and suggest that students familiar with HR metrics should be better equipped to prove and enhance the contributions of human resources to their organisations.

Some research has included aspects of HRA in studies examining and comparing reporting practices of a number of countries. A study by Subbarao & Zehgal (1997) gave a macro-level perspective to HRA disclosure in financial statements by analyzing the differences across countries in the disclosure of human resources information disclosure in annual reports across six countries. The authors found differences in disclosures of HR information across countries and provided accounting and financial professional insights on the HR information areas they need to focus on in their country. In another study, Boedker, Mouritsen & Guthrie (2008) examined contemporary trends from Europe, Australia, and the United States, in "Enhanced Business Reporting" (EBR), which includes aspects of HRA. The authors found a vast diversity in international EBR practice, including measurement and reporting models and suggested the need for further research about the barriers to and consequences of harmonization.

Like many other countries of the world, in India, concept of human resource accounting was also extensively studied by Mahalingam (2001), Patra, Khatik & Kolhe (2003), who had emphasised on human resource value approach based on the skills and the returns from such skills over a time period. In most of the cases, Lev & Schwartz (1971) model was used to evaluate HRA measures. Bhatt (2000) has defined human resource accounting as the process of depicting the human resources potential in money terms.

Based on the above discussions, we can sum up the underlying theories on HRA which are based on the following premises:

- Employees are valuable resources of any organisation.
- Consideration of human resources as organisational resources is determined by the way people are being managed in the organisation.
- HRA information substantially helps decision making process in the organisation.

Various Methods for Valuation of Human Resources

Different approaches to the valuation of human resources may be broadly grouped under two categories:

1. Non-monetary measurement
2. Monetary measurement

Non-Monetary Measurement

Such methods involve the classification of human resources in terms of skills (skills inventory), performance evaluation, potentiality for development and promotion, attitude surveys and subjective value.

Skill is a coordinated series of actions to attain some goal. Operationally, skills are defined widely as overt responses and controlled stimulation. Overt responses may either be verbal, motor or perceptual. Verbal responses typically stress on speaking (which requires memorisation of words). Motor responses stress on movements of limbs and body while perceptual responses stress on understanding of sensory responses. Controlled stimulation, on the other hand are energy inputs to the workers which we express in units of frequency, length, time and weight.

Basic concepts of rest of the methods except for 'subjective value' have already been introduced in relevant chapters. 'Subjective value' method indicates a subjective evaluation of approximation of the likelihood of an event.

Monetary Measurement

There are a number of monetary measurement techniques. Each such technique has its relative advantages and disadvantages. Here we will discuss such techniques very briefly, as under:

1. ***Capitalisation of Historical Costs Method:*** This method was developed by Likert. It capitalizes all costs of recruitment, hiring, training and other initial costs involved in the development of human resources, i.e. employees. The amount so capitalised is written off over the period an employee remains with the organisation. If he leaves before the expected service period, the amount remaining as an asset is written off in its entirety in the year of leaving.

2. ***Replacement Cost Method:*** This method measures the cost to replace an organisation's existing human resource. It indicates what it would cost the concern to recruit, hire, train and develop human resources to match the present level of efficiency.

3. ***Opportunity Cost Method:*** Under this method, the value of human resources is determined on the basis of the value of an individual employee in an alternative use. If an employee can be hired externally, there is no opportunity cost for him.

4. ***Economic Value Method:*** Under this method, human resources are valued on the basis of the contribution they are likely to make to the organisation during the period of their employment. The remuneration to be paid to an employee is estimated and discounted appropriately to arrive at the current estimated value.

5. ***Present Value Method:*** This method measures human resources by attributing an employee's value to the organisation as an equivalent to the present value of his remaining earnings. Organisations like; MMTC, ONGC, BHEL, ACC, Neyvell Lignite Corporate, etc. have already adopted this concept.

From the HRD point of view, Human Resources Accounting helps to understand many pertinent issues like developing skill inventory, performance appraisal, assessing the individual's capacity for development, attitude surveys and subjective appraisal, as discussed above. Hence, for designing a Human Resource Information Systems (HRIS), we need to consider the following factors:

1. *Personal Profile:* This includes name, sex, range, age, marital status, address and phone number, service date, etc.
2. *Career Profile:* Education, training, certificates, licences, degrees, skills, hobbies, requisite training, interests, etc., are combined in the skill profile.
3. *Benefits Profile:* Insurance coverage, disability provisions, pension, profit sharing, vacation, holidays, sick leave, etc., are covered in the benefits profile.

Details of some HRA Models

We have already discussed briefly various HRA models. Here, we will discuss some widely used models in details.

Present Value of Future Earning Model

As per this model, the value of human resources is determined in terms of their present value to the organisation. Present value can be determined using various approaches. Most popular approach is developed by Lev and Schwarts (1971). As per this approach, determination of the total manpower cost depends on the individual value of such manpower to the organisation. The model suggests division of total manpower of the organisation into some homogeneous groups like, skilled, unskilled, semi-skilled, technical staff, managerial staff, etc. in different classes and age groups. Average earnings from different classes and age groups are then computed for different categories of manpower and then separately, present value of the human capital is calculated. The aggregate present value of different categories represents the capitalized future earnings for the organisation as a whole. It is done based on the use of cost of capital rate for capitalising the present value of the future earnings of manpower. Thus according to this model, the present value of human capital is represented in terms of the age, keeping in mind, the future earnings potentiality during the tenure of employment. The formula for such computation as suggested by them, therefore, is as under:

$$V_r = TE(t)/t: r\ (1 + r)t - r$$

Where V_r = the human Capital value of a person r years old,

E(t) = the person's annual earnings up to retirement, represented by the earning profile,

r = discount rate (Cost of Capital)

T = Retirement age

Rewards Evaluation Model

This is what we call Flanholtz model. The model identifies major variables to determine individual's value to an organisation. This is the expected realizable value, i.e., the present worth of future services expected from the person during the period of his employment with the organisation. As per this model, individual manpower's value to an organisation depends on the positions occupied by him in the organisation. The movement of people from one role to another is accounted for with the stochastic process with rewards. Therefore, future roles of manpower are determined using the probabilistic approach. The model basically rests on a five steps approach for assessment of the human resource value to the organisation:

- Expected service life is pre-determined.
- Future job roles are determined, probabilistically.
- Estimated value is determined for a particular job position for a specified time frame.
- Each possible mutually exclusive state is determined at specified times.
- Discounting the value is done at a predetermined rate to compute the present value of human resources.

For obvious operational complexities, like; assessing the career movements, etc., this model, despite its simplicity, cannot be always appropriate in determining the future value and so also the present value of human resources.

Certainty Equivalent Net Benefit Model

This model was suggested by Pekin Ogan (1976). As per this model, the value of human resources is determined taking into consideration the certainty with which the net benefits in future will accrue to the organisation. Certainty factor helps us to assess the benefits that will be available in future. The certainty equivalent benefits are calculated by multiplying the certainty factor with the net benefits from all employees, which ultimately become the total value of human resource of the organisation.

HRD Audit

Personnel/human resources or HRD audit is a systematic survey and analysis of different HRD functions with a summarised statement of findings and recommendations for correction of deficiencies. Basically it examines and evaluates policies, procedures and practices to determine the effectiveness of HRD function in an organisation. HRD audit ensures that sound and cost-effective policies are implemented.

Objectives of HRD Audit

1. To determine the effectiveness of management programmes which facilitate the development, allocation and monitoring of human resources.

2. To analyse the factors involved in HRD and develop a statement of findings with recommendations for correcting deviations, if any, on the following issues:
   (a) The extent of deviation from HRD policies
   (b) To what extent objectives are spelt out
   (c) To what extent performance standards have been established
3. To seek explanations and information and answers to all such above questions as: What happened? Why did it happen?
4. To study the extent to which line managers have complied with HRD policies and as such the operational problems in implementing the existing HRD policies.
5. To study the current manpower inventory and identify shortfall or excess, if any.

Job/Role of HRD Auditor

From the above stated objectives, the job of the HRD Auditor can be enumerated as follows:

1. To get the current facts.
2. To study the effectiveness of the present system by answering the following issues:
   (a) Why was the practice introduced?
   (b) What would be the result, if the practice is discontinued?
   (c) What needs were intended to be fulfilled and have those been fulfilled or not?
   (d) What could be the best possible alternative for fulfilling such needs?
   (e) What changes can improve effectiveness of the existing practice?
   (f) Are such intended changes economically and operationally viable?
   (g) Are such changes sustainable from the union's point of view?
   (h) What should be the time-frame for introducing the change?

Importance of HRD Audit

To keep pace with the changing environment, the importance of periodic HRD audit has increased in recent years. The recent economic restructuring programme of the Government of India, as discussed earlier, prompted the need for restructuring of the organisation, which, *inter alia*, calls for restructuring of production, manpower, strategies, management practices and philosophies, etc. All such possible reasons for periodic HRD audit can be enumerated as follows:

1. Technological changes, inter alia, are calling for renewal of knowledge and skills of existing manpower. Training function, therefore, has assumed importance. Periodic HRD audit can help to identify the changing training needs and development of new training modules for effective utilisation of smanpower.

2. To keep pace with the environmental changes, management philosophy and practices at the organisational level also need to be changed, like participative management (through quality circles and value engineering team), employee empowerment, total employee, involvement, etc. Need for all these can be understood only when we periodically undertake HRD audit.

Similarly, changing role of trade unions (which are now more pro-active than reactionary), Government (which is now more liberal than restrictive), emergence of new working class (who are more enlightened than their predecessors), emergence of international quality system requirements (which call for scientific documentation of different corporate functions and infuse attitudinal changes), changing expectations of customers (which call for more customer orientation), new statutory requirements (pollution control), etc., are now influencing HRD functions at the corporate level, the effectiveness of which can only be understood by periodic HRD audit.

Scope of HRD Audit

For integration of personnel management with HRD functions, HRD audit now encompasses all the areas like review and integration of corporate mission, goals, policies and objectives, manpower planning, career planning and development, promotion and transfer policies, performance appraisal systems, training and development functions, recruitment and selection, etc.

Records Used for HRD Audit

Records provide ready reference and serve as future and guides. Reports, on the other hand, describe an incident, event or situation. Depending upon the organisation, the following records/reports are usually checked for HRD audit-time study records and time standards, cost records, records on scores obtained in tests and other examinations, medical and accident reports, attitudinal survey reports, grievance reports, turnover reports, data on work stoppages, performance reports, pay roll data, labour costs data, etc.

Methods and Techniques of HRD Audit

HRD audit can be carried out either by attitudinal survey or by interpreting data. Details of attitudinal survey have already been explained in a separate chapter. Interpretation of data can be done either by simple comparison over a period or by ratio analysis or by graphical or pictorial displays. The following examples illustrate the data interpretation method.

Checklists for HRD Audit

T.V. Rao and Udai Pareek (1996), to measure the effectiveness of people management, developed a set of 20 questions mostly to suggest linking of HRD to the corporate objectives, goals and strategies, effectiveness of free flow of HRD information down the ranks, application of knowledge of behavioural science and industrial psychology for HRD, etc.

For other HRD sub-systems too, they have developed similar sets of questionnaire, adding responses which can help an organisation to audit their HRD activities. However, using same general checklists for all organisations may not be very effective to audit human resources for its obvious uniqueness in functional practices and philosophies.

Advantages of an HR Audit

- To ensure effective utilisation of human resources.
- To comply with administrative regulations.
- To inculcate sense of confidence in management.
- To develop and sustain organisational reputation in the society.
- To perform a "due diligence" review for various stakeholders.

Prerequisites of an HR Audit

In a Human Resources audit, the aspects of HR practices in an organisation that are covered are:

- Legal compliance
- Compensation/Salary Administration
- Employment/Recruiting
- Orientation
- Terminations
- Training and Development
- Employee Relations
- Communications
- Files/Record Maintenance/Technology
- Policies and procedures (including employee handbook)
- Communications

HR Audit Questionnaire

Please answer the following questions about organisational HR functions using the following scale of 1 to 5:

1 Strongly Disagree	2 Disagree	3 Undecided	4 Agree	5 Strongly Agree

HR Functional Capacity Ratings

HR professionals in your firm are perceived to be business partners.	
Line staff complies with HR department's programmes as a part of protocol but do not fully buy into the value of such programmes.	
HR provides new and relevant solutions that address organizational needs in a proactive manner.	
HR processes are efficient and user-friendly.	
HR systems are up to date and make use of current technology.	
HR personnel are technically adept and apply their knowledge with impact.	
HR programs are viewed as a necessary evil and as a cost to be minimized.	
HR focuses mostly on processes and not enough on outcomes.	

HR Leadership Capacity

HR leaders understand the current business challenges and environment.	
HR professionals are perceived as technical and administrative experts.	
Leaders in HR possess good strategic thinking skills and can hold their own in conversations about corporate strategy.	
HR leaders think systemically about their programs before submitting them for review.	
HR leaders assertively advocate for the needs of employees, even in the face of opposition and resistance.	
HR leaders can show the business value of their proposals in concrete terms and that can be measured for ROI.	
HR leaders are strong role models for other leaders in the organization.	
HR leaders are willing to consider and try out new and untested approaches.	

Organisational Expectations and Support for HR

Senior executives hold their HR leaders to high expectations for performance and results.	
HR leaders are selected based upon a model that it relevant to business outcomes.	
HR is respected for its role and supported through leadership action and time.	
The organizations' senior leadership value programs that enhance corporate culture and intellectual capital.	
HR goals and deliverables are explicitly defined.	
HR is held accountable for results.	
Corporate sponsorship exists and resources are provided for innovative HR practices and technologies.	
HR leaders are treated as partners and are called to offer their opinions about corporate strategy.	

Value Added HR Activities

HR creates opportunities for process improvements and constructively offers suggestions to line personnel.	
HR ensures that employees are engaged and that they feel commited to their organizations through sound internal programs that bring awareness to employee needs and concerns.	
Leadership programs are offered that have a direct impact on improving employee morale.	
New systems are introduced that help employees communicate their needs and concerns in a productive and proactive manner.	
HR offeres solutions for job or work redesign to sustain employee motivation and reduce lethargy.	
HR advocates strongly for employee concerns and serves as an advocate for their needs when critical business decisions are made.	

HR Research

Information on HR can be made available in two forms; the first one includes facts, terms and concepts or ideas, while the second one is the form of predictions and explanations. The second form is the product of research. HR research is the detailed analytic study about people is the organisation by conducting attitudinal survey or direct interview with a structured, close ended questionnaire. By simple analysis of data also research can be carried out, but that may not give much insight on employees' attitude or intrinsic feelings.

There are different phases of HR research like, fact finding, hypothesis formation, valuation and interpretation and application of the results, etc. In India, many organisations carry out systematic HR research. However, systematic HR research can help organisations to combine people and procedures, study patterns of supervisory behavioural, supervisory skills, identify needs for changing policies and procedures, etc.

HRD and National Planning

Importance of HRD at the organisational level has already been highlighted in our introductory submission. At the national level also, focus on HRD activities is absolutely necessary to develop employable human resources. Development of employable human resources is possible once we go for developing infrastructural support for increasing literacy, developing graduates and postgraduates, professionals, scientists, etc., whose knowledge could be utilised in the organisations. Realising this importance, the Government of India has now even set up a Human Resource Development Ministry. However, at the national level, HRD does not mean only education and training. It encompasses health, housing, provision for drinking water, hospital and medical facilities, social security and other welfare measures, etc. Even though budgetary allocation for HRD in India is not up to the mark, the trend indicates HRD has started receiving priority like other national issues. A comparative analysis of human development data indicates that availability of employable people is relatively less in India, even though population growth is much on the higher side. By the employable or employability, it is meant that availability of adequate human resources with high technological literacy and managerial competencies. Realising this importance, recently the World Bank has sanctioned aid for ₹ 1,650 crores to India for revamping and upgradation of our education system, covering 539 polytechnics in 17 states and 2 union territories. As on date, we are having 300 recognised technical education institutes at the degree level and 750 polytechnics at the diploma with annual admission capacity of 65,000 and 90,000 students respectively. Besides this, facilities for postgraduate studies and research work benefit another 11,000 scholars.

Many organisations in India have of late started taking active interest in developing human resources by collaborating with technical and management institutes. As on date, we are having 185 universities, 42 deemed universities and 5 institutions of national importance, which have been established through state and central legislation. We have nearly 11,000 colleges in the country in addition to some unrecognised institutions. Polytechnics have been brought in an integrated development under the World Bank and Canada-India Institutional Cooperative Project.

Table 20.3 below indicates resultant human development efforts of the Government of India vis-à-vis comparison of such data with other Asian countries.

Table 20.3: Human Development Indicators for Some Asian Countries - 2000

Countries	Literacy Rate (in Percentage)	Life Expectancy at Birth (in years)	Infant Mortality (per '000)
Sri Lanka	90	75.6	16
China	80	72.3	48
Indonesia	84	67.5	43
India	62	60.9	72.2
Pakistan	38	65.6	73
Bangladesh	38	51.9	—

Sources: Economic Survey, 2000-2001; Asian Development Outlook, 2000.

Note: Literacy rate data relates to 1995, excepting India. Indian data relates to 1997.

- Data on life expectancy relate to 1998
- Data on infant mortality relate to 1995-2000

Table 20.3 above indicates, how poor is India's human development data in comparison with some of the Asian countries. On the contrary, India has an edge over others on GDP growth rate and value addition in agriculture, industry and services. Table 20.4 captures such trend in India vis-à-vis other Asian countries.

Table 20.4: Important Economic Indictors for Some Asian Countries - 2000

Countries	Growth Rate of GDP (in percentage)	Growth Rate of Value Added (in percentage)
Indonesia	4	3.77
India	7	5.00
Malaysia	6	2.73
Philippines	3.80	3.83
Pakistan	3.80	4.60
Republic of Korea	7.50	9.16
Singapore	5.90	4.10
Srilanka	5.00	4.70
Thailand	4.50	3.77
Bangaldesh	6.40	5.90

Source: Asian Development Outlook, 2000.

Notes: Value added percentages have been averaged for all the sectors together.

Above information, therefore, suggests shifting of priorities for Indian planners for developing human resources.

HRD from World Perspective

In New Delhi, during 19-23 January, 1995, labour ministers of non-aligned and other developing countries met to debate on human resources. In the said meet, the labour ministers took stock of the current world economic scenario vis-à-vis its impact on human resources in developing countries. The meet emphasised:

1. The need for effective workers' participation for enhancing productivity.
2. The need for adopting employment policy in congruence with the national economic and social development policy.
3. The need for education and training of workers and building economically valuable stock of technicians, scientists, technologists and management specialists by increasing access to education, making it equitable and affordable.
4. Need for vocational guidance and counselling.
5. Need for promotion of self-employment.
6. Need for striking a balance between labour protection through state intervention and market flexibility.
7. Need for eliminating gender discrimination and enhanced participation of women in all economic activities.

8. Need for elimination of child labour.

9. Need for safeguarding the interest of international migrant workers.

10. Need for establishing internal labour standards.

Regarding human resources and skill development, the meet reached to a consensus and adopted the following resolutions:

1. To establish policies and practices to secure investment requisite, proportion of the Gross National Income as government expenditure in education and training.

2. To study sub-sectoral priorities (between primary, secondary and tertiary levels of education), and analyse investment ratios between the sub-sectors and maximise the rate of return on investment.

3. To enhance access to and retention in education and training and thereby avert wastage of educational investments.

HRD in Asian Countries

Indonesia

In Indonesia, change in employment relationship for technology and consequent restructuring of the organisation is controlled by the government for obvious surplus of labour in the labour market. The employment matters being highly regulated in Indonesia, scope of organisation-wide HRD activities is limited.

Malaysia

Malaysian economy is now facing extreme recession. Termination and lay-offs are very frequent in industries, which obviously restrict the HRD activities.

Philippines

Philippines industries are facing the challenge of new technology, which resulted in large scale displacement of workers, skills-mismatch and redundancy. This situation is being settled by widespread training and development programmes in the industries.

Singapore

Singapore has established a Skills Development Fund to counter the effect of technology and train the workers.

Thailand

The extent of HRD activities in Thailand are limited. Retraining efforts to help the workers to make them adaptable to changes are also not that adequate.

SUMMARY

Human Resources Accounting helps in quantifying HR values in an organisation. While subjective skill assessment helps in one way to understand the skill inventory, quantified HRA data further reinforce it for successful HRP. Whether HR initiatives are correct or not or whether HRA value are appreciating or depreciating need to be periodically evaluated through a systematic HRD audit. Similarly, such assessment at the national level also helps us to understand the macro-level trend. Periodic research initiatives augment the total process.

KEYWORDS

Human Resource Accounting	Replacement Cost
Opportunity Cost	Economic Value
Present Value	HRD Audit
Checklist for HRD Audit	Skill Development

REVIEW QUESTIONS

1. Define Human Resource Accounting. What are the different methods of Human Resource Accounting?
2. For designing a Human Resource Accounting System, what are the factors that need to be considered?
3. Define HRD Audit. What are its objectives and importance?
4. What should be the role of an HRD Auditor?
5. What is the scope of HRD audit? What records need to be used for it?
6. Briefly explain methods and techniques of HRD audit.
7. What is the significance of HRD for national planning?
8. Write short notes on:
   (a) Personnel Research
   (b) Human Development Indices
   (c) Technology and HRD
   (d) Checklist and HRD
   (e) Checklist for HRD audit
   (f) Career Profile
   (g) Present Value Method

Case Study

SUPRAMENTAL – The Benchmarked HR Audit Systems

Periodic auditing of human resources function can strengthen the effectiveness of human resource utilisation in any organisation. To attract and retain talents are now considered crucial for any organisation aspiring to grow. Most conventional approach to attract and retain is to design suitable motivational reinforcers, pacing with the needs of the people. But there are many other issues that deserve attention. SUPRAMENTAL, a new-generation software developer focuses on systematic HR audit to identify such underlying issues and accordingly, design the HR systems and practices, which could help them to get results. SUPRAMENTAL is specialised in medical diagnostic software, and one of their core strength is telemedicine support systems. Medical diagnostic reports widely vary from laboratories to laboratories. It is for this new generation that physicians insist on diagnostic reports that use SUPRAMENTAL software. SUPRAMENTAL's newly designed USB port can collect the entire clinical data on patients' and can generate detailed diagnostic reports for much easier clinical diagnosis. The system requires no body invasion or blood collection; just fixing on arms. The company is now trying to innovate new medical diagnostic software for total diagnosis of diseases. What is more important is that the diagnostic reports also provide a suggestive line of treatment of ailments, going through which the doctors can understand whether their approach is right? Based in Pune, SUPRAMENTAL engages country's best talent in medicine, information technology, bio-chemistry, bio-technology, bio-physics, and electronics. Even for other management support functions, the company also settles for the best talents. Being in much specialised field of operation, the company now emphasises on long-term retention of employees. To realise such intents, the company focused on institutionalizing their HR audit systems.

The first level of study could identify the following areas of investigations:

- Understanding of best practices, emulating the experiences of world class organisations
- Understanding the extent of regulatory compliances with the identified best practices
- Understanding of the processes that can support HR in providing the highest quality service to employees

With the first phase focus on the above aspects, the company started collection of data and documenting the same, with side by side evaluation of HR policy manuals, HR benefits, communication systems with the employees and accordingly could identify and prioritise the following areas:

- Redesigning of HR structure
- Reframing of HR Policies and Procedures
- Detailed documentation of employee life cycle (attraction, recruitment, hiring, orientation, and termination)
- Developing the evaluation system of performance and training
- Developing Compensation and benefits administration
- Developing employee communication

SUPRAMENTAL's focus was strengthened by forming a special task force of top management people, who have been specially trained to document the entire HRD audit system and systematically carry out the audit to generate information that could substantially reduce the problem of talent attrition. SUPRAMENTAL also designed a detailed Employee Hand Book to incorporate all the new HR initiatives on career development, promotion, compensation designing, etc. The company periodically updates the HR handbook with time to time recommended best practices and communicates the same to the employees. With major changes in the HR processes, the HR audit functions of the company has become more streamlined and aligned with the core objectives.

The top management HR audit team reviews the following areas during their audit period:

- Status of Strategic initiatives
- Recruitment Process (sourcing, interviewing, hiring, record-keeping and orientation)

Contd...

- Retention and Succession Plans
- Training
- Communication
- Policies and Procedures
- Performance Management
- Compensation
- Administrative staff levels and functions
- Job Descriptions
- Regulatory Compliance
- Processes and Efficiencies

Question

HR specialists study the above line of actions and recommend whether SUPRAMENTAL requires reviewing of some more areas to make their HR audit foolproof to achieve their core objectives of attraction and retention of talents.

BLOCK EIGHT

EMPLOYEE RELATIONS

UNIT 21

Discipline and Grievance Handling

Learning Objectives

After completion of this unit, the students will be aware of the following topics:

- *Introduction*
- *Theories of Disciplinary Powers*
- *Different Approaches to the Problem of Discipline*
- *Disciplinary Problems*
- *Norms to Ensure Discipline in Organisations*
- *Causal Factors of Indiscipline*
- *Need for a Disciplinary Policy*
- *Role of Trade Unions in Discipline*
- *Steps to Enforce a Disciplinary Procedure*
- *Results of Survey on Disciplinary Problems*
- *Steps to Ensure Discipline*
- *Code of Discipline in Industry*
- *Grievance Handling*
- *Principles of Natural Justice*

WORKPLACE BULLYING

Workplace bullying is very common in organisations. Often, managers use this to create pressure on employees to leave the job. Although we have other mechanism to fire, managers prefer the bullying route to get results immediately. But bullying can spark industrial relations problems and can be a major issue of grievances. This was what happened in one of the leading organisations in India, engaged in educational services.

Ashoke, the Director of the unit is the first batch alumnus of IIM, Kolkata. His style of doing job is to confuse others. Less bothered for his achievement; as his past trend indicates, his average presence in one job is less than one year. Ashoke envies his other senior level employees, who are more qualified and who often earn more than Ashoke from their consultancy and other creative pursuits. Most of the senior level employees are in their declining or settlement age-group, despite being reasonably more qualified than Ashoke. Ashoke can easily make them the prey and in meetings sold them to give message to others, whom Ashoke envies, for the reasons explained above. Always busy with his tour in the name of network building, Ashoke remains absent from his workplace for almost half of the month and his soaring travelling allowances have now become a major audit issue. Ashoke believes in managing the show with phonies (chamchas). Based on his phonies' information, Ashoke started scaring those, whom otherwise, so far, he used to spare for their superiority (as perceived by Ashoke).

Dipak, one such person, who rose through the ladder with sheer efforts and dedication was the target of Ashoke. Dipak was incidentally persuaded by Ashoke to join the organisation and was known as one of the admirers of Ashoke.

In one of the meetings, Ashoke reprimanded Dipak on flimsy ground, alleging Dipak is not listening to him, which he feels is a gross misconduct and a fit case for taking disciplinary action. Dipak enquired what special work Ashoke has given that prompts him to believe has not been carried out. Dipak also asked Ashoke what makes him to believe that orders that have not been given at all and non-carrying of the said purported order could be an issue of misconduct. With this, Ashoke got infuriated and started scolding Dipak in the meeting. Dipak also argued with Ashoke with equal pitch and tone. Others remained mute watchers in the incident.

Ashoke then started exerting pressure on Dipak in the name of disciplinary action. Dipak also alleged the case of workplace bullying.

INTRODUCTION

In a broad sense, discipline means orderly and systematic behaviour. Every organisation, for operative efficiency, frames certain codes of behaviour for employees, under normal practice, contract or statutes or under mutual understanding. Breaking of such behavioural norms creates disciplinary problems.

1. Early intervention
2. Identification of problem
3. Clear expectations
4. Feedback
5. Positive reinforcement
6. Follow-up

Corrective discipline is ideally suited to solve continual performance problems, rather than isolated ones. Discipline again may be classified as positive and negative discipline. When a person spontaneously abides by the required norms, it is called positive or constructive discipline. But when he is compelled to behave in a desired way under threat or fear of punishment, it is termed as negative, punitive or autocratic discipline.

Positive discipline is achieved through education and training and negative discipline is enforced by punishment. Indiscipline may be of two types: individual or Collective. Individual causes are basically problem of attitude, while industrial relations are responsible for collective indiscipline.

Walter Kiechel (1990) developed the concept of 'hot stove rule' to administer discipline in an organisation. By touching a hot stove we get burnt, thus we get immediate response and it leaves no question of cause and effect. This analogy keeps the discipline impersonal, i.e. penalties for a given violation is independent of the personality of the violator.

Theories of Disciplinary Powers

Employers derive their disciplinary power presumably from two theories: institutional theory and contractual theory.

1. ***Institutional Theory:*** Organisation structure is designed in a hierarchical manner. Employers being the heads assume highest responsibility to look after the interests of such an organised community. As such, they feel that they have the power to make regulations, direct operations and exercise disciplinary control.

2. ***Contractual Theory:*** This theory, however, considers that employers' disciplinary powers stem from the contract of employment. Employment contracts subject employees to subordination and thereby vest employers with necessary authority to ensure performance, which again is possible by enforcement of disciplinary powers.

Different Approaches to the Problem of Discipline

Indiscipline and violence can be diagnosed from the following approaches:

1. Legalistic approach
2. Humanitarian approach
3. Human resource Approach
4. Behavioural approach
5. Leadership approach

Legalistic approach being too formal and rigid can hardly bring about changes in workers' mind. The concept is somewhat like progressive discipline. Other approaches are important as by taking care, we can minimise the recurrence of such ill-fated behaviour, subject or its proper enforcement. The other four approaches are interlinked, hence, we are not desegregating the approaches, rather we are trying to analyse them from an aggregative angle.

Causes of indisciplined behaviour are usually:

1. Excessive job pressure,
2. Improper training,
3. Ignored complaints,
4. Unfair treatment,
5. Favouritism,
6. Poor management-labour relations,
7. Lack of confident leadership,
8. Lack of recognition and lack of opportunity for initiative.

V.K. Calla, in his *Discipline in Industry*, has identified seven reasons for disobeying as follows:

1. Ignorance,
2. Physical or mental incapacity,
3. Inadequate training,
4. Dissatisfaction with work,
5. Misguidance of Union,
6. Desperate attempt to claim self-leadership by deliberate dissonance, and
7. Absence of standard or uniform disciplinary policy.

To identify indiscipline in the organisation, Calla further mentioned some indicators, like:

1. High rate of absenteeism
2. High rate of labour turnover
3. High rate of sickness and accidents
4. Multiple unresolved grievances
5. Industrial relations state
6. Low output, faulty out-turn and lower productivity
7. Low motivation and morale
8. Prevalence of 'we-feeling' in the work-group, etc.

We-feeling in a strict sense means dominance of individual identity over organisational identity.

Disciplinary Problems

Poor handling of disciplinary action may cause serious problems to the organisation. Although nature of the problem varies from organisation to organisation (due to difference in size, structure, management style and ownership), common problems may be summed up as follows:

1. Increase in the number of cases to arbitration (including cases hard to defend), thereby raising cost both in terms of arbitration fees and work stoppages (due to loss of working hours of both the aggrieved employees and their witnesses).
2. Increase in the cost of training and recruitment for high labour turnover. Failure of the organisation to set right grievances with proper intervention frustrates the employees and at times they withdraw from the organisation either on their own or on organisational order. This leads to colossal loss, particularly in terms of training cost, which the organisation sustains either in a formal way (through training in outside institutions) or in an informal way (learning while at work).
3. Increase in frequent work disruptions cause production loss, create an adverse impact on market for non-compliance of purchasers' delivery schedules and thereby affects profitability.
4. Increase in hostility and loss of self-respect vitiate organisational culture, develop mistrust, which in turn seriously impedes productivity.

This necessitates proper handling of employee complaints, a checklist of which maybe devised as follows:

1. Put the aggrieved employee at ease.
2. Communication your gladness for his coming
3. Ask what he or she would like to discuss
4. Listen attentively
5. Sympathise with the employee
6. Explain what you expect to do
7. Set a follow up date.

Norms to Ensure Discipline in Organisations

By now it is clear that to ensure discipline in an organisation, a set of norms need to be followed. Such basic prerequisites are as follows:

1. The goals or objectives should be stated clearly. The rules must be in clear and unambiguous terms, with special mention of the standards expected of the workmen.

2. Such rules and regulations should be properly communicated and must be understood.
3. The authority to enforce rules must be specified.
4. The procedure for appeal by an aggrieved party should be specified.
5. The punishment prescribed should be made known.
6. The rules of conduct must contain provisions for investigation and settlement of grievances.

Causal Factors of Indiscipline

The problem of indiscipline is the culmination of multiple factors; for precisive solutions we need to consider the exact causal factor instrumental for indisciplinary behaviour of employees. In fact the causal factors may be:

1. the employee himself,
2. the supervisor, or
3. the organisation.

Employee indiscipline largely stems from the organisation itself. However, such employees too are not uncommon who, because of their intrinsic characteristics (which build their habits, strength and personality) by nature are aggrieved easily and nurture indiscipline, whose percentage though minute may influence the attitudes of other members of the organisation (at the conscious or unconscious level) and thereby threaten the smooth functioning of the organisation.

The supervisor may be the causal factor for inappropriate method of supervision and giving improper assignments and orders. The organisation becomes a causal factor with the use of unsound and unnecessarily restrictive policies and regulations and with improper expectations from the employees.

The organisation, to mitigate this problem, should:

1. Apply its rules with fair objectivity or uniformity.
2. Communicate to employees the consequences of their actions.
3. Adopt fair rules and directives and have reasonable expectations from employees.

Similarly supervisors, to minimise the problem of indiscipline should:

1. avoid inappropriate action in matching offences with sanctions,
2. ensure due process and equal protection as means of creating an organisational culture that supports employees' dignity and rights,
3. minimise the need for employees to pursue their rights through external channels such as arbitration, government and courts.

NEED FOR A DISCIPLINARY POLICY

To obviate the problem of indiscipline, every organisation should have a well defined disciplinary policy. A well defined disciplinary policy avoids management inconsistencies and promotes a climate of mutual respect, fair play and clear standards throughout the organisation. Disciplinary policy to a great extent stands on prevailing norms and legal requirements. But to make it more effective, management can instill its own philosophy (with a more humanitarian approach). Such a step will make the policy more flexible than a rigid or formal one, which perceives man as a passive organism. While framing a disciplinary policy, following principles should be adhered to:

1. A searching examination for the cause of indiscipline should always be made.
2. Disciplinary rules should be framed after due consultation with the workers or their representatives.
3. If any particular rule is infringed frequently, its causes should be investigated.
4. Rules should be considered as means and not as ends. Thus, rules should not be rigid.
5. Periodically rules should be checked up to understand whether changes are necessary in the light of the experience.
6. Rules should be enforced without any bias.
7. Rules should be strictly complied by the management people to set an example before others to emulate.

ROLE OF TRADE UNIONS IN DISCIPLINE

Trade unions to a great extent are responsible for indiscipline and violence, particularly in organisations which are unionised and where multiple unions exist. Different philosophies of trade unionism or different schools of thought perceive management effectively. Their expectations too at times vary. Thus, the 'economic advantage school' believes in maximisation of wage gains. The 'job security school' believes that long term security of employment is more important than short run maximisation of wages. The 'Marxist school' perceives conflict between capital and labour is inherent. The 'political school' emphasises the power conflict between management and labour over different basic issues such as the recognition of unions, collectively concerned with power and status. Such divergent schools of thought widely differ in their approaches. Unless management tries to integrate their own philosophies with trade unions, industrial relations are likely to deteriorate, which subsequently give rise to indisciplined and violent behaviour.

However, the influence of affiliated trade unions in industrial disputes in India does not seem to be a major problem, when we try to corroborate it with statistical data. Unaffiliated unions and others percentage share to total disputes in India, on an average is 85.23 per cent, percentage share of workers involved is 84.37 per cent and finally percentage share to total man-days loss is 93.7 per cent.

STEPS TO ENFORCE A DISCIPLINARY PROCEDURE

A systematic disciplinary procedure is essential to maintain established standards of work. Following steps are followed to enforce discipline in an organisation:

1. Calling for explanation
2. Consideration of explanation
3. Show-case notice
4. Notice of holding the enquiry
5. Punishment
6. Follow-up

Discipline without Punishment

John Huberman in his famous article *Discipline without Punishment* spelt out the methodologies to handle disciplinary problems in organisations with a positive disciplinary approach. He has suggested the following courses of action to rectify the indisciplined behaviour of employees in organisations:

1. No disciplinary demotions, suspensions or other forms of punishment be applied.
2. In case of disciplinary problems which may consequently give rise to unsatisfactory work performance (e.g., carelessness in handling materials, less attention to duty) or break of discipline (e.g., overstaying rest or lunch periods, absenting from duty, etc.) following steps should be followed:

   (a) The immediate superior will offer the worker a casual and friendly reminder on the job.

   (b) If the incident continues to recur, the boss will again try to correct it calling the individual to his office for a serious but friendly chat. The boss at this stage will explain the need for and purpose of the rules, and make sure the employee understands the same.

   (c) In case of further repetition of the incidents, the earlier step should further be repeated with some variation like verifying from the employee whether he is disliking the work. If that be the case, the employee may be told that it is better for him to look for some other job or line of work. This conversation may be further confirmed in a letter to the employee's home.

   (d) If the employee continues to be indisciplined even after 6 to 8 weeks from this period, he should be asked to go home with pay to consider seriously whether he does or does not wish to abide by the company standards. At this time he should be informed that recurrence of such behaviour will result in his termination.

   (e) If another incident occurs even after this, the employee's services are terminated.

Huberman contended that this approach to a significant extent changes the indisciplined behaviour of the employee and thus without directly taking any punitive measures, rectification/correction of the employees indisciplined behaviour becomes possible.

Opposed to this approach, we have McGregor's 'hot stove rule', which suggested infringing discipline should invite direct punitive measures to rectify the behaviour. Since we do not have sufficient studies to authenticate which disciplinary action is more appropriate, it is difficult to suggest a particular approach to handle disciplinary problems in Indian organisations.

Results of Survey on Disciplinary Problems

The author is his individual capacity has carried out a survey on disciplinary policy, at it is still now a dreaded causal factor of industrial disputes in India claiming maximum number of loss of man-days. The survey was carried out during 1995 covering 25 personnel managers, 50 supervisors and 100 workers of different trades drawn from 17 organisations, including public sector organisations. For the purpose of the survey separate set of structured questionnaires were made covering following areas:

1. Relations with fellow workers
2. Co-operation that they receive from co-workers
3. Perception about working conditions
4. Feelings about pay packets
5. Job satisfaction
6. Independent responsibility in job
7. Extent of agreement with management's idea
8. Whether suggestions are honoured by management
9. Feelings about the style of supervision
10. Knowledge and attitude towards company's disciplinary policies
11. Uniformity of policies – whether some get special privilege
12. Grievance handling procedures
13. Time usually taken for grievance redressal
14. Attitudes towards union
15. Perception of *gherao* and use of abusive language
16. Distribution of domestic hours and holidays.

Survey results have been grouped into two aspects: positive and negative. A note on public sectors has been given separately for obvious differences in work culture and organisational pattern with private sector. Management-union-worker relationship has also been shown separately and finally a conclusion has been drawn in the light of the survey to ensure discipline in an organisation.

Positive Aspects of Survey

1. A sense of belonging develops even in organisations where workers are not well paid because of their association with the company over a long period. Such feelings debar workers from being violent or agitated.
2. If the company can fruitfully convince workers about the present situation, which prevents management from acceding to workers' demand for higher wages, workers are prepared to sacrifice their present for future betterment.
3. A positive behavioural reinforcement helps management to accept workers' demand with some deviations without any effect on workers' discipline.
4. Institutional culture and prevalence of family hierarchical relations have positive effect on workers' discipline.
5. Friendly relations with an open door policy dissuade workers from being indisciplined.
6. An intrinsically indisciplined worker cannot remain in the group for long. The group in such cases often creates pressure on management to isolate such an element.
7. Communications in workers' language have positive effects on workers' behaviour.
8. Quick disposal of grievances is possible by forming joint worker-management committees at every operational level. Settlement of disputes at the originating level does not allow indiscipline to spread.
9. Absence of hierarchical barrier has positive effect on workers' discipline.
10. Slackened disciplinary policy, if followed uniformly, boosts a worker's loyalty towards the organisation and keeps them from being indisciplined on future issues.

Negative Aspects

1. Improper job distribution (where some are allowed to remain idle or given minimum job while some others are burdened with job pressure) aggressive workers in general.
2. Frequent changes of executives confuse workers as they are subjected to divergent approaches. This situation negatively affects workers' behaviour.
3. Workers view seriously when they are not allowed to approach higher officials for redressal of their grievance but receive orders directly from the top to execute jobs. This induces them to be indisciplined by disobeying orders or to justify their importance.

4. Simultaneous orders from different levels confuse workers and adversely affect discipline.
5. Young educated workers are more indisciplined than old illiterate ones.
6. A sense of insecurity regarding the future of the organisation impairs productivity and depresses workers. Such depression, if it is acute, takes the shape of violence.
7. Incomplete communication about the company's rules and regulations confuses workers and supervisors exercising their discretion in matters of leave sanction, overtime or acceptance of late comers. Disfavoured employees for obvious reason get dissatisfied and consequently nurture indiscipline.
8. Workers do not tolerate management's high-handed attitude indefinitely. They react on continuance.
9. Casual and *badli* workers are more indisciplined and violent in nature.
10. Workers in general become indisciplined due to prevalence of excessive noise, bad sanitation and improper humidification (causing much discomfort due to intolerable heat) in workplaces.
11. Workers, satisfied financially, look for other comforts in workplaces and such issues, if not considered by management, cause dissatisfaction. Such dissatisfaction develops indiscipline.

Some Points about Public Sector

1. Workers in public sector, for the obvious sense of service security, face the management even with minor discords. They, however, feel management can do nothing beyond defining rules and regulations.
2. Management is more biased in the public sector. 'Robbing Peter to pay Paul' recurs often, causing great harm to industrial relations.
3. Public sector seriously lacks in management expertise or professionalism to handle employee grievances. Even problems which can be solved within the organisation are left unattended, allowing aggravation of the situation and employees are virtually forced to take resort to the long-drawn legal system.

Steps to Ensure Discipline

1. Delegate authority for grievance handling (minor in nature) at the operation level, forming groups or committees with workers, unions and management's representatives.
2. Allow dissatisfied employees to represent their case in person to higher authorities (with suitable control).
3. Introduce suitable training packages as a continuous process for in-job development. Such training should be value laden.

4. Follow a standing disciplinary policy strictly framed after discussion with workers and adequately complying with legal requirements. Such a policy should be communicated to each and every worker.
5. Supervisors should know the extent of their authority. Any exercise of discretion causing dissatisfaction among others should be strictly debarred.
6. Organisational environment, responsible for workers' disgruntlement should be immediately looked into. Changes in line with requirements should be undertaken. If it is impossible for any technical reason or paucity of funds, communication to that effect should be made to the workers.
7. Orders for job execution should flow to workers from one channel only.
8. Job distribution should be proper.

Role of Personnel Administrator in Enforcing Discipline

1. To advise and assist top and line management to adopt and develop constructive management philosophy regarding employees and their conduct.
2. To assist in formulation of effective and positive disciplinary policies and procedures.
3. To communicate the policies to all the employees in the organisation.
4. To ensure that disciplinary policies and procedures are conforming to the legal provisions.
5. To enforce the policies strictly in an unbiased manner.
6. To ensure that disciplinary action is consistent with the principles of personnel management.
7. To train executives and supervisors in handling disciplinary problems and cases.
8. To involve the union and employees in the formulation and implementation of disciplinary process and measures.
9. To help to develop standards of self-discipline among the employees.
10. To win the confidence of employees in company policies and discipline.

Disciplinary Proceedings (Domestic Enquiry) Steps

Complaint

A written complaint from the supervisor about the commission of the act of misconduct is the starting point. This should give details of time, place and the incident.

Framing of Charge-sheet

1. The charge-sheet should be drafted in a clear and unambiguous language.
2. If the charge relates to an incident, date, time and place of occurrence should be mentioned.
3. The charge-sheet calling upon the employee to submit an explanation must specify the period of time by which the employee has to submit his explanation.

Suspension Pending Enquiry

If the act of misconduct is very serious, the employee may be suspended pending enquiry. It has to be made clear that during the period of suspension, pending enquiry, he will not leave station. Subsistence allowance is payable to him under the rules. He should give a declaration that he is not employed elsewhere during that period.

Issue of Charge-sheet

The charge-sheet should be served personally with acknowledgement. If he refuses to accept, the same should be sent to his local and home address under Registered Post A.D. as well as under certificate of posting. If the charge-sheet is returned undelivered, the envelope should be kept without opening. In this situation a copy of the charge-sheet should be displayed on the notice board.

Consideration of Explanation

1. The charge-sheeted employee may admit the charge and request for mercy; or
2. He may deny the charge and request for enquiry; or
3. He may not reply at all.

Enquiry Proceedings

1. If the charge is minor and the workman begs to be excused, no enquiry is required.
2. If his misconduct is serious enough to warrant discharge or dismissal, a proper enquiry is to be held before awarding punishment.
3. If he fails to submit the reply within the specified time-limit, steps should be taken to hold the enquiry. While issuing the notice for the enquiry, the employee should be requested to submit his explanation.
4. The Enquiry Officer should give full opportunity to employee to defend himself by cross-examining the witnesses produced by the management.
5. It is for the management to prove the charges against a workman and it is not the workman who has to prove his innocence.

Co-worker's Assistance

Depending on the provisions of standing orders and service rules a co-worker may be allowed to help the employee in domestic enquiry.

Exparte Enquiry

If the employee fails to turn up for the enquiry after being given sufficient notice, the enquiry officer may conduct the enquiry and take evidence as required.

Enquiry Report

The enquiry officer, after having gone through the entire records of the proceedings and giving his reasons for accepting or rejecting the evidence tendered in the course of enquiry, has to categorically state whether the charges are proved or not proved. He has to submit a written report giving his verdict and recommendation together with the reasons.

Final Action

The Competent Authority will go through the enquiry report and all connected papers/ exhibits and has the options to agree or disagree with the findings of the enquiry officer. If he does not agree, he has to give reasons before drawing his conclusions and awarding punishment. The employee should be informed in writing of the punishment.

CODE OF DISCIPLINE IN INDUSTRY

To maintain Discipline in Industry both in public and private sector there has to be (i) a just recognition by employers and workers of the rights and responsibilities of either party, as defined by the laws and agreements (including bipartite and tripartite agreements arrived at all levels from time to time) and (ii) a proper and willing discharge by either party of its obligations consequent on such recognition.

The Central and State Governments, on their part, are required to examine and set right any shortcomings in the machinery they constitute for the administration of labour laws.

To ensure better discipline in industry.

Management and Union(s) Agree

1. That no unilateral action should be taken in connection with any industrial matter and that should be settled at appropriate level.

2. That the existing machinery for settlement of disputes should be utilized with the utmost expedition.

3. That there should be no strike or lock-out without notice.

4. That affirming their faith in democratic principles, they bind themselves settle all future differences, disputes and grievances by mutual negotiation, conciliation and voluntary arbitration;
5. That neither party will have recourse to (a) coercion, (b) intimidation, (c) victimization or (d) go-slow.
6. That they will avoid, (a) litigation, (b) sit-down and stay-in strikes and (c) lock-outs.
7. That they will promote constructive co-operation between their representatives at all levels and as between workers themselves and abide by the spirit of agreements mutually entered into.
8. That they will establish upon a mutually agreed basis, a grievance procedure which will ensure a speedy and full investigation leading to settlement.
9. That they will abide by various stages in the grievance procedure and take no arbitrary action which would by-pass this procedure.
10. That they will educate the management personnel and workers regarding their obligations to each other.

Management Agree

1. Not to increase work-loads unless agreed upon or settled otherwise.
2. Not to support or encourage any unfair labour practice such as (a) interference with the right of employees to enroll or continue as union members, (b) discrimination, restraint or coercion against any employee because of recognized activity of trade unions and (c) victimization of any employee and abuse of authority in any form.
3. To take prompt action for (a) settlement of grievances, and (b) implementation of settlements, awards, decision and orders.
4. To display in conspicuous places in the undertaking the provisions of this code in the local language(s).
5. To distinguish between actions justifying immediate discharge and those where discharge must be preceded by warning, reprimand, suspension or some other form of disciplinary action and to arrange that all such disciplinary action should be subject to an appeal through normal grievance procedure.
6. to take appropriate disciplinary action against its officers and members in cases where enquiries reveal that they were responsible for precipitate action by workers leading to indiscipline.
7. To recognize the union in accordance with the criteria (Annexure-I) evolved at the 16th Session of the Indian Labour Conference held in May 1958.

Union(s) Agree

1. Not to engage in any form of physical duress.
2. Not to permit demonstrations which are not peaceful and not to permit rowdyism in demonstration.
3. That their members will not engage or cause other employees to engage in any union activity during working hours, unless as provided for by law, agreement of practice.
4. To discourage unfair labour practices such as (a) negligence of duty, (b) careless operation, (c) damage to property, (d) interference with or disturbance to normal work, and (e) insubordination.
5. To take prompt action to implement awards, agreements, settlements and decisions.
6. To display in conspicuous places in the union offices, the provisions of this Code in the local language(s).
7. To express disapproval and to take appropriate action against office-bearers and members for indulging in action against the spirit of this code.

Grievance Handling

ILO defined grievance as a "measure or situation, which concerns the relation between the employer and the worker or which affects or may affect the conditions of employment of one or several workers in the undertaking when that measure or situation appears contrary to provisions of an applicable collective agreement or of an individual contract of employment…." It may raise a questions of discipline and dismissal, the payment of wages and fringe benefits, working time, overtime, promotion, demotion, transfer, safety, job description and many other work related issues.

Grievance is defined as 'cause for complaints or annoyance'. Initially grievance handling was a one-step procedure. The worker directly approached the employer and a decision was given immediately. However, with the development of mass production facilities, increased number of workers and supervisors and complication of multi-tier organisational structure, the number of grievances in organisations have gone up considerably making it difficult to sustain grievance handling as a one-step procedure.

The best way to handle grievance is to deal with it in the shortest possible time and at the lowest possible level. Unfortunately not many establishments have a formal, laid-out procedure for dealing with grievances. In grievance handling, the role of personnel manager should be purely advisory and every effort should made to induct and train each supervisor in handling the grievances of his subordinates effectively.

Grievance Handling Procedure

The step-ladder procedure of grievance handling is a widely used technique. The stages are as follows:

1. The aggrieved employee approaches the immediate supervisor either in person or through a written application in a standard form within a week's time, i.e. from the period when he feels certain action of the management has resulted in a sense of grievance in him. The immediate supervisor (in accordance with the delegated authority and the type of grievance) discusses the grievance with the employee and gives his decision. A time-limit of two weeks can be given for this stage.

2. If the employee is not satisfied with the decision in the first stage, he may approach the departmental head with a written application in a standard form, for reconsideration of his case. The employee may be allowed to personally represent the case along with the co-worker. The departmental head should give his decision in 15 days' time.

3. The appeals at this stage would be handled by a joint committee consisting of an equal number of representatives of the union and management. A secretariat is provided to process the cases at this stage. This committee should also have a time-limit for appeals as well as for disposal of the grievance referred to it. This committee shall give its recommendation by consensus and agreement. Unanimous recommendations of the committee shall be accepted by the management who must issue orders accordingly. The union and management may also reverse the right not to accept the recommendations. Otherwise, it should be deemed to have been accepted by both. In the event of non-acceptance of the recommendations by either party or non-unanimity in the committee at this stage, the grievance may be forwarded by the committee to a high-level joint commitment.

4. At this stage the joint committee shall consist of top management and union representatives. Cases spilling over from the above stage as well as those brought up by either side will be considered and decisions taken for implementation. If disagreements still prevail, both the sides may refer it for arbitration.

With sincerity of purpose and an intention to resolve disagreements across the table a formalised procedure as above is bound to result in achievement of industrial harmony.

The above model of grievance handling procedure was adopted in the 16th Session of the Indian Labour Conference in 1958 as part of the Code of Discipline in a voluntary measure. Many progressive organisations have adopted the system with suitable modifications.

PRINCIPLES OF NATURAL JUSTICE

In a series of decisions, the Supreme Court made certain observations in dealing with delinquent employees. These are known as Rules of Natural Justice and require that:

1. The employee proceeded against must be informed clearly of the charges levelled against him.

2. The witness must be examined ordinarily in the presence of the charge-sheeted employee, in respect of the charges.

3. The employee must be given fair opportunity to cross-examine the witness.
4. The enquiry officer has to record his findings along with the reasons for the same in his report.

SUMMARY

Discipline means orderly and systematic behaviour, which is an important pre-requisite for organisational harmony. Absence of discipline or indisciplined behaviour may stand against achievement of organisational objectives. Every organisation, to enforce discipline, lays down certain procedures and norms, which employees are required to comply with.

Approaches to discipline differ from organisation to organisation. But most of them prefer to adopt a legalistic approach. Disciplinary proceedings follow certain well-defined steps. Problem of discipline can be avoided by adopting a well defined Grievance Handling System or else it can culminate to a collective problem of discipline in an organisation. Principles of natural justice should receive attention while handling grievances or a problem of discipline in an organisation. Handling discipline problems in an organisation requires specialised knowledge and skill. Hence a simulation game in the form of a role play has been appended for practice.

KEYWORDS

Progressive Discipline	Discipline without Punishment
Corrective Discipline	Positive Discipline
Negative Discipline	Grievance Handling
Hot Stove Rule	Step-ladder Procedure
Institutional Theory	Natural Justice
Contractual Theory	

REVIEW QUESTIONS

1. What are the steps necessary for corrective discipline? How positive discipline approach is different from negative discipline? Which approach you consider to be the best?
2. What are the causes of indisciplined behaviour in an organisation?
3. Briefly state common disciplinary problems. Prepare a checklist for resolving such problems.
4. Develop a disciplinary policy for an organisation covering at least four important areas.
5. What are the steps one should follow in initiating disciplinary action against an employee?
6. Discuss step-ladder system in grievance handling.

CASE STUDY

DISCIPLINE ROLE PLAYS

The use of disciplinary procedures in the workplace is one of the most fraught tasks that managers have to carry out. Not only managers are forced to take unpleasant action for the person being in disciplined, and unpopular with other members of the staff, they are also governed by different aspects of labour law which may even call for legal action for a wrong decision.

The basic purpose of a disciplinary procedure is not to punish but to bring improvement in performance or adherence to the rules. There are different ways of doing this. It can be very informal in the day-to-day course of events or strictly formal as per the laid down norms (recognised company procedures). The formal process starts with investigation of facts, setting of standards and defining the future course of action.

In any disciplinary interview the facts must be established. The reasons for the poor performance (or failure to comply with rules) and the degree to which the rules or standards were understood must be investigated. The process of disciplinary interview is very similar to any other formal interview but the degree of skills is different.

Some of the identified skills for disciplinary interview are:

- Assertiveness
- Questioning and probing for information and feelings
- Listening
- Establishing the facts
- Judgement on appropriate sanctions within the laid down procedure
- Judgement on degree of assistance required
- Judgement on the standards or targets for improvement
- Judgement on reliability of evidence and veracity of witnesses
- Control and dealing with emotion
- Influencing
- Control of conversations
- Gaining commitment and agreement.

By doing a discipline role play, we can practice following learning points and enrich following skills.

- General interviewing and communication skills, which cover questioning, listening, probing, summarising and observation of non-verbal signals.
- Investigating of the facts.
- Ensuring the employee has the chance to put their case.
- Possible dangers of making snap judgements and the need to make a judgement about the truth.
- The concepts of fair and unfair dismissal.
- The importance of dealing in facts and evidence, not opinion or hearsay.

Those who will be observing the role play (non-participating members) should try to answer the following questions as part of the review:

- What was the manager's attitude? Was it appropriate?
- How well did the manager establish the facts of the case?
- Was the employee given the chance to put his case?
- Was the procedure to be followed next, or for an appeal, made clear?

Contd...

General Information for All

Guru Transport is a established parcels carrier for several years with depots in all parts of the country. In these depots parcels are sorted as per delivery areas and reloaded during night shift on to delivery vehicles to ensure deliveries by next day.

At the Khidderpore depot there is a night shift of 16 people who work from midnight to 8 a.m., 5 nights a work. The depot is closed on Saturday night. A fleet of 20 vehicle operates daily from the depot. They deliver their loads in the morning and collect parcels for delivery elsewhere during the afternoon. These are returned to the depot, sorted and loaded out on the night truck vehicles.

The night shift is run by Debnil, an ex-driver, who has been night shift foreman for the last 5 years. The 16 staff have been there for several years although there are a few who are recent recruits. The company has never managed to recruit 16 staff who are happy to work permanently in night shifts. There are, therefore, 4 or 5 posts that are constantly turning over to the new staff.

On Saturday morning, Debnil rang the Depot Manager to say that he had suspended, with pay, one of the shift members and sent him home on the suspicion of theft. He has been told to return today for a disciplinary hearing with the Depot Manager. The man suspended is called Anil. The company disciplinary policy states that theft of company property or property of the company's customers is gross misconduct and is likely to result in summary dismissal. A digest of the company's disciplinary policy and rules is issued to all new starters and is occasionally re-issued with wage packets as a reminder. The last occasion it was re-issued was 6 months ago. The whole policy is available in the general office and a permanent notice is displayed on two notice boards in the depot, drawing attention to its availability to anyone wishing to see it or any of the other company policy statements that are held in the same place.

Brief for the Depot Manager

You are the manager of Khidderpore depot of Guru Transport. You have held the post for nearly 3 years. On Saturday morning you were phoned by Debnil, the night shift foreman, to be told that he had suspended one of his men for suspected theft and sent him home on full pay. You heard brief details and agreed that he appeared to have acted correctly.

You have investigated as much as you can, mostly by talking to Debnil, but also one or two of the night shift workers were able to confirm this morning what happened after Debnil had challenged the accused employee, Anil.

As far as you can determine, Debnil came out of the rest room at the end of a break period at about 3.30 a.m. ahead of the rest of the shift. Apparently, Debnil had left the room a few minutes earlier. Everyone else was in the rest room and began to follow Debnil out. Debnil tends to signal the end of the break by getting up and leaving. The staff then follow within the next couple of minutes, having packed away lunch boxes.

As Debnil came out on to the loading bay he saw Anil with his hands in a large parcel that had been ripped open. Debnil asked Anil what he was doing and he said that he had been trying to repack it. Debnil then noticed that Anil had some cameras sticking out of his pocket. The broken case was found to contain five similar pairs of cameras and the bent and torn packaging from another pair. The consignment note inside referred to the contents of the box as being 6 pairs of cameras. Debnil concluded that the cameras in Anil's pocket were the ones missing from the parcel.

Debnil was very suspicious and was fairly sure that Anil intended to steal these cameras. It was only because he had decided to come out of the same rest room in good time (because there was still a lot of work to be done), that he caught Anil at it. Anil had left the rest room early, Debnil thinks, to have the chance to open his box he thought might have contained something valuable.

Anil was told to go to the rest room while Debnil considered what to do, and was then sent home, at about 3.45 a.m., having been told by Debnil to be back on Tuesday for a hearing with you. There had been a few heated words, but Anil had eventually decided to comply, and one of the other men on the shift heard Anil saying, 'I will sort it out on Tuesday. You won't .... listen, you vindictive old.......!' as he left the rest room.

Contd...

Anil is comparatively new to the shift, having been taken on 12 weeks ago. He came from the local Employment Exchange with some good references. Debnil says his work is all right, but his attitude is a bit ill-mannered and hostile, and he does need a bit of chasing.

The disciplinary hearing is due to start shortly. You have invited Anil's shop representative (nominated by the union) to attend.

Brief for the Accused Employee

You are Anil and you have been employed for the last 12 weeks on the night shift at Khidderpore depot of Guru Transport. You came from working for the company, where you had been for the last 12 weeks, to earn more money by working nights.

You quite like the job. But the foreman, Debnil gets on your nerves. He never leaves you alone. Every time you straighten your back, it seems that Debnil is there telling you to get on with it. You have talked back a few times, accusing Debnil of picking on you.

On Friday night, you worked as usual and at about 2 a.m. you went to the toilet. On your return (and you had not been hiding or having a smoke or anything), Debnil came up to you and asked you where the hell had you been, and accused you of skiving when you told him. It was another example of Debnil's attitude to you.

During the break later, you had finished your snacks and, having left your newspaper at home, decided to get straight on with loading the van you were on before break. You knew there were plenty more vans to load before the end of the shift and the break was nearly over anyway. As you moved the first trolley to the back of the van a pair of cameras started to fall out of a damaged box in the piles. They looked a bit unsafe so you lifted the box out of the pile to put it to one side to mend them in a moment. You were examining what needed to be done, before fetching the tape dispenser, when Debnil came to the place and jumped to the conclusion that you had ripped the box and stolen the cameras.

A few heated words were exchanged, you shouted at him about all the times he had been picking on you for no apparent reason and Debnil, became all formal and told you to go and cool off in the rest room. The other blokes suggested you had better do as he said and a few minutes later Debnil came in, told you to get your things and go home. He said you were suspended on full pay and asked you to come in again on Tuesday to see the Depot Manager.

Brief for Debnil, the Night Shift Foreman

You have been the night shift foreman for the last 5 years. Most of the men on the shift have been with you for sometime. The turnover among the rest of the shift is quite high and when you get a new employee you like to make sure that they know who is the boss and get into the habit of doing a good night's work.

Your latest member of the shift, Anil, has been difficult. You have let him know what is required, but he has to have the last word and does not seem to accept that your job as foreman means that you have to supervise what people are doing. You have had arguments with him a few times. He seems to work reasonably well, but you don't think he really fits in your team.

On Friday, as you came out of the rest room after the break you found Anil with his hands in a ripped box and a pair of cameras in his pocket. He had left the rest room some time before and not returned. You asked him what he was doing and he came up with all sorts of excuses about mending the box. But he had the cameras in his pocket, not tape, and you checked that there was a pair missing from the box according to the consignment note on the inside. There was also a damaged package still inside the carton that was empty. Anil must have ripped it to get the cameras out.

He started shouting at you, calling you all sorts of things and you decided that now was not the time to start an argument with him and sent him off to the rest room. A few minutes later you had decided that the only thing you could do was to suspend him and then the manager would have to deal with it.

The chances are he will have to be sacked. That does not worry you too much, his reaction on Friday night was such that you would find it difficult to work with him again.

The hearing is in the Depot Manager's office in a few minutes.

Contd...

Brief for the Section Representative

You are the shop steward/section representative for the Khidderpore depot. You work in the warehouse during the day as a fork-lift truck driver.

Anil is a member of the union and when you spoke to him this morning you gathered that he intends to deny vigorously the accusation of theft raised against him. You don't really know the man, since he works at night.

His story is that he had moved a trolley with his broken parcel and several others on it and as he did so the cameras had fallen out. He said he had put them in his pocket for safety and extracted the box from the pile so that he could repair it. He would then have returned the cameras to it before taping it up again.

According to Anil, his foreman, your old friend Debnil, then went off the deep end and jumped to the conclusion that he was trying to steal the cameras. Anil also told you that Debnil has had it for him ever since he arrived to work here 12 weeks ago. An argument followed and Debnil suspended him tolling him to go home.

Theft is clearly described in the company's disciplinary policy as gross misconduct, so if Anil was stealing then he will probably be asked and there is not much you can do about it, but you will do your best to see that he gets a fair hearing and that there should be good reason to dismiss him if that is what is decided.

The Depot Manager has always been fair and you have never had to challenge a disciplinary decision before. This is, however, the first time that you have been involved in a case of gross misconduct with summary dismissal as the likely outcome.

Start the role play session, dividing your team into several groups. Each team member assuming some specific role, must read the scripts thoroughly and limit their discussions within the given information. You cannot stretch your imagination to unrelated areas. Separately keep a group of people to observe your discussions and give feedback on various aspects listed under review head at the end of the session. You can rotate the presentation group for getting new dimensions to this case. Also practice reversing your role in subsequent presentations.

Observation Sheet

Note both positive and negative observations below:

Points to Consider	Examples and their effect
Opening • Putting at ease. • Venue, seating, formality • Clarity; was the purpose explained?	
Middle • Sensitivity, use of questions, listening. • Control of pace. • Structure and direction. • Body language, approach and style. • Rapport and agreement. • Who is doing all the talking?	
Editing • Outcome, feeling at the end, acceptance or agreement. • Summary	
Overall effectiveness • Was the aim achieved?	

APPENDIX 1

Table 1: Number of Industrial Disputes in Public and Private Sectors during 1989 to 1998

Year	No. of Disputes			Number of Workers Involved			Number of Man days Lost			Average No. of Workers Involved per Dispute
	Public	Private	Total	Public	Private	Total	Public	Private	Total	
1	2	3	4	5	6	7	8	9	10	11
1989	615	1,771	1,786	918,400	445,854	1,364,254	5,739,612	26,923,765	32,663,377	764
1990	628	1,197	1,825	884,184	423,679	1,307,863	5,735,541	18,350,629	24,086,170	717
1991	653	1,157	1,810	787,921	554,101	1,342,022	4,144,505	22,283,587	26,428,092	741
1992	617	1,097	1,714	565,935	686,290	1,252,225	1,924,376	29,334,368	31,258,744	731
1993	359	1,034	1,393	565,152	388,715	953,867	2,291,547	18,009,106	20,300,653	685
1994	316	885	1,201	523,152	323,058	846,429	1,315,872	19,667,210	20,983,082	705
1995	343	723	1,066	725,227	264,468	989,965	4,793,516	11,496,053	16,289,569	928
1996	381	785	1,166	606,561	332,743	939,304	3,151,038	17,133,765	20,284,803	806
1997	448	857	1,305	618,360	362,907	981,267	2,180,565	14,790,824	16,971,389	752
1998	283	814	1,097	900,882	388,041	1,288,923	7,576,289	14,485,695	22,061,984	1,175

Source: Indian Labour Year Book, 1998.

Table 2: Number of Disputes by Strikes and Lockouts during 1989-1998

Year	Strikes			Lockouts		
	Number	Number of Workers Involved	Man days Lost	Number	Number of Workers Involved	Man days Lost
1	2	3	4	5	6	7
1989	1,397	1,158,107	10,695,112	389	206,147	21,968,265
1990	1,459	1,162,303	10,639,687	366	145,560	13,446,483
1991	1,278	872,482	12,428,333	532	469,540	13,999,759
1992	1,011	767,484	15,132,101	703	484,741	16,126,643
1993	914	672,024	5,614,515	479	281,843	14, 686,138
1994	808	626,326	6,651,054	393	220,103	14,332,028
1995	732	682,595	5,719,961	334	307,100	10,569,608
1996	763	608,673	7,817,869	403	303,631	12,466,934
1997	793	637,480	6,295,365	512	343,787	10,676,024
1998	665	800,778	9,349,108	432	488,145	12,712,876

Source: Indian Labour Year Book, 1998.

Contd...

Table 3: Industrial Disputes during 1997 and 1998 (By Industry Divisions)

Industry Code	Industry Division	1997			1998		
		Number of Disputes	No. of Workers Involved	No. of Mandays Lost	Number of Disputes	No. of Workers Involved	No. of Mandays Lost
1	2	3	4	5	6	7	8
0	Agriculture, Hunting, Forestry and Fishing	33	17903	544039	36	29200	427565
1	Mining and Quarrying	375	274144	891704	211	692775	5622913
2&3	Manufacturing	743	307730	13212990	676	266815	12168479
4	Electricity, Gas & Water	6	2809	29347	8	2844	11444
5	Construction	13	4584	53985	2	468	7542
6	Wholesale and Retail Trade and Restaurants & Hotels	17	1805	299463	17	2231	276652
7	Transport, Storage and 9 Communications	9	1430	93948	19	237994	1658358
8	Financing, Insurance, Real Estate and Business Services	20	349461	545875	13	11944	43797
9	Community, Social and Personal Services	43	6256	294398	50	5981	213612
10	Activities not Adequately Defined	46	15145	1005640	65	38671	1629622
	Total	1305	981267	16971389	1097	1288923	22061984

Source: Indian Labour Year Book, 1998.

Table 4: Industrial Disputes Trend

ITEM	2002	2003	2004	2005
A. No. of Strikes	295	255	236	227
No. of Workers Involved	900,386	1,010,976	1,903,054	2,722,784
No. of Man-days lost	9,664,537	3,205,950	4,828,737	10,800,686
B. No. of Lockouts	284	297	241	229
No. of Workers Involved	179,048	804,969	169,167	190,817
No. of Mab-days lost	16,921,382	2,70,49,961	19,037,630	18,864,313

Source: Labour Bureau, Shimla

Note: (P) = Provisional

N.B: Only those work stoppages which are on account of industrial disputes and which involve 10 or more workers, whether directly and/or indirectly are included in the statistics of Industrial disputes.

UNIT 22

Trade Unions and Labour

Learning Objectives

After completion of this unit, the students will be aware of the following topics:

- *Introduction*
- *History*
- *Importance of Unemployment and Balance of Payment Problems*
- *Rural Labour in India*
- *Absenteeism*
- *Labour Turnover*

PARTNERING WITH TRADE UNIONS – TIME FOR RECONSIDERATION

The economic slowdown subsequent to Lehman Brother's collapse in September, 2008 was a great challenge for the Airlines Industry and so also the trade unions in India and abroad. Jet Airways in India had to face the Pilots' strike for five days, causing huge loss for the company as well as for the nation. Jet Airways labour dispute in 2009, raises the question, can we sustain with this labour laws which are not in tune with the economic reforms and the changing business scenario. Like Jet Airways in India, British Airways also faced trade unions protests first on the cost cutting decisions of management and subsequently, on job cutting of 1000 administrative and 2000 cabin crew. To recover the financial crisis and to get back in full operations, the company decided to raise the fund through issuance of bonds. Both these plans of manpower rationalisation by right sizing and financial restructuring could encounter problems because of trade unions' protest. With crippling financial position, posting a recorded annual loss of £401 million, the company was in a fix.

Trade unions in both the above cases played the positive roles in accepting the pay cuts and compromising on several issues. While in the case of Jet Airways, the process was much easier, in the case of British Airways, it was not so easy. However, in both the cases, trade unions' preparedness to co-operate raises the question are our unions prepared to face the challenge of economic slowdown.

INTRODUCTION

Trade unions are voluntary organisations of workers. Through joint action, they protect and promote the interest of workers. With the setting up of large-scale industrial units, a new class of workers, dependent solely on wages for their livelihood, have emerged in India. In the absence of collective action, this working class had to be satisfied with wages, which they could individually negotiate with the employers. In such a circumstance, individual workers had virtually no bargaining power, perhaps for reasons of abundant supply of labour. Hence, the need for joint action at least to sustain, if not to improve, their bargaining power against the employers has been strongly felt. The pace of such action has been accentuated with the recognition by the community to form unions to institutionalise workers' rights to organise, to press for their demand collectively and to go for strike when their claims are not accepted.

HISTORY

The earliest known trade unions in India are:

1. The Bombay Mill Hands' Association, formed in 1890 for the purpose of urging the Government of improvements in factory law. However, it soon became defunct after the passing of the 1891 Act.

2. The Amalgamated Society of Railway Servants of India and Burma formed in 1897 by Anglo-Indians and domiciled Europeans employed in the Railways. This, however was more of a friendly association than to secure concessions.

3. Printers' Union started in Calcutta in 1905.

4. The Bombay Postal Union formed in 1907.

5. The Kamgar Hitwardhak Sabha, Mumbai in 1910. This was a body of social workers and not workers of the organisation. They were interested in general welfare of labour.

In the decade following the end of the First World War, we have witnessed in India rapid developments in the field of trade unionism. These were the beginning of the trade union movement in India. Within a period of five years (1919-1923) large number of unions were formed in different parts of the country. The movement initially had made an inroad in the Railways, in Postal and Telegraph Department, among seamen and in the Textile Industry in Ahmedabad city and also in some other centres.

Although individual unions were well accepted by the society almost since their stage of formation, employers in majority of the cases refused to recognise the unions on the plea that union executives consisted of outsiders. Workers interested in trade union activities were victimised by the employers. To thwart the trade union movement, the then employers succeeded to get an amendment passed in the Indian Penal Code in 1913, declaring trade unions as illegal bodies. The Buckingham & Carnatic Mills case of 1921 in Madras High Court, granting an interim injunction against the Madras Labour Union, further added to this fuel. At this point of time trade union leaders suddenly found that they were liable to prosecution and imprisonment even for bonafide trade union activities. In March, 1921, the Legislative Assembly of the Government of India, on the motion of Late N.M. Joshi, the then General Secretary of the All India Trade Union Congress (AITUC), passed a resolution for the registration and protection of Trade Unions. Since then, the pace of the Indian trade union movement continued unabatingly and reached its height during 1928-29, when communists wooed the world of Indian labour.

After the World War II and independence of the country in 1947, political considerations led to the division of trade union leadership. In 1947, Indian National Trade Union Congress (INTUC) was formed. The differences with the socialist workers inside AITUC, led to the formation of Hind Mazdoor Sabha and subsequently to the Central Indian Trade Union Congress (CITU), representing leftists. The socialists under the leadership of Dr Ram Manohar Lohia formed the Hind Mazdoor Panchayat and the Jan Sangh set up the Bhartiya Mazdoor Sangh. Since then four more Central Trade Union Organisations have been formed to accelerate the pace of Indian trade union movement.

Trade unions in India are associated mainly with the two international trade union federations, viz., the World Federation of Trade Unions (WFTU) and the International Confederation of Free Trade Unions (WFTU). In matters of industrial reactions and workers' productivity, trade unions play a crucial role. Relative strength of any particular union is determined from its membership details.

In the Table 22.1, we have furnished verified membership details of ten major Central Trade Unions in India.

Table 22.1: Ten Major Central Trade Unions in India

S. No.	Name of Trade Union	Membership as on 31.12.1980	Membership as on 31.12.1989
1.	INTUC	22,36,128	26,92,388
2.	BMS	12,11,345	31,16,564
3.	HMS	7,62,882	14,80,963
4.	UTUC (LS)	6,21,359	8,43,256

Contd...

5.	NLO	2,46,540	1,38,877
6.	UTUC	1,65,614	5,84,523
7.	TUCC	1,23,048	2,30,139
8.	NFITU	84,123	5,29,762
9.	AITUC	3,44,746	9,38,486
10.	CITU	3,31,031	17,75,220
11.	HMKP	-	3,516
12.	IFFTU	-	428
	TOTAL	61,26,816	1,23,34,142

Source: *Different Issues of Indian Labour Journal.*

In a very recently concluded survey, it has been indicated that BMS is having the highest membership followed by INTUC, CITU, HMS and AITUC. The latest membership details of the above five major Central trader union organisations are presented below:

Table 22.2: Major Central Trade Union Organisations

Organisation	Membership Claimed	Membership Verified
INTUC	54,35,705	25,87,378
AITUC	29,73,933	9,05,975
HMS	43,56,034	13,18,804
CITU	23,86,242	17,68,044
BMS	40,81,424	27,69,556

Source: *Business India*, August 29-September 11, 1994.

To authenticate the membership claim of different trade union organisations, Government is now urging the employers to affect deduction of membership fees from the pay of those employees who give such instruction in writing to them. Fees, thus, collected will then be diverted to the respective trade union organisations.

Number of registered unions (workers and employees) and their respective membership, verified from returns submitted by them for the years 1986 to 1996 are presented in the Table following:

Table 22.3: Registered Unions and their Respective Membership

Year	Number of Registered Trade Unions(E)	Number of Unions Submitting Returns	Membership of Unions Submitting Returns (In thousands)			Average Membership per Unions Submitting Returns
			Men	Women	Total	
1	2	3	4	5	6	7
1986	48,030	1,1365 (39.6)	7,370 (90.0)	820 (10.0)	8,190	721
1987	49,329	1,1063 (36.9)	7,211 (90.6)	748 (9.4)	7,959	719

Contd...

1988	50048	8,730	6,334	739	7,073	810
1989	52,210	9,758	8,207	1,088	9,295	953
1990	52,016	8,828 (46.4)	6,181 (88.1)	838 (11.9)	7019	795
1991	53,535	8,418 (36.8)	5,507 (90.3)	594	6,100	725
1992	55,680	9,165	5,148	598	5,746	627
1993	55,784	6,806 (26.3)	2,636 (84.1)	498 (15.9)	3,134	460
1994	56,872	6,277 (25.3)	3,239 (79.1)	855 (20.9)	4,094	652
1995 (P)	57,952	8,162 (24.6)	5,675 (86.8)	863 (13.2)	6538	801
1996(P)	58,805	7,309 (20.4)	4,259 (75.9)	1,354 (24.1)	5,613	768

Source: *Indian Labour Year Book, 1998*
Note: (E) Estimated
(P) Provisional

It is evident from the table percentage of registered unions submitting returns, over the years, have declined considerably. This also indicates dwindling trade union activities in the country.

Beginning from 1928-29 till 1970s, trade unions in India reached a commanding height. Almost all public sector units and major private sector organisations by this time have been unionised. However, since early 1980s we have seen the declining phase of trade unions in India. In fact from this period onwards the industrial restructuring process began in India.

With the announcement of the new economic policy of the Government of India in 1991, labour institutions and trade unions in India are now facing a challenging task ahead. The new economic policy poses following challenges to the trade unions:

1. Gradual shift of employment from the organised sector to unorganised sector. Out of the total labour force of 317 million in the country, the organised sector employs merely 26.8 million, i.e., only 8.5 per cent. Such shift in employment is a major phenomenal trend during post industrial restructuring process (began in 1980s). This trend obviously gives employers of the unorganised sector the advantage to flout labour laws.

2. The increasing emphasis on exports and emergence of free exporting processing zones in different parts of the country is again a major source of threat to the trade unions as such units are also getting the advantage to immune them from labour laws.

3. The growth of employment over the last few years has severely affected the industrial restructuring process. Added to this is the burden of unemployment as nearly four million people from the organised sector are likely to lose their employment in the process of the structural adjustment programme.

4. Closure of sick industrial units which employ 45 lakh people, sooner or later, will further add to the burden of unemployment. Government of India even though initiated to provide safety net under the Voluntary Retirement Scheme (VRS) to give some benefits to the workers thus losing their jobs, in reality, is yet to come out with any concrete proposal (excepting mooting of the idea). In a national level seminar organised by the

Indian Society of Labour Economics during 1992, the Department of Industries closely circulated a paper on proposed VRS, giving the details of the government's resolution on such count taken during February, 1992. However, the said scheme is yet to be operationalised, excepting in some select PSUs, who are going for disinvestment and private sector organisations. In both the cases, NRF money, which is primarily for helping organisations to withstand the pressure of liberalisation (by technological changes), is being unduly used, without any governmental intervention. There are wide variations in the VRS modalities. Only recently, government has proposed VRS in departmental undertakings.

5. To keep pace with the global competition accentuated by the market globalisation programme (an outcome of economic liberalisation policy), Indian industries are now required to introduce new technology. In industrial units conventional machines are now being replaced by Numerically Controlled (NC), Computer Numerically Controlled (CNC), Direct Numerically Controlled (DNC) Machines, Flexible Manufacturing System (FMS), etc. Such introduction of new technology is now making the traditional skills redundant, which necessitates redeployment of the workers after suitable retraining or replacing the workers (who cannot be retrained) by the new working force. This new working force being educated and skilled are mostly inducted in managerial or supervisory grades, resulting in reduction in employment of workers. In addition, new technology being more systematic is enabling the management to have greater control over the labour process. All these, therefore, severely erode the powers of the unions.

It is evident from the analysis of industrial dispute figures over the last few years that lockouts are responsible for more number of loss of man-days. This clearly indicates the reduced power of unions to influence the employment relations in the industrial units. The fact that the trade unions are losing their powers is evident from the fact that in many units, enterprise level unions are emerging. Such enterprise level unions are internal or independent unions having no political affiliation. Hence, in the context of the present scenario, it is expected that trade unions in India will have to make them more transparent and responsible to survive in the coming years.

Importance of Unemployment and Balance of Payment Problems

Ever since it started developing on a planned basis (since 1950-51), Indian economy is ailing from certain chronic economic problems. Among these problems, unemployment and rising balance of payment crisis have assumed critical proportions, especially since 1970. Without solving these two problems or at least reducing the acuteness of these problems, the Government of India or the Planning Commission cannot pay attention to the other more general problems. When unemployment is confined to only a section of the rural populations, government can give some dole to pacify the unemployed. But when the urban population also becomes unemployed to a substantial extent and particularly when they are educated unemployed, it becomes difficult to contain the situation; the situation becomes grave. Similarly, when the balance of payments deficit remains within reasonable proportion, government can pay attention to other internal problems. When the deficits increase over time, government has to borrow from agencies as India has drawn from IMF or government can see no way of either reducing the deficits or to find means for paying back the foreign money. Moreover, indebtedness creates psychological phobia both in the government and among the people whom the government serves. Therefore, the question of indebtedness gets top priority in the thinking of planners, policy makers and economists. There is an inherent difficulty in the situation. The problems of unemployment and balance of payment deficits cannot be taken up separately. It must be tackled together. Inter dependence between the level of employment and the extent of deficit is such that if the government takes a policy on reducing unemployment, deficit is likely to increase (as they are inversely related).

Interrelation between Unemployment and Balance of Payment Deficit

Let us now consider the following simple Keynesian income generation model. Let national income be denoted by 'Y' (a variable), C = consumption depending on 'Y' is also a variable. I = investment (autonomous and given). Investment is unpredictable because it is influenced by investors' behaviour. X = exports of the country also autonomous and given (depends on foreigners' demands for our goods). M = imports, a variable depending on Y, a part of the total consumption of good by countrymen.

Then $Y = C + I + X - M$

Since, I and X are constants we use bars on them. 'Y' or national income is measured as the total value of domestic outputs of final goods. Outputs of intermediate goods and raw materials are embodied in the calculation of final goods output. To avoid double counting, such outputs of intermediate goods and raw materials are not separately added again.

Thus, output of final goods consists of total consumption by the people of domestic goods, total investment, i.e. total purchase of machinery and any exports that have taken place out of the domestic output. All final goods, therefore, can be presented as below:

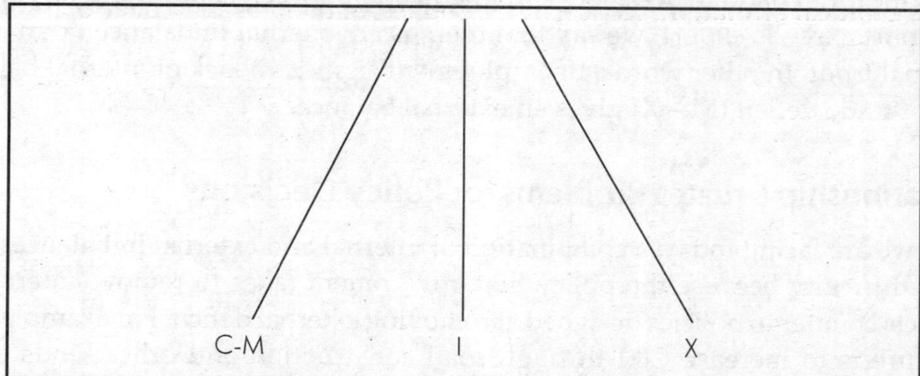

C – M = Consumption of domestic goods

In the above presentation, we have assumed that imports consists of only consumables, alternatively if there is some import of machinery that has been included in $\hat{I}$ (investment), then such imports are also substracted and the total subtraction is again M (imports) Now we can write final goods produced:

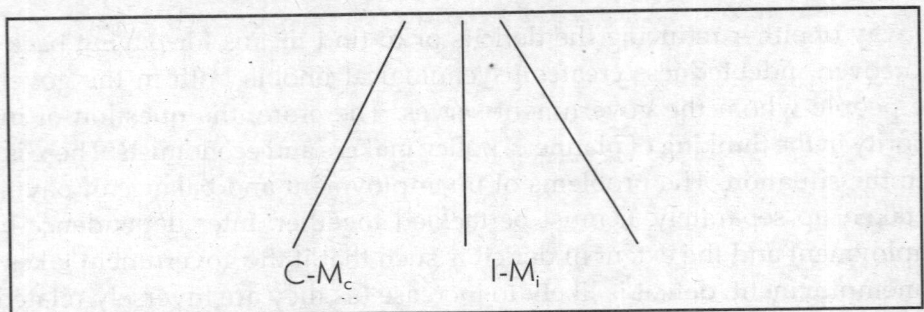

$C - M_c$	=	Consumption of domestic goods
$I - M_i$	=	Investment of domestic machinery
$X - M_i$	=	Investment of domestic machinery
M_c	=	Import of consumables
M_i	=	Import of consumables
Entire	=	$M = (M_c + M_i)$ to be subtracted

National output (finished goods) = National income

Y	=	$C + I + X - M$
C	=	Consumption of domestic goods and imports
I	=	Investment of domestic machinery and imported machinery
X	=	Exports
M	=	Subtract imported consumption and investment from C + I

When the national output produced (y) and spent for consumption, investment and exports cannot employ even a reasonable part of the country's resources, we say that there is imbalance in the economy. This imbalance is an 'internal imbalance', i.e. an imbalance on the domestic front. On the other hand, when there is an inequality between exports and imports, especially when import exceeds export, we say that there is an external imbalance or an imbalance on the external front. In other words, unemployment signifies a lack of internal balance and the balance of trade deficit ($M - X$) gives an external balance.

Interrelationship Creates Problems for Policy Decisions

In India, we are facing today, a combination of internal and external imbalances. This creates a special difficulty because the policy that government takes to remove internal imbalance usually acts counter to policies designed at removing external deficit. For example, government expenditure is to increase C&I through road construction and other kinds of short-term investment, even flood-relief, food for work programmes and the usual social benefit measures increase national output and level of employment. However, out of the new incomes created by these schemes a part go to increase income further in the hands of businessmen who sell the consumption and investment goods. With the extra incomes the businessmen in turn buy goods partly from the domestic market and partly from foreign market. Now there is already a deficit in the Balance of trade - $M < 0$ (negative). Now with M rising and stagnating, the balance of trade deficit or the imbalance on the external front worsens as a result of policies aiming at reducing unemployment.

In short unemployment cannot be reduced without raising incomes, a part of which must go to rich people also through increased business and imports tend to rise even if by a small amount. There is nothing in the mechanism that can close or improve the deficit on the external front.

The major difficulty in taking an anti-unemployment policy is, therefore, the existence of an external deficit which tends to get worse when income and employment increase. The standard fiscal (budgetary) and monetary (RBI's) methods are designed to boost the overall level of activity in a country so that both employment and national income increase. These methods are called the macroeconomic methods of raising employment. As we have seen, the existence of an external deficit in India discourages to some extent the macro-economic income raising policies taken up by the government.

There are, however, other methods of raising employment which are less harmful to the external balance. If a given output is produced by a labour intensive method rather than by an automatic and capital intensive technique, then the likelihood of increased business income and the resultant import diminishes. In the diagram, we have curved the various alternative methods of producing a fixed output. The equal output curve is called an iso-quant because output remains fixed as we move along the curve.

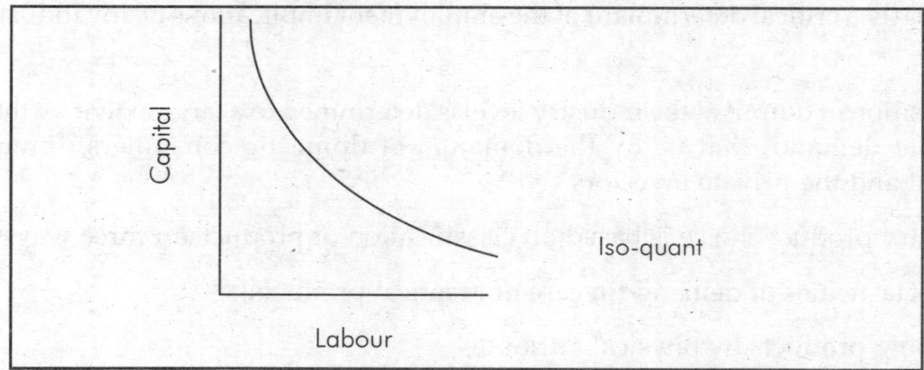

Figure 22.1: Equal Output Curve

As we go down less and less capital is used, more and more labour is used in substitution for capital and output neither increases nor diminishes. Clearly there is not one iso-quant but many iso-quants for various levels of output. At each level of output the capital-labour substitution possibilities are shown by one curve (and at another level of output by another curve).

If employment is raised through substitution of labour for capital without raising the output then the multiplier effect on national income may not operate strongly. Furthermore, though wage incomes increase, the owners of capital may receive less because less capital is used and it is not likely that imports should increase and balance of trade deficit should get worse.

We have seen that the first micro-economic cause of continued unemployment problem in India is a wrong choice of the technique of production, where labour can be substituted for capital without loss of efficiency, the businessmen should be induced to make such substitution. Left to themselves, the owners of the first do not always make such substitution because they are concerned about their own profits rather than the overall level of employment in the country. If the government takes a tax-cum-subsidy policy on the use of labour, wherever possible, then labour intensive techniques will be used by the producers. The tax-cum-subsidy policy will be designed to increase the effective price of capital by tax and to reduce the effective price of labour by a subsidy financed by the proceeds of tax.

The second cause for continued unemployment, also micro economic in nature, is the changing product-mix in the country. With the industrialisation, there is a natural tendency for employment to increase rapidly in all sectors. All industries grow, though at various rates and each industry employs more labour than before. The overall level of employment, therefore, should increase at a reasonably good rate.

In our country, however, the growth of national income is not accompanied by a satisfactory rate of growth in employment. The reasons for such decline in employment are:

1. Composition of the industrial production may have changed and new composition may be proportionately less employment potential than the previous composition.

2. Within an industry, technology may have changed and technology with much less employment potential may be much more common now than before.

The particular product-mix to be manufactured, at both inter-industry and intra-industry levels, is clearly a critical determinant of the employment implications of any industrialisation strategy.

The composition of output at the industry level is determined to a large extent by the structure of aggregate demand, that is, by the demands of domestic consumers, foreigners, the government and the private investors.

Intra-industry product choice is based on classification of products in three ways:

1. Cross-elasticities of demand (in case of identical products);
2. Grouping products by physical attributes;
3. Classification as per characteristics.

After deciding which goods should be produced or more realistically, in conjunction with that decision, a decision still has to be made as to how they are to be produced, with what technology and factor proportions.

Appropriate technology may be defined as the set of techniques, which makes optimum use of available resources in a given environment. Detailed product-by-product studies are the surest way of estimating the extent to which the adoption of more appropriate techniques can be expected to increase labour use. At least, it should not be forgotten that as long as the marginal productivity of labour is positive, every increase in employment increases the productivity of capital and, therefore, increasing employment always raises output.

The concept of labour intensity is used in three senses:

1. Share of labour input in the total value of output;
2. Wages as percentage of the value added;
3. Employment component of productive capital or of output.

The rates of substitution between capital and labour are different in different industries and are different at different levels of output. Let us consider the technology equilibrium below:

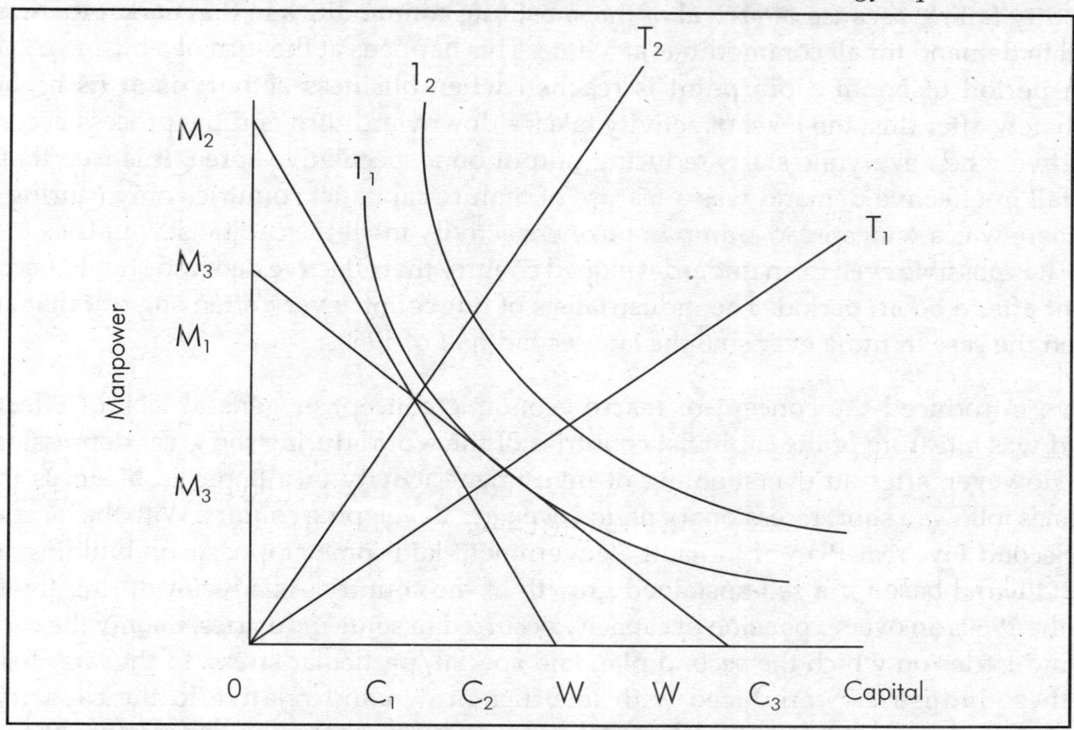

Figure 22.2: Technology Equilibrium

I_1, I_2 are different iso-quants for different levels of production. The entrepreneurs would be indifferent to the factor-mix at each of these curves but he would always try to move on to the higher curve so long as economies of scale will allow. The actual decision about the level of production would be guided by technological possibilities and factor endowments. On iso-quant I_1, all points, such as a,b,c, are of equal significance to the entrepreneur, but the alternative technologies may not be available on all of them. If only two technologies, namely, OT_1 and OT_2 are feasible, the considering X axis to represent capital and Y axis manpower, OT_1, would be a capital intensive technology whereas OT_2 would be a labour intensive technology. Suppose OC_2 is the invisible capital resource available in the economy under technology OT_1 then only OM_1 amount of manpower could be employed. In case OM_3 represents the available manpower in the community, then $M_1 - M_3$ would be the quantum of unemployment. To provide full employment, technology OT_2 may implies that C_1C_2, the surplus capital resource, may depress the rate of interest thus making substitution of labour more plausible. For obtaining full employment with OT_1, the amount of capital required would be OC_3, indicating the need for additional technology OT_1 to technology OT_2 would require much capital judgement on economic parameters and considerable administrative re-organisation. Such changes to be stable and effective will have to be supported by technical training, managerial improvement, appropriate fabricating equipment, better entrepreneurial motivation and the workers' adoption to the new production organisation; restraint on militant trade unionism, changes in labour laws, readjustment in rates of interest and wage and elimination of artificial support to one factor against another will also be essential. Much political overtones are in-built in these considerations, which make the decision very sensitive to various non-economic influences.

The third reason for unemployment is macro-economic in nature. J.M. Kenes, in 1930, brought into economics the concept of lacking effective demand. Instead of the demand for one commodity falling because of arrival of the substitute commodities in the market there may be a fall in demand for all commodities at a time. This happens at the turn of a business cycle. After a period of boom a pin point is reached when business activity is at its highest. Immediately after this, the level of activity takes a downward turn and the process becomes cumulative when everyone starts reducing output on a speculative spree. It is true that an actual fall in effective demand was a feature of mature capitalist countries only (during the 1930s there was a widespread slump in business activity in all the capitalist countries in the world). It is possible even in an underdeveloped country that effective demand should become stagnant after a boom period. The industrialists of our country very often suggest that such has been the case in India ever sine the late second half of 1960s.

We have introduced the concept of macro economic concept or general lack of effective demand was a feature of the capitalist countries of the world during the great depression of 1930s. However, after an overshooting of investment activity or a boom in business there sometimes follows a short recessionary period even in a developing country. With the inception of the Second FiveYear Plan of India, the government laid some emphasis on building up a good industrial base for a self-sustained growth of the country. As a result during the first half of the 1960s an over expansion of capacity occurred in some industries, mainly the capital goods industries on which the second plan laid special/particular stress. In the later half of 1960s these industries were faced with insufficient demand relative to the capacity of production. A general recession in all capital goods industries set in. In this manner at a very early stage of development the Indian business community was faced with what is usually a feature of mature capitalist countries alone. During the 1970s there was some revival from the recession even in the capital goods industries. The consumer goods industries on the other hand were faced with a different kind of demand problem. The prices fixed for many durable consumer goods are such that even in a vast country like India, there cannot be much demand for these goods. The demand comes from an exclusive class of people which has very few members.

Capacity under utilisation may also be attributed to as an important economic cause for unemployment in India. Capacity under-utilisation has increased from 20 per cent to 30 per cent during the fourth plan period alone. Labour unrest, material shortages, transport bottlenecks, power failures, managerial shortcomings, shortage of demand, ambitious project planning, etc., may be held responsible for capacity under-utilisation. Apart from these, structural characteristics of the Indian industries, i.e. monopoly, oligopoly structure may also be held responsible for widespread unemployment. Monopolists restrict their output to reach high profits in the protected market.

The above being the main causes of unemployment in India, the appropriate policies for reducing unemployment should be as follows:

1. The first and foremost cause was a wrong choice of technique of production. The government policy should be a combination of subsidy and tax to favour the labour intensive method of production in preference to an equally efficient capital intensive one.

2. The second cause is the development of a product-mix in which the weight of those goods is increasing which are naturally less labour intensive than the industries which they are replacing. The government policy under plan perspective should be based on a comparison between two different goals of increasing national income and increasing employment. If it is considered that reducing unemployment is more important than national income then some of the highly productive modern industries should be given disincentives and traditional labour intensive industries should receive encouragement from the government. This can also be done by means of taxes and subsidies selectively applied.

3. The third or macroeconomic cause is more difficult to cure. In this case, a tax-cum-subsidy method will not work because there exists a general lack of demand not for selected industries which can be helped by the government but for many industries at a time. One method of tackling this problem is a redistribution of income in favour of those people whose propensity to save is low. From the circular flow of income and demand from goods the saved parts of income are withdrawn. If income is re-distributed in favour of those who save less and consume more then the withdrawn part diminishes and most of the income flows back to the industrialists in the form of fresh demand for goods and as a result new employment is created. This situation is for generating mass incomes, which create demand for commodities consumed by the common people, for example, coarse clothes, bulk drugs, commercial vehicles, railway wagons, bushes, cheap radios, bicycles, electronic gadgets, etc., and the unemployment can be substantially reduced by means of mass production of these commodities. The erstwhile socialists countries, in spite of similar problems as we are facing, have made good progress in increasing the level of employment by keeping income distribution fair. Their recent political change-over, however, aggravated the problem of unemployment.

Table 22.4: No. of Units effecting lay off and Workers laid off by different causes during 1987-1992

	1987		1988		1989		1990		1991		1992	
Cause	**Units**	**Workers**	**Units**	**Workers**	**Units**	**Workers**	**Units**	**Workers**	**Units**	**Workers**	**Units**	**Workers**
Shortage of power	333	100593	225	60727	206	41283	178	35933	131	28661	166	60187
Shortage of raw material	128	14533	123	15856	141	13076	107	8246	127	18854	72	12882
Breakdown of machinery	47	4246	35	4466	31	2882	27	1576	29	3577	40	6221
Lack of demand	113	8800	103	3859	76	2929	63	1817	82	3157	60	2391
Financial Stringency	35	8524	38	6025	36	3973	24	2771	36	2235	16	3973
Off season	0	0	1	78	1	19	1	10	0	0	0	0
Others	53	8229	52	14098	47	6491	42	13718	56	14576	54	10261
Total	709	144925	577	105109	538	70653	442	64080	461	71060	408	95915

Source: Labour Bureau, Shimla

Table 22.5: Cause-wise Number of Units effecting Retrenchment and Workers Retrenched during 1987-1992

	1987		1988		1989		1990		1991		1992	
	U	W	U	W	U	W	U	W	U	W	U	W
Financial Stringency	50	618	60	687	32	529	77	958	40	611	29	1632
Shortage of Raw Materials	21	470	17	320	14	192	14	318	11	173	4	83
Shortage of Power	2	29	2	237	3	20	2	16	0	0	1	16
Breakdown of Machinery	0	0	1	33	1	13	0	0	2	9	1	10
Lack of demand	149	1210	186	1957	69	518	100	1073	100	1345	97	810
Off Season	103	2566	101	1607	50	1962	69	615	69	2035	40	711
Not known	29	267	12	173	5	24	5	55	13	223	3	16
Total	356	5202	379	5014	174	3258	268	3037	235	4369	175	3338

Source: Labour Bureau, Shimla
Notes: U = Units, W = Workers, P = Provisional
Data of 1992 is from January – November,

Table 22.6: Distribution of Strikes and Lockouts by Different Causes during 1987-1992

	1987		1988		1989		1990		1991		1992	
Causes	S	L	S	L	S	L	S	L	S	L	S	L
Wages and Allowances	423	61	413	60	391	34	406	36	367	68	167	44
Bonus	94	41	83	34	92	16	64	8	58	12	9	10
Personnel	209	27	202	27	274	26	225	11	212	58	65	29
Retrenchment	61	3	58	1	36	3	46	8	35	4	9	3
Leave & Hours of Work	18	4	17	11	18	3	26	1	50	2	5	9
Indiscipline and violence	62	184	72	196	100	175	114	171	111	223	29	165
Others	447	122	424	101	446	112	552	107	456	151	192	96
Not Known	34	9	35	11	40	20	30	24	24	40	11	8

Source: Labour Bureau, Shimla
Notes: S = Strikes, L = Lockouts, P = Provisional 1992 data is upto November

Table 22.7: Growth of Registered Trade Unions and their Membership, 1991 to 2002

Year	No. of registered Trade Unions	No. of Unions submitting returns	Membership of Unions submitting Returns					Average membership per union
			Men		Women		Total Membership ('000)	
			Number ('000)	Percentage to total	Number ('000)	Percentage to total		
1	2	3	4	5	6	7	8	9
1991	53535	8418 (15.7)	5507	90.3	594	9.7	6100	725
1992	55680	9165 (16.5)	5148	89.6	598	10.4	5746	627
1993	55784	6806 (12.2)	2636	84.1	498	15.9	3134	460
1994	56872	6277 (11.0)	3239	79.1	856	20.9	4095	652
1995	57952	8162 (14.1)	5675	86.8	863	13.2	6538	801
1996	58988	7242 (12.3)	4250	75.9	1351	24.1	5601	773
1997	60660	8872 (14.6)	6504	87.8	905	12.2	7409	835
1998	61992	7403 (12.0)	6104	84.2	1145	15.8	7249	979
1999	64817	8152 (12.6)	5190	81.0	1218	19.0	6407	786
2000	66056	7253 (11.0)	4510	83.2	910	16.8	5420	747
2001	66624	6531 (9.8)	4392	74.8	1481	25.2	5873	900
2002	68544	7812 (11.4)	5102	73.2	1871	26.8	6973	893

Source: Labour Bureau, Shimla

N.B.(1) Figures in brackets in column 3 denote percentages of Unions submitting returns to total number of registered Unions.

(2) The figures of Trade Unions are exclusive of Federations in all the Statements.

(3) Figures in Col.2 are estimated by incorporating the latest available information of the non-responding States.

Rural Labour in India

In India more than 219 million people are engaged in agricultural activities. Adding the non-agricultural employment in the rural areas, the percentage of employment in the rural sector is as high as 65.5 per cent of the total workforce of the country.

The National Commission on Rural Labour submitted its report to the government in July, 1991. The economic reforms programme of the Government of India hardly gave any emphasis on the prospectus for agricultural and rural labour. The major features of the rural labour scene in India may be enumerated as follows:

1. The rural force, whether in agriculture or in non-agriculture is growing at a faster rate than the population growth in rural area. This is particularly for reasons of decline in the proportion of self-employed households in agriculture, which is primarily for reasons of continued sub-division of holdings. This renders self-employed labour force in rural area redundant compelling them to join the ranks of wage labour. In non-agriculture, employment in rural areas (household industries) is declining under the impact of technologically efficient modern industries.

2. Substitution of capital for labour in agricultural is also responsible for decline in rural employment.

3. Slow rate of public investment in agriculture is also responsible for deceleration in employment of rural labour. Government level survey in 1991 indicates growth of employment in rural areas decelerated from 2.5 per cent per annum during the seventies to less than 1 per cent over the eighties.

4. Rural labourers in India have very little access to the minimum needs like education, health care, drinking water, fair price shops/public distribution system, social security benefits, etc. Thus living conditions of rural labour have not improved even though socio-economic development process improved the levels of living conditions of a small section of working class, i.e. the urban workers in organised sector.

5. The economic reform process by reducing the farm subsidies is further affecting the rural employment as farm owners will henceforth be more interested to employ technology efficient systems to increase the agricultural output replacing agricultural workers.

6. There is an increasing trend to corporatise the agriculture under large industrial units both by employing technology efficient production system and by using improved variety of seeds. Such corporatisation process on one hand resulted in taking over of small landholdings, replacing the workers engaged therein and on the other reduced the overall rural employment substituting capital for labour.

7. Another recent phenomena is to emphasise on the selection of crops. It is evident that most of the agricultural land is now embarking on production of commercial crops, which are used as inputs of industries. Long range reaping of benefits by shifting the cultivation from food crops to teak wood is also a major phenomenal change in Indian agriculture. Since such crops, i.e. commercial crops and teak wood relatively require less labour inputs (as they require more technology-efficient monitoring system), overall employment in the rural areas is significantly decreasing in the recent years.

The economic reform programmes of Government of India utterly ignored the importance of rural or agricultural employment which still enjoys a high percentage of total employment share in India. The National Commission on Rural Labour emphasised on the need for developing rural human resources, providing social security to the rural workers, provisioning employment guarantee and also strengthening public distribution of essential commodities, in line with the on-going economic reforms programme to improve the living standards of rural labour.

Very recently, government has instituted Employment Assurance Scheme (EAS) to ensure wage employment to the rural labour at least for 100 man-days during the lean agricultural season. To start with, the scheme has been implemented in 1,700 backward blocks, primarily situated in drought prone desert, tribal and hill areas. A Revamped Public Distribution System (RPDS) is also in operation. Water and soil conservation, afforestation, agro-horticulture, silvipasture under watershed development and minor irrigation works are also on the priority agenda of the government. To promote equity, social justice and human resource development, it is, therefore, necessary to augment government sponsored activities in the rural areas as a part of the on-going reform process. We have discussed some of the recent schemes, in the chapter on Human Resource Planning.

Absenteeism

Absenteeism is a total man-shifts lost because of absences of the total number of man-shifts scheduled to work. It, therefore signifies unauthorised, unexplained, avoidable and willful absence from work. Normal absence is excluded from this category as an employee usually takes leave of absence with prior permission of the authority to meet his own personal exigencies. Such exigencies may be on the ground of sickness, certain domestic eventualities, accidents, etc. In all the cases, an employee may not take prior permission from his employer but may regularise his absence giving an intimation within a scheduled period of absence. In most of the cases, if an employee remains absent from work for more than three consecutive days without any intimation, it is considered as willful or unauthorised absence. This, therefore, makes an employee liable to give intimation within three days from the date of his absence to regularise his leave. Absenteeism is, therefore, a willful or habitual absence from work and not any other types of absence.

Willful or habitual absence contributes to production loss and, therefore, it is a major problem for the management. The problem of absenteeism at macro level in India varies from industry to industry. Such rate normally varies from 7 per cent to 30 per cent in mining, textile, jute plantation and engineering.

Although there are a number of studies on problems of absenteeism at unit level, macro-level data on absenteeism in India is yet to be available to study the phenomenon both behaviourally and economically.

National Productivity Council carried out a survey to understand the magnitude of absenteeism and found that personal sickness, family sickness, domestic and social exigencies are the most important factors for absenteeism in Indian industries. Other factors of absenteeism like drunkenness, poor interpersonal relationships, genuine transportation problems, need for leisure, etc. are responsible for relatively less percentage of absenteeism. Whatever may be the factors for absenteeism, any organisation needs to ensure better working environment, good interpersonal relationships, less industrial fatigue, adequate welfare facilities, motivation, quick redressal of grievances for reducing the rate of absenteeism. If all the above measures do not succeed, organisations need to educate workers and give counselling to make them aware of the effect of absenteeism, duly mentioning the financial loss sustained by them (in terms of wage-loss) and problems which the organisations suffer.

Labour Turnover

Labour turnover is the rate of change in the working hands of a particular organisation during a given period. It, therefore, signifies the shifting of workforce from one organisation to another and also the loss of manpower due to discharge, retirement, death, etc.

The rate of labour turnover is expressed in terms of accession and separation rate. Accession is addition to the workforce while separation is deletion from the workforce, for any of the reasons mentioned above. Labour turnover is a serious problem for the industry because of the following reasons:

1. High cost of recruitment to effect replacement;
2. High training cost;
3. Loss of supervisory and managerial time;
4. Slow rate of output of the new incumbents;
5. Damage to the plant and machinery;
6. High rate of scrap and waste, etc.

In India due to less scope for job-mobility, labour turnover, job change or job switch is not a serious problem except in some particular occupations where knowledge and skill of workers is relatively more. In high profile jobs, turnover is more for the obvious increased scope of job switch.

To encounter the problem of labour turnover, it is necessary for the organisation to initiate same action as pointed out in the case of managing the problem of absenteeism earlier. However, little more attention is required to sustain employee motivation fulfilling both their intrinsic and extrinsic needs.

Summary

Economic inequality in India is a perennial problem, leading to poverty and unemployment in India. Along with the initiatives of the Government to bring order at the macro level through required initiatives, side by side, trade unions are also playing their role at the organisation level. Trade unions as institutions today are recognised worldwide, not just to fight against inequality in employment practices at the organisation level but also to bring social order. The trade unions in India celebrated its centenary in 1992. Characteristically, Indian trade unions can be grouped under two main categories: politically affiliated unions and the independent unions. The politically affiliated unions are those who are having links with one or more political parties. Characteristically, such unions federate themselves industry wise, and also geographically.

With the changing economic order, globalisation and change in the structure of employment, including the new generation of knowledge workers, trade unions membership is day by day decreasing. In many organisations, however, trade union actively partners with the management and with joint effort, extends the support to the organisation to survive the economic challenges. Human resource managers need to understand the dynamics of managing the trade unions.

KEYWORDS

Trade Unions	Absenteeism
Rural Labour	Employment
Unemployment	

REVIEW QUESTIONS

1. Briefly point out the history of trade union movement in India.
2. Do you think trade unions in India are becoming defunct institutions? Give adequate justification for your answer.
3. What are the challenges being faced by the Indian trade unions in recent years? Briefly discuss in the context of the recent economic liberalisation programme of the Government of India.
4. In what way unemployment is related to balance of payment problems? What are your suggestions to solve such problems?
5. Briefly discuss Keynsian Income Generation Model in relation to unemployment and balance of payment deficit.
6. What are the different types of unemployment? In India what types of unemployment are more prevalent and why?
7. Briefly discuss the present employment situation in India in relation to the current economic liberalisation programme of the Government of India.
8. Do you think that in India we are experiencing a change in the occupational pattern? Give justification for your answer.
9. In what way technology upgradation influences employment in India?
10. What are the problems of rural labour in India? What major roles the National Commission for Rural Labour has played to alleviate such problems?
11. Briefly discuss the problems of absenteeism in Indian industries.

12. Write short notes on:
    (a) Human Capital
    (b) Internal Labour Market
    (c) National Renewal Fund
    (d) Voluntary Retirement Scheme
    (e) International Economic Imbalance
    (f) Technology Equilibrium
    (g) Educated Unemployment
    (h) Economically Active Population
    (i) Labour Turnover
    (j) Knowledge Workers.

CAE STUDY

TKML – THE CASE OF MANAGEMENT SPARKED INDUSTRIAL RELATIONS PROBLEMS

Toyota Motor of Japan and Kirloskar Group, India entered into a joint venture to start car-manufacturing unit near Bangalore, Karnataka in 1997 with a whooping investment of ₹ 7 billion. Although the joint venture was initially started with equal shares of both Toyota and Kirloskar, gradually in a phased manner it was taken over by Toyota, resulting in increase of Toyota's holding of 99% against Kirloskar holding of 1% in 2003. Kirloskar's miniscule holding gradually reduced its control over the venture, and gradually Toyota took over the venture for increasing the market presence. The Toyota Kirloskar Motors Limited (TKML) employs 1,819 workers, both on regular and contractual pay roll.

Japanese managerial practices are highly culture specific and literally, a mismatch for many other countries of the world, including India. Much before Toyota Motor's entry into the U.S. market, Mazda of Japan did enter into the U.S. market, but for imposing the Japanese managerial practices, had to withdraw and close their units. However, Toyota Motors in the U.S.A today is a success story, for embracing the American management practices and matching the same with the Japanese managerial practices, the resultant effect of which is the development of theory 'Z'. In TKML venture, however, Toyota did not follow their success lessons in the U.S. market, causing incongruence in the work environment. The major causes of strike and so also the labour unrest in TKML can be attributed to preferential treatments and favourable managerial practices for the Japanese workers, against the local recruits.

Automobile and auto component manufacturing receives high-priority sector status in India. To make the state more industry friendly and attract foreign investment, the government of Karnataka conferred automobile sector-the status of a Public Utility Service (PUS) and accordingly, brought new amendment to the Industrial Dispute Act, debarring workers from any strike. Simultaneous amendment to the Contract Labour Act, also empowered TKML to outsource its activities without any restriction and even provided the unfettered right to appoint on contractual terms. All these are in addition to other usual benefits for the investors in the State of Karnataka.

The TKML, right from the beginning, imposed the Toyota Production System (TPS), in-built with the Japanese 'kanban' or 'Just In Time' production strategy with higher work load and job related stress. The pull production strategy at the TKML, is a discretionary work time, computed based on the ratio of total available task time to the total demand for the output. This is conventionally known as tact time, which leads to multi-tasking, and requires overwork of workers. TKML made this as the measure of efficiency, i.e., ultimately a compelling pressure on workers to overwork. Every worker at the TKML has to comply with tact time. The second compelling reason for workers' unrest at the TKML was the system of performance appraisal. Most of the performance criteria like; teamwork, attitude, behaviour, adaptability, etc. are difficult to define and according to workers, can be manipulated. Tangible performance criteria like, attendance, quality, etc. are non-discretionary being verifiable. The system of performance appraisal being more subjective conferred the discretionary power to the supervisors and managers to discriminate the management practices. The TKML management enjoys the right to terminate the workers on poor performance ground. The spirit of performance appraisal system, therefore, is to develop the hierarchy among workers, working in the same position and doing the same nature of jobs, resulting in weakening of the class-consciousness, vitiating the minds of the workers. In addition to the above, poor wages, disciplinary actions, punitive measures, etc., culminated to successive workers' unrest at the TKML in 2001, 2004, 2005 and 2006 and subsequent lockout of the company. The case of TKML, therefore, sparked typical industrial relations problems.

Question:

1. Critically evaluate the HR policies of the company.
2. Do you think TKML could avert such problems of workers' unrest with proactive HR policies?

UNIT 23

Collective Bargaining

Learning Objectives

After completion of this unit, the students will be aware of the following topics:

- *Introduction*
- *Important Assumptions to Achieve Stable Collective Bargaining*
- *Role of Government in Collective Bargaining*
- *Characteristics of Collective Bargaining*
- *Importance and Need for Collective Bargaining*
- *Prerequisites for Collective Bargaining*
- *Collective Bargaining in India*

INTRODUCTION

Collective bargaining is a method to determine working conditions and terms of employment through negotiations. Negotiations take place between 'employers' organisations and one or more workers organisations. Negotiations helps to reach an agreement. Collective bargaining is considered as an economic institution and trade unionism by forming a labour cartel restricts the entry into the trade. This theory of industrial democracy was advocated by Webbs. Alan Flanders (1975) discarding this concept advocated that collective bargaining is basically political as it aims to protect dignity rather than economic interest. Marxist school considers the collective bargaining as a means of social control. The marketing concept considers collective bargaining process as a constitutional system to determine relations between management and trade unions. Finally industrial relations concept views collective bargaining as a system of 'industrial governance'. In practice, however, we do not consider any theoretical distinction. All these theories converge on three basic issues, which define collective bargaining. It is (i) a means to contract for sale of labour, (ii) a form of industrial government, and finally (iii) a system of industrial relations.

ILO defines the term collective bargaining as 'negotiations about working conditions and terms of employment between an employer, a group of employers or one or more employers' organisations, on the one hand and/or more representatives of workers organisation on the other hand with a view to reach an agreement.

In collective bargaining, the object is to arrive at an agreement on wages and other conditions of employment about which the parties start with divergent viewpoints, but ultimately attempt to make a compromise. As soon as the bargain is made, the terms of agreement are put into operation. On the other hand, the major task of the latter relates to sharing the information and suggestions with regard to issues of common interests including health, safety, welfare and productive efficiency.

Mary Sur observes, collective bargaining starts with claims advanced by both sides – demands from the union and statements by the management on how far they can concede these demands and what they want in return, just as the bazaar vendor and buyer start by quoting prices which are at variance, each knowing that he will have to make some accommodation in the end in order to reach a final agreed price. According to the Encyclopaedia of Social Sciences – 'Collective bargaining is a process of discussion and negotiation between two parties, one or both of whom is a group of persons acting in concert. The resulting bargain is an understanding as to the terms and conditions under which a continuing service is to be performed.....More specifically, collective bargaining is a procedure by which employers and a group of employees agree upon the conditions of work'.

The most comprehensive definition of collective bargaining has been provided by TULRCA 1992 s. 178 (1) & (2) of U.K. employment law programme. It is a negotiation connected with one or more of the following:

1. Terms and conditions of employment, or the physical conditions in which workers are required to work,

2. Engagement or non-engagement, or termination or suspension of employment or the duties of employment, of one or more workers,

3. Allocation of work or the duties of employment between workers or groups of workers,

4. Matters of discipline,

5. A worker's membership or non-membership of a trade union,

6. Facilities for officials of trade unions, and

7. Machinery for negotiation or consultation, and other procedures, relating to any of the above matters, including the recognition by employers or employers' associations of the right of a trade union to represent workers in such negotiation or consultation or in the carrying out of such procedures.

Important Assumptions to Achieve Stable Collective Bargaining

1. While employers and employees have different interests, these differences are not irreconcilable. Instead they are somewhat the same as the difference between buyers and sellers in general. Therefore, through bargaining, a deal can be cut which sets the price and regulates the conditions under which employees sell their labour.

2. Each side accepts the legitimacy of the other and its right to survive.

3. The sides are roughly equal in strength; otherwise one side will dominate rather than bargain with the other.

4. The union legitimately represents the interests of all of those it claims to represent (a claim sometimes questioned by women and members of minority groups).

5. Both parties are willing to negotiate seriously with the aim of reaching agreement.

6. If agreement can not be reached it is legitimate for either side to exert economic pressures (even as strike or lockouts) in order to induce the matter to make concessions. The type of pressure, which is usually regulated by law or generally accepted rules of fair play, differ among countries.

7. The Government plays only a limited direct role in bargaining.

Role of Government in Collective Bargaining

The government may influence collective bargaining and employment conditions in ways which differ greatly among countries:

1. It may determine employment conditions by law, for example, through setting minimum wages, legislating the length of holiday or preventing ethnic discrimination.

2. It may provide some benefits directly, for example, pensions.

3. It may set the ground rules which govern the parties conduct, for example, through giving unions the right to bargain, restricting the conditions under which strikes may occur or determining the scope of bargaining.

4. It may settle disputes which the parties are unable to settle themselves often through mediation or arbitration. In Australia conciliation and arbitration play major role in determining the conditions of employment.

5. Through its macroeconomic and social policies it affects the terms of bargaining agreements.

6. The government is a major employer itself and often bargains with unions representing its employees, frequently setting a pattern for the entire economy. In fact, union density is higher in the public than in the private sector in most countries today.

Further more, as the presumed representative of the public interest, the government is interested in industrial peace. Price stability, increase productivity and non-discriminatory employment patterns. To achieve these objectives it can pressure the parties (often through legislation). On the other hand, the parties can pressurise the government (often through political action). Thus the government is a third party in collective bargaining combining the often conflicting roles of neutral and bargainer.

Three examples illustrate the range of governmental roles; in the USA Government is primarily (and perhaps ineffectively) a referee in collective bargaining. In Latin American countries, where collective bargaining is poorly developed, the parties pressure the state to obtain conditions which in countries (including India) might be obtained through bargaining. However, if government participation is more, the collective bargaining process would not be voluntary.

Characteristics of Collective Bargaining

From the foregoing definitions of collective bargaining, some essential characteristics may be enumerated as follows:

1. It is a group action as opposed to individual action and initiated through the representatives of workers and delegates of the management at the bargaining table.

2. It is flexible and mobile and not fixed or static. It has flexibility and ample scope for compromise for a mutual give and take before the final agreement.

3. It is a two party process. It can succeed only when labour and management want to succeed. There must be a mutual eagerness to develop the collective bargaining procedure and result in a harmony and progress. It can flourish only in an atmosphere which is free from animosity and reprisal.

4. It is a continuous process, which provides a mechanism for continuing and organised relationships between management and trade unions. The heart of collective bargaining is the process for continuing joint consideration and adjustment of plant and problems.

5. The term is dynamic itself because the concept is growing, expanding and changing.

6. It is industrial democracy at work.

7. It is not a competitive process by a complementary process, i.e. each party needs something that the other party has, viz, labour can make a greater productive effort and management has the capacity to pay.

8. It is an art, an advanced from of human relations. To substantiate this, one need only witness the bluffing, the oratory, dramatics and coyness mixed in an inexplicable fashion which may characterise a bargaining session.

Importance and Need for Collective Bargaining

It is evident from the foregoing discussion that to settle differences on the work related issues, collective bargaining as a process is perceived both by employers and employees as an important machinery. We have adequately covered the general issues which are usually settled through collective bargaining.

The need for collective bargaining in India arose due to some controversial problem which the Indian industry had to face after the termination of the Second World War. One of the most important among these is that of modernisation. The problems of modernisation and productivity are to be viewed in a proper light in the context of industrial development on planned lines. Indian industry cannot compete in foreign markets if it does not follow modern methods of production. Since modernisation causes displacement of workers, it naturally invites hostility and the workers and management must, therefore, come together in their viewpoint through collective bargaining. The solution of common problems can come from legislative measures. Collective agreements provide the climate for smooth progress as there is ample scope for a synthesis between demands from one side and concessions from the other.

1. In individual bargaining the workers may be tempted to accept undesirable conditions and may thus bring down the general level of remuneration. Due to immobility of labour, all workers are not in a position to desert a wage cutting employer. This immobility may be due to ignorance and illiteracy and industry specific skill factors.

2. The speedy workers may accept a lower rate of payment which may yield them a reasonable amount of wages, but such a low rate of wages would yield insufficient earnings to a great majority of workers.

3. Sometimes employers are in a position to control the bulk demands for the labourers and they may through combined action, force the workers to accept low wages. Collective bargaining is the only device which can avert such combined action and prevent the creation of such monopolistic tendencies.

4. The market apparatus consisting of the two forces of demand and supply can settle only the problem of determination of wages, some of the non-wage issues like the length of working day, health and safety of workers, speed operations, introduction of rationalisation measures of security of job have to be settled by personal decisions and not by the forces of demand and supply.

5. Collective bargaining also provides some voice in the conduct and management of the industry. Workers have now a definite place in the exercise of a real influence in the determination of labour matters affecting them every now and then.

6. To ensure continuity of production, workers and employers must shake hands and this makes it inevitable to make collective bargaining a regular feature of industrial life.

7. The problem of good human relations can be tackled successfully by the collective bargaining process.

Prerequisites for Collective Bargaining

The success of collective bargaining machinery largely depends on the respective attitudes of workers in general and union in particular on one hand and the attitude of management of employer on the other. However, if collective bargaining is to exist in the country successfully the following factors are essential:

1. It is necessary for the management to recognise the union and to bargain in more good faith, in the unionised situation. This is also pressure on the union to formulate plans and demands in a systematic manner.

2. There should be a change in the attitude of employers and employees. They must realise that collective bargaining approach does not imply litigation as it does under adjudication. Both should be keep in mind that, they are to resolve their differences on their respective claims quietly and calmly, with their own resources, reducing their dependence on the third party intervention.

3. For the purpose of collective bargaining, employers should be represented by the management and workers by their union representatives. Careful thought and selection of the negotiating team is very much essential. For the management team, it is better to have a mixed composition, such as production, finance, industrial relation experts and headed by a personnel expert.

4. It is also appreciable to have open minds, listening to others' concern and point of view and to have some flexibility in making adjustments to the demands.

5. To ensure collective bargaining, unfair labour practices should be avoided and abandoned by both otherwise atmosphere and confidence will be vitiated by malpractice if either side takes advantage of the other by resorting to unfair practices.

6. Either side should avoid putting forth any irrational or unreasonable demand.

7. Negotiations can be successful only when the parties rely on facts and figures to support their points of view. That is why trade union should be assisted by specialists, viz., economists, productivity experts, etc.

8. Trade union should encourage the internal union democracy and periodic consultation with the general rank and file of the union members.

9. The negotiation results, the terms of contract should be in writing and embodied in a document. If no agreement is reached the parties should proceed to conciliation, mediation or arbitration.

   If no settlement is arrived at even then, the workers should be free to go in for strike and the employers on lockout. But utmost care should be taken to resolve differences mutually.

10. Strikes and lockouts should be the last resort. Periodic discussions may be necessary between management and unions to interpret the provisions of the contract and clarify doubts.

11. Trade unions should be equally concerned with both, quality of work, leading up to a consistent concern for the viability of the firm and its products and services.

12. Once the agreement is reached, it must be honoured and fairly implemented.

Collective Bargaining in India

There are certain differences in union characteristics in developed and developing countries. In UK, workers are unionised as per their respective trades. Such unionisation which is more concerned for the group's well-being in reality provided the base for bargaining with management on different employment issues.

The term collective bargaining in fact originated from Great Britain and was coined by Beatrice Potter as is evident from her book *'The Co-operative Movement'* in 1891 and *'Industrial Democracy'* in 1897, where it was regarded as the alternative to individual bargaining.

In India, however, collective bargaining is a late development and has marked its presence only in the year 1918, in Ahmedabad. Voluntary collective bargaining in industry and commerce has developed in India since independence.

The textile industry in Ahmedabad has the longest history of settlement of disputes by mutual negotiation and voluntary arbitration can claim to have paved the way towards modern collective bargaining although the experiment at Ahmedabad was not directly followed elsewhere.

The inspiration of peaceful settlement of differences between management and labour at Ahmedabad came from Gandhiji, who set out his philosophy of industrial relations in his autobiography.

In 1918, Gandhiji was leading the textile workers of Ahmedabad in their demand for better working conditions, but even though he had supported their strike, he was advocating the resolution of conflict by negotiation and mutual discussion between the accredited organisations of labourers and employers. Where negotiation failed, the recommended conciliation, he suggested, is reference to an agreed arbitrator or board of arbitrators whose decision would be binding. In 1918, when the wage disputes were eventually settled at Gandhiji's intervention by reference to an arbitration board representing both employers and workers he declared that he did not see why all future differences should not be settled in the same way.

Gandhiji was successful in bringing the Ahmedabad Mill Owners' Association round to his point of view and in 1920 it was agreed that any dispute or difference of opinion which the workplace could not themselves settle should be referred to Gandhiji and Seth Mangal Das, the President of the Association, as arbitrators. In case they could not reach agreement, provision was made for reference to an umpire whose award would be final.

This system prevailed until 1939 in Ahmedabad. The system of voluntary arbitration could hardly be called collective bargaining. Usually they were able to reach agreement, but on several occasions they had to recourse to an umpire on some unresolved points. In the first 16 months of its existence, the Board gave 23 awards but not all the questions which came before it were the subject of actual disputes.

Just before the Second World War the system of arbitration at Ahmedabad seemed to be breaking down and in 1940, under war time conditions, a reference was made to compulsory adjudication under the Bombay Industrial Regulation Act, 1946.

In 1952, after a lapse of about 14 years, the Ahmedabad Mill Owners' Association and the Textile Labour Union signed two agreements, initially for two years, by which the machinery of voluntary arbitration was revived. This was a proper collective bargaining between the two representative organisations, who agreed that in future all disputes between mills and their employees should be settled out of the court.

Collective bargaining in Ahamedabd textile industry is now carried out at two levels, viz.

1. Between Mill Owners' Association and Textile Labour Association, and
2. Between individual mills and Textile Labour Association.

In 1955, a general agreement on the subject of annual bonus was reached for the years 1953-57, covering all the mills. In 1957, a joint productivity council was set up for Ahmedabad textiles.

From the above discussion, it is clear that a continuing collective bargaining process has come into being in Ahmedabad textile industry.

There was, however, another early instance of an employers' association and an industrial union coming together to solve their problems. This was in the coir industry in Tranvancore (Kerala). However, both in Ahmedabad and Kerala, collective bargaining process was for groups of employers.

The earliest example of collective bargaining within an individual concern was that of Joint Steamer Companies in Calcutta. Their first written agreement with Bengal Mariners Union was in the year 1946. Among the manufacturing enterprises the earliest record of the post-war collective agreements was made by Dunlop Rubber Company at Shagunge in West Bengal in 1947. The Bata Shoe Company in West Bengal made its first agreement in 1948. In 1951,

Indian Aluminium Company, in 1952, the Imperial Tobacco Company, in 1953, the Mysore Iron and Steel Company, in 1955 TISCO, Jamshedpur, in 1956, National Newsprint and Paper Mills at Nepanagar (M.P.) have singed their collective agreements with their workmen.

Form the above discussions, it is, therefore, clear that from 1950 onwards collective bargaining has acquired importance in India. The new industry groups, engineering, chemicals, etc., with a higher degree of professionalisation in management have developed collective bargaining as an institution. In India, collective bargaining is taking place at various levels, viz., plant level, industry level and national level. We have illustrated above certain plant level and industry level collective bargaining agreements in the past. The agreements at the national level are generally bipartite agreements and are finalised at conferences of labour and managements convened by the Government of India. The Delhi Agreement of 7th February, 1951 and Bonus Agreement for Plantation Workers of January, 1956 are examples of such bipartite agreements in the past.

The issues of bargaining in India are generally wages, dearness allowance, retirement benefits, bonus, annual leave, casual leave, paid holiday, etc., Study of Employers' Federation of India shows that 'wages' issue is most prominent among others. Information about collective bargaining settlement, compiled by Labour Bureau, Shimla for the quarter ending December, 1994 shows that 115 settlements have been arrived through collective bargaining agreements during the period in India. Out of these, only one settlement relates to the State sphere while 114 fall in the Centre sphere. We have illustrated the position in the following Table.

Table 23.1: Month-wise Collective Bargaining Agreements during the Quarter ending 31st December, 1994

S.No.	Subject	Number of Agreements						Total	
		October 1994		November 1994		December 1994			
1.	Wages/DA	09	-	13	-	05	-	27	-
2.	Bonus	17	-	11	-	02	-	30	-
3.	Overtime	02	-	02	-	02	-	06	-
4.	House Rent	04	-	04	-			08	-
5.	Health	01	-	02	-	01	-	04	-
6.	Welfare	01	-	04	-	02	-	07	-
7.	Hours of Work	02	-	-	-	-	-	02	-
8.	Conveyance	03	-	02	-	-	-	-05-	-
9.	Leave	04	-	03	-	02	-	09	-
10.	Liveries	04	-	06	-	-	-	-10	-
11.	Service Matter	32	01	20	-	19	-	71	01
12.	Others	07	-	09	-	01	-	17	-
	Total	48	01	09	-	23	-	114	01

Politicisation of trade unions, failure of both parties to devote adequate time, third party intervention, etc., are some of the problems of collective bargaining in India. Mary Parker Follet criticised the collective bargaining process particularly for absence of workers' rights and privileges which itself stand against their bargaining power. Workers being weak bargainers, can never expect to gain from the collective bargaining process.

SUMMARY

Collective bargaining is a voluntary process of negotiation between employers and employees to determine various terms of employment. The process ensures organisational democracy. However, it often transpires as an ineffective process of reaching an agreement. Over the years, the importance of collective bargaining is receding globally. Most of the organisations prefer to have enterprise-wide bargaining rather than industry-wide bargaining. Even industry-wide bargaining agreements are not implemented by many organisations within the same industry group. The banking industry example is relevant in this context. In a collective bargaining situation, HR managers need to play a crucial role to strike a win-win deal. To achieve this they have to enrich their negotiation skills, practicing on a regular basis collective bargaining simulation games. Here we have discussed one for practice.

KEYWORDS

Industrial Democracy
Economic Institution
Political Institution
Industrial Governance

REVIEW QUESTIONS

1. Define collective bargaining. What are its important characteristics and what are the important pre-requisites of its success?

2. Considering Indian industrial environment, do you think, collective bargaining Process is at all helpful to sustain good worker-management relations?

3. Make a review of the collective bargaining scenario in India.

4. To make collective bargaining process a success, what are the roles of workers and management representatives.

CASE STUDY

SONAJULI TEA ESTATE – BACKGROUND

Sonajuli Tea Estate is a famous CTC tea manufacturer in Tezpur District of Assam. It is located almost 40 kilometers away from Tezpur Airport in a place known as Rangapara. The nearest town and Rangapur Railway Station is 5 kms away from the Tea Estate. The Tea Estate is spread over 2 kilometers, divided by number of sections. The annual yield from the Estate is over 14 tonnes. CTC tea manufactured in Sonajuli realises good price at Guwahati, Siliguri and Calcutta Auctions over many other Tea Estate of the region. However, there always exist a feeling that the resources of Tea Estate are grossly under-utilised and there are tremendous scope for further development.

The business is typically run by family members with little or no professional knowledge, which is often considered as detrimental to further development of the Estate. Mr. Ayush Bagla, the new CEO of the Company, is a present generation young professional family member, who has taken over the charge from his grandfather to run and manage the Estate. Ayush after taking over the charge at Calcutta Corporate Office retained a consultant to study the present condition of Sonajuli. He had also in mind to go in for ISO certification to bag export orders and to achieve further internal efficiency. Ayush being quite new in Tea Industry he was briefed about the company as below:

1. *On Workers:* In Tea Industry, typically same workmen is put into different activities at different point of time and such interchangeability even exist between Garden and Processing Unit. It means same worker at time plucks the green leaf from the garden and also at times work in different divisions of the processing unit. Factory Manager attributes this due to high rate of absenteeism, when they are compelled to interchange workers between garden and processing unit. He had also stated that tea manufacturing is a seasonal activity and requirement of worker varies depending on leaf availability. Being a low technology activity, he feels such use is not at all detrimental to the interest of the organisation.

2. *On Manufacturing/Processing:* Processing activities start after receipt of green leaf from the garden. During full bloom season, green tea leaf are received thrice in a day at different point of time. Otherwise, such leaf are received twice a day during plucking season, which normally starts from February and continue till October or even till November. In the first two months of flushing, they get good quality of leaf, which ensures good price realisation in the Auction Markets.

   (a) *Withering Operation:* After receipt of green leaf from the Garden, leaf are spread over withering troughs. Sonajuli has a few withering troughs which are enclosed, i.e., totally covered, while a few are open. Normally green leaf are withered for 16-18 hours, depending on the weather condition. In enclosed troughs, however, time requirement is less. Decision on withering time is taken by the Factory Manager, which is recorded on a small board, indicating Lot No., Section (from where the leaf has been plucked), start time and date, end time and date. Withering time depends on humidity and temperature and for that purpose one Thermometer with dry and wet bulbs is fixed in the Withering Division for time to time monitoring. Proper withering is necessary for loosing of moisture. Hence decision on timing depending on weather, is very crucial. However, Factory Manager after deciding on the Withering time and recording the details on the board, leave it to the workman in-charge to transfer the withered leaf in the adjoining processing unit. Before such transfer, he, however, inspects manually the extent of withering.

   If the leaf transpired (to him) to be under withered, he may decide to extend the withering time, which, however, may not be always possible for obvious queuing problem, as plucked leaf thereby will have to be dumped till the earlier lots in the troughs are cleared. In case the leaf are over-withered, he has to be careful in subsequent operations to retain the quality of the make tea.

   (b) *CTC Operation:* After withering, withered leaf are run through CTC machine, which actually crush, tear and curl the withered leaf in a few minutes (which depend on machine rotation) and transfer the output to plastic containers. During CTC operation, the supervisor and even at times the Factory Manager manually inspects the output and time to time adjust the machine. However, such

Contd...

inspection/checking being infrequent, output nature varies. CTC operation has remote relation to final grading (as the sizes or grade of make tea are important for better price realisation). After CTC, withered leaf form granules. While one worker is responsible for pouring the withered leaf on CTC mouth, other one transfers the output to plastic containers and help in carrying those to fermenting room through wheeled trawlers.

Another worker sweeps the left out output and re-transfer those to plastic containers. During this process, the noise level being too high (far exceeding 65 decibel), workers carryout their jobs on signals and body language.

(c) *Fermenting:* After CTC operation, fermenting job starts, when output is spread over fermenting bays with 1 or 1-1/2 inch thickness evenly inside enclosed room for 2-3 hours, again depending on humidity and temperature inside the room. Fermenting process helps in deoxidation and natural colouring, when output become brownish. Since bacterial infection may create quality problem, adjusting the fermenting time is very crucial, hence such operation requires constant monitoring. Both the supervisor and the Factory Manager, therefore, monitor this operation. However, their non-availability leaves this job to the attending workmen.

(d) *Drying:* In the drying stage, fermented leaf are transferred to the dryer mouth and allowed to be dried to the extent required to reduce significantly the moisture content to make the bulk tea. Drying time depends on both the inlet and outlet temperature and decided again by the Factory Manager and the Supervisor. Inspection is carried out time to time to verify whether the lot is getting properly dried or not. Under drying creates moisture formation and over drying develops burnt smell. Both, therefore, deteriorates quality. Since there exist no auto mechanism, inlet and outlet temperature indicators require constant monitoring to adjust the drying time. After drying operation, bulk tea is spread over on a cloth to allow the same to come to normal temperature.

(e) *Grading:* After completion of drying operation, bulk tea are graded, passing it through wire meshes of different sizes. Grading depends on the granules size and accordingly different names are given to the make tea like:

(i) Broken Orange Pekoe (BOP)

(ii) Broken Pekoe (BP)

(iii) Broken Pekoe (Small) (BPSM)

(iv) Small Broken Pekoe (SBP)

(v) Pekoe Dust (PD)

(vi) Dust (D)

(vii) Churamani Dust (CD)

(viii) Dust - 1 (D-1)

(ix) Broken Pekoe - 1 (BP-1)

(x) Pekoe Fanning-1 (PF-1)

(xi) Orange Fanning-1 (OF-1)

(xii) Pekoe Dust - 1 (PD-1)

(xiii) Red Dust (RD)

(xiv) Churamani Dust - 1 (CD-1)

(xv) Dust - 1 (D-1)

Contd...

After every cycle of operation, wire meshes need to be thoroughly brushed to get the make tea properly graded. Wire mesh holes also need to be visually inspected and time to time replaced to make sure that the holes are in proper size. During the grading operation, fibres and dust mix accumulate on the floors, which are collected by sweeping and again sorted using a conventional methods, i.e., passing through a blower to segregate dust from fibres. At this stage some tea waste (both the fiber and blown out dust, which accumulate on the floor) are collected and stacked on roof top separately to dispose as per government directives.

Graded and sorted tea then stacked in separate bins, especially made from aluminium sheets to retain their essence. Based on the dispatch advice, tea are dispatched time to time, collecting from the bins. Grading operation is monitored by the supervisor or by a senior worker.

(f) *Packing and Dispatch:* Packing of graded make tea is done in plyboard cartoons, commonly known as tea chest. Plyboards are separately purchased and chests are made by the factory workers. Depending on the customers' requirement, jute bags, with plastic lining inside are also used. Since the Factory only sells through auction route, small tea packets are not made. If the make tea remain in the graded bins for a long, it gives a tainted smell and to prevent that, before dispatch, it is necessary to inspect and if require, it may be refined or re-dried once again.

With these, the manufacturing/processing operation comes to an end. However, to appreciate the entire operation in its totality, the consultant also briefed the CEO on other activity areas of the units, that support the tea manufacturing process.

1. *Stores:* Every year, the Factory Manager draws list of the items he requires for the factory and accordingly procurement is made. Store is controlled by a Store Clerk, who records all the receipted items in bin cards and stack those in appropriate places. Materials are issued to the user sections against requisitions, approved by the Factory Manager, and signatures of the persons receiving the materials are endorsed on the bin cards. Stores clerk informs Factory Manage time to time his stock position.
2. *Inspection of Incoming Materials:* For standard items, purchased from established suppliers, only visual inspection and counting are made and properly stacked in appropriate racks with records in bin cards. Receipt advice is then sent to the Factory Manager for his reference and record. For certain standard items like electric bulbs, etc., some sample pieces are tested to verify whether the same are in order or not. Non-standard items are classified as those which are procured time to time based on user section's requirements. Maintenance spares, machinery, inspection and testing kits, measuring instruments are classified under this category. All such items on receipt by the stores are sent to the Factory Manager who inspects the quality either by testing functionality or by fitment trial. Only after receiving his clearance, stores clerk takes those items in stock duly recording in his bin cards and stacking in appropriate racks.
3. *In-process Inspection:* This inspection is carried out at different stages during tea processing by the respective supervisors or by the Factory Manager. While for withering, CTC and fermenting operations, visual inspection is considered as adequate, in other cases like moisture testing, fiber content analysis, some inspection gadgets are used.
4. *Final Inspection:* Tasting of make tea is done by the Factory Manager at the end of the day to verify liquor, colour and flavour. He endorses the results on a note sheet and send the report every day to Calcutta H.Q. Based on the results, make tea are sentenced as good, bad, poor, fair or certain other internal marks.

   This Tasting is very crucial as it decides the ultimate quality and the likely price offer in the auction market. After tasting, if the Factory Manager feels, he may direct required corrective action at different stages of operation.

   In addition to the above, the factory manager has a few maintenance crew who attends time to time the breakdown problems.

   During the off-season, total overhauling of the machinery is done in the form of Preventive Maintenance to avert any major breakdown during the peak operation time.

Contd...

The Factory has also a Labour Welfare Department, one Medical Unit-cum-Hospital, to fulfil the statutory requirements.

Draft Agreement

This AGREEMENT made this FIRST date of June, 2001, between the undersigned firm of Assam (hereinafter referred to as the employer), party on the first part, and the Tea Workers' Local Union No. 3, Guhawati (hereinafter referred to as the union), parties on the second part, as representative of the employees covered by this Agreement.

Therefore, in consideration of the mutual covenants hereafter set out, the parties hereto covenant and agree as follows:

Article 1: Union Recognisation

(a) The EMPLOYER recognizes the UNION as the sole Collective Bargaining agent for its employees in SONAJULI TEA ESTATE, as hereinafter more specifically stated.

(b) The EMPLOYER will not interfere with the right of employees to become members of the Union. The UNION will not intimidate or discriminate against employees who choose not to join the UNION.

(c) The term 'Employee' or 'Employees' as used in this agreement, shall be construed to include only the classifications of employees specifically listed in this agreement and employed in the employer's Estate.

Article 2: Hiring of New Employees

(a) For hiring of new employees up to the level of Supervisor, the employer would consider local candidates and wherever possible recruitment would be made from the employees' wards. In this case preference would be given first to wards of those employees, who have died before completion of their total service tenure.

(b) For employees above the supervisory level, recruitment would be made open to attract best available talent.

(c) All recruitment would be on contractual terms for initial 5 years and thereafter the terms would be renewed subject to mutual acceptance.

(d) Internal hiring, wherever possible would be made by job restructuring.

(e) Any employee, who may opt for internal transfer for his own convenience, would loose his seniority.

(f) For meeting temporary requirements, the company can go for temporary hiring.

(g) In all cases of hiring (except for the managerial level), the company would give preference to previously laid-off employees.

(h) In recruitment decisions, employer's decision would be final and unions can not interfere in the matter.

Article 3: Layoffs and Re-hiring

Should it become necessary to lay off employees, they should be laid off impartially according to job security. Upon re-hiring, the last employee laid off shall be the first re-hired and the first laid off shall be the last re-hired.

Article 4: Discharge

Unions have right to investigate causes of discharge, dishonesty, etc. No wages for time not worked shall be paid to discharged employees if the union does not make its investigation within 3 working days. If no investigation is made, the discharge shall be considered as accepted by the union.

Contd...

Other Articles: 5-18

All other Articles, i.e., Articles 5-18, would remain unchanged, all of which have duly been agreed by the employer and the employees in earlier Collective Bargaining Agreement of 1998. However, for quick reference, those clauses in the Agreement are listed as under:

(a) Discrimination and Union Activity

(b) Injuries and illness

(c) Reporting Accidents and Injuries

(d) Safety

(e) Hours of Work

(f) Holidays

(g) Vacation

(h) Insurance

(i) Wages

(j) Limitation of Union Responsibility for unauthorised strikes

(k) Separability

(l) Arbitration of Grievances

(m) Termination of agreement date effective and its continuance till further finalisation of agreement

(n) Preferential price to employees for purchasing company made products.

Question

Practice this simulation game and record your observations in the observation sheet. List out negotiation strategies followed by each participating party and critically examine those.

Observation Sheet

Note both positive and negative observations below:

Points to Consider	Examples and their effect
Opening • Putting at ease. • Venue, seating, formality • Clarity; was the purpose explained?	
Middle • Sensitivity, use of questions, listening. • Control of pace. • Structure and direction. • Body language; approach and style. • Rapport and agreement • Who is doing all the talking?	
Editing • Outcome, feeling at the end, acceptance or agreement. • Summary.	
Overall effectiveness • Was the aim achieved?	

UNIT 24

Introduction to Labour Laws

Learning Objectives

After completion of this unit, the students will be aware of the following topic:

- ❑ *Introduction*
- ❑ *Industrial Relations and Labour Welfare in India*
- ❑ *Factories Act, 1948*
- ❑ *Industrial Disputes Act, 1947*
- ❑ *The Industrial Employment (Standing Orders) Act, 1946*
- ❑ *The Trade Unions Act, 1926*
- ❑ *The Minimum Wages Act, 1948*
- ❑ *The Payment of Wages Act, 1936*
- ❑ *The Payment of Bonus Act, 1965*
- ❑ *The Employees' Provident Funds and Miscellaneous Provisions Act, 1952*
- ❑ *The Payment of Gratuity Act, 1972*
- ❑ *The Employees' State Insurance Act, 1948*
- ❑ *The Workmen's Compensation Act, 1923*
- ❑ *Other Mandatory Acts*
- ❑ *Industrial Relations (Policy General)*

WTO THE INTERNATIONAL LABOUR COPS

Article 19 of the Constitution of India, inter alia, guarantees the right to form associations or unions and freedom to practice any profession or to carry on any occupation, trade or business, subject to restrictions imposed by law on the exercise of these freedoms. Along with this, The ILO declaration on Fundamental Principles and Rights at Work, adopted by the International Labour Conference in June 1998, emphasise on respecting the principles of the constitution pertaining to such fundamental rights. ILO made it mandatory for the member countries to ratify these provisions. Irrespective of ILO's membership, it has now become essential to accept ILO's mandates in international trade. As international labour cops, ILO, therefore, validates the country specific legal provisions on labour. ILO's prime concern is now to ensure following rights and privileges to the workers, irrespective of their country of origin, and irrespective of membership of ILO of those countries, from where the worker hails. Such provisions can be listed as under:

- Freedom of association and the effective recognition of the right to collective bargaining;
- Elimination of all forms of forced or compulsory labour;
- Effective abolition of child labour; and
- Elimination of discrimination in respect of employment and occupation.

Valuing workplace diversity, equity, security and dignity, creation of decent jobs, keeping pace with the new economic order, have now been mandated by ILO, for organisations across the globe to mandate. As international labour cops, ILO's mandates are binding, else export market opportunities are shunned for the organisations. India is considered as ILO resolutions compliant country.

INTRODUCTION

Industrial Relations is an interdisciplinary behavioral science that focuses on the study of people in the workplace. It is employer-employee relation, i.e., relationship between management and individual or group of employees. It covers:

- Nature of work
- Management of human resources
- Labour-union-management relations nature of organisations
- Worker motivation & behavior
- Impact of public policy on workers & work place
- Labour supply and demand
- Compensation

There are number of theories on industrial relations. All these theories help us in analysing industrial relations and develop a framework of industrial relations in India. Such theories can be broadly classified into two areas:

- Political
- Apolitical

Political theories focus on macro level issues concerning political-economic purposes of society, like; class characteristics of the state, conflict between the classes, the exploitative element of economic and industrial structures and systems, issues concerning ownership, role of working class, political power, etc. Apolitical theories, on the other hand are concerned with micro organisational questions at the strategic, functional and operational levels of the firm or the industry. All procedural issues like law and rules regulating work are covered under this category.

Industrial Relations depend on number of factors. Macro level industrial relations depend on factors like; labour market reform, unemployment and poverty, national development priorities and international standards. Micro level industrial relations on the other hand depend on factors like; works organisation, skills formation, compensation, workplace governance, etc.

Labour Welfare defined as the work for improving the health, safety, general well being and industrial efficiency of the workers beyond the minimum standards laid down by various Acts and Legislations. International Labour Organisation (ILO) defined Labour Welfare as "Workers' welfare….such services, facilities and amenities which may be established in or in the vicinity of an undertaking to enable the persons employed in them to perform their in healthy, congenial surroundings, and provided with amenities conducive to good health and high morale." Some labour welfare measures in our country are statutory, like; Factories Act, 1948, which require employers to abide by the provisions of various welfare activities, while some other are voluntary. It can also be classified as intramural and extramural. While intramural includes those welfare activities, which ensures better quality of work like; scientific selection, training, good work environment, prevention of accidents, canteens, rest-rooms and refreshments, etc. extramural other welfare issues, which also indirectly affect the quality of work life. Such issues cover; housing accommodation, medical services, recreation facilities, conveyance, social insurance scheme, provident fund benefits, pension, sickness and maternity benefits, school-education for children, etc.

Industrial Relations and Labour Welfare in India

Labour legislation in India can be traced back to 1850's with the enactment of Apprentices Act. This Act was initially intended for destitute child to enable them to develop their skill base and get a job when they grow up. This was followed by the Fatal Accidents Act, 1955, Employers and Workmen (Disputes) Act, 1860, Factories Act, Mines Act, Plantation Labour Act and series of other legislations. Labour is a common central and the state subject. The Constitution of India (Article 246/4) empowers both the central and the state governments to legislate on issues related to labour, encompassing issues on trade unions, industrial disputes, social security, social insurance, employment and unemployment, welfare related issues, covering working conditions, provident funds, pensions, maternity leave and benefits, workmen's compensation, etc. The state governments are empowered to change and modify labour laws, enacted by the central government considering the specific issues and conditions of labour prevailing in the states.

As HR manager, one has to understand the basics of relevant labour laws, so as to ensure that any decisions are not taken in contravention of the prevailing norms, which may otherwise become a subject of adjudication.

FACTORIES ACT, 1948

This Act is divided into twelve chapters covering 141 sections, which again are supplemented by three schedules. The first Act was enacted in 1881 to regulate working conditions in factories primarily for women and children and to provide them health and safety measures. In 1911 the new Factories Act was enacted, replacing the old one, covering also the hours of work for adults. The Act was further improvised in 1934, incorporating recommendations of the Royal Commission of Labour. The new Act of 1948 replaced the earlier one and through a series of amendments made from time to time, the Act is now more comprehensive covering all areas of working conditions of labour.

The main objectives of the Factories Act are two-fold. First it regulates working conditions in factories and secondly it ensures fulfillment of basic safety requirements, health and welfare, regulates working hours, leave, holidays, overtime, employment, etc. The scope of the Act extends to all factories in India. Section 2 (m) of the Act defines factories as 'any premises where manufacturing process is carried out using power and which employs 10 or more workers on any day of the preceding 12 months. In cases where power isn't used, such number would be 20 or more.

Under the Factories Act, employers have following obligations:

- Compulsory approval from the State Government or the Chief Inspector of Factories.
- Sending the notice of registration/licence to the Chief Inspector of Factories within seven days from the date of his taking over of charge.
- Conform to general duties concerning health, safety and welfare of workers.
- Conform to general duties regarding articles and substances for use in factories.
- Provide required health measures.
- Undertake safety measure.
- Provide stipulated welfare measures, the degree of which varies with the number of workmen employed.
- Conform to stipulations on working hours, holidays and overtime.
- Conform to provisions concerning leave and wages.
- Display notices, maintain registers and submit returns.
- Send notices on accidents, dangerous occurrences and diseases.
- Fulfill obligations regarding hazardous process/substances.

Factories Act also provides for certain obligations of employees, rights of employees and employers and penalties for offences.

Every HR manager must know the basic tenets of the Act to guard against any decision, which may not be tenable.

INDUSTRIAL DISPUTES ACT, 1947

This Act primarily regulates industrial relations in India. The Act provides a machinery and procedure for settlement of industrial disputes by negotiation, without resorting to strikes and lockouts. The scope of the Act extends to the whole of India for every industrial establishment carrying on any business, trade, irrespective of the number of people employed. However, the Act is not applicable for people employed in managerial or administrative capacity and for those who are employed in Army, Air Force and Navy, Police Services and Prison Services. The Act defines industrial dispute as any dispute or difference between employers and employees or between workmen and workmen, which is connected with the employment or non-employment or the terms and conditions of employment. A tentative list of disputes, covered under this Act is reproduced below:

1. The propriety or legality of standing orders.
2. Discharge or dismissal.
3. Matters pertaining to reinstatement or grant of relief for wrongful dismissal.
4. Matters pertaining to withdrawal of any concession or privilege.
5. Matters pertaining to strike or lockout.
6. Payment of wages, including periodicity and mode of payment.
7. Leave and hours of work.
8. Holidays
9. Bonus
10. Retirement benefits
11. Discipline
12. Non-implementation of award, etc.

Labour Bureau, Shimla has classified the disputes under several heads indicating their incidences on total disputes in percentage terms.

The HR manager has to comply with the laid down obligations under the Act, which broadly cover service conditions, constitution of works committee, implementation of agreements, settlements and awards, avoidance of illegal lockout and non-indulgence in unfair labour practices.

THE INDUSTRIAL EMPLOYMENT (STANDING ORDERS) ACT, 1946

This Act requires employers to clarify conditions of employment so as to enable the workmen (employed by them) to understand the rules of conduct pertaining to working hours, holidays, attendance, leave, termination of employment, suspension or dismissal, misconduct, etc. The

Act is applicable to industrial establishments, employing 100 or more workmen. Under this Act, employers are required to submit a draft of standing orders to the certifying officer for certification. Upon certification it receive the force of law and employers are required to display the text in the language of the workmen and in English prominently. Once certified, employers cannot modify the standing orders without the approval of the certifying officer. Model standing orders cover following areas:

1. Basis of classification of workman – permanent, probationers, temporary, casual, apprentices, *badlis*
2. Information on working time
3. Information on holidays and paydays
4. Wage rates
5. Shift work
6. Attendance and late coming
7. Leave
8. Payment of wages
9. Stoppage of work
10. Termination of employment
11. Act of misconduct, which is liable for disciplinary action, etc.

Standing orders are guidelines for HR decisions, hence HR managers must know legal interpretation of standing orders.

The Trade Unions Act, 1926

Trade unions are primarily formed to regulate the relations between workmen and employers. The Act provides for registration of trade unions, which also includes association of employers. Upon registration, trade unions enjoy certain protection and privileges under the law. In addition, the Act also provides for imposing restrictions on the conduct of any trade or business. Registration of a trade union is not compulsory but a registered union enjoys certain rights and privileges under the Act, it is always desirable to get a trade union registered. The Act requires that at least 50 per cent of the office bearers of a union should be actually engaged or employed in the industry. A registered trade union is a body corporate with perpetual entity under a common seal. It can acquire, hold, sell or transfer any movable or immovable property and can be party to contracts. It can sue or can be sued in his own name. From the HR manager's point of view, it is essential to invite registered trade unions of the unit only for collective bargaining and also form participative forums like works committee, etc., from their nominated representative.

The Minimum Wages Act, 1948

The Act provides for minimum statutory wages for scheduled employment. The Act also stipulates maximum daily working hours, weekly rest and overtime. It prevails over the rates fixed under any award agreement. The Act empowers the State Government to fix minimum wages, failing which they cease the right to engage labour and run the industry. Wages, as per the Act, include all remuneration capable of being expressed in terms of money including house rent allowance. However, it excludes the value of housing accommodation, supply of light, water, medical attendance, employer's contribution to provident fund and pension fund, travelling allowances or the value of travelling concession, gratuity payable on discharge or any other payments made to defray special expenses. For HR managers it is important to consider all these aspects while designing compensation package.

The Payment of Wages Act, 1936

The Act is intended to regulate payment of wages in a particular form at regular intervals without any unauthorised deductions. It is applicable to the employees receiving wages below ₹ 1,600 per month. As per the Act, employers are responsible for payment of wages to the employees duly fixing the wage periods (which in no case should exceed one month), deciding about time of payment as per the norms (which requires payment within seven days of the expiry of the wage period for establishment where less than 1,000 people are employed and in other cases within ten days of the expiry of wage period), mode of payment (in cash or by cheque or by crediting to employee's bank account with prior consent) and ensuring no unauthorised deductions. All these aspects must be known to the HR manager.

The Payment of Bonus Act, 1965

The Act imposes statutory liability on employers (covered under the Act) to pay bonus to employees according to the prescribed formula, linking the bonus with profits or productivity. Bonus is payable to every employee receiving salary or wages up to ₹ 3,500 per month, provided the employee has worked at least for 30 days in that year, save and except those employees who have been dismissed from service for fraud, riotous or violent behaviour, or theft, misappropriation or sabotage of any property of the establishment. Such employees ceases the right to get bonus even for previous unpaid years, irrespective of the fact that they have committed such acts in the present year. Employers can deduct from the bonus any customary payment made to the employees (festival or interim bonus) earlier. Employers can also recover any financial loss caused for the misconduct of the employees.

The Employees' Provident Funds and Miscellaneous Provisions Act, 1952

The Act provides for compulsory contributory fund for social security of the employees and their dependents (in case of death). It extends to every factory, establishment employing 20 or more persons. The Central Government, however, by notification, brings any establishment under the purview of the Act even in cases where such establishments employ less than 20 persons. However, cooperative societies employing less than 50 persons and working without the aid of power, newly set up establishments (for initial 3 years), and State/Central Government establishments (where they have their own schemes) are immune from the provisions of this Act. The Central Government has framed three schemes under the Act, i.e. Employees' Provident Fund Scheme, 1952 (for provident funds), Employees' Family Pension Scheme, 1971 for providing family pension and life assurance benefit, which been merged with, Employees' Pension Schemes, 1995 and the employees' Deposit Linked Insurance Scheme, 1976. The Act requires employers to contribute amount @ 12 per cent of the Wages, D.A. etc. (10% in case of BIFR referred establishments or establishments employing less than 20 persons or any establishments in the jute, beedi, brick, coir or gaur gum industry) and ensure similar deduction from employees and deposit the same together with administrative charges and required returns/attachments to the regional provident fund office or to their own private provident fund scheme (approved by the Provident Fund Commissioner).

The Payment of Gratuity Act, 1972

This Act is also a social security measure to provide retirement benefit to the workmen, who have rendered long and unblemished service to the employer. Employees are entitled to receive gratuity under the Act, provided they have rendered continuous 5 years service or more at the rate of 15 days wages for each completed year, subject to a maximum of ₹ 3,50,000. The gratuity may be wholly or partly forfeited by the employer if termination of services of an employee is due to his riotous or disorderly conduct or any other act of violence or any offence, including moral turpitude committed in the course of his employment.

The Employees' State Insurance Act, 1948

The principal objective of this Act is to provide to the workers medical relief, cash benefits for sickness, compensation for employment injuries (which also covers occupational diseases), pension to the dependents of deceased workers and maternity benefits to women workers. All these benefits are given from a contributory fund. Once workmen are covered under ESI Scheme, compensation under Workmen's Compensation Act for employment injuries are not payable. The Act is applicable to all factories (excluding seasonal factories) employing ten or more (when manufacturing process is carried out using power). For factories carrying out the manufacturing process without the aid of power, the said number is 20 or more persons. The scope of the Act covers every employee, including those engaged as casual or by a contractor, provided they do not receive wages not exceeding ₹ 6,500 per month. Apprentices engaged under the Apprentices Act are not eligible for ESI benefits. The Act requires registration of eligible factories and establishments within a prescribed time limit. Similarly entitled employees are also required to be insured in a prescribed manner under the Act. Since the nature of insurance is contributory, employers are required to pay @ 4.75 per cent and employees are required to contribute @ 1.75 per cent of the wages. However, such employees who are drawing less than ₹ 40 as daily wages are exempted from the requirement of contribution. The Act provide benefits at prescribed rate and imposes penalty for violation up to 5 years imprisonment and fine upto ₹ 25,000.

THE WORKMEN'S COMPENSATION ACT, 1923

Factories and establishments which are not covered under the Employees State Insurance Act, are covered under this Act to provide relief to workmen and/or their dependents in case of accidents arising out of and in the course of employment causing either death or disablement of workmen. The workmen's compensation (Amendment) Act, 2000 w.e.f. 8-12-2000 has brought all the workmen within the limit of this Act, irrespective of their nature of employment. Under the Act, the employers are under obligation to pay compensation for any accident suffered by an employee in the course of employment, failing which the Act provides for penalties. There must be some causal connection with employment to become eligible for compensation, which may not necessarily be inside the workplace. Causal relationship is established by the circumstantial evidence, which my be even in cases where workmen sustain injury while coming to work or while going to his house after completion of work.

These apart, there are many other acts, governing industrial relations and labour welfare in India. Some of those are as under:

Shops and Establishment Act

The Act in essence a state legislation. It seeks to regulate the working conditions of workers in the unorganized sector, including shops and establishments which do not come under the Factories Act Regulations for working hours, rest intervals, overtime, holidays, termination of service, maintenance of shops and establishments and other rights and obligations of the employer and employees are laid down.

Maternity Benefits Act

This provides maternity benefits to women employees. It sets out that a woman may avail three months leave with full salary before or after the birth of her child.

Workmen's Compensation Act

According to this Act workers and/or their dependents are provided with relief in the event of accidents arising out of or in the course of employment, causing death or disability.This Act extends to the whole of India.

Group Insurance

According to this, public liability insurance for installations that handle hazardous substances is mandatory to ensure that minimum relief may be given to victims. This is based on the principle of strict liability. Every owner is required to take out an insurance policy for an amount not less than the paid up capital (or market value of all assets and Stock) of the establishment subject to a ceiling. The owner is also required to contribute an amount equal to the amount of the premium to an environmental relief fund. A company newly set up is exempt from the Employee's Provident Fund and Miscellaneous Provisions Act for the first three years of operation. Certain other amenities, such as canteens, rest shelters, first-aid centres, crèches (day-care centres for female employees' children), and educational and recreation centres, are to be provided by the employer in factories, mines and plantations. Large industrial Units located away from the main cities sometimes provide subsidised housing for their workers. Some states require the setting up of a welfare fund with contributions payable by the employer, employees and the concerned government for promoting activities connected with the welfare of labour.

Coverage

All social benefits are available to a worker irrespective of nationality. A worker may not decline coverage. Foreign nationals employed in India at a relatively high level may not be covered by the Act, depending on their terms of employment.

OTHER MANDATORY ACTS

In addition to the employees direct benefits fund Acts mentioned above, other acts constituted in India are the WATER (Prevention & Control of Pollution)Act and the WATER Cess Act, AIR (Prevention & Control of Pollution)Act, the Environment Protection Act & FOREST conservation Act (concerned with the pollution and improvement of the environment).

Environment Act

This provides a framework for the Central Government to coordinate environment related activities of the central and state authorities. Limits on industries effluent and emission discharges have been prescribed. Boards constituted under these Acts are empowered to make an application to the court to restrain the potential pollution of air, water or land and also to take emergency measures in case of actual pollution. Under the environment law discussed above, penalties of both fine and imprisonment which are very high may be enforced for the contravention of the Act. Some of the recent amendments of important Acts have been discussed here in brief to understand the process of changes in industrial relations and labour Welfare in India.

Trade Unions (Amendment) Act, 2001

The Trade Unions Act, 1926 provides for registration of trade unions of employers and workers and in certain respects, it defines the law relating to registered trade unions. It confers legal and corporate status on registered trade unions. The Act is administered by the concerned State Governments. Certain provisions of the Act were amended and given effect to w.e.f. 9.1.2002.

Some of the salient features of the Trade Unions (Amendment) Act, 2001 are:

1. No trade union of workmen shall be registered unless at least 10% or 100, whichever is less, subject to a minimum of seven workmen engaged or employed in the establishment or industry with which it is connected are the members of such trade union on the date of making of application for registration.

2. A registered trade union of workmen shall at all times continue to have not less than 10% or 100 of the workmen, whichever is less, subject to a minimum of 7 persons engaged or employed in the establishment or industry with which it is connected, as its members.

3. A provision for filing an appeal before the Industrial Tribunal/Labour Court in case of non-registration/restoration of registration has been provided.

4. All office bearers of a registered trade union, except not more than one-third of the total number of office bearers or five, whichever is less, shall be persons actually engaged or employed in the establishment or industry with which the trade union is connected.

5. Minimum rate of subscription by members of the trade union is fixed at one rupee per annum for rural workers, three rupees per annum for workers in other unorganized sectors and 12 rupees per annum in all other cases.

For the promotion of civil and political interest of its members unions are authorized to set up separate political funds.

Criteria for Recognition of Unions

Where there is more than one union, the union claiming recognition should have been functioning for at least one year after registration. Where there is only one union, this condition would not apply.

The membership of the union should cover at least 15% of the workers in the establishment concerned. Membership would be counted only of those who had paid their subscriptions for at least three months during the period of six months immediately preceding the reckoning.

A union may claim to be recognized as a representative union for an industry in a local area if it has a membership of at least 25% of the workers of that industry in that area.

When a union has been recognized, there should be no change in its position for a period of two years.

Where there are several unions in an industry or establishment, the one with the largest membership should be recognized.

A representative union for an industry in an area should have the right to represent the workers in all the establishments in the industry, but if a union of workers in a particular establishment has a membership of 50% or more of the workers of that establishment it should have the right to deal with matters of purely local interest, such as, for instance, the handling of grievances pertaining to its own members. All other workers who are not members of that union might either operate through the representative union for the industry or seek redress directly.

In the case of trade union federations which are not affiliated to any of the four central organisations of labour, the question of recognition would have to be dealt with separately.

Only union which observe the Code of Discipline would be entitled to recognition.

Scheme For Participation of Workers in Management

In December 1983, following a review of the progress of participative schemes in industry, a new scheme was prepared and notified.

This scheme is applicable to all central Public Sector enterprises, except those specifically exempted. It envisaged constitution of bipartite forums at shop and plant levels. In enterprises considered suitable, it was also to be implemented at the Board level. The mode or representation of workers' representatives was to be determined by consultation with the concerned unions, any parity in representation between the management and unions continued to be the norm.

The scheme brought within the ambit of the councils a wider spread of work-related issues. At the plant level, the council could discuss issues relating to personnel, Welfare, environment and community development, plant operations and functioning, and also take up financial matters relating to profit and loss statements, balance sheets, operating costs, plant financial performance, labour and managerial costs, etc.

INDUSTRIAL RELATIONS (POLICY GENERAL)

- Monitoring of Industrial Relations (Mandays lost in strikes and lockouts/workers affected by closure/retrenchment, reasons for labour unrest and industrial sickness etc.)
- Convening of meetings of Industrial Tripartite Committees and Special Tripartite Committee.
- Decisions on closure, retrenchment and lay-off applications submitted by Central Public Sector Undertakings (CPSUs).
- Policy matters relating to employees in Central Public Sector Undertakings on payment of statutory dues of workers, impact of disinvestments and restructuring of PSUs on employees, improvements in Voluntary Retirement Scheme/Separation Scheme, etc.

Special Tripartite Committee/Industrial Tripartite Committees

Seven industrial tripartite committees have been constituted with the view to promote the spirit of tripartism. These tripartite bodies aim at solving the industry specific problems related to workers in the Sugar industry, Cotton Textile industry, Electricity Generation and Distribution, Jute industry, Road transport, Engineering industry and Chemical industry. In addition a Special Tripartite Committee has been constituted to discuss general matters pertaining to Government reforms policies and their impact on workers.

SUMMARY

Industrial Relations and Labour Welfare are two important areas governing employer – employee relations and benefits. For efficient management of an organisation, it is essential to nurture healthy industrial relations and provide benefits to workers, both statutory and non-statutory. In India, we have several acts and legislations concerning these two areas. We have briefly introduced these here. Many organisations, to derive motivational benefits provide welfare benefits beyond what are statutorily required. For example, TISCO much before formal enactment of various rules and regulations provide welfare benefits to workers. They even provide some benefits and services to employees beyond statutory requirements. These are healthy practices.

KEYWORDS

Industrial Adjudication	Safety and Welfare
Working Hours	Industrial Disputes
Industrial Relations	Standing Orders
Bonus	Wages
Trade Unions	Shift Work
Gratuity	

REVIEW QUESTIONS

1. Discuss, why it is so important for HR managers to understand labour laws?
2. Identify four important Labour Laws and discuss how the provisions of these laws can influence HR decisions?
3. What are the basic differences in Factories Act and Industrial Disputes Act? Why both the Acts are relevant for managing human resources?
4. Define Industrial Relations and Labour Welfare.
5. Briefly discuss various Labour Welfare measures, which are statutorily required to be complied with by an organisation.
6. What are the recent amendments to Trade Unions Act? How these amendments help in better industrial relations?
7. Discuss the code of discipline and its significance to Industrial relations.
8. Briefly point out the process of workers' participation to management.
9. Write short notes on:

   (a) Trade Unions Act

   (b) Payment of Gratuity Act

   (c) Payment of Bonus Act

   (d) Standing Orders

   (e) Apprentices

CASE STUDY

DISCIPLINING WORKERS – THE CASE OF ZENON

Organisations cannot alter existing service conditions unilaterally unless 21 days notice is served to the unions and workers of the unit. The other interesting feature is that if during the pendency of an existing dispute, organisations alter the service conditions, which may prejudice the dispute, putting workers into the disadvantageous position, and the same can be construed as void. Although industry circle considers that this rigidity weakens the competitive position of an organisation in this era of globalisation, it has now become the practice in discipline and grievance handling, and also in industrial disputes.

A permanent worker of Zenon has recently been removed from the service on the charge of gross misconduct. The charged employee was removed from the service on the charge of habitual absenteeism. The contention of the charged employee during disciplinary proceedings was that due to his ill health, his schedule of attendance got disturbed since the last six months and he had produced all the relevant documents to substantiate his case. His contention was negated by the disciplinary committee which heard his case and finally concluded that absence due to illness can also be construed as misconduct.

The aggrieved worker then, went to the Labour Court appealing for his reinstatement. The court after hearing the case ordered for his reinstatement, alleging in the standing order of the company, absence due to illness is not defined as misconduct; hence removal from the service on the charge of misconduct for absenteeism due to illness is not in order. Zenon contended absenteeism as a misconduct is already documented in the Standing Orders. Hence, decision for his removal does not infringe the provisions of the law.

Question

As an HR expert, explain what could be right approach for Zenon to remove the worker from the service, without prejudicing the legal provisions?

UNIT 25

Work Environment Management

Learning Objectives

After completion of this unit, the students will be aware of the following topics:

- *Introduction*
- *Internal Task Environment Issues*
- *Fatigue at Workplace*
- *Boredom at Workplace*
- *Hazards at Workplace*
- *Accidents and Safety Issues at Workplace*
- *Employee Morale*
- *Personnel Records-keeping for Better Work Environment Management*
- *Whistle Blowing*
- *Ethics and Values for HR*

WHISTLE BLOWING FOR GOOD CORPORATE GOVERNANCE

Blowing whistle against corruption and unethical business practices substantially reduces the risk of organisational failure to sustain in the long run. Even though many organisations proclaim that they encourage whistle blowing against wrong practices, we really do not have adequate evidences to authenticate so. We all know the unpleasant experience of Enron's whistle blower-Sherron Watkins. She had to face all the odds after she blew her whistle against the accounting scandal. Enron had collapsed. Unfortunately, we did not have any whistle blowers in case of Lehman Brothers which could have ultimately saved the situation of global economic meltdown. Even for Satyam in India, we did not have any whistle blower. Corporate governance is now a global issue. Deteriorating corporate governance gradually cripples the organisation and even leads to its closure or liquidation. While it is possible to enforce corporate governance through institutionalised systems and practices, there always exist some loopholes in detecting the right scenario. In such cases, whistle blowers can play the effective role.

INTRODUCTION

The term work environment has two dimensions: the task and mega environment. Task environment is internal to an organisation, while the mega environment is exogenous to organisations, yet they influence the task or internal environment. We can clarify the issue using an example. Change of work process through organisational re-engineering, is a construct of task or internal work environment. On the other hand, increase in global competition is a component of mega environmental issues. Both have strong influences in changing the organisational work environment. However, in this unit, we are more concerned with internal or task environmental issues, which have strong linkage with the human resource management issues.

Globally, the work environment is undergoing constant change. In factories, manufacturing units, production houses, the work scenario and working condition is changing. Some of the changes like, prolonged working hours, specialisation of job profiles, technical complexities for jobs, increase in work pressure, etc., are globally visible. All such changes, organisations are required to manage to survive in a competitive business. Achieving increased production, maintaining quality requirements; by ensuring long working hours, managing safety and welfare of the employees and reducing fatigue, have now become almost essential business imperatives to stay ahead in competition. Some aspects of work environment can exert positive effect on working capacity of the employees, while some other may have negative effects. A better working environment, for example, may exert positive influence. But, unhygienic physical environment may exert negative influence on employees.

INTERNAL TASK ENVIRONMENT ISSUES

Some of the internal or task environment issues are discussed below:

1. ***Hours of work and its effect on production:*** It is our general belief that by increasing the working hours, organisations can achieve increased production. But, this may not always be true. Even, by analysing the ratio of total working hours and the total production, either in value or volume terms, we cannot establish this. This is because of the difference between the real working hours and nominal working hours. Working capacity of

employees are limited to the real working hours, stretching the working hours (nominal) may require employees to contribute more, but with reduced work energy, change in production value and the volume, may not be matching. Therefore, increasing working hours may not always be the right choice. During the extended working hour period, employees' unproductive working time, rest pauses, work pace significantly changes. Hence, it creates the difference between actual hours of work and nominal hours of work. For industrial workers, payment of overtime is a statutory obligation. Many organisations, to keep pace with their increased production plan, often feel compelled to retain such workers on overtime. However, globally, it has been established that in overtime period, production actually reduces.

Various psychological studies conducted in industrial organisations suggest that breaks or work pauses during working time enhances the working capacity of employees and assists in increasing production. Hence, HR managers need to study the implications of the length and frequencies of the breaks, particularly, its impact on performance of the employees. For example, in call centers, tele-callers cannot leave their workstations in between. Thus, the system of giving one break in between eight working hours may not be the right approach. Rather, they may be given staggered break, batch-wise to ensure manning of workstation, every two hours or so, limiting the total breaks timing as per organisational policies. This renews the work energy of workers, reducing their work related fatigue. Thus, regular rest pauses to employees' decrease fatigue or monotony, enhance production and productivity and also develop good corporate image. The type and nature of work determines the duration and the frequencies of the rest pauses. Organisations should ensure that during rest period, employees are allowed to change their posture, for instance, if the work requires seating, then, during rest period, employees should be allowed to stand and walk around or vice-versa. This would decrease the level of fatigue. Prolonged working hours also increases absenteeism and increased absenteeism affects the level of production. Although there are many other reasons for absenteeism, but work-related fatigue due to prolonged working hours, can be construed as one of the important cause.

2. ***Music at work:*** Music at work is one of the most popular work environment changes. However, a decision on its intensity and variety is crucial. Instrumental, classical, jazz, pop, etc., are the examples of variety, while the volume is an example of intensity. During lunch break, in industrial production unit, plying of pop songs with increased intensity is a normal practice. Jazz and instrumental music with low intensity during working hours, on the other hand, is a popular practice both in offices and factories. HR managers must ensure that music should not conflict with the work efficiency of employees, diverting their attention. Some organisations, instead of playing music uniformly throughout the working time, may play it at synchronized interval, may be 10 minutes, every one hour, strategically to use it as a fatigue busters. In some complex nature of jobs, use of music often may be counter-productive. Hence, decision on exerting positive work environment changes through music at work should be taken very carefully. Psychological researches on music at work suggest usage of music as a rhythm, keeping pace with the work rhythm.

3. ***Noise level at work:*** Any voice that sounds unpleasant to ears is considered as noise. Noise is generally an annoying sound, which distracts our attention and interferes with our work. In some workplaces, machine operation related noises are steady in nature. It may even exceed the required 65-decibels limit. Good example is a jute mill. In such cases, workers adapt themselves to the noise level. Since they become used to it, barring their impaired hearing, it may not interfere with their work efficiency. But intermittent noise may act as distracter and interferes with the work efficiency. In a steadily noisy work environment, sudden silence at work place may be a distracter. In such an environment, if the noise level exceeds the permissible limit, employees should be protected with the earplugs or earmuffs, to protect their hearing capacity.

4. ***Illumination:*** Illumination is maintaining daylight or daylight equivalent brightness in workplace. Actual daylight is the best source of illumination for work. However, in all work places, natural daylight may not be available. This may be for reasons like; nature of work (which may require to be done in close environment), night-work or even the particular layout of the office or the production unit. Wherever, artificial lighting is required, organisations should ensure that it is more proximate to daylight, both in colour and composition. While installing the lighting system in the workplace, it is important to emphasise on factors like distribution, location and glare of the lights, so that it properly illuminates the workplace. To the extent possible, illumination should combine the daylight and the artificial light. Artificial light should be free from colours. However, where it is difficult to avoid colourful lights, Mazda or yellow light should be the best choice. Unbalanced or unmatched colour put hindrances in the workplace. Again artificial lighting should have the adequate property of diffusion, i.e., it should have minimum glares. Excessive brightness leads to visual discomfort.

5. ***Miscellaneous Factors:*** To make the work environment free from dullness, monotony and physical discomfort, we also take some other measures. One such measure is building cafeterias, which provides opportunity to employees not only to feel relaxed but also to further their thought process either in discussions with other team members or in isolation over a cup of tea or coffee.

   Another important aspect of work environment is availability of proper rest room. Also, hygienic sanitary facilities, appropriate temperature and humidity level, ventilation, etc., significantly contribute to inculcate positive attitude to workers and improve the overall productivity and efficiency in work place. Therefore, organisations should not limit their focus on those workplace environment aspects, which are statutorily required, rather provide more, to develop the work place, a compelling one to the employees.

Practice Assignment

Visit any organisation in your locality and study their internal work environment. Relate your identified work environment issues as per our given list and suggest possible remedial actions to the organisation.

FATIGUE AT WORKPLACE

Fatigue is physical and/or mental exhaustion that can be triggered by stress, medication, overwork or mental and physical illness or disease. Everyone experiences fatigue occasionally.

It is the body's way of signaling its need for rest and sleep. But when fatigue becomes a persistent feeling of tiredness or exhaustion that goes beyond normal sleepiness, it is usually a sign that something more serious is amiss.

Physically, fatigue is characterised by a profound lack of energy, feelings of muscle weakness and slowed movements or central nervous system reactions. Fatigue can also trigger serious mental exhaustion. Persistent fatigue can cause a lack of mental clarity (or feeling of mental "fuzziness"), difficulty in concentrating, and in some cases, memory loss.

Causes and Symptoms of Fatigue

Fatigue may be the result of one or more environmental causes such as inadequate rest, improper diet, work and home stressors or poor physical conditioning, or one of the symptoms of a chronic medical condition or disease process in the body. Heart disease, low blood pressure, diabetes, end-stage renal disease, iron-deficiency- anemia, narcolepsy, and cancer can cause long-term, ongoing fatigue symptoms. Acute illnesses such as viral and bacterial infections can also trigger temporary feelings of exhaustion. In addition, mental disorders such as depression can also cause fatigue.

A number of medications, including antihistamines, antibiotics, and blood pressure medications, may cause drowsiness as a side effect. Individuals already suffering from fatigue who are prescribed one of these medications may wish to check with their healthcare provider about alternative treatments. Extreme fatigue, which persists, unabated, for at least six months, is not the result of a diagnosed disease or illness, and is characterised by flu-like symptoms such as swollen lymph nodes, sore throat, and muscle weakness and/or pain may indicate a diagnosis of chronic fatigue syndrome. Chronic fatigue syndrome (sometimes, called chronic fatigue immune deficiency syndrome), is a debilitating illness that causes overwhelming exhaustion and a constellation of neurological and immunological symptoms. Between 1.5 and 2 million Americans are estimated to suffer from the disorder.

Building/work-related fatigue may have a variety of causes. Conventional wisdom says that it is due to work-related stress or ergonomic concerns such as working at a computer/ computer terminal for extended periods of time. There is no doubt that the strain of working at a computer 4-8 hours a day can result in headache and fatigue, which is particularly noticeable late in the day. Work-related stress may also be expected to cause late afternoon fatigue and headache. It is not unusual for office workers to experience fatigue as early as 10 o'clock in the morning. Such fatigue is not likely to be work-induced. There must be some other cause. In most cases, such symptoms appear to be related to ventilation deficiencies. Buildings need to be ventilated to remove contaminants that we ourselves produce. These contaminants are referred to as bioeffluents. They include carbon dioxide (CO_2) acetone, ammonia, methane, a large number of volatile fatty acids, solvents previously inhaled, etc. These bioeffluents are not believed to be individually harmful. However, as bioeffluent levels increase (as determined from CO_2 concentrations) building occupants increasingly begin to complain of unpleasant human odor, stale, unpleasant air, lack of air movement, and yes, fatigue and headache.

The wide range of causes that can trigger fatigue include:

1. Undiagnosed medical conditions
2. Unhealthy lifestyle choices
3. Workplace issues
4. Emotional concerns and stress
5. Fatigue can also be caused by a large number of other factors working in combination.

Medical Causes

Many diseases and disorders can trigger fatigue. From HR managers' point of view, such medical causes of fatigue are difficult to measure. However, keeping a track on medical status of individual employees, HR managers can ascertain possible link of employee fatigue with medical reasons.

Workplace related Causes of Fatigue

Common workplace issues that can cause fatigue include:

- *Shift work:* The human body is designed to sleep during the night. This pattern is set by a small part of the brain known as the circadian clock. A shift worker confuses their circadian clock by working when their body is programmed to be asleep. Sleeping during the day is usually difficult, because the person's brain chemicals (neurotransmitters) are naturally set to 'wakefulness' mode.
- *Poor workplace practices:* It can add to a person's level of fatigue. These may include long work hours, hard physical labour, irregular working hours (such as rotating shifts), stressful work environment (such as excessive noise or temperature extremes), boredom, working alone with little or no interaction with others or fixed concentration on a repetitive task.
- *Workplace stress:* It can be caused by a wide range of factors including job dissatisfaction, heavy workload, conflicts with bosses or colleagues, bullying, constant change, or threats to job security.
- *Burnout:* It can be described as striving too hard in one area of life while neglecting everything else. 'Workaholics', for example, put all their energies into their career, which puts their family life, social life and personal interests out of balance.
- *Unemployment:* financial pressures, feelings of failure or guilt, and the emotional exhaustion of prolonged job hunting can lead to stress, anxiety, depression and fatigue.

Psychological Causes

Studies suggest that psychological factors are present in at least 50 per cent of fatigue cases. These may include:

- *Depression:* This illness is characterised by severe and prolonged feelings of sadness, dejection and hopelessness. People who are depressed commonly experience chronic tiredness.

- ***Anxiety and stress:*** A person who is chronically anxious or stressed keeps their body in overdrive. The constant flooding of adrenaline exhausts the body, and fatigue sets in.
- ***Grief:*** losing a loved one causes a wide range of emotions including shock, guilt, depression, despair and loneliness.

Diagnosis of Fatigue

Since fatigue can present a vast range of symptoms and be caused by many different factors working in combination, diagnosis can be difficult. Your doctor may diagnose fatigue using a number of tests including:

- ***Medical history*** – recent events such as childbirth, medication, surgery or bereavement may contribute to fatigue.
- ***Physical examination*** – ensures identification of signs of illness or disease. The doctor may also ask detailed questions about diet, lifestyle and life events.
- ***Tests*** – this may include blood tests, urine tests, x-rays and other investigations. The idea is to rule out any physical causes, such as anaemia, infection or hormonal problems.

Implications of Fatigue

Fatigue is one of the most critical safety issues. While not all of the physiological reasons for fatigue have been fully quantified and categorised, one thing is clear -fatigue has a detrimental impact on human performance. Additionally, it has been recognised that the lack of basic knowledge or misconceptions about fatigue among management, employees and government regulators has prevented implementing substantial changes in existing attitudes concerning the critical relationship between fatigue and safety.

While physical fatigue is a major concern in industry, managers and executives largely suffer from cognitive fatigue. Cognitive fatigue is the degradation of mental capacities in regard to decision-making, reason and judgment and the ability to remember and process contextual information. This degradation can be caused by either acute or cumulative loss of meaningful sleep. Hence, fatigue is more than being tired. Some of the causes are:

- Conflict between work schedules and body time (an individual's normal circadian sleep time)
- Continuous circadian disruption
- Extended, frequent and/or unpredictable work periods
- Prolonged wakefulness
- Fatigue from continuous operations
- Boredom/complacency

- Shift work - any schedule that requires people to be awake and active when they would normally be asleep. It requires overriding the circadian clock, which pre-programmes daytime activity and night time sleep. Hence, shift work creates conflict between environmental synchronizers (reset) and work/rest schedules, day/night cycles, etc.

Fatigue is a physiological condition, which, in an operational environment cannot be eliminated, but can be managed if the proper set of tools is put in place. Sleepiness is not an indicator of laziness. Sleep is a physical requirement just like eating, drinking, and breathing. Failure to recognise this requirement and effectively manage it, results in a degradation of human performance and an increased risk of incidents (i.e., rules violations, collisions, personal injuries, fatalities, etc.). Individuals can improve their alertness on the job by learning more about the science of sleep and by developing good sleeping habits. Organisations can improve the alertness of their membership and workforce by working in partnership to develop science based fatigue counter measure policies and programs. Organisations and individuals need to analyse the various fatigue countermeasures currently available; determine which ones are effective in their operational environment; and implement those countermeasures. There is no quick fix or magic bullet. Organisations need to build a package of countermeasures into a comprehensive programme and then, implement the same to manage fatigue.

Fatigue is a symptom, rather than a specific disease or disorder. People who are fatigued feel tired all the time-in both body and mind. An employee with fatigue syndrome suffers from reduced reflexes and functions at less than the level of efficiency. Fatigue can cause a vast range of other physical, mental and emotional symptoms, including:

- Chronic tiredness or sleepiness
- Headache
- Dizziness
- Sore or aching muscles
- Muscle weakness
- Slowed reflexes and responses
- Impaired decision making and judgement
- Moodiness, such as irritability
- Impaired hand to eye co-ordination
- Appetite loss
- Reduced immune system function
- Blurry vision
- Short-term memory problems

- Poor concentration
- Hallucinations
- Reduced ability to pay attention to the situation, at hand
- Low motivation

Practice Assignment

In the same organisation, where you have visited earlier, identify work related fatigue and suggest your action plan to remove work related fatigue.

BOREDOM AT WORKPLACE

Boredom is a condition characterised by a perception of one's environment as dull, tedious, and lacking in stimulation. There is an inherent anxiety in boredom; people will expend considerable effort to prevent or remedy it, yet, in many circumstances, it is accepted as a suffering to be endured. Common passive ways to escape boredom are to sleep or think creative thoughts (daydream). Typical active solutions consist in an intentional activity of some sort, often something new, as familiarity and repetition lead to the tediousness.

The first record of the word boredom is in the novel, Bleak House, by Charles Dickens, written in 1852, although the expression to be a bore had been used in the sense of "to be tiresome or dull" since 1768.

Definition of Boredom

There is no consensus on the definition of boredom, although some common themes exist in the various attempts at defining the construct. These include the following features:

- *The Environment:* A monotonous, repetitive, low stimulation environment (perceived or real)
- *Arousal:* Less than optimal (low) levels of physiological arousal
- *Affect:* A dissatisfying emotional state
- *Cognition:* Concentration, attention deficits
- *Perception:* One-dimensional perceptual tendencies
- *Time:* Inefficient use of time and perception of time as passing slowly.

Review of various definitions of boredom, presented in tabular form below, indicate the term has been used and described by various authors differently.

Table 25.1: Definitions of Boredom

Author(s)	Definition
O'Hanlon (1981)	"... unique psychophysical state that is somehow produced by prolonged exposure to monotonous stimulation" (p. 54)
Hill and Perkins (1985)	"... boredom occurs when stimuli is construed as subjectively monotonous" (p. 237)
De Cheene and Moody (1988)	a "...sense of inadequate stimulation from the environment" (p. 20)
Geiwitz (1966)	"... that monotony objectively defined as an attribute of the situation is less important than the subjective feeling of repetitiveness" (p. 593)
Csikszentmihalyi (1975, 1990)	Boredom occurs when an individual's ability exceeds environmental demands.
Barmack (1937)	Boredom is due to an individual having to work on a task that is no longer gratifying.
Fenichel (1951)	boredom "... arises when we must not do what we want to do, or must do what we do not want to do" (p. 359)
Mikulas and Vodanovich (1993)	"A state of relatively low arousal and dissatisfaction which is attributed to an inadequately stimulating environment" (p. 1)
Leary, Rogers, Canfield, & Coe (1986)	"... an affective experience associated with cognitive attentional processes" (p. 968)
Damrad-Frye & Laird (1989)	the product of a "...metacognitive judgement about one's attentional capacity" (p. 320)
Fisher (1987)	"...an unpleasant, transient affective state in which the individual feels a pervasive lack of interest in and difficulty concentrating on the current activity" (p. 396)
Perkins and Hill (1985)	The onset of boredom occurs by perceiving stimuli as unidimensional. "...cognitive changes in the direction of less differentiated and more homogeneous construing give rise to a state of subjective monotony which induces, or perhaps even represents, the state we call boredom..." (p. 231)
Waugh (1975)	Boredom occurs "...our attitude toward time is altered...Time seems endless, there is no distinction between past, present, and future. There seems to be only an endless present." (p. 541)
Iso-Ahola & Weissinger (1987); Iso-Ahola & Crowley (1991)	The inability to adequately organise one's time increases the likelihood of boredom
Phillips (1993)	It is incorrect to consider boredom to be a single construct but rather "... the boredoms, because the notion itself includes a multiplicity of moods and feelings ..." (p. 78).

Practical Effects of Boredom

Workplace boredom can have major negative impacts on people. It hurts people's sense of self-worth, which can cause them to work less effectively or even to not work at all. On the other hand, boredom may be beneficial in some ways. Boredom is a natural feeling that comes about when the person feels as though there is nothing new or nothing to inspire their thought in that situation. To relieve boredom, then, that person may take up a new hobby or come up with an interesting idea by thinking creatively.

Monotony at Workplace

The word boredom is related with the term monotony. Monotony is defined as the tedious lack of variety or dullness arising from the fact that nothing different ever happens. It is an unvarying condition of work (repetitiousness). Since the root of monotony is the boredom at workplace, which we have discussed extensively in the foregoing sections, here we are not discussing the same again. However, job enrichment can be the best option to avert monotony at work. Among others, job enrichment requires adding new variety of job so that an employee can get respite from the monotonous daily routine.

Practice Assignment

It is often stated that boredom and monotony are the natural outcomes of protocol (standardised) bound job. Some organisations are however, able to address this by their innovative practices. Collect some industry examples and illustrate.

HAZARDS AT WORKPLACE

A hazard is a source or potential source of human injury, ill health or disease. There is a range of hazards which need to be identified, assessed and controlled before starting the relocation or closure process. These include physical, psychological and social hazards.

Physical Hazards

Physical hazards are perhaps the most readily identifiable and increase during a relocation or closure process. These hazards are numerous and include:

- Clutter from boxes, furniture and trolleys
- Obstruction of thoroughfares where corridors and passageways are used as temporary storage areas
- Manual handling risks associated with lifting, shifting, packing and moving,
- Cleaning products.

EXAMPLE OF WORK PLACE HAZARDS

During the packing process, the office environment can become cluttered with boxes and additional waste disposal bins. It is important to ensure that there are designated areas for these items so that they are easily accessible (to reduce manual handling hazards) but do not obstruct traffic flow or emergency exits and firefighting equipment.

Social or Psychological Hazards

Social and psychological matters, contribute to psychological hazards, which stem from individual employee's perceived feeling that they are going to loose their jobs or when there are relocated or redeployed, or when they are required to adjust them with the organisational changes. Organisation can support its employees through the various processes, as outlined below to help them to overcome psychological hazards.

- Ensuring that lines of communication are open
- Ensuring that there are consultative mechanisms in place
- Recognising and addressing staff uncertainty
- Creating an atmosphere of support in the workplace.

Hazard Management

Hazard management aims to reduce the risk of injuries and illness associated with work. It is a systematic, sequential process for making an environment as safe as possible. The steps in the process are:

1. Identify the hazard by determining what has the potential to cause injury or illness.
2. Assess the risk understanding the likelihood of hazard, injury or illness and its consequences.
3. Control the risk duly identifying health and safety issues and establishing the control systems to eliminate or minimise the same.
4. Monitor and evaluate, ensuring that the control measures are effective.

For example, Let us assume that your organisation wants to identify the hazard involved in moving archive boxes and you have been asked to do the job. In what way you would like to perform the job?

Suggestions

1. Assess the risks to determine the likely weight of the boxes and how many are there to move.
2. Control the Risk by hiring or borrowing a trolley suitable to the task.
3. Monitor and review the hazard on a regular basis, taking stock of the number of archive boxes that are being moved to minimise double handling. Also, ensure that the type of trolley acquired is the right one for the job and that it is resolving the entire manual handling risks involved.

4. Evaluate the controls by determining whether the trolley will be available whenever the boxes need to be moved, and the staff is aware of safe loading and handling precautions and that it is the most appropriate way to do the job.

Common Hazards and Examples of Control Measures

Some of the examples of control measures for common hazards are as under:

1. Physical hazards control measures like: controlling of bending and stretching while packing/unpacking. Such bending or stretching control during the process of packing and unpacking can be ensured using the following preventive actions:

   (a) Reduce the excess load prior to move.

   (b) Use surfaces when packing/unpacking to eliminate the need to bend.

   (c) Ensure appropriate aids, for example, step ladder to reach items above shoulder height

   (d) Ensure adequate storage space at the new location which enables storage between knee and shoulder heights

   (e) Provide training for relevant staff

2. Lifting or moving boxes/equipment/furniture

   Allocate adequate resources to pay for professional removalists where appropriate.

3. Exposure to dust

   Arrange monitoring of the area. If dust is an issue, ensure quality cleaning. While doing this, it is important to deploy only those staff members who do not have respiratory complaints. Provide dust coats and gloves to the staff members.

4. Psychological Factors Control measures

   (a) Consultation, communication, access to an Employee Assistance Programme.

   (b) Implement transition programme including application/interview skills, financial and vocational advice.

Hazard Audit

Managing hazards at workplace requires systematic managerial intervention, more particularly from the HR department. The principal action in managing the hazards of the closure or relocation is to undertake a hazard audit. A hazard audit is a formal examination and documentation of the hazards identified and the control measures selected. A small team of suitable staff should undertake the hazard audit.

ACCIDENTS AND SAFETY ISSUES AT WORKPLACE

Accidents and Safety issues in organisations, both in India and abroad is a major area of concern for HR professionals. Accidents cannot be measured only in terms of frequency, i.e., number of times it occurs. It is measured in terms of severity. Accidents increase the number of mandays loss and compensation payment (both statutory and voluntary, more on humanitarian ground due to pressure of trade unions, etc.). Because of such enormity of situation, accident prevention, taking into account, safety measures is very important for organisations.

Before we analyse what causes accidents, let us try to understand the definition of accidents. An accident is an event which occurs without any predictable reason and leads to personal injury of workers and damage to the equipments or property of an organisation. Industrial accidents arise directly out of the work situation, which may be for faulty equipment or the inadequate performance of an individual worker or group, complexity of process and methods (when the operation itself is hazardous), etc. Whatever may be reasons for accidents, we can classify accidents based on three important dimensions, i.e., the nature of accident, the causes of an accident and the effect of an accident. We are illustrating these dimensions in the box below:

CLASSIFICATION OF ACCIDENTS

1. Nature of the event (assuming the accidents occurred during movement of materials in a forklift inside the factory)
   a. Collision with workers walking through the factory road
   b. Collision with other forklifts and light vehicles and trucks moving through the factory road
   c. Collision with fixed objects lying on the road
2. Causes of the event (assuming a machine operation)
   a. Catching of fingers, arms, clothing, etc., in machines
   b. Catching of tools, guides, etc., in machines
   c. Flying objects and particles

   (assuming a non-machine operation)
   I. Falling objects
   II. Objects on floor
3. Effects of an event (assuming accidents took place in a warehouse)
   a. Damage to stored items
   b. Damage to material handling equipments
   c. Personal injuries

Whatever may be the nature, causes and effects of accidents, results of accidents principally involve costs, industrial relations, human resource management problems, social consequences, etc.

Accident Prevention

Accident prevention requires investment for both employees and employers. Accidents are not only expensive, but they also lower the morale of the workers and in addition, result in lower production rates. As a group, companies with excellent safety records probably have more satisfied workers than companies with high accident severity and frequency. There is an interaction here. Just as accidents lower morale, poor morale appears to be a cause of accidents. Any accident prevention requires a consideration of the human element in the occurrence of accidents. Causation of accidents, like any problem of causation is a complex matter. Human errors are important cause of accidents and the mechanical failures. Two most important aspects of the human element in accident prevention are equipment design and training.

Safety – Definition and Concepts

The word safety can be defined as freedom from danger. Any workplace needs to be safe and without risk to health. Although there are various legal provisions for safe work place, normally we consider a work place to be safe one, when it satisfies the following conditions:

1. Foolproof maintenance of equipments, devices and systems in the work place
2. Effective and suitable provisions for ventilation
3. Provision for maintenance of a reasonable temperature
4. Provision and maintenance of suitable and sufficient lighting
5. Cleanliness of the workplace, furniture, furnishings and fittings
6. Provision of adequate facilities for the storage of waste
7. Prevention of overcrowding in the workplace
8. Provision of suitable workstations and seating
9. Maintenance of safe floors and traffic routes
10. Measure to prevent falls of people and falling objects
11. Installation of safe windows doors and gates
12. Ensuring safety of windows, skylights and ventilators
13. Ensuring control of movement of materials using fork lift
14. Safe doors and gates
15. Safe escalators and moving walkways.

Organisations develop a safe system of work by integrating people, machinery and materials in a safe environment and workplace to produce and maintain an acceptable standard of safety. To understand whether safety requirements are adequate, organisations systematically undertake safety audit. A safety audit is the systematic measurement and validation of an organisation's management of its health and safety programme against a series of specific and attainable standards. A safety audit subjects each area of an organisation's activities to a systematic critical examination with the principal objective of minimising loss. It is an ongoing process aimed at ensuring effective health and safety management.

Safety Culture

To ensure safe workplace, every organisation has to promote a safety culture. Some of the important issues to promote a safety culture can be listed as under:

1. Leadership and commitment from the top, which is genuine and visible.
2. Accepting safety as a long-term strategy, which requires sustained effort and interest.
3. A policy statement of high expectations and conveying a sense of optimism about what is possible supported by adequate code of practice and safety standards.
4. Health and safety should be treated as other corporate aims, and adequately resourced.
5. It must be a line management responsibility.
6. Ownership of both health and safety must permeate at all levels of the work force-this involves employee involvement, training and communication.
7. Realistic and achievable targets should be set and performance measured against them.
8. Incidents should be thoroughly investigated.
9. Consistency of behaviour against agreed standards should be achieved by auditing and good safety behaviour should be conditions of employment.
10. Deficiencies revealed by an investigation or audit should be remedied promptly.
11. Management must receive adequate and up-to-date information to be able to assess performance.

Practice Assignment

Visit a chemical processing unit and study their safety and accident prevention issues. Critically evaluate the same.

Legal Provisions for Occupational Health and Safety

Workplace safety has its relation with employee motivation, morale and productivity. With poor safety management, organisations not only suffer financial loss, but also deprive them from the benefits of productivity rise. Thus, safety issues are now considered voluntary and strategic initiative of an organisation. However, Indian organisations still lack in their safety initiatives. Indian labour laws have laid down certain provisions, requiring organisations to comply with those to ensure safe work place, free from occupational health hazards. The Factories Act, 1948, to give effect to some of the ILO conventions and recommendations, in its 1976 amendment, made compulsory appointment of safety officer. The stringent requirements have further been reinforced with the 1987 amendment of the Factories Act, extending the safety issues even outside the organisational boundary. All organisations are now bound to disclose information about their safety preparedness to the statutory authorities.

Similarly the Mines Act, 1952, also spelt out occupational health and safety issues. Likewise, The Dock Workers (Safety, Health and Welfare) Act, 1986, The Plantations Labour Act, 1951, The Shop and Establishments Act, The Explosives Act, 1884, The Petroleum Act, 1934, The Insecticides Act, 1968, Indian Boilers Act, 1923, The Dangerous Machines (Regulation) Act, 1983, The Environment (Protection) Act, 1986, The Indian Atomic Energy Act, 1962, etc. have some provisions or the other concerning occupational health and safety issues in organisations.

EMPLOYEE MORALE

Employee morale is a crucial component in the overall success of any company or organisation. When the work environment is demotivating, the employees loose their morale. Various studies indicate that high employee morale equates to high productivity. Linking between employee morale and motivation is a subject of qualitative measurement. However, degree of motivation, being quantitatively measured and motivation is the outcome of certain good HR practices like, competitive compensation, recognition, personal drive and loyalty to the organisation, organisations focus on measuring employees' morale through pro-active HR initiatives. Effective communication often considered as the log-lasting strategy to sustain employees' morale.

Morale is defined as the end result of many factors. Some of these factors are the work environment itself, worker satisfaction and action, compensation, supervisory style, working culture issues, status, etc. However, this list is not exhaustive. Some of the signs of decreased morale are: tardiness, absenteeism, apathy, backstabbing, decreased quality, decreased productivity, increased errors, accidents or injuries. HR managers must appreciate that morale is not a cause, but rather the effect or result of many factors.

Steps to Improving Morale

Since causes of reduced employees' morale are difficult to measure, it is difficult to come up with some prescribed morale improvement strategy from organisational point of view. It is first important to understand the reasons for poor morale. If not directly measurable, organisations take initiative to improve the morale through several motivational reinforcements. Some of the widely practiced measures to improve morale could be: showing concern to employees, inculcating a sense of feeling in the minds of the employees that organisations are committed to care for them; providing appropriate feedback; creating goals; recognising the employees' efforts; providing challenging tasks, etc. Morale exists when people know their jobs and understand how their jobs help to accomplish the mission of the organisation. Employees with high morale willingly sacrifice their goals for the goals of others and the organisation. This approach recognises that the customer is first. To ensure high morale, professional organisations develop employees to feel more responsible for their performance and quality of jobs, empower them, reward them and inculcate a sense of fearlessness.

Practice Assignment

Do you believe that increased level of employee morale can lead to higher performance and productivity? Elucidate your answer with an industry example.

Personnel Record-keeping for Better Work Environment Management

Personnel Records, also called personnel files, are recorded information about employees, which are kept by an employer, usually in the form of and under the name "personal files".

Information is one of the most important inputs for an organisation. A boundary spanning sub-system of open organisation collects information inputs from outside the organisation, to bring changes in technical and managerial sub-system. This process enables an organisation to remain competitive in the market. In-house information, more particularly, those pertaining to employees can also serve as valuable inputs for decision making. Some of the personnel records are maintained more for statutory reasons. However, true benefits of maintaining personnel records can be derived, only when these are used for both routine and strategic decision-making. Personnel records can be maintained in one of the following basic systems:

- Manually (in file cabinets without a computer);
- With an integrated Payroll/Human Resources system;
- With a standalone Human Resource Information System (HRIS);
- Any combination of the three.

Manual personnel record systems exist in almost all companies. Organisations, which are not fully computerised, integrate such manual personnel record system in conformity with the computer systems requirements. This type of organisations maintains their integrated computerised payroll or HR systems. Some organisations, however, maintain stand-alone Human Resource Information Systems, to ensure that HR information become effective input for routine and strategic HR decisions.

Personnel records thus include all information collected, assembled or maintained by the organisation and relevant to the employment relationship of the individual with the organisation. Organisations maintain Personnel Files for individual employees to record and document relevant events and discussions with the employees regarding performance, recognition, promotion, demotion, compensation, leave, absence, disciplinary issues, training and conduct. Routine documentation in personnel files pertains to personal demographics of the employees. Maintaining some personnel records are statutory and such records need to be preserved for a longer time frame; while some other personnel records may be voluntarily maintained by an organisation to derive the benefit of strategic decisions like succession planning, competency mapping, etc.

Recommended retention periods (i.e. where no statutory retention periods exist) based on organisational practices are illustrated in table below:

Table 25.2: Recommended Retention Periods

Records	Recommended Retention Period
Human Resource valuation reports	Permanently
Application forms and interview notes (for unsuccessful candidates)	One year
Assessments under Health and Safety Regulations and records of consultations with safety representatives and committees.	Permanently
Money purchase details	6 years after transfer or value taken
Maternity/Parental Leave Records	5 years from birth/adoption of the child.
Pension scheme investment policies	12 years from the ending of any benefit payable under the policy
Pensioners' records	12 years after benefit ceases
Personnel files and training records (including disciplinary records and working time records)	6 years after employment ceases
Redundancy details, calculations of payments, refunds, notification to the Secretary of State	6 years from the date of redundancy
Senior executives' records	Permanently for historical purposes
Time cards/Attendance Records	2 years after audit
Trade union agreements	10 years after ceasing to be effective
Rules	Permanently
Board Meeting minute books	Permanently
Works council minutes	Permanently

List of Personnel Records

For organisational convenience, a tabular list of personnel records, which should be maintained in employees' personnel file, is reproduced as shown in Table 25.3.

Table 25.3: Tabular List of Personnel Records

Personnel File Contents	Document/File
A. Application Details	Yes ¨ No ¨
• Application for employment form • Employee CV • Employee I.D. document or permanent residency (Photostat) • Employee driver's license (Photostat) • Interviewing Notes • Interview Correspondence • Offer of Employment • Employee Acceptance • Employee Orientation Checklist • Employee Contact Numbers, Address and next of kin	
B. Salary Details	Yes ¨ No ¨
• Employee Salary Advice • Monthly salary advices • Complaints of indebtedness • Stop Order and other salary deduction authorization forms • Retirement Fund and Medical Aid membership forms • Beneficiary forms.	
C. Leave Record	Yes ¨ No ¨
• Leave schedules • Annual • Casual • Sick • Study/Sabbatical • Others	
D. Performance and Development	Yes ¨ No ¨
• Position Descriptions • Training records, including Formal Training Plans • Performance Plans • Performance Ratings	
E. Disciplinary Procedures	Yes ¨ No ¨
• Pending personnel actions, awards recommendations, etc. • Disciplinary/adverse action backup materials • Disciplinary File Documentation Checklist • Objective: To provide a clear audit trail of all actions taken and leading up to a formal disciplinary action. 1. Copies of notice of proposed action • Employee response (or notation that no written response made) • Summary of response when made orally (including employee's or representative's signature as to accuracy of memorandum) • Notice of decision and reasoning behind decision (specifically addressing Douglas factors)	

Contd...

Supporting documentation such as: 1. Witness statements 2. Affidavits 3. Documents 4. Investigative reports or extracts of them 5. Pertinent regulations 6. Personnel actions 7. Reports on personal interviews/group meetings 8. Evidence of delivery of notice letters 9. Completed case sheets, with all items filled in (noting "N/A" if necessary)	
F. Grievance Procedures	Yes ¨ No ¨
Objective: To provide a clear audit trail on all actions taken and leading up to a final decision on each grievance. This checklist applies to both negotiated and administrative grievances. Written grievance. Designation of representative. Witness statements. Memos on discussions with grievant/supervisor/rep/witnesses. All Grievance forms and Notices. Chairperson (all levels) report of findings and recommendations. Union letter invoking dispute Request for arbitration or application to Labour Court (Memos regarding meetings with union to select arbitrator/schedule arbitration, etc.) Brief. Arbitration notes. Post-hearing brief. Arbitrator's or Labour Court decision. Record of implementation of arbitrator's decision. Other supporting documentation such as: Applicable regulations Official documents (e.g., performance plans, performance ratings) Documentation regarding requests for and approval of extensions/waivers of any steps in the process.	
G. Personal Medical Information	Yes ¨ No ¨

Note: Medical documentation, including injury compensation forms, suitability and/or security information should not be maintained in this folder. Other official folders must be established for this purpose.

Recommendations for Personnel Record Keeping

- Review applicable laws with regard to required records.
- Review employment application forms, evaluation forms, and other similar documents to be sure that they are non-discriminatory.
- Review with supervisors, the kind of disciplinary documentation, which should be maintained in all employee files.

- Know to what extent state laws mandates employee access to personnel files and establish a system for controlling such access.
- Do not disclose information on employees except to those who have a legitimate need to know the information.
- Do not discuss charges or complaints against individual employees with more people than absolutely necessary.
- Get consent before disclosure where possible.
- Have one person responsible for all disclosures to ensure consistency of treatment.
- Provide "neutral" references for former employees.
- Maintain adequate security overall employment records.

Use of Human Resource Information System (HRIS) for maintaining Personnel Records

An HRIS is a systematic procedure for collecting, storing, maintaining, retrieving and validating data needed by an organisation about its resources. The HRIS is usually a part of the organisation's larger Management Information System (MIS). The HRIS need not be complex or even computerised. But computerisation has its own advantage of providing more accurate and timely data for decision making. Thus, Human Resource Information Systems (HRIS) are defined as the range of computerised technology that is used to store, record, link, analyze and present data about the human element within the business. Connections to the external environment through the Internet are significant in this definition, as are Intranets which allow organisations, the potential to communicate from within, more rapidly and effectively. HRIS will assist in the provision of high-level customer focus and lowering an organisation's operational costs. Although HRIS includes hardware and software, it also includes people, policies, procedures and data. The areas of application of HRIS are many. Some of them include training management, risk management, turnover analysis, succession planning, flexible benefits, compliance with government and legal requirements, attendance with governments and legal requirements, attendance reporting and analysis, HRP, accident reporting and prevention, strategic planning, financial planning and other related areas.

WHISTLE BLOWING

Whistle blowing is raising the voices usually by the members of the organisations, who are presently serving or who had served earlier against the illegal, immoral or illegitimate practices, detrimental to the interests of the organisation in the long run. The concept is often institutionalised by the organisations with a documented policy, both in the interest of the organisations and the whistle blowers. In organisations, many sensitive issues may encompass the role of some employees, even in their day to day work. For example, internal auditors, inspectors, etc., play the most crucial roles in company's finance functions. Even marketing managers' unethical products campaigning go against the interests of the organisations. Sometimes, managers and executives may, at times, be biased in many employment related decisions, like, recruitment, promotion, transfers, compensation design and even in decisions pertaining to dismissals. It may not always be possible for the management to gauge the justification of decisions as many such decisions are subjective and often influenced by the personal prejudices and bias of the managers and executives. In such cases, whistle blowers can play the most effective role in giving the warning signals. But whistle blowers often require revealing their observations to the managers who are outside their normal chain of command. Even at times, they go out of the organisational hierarchy and make such information available to various regulatory bodies for positive action. In such situations, whistle blowers may even have untoward experience, to the extent of threatening of their security and safety. It is for this reason that those organisations which believe in good corporate governance always prefer the structured whistle blowing policy.

Factors that Influence Whistle Blowing

A whistle blower in organisations perceives the following factors:

1. Occurrence of some misdeeds or illegal activities - The whistle blower perceives that such things can be prevented by the top management of the organisation.
2. Whistle blowers believe that some action can control such illegal or immoral activities.
3. Whistle blowers follow a process to expose the problem to the top management, expecting some action that leads to correction.

Careful examination of the above factors indicates that whistle blowing involves organisational and individual dependence. Often, we observe in organisations that some employees play the role of whistle blowers. This may be partially attributable to the accessibility to the information, which is obviously restricted to some employees. Other reason may be the prevalence of organisational culture that dissuades employees to indulge in whistle blowing. Whatever may be the reason, employees do whistle blowing, out of their sense of moral responsibility, guts and concern for the organisation and society.

In organisations, whistle blowing per se was all along the domain of trade unions. But trade unions' whistle blowing was often construed as a perennial opposition of managerial activities. With more institutionalised approach, today, whistle blowing has become the responsibility of all cross-sections of employees, whosoever has the access to the sensitive information. It is not always essential that every whistle blowing will lead to detection of some disorder in the activities of the organisations. Therefore, organisations that believe in good corporate governance must not discourage those whistle blowers, whose information leads to no results; rather try to appreciate their concern for the organisations. At the same time, organisations must also take positive steps for the security and safety of the whistle blowers, after the information leads to results.

In Enron's case, the whistle blower Sherron Watkins, had to face lot of opposition from the co-workers, top management, etc. By promoting the befitting culture of the organisation, it is possible to get better results from whistle blowing.

Whistle Blowing and the HR Department

HR Department can play the most crucial role in instutionalising the whistle blowing. But in some cases, when whistle blowing issues pertain to HR department's issues, it may be often difficult for the whistle blowers to take HR head into confidence, fearing he/she may be party to the irregularities. Nevertheless, HR departments of the organisations, in most of the cases, facilitate in managing the whistle blowing. HR must focus on setting up the channels and appropriate mechanisms for healthy and open communication to dispel the fear of the whistle blowers. Apart from developing a documented systems and procedures, HR may train the employees, to make them aware on the process of handling the whistle blowing issues.

Ethics and Values for HR

Values and Ethics are two moral principles which today's organisations need to integrate with the behaviour of all cross-sections of employees, so that it reflects in all their actions. To ensure this in organisational practices, most of the organisations adopt certain code of ethics. Both the terms are used interchangeably and construed as the science of conduct or the values of management. Moreover, values are considered as the important constructs of ethics. In organisations, moral values are reflected through mutual respect, honesty, fairness, sense of responsibility, etc. Through some documented code of ethics, organisations, make their employees aware about right or wrong in their decision making and in all other organisational practices. Operationally, therefore, we can define ethics as the framework of values for moral behaviour. Again, ethics encompass both the business and profession. While business represents application of ethics in our decisions and actions, profession requires adherence to certain code of ethics specific to the profession. Historically, in India, guild systems laid down the ethics of business or profession. Codes of ethics are documented guidelines for compliance and every employee of the organisations, by virtue of his membership with the organisations are expected to comply with such code of ethics. Code of ethics and the perceived values vary between individuals and across the cultures.

We have four key ethical principles: egalitarianism, utilitarianism, individual right and distributive justice. With a utilitarianism approach in ethics, organisations take decisions based on the perceived decisional outcomes.

Code of ethics is different from the code of conduct. Code of ethics is the statement of values and beliefs, while the codes of conducts are translating the values into some specific behavioural standards. In other words, codes of conduct are the outlines of some fundamental set of principles. Ethical values are critical to the performance of individual employees and the organisation as a whole. Ethics and values are considered integral part of organisational functioning. Perceived ethical values exert impact on organisations in the following ways:

- Influence the efficiency and effectiveness of individual level and organisational performance
- Influence the decision-making processes
- Influence employees' commitment and job satisfaction
- Influence employees' stress in workplace
- Influence employees' turnover.

Through ethical practices, organisations can also get the benefit of favourable public image. People always repose their confidence on ethical organisations and buy their products and services without questioning. Many Indian organisations like, TAYA, ITC, Murugappa Group, Grasim, etc. are today favourably considered by the people for their focus on ethical business practices and social responsibilities.

SUMMARY

This unit elaborates on several HR applications area in an organisation. For HR manager, understanding organisational environment, both in the context of internal and task related issues and external environmental issues are now considered very important. Organisational environment per se affects performance and productivity of the employees. Hence, its effective management is now an important priority for HR managers. Many organisation environmental issues (more particularly task related) contribute to employees' fatigue, monotony, boredom, accidents, safety, morale and grievances. As HR manager, each micro effect needs to be managed, or else organisation will loose its business focus and nurture unproductive and demotivated workforce, which only add to the financial burden of the organisation. The chapter finally concludes with elaborate discussions on personnel record keeping, duly focusing on both statutory and voluntary perspectives. The unit also discusses on Personnel Record Keeping, as it helps efficient management of human resources in organisation.

KEYWORDS

Personnel Records	Employee Morale
Boredom	Monotony
Work Place Safety	Work related stress
Whistle Blowing	

REVIEW QUESTIONS

1. Define Human Resource Accounting. For designing Human Resource Accounting System, what are the factors you need to be considered?

2. Define Personnel Audit. What are its objectives and importance?

3. What is the scope of Personnel audit? What records need to be used for it?
4. Briefly explain methods and techniques of Personnel audit.
5. Discuss stepladder system in Grievance Handling.
6. Define the term work environment. What internal work environment factors influence employees' performance and productivity?
7. What is wok-related fatigue? How can it be managed in an organisation?
8. Explain the term boredom. Is it different from monotony? How boredom can be avoided in an organisation?
9. For HR professionals how safety issues are important? What steps do you recommend as HR manager to avoid industrial accidents in an organisation?
10. Explain the nature of personnel records. What type of personnel records do you recommend for an organisation?
11. What is employee morale? How can it be measured? In what way can increased level of employee morale benefit an organisation?
12. Write short notes on:
    (a) Checklist and Personnel Audit
    (b) Music at work
    (c) Shift work
    (d) Safety culture
    (e) Hazards Audit
    (f) Workplace stress

CASE STUDY 1

UNITED TECHNOLOGIES CORPORATION (UTC) - ENSURING GLOBAL PRESENCE THROUGH ETHICAL PRACTICES

With more than 2.5 lakhs employees having presence in 62 countries, UTC today is a global conglomerate. UTC's business units are: Carrier Corporation, Hamilton Sundstrand, Otis Elevator, Pratt & Whitney, Sikorsky, UTC Power and the Chubb. Obviously, for its global presence, UTC's most challenging task is to make their new recruits understand their global ethics programme, integrating cross-cultural and cross-country work environment. UTC's ethics programme conforms to the global workplace. Most of the UTC's business units are almost a century old. UTC's business ranges from aircraft engines, helicopters, security and fire protection, air control systems, detector lock to machine tools. Compliance with ethical issues are especially important, as many regulatory norms embrace UTC's manufacturing ventures. As a major vendor to US Government Department of Defense in 80s, in one of the UTC units, there was serious allegation of ethical violation, which was like making super-normal profit in Defense contracts. All these prompted UTC to increase their self-regulation through formal Code of Ethics, which UTC had adopted since 1990. UTC's Code of Ethics is articulation of standards of conduct surpassing even the legal requirements. UTC successfully embraced the Code of Ethics in their corporate culture and business practices.

At the corporate level, UTC's code of ethics shows commitment to the highest standards of ethics and business conduct, encompassing their relationships with the customers, suppliers, shareholders, competitors and the communities, including its own employees.

Source: Web-site reference: http://www.utc.com

CASE STUDY 2

SAMPLE CODE OF ETHICS OF INFOSYS, INDIA

Sample Code of Ethics on Corporate Governance of Infosys, India is reproduced below:

We believe that sound corporate governance is critical to enhance and retain investor trust. Accordingly, we always seek to ensure that we attain our performance rules with integrity. Our Board exercises its fiduciary responsibilities in the widest sense of the term. Our disclosures always seek to attain the best practices in international corporate governance. We also endeavour to enhance long-term shareholder values and respect minority rights in all our business decisions.

Our corporate governance philosophy is based on the following principles:

1. Satisfy the spirit of the law and not just the letter of the law. Corporate governance standards should go beyond the law.
2. Be transparent and maintain a high degree of disclosure levels. When in doubt, disclose.
3. Make a clear distinction between personal conveniences and corporate resources.
4. Communicate externally, in a truthful manner, about how the Company is run internally.
5. Comply with the laws in all the countries in which the Company operates.
6. Have a simple and transparent corporate structure driven solely by business needs.
7. Management is the trustee of the shareholders' capital and not the owner.

At the core of our corporate governance practice is the Board, which oversees how the management serves and protects the long-term interests of all stakeholders of the Company. We believe that an active, well-informed, and independent Board is necessary to ensure the highest standards of corporate governance. The majority of the Board, 8 out of 15, are independent members. Further, we have audit, compensation, investor grievance, nominations, and risk management committees, which comprise independent directors.

As a part of our commitment to follow global best practices, we comply with the Euro shareholders Corporate Governance Guidelines 2000 and the recommendations of the Conference Board Commission on Public Trusts and Private Enterprises in the U.S. We also adhere to the UN Global Compact Programme.

Question

Read the above two Code of Ethics. Identify the differences. Develop your answer with suitable logic.

Source: http://www.infosys.com/investor/corporategovernance.asp. Accessed on 16th August, 2007

BLOCK NINE

EMERGING ISSUES

UNIT 26

International Human Resource Management

Learning Objectives

After completion of this unit, the students will be aware of the following topics:

- *Introduction*
- *Definition and Concepts*
- *Different Aspects of IHRM*
- *Difference between IHRM and Domestic HRM*
- *Reasons for the Emergence of IHRM*
- *Components of IHRM*
- *A Model of IHRM*
- *Human Resource Planning (HRP)*
- *International Human Resource Staffing – The Mix of PCNs, TCNs, and HCNs*
- *IHRM Policies and Practices*
- *IHRM and Managing Diverse Culture*
- *Managerial Practices in China, Korea and Japan*
- *International Manners*

Lehman Brothers – The Collapse that Challenged the Global HR

The WorldCom, Enron and then, the Lehman Brothers: three large corporate disasters literally challenged the global HR practices. The first casualty of any corporate collapse is the people, whom we consider as the most precious resources, for their inimitable characteristics to benefit organisations with sustainable competitive advantages. Most of the times, effect of such collapse restricts to the organisation itself. This was also for WorldCom and Enron. But Lehman's collapse had cascaded to the landscape of global business. It was on September 15, 2008, when Lehman Brothers officially announced its bankruptcy, the largest in the history. When Lehman declared its bankruptcy, it had $639 billion in assets and $619 billion in debt. With 25,000 employees in its roll, Lehman's demise literally sparked financial crisis globally; so much so, it literally had adverse effects on global economy. This was because of Lehman's typical nature of business, i.e., the subprime mortgage. With its humble beginning in 1850, the company gradually became the international powerhouse. The subprime mortgage business vertical of Lehman was to captivate the opportunities of U.S. housing boom. From a sky rocketing stock value of $86.18 in February, 2007, suddenly Lehman started realising its fall. The first quarter of 2007 was the beginning of negative results, side by side with the crackdown of U.S. housing market and consequent rise in the cases of defaults on subprime mortgages. This is what we call the syndrome of home delinquencies. The subprime crisis gradually engulfed the entire housing market and then, even cascaded to the U.S. economy and then, to the global economy.

To recover from shock, the CEO of the company, Mr. Richard Fuld took series of measures like, part selling of assets, hiding of commercial real estate assets, etc. Fuld did all these to get a stake from Korea Development Bank, who later put the discussion on hold.

With Lehman's collapse, the corporate world started large scale downsizing of human resources, restructuring and scaling down their operations, in their disparate attempt to survive. But many could not survive and had to close their operations. Apparently people became the liability for the organisations. The worrisome business scenarios further sparked the age-old practices of contractual short-term employment, reducing human resources, like another passive inputs to a production process. HR gradually became the most challenging function, as HR managers from their strategic role had to belittle them to the firefighting role.

Introduction

Emergence of trade blocks with the formation of different economic and political forums like; European Union, North America Free Trade Association, Asia Pacific Economic Conference and expanding role of World Trade Organisation have now significantly changed the global business environment. Internationalisation of business now exerts influence not only on labour markets and staffing requirements but also on HR practices. Multi-domestic operations, joint ventures and strategic alliances are common forms of business structures across regions. Changes in organisational structures, relationships with overseas operations, state-of-the-art communications technology and global market now demand different HR approaches for managing MNCs.

Definition and Concepts

International human resource management (IHRM) is the process of sourcing, allocating, and effectively utilising human resources in a multinational organisation. In global organisations human resource managers are required to achieve two conflicting strategic objectives. First to integrate human resource policies and practices across a number of subsidiaries in different countries and second to make HRM practices sufficiently flexible to accommodate different business and cultural settings. Such problem of balancing integration and differentiation is a common dilemma facing international HR managers and other functional managers in global organisations.

International human resource management (IHRM) is about the worldwide management of human resources. The purpose of international human resources management is to enable the firm, the multinational corporations (MNCs), to be successful globally. Some of the important objectives of IHRM are: (a) remaining competitive throughout the world; (b) efficient; (c) locally responsive; (d) flexible and adaptable and (e) capable of transferring learning across their globally dispersed units.

For many organisations, IHRM is the most important critical success factor. IHRM requires a much broader perspective even for the most common HR activities. Even when dealing with one particular HR function area such as compensation, the international HR manager is faced with a great variety of national and international pay issues. For example, while dealing with pay issues, the HQ-based HR manager must coordinate pay systems in different countries with different currencies that may change in relative value to one another over time. In the case of fringe benefits provided to host company employees, some interesting complications might arise. A final aspect of the broader scope of IHRM is that the HQ-based manager deals with employee groups that have different cultural backgrounds. The HQ manager must coordinate policies and procedures to manage expatriates from the firm's home country. Parent Country Nationals, (PCNs), Host-Country Nationals (HCNs), as well as third country nationals (TCNs, e.g. an Indian manager working for a German MNC in the firm's Mexican subsidiary) in subsidiaries around the world.

Although such issues are important for the HQ-based manager, they are also relevant to the HR manager located in a subsidiary. This manager must develop HR systems that are not only acceptable to the host country but also compatible with company-wide systems being developed by his or her HQ-based counterpart. These policies and practices must effectively balance the needs and desires of local employees, PCNs and TCNs.

Different Aspects of IHRM

International Human Resource Management (IHRM): encompasses strategic and operational aspects of international HRM. According to Schuler et a1., 2002, IHRM covers following areas:

- Understanding international HRM strategies and practices in relation to changing strategies of the international business firm.
- Exploring the links between the implementation of international strategies and international HRM policy and practices.
- Developing comprehensive frameworks to reflect the complex set of environmental factors.
- Examining international HRM activities to recognise their systematic interaction.

It is now recognised world wide that HRM is strategic to business success. IHRM is the internationalisation of business, and the HRM strategies, policies and practices, which organisations pursue to meet the requirement of internationalisation of business (Scullion,

1995). It is now agreed globally that IHRM is essentially concerned with some core activities of recruitment and selection, training and development, compensation and repatriation of expatriates, managing multicultural teams and international diversity and performance management.

Difference between IHRM and Domestic HRM

There are some commonalities in IHRM and domestic HRM practices, particularly in areas like: HR planning and staffing, recruitment and selection, appraisal and development, rewards, etc. The main distinction, however, lies in the fact that while domestic HRM is involved with employees within only one national boundary. IHRM deals with three national or country categories, i.e., the parent country where the firm is actually originated and headquartered; the host country where the subsidiary is located; and other countries from where the organisation may source the labour, finance or research and development. This is because there are three types of employees in an international organisation, i.e., Parent-Country Nationals (PCNs); Host-Country Nationals (HCNs); and third-country nationals (TCNs). There are two major factors therefore which differentiate domestic HRM from IHRM. First, the complexities of operating in different countries (and therefore in different cultures), and secondly, employing different national categories of workers. This suggests that international HRM is concerned with identifying and understanding how MNCs manage their geographically dispersed workforces in order to leverage their HR resources for both local and global competitive advantage (Schuler et a1., 2002). Globalisation has brought new challenges and increased complexity such as the challenge of managing newer forms of network organisation. In recognition of such developments, new requirements of IHRM is to play a key role in achieving a balance between the need for control and coordination of foreign subsidiaries, and the need to adapt to local environments.

Reasons for the Emergence of IHRM

Main reasons, for the rapid growth of interest in the field, over the last decade and a half, have been outlined by Scullion (2001) as under:

1. The rapid growth of internationalisation and global competition has increased the number and significance of MNCs in recent years, resulting in the increased mobility of human resources (Black et a1., 2000).

2. The effective management of human resources and the quality of management is now recognised as a major determinant of success or failure in international business (Black et a1., 1999; Harris et a1., 2003).

3. The performance of expatriates is crucial for achieving success or else the indirect costs of poor performance of expatriates may affect the market share and damage to foreign customer relations.

4. Shortages of international managers now stand against implementation of global strategies. This implies an increasing need for international managers with distinctive competences to manage culturally diverse work force in MNCs.

5. Traditional hierarchical organisational structures are now becoming redundant and MNCs are going for network of personal relationships and horizontal communication channels. In network organisation, HR plays a pivotal role.

6. HR strategy now plays a more significant role in implementation and control in the international firm, which requires developing different organisational cultures. This has significantly enhanced the role of IHRM.

7. Increasing number of strategic alliances and cross-border mergers and acquisitions has further increased the strategic importance of IHRM as global business is increasingly shifting from formal, developed and matured markets to informal, emerging and culturally distant markets (Harvey et a1., 1999a).

8. Learning, knowledge-acquisition and adaptation have been identified as important potential sources of competitive advantage for MNCs. This has also enhanced the role of IHRM to meet the key strategic challenge of objectives.

9. Similarly, knowledge management is also an important source of competitive advantage for multinational firms. Knowledge management requires organisation's ability to create, transfer and integrate knowledge across borders. IHRM in this context play a central role.

10. Growing importance of expatriation in international firms; that is, the practice of developing host-country managers or third-country managers through developmental transfers to corporate headquarters has also enhanced the role of IHRM. Such developmental assignments for local managers provide the means for them to develop the skills and knowledge they will need to manage a global business.

COMPONENTS OF IHRM

HRM has several components:

1. Acceptance of plurality – different approaches may be appropriate in different regions, under different market conditions, and at different stages in the life of an organisation.

2. Acceptance that migration is a key global phenomenon of the second half of the twentieth century, and that culturally diverse workforces are the result of this great movement of people around the globe. Organisations are now increasingly recognising the need for a cross-cultural approach to HRM.

The benefits of cross-cultural HRM are:

- It enables organisations to overcome language barriers.
- It avoids misunderstandings when representatives do business overseas.
- IHRM prepares people to work overseas, as it develops people beyond outdated stereotypes.
- Managers can work and manage diverse workforces which widens clientele base.

Effective cross-cultural HRM is based on a recognition of intercultural differences. People who have been trained for working across cultures are able to avoid misunderstandings based on differences in:

- Attitudes to time
- Degree of individualism
- The amount of personal space around people, stepping inside which creates discomfort, or maintenance of which gives an impression of unfriendliness
- Communication style (for example direct/indirect, plain/flowery)
- Power distance (the degree to which people of different ethnic background expect to be treated with different levels of respect
- Competitiveness – the degree to which competition is a significant motivator
- Orientation to action or to waiting or listening.

Managing cultural diversity, whether overseas or in a multicultural workplace, requires the following preparatory steps:

1. ***Cultural audit:*** Managers can audit their own cultural assumptions and those of their organisation.
2. ***Briefing from cultural expert:*** Briefings about customs, laws and regulations in the overseas host country should draw on the expertise of nationals from that country; similarly within multinational workplaces intercultural briefings may be useful.
3. The management initiative needs to be checked for cultural assumptions:
   (a) *Goal setting or management by objectives:* is this the best approach in cultures where there is less belief that the actions of individuals can make an impact on outcomes?
   (b) *Performance appraisal:* is this a system of feedback-giving? In some countries praise or criticism are not offered directly.
   (c) *Performance pay:* individual performance pay may be inappropriate in cultures where collectivism and community are more valued than individualism.
   (d) *Grievance procedures:* these may not be appropriate in cultures where it is not common to confront conflict explicitly.
4. Training is seen as the most important preparation for an overseas assignment, and cross-cultural training is also important in culturally diverse workplaces.
   (a) Information sessions may be enough for shorter visits.
   (b) Affective education - for example role plays and discussion sessions will be needed where attitude change is important.

(c) Immersion techniques such as months of intensive language and cultural training are required for situations where staff are going to live and work overseas for a year or more.

A Model of IHRM

Model of IHRM is based on the framework offered by Schuler, Dowling, and DeCieri (1993). According to Sundaram and Black (1992), MNC is:

"any enterprise that carries out transactions in or between two sovereign entities, operating under a system of decision-making that permits influence over resources and capabilities, where the transactions are subject to influence by factors exogenous to the home country environment of the enterprise".

This definition serves to highlight the differences between managing global firms and domestic firms and thus establishes the basis for conceptualising IHRM as substantially more encompassing than domestic human resource management. A consequence of this for most MNCs is a human resource department that develops and administers the following policies and practices but across a wide variety of nations, each with its own social, cultural, legal, economic, political, and historical characteristics (Morgan 1986):

- Human resource planning
- Staffing
- Performance evaluation
- Training and development
- Compensation and benefits
- Labour relations/safety and health

With strategic perspective, today's model of IHRM incorporates the broader, contextual reality encompassing a strategic perspective.

Human Resource Planning (HRP)

In IHRM, Human resource planning is an indispensable means of effective inter-unit linkage. It involves synchronising the staffing, appraisal, and compensation sub-systems of IHRM. HRP in IHRM needs to be comprehensive and responsive to the MNC's industry characteristics, product stage, organisational phase of international development, global structure and competitive strategies (Bartlett and Ghoshal 1991, 1998). These considerations are reflected in the following critical human resource planning issues facing MNCs:

- Identifying top management potential at the earliest possible career stage.
- Identifying critical success factors for the future international manager.
- Providing developmental opportunities.

- Tracking and maintaining commitments to individuals in international career paths.
- Tying strategic business planning to human resource planning, and vice versa.
- Dealing with the organisational dynamics of multiple (decentralised) business units while attempting to achieve global and regional strategies.
- Providing meaningful assignments at the right time to ensure adequate international and domestic human resources.

Specific focus in HRP of MNCs, as highlighted by Wong (2000) are:

1. Assignment and cost planning,
2. Candidate selection,
3. Assignment terms and condition documentation,
4. Relocation processing and vendor management,
5. Cultural and language orientation/training,
6. Compensation administration and payroll processing,
7. Tax administration,
8. Career planning and development,
9. Handling spouse and dependent matters, and
10. Immigration processing.

To perform these tasks through an integrated HRP initiative is the major challenge for MNCs.

International Human Resource Staffing – The Mix of PCNs, TCNs, and HCNs

Staffing is a major IHRM practice that MNCs are required to coordinate. It is MNCs tradition to send parent-country nationals abroad to ensure that the policies and procedures of the home office were being carried out in foreign operations. However, for prohibitive cost and career issues, MNCs are now increasingly turning to third-country and host-country nationals to satisfy international staffing needs. Some of the critical dimensions for foreign assignment selection are; providing support to family, receiving support from family, knowledge of foreign language, adjustment to living abroad, sensitivity to and acceptance of cultural differences, acceptance of different mores (values, behavior, attitudes), developing/maintaining relationships, involvement in host community, coping with different/difficult living circumstances, locating resources (housing, food, etc.) in foreign countries, adjustment to foreign business practices, sensitivity to appropriate business protocol/practices, interacting with business contacts, clients, and staff in a socially acceptable manner, establishing and maintaining business contacts, etc. These apart, technical competences, maintaining smooth and effective working relationships with management and coworkers, working as an effective team member, communicating and persuading are also significantly different in MNCs.

For all these, it is important for international HR managers to develop a global work force and global managers.

Appraising Performance

Managing performance of expatriates also require evaluation of some performance dimensions which may not specifically be job-related. This encompasses cross-cultural interpersonal qualities; sensitivity to foreign norms, laws, and customs; adaptability to uncertain and unpredictable conditions; and the host location's integration with other MNC units, etc. The significance of these factors will vary by the type of expatriates.

Compensating the Expatriate

Expatriate compensation issue is also as significant as appraisal in fostering inter unit linkages and the attainment of international strategic objectives. The reality is that expatriates tend to have greater income security because performance evaluations usually are a rather modest determinant of their total compensation package. While PCNs may have fewer opportunities to invest in tax shelters and other economic amenities than their functional equivalents at home, the former can cost MNCs up to five times. A side effect of this cost differential is the substantial disparity between the salary of PCNs and that of HCNs or TCNs. This disparity has the potential to create status distinctions in an MNC's global workforce, thereby inhibiting inter unit linkages. Similar patterns are evident in the provision of benefits. Some of the key issues in compensating the expatriates are:

- How can MNCs develop pay structures that are cost-effective, fair, and adaptable to different employee groups?
- How can MNCs develop more culturally sensitive compensation schemes that recognize country differences, yet are equally motivating and still equitable?
- How can international-assignee compensation be better linked to the strategy and industry characteristics of a given MNC?

Training and Development

This aspect of IHRM presents another means of linking the dispersed units of an MNC. Increasingly, scholars and professionals are casting the training and developing of international assignees into a much larger frame, one consistent with broader, more theoretical, and systematic description of IHRM. For example, the family is now recognised as a very significant factor in expatriate's success. International HR planning is seen more often as a key orchestrator of expatriate career development, incorporating expatriate assignment decisions and the repatriation process. Perhaps most indicative of this shift in perspective is the contention that training and development is no more important for PCNs than it is for individuals from other parts of the world (Adler and Bartholomew, 1992). In fact, global firms can enhance their inter unit linkages by creating a pool of global managers with citizenship from anywhere in the world. Management development activities could be housed in corporate or global headquarters with local, regional, and other HR units assisting in programme design and delivery.

Internal Operations in IHRM

Internal operations require the same degree of research attention as inter unit linkages, since both have an influence on MNC effectiveness. Local units must recognise and abide by indigenous employment law, tradition, and custom, unless variances or exemptions have been granted by the host government, thus, overseas units need to be given some autonomy to adapt HR practices to local conditions. Yet, because they need to be co-ordinated with the rest of the MNC (e.g., to facilitate the transfer of local managers) some commonality must exist regarding human resource policies. The local unit needs to develop HR practices that advance its competitive strategy as well. They need to transcend mere conformity with indigenous culture.

IHRM Policies and Practices

There are at least three ways of enhancing internal operations through IHRM policies and practices. The first entails matching and adapting HR practices to closely accommodate the unit's competitive strategy, local culture, and governing legal system. The second necessitates creating a modus operandi whereby HRM practices can be modified swiftly to respond to changing host conditions. The third calls for a set of IHRM policies at the MNC level that can encompass and legitimise the HRM practices of the local units.

Matching and Adapting HR Practices

One means of ensuring that HR practices are consistent with labour-market requirements would be to staff the HR function with host-country nationals. In fact, this is one of the positions that MNCs seem most prone to fill with indigenous persons. To complement this fit, the location manager, in turn, needs to inform the HR manager of the unit's business needs, in particular its competitive strategy.

The process of systematically aligning human resource practices, policies, and philosophies with each other and the unit's strategic needs is similar for domestic corporations and MNCs. A major difference, however, lies in the need to balance the competitive strategy and cultural imperatives. The cultural imperative is an encompassing term that can include aspects of the local culture, economy, legal system, religious beliefs, and education. Its importance to IHRM resides in the definition of acceptable, legitimate, and feasible work practices and behaviors. Acceptable in terms of questions such as "Can we pay workers different rates, and thereby differentiate them, according to performance?" Legitimate in terms of questions such as "Are there any legal statutes prohibiting us from not paying workers overtime for work done on Saturday and Sunday?" Feasible in terms of questions such as "While this society espouses hierarchical, authoritarian, and paternalistic values, can we empower the workforce to make workplace decisions in order to facilitate our quality strategy?"

All of these components should influence decisions about where to locate units and which HR practices to use therein. The extent to which MNCs deliberate on these matters prior to host entry has not been examined in previous studies.

Local units also must be ready to ensure that HR practices, once developed, can be adapted to fit MNCs' evolving needs and goals. For example, host management might institute much more comprehensive succession planning and development schemes than are warranted in the host environment to accommodate the larger multinational's potential staffing and transfer needs. In all likelihood, this will be done for a limited pool of individuals (i.e., persons targeted as global managers). Another key issue is the relative impact that organisational and personal factors have on the lag period within MNCs for responsive adaptations in HR practice.

Key IHRM Issues in International Joint Ventures (IJVs)

In today's globalised world, partnerships, alliances and international joint ventures among two or more firms are becoming increasingly common. The existing IHRM literature highlights issues such as importance of IJVs, reasons for the formation of JVs, success and failures of JVs, conflict in IJVs, culture and control, IJVs and learning in and from IJVs. All these issues have implications for the management of HRs in IJVs. Of most reasons for the formation of IJVs, the reason that appears to gaining substantial momentum involves learning and knowledge, sharing and transfer. In this regard, the role and importance of HRM issues and activities in IJVs become of prime importance.

More specifically, within the IJV context there are a multitude organisational issues that are at the same time human resource issues. Broadly presented they can be categorised by organisational level and individual/group level.

Organisational Level

At this level the organisational/HR issues involve:

- ***Parent-to-Parent Relationships:*** such as seeking and selecting; building trust and cooperation; and learning about each other and from each other.
- ***Parent-to-IJV Relationships:*** such as identifying the reasons to establish the IJV, the appropriate structural relationship, e.g., degree of control vs. autonomy, methods of integration, the assignment of managers and non-managers for and to the IJV, and the management and transfer of learning and knowledge.
- ***IJV-Environmental Context Relationship:*** such as the identification of the relevant stakeholders and their objectives; and acquiring knowledge of the relevant laws, political system, social system, culture, customs, language, tradition and labour market.
- ***Parent Characteristics:*** including such issues as the values, vision, culture, practices, structure and strategy that will enable the parent to learn from the IJV itself and the other parent, in other words, organisational capability. Developing and utilising an

organisational-level capability appears to be more important for competitive partners that engage in IJVs.

Individual/Group Level

Several organisational/HR issues at the individual/group level in IJVs are:

- ***Learning, sharing, and transferring of knowledge*** to enable the other employees and team to learn and grow.
- *Competencies* (knowledge, skills, abilities, personality and habits) to perform the organisational roles.
- *Behaviours, actions and attitudes* that are consistent with needs of the business, customers and colleagues.
- ***Motivation and commitment*** to be productive, stay with the firm and attract others to the firm.
- ***Lack of business success in the IJV*** due to human resource issues such as lack of competent and motivated staff; staff not matched with the requirements of the competitive strategy, or staff not socialised and committed to the IJV itself; or staff not able to manage dual loyalties.

Virtually all of the issues listed above are significant in the IJV process and involve and depend upon HRM. These issues have significant HR implications for HR activities in IJVs.

HR Activities

The HR activities included here relate to, are associated with, and impact the organisational level and the individual/group level human resource issues indicated above. These include policies and practices associated with:

- Environmental analysis
- Organisational structure, design, strategy, values, mission and culture
- Human resource planning
- Job design and job analysis
- Recruitment, selection and orientation
- Training, socialisation and assimilation
- Performance and career management
- Remuneration (compensation)
- Employee welfare
- Communications

Auditing IHRM Initiatives

To ensure that all the HR related challenges are met, MNCs need to systematically evaluate their functional capacity and responsiveness in IHRM. Auditing strategic IHRM activities from multi-constituent, strategic fit, and efficiency-effectiveness perspectives is essential in IHRM. This synergistic approach examines the potential for conflict among the audit's stakeholders; the need to differentiate its contents based on competitive strategy, organisational lifecycle stage, and national culture; and the ways that effectiveness can be operationalised in multinational settings. Several propositions were developed that require close empirical scrutiny. There are also other ways of conducting IHRM audits. Ulrich (1999) suggests that HR audits can be conducted by assessing: (1) HR practices (i.e. assessing the array of services offered by an HR department), (2) HR professionals (for example, doing a 360 feedback on the extent to which an HR professional demonstrates competence), and (3) HR function or department (such as by computing functional competence, by investigating overall indicators of HR functions, or by measuring the competence against established benchmark standards).

IHRM and Managing Diverse Culture

Due to global business alignment, it has now become imperative to develop organisational culture with some unique characteristics. Culture is country specific belief, values and norms of a social group shared by its members and distinct from other social groups (Lytle, Brett, and Shapiro 1999). Culture concerns economic, political, social structure, religion, education, and language. Ruben (1983) defines culture as "... the extent that members of a social system share particular symbols, meanings, images, rule structures, habits, values, and information processing and transformational patterns they can be said to share a common culture." Hofstede (1980) reinforces this image of the group by stating, "the essence of culture is the collective programming of the mind." This dynamic of sharing as a central element to culture is well supported by many experts (Kroeber & Kluckhohn, 1963; Munter, 1993; Porter & Samovar, 1994; Ronen, 1986). The broad definition of culture therefore provides a framework for understanding differences among cultural groups in organisations and societies.

Obviously country specific and organisation specific culture requires careful attention of international HR professionals, which otherwise may stand against effective management of international operations. Some of the corporate examples can elucidate this concept.

Hewlett-Packard (HP) has successful to create a conscious corporate culture, which they call 'The HP Way'. HP's corporate culture is based on (1) respect for others, (2) a sense of community, and (3) plain hardwork (Fortune Magazine, May 15, 1995). This conscious culture they have developed and they are sustaining through extensive training of managers and all cross-section of employees. Today HP's growth and success internationally may be traced to their conscious corporate culture.

Another illustration of corporate culture is Southwest Airlines. It is one of the most profit making Airlines in the U.S.A. Southwest's CEO, Herb Kelleher, defines Southwest culture as under:

"Well, first of all, it starts with hiring....If you start with the type of person you want to hire, presumably you can build a work force that is prepared for the culture you desire. Another important thing is to spend a lot of time with your people and to communicate with them in a variety of ways. ... the way you appear and the way you act—is a form of communication. We want our people to feel fulfilled and to be happy, and we want our management to radiate.....that we are proud of our people, we are interested in them as individuals and we are interested in them outside the work force, including the good and bad things that happen to them as individuals."

Most important example from international perspective is Advanced Micro Devices (AMD). AMD is located in Dresden of East Germany and a composite of three cultures—American, West German and East German. The Americans are "go-getters", who believe in shooting first and aiming later. West Germans are analytical, thorough and correct, whereas the East Germans have mastered the art of innovation with limited resources. AMD became an ideal convergent point for Americans and West Germans to make computer chips, after the Berlin Wall fell. However, soon it became evident that culture clashes hindered success. Americans believed that everyone would want to follow their best practices and Germans found the Americans patronising. West Germans viewed the plant as an opportunity to help their East German brethren. East Germans felt that their unique talents for ingenious solutions were being ignored. These feelings were reflected everywhere even in the way meetings were conducted. American managers preferred freeform brainstorming sessions in English, wherein ideas could be developed spontaneously. The Germans did not want to present their thoughts without any preparation. The Dresden start-up team designed a meeting format, which opened with American-style brainstorming sessions. However, a formal reflective process took place between meetings and language barriers came down once members were given choice to present their ideas either in English or in Germany, depending on his comfort level. In this dilemma process the Americans learnt the art of deliberation and the Germans off-the-cuff dynamism.

As a result, this multicultural style gave AMD the much-needed competitive edge. AMD's Dresden factory broke production speed records, in less than two years and went through three generations of chip redesign without major errors in a year. The AMD dilemma suggests that success depends on the willingness of employees to let down their defences and talk about ethnic and national personalities and the way they learn from each other. AMD's case has developed Dilemma Theory (Trompenaars, F., Hampden-Turner, C., 1998) a much discussed theory now worldwide and commonly known as THT Theory. According to this theory, insidious culture clashes and most management problems are a result of the human habit of viewing life in terms of all-or-nothing choices. It is always winning versus losing strategies, right versus wrong answers and good versus bad values. Business issues must not be approached as a contest between good and evil, or the potential benefits of "evil" might be lost. It is better to interpret clashes as a reconcilable dilemma.

An example of more down to earth corporate culture can be of Sears, the second largest retail chain of the world. Sears emphasise on three Cs. Compelling place to work, compelling place to shop and compelling place to invest. Sears believe these cultures when practiced takes into account overall growth and prosperity of their organisation. Incidentally, they also align their performance management system with three Cs. Similarly Wal-Mart, the largest retail chain of the world also believe their all employees are their Associates and hence as a matter of corporate culture and practices. Wal-Mart shares all strategic information with employees to get the benefit of empowerment and motivation. Wal-Mart achieves significant rate of growth every year.

All these international examples, therefore illustrate how successfully managing culture of an organisation, it is possible to be effective in international operations.

Some of the Indian examples here also will authenticate the international experiences. We have the most successful stories of organisational transformation, i.e., Aditya Birla Group under Kumar Mangalam Birla, which metamorphoses itself into a modern multi-cultural transnational with more than 72,000 people drawn from 20 different countries. In his words transformation is about turning aspirations into reality, converting setbacks into opportunities. It is about courage of conviction. It is about what Charles Handy calls "the creation of new alchemists from ordinary people". Transformation is the end result of a highly energised process that combines human ingenuity with its indomitable spirit to make new things happen and create value.

Therefore, all these examples illustrate how developing and sustaining a conscious culture in the work place can contribute to the growth and prosperity of a global organisation. Work culture as a separate branch has received priority due to globalisation.

To illustrate we can site the example of Jack Welch, CEO, General Electric, who created a new corporate culture to meet the business objectives. Key elements of GE's corporate culture are as under:

- Redesigning the role of the leader in the new economy: creating followers through communicating a vision, and establishing open, caring relations with every employee.
- Creating an open, collaborative workplace where everyone's opinion is welcomed.
- Empowering senior executives to run far-flung businesses in entrepreneurial fashion.
- Liberating the workforce; making everybody a participant through improving vertical communication and employee empowerment.

Managing culture is an important IHRM issues, is evident from the above examples. All the above corporate examples provide some guidelines for international HR managers.

Managerial Practices in China, Korea and Japan

It is important for HR managers to appreciate the differences in managerial practices in different countries. Here we have very briefly outlined the managerial practices of three different countries.

Chinese Management

The opening of the People's Republic of China (PRC) to the external world, subsequent to China's membership of World Trade Organisation (WTO) has changed the economic landscape around the world. With more than 25 per cent of the world's population, China is a market that promises exciting opportunities for all multinational corporations. Quite expectantly today many international organsations are in China. The leading companies in the major sectors in the domestic economy to date are all Chinese domestic firms. For example, Legend dominates the computer industry, Haier dominates the home appliances sector, and China Mobile has the majority market share in the mobile communications industry. With foreign direct investment, now in China, private sector participation is increasing. Today in China private sector contributes to two-thirds of the annual GDP. Even though China has adopted a corporation model, there is no real separation of ownership and control in Chinese organisations. Moreover, the managers are officials, not entrepreneurs. They may not be able to function like professional managers. There is no real incentive for them to behave like entrepreneurs, even though they have the capabilities. Thus, they are ineffective governance agents. Since the legal environment is not yet mature for business operations, managers have room to shirk responsibilities and pursue their own interests. This situation is complicated by the existence of corrupt officials, which results in loss of state assets. The focus of reform in China is primarily on the State Owned Enterprises (SOE). The current labour, social security, and housing reform provide a more favourable environment for these firms' management of their resources. Nevertheless, China currently still lacks an efficient capital market. Proper development of the capital market would facilitate the governance and growth of SOEs.

However, successful SOE reform also requires strong managerial leadership. The current leaders of SOEs have not taken on leadership roles out of personal desire. Instead they have had to assume managerial leadership because of their official capacity. While they focus their energy on the survival and growth of their firms through competitive strategies, new product development, and alliances with foreign firms, they may have overlooked the importance of managing human resources and developing effective teams. Their learning and managerial behaviour with foreign partners are also critical in acquiring organisational knowledge for future development. The high productivity of the non-state-owned sector has presented a number of challenges to SOEs. How SOEs respond and work with these "new" enterprises is a challenge to many business leaders and entrepreneurs. Their social and political network offers competitive advantage for these SOEs in many sectors.

At a relatively micro level, the internal management system of Chinese firms (both state and non-state firms) in a globalise context is worth investigation. Moving from a planned to a market economy and from a domestic to a global focus, most firms are faced with the integration of Western and Eastern management styles and ways of doing business This has become more important in international joint ventures and foreign-owned firms since entry into the WTO. Top managers therefore have to understand the cultural and social characteristics of their partners, and they themselves must also develop a global vision. Doing this, will increase Chinese firms' ability to change in the future.

In recent research, increasing attention has been given to firm strategies in transitional economies such as China and the former Soviet Union. According to the market transition perspective when traditionally planned economies are in the transition process, their modes of resource control and allocation shift from political disposition to marketisation. Such marketisation and privatisation trends have significant implications for firms needing to adapt to environmental changes or to develop proactive strategic responses to change their environments. Several theoretical frameworks have been used to explain firms' strategic choices in transitional economies. For example, from an institutional perspective, a networkbased growth strategy would be more viable in transitional economies because institutional constraints limit the use of internal growth strategies. Resource based view to investigate why Chinese high-technology ventures tended to adopt agency business activities (e.g., helping to sell and distribute foreign firms' products in the Chinese market) rather than focus on product innovation, as their foreign counterparts do is also not very clear. Another theory argued that in transitional economies, where well-developed price systems and legal frameworks are lacking, transaction costs are high in terms of measurement and enforcement. High transaction costs suggest that firms in transitional economies can use networking as a hybrid strategy rather than acquire or merge through the markets.

Korean Management

The Korean economy came to be widely regarded as a possible 'role model' to be followed by other newly industrialising economies. The 1997 'Asian Crisis' shattered this image. The economy faced a competitive squeeze between lower-cost and rapidly growing economies, such as China, on the one hand, and higher knowledge/technology-based economies, such as Japan, on the other. This situation is a result of structural economic problems, such as high cost but rigid systems and widespread bureaucratic intervention. It is believed there is a need to build up a new economic paradigm, one based on market-led, global and transparent systems, giving the potential to combine the best of both worlds. It is argued that a principal reason for the financial collapse was a failure of Korean management to adjust to changing business conditions. As Korean firms grew in size and scope, many of the entrepreneurial characteristics that supported their early successes were replaced by bureaucratic, nonresponsive management structures that proved unable to cope with emerging external opportunities and threats. A central question at issue here is what Korean firms must do to re-invent themselves in ways that will enhance their competitive edge in the future. Since the mid-1980s, many Korean companies have adopted a unique approach to managing their organisational culture, that is, the so-called 'culture change campaign'. This contribution examines how effective the campaigning approach to managing organisational culture was in Korea. Although many Korean companies made substantial investments in their campaigning efforts, empirical data indicate that the campaigning approach overall was not successful. The possible reasons for the failure are identified, and suggestions for improvements made. Implications for culture change management are made from the lessons of the Korean experiences. The government, the majority stockholder and major institutional force, played a critical role as an initiator of change, but turned into an inertial force in the later phases of change. The change of organisational structure that was strongly supported by top management was successful, while the momentum for HRM change, without such support, was not enough to overcome trade union opposition and employee resistance.

Concept of Korean business management has a tendency to "individualism" in comparison with Japanese social collectivism forgetting family. It is also described as "family egoism". Korean people are said to find their identities in their family groups. So in other words their individualism can possibly run on their egoism of family. In every factory or office, and people work through till the last with strong responsibility. However Korean style of production in their workshop is open for everything, but it can't be well done by them with rough spirits on their half way with their moderate responsibility. The concepts of business management in Korean companies are almost similar to the companies in Japan and USA.

Japanese Management

From the early 1990s, the Japanese companies seemed to be the losers in most global industries. The erosion of the competitive position of the Japanese corporations has led a number of strategists to question whether they have a competitive strategy. Haslam et al. (1996), for instance, attribute the startling performance of the Japanese companies in the 1970s and 1980s to output expansion at home and favourable labour settlements (wages, hours of work) rather than to sustainable competitive advantages. In the 1970s and the 1980s when the Japanese were feared competitors, they benefited structurally from a combination of low Asian wage costs and high Western prices which generated large cash surpluses as they increased their share of Western high income markets (Haslam et al. 1996, p. 24). Michael Porter is even more assertive: "Japanese companies rarely have strategies", he argues in a 1996 Harvard Business Review article where he addresses alternative approaches to the concept of competitive strategy: The dangers of Japanese-style competition are now becoming easier to recognise. In the 1980s, with rivals operating far from the productivity frontier, it seemed possible to win on both cost and quality indefinitely. Traditionally business strategists in Japan have identified three alternative forms of competition: operational effectiveness (cost and quality competition); development of different products (product competition); and an in between strategy, market focus (focus competition). Technology and market information is scattered both inside and outside Japanese organisations. Training programmes, team production, and job rotation, for instance, have become standard practice in every company. However, company vision and governance structure to exploit new business opportunities ahead of competition is somehow not very evident from Japanese organisations. The same applies for corporate governance, especially corporate alliances.

The successful expansion of Japanese companies in the world economy from the late 1960s to the late 1990s has created an enormous literature that provides a variety of explanations for the success of Japanese companies. A substantial part of this literature focuses on three kinds of organisational arrangements that have given them a competitive edge against their Western counterparts: (1) Operational logistics such as the just-in-time inventory control method and shop floor organisation, such as teamwork, flexible floor assignments, job rotation and regular transfers to different divisions and corporate affiliates – practices that are often credited for total quality. (2) Corporate governance, such as the development of corporate alliances and keiretsu relations that allow their members to share R&D information and develop cost cutting techniques. (3) A "community of fate" environment that is based on participatory management, job security, joint consultation between labour and management, horizontal communication, team incentives, and a relatively small gap between the highest and the lowest salaries. Of these organisational arrangements, operational logistics are about hardware technologies and software technologies that can be imitated by other companies. Corporate governance and "community of fate" are company-specific assets and, therefore, they cannot be imitated.

As US and European companies are striving to model their management operations after those of their Japanese counterparts, the Japanese themselves are moving to a new orbit of management that includes reengineering of products and resources rather than processes, world-class inventory systems, and "bullet train" teams: They are redesigning products, redeploying workers, reconfiguring distribution systems, and generally retooling some of their most storied management practices, from just-in-time production to consensus decision making, from flexible manufacturing to continuous improvement. Some companies, for instance, make products simpler with the use of standardised parts. Mabuchi Motors, a small electric carmaker, makes 70 per cent of its products with only 20 different parts. Kyocera Corporation and Higashimaru Shoyu go even further: The K yocera Corporation, a technology company, has divided itself up into 800 small companies (referred to as amoebas) that expected to trade both internally and externally. Higashimaru Shoyu, soy-sauce maker, has turned each stage in the production process into a separate profit center, telling the separate profit centers, to buy and sell parts from each other. The company has created its own internal currency. In short, a number of Japanese management practices, that can be classified as operational logistics, have already become standard practice around the world, so no longer constitute a competitive advantage for Japanese companies.

International Manners

For obvious globalisation, it is now essential to familiarise ourselves with different international manners, which vary across the nations due to specific culture and value systems prevailing in respective countries. Here we have discussed briefly those for a general appreciation.

Africa - General Etiquette

Aftica - Greetings & Forms of Address: A light warm handshake is the acceptable form of greeting when you meet and when you leave.

Africa - Business Cards: Present the card with your right hand.

Africa - Meetings & Presentations: Be prepared for a large number of people at meetings and during negotiations

Africa - Home Invitations & Gifts: Avoid giving flowers as a gift in Kenya, as they symbolize sorrow and condolence.

Africa - Topics to Avoid: Refer to people as Africans not blacks.

Africa - Gestures to Avoid: In rural areas, avoid strong eye contact.

Asia - General Etiquette: Asia - Greetings & Forms of Address. Most East Asians (people from Japan, Korea, Thailand, Brunei, Malaysia, Myanmar (Burma) and Vietnam) bow to each other.

Asia - Business Cards: Offer your card and important papers to the Chinese, South Koreans, and Japanese with both hands, and accept theirs the same way.

Asia - Meetings & Presentations: Decide beforehand what technical information you are willing to share with your Asian counterparts, and be sure everyone on your team knows.

Asia - Negotiation Tips: Don't get too personally involved with your counterparts. Keep some distance. The Asians will respect you more if you are a little aloof.

Asia - Table Manners: Cover your mouth with your hand when you use toothpicks.

Asia - Dress Code: Both men and women should avoid "going native" in their clothing choices.

Australia & New Zealand - General Etiquette

Australia & New Zealand - Greetings & Forms of Address: At parties, your host will introduce you to the other guests. It is also acceptable to introduce yourself if you wish.

Australia & New Zealand - Appointments & Punctuality: In Australia, use any connections and introductions you have, as there is an old boy network of senior executives and major players.

Australia & New Zealand - Negotiations: Be prepared for different people showing up at the negotiating table. Bargaining is not the norm.

Australia & New Zealand - Corporate Gifts: Australians and New Zealanders do not expect gifts from foreigners doing business with them.

Australia & New Zealand - Table Manners: Australians and New Zealanders eat Continental-style.

Australia & New Zealand - Gestures: British gestures are understood and used.

Europe (Eastern & Western) - General Etiquette

Europe (Eastern & Western) - Greetings & Forms of Address: Shake hands with a firm grip when you meet and when you depart. If you meet the same person more than once in a day, shake hands each time.

Europe (Eastern & Western) - Appointments & Punctuality: Never try to make a cold call to get an appointment; it is just not done. Europeans do not like to conduct business on the phone.

Europe (Eastern & Western) - Meetings & Presentations: Good manners are critical and ignorance is no excuse for bad behaviour. Europeans are very class conscious. They have a distinct notion of what refined conduct should be.

Europe (Eastern & Western) - Negotiations: Europeans are conservative in their approach. Negotiators are older and experienced. They are careful in decision making and not willing to take too many risks.

Europe (Eastern & Western) - Dress Code: Europeans dress well and expect others to do the same. Their first impression of your appearance, good or bad, will often help form a lasting opinion of your character. Finely tailored clothing of classic cut and style predominate in the business world. Shoes should be polished and of good quality and style.

Europe (Eastern & Western) - Business Entertaining: Although power breakfasts are becoming more popular (in France, Switzerland, Monaco, and England) business lunches are far more common and may take place in a cafe.

Middle East & Gulf States - General Etiquette

Middle East & Gulf States - Greetings & Forms of Address: Arabs are elaborate with greeting. In addition to a handshake, they may touch your arm or shoulder, and after several meetings will embrace you. Consider this an honor.

Middle East & Gulf States - Negotiations: If you can negotiate in a souk (a marketplace in a Muslim country) you will be able to negotiate with any Arab businessperson.

Middle East & Gulf States - Corporate Gifts: Corporate gifts should be presented publicly to the group after a deal is closed. Wait for your host to present you with a gift first.

Middle East & Gulf States - Table Manners: Meals are large and lengthy, so make sure you have a good appetite; eating large quantities shows your appreciation. It is very common for women to eat separately from men, even in their own homes.

Middle East & Gulf States - Gestures to Avoid: Do not walk in front of an Arab while he is praying and never step on a prayer mat.

Middle East & Gulf States - Dress Code: Your approach to dressing should be modest. The body must be covered at all times for both genders, even when it is hot.

Israel General Etiquette

Israel - Greetings and Forms of Address: A warm handshake followed by "Shalom" is the acceptable form of greeting when you meet and depart. Titles are not considered important. Do not be offended when you are called by your first name.

Israel - Appointments & Punctuality: You are expected to be punctual. However, Israelis are casual about time, and it is not unusual for your associates to be up to half an hour late.

Israel - Business Cards: To impress your host, have your business cards engraved. It is a sign of status in Israel.

Israel- Meetings & Presentations: Business is conducted at a similar pace to that of a large American city such as New York.

Israel - Negotiations: Decision making takes more time than in the West. Top executives make the final decisions in private companies. Companies owned by a group of people make decisions collectively.

Israel - Photography: Do not photograph altercations between Jews and Arabs.

North America (Canada & United States) - General Etiquette

North America (Canada & United States) - Greetings & Forms of Address: A proper North American handshake is a full-hand grip that is firm and warm with an understated downward snap.

North America (Canada & United States) - Appointments & Punctuality: In North America, it is acceptable to make a cold call (calling a person without making an introduction or an appointment).

North America (Canada & United States) - Meetings & Presentations: Meetings begin and end as scheduled. There is very little small talk at meetings. North Americans like to get down to business immediately and follow the agenda.

North America (Canada & United States) - Negotiations: Negotiations are approached in a problem-solving manner. Decisions are made after requested information has been gathered and pondered over for accuracy and effectiveness.

North America (Canada & United States) - Table Manners: In Canada, both North American and Continental styles of eating are followed. In the US., the North American style is mostly used, which consists of switching the fork from the left hand to the right hand after cutting the food.

North America (Canada & United States) - Gestures: Standing too close to a North American may be perceived as an invasion of one's personal space.

Latin America (Including Mexico) - General Etiquette

Latin America (Including Mexico) - Greetings & Forms of Address: Latin America (Including Mexico) - Meetings & Presentations.

Latin Americans consider the North **American approach** of getting to the point and leaving the details for later too straightforward.

Latin America (Including Mexico) - Negotiations: Executives may play up the drama of negotiations to bide their time. Patience and diplomacy are critical so avoid showing anger at interruptions or delays.

Latin America (Including Mexico) - Corporate Gifts: Do not give corporate gifts until after a deal has been closed. Present them in a social setting rather than a business environment. Gifts will be opened after you have left.

Latin America (Including Mexico) - Table Manners: Never pick up food with your fingers, even fruit and chicken should be eaten with utensils.

Latin America (Including Mexico) - Customs & Traditions: Honour is of great importance to the Latin American people: never criticize, pull rank, or embarrass someone in public.

SUMMARY

Internationalisation of business due to globalisation and formation of different trade blocks and increasing role of WTO, has now started creating an impact on HR practices. In fact a new branch of HR, i.e., international HRM has now emerged and become an essential part of study for all HR professionals. IHRM practices now encompass not only understanding the basic differences in HR practices across the country but also the cross-cultural issues, which greatly influence the work related behaviour of people. To grab the international market, all MNCs and TNCs now focus on IHRM and train their manpower accordingly. HR administration part in IHRM also significantly differs due to variation in labour laws and other legislations globally. IHRM is now the important critical success factor for global presence of organisation and it requires a much broader perspective even for the most common HR activities.

KEYWORDS

MNC	TNC
International Manners	International Joint Ventures
Cultural Diversity	Globalisation

REVIEW QUESTIONS

1. Define IHRM and explain why it is important for the organisations.
2. Explain different aspects of IHRM and how IHRM differs from domestic HRM.
3. What are the main reasons for emergence of IHRM? Give your answer with some organisational examples.
4. Discuss how IHRM influence HR practices. Illustrate your answer selecting at least two HR areas.
5. What are the key IHRM issues in international joint ventures? How you as HR manager can address such issues?
6. Why IHRM issues are influenced by culture? Explain the management practices of a country and illustrate how IHRM is influenced by their culture.
7. Write short notes on:
   (a) Community of Fate
   (b) THT Theory
   (c) Individualism
   (d) PCN
   (e) TCN
   (f) SOE
   (g) IJV

CASE STUDY 1

CHINESE DRAGON – THE WTO AND INDIA

Since the reform initiative in 1979, the Chinese Government has promoted an aggressive policy of export led growth that has been exceptional gains. Currently, China has boasted on average an eight per cent growth rate since the late 1980s. As the Chinese Government struggler with the adaptation from a central economy to one that is dictated by market forces, they have been under the careful scrutiny of the international community.

Many members of GATT and the WTO are somewhat apprehensive when they ponder the thought of a twenty-first century dominated by China. Despite this, many of the current economic powers have attempted to negotiate in an effort to bring China into the ranks of the World Trade Organisation.

With China's accession to WTO many countries of the world are likely to experience imbalance in their foreign trade, including India. Experts, however, say, these will be short-term implications. In the long-run, consumers of the world as a whole will gain.

For nearly fifteen years, China has been seeking entry into the World Trade Organisation. With the successful completion of all bilateral Accession Protocols necessary for membership, in the recently concluded Doha Ministerial Conference (2001), China's membership to WTO has finally been accepted. For many China's entry into the WTO is a source of consternation, sparing fear of job losses in domestic home markets. Others worry that such a large, yet still highly regulated economy will disrupt the WTO, an institution committed to the principles of free trade. Politically, China preferred to join WTO to sort its dispute with trade partners rather than to take a bilateral negotiation approach, as the latter is usually vulnerable to political intervention. For example, China has had to obtain the Most Favoured Nation (MFN) status from the U.S. on a yearly renewable basis. Despite its success in getting the renewal, China has always been tormented over its poor record in Human Rights and Missile Non-Proliferation even as the U.S. Congress inter linked these issues with the renewal of MFN status. By joining the WTO, China hopes to avoid such conflicts with individual countries under the commonly agreed principles of the WTO and obtain permanent MFN status from its major trade partners. The second political consideration relates to the unification of China. After the hand-over of Hong Kong and Macao, Taiwan remains as the sole territory that the Chinese Government is committed to integrate with. The membership of both China and Taiwan in the WTO will accelerate these linkages for two main reasons. First membership is almost certain to end Taiwan's long standing ban on direct shipping and air travel between Taiwan and the mainland. Second Taiwan will have to eliminate important non-tariff barriers on Chinese goods, notably the import ban imposed on a large number of goods of Chinese origin. The increased inter-dependence on each side is likely to facilitate the future peaceful unification of China.

Another political reasons is to enhance China and other developing economies' bargaining power over global trade issues. If China thinks that a drafted rule might handicap its interest or that of developing economies as a whole, it might align with other developing economies, together with Hong Kong and Macao, to veto the agreement. In this way, China hopes to replicate its current influence in the United Nations at the WTO as well.

The determination of the Chinese government to transit China's highly centralised planning economy into a socialist market economy is also one ofthe most powerful drivers behind China's desperate bidding for the WTO.

Finally, China has for a long period believed in an export oriented strategy. Therefore, in order to gain access to world markets. China has been vigorous pursuing the WTO, even if it meant opening up its own markets.

Impact on India

On the positive side, China's entry into WTO may provide some relief to the Indian Industry. As a member of WTO, China will have to abide by the multilateral rules and the agreements and make its policies transparent.

Contd...

All these may lessen the anxieties of the Indian industry about infiltration of exceptionally low cost products from China into the Indian market. China is likely to lose several of its existing advantages in the process of being WTO compliant. Substantial lowering of tariffs, reduction of subsidies etc., should provide significant opportunities for accessing the Chinese market. Removal of quantitative restrictions (since China is not a country with BOP difficulty) is also expected to widen export opportunities. Further with transparent economic and trade policies, it should be easier for the Indian industry to understand this complicated and vast market, establish their presence and develop long-term strategy.

On the negative side, China's accession in the WTO has created new challenges for India in the sphere of trade and foreign policy. India will come under increased pressure to further liberalise, particularly because China's offers on trade liberalisation go well beyond India.

Chinese entry into WTO is also likely to create impact on some sectors of Indian industry as under:

1. On manufacturing China has developed an excellent competency over Indian industries. Further India cannot impose anti-dumping duties on Chinese imports without discretion.
2. In Textile Sector, China will capture India's market share in the EU and other countries because of their much higher productivity.
3. Indian Auto Industry also, more particularly 2 wheeler industry will get adversely affected for China's relative cost advantage. For example, China can manufacture scooters for as little as $100.

Following Indian companies to reap the advantage of post-Doha conference and subsequent China's accession to WTO decided to set up joint venture with Chinese Companies:

1. Bajaj Auto Ltd.
2. Aianta Clocks
3. Videocon

Overall, it is felt by various trade associations and Confederation of India Industry that trade between China and India will increase after China's accession to WTO.

Questions

1. On reading the news about accession of China to WTO, your Organisation, an internationally well known name in manufacturing of white goods, who had just two years' before started operation in India decided to relocate its manufacturing base in China. Discuss the likely benefits your Organisation can reap out of this move. What are the likely problems your organisation may encounter in such move?
2. What would be the macro level impact on Indian economy with China's accession to WTO? As a President of a Trade Association (dealing with Textiles) what would be your role to protect the interest of your affiliated units?
3. On what count, you may consider China's entry to WTO is a boon to India?

Case Study 2

General Electric

Today, General Electric succeeds in dozens of diverse businesses, and is continuously at the vanguard of change. Some years ago, however, in locations throughout GE, local managers were operating in an insulated environment with walls separating them, both horizontally and vertically, from other departments and their workforce. Employee questions, initiatives, and feedback were discouraged.

Determined to harness the collective power of GE employees, create a free flow of ideas, and redefine relationships between boss and subordinates, Jack Welch, CEO, General Electric, created a new corporate culture. It's key elements are:

- Redesigning the role of the leader in the new economy: creating followers through communicating a vision, and establishing open, caring relations with every employee
- Creating an open, collaborative workplace where everyone's opinion is welcome
- Empowering senior executives to run far-flung businesses in entrepreneurial fashion
- Liberating the workforce; making everybody a participant through improving vertical communication and employee empowerment.

The Need for Change

In the new knowledge-driven economy, Jack Welch, CEO, General Electric, "viewed this as anathema. He believed in creating an open collaborative workplace where everyone's opinion was welcomed." He wrote in a letter to shareholders: "If you want to get the benefit of everything employees have, you've got to free them make everybody a participant. Everybody has to know everything, so they can make the right decisions by themselves."

Improving Connectivity: Creating a Seamless Link between Strategy, Management, and Employees

Determined to harness the collective power of GE employees, create a free flow of ideas, and redefine relationships between boss and subordinates, Welch developed Work-Out, a series of town hall meetings conducted by GE management and designed to encourage employee feedback, cross-pollination of ideas, and employee empowerment "In the Welch-led GE culture, traditional barriers dividing employees, co-workers, and management give way to tethers of interdisciplinary and interdepartmental cooperation".

Reassessing Performance and Benchmarking Employees Continuously

Jack Welch does a good job of illustrating the need for proactive change management and constant reassessment when he says, "If the rate of change inside an organisation is less than the rate of change outside... their end is in sight". One of the tools used by Welch to ensure constant reassessment and benchmarking is the annual review undertaken by every GE executive and staff member. Once a year, every employee's performance evaluated and awarded a numerical ranking of between 1 and 5. "The implicit understanding is that both the individual and his or her score are moving up or it's time to leave the company".

Building Effective Top Management Team: GE's Ways

1. Selecting superior managers, dedicated to eliminating bureaucracy and building businesses, to run GE's operating units in entrepreneurial fashion.
2. Creating a transparent financial reporting structure that enables CEO to monitor the manager's individual performance by the numbers. Under the CEO's watch, managers have wide latitude in building their GE units, as long as the numbers demonstrate the wisdom of their ways.

Contd...

Redefining Relationships between Management and Employees

The Four Key Goals of GE's Work-Out Meetings

1. Encourage employees to share their views in a collaborative culture.
2. Vest greater responsibility, power, and accountability with front-line employees.
3. Eliminate wasteful, irrational, and repetitive steps in the work process (which would come to light through employee feedback).
4. Dismantle the boundaries that prevent the cross-pollination of ideas and efforts.

Leading Change through the GE's Organisation: The Jack Welch's Way

1. Redesigning the role of the leader in the new economy: creating followers through communicating a vision, and establishing open, caring relations with every employee.
2. Creating an open, collaborative workplace where everyone's opinion is welcomed.
3. Empowering senior executives to run far-flung businesses in entrepreneurial fashion.
4. Liberating the workforce; making everybody a participant through improving vertical communication and employee empowerment.

Question

List out the important lessons, which you as HR Manager can emulate from the case study.

IHRM WITH A SOLVED CASE ANALYSIS

MACQUARIE BANK

Macquarie Bank is an excellent example of a highly successful organisation, which has been able to maintain its success using an incremental adjustment process while operating in a rapidly changing environment. During the 1980s and 1990s changes occurred in the environment of Australian financial institutions. These included rapid deregulation of the financial services sector by the Australian Labour Government. The critical moves involved were the floating of the Australian dollar; progressive removal of restrictions on competition between banks, building societies, merchant banks and other institutions which offer financial and financially related services; approval of new banking licences including licences to 16 foreign-owned banks to operate in Australia.

From its inception as Hill Samuel Australia in the early 1970s, the bank's strategic focus was merchant banking (investment banking). In 1980 the bank commenced a process of diversification. But with deregulation in the 1980s, it diversified further, building up strength in specialist markets, particularly in high value-added niches (market segments) like corporate services, bullion and commodities. The pace of diversification quickened by the mid 1980s with the bank entering a range of new areas including retail domestic banking, equity investments, property and leasing. Growth was both by development and by acquisition. Macquarie remains one of Australia's most successful and profitable banks. So how was the needed organisational change managed by Macquarie executives?

Change in Macquarie has been a process of constant adjustment. One executive described it this way: 'We never stay still, but we don't change in quantum leaps - our corporate culture would preclude that - running a business on partnership concepts means that policy decisions are not dramatic, they evolve.' The rapid growth in Macquarie's product range was accompanied by a quadrupling of staff numbers in the 1980s. Business product units, or 'clusters', grew in number to almost 30 by the late 1980s, presenting an increasing problem of co-ordination in a collegial/partnership system where unit heads nominally report to the managing director.

The greater size and complexity created problems of co-ordination. The obvious answer was to create additional structures, systems and controls, but this was foreign to the collegial values of the bank which is staffed mainly by highly qualified professionals. The answer actually chosen was to produce a 'goals and values' statement, an articulation of deeply held values about cultural and business behaviour, including how the process of change should be managed. The values statement is essentially a set of values and norms; internal controls, that substitute for external control systems. This was supplemented by developing business units into highly autonomous profit centres and then creating cross-functional synergies through more systematic communication by management across these centres.

But what were the methods adopted at Macquarie to bring about these changes? There was increasing convergence on a consultative style of management. The consolidation of the style reflects the frequent use of the executive committee as a forum for discussion of major issues and decisions. The collegial style was symbolized by the fact that the managing director shared the same open-plan office.

Interestingly enough, when first-line and middle-level managers were asked for their perceptions of the bank's leadership style, they saw it as substantially more directive than consultative. All 15 respondents who rated the managerial style this way indicated that they thought this directive style was appropriate. 'We need strength and decisiveness at the top', one commented. Consistently, some who rated the leadership style as consultative believed that the style was not directive enough for the present environment. This is an interesting comment because it challenges one of the basic assumptions of the organisational development movement, which is that people want consultation about organisational strategies. In a turbulent external environment, however, they may prefer decisive leadership.

Macquarie does not have the all-encompassing human resource systems typical of some organisations. It follows an organic, developmental approach, aptly summarized by one executive as follows: 'We recruit the best from universities and graduate schools; train on the job and pay top money—we are a meritocracy. We

Contd...

try to provide a flexible organisational environment where people can achieve.' The policies are well suited to a flat organisational structure where specialist skills can be developed within small work teams, closely related to the product-market interface. It is not expected that Macquarie will change the basic tenets of the meritocracy system. However, there was sufficient evidence during the study to indicate that the bank may need to consider more systematic approaches to its human resource policies in the future.

The priority areas in human resources practice were:

- recruitment and selection (corporate image as an employer is important; use of psychological tests, and policy of 'growing our own' from graduate trainees is a key strategy);
- performance appraisal (an essential mechanism for tracking goal achievement and help in determining rewards);
- rewards and compensation ('We pay well');
- organisation and development (goals and values statement, team building, monthly newsletter).

In such a dynamic environment how was the bank able to maintain an incremental strategy and achieve such outstanding performances? Its success appears to have been mainly a function of its small size relative to other banks and its combination of diversified niche strategies with a loosely coupled flexible organisation. Its short communication chains and collegial workforce culture led to considerable flexibility in responding to changing market demands. These are strengths which in any larger organisations seek to emulate through the formation of decentralized, strategic business units.

Macquarie Bank has been successful in operating this way so far. As the bank grows further the executives will have to assess whether these strategies can continue to work. Nevertheless the case demonstrates that participative evolution can be an effective change strategy even in a turbulent environment, at least for a relatively small, highly specialized and successful niche player such as Macquarie.

Source: Extracted from John Storey

SOLUTION (THIS SOLUTION IS ONLY A TENTATIVE GUIDE FOR HR STUDENTS)

This case study illustrates how Australia based Macquarie Bank could achieve success in a rapidly changing environment making use of incremental adjustment process. Between 1980s and 1990s financial sectors' reforms in Australia, intensified competition between domestic banks. The spate of competition further got accentuated for entry of foreign banks in Australia. To keep pace with such competitive spree, Macquarie Bank, leveraging the advantage of deregulation, changed its business focus, shifting from their core merchant banking operation to value added niche specialist markets, like; corporate services, bullion and commodities. The pace of diversification further extended by the bank to new areas like equity investments, property and leasing. Such incremental adjustment process further got a boost by acquisition, which took Macquaire Bank, to the status of one of the most successful and profitable banks of Australia. Obviously experience of Macquaire Bank is now an important example before us to emulate.

Incremental adjustment process in a changed environment would not have been possible for the bank without strategic management of human resources. In any change process it is inevitable. During the process of adjustment, Macquarie bank sustained the partnership concepts making their policy decisions as evolving one. To sustain rapid growth Macquaire Bank had to quadruple its staff members, increase its business product units to 30 clusters and then faced the challenge of increased co-ordination. Instead of going through the normal process of creating additional structures and systems, taking the advantage of qualified professionals, the bank chose to produce 'goals and values', enunciating certain values and norms to develop a corporate culture and business behaviour, for autonomous internal control. This was further supplemented by developing strategic business units (autonomous profit centers) and cross-functional synergies, i.e., converging to a consultative style from their erstwhile collegial style.

Methods adopted by Macquaire Bank to bring about the changes, keeping pace with the changing deregulatory environment can be identified firstly as managing by consultation. This is opposite to directive style. This style primarily reflects extensive use of committee for discussion and decisions on major issues. In any organisational change process, more particularly in alike situation of Macquaire Bank, it is quite likely that people would like consultation in organisational strategies. This however, may not be correct when external environment is turbulent. In such cases decisive leadership may be a better option.

HR practices of Macquaire Bank during the process of change was also strategic. It not only focused on sustainability in a changing competitive environment but also on growth. This the bank defines as organic development approach. They not only recruited the best from universities and graduate schools but also trained them on the job and paid them 'top money.' Such practice of meritocracy further got reinforced by creating a culture of achievement. Flexible organisational environment, flat organisational structure, small work teams also furthered the meritocracy.

Despite all these achievements, responding to the changed environment, the bank is needed to re-look into their HR practices, as some of the HR practices need to be more strategic. In recruitment and selection, corporate branding or image building is very important. Recruitment process needs to be reinforced making use of psychological tests. Graduate trainees should have career progression path, so as to give a message 'growing our own.' Even though they pay top money, there is no indication whether the bank track goal achievement and align the same to determine rewards, making use of an effective performance appraisal system. Hence just telling 'we pay well' do not spell out how strategic is their rewards and compensation structure. Similarly, organisation development initiatives also do not indicate about creating a culture of shared value, extending the scope of consultative decision making beyond the executive committee (by developing team culture), introducing a monthly news letter are some examples of required HR strategies.

Even though the bank could achieve outstanding performances by incremental strategy, so far, which could be attributed to its relative small size (compared to their competitors) and diversified niche strategies in a flexible organisation and collegial workforce culture, to sustain it in the long run, the bank require to be more strategic in their HR practices.

Special Notes on Globalisation Impact Study on India

Introduction

This special note is intended to help HR students to understand India's stand in a globalised economy and appreciate the degree of preparedness, which may be required for a HR person to work in MNCs.

Stephen Gill defines globalisation as the reduction of transaction cost of trans-border movements of capital and goods thus of factors of production and goods. Guy Brainbant says that the process of globalisation not only includes opening up of world trade, development of advanced means of communication, internationalisation of financial markets, growing importance of MNC's, population migrations and more generally increased mobility of persons, goods, capital, data and ideas but also infections, diseases and pollution.

It is therefore evident that the term globalisation has no universally acceptable definition. Impact of globalisation practically encompasses every aspect of human life like; politics, economics, religion, culture, knowledge and science. However, we will primarily focus on economic issues and while studying the impact also consider different cross-border cultural and managerial issues.

From the economic point of view globalisation is like any other external phenomenon and therefore can be described and analysed. The process combines economic or monetary policies which increases the spate of globalisation. Because of its multi-dimensions, for some, it may be the expansion of international trade, migration of human resources to various parts of the world. For others it may be the flow of cash and other investments amongst nations, capital investment of one nation in another for purposes of producing and then marketing either in the country where investment has been made or in other countries. The other aspect is the exchange of capital between nations or regions. The next aspect is the impact and influence of Multinational Companies or Trans-national Corporations (MNCs/ TNCs) on trade, investment and production. Next is the exchange of technology between countries. And finally there is the expansion of international communication networks and the impact of electronic technology on the media in different nations.

The term multinational and transnational corporations require clarifications. Although in many literatures they are used interchangeably, we can still make technical differentiation. Multinationals or MNCs suggest that a company spreads its activities equally among several countries. However in reality this may not be the case. Transnationals or TNCs have their head offices in their respective country of origin or home country, with management, control and majority shareholders there. They have branches, subsidiaries and production units in other countries, but they retain decision-making power in their 'home' base. They do not spread their activities and power equally between countries. However, for some MNCs also we find similar practices. Hence both the term MNCs and TNCs are interchangeably used.

The influence of MNCs and TNCs in the spate of globalisation can be understood if we review their influence in the global economy. Here we have presented some bullet points to understand their relative importance.

- The top 300 corporations own or control more than one quarter of all the productive assets of the world.
- There are about 37 000 TNCs in the world, and they have over 200000 foreign affiliated companies.
- Five advanced capitalist countries (USA, Japan, France, Germany and the UK) account for 172 transnationals out of the top 200 and for US$ 2,000000000000 (two trillion dollars) worth of foreign direct investment (in 1992). Fewer than one in ten TNCs come from newly-industrialising countries like Korea and Brazil.
- Transnational corporations control about 70 per cent of all world trade. Almost 40 per cent of world trade takes place between the companies of individual corporations.
- Some goods are controlled by only a handful of TNCs. For exomple just six corporations control 90 per cent of the world's trade in wheat. TNCs control 80 per cent of all land farmed for export crops.

Contd...

- The biggest TNC is General Electric, with assets worth over US$251 billion (251,000000000 US dollars).
- The TNC that employs the most workers is General Motors: about 750,000 people worldwide.
- The sales of the Ford motor company each year are greater than what the country Norway produces in a year (Gross Domestic Product, GDP). Philip Morris's tobacco sales every year total more than the GDP of New Zealand.
- The top six corporate groups in Japan together make up four-fifths of Japan's gross national product (GNP).
- Most foreign direct investment is exchanged between the big three industrialised blocs: the USA/ Canada/ Mexico (the North America Free Trade Area - NAFTA), the European Union (EU), and Japan/Asia.

In the 1980s, most foreign investment going to the Third World went to Brazil, Mexico, Singapore and Malaysia. In the 1990s China leapt into first place, with foreign investments worth US$ 26 billion a year. By contrast, the whole continent of Africa receives only US$ 3 billion a year, even though African governments have adopted pro-investment policies and profits rates are often higher than in Europe. Central/Eastern Europe get about US$ 5 billion a year.

Foreign investment today goes more into services such as banking, communications, transport, electricity supply and tourism and less into manufacturing goods. Privatisation of the public sector is encouraging this trend.

India is Global

The new policy regime radically pushed forward in favour of a more open and market oriented economy. Major measures initiated as a part of the liberalisation and globalisation strategy in the early nineties included scrapping of the industrial licensing regime, reduction in the number of areas reserved for the public sector, amendment of the monopolies and the restrictive trade practices act, start of the privatisation programme, reduction in tariff rates and change over to market determined exchange rates.

Over the years there has been a steady liberalisation of the current account transactions, more and more sectors opened up for foreign direct investments and portfolio investments facilitating entry of foreign investors in telecom, roads, ports, airports, insurance and other major sectors.

The Indian tariff rates reduced sharply over the decade from a weighted average of 72.5% in 1991-92 to 24.6 in 1996-97. Though tariff rates went up slowly in the late nineties it touched 35.1 % in 2001-02. India is committed to reduced tariff rates. Peak tariff rates are to be reduced to the minimum with a peak rate of 20%, in another 2 years most non-tariff barriers have been dismantled by march 2002, including almost all quantitative restrictions.

The liberalisation of the domestic economy and the increasing integration of India with the global economy have helped step up GDP growth rates, which picked up from 5.6% in 1990-91 to a peak level of 77.8% in 1996-97. Growth rates have slowed down since the country has still been able to achieve 5-6% growth rate in three of the last six years. Though growth rates has slumped to the lowest level 4.3% in 2002-03 mainly because of the worst droughts in two decades the growth rates are expected to go up close to 70% in 2003-04. A Global comparison shows that India is now the fastest growing just after China.

This is major improvement given that India's growth rate in the 1970's was very low at 3% and GDP growth in countries like Brazil, Indonesia, Korea, and Mexico was more than twice that of India. Though India's average annual growth rate almost doubled in the eighties to 5.9% it was still lower than the growth rate in China, Korea and Indonesia. The pick up in GDP growth has helped improve India's global position. Consequently India's position in the global economy has improved from the 8th position in 1991 to 4th place in 2001. When GDP is calculated on a purchasing power parity basis.

Contd...

Where does Indian stand in terms of Global Integration?

India clearly lags in globalisation. Number of countries have a clear lead among them China, large part of east and far-east Asia and eastern Europe. Lets look at a few indicators how much we lag.

Over the past decade FDI flows into India have averaged around 0.5% of GDP against 5% for China 5.5% for Brazil. Whereas FDI inflows into China now exceeds US $ 50 billion annually. It is only US $ 4 billion in the case of India.

Consider global trade – India's share of world merchandise exports increased from .05% to .07% over the past 20 years. Overthe same period China's share has tripled to almost 4%.

India's share of global trade is similar to that of the Philippines an economy 6 times smaller according to IMF estimates. India under trades by 70-80% given its size, proximity to markets and labour cost advantages.

It is interesting to note the remark made last year by Mr. Bimal Jalan, Governor of RBI. Despite all the talk, we are now where ever close being globalised in terms of any commonly used indicator of globalisation. In fact we are one of the least globalised among the major countries – however we look at it.

As Amartya Sen and many other have pointed out that India, as a geographical, politico-cultural entity has been interacting with the outside world throughout history and still continues to do so. It has to adapt, assimilate and contribute. This goes without saying even as we move into what is called a globalised world which is distinguished from previous eras from by faster travel and communication, greater trade linkages, denting of political and economic sovereignty and greater acceptance of democracy as a way of life.

Consequences

The implications of globalisation for a national economy are many. Globalisation has intensified interdependence and competition between economies in the world market. This is reflected in Interdependence in regard to trading in goods and services and in movement of capital. As a result domestic economic developments are not determined entirely by domestic policies and market conditions. Rather, they are influenced by both domestic and international policies and economic conditions. It is thus clear that a globalising economy, while formulating and evaluating its domestic policy cannot afford to ignore the possible actions and reactions of policies and developments in the rest of the world. This constrained the policy option available to the government which implies loss of policy autonomy to some extent, in decision-making at the national level.

Macro-economic review of Indian Economy in the Spate of Globalisation

India is one of the sixth fastest growing economies of the world and ranked fourth in terms of Purchasing Power Parity (PPP) in 2001. The business and regulatory environment is evolving and constantly improving. It has highly talented, skilled and English-speaking human resource base and it is the backbone in a globalised economy. The economy has transformed into a vibrant, rapidly growing consumer market, comprising over 300 million strong middle class with increasing purchasing power. The country provides a large market for consumer goods on the one hand and imports capital goods and technology to modernize its manufacturing base on the other. Such important features which are crucial for globalisation can be listed as under:

- An abundant and diversified natural resource base.
- Sound economic, industrial and market fundamentals.
- Highly skilled and talented human resources.
- Potential for attractive returns.
- Positive Government Attitude and Policies, etc.

The Government of India has adopted far-reaching measures to liberalise the Indian market and integrate the same with the global economy. The tenth five year plan document (2002-2007) targets a healthy growth rate of 8% Per annum.

Contd...

Globalisation Ranking and India

Ranking of the extent of globalisation in a country is done every year based on certain parameters by leading international agencies. We have presented here overall ranking of globalisation and some country specific details. It is a matter of interest for studying impact on Globalisation. India being ranked very low, 61 out of 62 countries of world, we have to understand whether India's economic progress in any way gets sluggish due to this. However, this only serves macro-level purposes. However, while studying globalisation impact on specific industry sector, we may have to relate these data in case of India.

UNIT 27

Current Trends in Human Resource Management

Learning Objectives

After completion of this unit, the students will be aware of the following topics:

- *Introduction*
- *Skill Shortage*
- *Quality Systems*
- *Competency Mapping*
- *Shamrock Organisation*
- *Six Sigma Practices*
- *Innovation and Creativity*
- *Supply Chain Management*
- *Business Process Outsourcing and Human Resource Outsourcing*
- *Knowledge Management*
- *WTO and Indian Labour*

GENERAL ELECTRIC – ACHIEVING EXCELLENCE THROUGH SIX-SIGMA

General Electric Company (GE) is one of the largest diversified companies in the world. Even some of the GE's Strategic Business Units (SBUs), because of its size and volume of activities can independently figure out among Fortune 500 companies. With business volume of almost $ 150 million, the company operates in more than 100 countries, having over 250 manufacturing facilities across the globe. With diversified product portfolio, ranging from plastics to locomotives, GE could also transform into the business of services and solutions. GE, a quality in name itself, is powered by the world's largest scientist's pool, whose R&D work continuously give GE the edge over other competitors. GE's R&D is the centre point for strategic cost effective technical innovations. Jack Welch, the legendary ex-CEO of the company never used to believe in quality programmes, branding it as theoretical. His quality philosophy rather was more deep-rooted as he used to consider quality an integral part of any business. However, Motorola's six-sigma quality initiatives impressed him and for obvious opportunity of objective assessment of achieved quality level, he had embraced the six-sigma practices in the company in 1995.

Six-sigma per se is a structured data-driven approach to eliminate defects, wastage, etc., recreating the process. While recreating the process, six-sigma emphasised on critical-to-quality factors as perceived by the customers. Primarily, it is based on a combination of statistical quality control techniques, assuming that the output of most of the physical processes follows a normal distribution, with the processes centered at the mean. Theoretically, any process would have a natural spread of 3 Sigma (standard deviation) from the normal distribution mean on either side of the center. This spread contains 99.9999998% of the process output. Thus, only 0.002 parts per million are out of the design specification. At six-sigma level, defects get reduced to 3.4 per million opportunities.

While introducing the six-sigma in GE's operations, it was observed that GE could achieve 3-4 sigma level, i.e., about 35,000 defects per million opportunities, which per se indicates that almost $ 7-10 billion are avoidable expenditure for the company, which can be saved in introducing six-sigma.

However, GE's premise for implementation of six-sigma was getting ready from 1988 onwards for its `Work Out' programme. Even though, it was not theoretically known as six-sigma programme, this programme gave every employee the opportunity to influence and improve GE's operations. Among others, GE's `work out' programmes emphasised on building trust, employee empowerment, etc. Therefore, six-sigma implementation in GE was relatively much hassle free.

Within few years of six-sigma implementation, GE's annual savings went up to $2.5 billion and over and above. GE could achieve customer satisfaction and improve the stakeholders' value.

INTRODUCTION

Importance of HRM, both at national and at organisational level, has been discussed throughout this book with a suggestion to integrate this with national and corporate strategies for overall development. In this unit, we have discussed the global scenario to further reinforce our arguments.

SKILL SHORTAGE

Shortage of critical skills is now a global phenomena. While for the developed countries, this is primarily because of aging population, for developing countries like India, the problem is absence of proper initiative at the national level. Whatever is being done now, could have been done at least a decade ago. The shift in skill requirements in India was witnessed from 1981 census reports. There was a massive shift in employment from secondary and primary sectors to service sector. Service sector alone now accounts for 22.45 per cent of total employment (as per 1991 census). This must have increased considerably by now. Unfortunately whatever national level initiatives taken by Directorate of Employment and Training to ensure regular supply of skilled manpower to industry were mostly to cater to the requirements of manufacturing sector. And importance of manufacturing sector is dwindling both in terms of share in employee (10.18% in 1991) and contribution to national income. Requirements of development of soft skills and state-of-art knowledge never received the priority of the Government. While there is a need for developing mass literacy, equally important is to focus on developing critical skills for sustaining the global competition. With a 7 per cent growth rate in GDP and 5 per cent growth rate in value addition (all sectors together), India is much ahead of many developing countries in the world. Still our quality of life is in shamble. We are ranked as 115th out of 162 countries of the world for investment in technology creation. This is an indicator of Human Development Index (HDI), which is compiled by the UNDP.

The problem of skill shortage in the developed countries, as was mentioned above, is primarily for aging population. But for India, it is for deficiency in our national level planning and implementation. National Renewal Fund (NRF) was especially created by the government, initially from a budgetary allocation and later by transferring proceeds from the disinvestment of PSU shares. The major thrust of NRF was to make fund available to organisations on soft interest terms to invest in skill renewal. Till recently the report indicates, the fund was grossly misused for disbursing voluntary retirement benefits. A news clip on NRF published by Free Press Journal on 5th January, 2000 is appended below:

FREE PRESS JOURNAL

New Delhi: Experts on Tuesday criticised the government for using the National Renewal Fund for disbursing voluntary retirement benefits, saying that the manner or the procedure was "short-sighted and anti-labour", reports UNI.

They told UNI that empirical evidences showing that the funds which should have been used for retraining and in assisting labour set up, its own businesses or in new jobs, were now being used for consumer spending and paying debts. This left people without a vocation, they said.

The experts, who included economists, and trade unionists were in the capital to attend a three-day conference on 'crises, reforms and recovery' organised by the International Management Institute. Dr B O Jonsson, a professor at the Runo Folk High School in Stockholm, observed that it was of utmost importance that money should be used for development of skilled labour. "India urgently needs skilled labour. But the enterprises are taking the easy option of dispensing off labour by giving lump sum," said Dr Jonsson, who also teaches at the Swedish College for Training of Trade Unions.

The workshop suggested setting up a labour market authority in India on the lines of those prevailing in Europe. The authority does the job of matching labour requirements of firms and helping placements. Such an authority would be useful and could ensure that labour is not mismatched or redundant.

The experts said it was of utmost importance that sufficient wages are passed to labour to ensure productivity, so that enterprise is able to compete internationally. "Our experience is that with low wages, productivity is low. So you must have an effective trade union movement to be competitive. It is the presence of strong unions which forces firms to be competitive," Jonsson said. The workshop emphasised that workers should undergo regular skill development and training. Jonsson said productivity in an enterprise depends upon management decisions like the price of a product, productivity and marketing and sales. Unions need to understand management decisions and appreciate what are good decisions.

The Institute of Applied Manpower Research, under the agies of the Planning Commission has done some studies in some sectoral and occupational categories. But these are far from adequate. Decision on skill development at national level can not be taken in isolation. This requires shift in plan priorities also. Social sector spending (both plan and non-plan, which includes spending an education also), in India, as percentage to total expenditure, shows a declining trend. From 11.14 per cent in 1996-97 to 10.72 per cent in 2000-2001. This itself speaks lackadaisical attitude of the Government in developing human resources.

However, initiatives at national level unless reinforced by organisations at micro level, through regular skill renewal efforts, we cannot achieve the desired results. Disclosure of information on expenditure on training by organisations is yet not a statutory requirement.

Another important aspect which deserve attention of HRM is demographic change process. For developed countries, the problem is aging populations, but for a developing country like India, the problem is just reverse. Our working population is increasing at the annual rate of 1.09 per cent. By the year 2015, we will have more population in working age group (15-64 years), which would be 66.7 per cent of total population against the present rate of 61.2 per cent. Therefore, we need to concentrate on human resource development in a planned manner, duly identifying the skill requirement.

Occupational Distribution of category-wise Workforce in India is presented below:

Categories	1961	1993-94	1999-2000
Professional and technical and related services	3236(17)	13707(37)	14547(37)
Administrative, executive and managerial workers	1812(10)	7132(19)	2218(31)
Clerical and related Workers	3866(21)	11070(30)	12533(32)
Service workers	5558(30)	12752(34)	1 6336(41)
Farmers, fishermen, hunters, loggers and related workers	137590(731)	237915(636)	35647(594)
Production and related workers, transport equipment operators and labourers	29286(156)	65934(176)	8141 (197)
All occupations	188244	373826	97021

Source: Economic and Political Weekly, August 11, 2001, Page: 3044

Note: Figures in brackets relate to share (per 1000) of the occupation group to the corresponding total workers in all occupations.

Interpreting the table we can understand better the present occupational structure in India and its trend. Over the years, skilled and knowledge-based jobs are increasing, while low-skilled jobs are decreasing. This further calls for future skill mapping through proper HRM initiative in India.

With the increase of global job mobility, recruiting competent people is also increasingly becoming difficult. The problem is more acute in India. Therefore by creating an enabling culture, organisations are also required to work out a retention strategy for the existing skilled manpower. Similarly to attract talent, organisations need to focus on compensation strategy with enabling work culture.

Indian organisations are also witnessing a change process in systems, management culture and philosophies and management practices. Apart from economic compulsion, such change process is the outcome of global aligning of Indian organisations. To sustain the competitive pressure, we now need to have better skill and knowledge edge over others. Fortunately, multi-skill development, even though considered globally not very successful in other countries and even at times counter productive to them, for India it is very successful for its obvious root to our age-old social stratification theory. This we have discussed earlier. Therefore, what is impediment for the others, is the advantage for us. Proper organisational initiatives can ensure skill-enhancement. Role of HRM is now all the more important.

QUALITY SYSTEMS

The revised Quality Management Standard ISO 9001 and ISO 9004 of 2000 focussed more on people-centric organisation. We will discuss its features in brief and then delineate how it influences HR issues in an organisation.

Main Features

Major changes in the revised ISO 9000 standards are the increased focus on top management commitment and customer satisfaction, the emphasis on processes within the organisation, and the introduction of continual improvement concepts.

The revisions of ISO 9001 and 9004 are based on eight quality management principles that reflect best management practices.

These eight principles are:

- Customer-focused organisation
- Leadership
- Involvement of people
- Systems approach to management
- Continual improvement
- Factual approach to decision-making
- Mutually beneficial supplier relationship

Features include the continuity and compatibility between the old and new version of the standards. With the revised ISO 9001, the Quality Management System covers those activities of an organisation that provide assurance to customers that their needs are being addressed.

The enhancement in the revised ISO 9001 of the "continual improvement" concept is intended to help an organisation respond to the changing needs of its customers, while stimulating the efficiency of the organisation and improving its competitive position.

The consistency of the two standards also support a smooth transition for the organisation wishing to go beyond ISO 9001 to ISO 9004.

Changes Introduced: The revision of the ISO Quality Management Standards includes a significant change to the structure of ISO 9001 and ISO 9004, which, while retaining the essence of the original requirements, reposition the 20 elements of the current ISO 9001:1994 and the guidelines of ISO 9004-1 : 1994 into four main sections:

1. Management Responsibility
2. Resource Management
3. Product realisation
4. Measurement, analysis and improvement

Sequence: There is more logical sequence of requirements and guidelines due to the process orientation of the new standards.

Top Management: More emphasis has been placed on the role of top management, which includes its commitment to the development and improvement of the quality management system, with a customer focus, consideration of statutory and regulatory requirements, and establishment of measurable objectives at relevant functions and levels.

Continual Improvement: An enhanced requirement for 'continual improvement' has been introduced, as anticipated, into ISO 9001, defining a complete cycle to improve the effectiveness of the quality management system.

Application: The concept of exclusions to the requirements of ISO 9001:2000 has been introduced as a way to cope with wide spectrum of organisations and activities that will be using the new standard, via clause 1.2, i.e. "Application".

Customer Satisfaction: Another new item that has been introduced into ISO 9001:2000 is the requirement for the organisation to monitor information on customer satisfaction as a measure of system performance.

Resources: Attention has been placed on top management to provide and make available the necessary resources. Requirements now include evaluation of the effectiveness of training, provision of relevant information, internal and external communication, facility needs, and human and physical factors of the work environment.

Terminology: Changes have also occurred in terminology. The most important changes concern the use of the term "organisation" instead of "supplier", still used in the current standards, and the use of the term "supplier" instead of "sub-contractor". These changes respond to the need of being more consistent and friendly with the normal use and meaning of the words.

Documentation: The number of requirements for documented procedures has been reduced in ISO 9001:2000, and the emphasis placed on the organisation demonstrating effective operation.

Other Changes: Other detailed changes of a less strategic nature have also been made with the intention to simplify or clarify requirements of the existing standards, and to make them more "user-friendly".

It is amply clear from the revision that organisations now need to prepare themselves addressing people centered issues with commitment from the top management with renewed thrust on HR issues, more particularly on Training.

Competency Mapping

Another important emerging HR issue is to build organisation in line with capability profile, pioneered by Dr. David Cohen and others. We have briefly introduced this concept here.

Competencies are attributes, some professional skills, or a combination of skills and knowledge and behaviours. Competency models suggest integration of business plan of the company with selecting the right individual for the job. An integrated system of corporate values, vision, mission statement, goals/objectives, action planning and support systems are needed to put it all together. A competency is defined as the smallest unit of on-the-job behaviour that is observable, measurable, and changes over time. Behaviour is a function of consequence.

Competencies matter because past performance is the best predictor of future performance, good current performance builds from past performance and the more recent the effective behaviour, the more appropriate fit to the job. The organisation needs to create an integrated human resources process by looking at not only the skills and knowledge but also the behaviour required by an employee to be successful in any job. This results in a capability profile. Capability is a combination of skills, knowledge and behaviour. Once this profile is in place, we can use the behaviours for selection and recruitment, for employee development, reward management, performance management, training, succession planning and career development. Rewards do not have to be financial they can be recognition or paid time off or a simple thank you.

Once this is in place we enable our people in true sense or make our organisation an enabling organisation and this way the organisation flourishes.

Some Lessons

1. Competency based models need to be applied first to human resources staff.
2. There must be full commitment from senior management.
3. Competencies must be designed and endorsed by the people who are going to use them.
4. Good competency profiles reflect the commonality of the work.
5. Partnerships with unions is critical – they must be involved early and often.
6. Many of the competencies that have painstakingly been identified are actually manifested in many other organisations – the work done by others could be helpful.

7. We must define the business that we are in.
8. Network with other organisations – excellent models others have developed will be of help.
9. We must anticipate emerging shifts to competencies - don't just focus on the present.
10. Our competency human resources model must be affordable – the more integration of human resources services we can complete the more affordable the model will be.
11. The cornerstone of this model is the relationship between the employees and their supervIsors.
12. If performance measurement information is to be used in the staffing process it must be absolutely clear when we establish our model and must be of the highest quality when gathered.
13. We must have a sound communication strategy with the stakeholders.

Results

1. Quick and cheaper staffing process – savings.
2. Decreased appeal rates.
3. Career management results in a selection process that is generally well received by managers, staff and union for its free and more transparent approach using competency.
4. Reduced training delivery costs through self-study and coaching.
5. Reduction in grievances.
6. Competency performance assessment results are easily transferable to the competency-based staffing process.
7. Career planning is taken far more seriously by employees.

Charles Handy also advocated future organisational models like; Shamrock, Federal and Triple-I. Such Organisational Models also refocus on people centric issues and call for redefining the future role of HR Professionals. We have also discussed these models briefly here.

Shamrock Organisation

A type of organisational structure based around a core of essential executives and workers supported by outside contractors and part-time help. This model has been conceived by Charles Handy. It describes a type of organisational structure with three parts or leaves – "a form of organisation based around a core of essential executives and workers supported by outside contractors and part-time help". The consequence of such an organisational form as perceived by Handy was that companies in the future are likely to resemble consultancy firms, advertising agencies, and professional partnerships in their structure.

This model, or variations of it, are often used to explain the move to outsourcing non-core functions. In Handy's analogy, the first leaf of the shamrock represents the core staff of the organisation. These people are likely to be highly trained professionals who make up the senior management. The second leaf consists of the contractual fringe either individuals or other organisations – and may include people who once worked for the organisation but now provide it with services. These individuals operate within the broad framework set down by the core but have a high level of discretionary decisionmaking power to complete projects or deliver contracts. The third leaf includes the flexible labour force. More than simply hired hands, in Handy's model, these workers have to be sufficiently close to the organisation to feel a sense of commitment that ensures that their work – although part-time or intermittent – is carried out to a high standard.

The second emergent structure identified by Handy was the "Federal Organisation" another word for decentralisation. He provided a blueprint for federal organisations in which the organisational centre co-ordinates, influences, advises, and suggests. It does not dictate terms or make short-term decisions. The centre is, however, concerned with long-term strategy.

The third type of organisation Handy anticipated is what he called "the triple I" information, intelligence, and idea. In such organisations the demands on Human Resource Management are large. Handy explained: "The wise organisation already knows that their smart people are not to be easily defined as workers or as managers but as individuals, as specialist, as professional or executives, or as leader (the older terms of manager and worker are dropping out of use), and that they and it need also to be obsessed with the pursuit of learning if they are going to keep up with the pace of change. "

More recently, Handy has suggested that successful organisations of the future will be what he calls "membership communities". His logic is that in order to hold people to organisations that can no longer promise them a job for life, companies have to offer some other form of continuity and sense of belonging. To do this, he suggests, companies have to imbue members with certain rights.

What Handy is advocating, in fact, is a notion of the federal organisation built on the principle of subsidiary. This places a large degree of thrust in its core professionals and other knowledge workers. Under Handy's membership community model, the centre is kept small and its primary purpose is to be "in charge of the future". Only if the organisation is severely threatened does decision-making power revert to the centre. This allows a company to react quickly in a crisis. The rest of the time, decision making is highly decentralised.

Six Sigma Practices

To leapfrog ahead of competition in this world of uncertainty, corporate world is experimenting with one after another processes. From 'Conformance to Standards' to achieve total quality, the focus has now been shifted to add economic value and practical utility to both the organisation and the customer. Realising Value entitlement both by the customers and the organisations is now the determinant of business relationship. It is now a win-win situation for the both. For customers, it is their rightful expectation to buy quality products at competitive cost, while for organisations, it is to produce at highest possible profit. This synergy is what everybody tries to achieve in this corporate world. Rejection Allowance, Unavoidable Rejection (UR) are now the forbidden words. Six sigma as a business process is now allowing organisations to improve their bottom line by designing and monitoring business activities in a way that minimises wastes and resources without, however, compromising with customer satisfaction. Six Sigma process is broader than Total Quality Management (TQM) programmes. While TQM focuses on detecting and correcting defects, six sigma recreates the processes to ensure defects never arise right from the beginning. From organisations' point of view, it provides maximum value in the form of increased profits and from customers' point of view, it provides maximum value in terms of high quality products and services at competitive costs.

Higher Sigma values indicate better quality products and lower sigma values represent less quality products. At six sigma level, products are virtually defect free, i.e., only 3.4 Defects Per Million Opportunities (DPMO).

Six sigma concept is different than TQM. TQM, per se, focuses on improvements in individual operations, without relating it to the processes. It emphasises on the use of statistical tools and due to absence of integration of operations and processes (which is a series of activities or steps to create a product or service in its totality), it takes long time for an operation to improve. While six sigma, using rigorous analytical tools with the leadership from the top, develops a methodology for sustainable improvements. Six sigma is a more integrated approach with commitment to achieve success by way of quality improvement that increases profitability and customer satisfaction. Six Sigma, therefore, is a break through strategy that improves organisational values, infusing changes in the processes, which go into creating defect free product or service at minimum cost. For introducing six sigma, it requires improvement in following areas:

1. Improvement of process
2. Improvement of product and services
3. Improvement in investor relationship
4. Improvement in designing
5. Improvement in supplier relationship
6. Improvement in training and recruitment.

Mickel Harry (1994) in his Six Sigma Academy, emphasises on all these areas, which prepare the ground work for achieving excellence in an organisation. Every member of the organisation needs to be trained, following the system and then the players in the break through strategy need to be identified to play the role of catalysts in the change process. In the change process customer is the king. Customers define quality and set expectations and hence, they figure out at the top among change agents. Other change agents being internal to the company, they are graded through training process. A typical inverted relationship in six sigma break through strategy is explained in Figure 27.1 below:

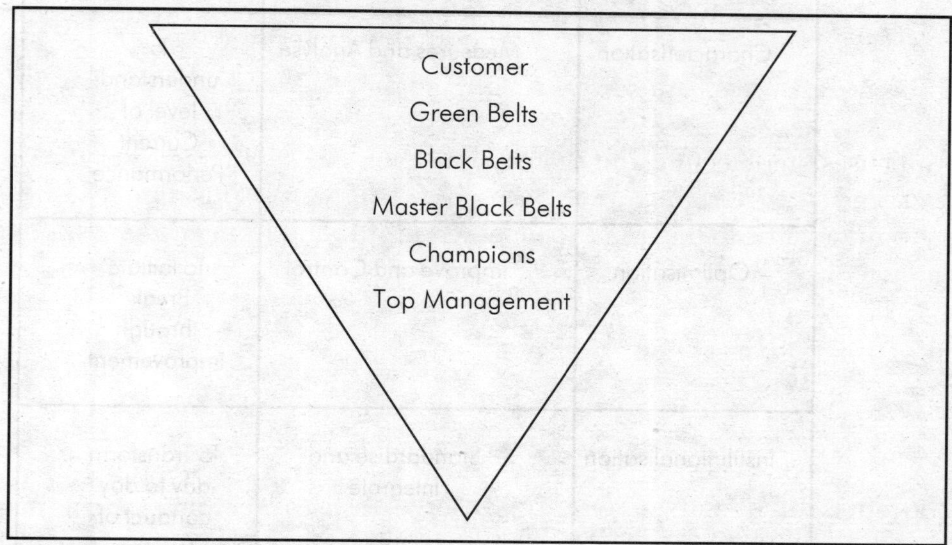

Figure 27.1: Six Sigma Break Through Strategy

Like customer at the top, at the bottom of the inverted pyramid is the top management, who supports and balances the six sigma change process. Champions are also executive leaders who identify individual leaders to ensure that key functions are connected to six sigma. They are the grounding force to make the strategy work. Master Black Belts are selected by the Champions to assist in dissemination of break through strategy and for identifying projects for improvement. They train and coach Black Belts and Green Belts, organise people, design cross-functional, experiments, structure and co-ordinate projects and meetings, collect and organise information. Black Belts work under the Master Black Belts and apply six sigma tools and knowledge to specific projects. Green Belts on the other hand are employees of the organisation who execute six sigma as part of their overall jobs. Green Belts dedicate only part of their overall jobs to six sigma projects. Master Black Belts and Black Belts dedicate 100 per cent of their time in working on six sigma projects.

Steps for Six Sigma

By now it has been made clear that six sigma is a problem-solving tool. Six sigma breakthrough strategy aims to achieve excellence by properly identifying issues pertaining to business, technology, manufacturing/services, quality, production and delivery system. There are eight fundamental steps to achieve six sigma quality in a process division of an organisation. These eight stages are: Recognise, Define, Measure, Analyse, Improve, Control, Standardise and Integrate. Such eight stages can be broadly categorised under four heads, as illustrated in Figure 27.2.

	Stages	Strategy Phase	Objectives	
BREAKTHROUGH STRATEGY	Identification	Recognise and Define	To identify Key Business Issues	BLACK BELTS
	Characterisation	Measures and Analyse	To understand level of Current Performance	
	Optimisation	Improve and Control	To initiate Break-through improvement	
	Institutionalisation	Standardise and Integrate	To Transform day to day conduct of business	

Figure 27.2: The Six Sigma Map

At each stage, organisations are required to perform specific tasks to finally institutionalise the six sigma breakthrough strategy. In identification phase, companies recognise in what way processes affect their profitability and what process are critical to business. Similarly characterisation phase helps to benchmark and provides the inputs to measure improvements. At this stage, action plan is charted to close the gap between the current and the future, matching company's goals for product and services. It is at this stage Black Belts select key characteristics of one or more products/services and develop a detailed description of each and every step in their processes. Using process control cards, Black Belts estimate the short-term and long-term process capability.

Using specific statistical tools, organisation, at this stage, try to analyse reasons for defective products/services, nature of problem – sporadic or persistent, technology or process related, etc.

In the optimisation phase, Design for Six Sigma (DFSS), is used to reconfigure products and services right from the beginning in a way that conforms to six sigma quality. This is done by discovering the key variables that lead to the problem and then designing the products and services eliminating such problem generating variables. Apart from such improvement initiative at optimisation phase, proper control is ensured by strict monitoring of the processes to avoid recurrence of similar quality problems in products and services. Thus optimisation ensures improvement of a process by reducing the variation using statistically designed experiments. Optimisation also controls the key variables ('vital few') to ultimately improve profitability and customer satisfaction.

In the final stage of institutionalisation, standardisation and integration of six sigma practices are done to run the day to day business of an organisation. Six sigma is a learning continuum, therefore, it reinforces the intellectual capital to identify the best practices continually and standardise those within and across the business to create a win-win situation in a competitive world. It is 'I am O.K. you are O.K.' situation for mutual satisfaction of customers and organisations.

How to Calculate Sigma

As has been explained earlier, six sigma break through strategy leads to defect free products and services, adding profit to the organisations and satisfaction to the customers (by way of quality products/services at lowest possible cost). However, no organisation can achieve six sigma level right at the beginning. It requires relentless efforts to achieve each sigma level and then ultimately the desired six sigma level, at which products/services are virtually defect free. For calculating sigma level, we use the Defects Per Million Opportunities (DPMO) formula, duly defining the customers' perceived Critical to Quality (CTQ) factors. Since this is a quantitative measurement, we also need to have discrete information about following three items:

1. ***UNIT:*** The item produced or being serviced
2. ***DEFECT:*** Event that does not conform to customers' requirements
3. ***OPPORTUNITY:*** Chance for occurrence of a defect

To illustrate, let us take the example of examination services of an Educational Institute. Students consider a defect in the system when results declared beyond three weeks. Students have four perceived CTQs, i.e., speed of delivery, correct transcript of marks, adequate information about incomplete or withheld results, proper computation of grades. These, therefore, make four opportunities in discrete terms. Once quantitative details about number of units and defects are made available, we can use the following formula to calculate the sigma level:

$$\frac{\text{Number of Defects}}{\text{Number of Opportunities for error} \times \text{No. of Units}} \times 1{,}00{,}000$$

Suppose in our case, we have 2500 results, of which 10 were late due to non-availability of assignments grades and 5 were bad due to improper computation of grades. The calculation, therefore, would be as under:

$$\frac{15}{2 \times 2500} \times 1{,}000{,}000 = 3000$$

3000 DPMO almost corresponds to 4.25 sigma level, which indicates, the hypothetical institution need to identify further the process flaws and improve upon the quality of service. At six sigma level, DPMO should be 3.4. Six sigma chart for corresponding DPMO is available in any standard book on statistics.

Relating Six Sigma to HR Strategy

Strategy is the direction and scope of an organisation over long term, matching its resources to its changing environment and in particular its markets, customers or clines, so as to meet stakeholders' expectations. HR strategy is the pattern of decisions concerning policies and practices associated with the HR system. Strategic Management of Human Resource Management (SHRM) is a competency-based approach to develop HR for sustainable competitive advantage. Environmental, Organisational, Institutional and Technological factors are potential influencers in HR strategy. For implementing six sigma break through strategy, we need to take cognizance of each such factor, right from identification to institutionalisation. Integrating six sigma to HR strategy reduces the time lag significantly and thereby helps in achieving excellence' in quality of product and services within minimum time frame.

Let us first try to understand the basic requirements for achieving six sigma.

At the outset, it requires to sell organisational values to its internal customers, i.e., the employees. A clear vision and mission do the job when successfully percolated to all cross section of employees. Mere documentation will not help. It requires practices by all through personal selling (behaviour). Vision and mission should reflect commitment to quality – a defect free product/services to the customers. It should further extend to explaining goals, objectives, strategies and action plan. Subsequently in all HR practices such strategic intent should be evident. In recruitment and selection, focus should be to select those who have multiple skill sets and who can be utilised interchangeably by cross lateral movement. This requires foreseeing the future skill sets with the changing technology or process. Similarly regular competency mapping and a synergy between individual and organisational competencies need to be achieved through training and development intervention. Training employees on six sigma requires both technical and behavioural reinforcements. Any skill gap requires repeated training till they all fit for the purpose. All cannot be black belts. It is also not required. But all should understand how important it is for them to improve their workmanship for defect free products and services. Ranging from product to process familiarisation, the training should focus on basic understanding of using statistical and analytical tools to help them to measure the variability and attribute reasons for failure.

Similar importance to compensation planning, motivation and retention should be given to ensure commitment and loyalty to the organisation. There are many ways to design compensation innovatively and also for employees' retention.

To conclude, six sigma, even though a top down approach, its success largely depends on the players, who are catalysts for such change. It makes no sense to engage a consultant and expect results, unless the initiatives are properly integrated with HR strategy of the organisation.

INNOVATION AND CREATIVITY

Innovation is a new technique or idea encompassing product/services, process, managerial styles and even organisational structure. It may be technology push or demand pull or even combination of both. Research and Development (R&D) activities of an organisation are examples of such innovation. In any organisation need for innovation is primarily felt to keep pace with the competition. It has to be essentially customer focussed as this backward linkage facilitates process-centered innovative changes. Whether it is just-in-time (JIT) inventory, Supply Chain Management (SCM), Business Process Outsourcing (BPO), Flexible Manufacturing Systems (FMS), Product/Service customisation, strategic backward or forward integration, synergy through merger or acquisition, alliances or collaboration, organisational re-engineering TQM or Six Sigma Practices, new work culture as facilitator of organisational change or any R&D initiative for value addition, which broadly encompasses innovation; all stem from customers' explicit or implicit needs. Mapping customers' needs and aligning the same to innovation initiative is what we need in this competitive world. Innovation is enabled by pro-active HR Practices. Subscribing to innovation without pro-active HR practices will hinder rather than fostering innovation in an organisation. Pro-active HR Practices, inter alia, call for creating a work environment that recognises creativity, inter-organisational co-operation rather than competition, working as cross-functional teams, productive meetings for innovative results, introduction of formal innovation programmes and finally organisation's receptivity to new ideas and perspectives. Fostering innovation requires a structured approach. It has to be broadly in the given context, leadership, values and culture. Contextual analysis helps in building required innovation teams. Leaders facilitate the teams. Values enable adoption of principles which foster innovation and finally the culture provides the playing field.

At this stage, it is pertinent to define creativity as innovation and creativity are often used interchangeably in work place. Webster Dictionary has defined creativity as "the ability or power to create, to bring into existence, to invest with a new form, to produce through imaginative skill, to make or bring into existence something new". Creativity is therefore, the core competency. It is the talent of employees of an organisation. Competitors can replicate the strategies of an organisation but not the creative talents of its employees. To encourage creativity, organisation first create the right environment where employees feel safe even to come up with 'dumb' or 'crazy' ideas. Creativity is often punished in organisation, as creative people spend more time to get ready for action. They are also more difficult to manage. Organisations, therefore, often see them as major time and money wasters and inhibit their creative thoughts. A review of creativity literature helps us to capture creative patterns in following ways:

- A creative process is a balance of imagination and analysis. It involves idea generation, analysis and evaluation.
- Creativity does not stems from subconscious process, as traditionally believed by the classical school of thoughts. It is a purposeful or directed attempt to generate new ideas under controlled situation to help organisation to leapfrog in competition. Paul E. Plsek (1997), used the term more appropriately as 'Directed Creativity'. It is a purposeful generation of creative ideas with seriousness of its implementation, whenever it matches with organisational requirements. Non-implementation of at least some ideas (that fit the purpose) will inhibit creativity.

Innovation is the implementation of creative ideas. Therefore, creativity is the sub-set of innovation. Innovation being a holistic concept, here we prefer to use the term interchangeably.

Competencies on the other hand are set of behaviours, which encompass skills, knowledge, abilities and attributes. Competencies are measurable and it changes over time. Hamel and Prahalad (1990) attributed business success only on innovative creativity, knowledge resources and the expertise, which together create the critical potential of an organisation, i.e., core competencies. Other proponents of core competencies like; Quinn (1992), Drucker (1992), Porter (1995), Waterman (1983), Peter (1988), Nonaka and Takeuchi (1955), Senge (1990), also show that developing core competencies help an organisation to build strategic power. Core competencies are difficult to duplicate by the competitors because of their distinctiveness. Core competencies are therefore critical success factors for any organisation. Although there exist widespread difference regarding constituents of core competencies and its relation with knowledge, skill, abilities and attributes of employees, there is agreement among its proponents about how it is created linking between organisation's goals, structure and culture. Innovation and creativity helps to develop core competencies supplementing knowledge and skill base for the employees. In this respect directed creativity, i.e., purposeful generation of new ideas matching with organisational requirements, is more relevant.

Innovation, creativity and competencies are important facilitators for organisational change. Imperatives for organisational change basically stem from redefining business focus, restructuring, customer orientation – all for competitive advantages.

How to Cultivate Innovation and align it to Competitive Strengths?

Innovation and Creativity in Indian Social System is embedded in the age old theory of Social Stratification. Social Stratification refers to principal mechanism of social order in society from which stems the concept of class categorisation. While caste, class, elite and professional occupational categories have been used for the analysis of social stratification in India, we find more use of occupational categories as an attributional property for class stratification. Among the occupational categories, professional and bureaucratic elites were those who had sustained training to acquire skill for performing the professional role in formal organisational set up and their nature of work was complex than others. Such brief historical note helps us to understand recognition of innovation and creativity in age-old Indian Social System.

Indian Gurukul System of learning also intended to reinforce innovation and creativity, recognising existence of core essence in each individual. Learning under Gurukul System was intended to help students to think independently and to understand the interdependence by exploring the nature. Over the years however, this has changed globally, reducing learning as a formal mechanism, where creativity and independent thought is punished as teachers do not like creative students' in the classroom as they make it harder for them to do their job.

The competitive compulsion in today's organisations now again put us back to the age old process of nurturing innovation and creativity, recognising its importance in gaining competitive strengths.

To cultivate innovation and creativity, we have to first understand the factors that inhibit innovation in an organisation. While introducing the concept, we have discussed about such factors. For recapitulation, here again, we briefly discuss those factors with some more inputs:

- Creating a congenial work environment is the most important pre-requisite: This requires major attitudinal and cultural change to provide the right playing field to foster innovation. The desired work environment to nurture innovation and creativity should be full of listening, speaking, evaluating questioning. Destructive way of questioning or questioning with cynical tone (e.g. Really?) may dampen the spirit of the innovators. Even giving negative non-verbal cue, i.e. diverting attention, falling asleep, etc., may vitiate the environment for cultivating innovation and creativity. Attitudinal and cultural change should also be reinforced by proper employee compensation, it also requires special reward for implemented ideas. If ideas are not at all implemented (at least some of them) it sends a wrong signal to creative people, who then start perceiving that their organisation inhibits creativity. Putting a suggestion box and rewarding employees for suggestions not implemented is also dangerous.

- Another important aspect for cultivating innovation in organisation is by fostering mutual cooperation. Creating SBU or IBU does not mean each SBU or IBU would compete with each other. By leveraging strength of each other, organisation should function as an integrated whole and work as cross functional teams. To illustrate, we find in most of the cases, customer database are common for SBUs in an organisation but SBU heads prefer to have proprietary control over these database, fearing clash of interest. Even within SBUs also we find executives compete with each other, by not sharing the information. Such competitive environment within the organisation, unless transformed to a cooperative environment, will not allow creativity to flourish. Even in B-schools also we find such trend, which transcends to the attitude of the students. Such students when enter the corporate world, they replicate their learning that foster inter-organisational rivalry and competition. We can correct this situation by forming cross-functional teams.

- Having productive meetings and brainstorming also lead to cultivation of innovation and creativity. Productive meeting and brainstorming does not mean that supremo will only speak and others will listen. It means true involvement of all members on issues, which may or may not pertaining to his/her area of activities. True productive meetings may not be time bound, it may run even for several days. This helps in process re-engineering and even at times helps in refocusing business to customers' expectation. Productive meetings help in capturing 'collective wisdom' of cross-section of employees toward the targeted goals. This, therefore, develops the innovative and creative response capability, which add to the competitive strengths.

  CHEVRON Corporation, a leader in the petroleum industry used 'Direct Participation (DP), involving employees in innovative thinking for designing and implementing change. In DP process, variety of stakeholders meet (for two to three days) to address a problem or issue that calls for change and produce detailed outputs which are quickly implementable. It brings multiple perspectives relating to the problem and facilitates identification of changes required to resolve it.

- The other major inhibitor for innovation and creativity is absence of formal innovation programmes and techniques in the organisation. Formal innovation programmes in an organisation should focus on generating ideas in relation to current and future customer needs, speed up idea generation with frequent meetings, funds quickly idea that fits the purpose and finally reduce the response time for implementation. Many organisations have adopted 'incubator' concept for nurturing innovation and creativity. Incubators in one of the leading Indian organisations are like small meditation halls, which allow employees to think in isolation, even taking a break from work and nurture issues for creative solution. Once the thoughts are matured then only those are put up for discussion by cross functional teams for implementation.

Finally, organisations should also be receptive to consider new ideas. Mere presence of formal innovation programmes will not help, unless organisation shows the concern for its implementation, at least some of them that fits the purpose. Quite often innovative ideas are thought as criticism of existing systems. In fact some employees, in the process of giving new ideas, often indulge unknowingly to criticise the existing system, hurting the sentiments and take a sense of pride, when it get accepted. This is dangerous and it requires proper training to all how to structure their ideas and present the same either in writing or in discussion forms.

For aligning innovation and creativity to competitive strategy, it is important to consider following aspects:

- Innovation should be focussed and need specific. We have already discussed the concepts of 'directed creativity' and current and future needs of the customers.
- There should be a clear documented policy about innovation and creativity. Like how it is captured, reward for best innovative ideas, if any, process of implementation, etc.
- Innovation and creativity can not be outsourced, hence emphasis should be on inhouse talent. If it is outsourced, it looses its competitive strength as others can replicate it.
- All innovative ideas should be subjected to brain storming and if acceptable should first be tried in pilot projects.
- For risk hedging, innovative ideas can be benchmarked with other organisations. HLL may succeed in repositioning their 'Lifebuoy' by changing its attributes (from carbolic soap with in-built health essence in it) but Colgate is struggling behind and trying desperately to retain market share by increasing product variety.
- Implementation should be closely monitored preferably by calculating ROI, and only after success in pilot projects, it should be institutionalised.
- Finally innovation and creativity need to be aligned to organisational values – which provide broad guidelines for adoption of principles, vision, mission and strategies.

Calculating ROI of Innovation and Creativity

After successful institutionalisation, duly aligning innovation and creativity to competitive strategy, it is important to calculate the ROI to quantify the results and understand, the variation to refine/modify or to strengthen or gain commitment from the employees. Two ROI systems widely in use are utility analysis and performance value. Nine step human capital ROI worksheet of Gordon (2001) even though basically intended to estimate monetary return of training can. also be utilised for calculating ROI of Innovation and Creativity Programmes of an organisation. Such steps with minor modification (customised for measuring ROI of innovation and creativity) is presented in following steps:

Step 1	Calculate all direct costs associated with Innovation and Creativity Programmes.
Step 2	Calculate cost of lost productivity while all participate in Brainstorming.
Step 3	Calculate the total cost of the innovation and Creativity Programmes.
Step 4	Estimate expected hourly, daily, weekly or monthly productivity benefits per employee, covered under the programme. This can be done by establishing control groups or by using a standard linear regression formula.
Step 5	Estimate the actual quality benefit from the programme.
Step 6	Estimate the time length effect of the programme, using a standard discount rate formula.
Step 7	Calculate profit per employee.
Step 8	Calculate benefits of the total programme.
Step 9	Calculate ROI.

Another seven-step model for calculating ROI was suggested by Stolovitch and Maurice (1998) based on Human Performance Technology (HPT) interventions. Using this model authors have even documented cases with 615 per cent growth of ROI in one year through HPT interventions. HPT is the method of measuring Human Capital, i.e., the sum total of human performance capability. Among others, HPT also focuses on Innovation and Creativity for enhancing human performance capability. This model can also be used for calculating ROI of Innovation and Creativity programmes of an organisation. The model is illustrated in with minor changes for Innovation and Creativity.

Step 1	Calculate potential value for improved performance through Innovation and Creativity interventions.
Step 2	Calculate estimated costs (both direct and overhead) of Innovation and Creativity interventions.
Step 3	Calculate the worth of interventions. Worth (W) is equal to the potential values (V) of improved performance divided by estimated costs of interventions. It means W=V/c.
Step 4	Develop and implement interventions.
Step 5	Calculate the true cost of the interventions and replace the estimated cost (as placed in Step 2) by the real estimates.
Step 6	Calculate organisational ROI considering change in sales figure, productivity gains, rejection rates, absenteeism figures, speed of order processing or any other relevant details, duly assigning monetary value. This can be done after allowing 6 months of implementation of Innovation and Creativity Programmes.
Step 7	Calculate individual increased value and study the trend

A study by Towers Perrin and his team (2001) indicated that technology induced new business environment has made innovation most important competitive strategy. Their research indicates by 2003, organisations globally have to emphasise on innovation, new markets, new products and services and finally e-commerce sales solutions. People Capability Maturity Model (P-CMM) of Software Engineering Institute, Carnegie Mellon University (1995) also emphasised on continuous workforce innovation for developing competency at both organisational and the individual level. This, however, preceeds other successful capability enhancement interventions, encompassing all contemporary HR practices, as a truly innovative organisation qualifies for level-5, i.e., the highest level of P-CMM Certification. Realising the potential of innovation and creativity, globally organisations are re-defining their core Human Resource Value with commitment to it.

Supply Chain Management

Supply Chain Management (SCM) is an integrated approach to outsource to derive customer satisfaction by cost optimisation. It cuts costs, reduces inventory, shares basic demand forecast with trading partners for mutual advantage, etc. Even though initial thrust of SCM was to integrate warehousing and transportation for efficient distribution at reduced costs, over the years SCM has become a strategic tool to increase market share and multiply customer satisfaction. The basic hypothesis on which SCM sustains is efficient interaction and interdependence of planning, people and processes i.e., three Ps which together reinforce output that satisfies customers, irrespective of their geographical dispersion, and increases market share and productivity. Out-source everything that's non-core – this is what Peter Drucker says for today's organisation. With IT interface, SCM has changed from its traditional Logistics management approach to many new areas of corporate outsourcing, even encompassing HR functions. Business Process Outsourcing (BPO), to be more specific, is relatively a new concept and an extension of SCM Philosophy, which is revolutionising the management practices of today's organisations. Take for example, British Telcom. In 18 months, they have re-defined their strategies 8 times. Or for that matter a Deshi organisation – Reliance, who had surpassed Du'Pont and Dow in terms of per employee profitability, yet with a HR strategy, which speaks more oriental and orthodox than trendy. These are the two extreme cases, where BPO and Human Resource Outsourcing (HRO) have different connotations.

Tracing history, we find that BPO and HRO was institutionalised in the name of Employee Leasing in developed countries. With its birth in the USA in 1982, by 1985, it had an annual revenue of $1 billion. Looking back to history we find that such firms started flourishing in the USA, especially after the enactment of the Tax Equity and Fiscal Responsibility Act (TEFRA), 1982. The 'top-heavy' Pension Plan in the USA disproportionately favoured company owners and senior executives (key employees) over lower level employees.

Till 1982, such practice was continuing and companies were also enjoying tax benefit for such a partisan policy. TEFRA instituted the requirements that such top heavy Pension Plan (the plan which provides more than 60 per cent of the accumulated benefits to key employees) will cease to enjoy tax benefits unless shared with all employees. But the exception clause allowed companies to exclude leased employees from their pension programmes if the leasing companies were having their own pension plan and contributed atleast 7.5 per cent of the salary in that scheme. This exception clause helped the employers to set up their exclusive Pension Plan and transfer their employees to leasing companies, and take them back under leasing agreement. To such exclusive pension plans, companies can contribute as much as 200 per cent of the salary and thus can shelter profit from taxes. Today leasing companies provide various services, absolutely relieving the client companies from personnel problems for a percentage of the pay roll, which generally varies from 5 per cent to 10 per cent. Such services include; recruiting, training, supervision, wage setting, handling of labour disputes, periodic performance appraisal, preparation of pay roll, maintenance of pay-records, administration of vacation and sick time, government paper work, preparation of employee-related reports and audits, etc.

Initially, leasing companies' main target as prospective clients was small business corporations, employing less than 50 persons. Such small companies' own benefits scheme being less attractive, they usually experience high rates of labour turnover. Moreover, as such companies are mostly owner-managed, their pension schemes disproportionately favour a handful of key employees, causing much discontentment amongst the rest of the employees. Because of their relatively poor benefit schemes, skilled manpower feels less attraction, which deprives them from quality labour services and workmanship. Again high cost of labour inputs fails to give them a competitive edge over big business corporations. All these factors, together with the TEFRA, made small companies target clients to leasing companies in the USA. From the USA, employee leasing concept, in more institutionalised form spread across the globe, including India. In India, high technology is gradually finding a place in organisations for increased productivity, decreased labour cost and for enhanced safety. Under utilisation of capacity, rising industrial disputes more lockout prone now than strikes) and consequent loss of mandays, surplus manpower, low labour productivity are some crippling characteristics of Indian industries. In distribution of total earnings, as percentage of value-added, Indian workers are sharing more than their counterparts in the developed countries like; UK, Japan and the USA. This justifies that Indian industries are burdened with high labour costs, even though in absolute terms, such costs may be quite low. These apart, Non-Wage-Labour Cost (NWLC) burden is globally rising. NWLC is a load on paid wage costs, in terms of deferred benefits to the employees and the personnel overhead cost. NWLC in UK is 40 per cent of the paid wage costs, in the USA it is 38 per cent, in Germany it is 82 per cent, while in France it is as high as 93 per cent. In India NWLC varies between 20 to 25 per cent of the paid wage costs. Retaining employees from leasing companies, therefore, substantially adds to labour cost savings and thus can enhance the profitability of the organisations.

C.K. Prahalad's core competency theory in 1990s, which suggests to identify core competencies and focus only on them and get out of everything that is non-core, was initially product/service-centric approach. Since then organisations were trying to reinforce their business strategies, aligning them to their core competencies. Over the years, this theory proved to have its renewed thrust in intra-organisational functions and operations, which calls for outsourcing all non-core or non-value adding activities and confining on core matters which are crucial to business.

In 1989, we get yet another mind-boggling idea from Charles Handy about future organisational model. Handy had predicted three different organisational models, which are distinctly different than what we are used to. His 'Shamrock' organisational model is based around a core of essential executives and workers supported by outside contractors and part-time help. This model explains the move to out-source non-core functions. The second emergent organisational structure identified by Handy was the "Federal organisation" - more improvised decentralisation where organisational centre co-ordinates influence, advises and suggests and does not dictate terms or make short-term decisions. The third type of organisation of Handy is known as 'Tripple-I', i.e. information, intelligence and ideas.

These apart, need for building organisation in line with the capability profile (David Cohen), shortage of critical skills, changing process, systems, culture and management practices, global competitiveness, need for cost control, need for flexibility and change, etc., are the issues which contributed to the need for outsourcing non-core activities of an organisation.

Business Process Outsourcing and Human Resource Outsourcing

The process of development of BPO and HRO, as an extension of SCM philosophy has been discussed from a historical perspective to appreciate its generic root. It is amply clear, over the years, the need for outsourcing was felt by the organisations both for economic and strategic compulsions. SCM, as a concept, though developed much later, it now integrates the outsourcing also along with customer service, demand flow and distribution. BPO is the long-term contracting of a company's non-core business processes to an outside service provider. BPO paves the way for global competition and ensures strategic focus on core capabilities for improving stakeholders' value, efficiency and reduced operating costs. Identified benefits of BPO are: quality improvement, enhanced access to technology, lower operating costs, greater efficiency and strategic focus on core competencies. Organisation in the USA, Canada, U.K., France, Germany, Netherlands, Spain, Switzerland, Sweden, Italy, Australia, Brazil, Argentina, Japan and also India are among some countries of the world, who have extensively gone for BPO to reap its advantages. BPO covers activities like; finance and accounts, human resources, real estate related matters, internal audit, tax compliance, applications process, procurement, etc.

Within an organisation, a supply chain encompasses all functions. Every organisation decides its own strategies for all functional areas, like accounting and finance, human resources, information technology, etc. Such functional strategies are integrated with supply chain strategies through a value chain. A strategic fit when ensured through a value chain, contributes to company's success. Proper mapping of customers' requirements and matching the same to supply chain responsiveness and the functional strategies within the value chain help us to achieve the strategic fit. Major drivers in a supply chain strategy are Inventory, Transportations, Facilities and Information. Responsiveness and efficiency of each driver determines the success of a supply chain.

SCM at the outset, emphasised on the importance of networking among component manufactures, service providers and distributors. With IT interface it has now assumed a broader perspective, leveraging competitive advantage for the organisations. Among others, SCM also helps in leveraging people by better use of human capital. BPO and HRO in that way are extension of SCM, which institutionalised the outsourcing of non-core activities for organisations. Like employee leasing, BPO and HRO also offer the same advantage to small companies, without requiring them to invest unnecessarily in costly insfrastructure, yet remain competitive in global market by substantial cost savings. With simultaneous changes in the organisational structure, as predicted by Charles Handy and the need for redesigning organisation in line with the capability profile, as advocated by David Cohen along with other changes concerning management practices and global economic environment, BPO and HRO are no longer confined within small business support services. With initial focus in call centres and medical transcription activities, it has now even been extended to expert knowledge services, facilitating organisations to outsource much more extensively their non-core activities and limiting their focus on core manufacturing, product management or marketing. The onus of identifying core and non-core activities lies within the oganisation. Examination may be a core activity for an educational organisation, while admission may be a non-core activity, which can be outsourced. This, however, may not, hold good for all. Some private players in education may consider both examination and admission as non-core and outsource it, by limiting their focus only on product (course-ware) development. The concept of educational franchisee, revolves around this philosophy. Similarly manufacturing may be a non-core activity for an organisation, while product development and marketing may be their core activities. There are many FMCG players who follow this model. An integrated SCM Model with HR BPO focus is presented in Figure 27.3.

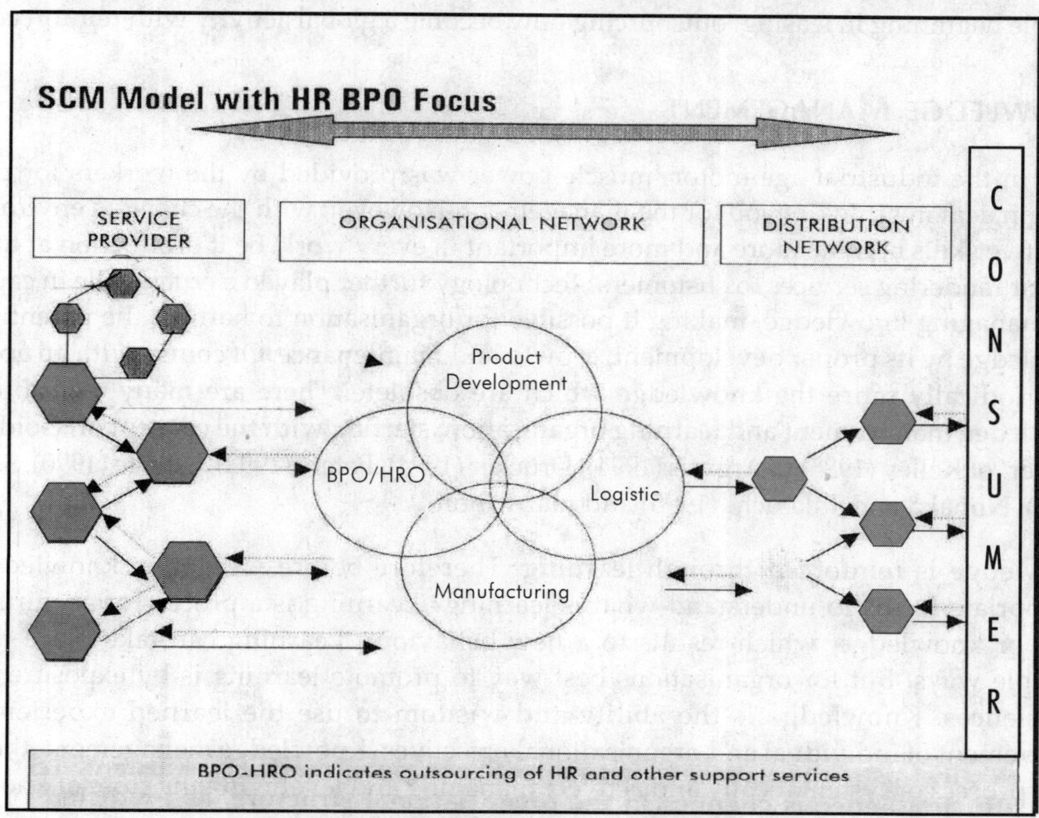

Figure 27.3: SCM Model with HR BPO Focus

After an organisation decides about outsourcing in the next phase, it is important for them to select the right vendors. Depending on the customers' expectations, vendors can be benchmarked on quality, price, delivery and service parameters based on market information, duly assigning weight for each such factor. Presently there are only handful of players in India in BPO market with employee strength as high as 12000 (GE, Gurgaon and Hyderabad) to as little as 25 (Accounts, Bangalore). But with the increase of global market in BPO from $ 208 billion in 1999 to $ 543 billion in 2004, as predicted by Gartner Group, more players are likely to crowd this sector. What is more likely that major IT giants like; Wipro, Infosys, Tata Consultancy Services (TCS), HCL Technologies, IBM Satyam are all joining the BPO bandwagon, redefining their business focus. With the passage of time even management consultants will make a foray into this segment, giving wide opportunities to the organisations to bargain for the best in terms of price, and quality. PWC, Accenture, Exult, Arthur Andersen, Loyds ISB are already in this business in a limited way. In BPO, HRO is a new accession, which makes a traditional, HR Department in an organisation as redundant. HRO initially started with payroll administration, but today it encompasses all HR functions. Gartner Group, for HRO alone, predicted a global business of $ 12 billion by 2003 from its present volume of $ 975 million (1999). Although outsourcing HR is still widely debated and there exists wide difference of opinions about its core or non-core characteristics, big giants are increasingly switching over to HR BPO, realising its potentiality beyond cost control. Exult, the international pioneer in HR BPO already roped in Bank of America, International Papers, BP Amoco and over the years predicts to spread their business in most of the fortune 500 companies. With humble beginning in leasing, outsourcing now become a global activity with reinforced SCM.

KNOWLEDGE MANAGEMENT

Early in the industrial age motor/muscle power was provided by the workers for product creation, leaving thinking job for the management. However, with the changed environment, cognitive skills became more and more important in every work, be it production at the shop floor or rendering services to customers. Technology further played a crucial role in capturing and managing knowledge, making it possible for organisation to harness the potentiality of knowledge by its proper development, growth and maintenance. Of course with an approach to periodically retire the knowledge which are obsolete. There are many contributors to knowledge management and learning organisation, starting with the concept of 'Gold-Collar Worker' of Kelley (1985) to Argyris (1994), Drucker (1994), Peters (1992), Senege (1990), Setewart (1997), Nonaka and Takeuchi (1995) and many more.

Knowledge is reinforced through learning. Therefore before we define knowledge it is appropriate for us to understand what is learning? Learning is a process of acquiring new skills or knowledge, which results to a new behaviour. Learning can take place through multiple ways. But for organisations best way to promote learning is by exposure to new experiences. Knowledge is the ability and wisdom to use the learned experiences for achievement of individual and organisational objectives. Knowledge management, therefore, is the process of systematically and actively managing and leveraging the store of knowledge in an organisation.

Any knowledge management initiative need to be first tested in the light of available guna dynamics, as advocated by Chakraborty (1987). It is not that he has contributed to knowledge management literature but because he has first espoused, knowledge and skills, when reinforced by values ensure better results. His characterisation of knowledge along three gunas, in the light of Indian-psycho-philosophy when reproduced as matrix (as below) indicates that mere rajas without the essence of sattwa cannot, per se, make a knowledge management and so also skill enrichment initiative successful in any organisation.

Table 27.1: Guna Dynamics of Knowledge and Work

	Tamasic	Rajasic	Sattwic
Knowledge	Small and narrow way of looking at things which has no eye for the real nature of the world	Seeing multiplicity of things only in their separateness variety	One imperishable, indivisible whole is becoming all and everything
Work	Action undertaken from delusion, in mechanical obedience to instincts, without regarding the strength or capacity, or its consequences, involving a waste of efforts or injury to others	Action performed under the dominion of desire, with an egoistic sense of own personality, done with inordinate effort	Action which is rightly regulated, done without attachment, without liking or disliking, without any desire of fruit (for himself)
Doer	Works with a mechanical mind, is stupid, obstinate, cunning, insolent, lazy and procrastinating	Eagerly attached to work, passionately desirous of fruit, impure, often violent, cruel, and brutal in the means used, full of joy and grief in success or failure	Free from attachment and egoism, full of a fixed personal resolution and a calm rectitude of zeal, un-elated or unrepressed by success or failure

Indian Social System had orientation towards developing and maintaining different social groups in terms of certain crafts. The quality elements in a particular craft and the necessary skill elements in the same, were the basis for social stratification. That is why, tracing history, we find, in India, there was a time, when carpenters, goldsmiths and weavers enjoyed the highest status. Over the years, however, such social stratification was aligned along caste-line, which also had the essence of occupational elements in it.

Lean Management Practices and HR

Lean management is all along institutionalised by the Japanese organisations, which helped them to achieve zero inventories and even zero wastage, leading to effective utilisation of resources. Operationally, lean management looks at the manufacturing of three primary processes that create value for the customers. These are product development, order to delivery and service through the products life cycle. It requires value creation from the standpoint of the customers, examining the current process and experimenting how it could perform better, understanding the requirement of the people and processes to support the value creation and aligning the purpose, processes and people in search of the perfect process.

To achieve the above intents, organisations focus on eight basic areas as under:

1. Strategic Vision and Core Values
2. Inspiring Leadership
3. Customer Orientation
4. Balanced Scorecard

5. People Involvement and Engagement
6. Process Innovation
7. Problem Investigation and Resolution
8. Organisational Processes

Strategic vision and core values are designed leveraging the collective expression of all the stakeholders of the organisation. We can call it shared vision and shared values. These need to be so designed so that all members of the organisation get the same direction and accordingly contribute. These also create a compelling work culture.

Inspiring leadership is also critical for lean management practices. Leaders persuade members of the organisations to deliver the compelling value to their customers. Inspirational leaders can get the required commitment from the people to the strategic vision and defined core values. They motivate, coach and guide the people and transform them to a true performer.

Customer orientation means designing or developing customer-centric products and services. In lean management customer centric approach in product design, keeping into consideration the cost, delivery, quality and overall customer satisfaction is very important. Customers' expectations are changing, it is for us to track such expectations and accordingly change our processes to deliver the best.

Balanced scorecard helps us to quantify the performance results of the employees from four major perspectives, i.e., learning and growth, internal processes, customer and finance. Each employee contributes to these four areas irrespective of the hierarchical level and functional areas. For effective lean management practices, balanced scorecard is the most effective instrument as it can scientifically track the development of the employees through incremental changes in their performance.

People involvement and engagement requires participation of all cross-sections of people of the organisation in the transformation process through lean management. Such participation of people is not so simple. It requires explaining to the people the need for transformation, giving them the indulgence to ask questions and get clarified on their doubts. Once people participate, they feel increasingly committed to deliver the results. An important prerequisite for people to participate is to create a compelling culture for competitive advantage.

Process innovation requires new thinking. It requires challenging the existing process, and managing the operations altogether from different perspectives. Let us take the example of Toyota Production System (TPS), which are actually institutionalised lean management practices. TPS renders our traditional percepts, i.e., by producing in bulk, we can achieve economies of scale as per unit cost of production reduces, wrong, making it obsolete. Instead, it recommends formation of productive cells and proves that even small assets can create low cost through flow, not the volume. Hence, in TPS, processes become cells, people become teams and products and services develop into value streams.

Problem investigation and resolution requires clear identification and understanding of the problems and solution of the problems using various problem solving tools. A structured model of problem investigation and resolution is DMAIC, which we use in organisational improvement strategy through six-sigma. DMAIC stands for Define, Measure, Analyse, Improve and Control.

Organisational processes put all the above elements of lean management practices together to achieve the intended results. Organisational process may be for human resource management, quality management or any other key business process.

From human resource management point of view, all these practices also add value both to the people and to the organisations and more specifically, it can make the process and people effective in achieving the business results balancing the needs of all stakeholders.

WTO AND INDIAN LABOUR

In Doha Ministerial Conference of WTO, (9-13 November, 2001) India had opposed the linkage between trade and labour standards. For developing countries, we all agree that, wage differentials is their major competitive advantage in international trade. Barring a few knowledge and technology intensive segments, where India has supremacy, India's international trade largely converges on this hypothesis, i.e., relative cheap labour. Obviously government is legitimate in protesting against such intervention of WTO that encompass labour and social issues. India in the long run needs to appreciate such requirement and improve the prevailing labour standards, yet can remain competitive internationally.

Global labour and environmental standards are two sticking points after 1999 Seattle fiasco. Western corporations along with consumer and human rights groups are the catalyst for such movement and trying to push through these issues under the banner of WTO. To attract and retain the orders from western companies, developing countries are increasingly falling into the prey of ILO, which is now a labour cop to monitor the implementation of internationally accepted labour standards. While WTO in the Doha round is practically silent over these issues, presumably to satisfy the member countries from developing nations, the United States and the Western European countries (European Union in particular) increasingly putting pressure on developing countries to comply with their code of conducts (which is now totaling to 240) on labour and environmental standards. India, Bangladesh, Philippine and Cambodia are already the casualties of such pressure. Adhering to local labour laws and ILO Principles (e.g. right to unionise) at aggregate level are construed as accepted labour standards. While India as a developing nation can boast to have elaborate labour laws comparable with international standards and India advocates the ILO Principles by and large, subscribing to most of the ILO resolutions, India has inherent problem to make these applicable widely, encompassing all the economic sectors, for its typical economic structure, which, without economic sectoral segmentation, still remains informal to the extent of 90 per cent. Contrarily, India's major export earnings still come informal sector.

Prevailing labour standard indices, in India is best understood from the pattern of industrial relations situation and QWL. QWL is the perceived important personal needs, which an individual tries to satisfy by working in an organisation. Growth and security, job re-design, formation of autonomous work groups, worker participation in management etc., are certain important QWL constructs.

While internal analysis of labour standards at macro level can be made more scientific using secondary sources data on Indian labour, QWL at macro level is best analysed from Human Development reports of UNDP. India is ranked as 115 out of 162 countries of the world in terms of Human Development Index (HDI). HDI is a composite index measuring average achievement in three basic dimensions of human development—a long and healthy life, knowledge and decent standard of living.

A decdal analysis of industrial disputes (1989-98) shows, 'mandays lost' have almost remained constant over the period but for marginal fluctuations. However, non wage related disputes are rising, questioning the compliance of labour standards. Human Development Report (2001) projects by the years 2008, 8 per cent of India's formal employment will be in the Information Technology Industry, with potentiality to earn $ 50 billion, which would then be 30 per cent of India's export. Such assessment undoubtedly vouches India's potentiality to develop human resources to withstand global competitiveness. Compliance with labour standards dictated by WTO, ILO, Western Europe, U.S.A., European Union or international human rights or consumer forums in no way dissuade India to loose competitive advantage rather contribute to better development of human resources for her inherent strength in Skill and Competencies. A temporal set back in some segments of the economy should not dissuade India from its implementation; keeping in view its long term efficacy.

States and the Western European countries (European Union in particular) increasingly putting pressure on developing countries to comply with their code of conducts (which is now totaling to 240) on labour and environmental standards.

Let us first examine the global perception on labour and environmental issues on multilateral trade under WTO dispensation. WTO declaration states "under WTO rules no country should be prevented to from taking measures for the protection of human, animal or plant life or health or for the environment at the levels it considers appropriate". The declaration, however, very emphatic for non-use of such measures for protectionist purposes. India firmly opposed any linkage between trade and labour standards. On environment issues also India opposed to the use of such measures for protectionist purposes. However, as Prof. Bhagwati (2001) rightly says, Indian needs to be "very clear as to what it is and what we are really objecting to". Issue of labour standards in multi-lateral trade regime is not yet dead. The International confederation of Free Trade Unions (ICFTU), with direct and indirect support of many Western Countries is still harping on trade-labour linkages ICFTU is blunt to enforce labour standards by the threat of sanctions. President George Bush, of the US, just after the Doha Ministerial Conference, assured the US Congress that labour and environment standards will be the centre of the Doha round, which is utterly contrary to the understanding at Doha. India may have temporary reprive, but reality is ILO, who was empowered by WTO, is yet to come out of the issues pertaining to social dimension of globalisation. The final declaration of Doha meeting, therefore, reaffirms the declaration made at Singapore ministerial conference regarding internationally recognised core labour standards. Bangladesh, India, Philippine, Cambodia, West African Cocoa farms, Malaysia, Thailand and Pakistan are already casualties of unilateral labour and environmental standards. 'Shrimp-turtle' or genetically modified food related issues are major environmental issues affecting the interest of developing countries.

Trade-labour debate is the outcome of Heckscher-Ohlin-Samuelson model. Stopler and Samuelson, based on the model argued about the impact of protective tariffs on the relative earnings of each factor of production. Protective tariffs on imported goods would increase its domestic price and therefore would increase the real return to the scarce factor of production in the importing country and reduce the real return to the factor abundant exporting country. This hypothesis therefore defeats the utilisation of cheap labour factor as competitive advantage in international trade by developing countries, including India. Therefore, linking labour with multi-lateral trade issues, would continue to be pressurised by developed countries for their obvious high labour factor cost, either due to their decline in baby boom or 'skill-based' economic change. What is silent at Doha, may spark a new debate at Mexico (in the next round). The way unilateral trade sanctions are negotiated by developed countries using these instruments, whether WTO labels it as protectionism or not, this will continue to dominate multi-lateral trade in years to come.

Why India Needs to Agree for Labour Standards?

Let us now examine, why India needs to appreciate such requirements and improve the prevailing labour standards.

The most widely used definition of core labour standards as found in the various conventions of the ILO, encompasses following four main protection for workers:

1. Guarantee of the right to organise and to bargain collectively
2. Prohibition of forced labour
3. Prohibition of child labour
4. Prohibition of discrimination against different categories of workers on the basis of gender, ethnicity, etc.

Indian trade unions are unanimously opposing any linkage between trade and labour standards in WTO, fearing this would lead to massive loss of employment, which tantamount to violation of human rights. Moreover, the argument is labour standards are intrinsically non-trade issues and any linkage would have protectionism in built in it. Ideologically, Indian trade unions labeled WTO agreement as imbalances and inequitable in favour of developed countries. However, Indian trade unions are vocal about labour rights violation and unanimous against deliberate exploitation and denial of wages, weak enforcement of legal machinery, use of obsolete technology, inadequate skill development initiative and denial of fair price. If we examine these labour rights issue, they are not very different from the core labour standards, excepting the last, point, which again a perennial trade related issue.

By now we have established that environment and labour will be used by the developed countries to raise non-tariff barriers to protect their markets against export by developing countries. Let us now examine the prevailing labour standards in India in the light of domestic industrial relations environment and wherever possible benchmarking it with other countries of the world. In Table 27.2, we have presented the trends of strikes and lockouts during 1965-1998.

Table 27.2: Trends of Strikes and Lockouts During 1965-1998

	1965-69	1970-74	1975-79	1980-84	1985-89	1990-94	1995-98
Average percentage of lockouts per year	10.6	11.9	13.4	16.4	29.6	31.1	36.3
Average percentage of mandays lost per year due to lockouts	29.3	25.9	36.3	a 36.4	58.8	59.0	61.4
Average number of mandays lost per year per worker involved in:							
(a) Strikes	7.8	9.2	10.6	b21.4	9.9	12.3	9.35
(b) lockouts	29.0	30.4	50.0	63.1	84.9	45.2	37.07

Source: Pocket Book of labour Statistics of relevant years, published by the labour Bureau, Shimla.

Analysing the trend it is evident that incidence of strikes have significantly reduced over the period with corresponding decrease in loss of mandays. While on the contrary lockouts are consistently increasing with corresponding rise in mandays lost. This clearly indicates a shift in the balance of power in favour of employers. With the economic adversity and rising competition with crisis in trade unionism, globally employers' militancy are on the rise. This was also documented in series of studies by Deyo (1989), Frenkel (1993), Wilkinson (1994), Frenkel and Harrod (1995) and Kuruvilla (1996).

The trend is common to both developed and developing countries.

In Table 27.3, classification of industrial disputes by causes have been made to understand how pattern of disputes are changing shifting from financial issues to non-financial issues.

Table 27.3: Cause-wise Analysis of Disputes

Course Group	YEARS 1994		1995		1997		1998	
	No. of disputes	Percentage to total	No. of disputes	Percentage to total	No. of disputes	Percentage to total	No. of disputes	Percentage to total
Wages and Allowances	354	29.4	320	30	305	23.4	233	21.2
Personnel	194	16.2	195	18.3	261	20.0	175	16.0
Retrenchment	19	1.6	10	0.9	7	0.5	8	0.7
lay-off	3	0.2	4	0.4	7	0.5	6	0.6
Indiscipline	185	15.2	145	13.6	246	18.9	225	18.9
Violence	20	1.7	14	1.3	13	1.0	7	0.6
Leave and Hours of work/shift workina	17	1.4	21	2.0	31	2.4	14	1.3
Bonus	92	7.8	79	7.4	112	86	123	112
Gherao	1	0.1	1	0.1	-	-	-	-

Contd...

Non-implementation of Agreements, Awards, etc.	37	3.1	43	4.0	43	3.3	32	2.9
Charter of Demands	55	4.6	61	5.7	68	5.2	97	8.8
Workload	10	0.8	10	0.9	9	0.7	6	0.6
Surplus labour	1	0.1	-	-	1	0.1	-	-
Betterment of Amenities	16	1.3	18	1.7	34	2.6	12	1.1
Suspension/Change of Manufacturing Process	1	0.1	-	-	-	-	1	0.1
Standing orders/ Rules/Service/ conditions/safety Measures	50	4.2	52	4.9	34	2.6	13	1.2
Others	118	9.8	57	5.4	85	6.5	89	8.1
Not Known	21	1.7	29.	2.7	37	2.8	49	4.5
Total	201	100	1066	100	1305	100	109	100

Source: Various issues of Indian labour Year Books, labour Bureau, Shimla.

Even though a special Tripartite Committee was constituted by the Ministry in 1992, we have not been able to address the issues pertaining to non-payment of statutory dues of workers employed in Central Public Sectors, problem of industrial sickness, increasing contractualisation of labour force, voluntary retirement schemes, etc. Even the number of industrial disputes and applications handled by the Central Government Industrial Tribunals-cum-Labour Courts in 1998 (latest published figure) is only 8.6 per cent, resulting huge number of pending cases awaiting adjudication. As on end 1998, there are 7683 cases pending before the tribunals. Even analysis of convictions for offences under the Factories Act, 1948, indicate gross violation of employment and hours of work, safety norms, heath and sanitation, welfare, not to talk about non-filing of returns and other miscellaneous causes. Details of such conviction obtained during 1997 (latest figure) are presented in Table 27.4.

Table 27.4: Convictions Obtained in 1997 for Offences under the Factories Act, 1948

Conviction Issues	No. of Convictions
Employment and Hours of Work	1759
Notices, Registers and Returns	1673
Safety Norms	806
Health and Sanitation including welfare	476
Others	1666
Total	6380

Source: Indian Labour Year Book, 1998. Based on information of 12 states only.

However, the only possible way to benchmark our data with other Asian countries could be made in case of hours of work per week and number of occupational injuries, using ILO sources. In Table 27.5, such data are presented, analysing which we find India comparably engages workers for maximum 47.9 hours per week, which is lower than many other Asian Countries.

Table 27.5: Hour of Work per Week in Asian Countries

Country	Hours of Work Per Week
Bangladesh	52
Hong Kong, China	45.2
India	47.9
Japan	46.4
Singapore	50.8
Thailand	51.7
Republic of Korea	47.9

Source: Indian Labour Year Book, 1998.

However, due to differences in methodology of data collection such figures may not be comparable in absolute terms as per ILO. What is encouraging to note, number of occupational injuries is comparably much lower in India than all other Asian countries. But this must not be construed as indicators of better labour standards in India, per se. India is progressive enough in labour standards, ratifying highest number of conventions than many other Asian and industrially advanced countries. As on 1998 India has ratified 38 ILO conventions against 19 by China, 26 by Philippines, 13 by Malasiya, 36 by Sri Lanka, 11 by Iran, 29 by Canada and only 12 by United States.

Beginning from 1928-29 till 1970s, trade unions in India reached a commanding height. However, since early 1980s we are witnessing the declining phase of trade unions in India In fact from this period onwards industrial restructuring process begun in India. The first and second generation reforms further culminated reduced role of trade unions in India with a significant drop in their membership. We have analysed earlier the trend in Trade unions membership from 1986 to 1996. The data shows a declining trend in membership over the decade. With the declining influence of trade unions, collective bargaining for determining working conditions and terms of employment through negotiations between an employers' organisations, on the one hand and one or more representative workers' organisations is loosing importance as institution in India. Such importance is also receeding globally. Organisations now prefer to have enterprise-wide bargaining. Even industry-wide bargaining agreements are not implemented by many organisations within the same industry group. Banking industry example is relevant in this context.

Regarding child labour, India has achieved remarkable progress by reducing it to 3.59 per cent in 1998 from 6 per cent in 1981. India has ratified six ILO conventions relating to child labour. National Child Labour Projects (NCLP) have been set up to rehabilitate child labour and India is determined to eliminate child labour and signed an MoD with ILO in this respect. Similar concern of India is also visible against discrimination in employment, equal remuneration, forced labour, right of association, etc., which culminated to ratification of all the relevant conventions in this regard.

Despite all the above achievements, India needs to improve upon in many respects to enhance quality of work life. In Table 27.6, important economic indicators for some Asian countries for the year 2000 is presented.

Table 27.6: Important Economic Indicators for Some Asian Countries - 2000

Countries	Growth Rate of GDP (in percentage)	Growth rate of Value added (in percentage)
Indónesia	4	3.77
India	7	5.00
Maloysia	6	2.73
Philippines	3.80	3.83
Pakistan	3.80	4.60
Republic of Korea	7.50	9.16
Singapore	5.90	4.10
Sri Lonko	5.00	4.70
Thoilond	4.50	3.77
Banglodesh	6.40	5.90

Source: Asian Development Outlook, 2000.

Notes: Value added percentages have been averaged for all the sectors together.

The table indicates India has achieved significant growth rate in GDP excepting Republic of Korea. Growth rate in value addition also is significantly higher for India excepting Republic of Korea and Bangladesh. However, human development indicators put India much behind many other Asian countries (Table 27.7).

Table 27.7: Human Development Indicators for some Asian Countries - 2000

Countries	literacy rate (in Percentage)	life Expectancy at birth (in years)	Infant Mortality (Per '000)
Sri Lanka	90	75.6	16
China	80	72.3	48
Indonesia	84	67.5	43
India	62	60.9	72.2
Pakistan	38	65.6	73
Bangladesh	38	51.9	-

Sources: Economic Survey, 2000-2001. Asian Development Outlook, 2000.

Notes: Literacy rate data relates to 1995, excepting India. Indian data relates to 1997.

- Data on life expectancy relate to 1998.
- Data on infant mortality relate to 1995-2000.

With the accession of China in WTO, India is required to concentrate in improving efficiency and productivity in manufacturing and services, without bothering for inclusion of labour standards in future WTO negotiations. Relative competitiveness of India vis-a.-vis other countries of the world put India much below than others. Even in key management effectiveness measures among emerging Asian countries India is way behind China and Malaysia. In terms of value addition per person (in US $), China is much ahead of India. India has to gain competitive strength through people. With a ranking of 115 out of 162 countries (2001) in terms of Human Development Index (HDI), India is way behind many others. Investment in technology creation, raising expenditure in Research and Development (from present 0.7% of GNP), long and healthy life, knowledge and decent standard of living, etc., should be the priority.

With the increase of global job mobility, recruiting competent people is also increasingly becoming difficult. The problem is more acute in India. Therefore by creating an enabling culture, organisations are also required to work out a retention strategy for the existing skilled manpower. Similarly to attract talent, organisations need to focus on compensation strategy with enabling work culture.

Let us not forget, 'India risks loosing the war for Indian talent'. Four out of ten Indian Software developers are now working in the USA India looses $ 2 billion per year for brain drain of Indian professionals to USA. Indian talents are recognised world-wide. What is required is to harness this and make its best use with managerial efficiency? If Reliance Industries can do better than DUPONT and DOW, Why not others!

With all the above initiatives, India can achieve supremacy and can look beyond present share of 0.7 per cent in global trade. By not agreeing to enforcement of labour standards for trade sanctions, India would indirectly create opportunities for other developing countries, including China, who are way behind India in achieving the desired labour standards.

Other emerging issues like Re-structuring, TQM practices, etc., have already been discussed in relevant units of the book.

HRM is now a holistic process of organisational strategy to gain competitive advantage.

Summary

Contemporary human resource management issues, among others, emphasise on changing HR's emphasis on value addition to organisation. In the process of value addition, HR has to first focus on attracting and retaining talents, and then, embrace those practices, which can truly make people effective in their performance. For today's organisations, the biggest HR challenges are managing multi-generational workforce, managing the changing legislation affecting workplace and various technological advances. These apart, HR today needs to embrace ethical practices, value diversity, embrace various quality management practices, six-sigma, lean management, innovation and creativity, outsourcing, etc.

KEYWORDS

BPO	HRO
SCM	Knowledge Management
Competitive Advantage	Innovation and Creativity
Direct Participation	Six Sigma Practices
Shamrock Organisations	Capability Profile
Quality Management Systems - revised version	-

REVIEW QUESTIONS

1. Discuss important changes in brief which may affect HRM functions.
2. Why as a HR Manager one has to understand the recent changes?
3. Do you think India has any potentiality in world BP HRO market?
4. To what extent revised version of Quality Management Systems influences the HR function?
5. Can HR play any role in inculcating Innovation and Creativity in an organisation?
6. What way six sigma practices bring changes in an organisation?

Case Study

Develop New Organisation Structure at Times of Need – The Experience of Bajaj Electricals

Bajaj Electricals Limited (BEL), a 1938 company in India, engaged in the business of manufacturing and marketing consumer electronics and luminaries, engineering and projects, is a well known household name. The company is recognised for quality and price effectiveness. However, the company experienced the brunt of economic downturn in the country since 2001. With economic down-turn, the company also had to face tough competition in most of its product lines, primarily for entry of multinational organisations in the country. As its consequential effect, the company had to experience significant down-slide in profits and its turnover.

It was at this time, the company went for total restructuring exercise to turnaround. To put it back to profits and growth, the company undertook various strategic, operational, distributional and marketing initiatives. At the same time, to get the best results from such initiatives, the company also changed its organisational structure from traditional vertical to a strategic business unit, along with revamping of its supply chains, matching with the competitive market situation. Side by side, the company also went for financial restructuring exercise, primarily to identify the possible cost cutting avenues to gain price efficiency. Simultaneously with the change in the organisational structure, the company could come up with innovative pricing and marketing strategies, which ultimately led to high rate of growth in 2003.

The company named this as 'Mission Excell' exercise which involved a comprehensive strategy simultaneously with the organisational and financial restructuring. Getting results from such exercise, subsequently the company adopted another slogan 'Operation Triumph 1001', i.e., to become a ₹ 1001 crore company by 2007, more than ₹ 2000 crore turnover company by 2009-10, and then, leapfrog to a quadruple turnover by 2014-15.

The success of Bajaj to converge to a winner from a total downturn trend in business through the change in organisational structure, financial restructuring and adoption of comprehensive business strategy, provides following guidelines to turnaround for others to emulate:

1. In business downturn, at the outset understand the challenges and issues involved in it.
2. Identify the need for change.
3. Initiate time bound change in the organisational structure and processes.
4. Understand the required strategic and operational initiatives to turn around the organisation.
5. Understand the effect of such initiatives on the top line (revenues) and the bottom line (profits) of the company.
6. Review the existing product portfolio and identify the need for change, if any, either by introducing new products or services, or by phasing out the existing products and services.
7. Develop pricing and market segmentation strategies focusing on business growth and increase in profitability.

Question

Can Bajaj's experience be replicated in each and every organisation? Justify your answer.

APPENDICES

- Skill Development
- Part - A: Management Exercises
- Part - B: 'Thinking on Constraint' for HR Problem Solving
- Part - C: Case Studies and Role Plays
- Part - D: Multiple Choice Questions for HR/HRM

Skill Development

This section is not an independent unit. It is intended to help HR students to apply their learned knowledge and skills, keeping in mind organisational requirements. This section is divided into several parts. Each part introduces some new application areas for the benefit of students.

Part - A: Management Exercises

Throughout the book, we have extensively covered various theoretical issues pertaining to human resource management functions. Now we are concentrating on application of various tools and techniques. HR students with such applications can use their learned knowledge, and gradually make them competent to groom as professional HR managers. Some of the tools and techniques are as under:

A. HR Games

The HR Games are a practical way of preparing HR students to gain application based knowledge in managing the real life HR related issues. HR games can encompass all HR functions like; recruitment, training and development, performance management issues, compensation design, labour relations, etc. HR games are conducted more in the form of questions and some practical issues, and the participants are asked to give correct answers within a given time. To conduct HR games, it is necessary to plan the entire programme, keeping in view the balanced use of routine and strategic HR issues. Through HR games, students not only learn the practical applications of their theoretical knowledge, but can also understand how team decisions become more effective. Students can also get the opportunity to network, and showcase their knowledge. Normally a coordinator or facilitator of HR games programme explains the objectives of the game to the participants and then divides the games in two parts viz., individual level HR games, and group HR games. Individual level HR games help us to assess the maturity level of the participants in HR decision-making. Group level HR games, however, explain how individual level HR decision making is affected (either improved or deteriorate) with the group involvement.

Effective Team Functioning Game

This game requires the following:

- *Time:* Approximately one hour to one hour fifteen minutes.
- *Items Required:* Each group should have multiple sheets of flipchart papers, different colour markers, and the handouts of the game issues.
- *Participants:* Total participants should be within the limit of 12-49, and divided into groups of four to seven.

- *Game Methods:* Ask participants to form groups, divisible with equal numbers and tell them that the purpose of the game is to determine what an effective team looks like. Give each team the flipchart papers, markers and handouts, and then read before them the following text:

  Underground reservoirs are designed to collect water coming out from the roof of a house, and then drain them out to a safer place. However, in the reservoirs other particles also accumulate, and in the process clog the drain pipes. Therefore, unless such particles are removed from the gutter, water may eventually get clogged, and adversely affect the foundation of the building. Similarly overflowing of water also may affect drain pipes, which may eventually collapse. Each team functions like a water reservoir. Such reservoirs are the team norms, which get distorted with the clogging with other particles. Till the time such particles are removed and regularly drained out, team effectiveness will suffer.

- *Exercise to the Participants:* Now ask the participants to develop a visual presentation, using the above analogy on the flipchart paper. Ask them to do mind mapping to identify, which behaviours can clog the reservoirs, and which can ensure smooth flow of the water, without affecting the foundation of the building, i.e., ultimately the achievement of the goals and objectives. At the centre of the reservoir, each group should draw the picture of their team, and then list the clogging particles (their behaviours) that may stop the draining out of water (against the achievement of their goals and objectives). They must explain to other members their line of action. Complete this game within 30 minutes.

Best Solution Hints

- Use the coloured markers to draw small picture (or a phrase) in the centre, indicating the issues that you want to solve.
- Draw lines from the main issue (that you have drawn in the centre), using different colours, to indicate manifestation of the issue. Explain what it represents.
- Connect the lines, indicating solution to the problems.

Suggestion: Perform this game in presence of your HR guides.

Slogan Writing HR Games

Purpose of this game is to give opportunity to individual participants to reflect on some HR issues. Number of participants should be within 10. Participants will be asked to understand some images and then reflect on the same individually. Various projective techniques can be used for this purpose.

After the listing of the slogans by all participants, the same may be circulated and then they will be asked individually to analyse the relevance of the slogan, and how the same differs from their own slogans. Ask them to select the best slogans, without naming who had contributed what? End the games in reviewing the best slogans.

Some of the best slogans identified by leading organisations of the world are:

In touch with tomorrow – Toshiba

Its all within your reach – AT&T

Where do you want to go today – Microsoft

Communicate for Better Decision Making Games

Divide the participants into convenient groups. Circulate to them some comic strips printed in a newspaper. Ask them to interpret, and accordingly, play their roles.

SWOT Analysis Games

First ask some participants to individually conduct SWOT analysis on their specific jobs. For students it must be hypothetical. Separately ask other participants to do the SWOT analysis individually on their departments. For students again, it must be hypothetical. For better results, restrict their choice of jobs and departments from a given list. Go for the reverse process. Those who have done earlier SWOT analysis on their job roles will now do SWOT analysis of groups and vice versa. Ask them to make the compatibility analysis and find the differences.

B. HR Simulations

Like HR games, HR simulations are also important to develop application based knowledge for the HR students to groom them as managers and executives. Particularly it is important for functional knowledge and decision-making skill development. Computer enabled business simulations are now available for human resource management areas. Compensation design, balanced score card, competency mapping, performance management, etc., can be taught to students using HR simulations, or computer enabled standard solutions. Particularly in compensation design, such simulation games, perform the quantitative analysis, and are more effective.

HR simulations can be both in the form of some open-ended exercises, like; developing HR mission statement, identifying the critical success factors for HR, drawing business plans in alignment with the HR, HR strategy mapping, negotiations and collective bargaining exercises, mock grievance handling, etc. These apart, HR simulations can be close-ended, i.e., giving the situations to the participants and asking them to reflect on within the ambit of information, Standard computer simulated HR games are made available by various professional bodies and vendors for use in training classes. For organisational use, however, it is always desirable to use HR games that meet the specific requirements. In some cases, however, managers can develop such games, keeping in view the purpose. For example, to develop the negotiation skill for effective collective bargaining, managers can develop the hypothetical scripts, and take the participants through the mock process, to enable them to gradually learn by practice.

We have included some collective bargaining examples in the book.

Let's try this game

A well known manufacturing organisation always believed in taking the consensus decisions to achieve the business goals. However, after the global meltdown, the company had to stop the practice of participative decision making, and most of the decisions they started imposing from the top. People down the line only need to comply with the decisions. This practice gradually distanced the people from the organisation. In general, people became restless as they are always left in hiatus. As a result, rumors, mistrust, and other vices gradually started vitiating the work environment in the company. Use a conceptual game; and help the company to gain the confidence of the workers.

(***Hints:*** Form small group of workers, without considering the functions and hierarchy, ask the workers to write their perceived goals in such a situation of turbulent business environment. Ask them to list at least ten such factors and arrange the same in order of perceived priority. After each worker individually write the points, ask them to discuss the same in their group and come out with five common factors, arranged in order of their relative importance. Fit their perceived goals with the goals of the management, using a goal congruence model; show the workers, the degree of commonalities, which invariably are high. Convince the workers that their interests and the interests of the management are common. Only in a turbulent business environment, management need to respond to the situation on time, which dissuades them to delay the decisions through established participative and consensus decision making.)

PART - B: 'THINKING ON CONSTRAINT' FOR HR PROBLEM SOLVING

No HR decisions can lead to hundred percent solutions to problems. However, risk of wrong HR decisions can be substantially minimized when we use the `Thinking on Constraint' (TOC) approach. TOC requires translation of intuitive plans to a format and discussion of the same rationally. Through rational discussion, plans are questioned and modified, and in the process, a common sense solution to problems is arrived at. TOC leads to common sense solutions to problems, and also facilitates communication, collaboration, and consensus to problem solution. With three generic objectives, like understand what to change, understand what leads to change and understand how to make the change happen; we use TOC approach.

Let's try this Problem?

You have been asked to design a compensation plan which motivates the good performers, without, however any incremental change in your compensation budget (TOC). Come out with your solution?

(***Hints:*** Introduce performance linked variable pay, make use of pay-band approach, introduce innovative compensation like; loyalty bonus with the time cap).

Organisation Chart of HR Department

This we have already discussed in our relevant chapters with illustration. Here we will show how Dabur, an Indian company could frame the HR Department, keeping in view its alignment with the business objectives of the organisation.

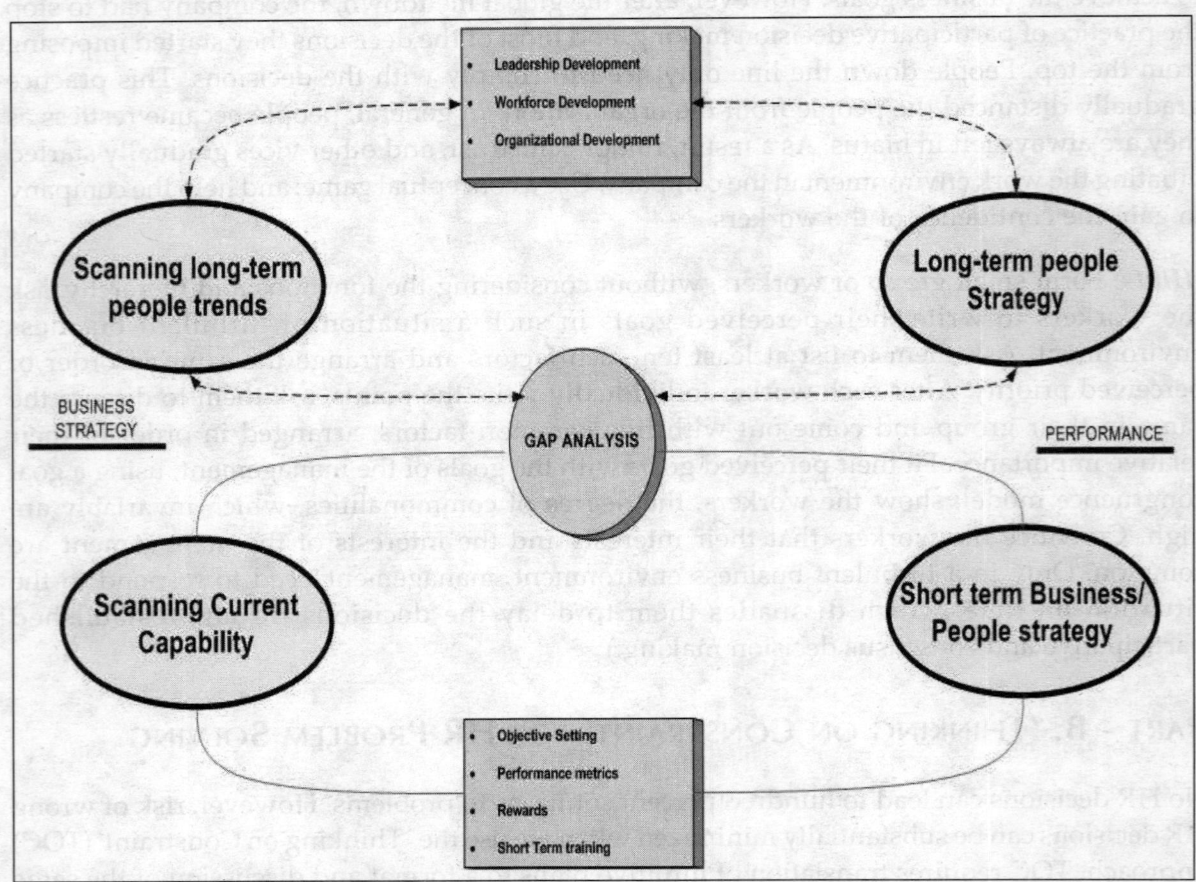

Dabur's HR Strategies support their business strategies through their short term cycle of HR activities of objective setting, performance appraisal, rewards/incentives and training. HR at DABUR is also able to align the workforce with the organisation by taking workforce development measures (Career development, Career Mapping initiatives as a part of action plan).

Go through the above chart and critically examine how it helps in aligning HR with the business? You can also study the best practices of other organisations for a better comparison.

Job Advertisements for Recruitment

The aim of advertising is to make people aware that a vacancy exists and to persuade them to apply for the position. Good advertising highlights the assets of the position and appeals to the career needs and concerns of the desired applicants.

Here we have illustrated three recruitment advertisements. First two advertisements are adapted from the downloaded templates while third one (more elaborate) is adapted from the detailed advertisement information of a large multinational. Going through these three samples, students must try on their own drafting job advertisements for different positions, understanding the job clearly.

Sample - 1

COMPANY PROFILE

Griffin Marine Travel headquartered in London is a 27-year-old company with 24 offices worldwide. GSC e-Services based in Mumbai is the Global Back Office of the Griffin Group and provides comprehensive 24/7 operations support to Griffin Global Network.

Job Title	Management Trainee
Job Code	CJ103767
Job Requirements	Generating new business, both domestic and international market. Liaisoning with various service providers – local & overseas. Product development/ tour programs/operational aspects/client handling
Location	Mumbai
Key Skills	Management
Post Advertisement Date	10 Apr '2007
Expiry Date	10 May '2007
Functional Area	Management
Job Role	Other
Compensation	Industry Standards
Work Experience	1 - 3 Yrs
Qualification	MBA/PGDM/PGDBA - Marketing
Employment Type	Permanent

Sample - 2

HRD, PERSONNEL, IR, RECRUITMENT, TRAINING AND DEVELOPMENT & ADMINISTRATION

Reference #	infas/Sumeet
Description of the Company	The company is today, among the India`s leading Apparel Manufacturers and Exporters, with an annual turnover of US$ 10 million, with the manufacturing facilities in Thane, Wada and Silvassa and has 38 years of expertise in serving an extensive clientele. IT exports to far flung markets that include the USA, France, Canada, Holland, Sweden and Australia. The Details of the Job are as follows:
Job Designation/Description	*Job Specifications:* Assisting Director in her area of work. Communicating with external as well as internal people on her behalf, Travel bookings, etc.

Contd...

	Must have: Good communication & interpersonal skills, Good organisational skills.
Job Location	MUMBAI
Candidate Attributes Required	Experience: 3-4 years of experience as personal assistant or executive assistant Qualification: Graduate. Salary: 9000 to 11000 per month. Reports to: Director Reportee: None.

Sample - 3

Job Specification: Personal Management Analysis

Job Description

Employees in this job complete and oversee a variety of professional human resource assignments in classification, compensation, labour law matters, recruitment and selection, testing, workforce planning, employee development, performance appraisal, occupational analysis, labour relations, and other human resource areas.

Position Code Title - Personnel Management Analyst

This is an executive level position and the selected employee carries out a range of professional human resources assignments while learning the methods of the work.

Job Duties

Note: The job duties listed are typical examples of the work performed by positions in this job classification.

1. Reviews recommendations for appointments, promotions, transfers, suspensions, and separations of employees.
2. Conducts interviews and recommends the hiring of new employees.
3. Reviews and approves selection criteria for filling vacancies.
4. Ensures compliance with and provides interpretation of legal issues.

Guidelines Relating to Personnel Processes

1. Prepares statistical reports regarding hiring practices and other selection data.
2. Plans, co-ordinates, and implements recruitment programmes; determines labour market conditions and recruitment strategies; prepares job bulletins and recruitment information; determines and places advertisements in appropriate media; and reviews and evaluates applications.

3. Counsels employees on rights, benefits, and opportunities for career advancement.
4. Determines class and level allocation of positions for establishment and reallocation purposes, and defends such allocations in redetermination, technical appeals.

Employment Relations related Jobs

1. Conducts job analysis and develops class specifications, including class concepts, knowledge, skills, and abilities, and education and experience requirements.
2. Provides technical assistance to the HR department and the organisation on issues related to the management of people.
3. Reviews, evaluates, and approves or disapproves requests for contractual personal services.
4. Evaluates selection methods and confers with resource persons to determine the best means of selecting and ranking applicants for specific jobs and positions.
5. Prepares test format, determines material to be covered, and develops test items; determines relative weight of test sections.
6. Conducts reviews of programmes and procedures to evaluate and improve the effectiveness, efficiency, and utility of operations.
7. Develops criteria for job performance evaluation, and ensures evaluations are conducted in accordance with organisational policy.
8. Collects and analyzes data relating to examination scores and job performance, and determines test validity.
9. Conducts and participates in surveys of public and private employment to analyze wages, pay practices, and other forms of compensation.
10. Responds to inquiries regarding the compensation plan to various statutory bodies.
11. Counsels management and employees on grievances and other complaints originating from individual work situations or work environment.
12. Develops and maintains comprehensive workforce plans and forecasts.
13. Co-ordinates human resource projects, programs, and special assignments.
14. Conducts occupational research studies; evaluates, analyzes, and classifies data.
15. Performs statistical analysis of employment data for publication in various occupational publications.
16. Conducts systematic searches for new job related information; reviews data and evaluates its usefulness and applications.
17. Provides technical assistance or information regarding the collection and evaluation of occupational information.
18. Assists in the development of equal employment opportunity programmes and affirmative action plans.

19. Identifies training needs of state departments and develops training materials and manuals.
20. Develops and modifies rules, regulations, policies, and procedures; provides interpretation to supervisors, personnel officers and other human resource professionals, individuals, and employee organisations.
21. Maintains records and prepares reports and correspondence related to the work.
22. Performs related work as assigned.

Additional Job Duties

1. Oversees the work of professional staff by making and reviewing work assignments, establishing priorities, co-ordinating activities, and resolving related work problems.
2. Performs on a regular basis professional human resource assignments, which are recognized by the organisation as more complex than those assigned at the experienced level.

Job Qualifications

Knowledge, Skills and Abilities

1. Knowledge of the principles and practices of personnel management.
2. Knowledge of state government organisation and structure, functions, and occupations.
3. Knowledge of interviewing techniques.
4. Knowledge of the methods employed to collect, analyze, and interpret data.
5. Knowledge of employment practices and related laws, rules, and standards, including applicable equal employment opportunity, affirmative action, civil rights, and other related laws and practices.
6. Knowledge of employee rights, benefits, and obligations.
7. Knowledge of labor relations, grievance, and appeals procedures.
8. Knowledge of personnel transactions and records.
9. Knowledge of personnel budgeting procedures.
10. Ability to interpret and apply laws, rules, and regulations.
11. Ability to collect, analyse, and interpret data.
12. Ability to complete projects independently.
13. Ability to provide guidance and train others in the work.
14. Ability to maintain records, and prepare reports, and correspondence related to the work.
15. Ability to communicate effectively with others.
16. Ability to maintain favourable public relations.

Additional Knowledge, Skills and Abilities

1. Ability to organize and co-ordinate the work of others.

2. Ability to set priorities and assign work to other professionals.

Working Conditions

None

Physical Requirements

None

Education

Professional PG level degree with Human Resource Management as major.

Experience

Three years of professional experience providing human resources services in any organisation of repute.

Special Requirements, Licenses, and Certifications

None

Job Code and Description

PERMGTALT - Personnel Management Analyst

Salary level

In the pay band of ₹ 6 lakhs to 8 lakhs per year all-inclusive.

Apply for the job downloading Blank Application from web site: www.exceelbooks.com.

Study all the job advertisement formats illustrated above. Now think of developing a job advertisement for a HR strategist, showing the KRAs, etc.

PART - C: CASE STUDIES AND ROLE PLAYS

We have discussed these in several unit. Students are required to practice the same. One has to bear in mind that we cannot have 100 solutions to cases and role plays, but at least we can develop our power for logical analysis.

PART - D: MULTIPLE CHOICE QUESTIONS FOR HR/HRM

Set 1

1. In an organisation, human resource development focuses on the development of:
   (a) Workers
   (b) Employees
   (c) Executives
   (d) Managers
   (e) All the above
   (f) None of the above
2. Which of the following is appropriate for human resource development function?
   (a) To relate to the objectives of the organisations
   (b) To relate to the expertise in the department
   (c) To be flexible enough to respond to sudden crisis
   (d) To function as part of HRM Department.
3. What type of training you recommend for a bank having branches in multi-locations?
   (a) e-learning
   (b) Class room Training
   (c) Outbound Training
   (d) All the above
   (e) None of the above.
4. In organisations, new employees are taken through:
   (a) Action learning
   (b) T-Group Training
   (c) On the job training
   (d) Induction
   (e) None of the above
5. A learning organisation represents:
   (a) An organisation which facilitates the learning of all members of the organisation
   (b) An organisation learning of managers is emphasised.
   (c) An organisation which facilitates learning to develop competencies of all cross-sections of employees

(d) An organisation which does training on ad-hoc basis
(e) All the above
(f) None of the above

6. Performance Appraisal is a type of:
(a) Planning Activity
(b) Organizing Activity
(c) Controlling Activity
(d) Leading Activity

7. Hawthorne studies established the work environment on:
(a) Human Behaviour
(b) Human Performance
(c) Human Satisfaction
(d) All the given options

8. Group behaviour is attributable to:
(a) Thermodynamics
(b) Group Dynamics
(c) Management by Objectives
(d) Group Behaviour

9. Organisational behaviour relates to:
(a) Psychology of people
(b) Behaviour of people
(c) Behaviour of people at work
(d) Man-machine interface

10. Which of the following is considered as the component of organisation?
(a) Team
(b) Structure
(c) Individual
(d) None of the given options

11. The term synergy indicates:
(a) Efficiency of organisation
(b) Integration of organisation
(c) Effectiveness of organisation
(d) Productivity of organisation
(e) Whole is greater than sum

12. Virtual teams indicate:
    (a) Physical meeting of team members
    (b) Information sharing among team members through communication links
    (c) Real-time interactions among team members
    (d) Bringing team members using technology intensive process.
13. Which aspect(s) of human resource management practices enhances the competitiveness of the organisation?
    (a) Compensation design function
    (b) Attracting and retaining talents
    (c) Managing the performance of people
    (d) Training and Development
    (e) Organisational Development
    (f) All the above
14. HRM encompasses implementation of all these variables except:
    (a) Design of Task
    (b) Managing People
    (c) Managing Compensation Design
    (d) Managing Performance
    (e) Designing organisation structure
15. Which process gets detailed information about jobs?
    (a) Job design
    (b) Job description
    (c) Job analysis
    (d) Job skills
16. Which HRM function ascertains the demand and supply of employees:
    (a) Skill Inventory
    (b) Programme implementation
    (c) Performance Evaluation
    (d) Assessment Centre
    (e) Human Resource Planning
17. Potential employees of an organisation can be identified through the process of:
    (a) Performance Management Systems
    (b) Recruitment and Selection

(c) Structured HR Policies

(d) Succession Planning

(e) HRIS

18. Scientific management was pioneered by:

(a) Eric Berne

(b) Chris Argyris

(c) Elton Mayo

(d) Henri Fayol

(e) F.W. Taylor

19. Which of the following is not the part of HR function?

(a) Routine administrative activities

(b) Transactional activities

(c) Transformational activities

(d) Day-to-day operational activities

20. Basic principles of organisational learning encompass:

(a) Participation

(b) Relevance

(c) Feedback

(d) Education

21. Career Development indicates:

(a) Career Planning

(b) Vertical progression of employees

(c) Horizontal expansion of jobs

(d) Career Anchor

(e) Facilitating employees to acquire knowledge and skill to rise through the ladder.

22. Which of the following can provide opportunity to the employee to develop their power of decision-making?

(a) Training

(b) Lectures and Seminars

(c) Assistant to Position

(d) Committee Assignment

(e) Empowerment

23. Organisational Training for a small group, which involves role-playing, simulation, encounter sessions, and also sessions on problem solving techniques, can be categorised as:
    (a) Career counseling
    (b) Succession Planning
    (c) Workshop
    (d) Career Development
    (e) On the job training
24. Top level managers of an organisation require high degree of:
    (a) Technical skill
    (b) Interpersonal skill
    (c) Business skill
    (d) Conceptual skill
25. HR is considered as:
    (a) Line function
    (b) Middle level managerial function
    (c) Top level managerial function
    (d) Public Relation function
    (e) Staff functions
26. Hawthorne studies attributed increased performance of workers to:
    (a) Increase in light
    (b) Decrease in light
    (c) Increased level of supervision
    (d) Increase in pay
    (e) Nurturing leadership
27. Organisational goals when assigned to individual level employees, we call it:
    (a) KRA
    (b) Performance Standards
    (c) Performance Metrics
    (d) Job Descriptions
    (e) KSA
28. Human resource planning in any organisation is performed through:
    (a) Demand forecasting
    (b) Supplies forecasting
    (c) Financial forecasting

(d) Sales forecasting
(e) All the above

29. Study regarding jobs within an organisation is represented by:
(a) Job analysis
(b) Job description
(c) Job specification
(d) Job evaluation

30. Manpower outsourcing is a part of:
(a) Organisational planning function
(b) Decentralization function
(c) Restructuring function
(d) Human resource planning function

31. Organisational behaviour represents:
(a) Human resource management function
(b) Collective behaviour of the organisation
(c) Social Behaviour
(d) Organisational culture
(e) All the above

32. In organisations, managers perform:
(a) Decisional roles
(b) Strategic roles
(c) Informational roles
(d) Interpersonal roles
(e) All the above

33. HR decision-making largely depends on:
(a) Rules & Policies
(b) Organisational Norms
(c) Internal Environment
(d) Legislations
(e) All the above

34. Technology enabled HRM function is facilitated by:
(a) E-recruitment
(b) E-Performance Management

(c) E-Training

(d) HRIS

(e) All the above

35. Aligning employees' goals with the business strategy and then assessing the progress there on is part of:

(a) Strategic Management Function

(b) Strategic Planning Function

(c) Strategic Control Function

(d) Diversification Function

(e) None of the above

36. Expectancy theory of motivation focuses on the relationships of:

(a) Needs, effort and persistence

(b) Needs, performance and inputs

(c) Inputs, performance and outcomes

(d) Needs, performance and outcomes

37. Horizontal expansion of job is known as:

(a) Job evaluation

(b) Job enrichment

(c) Job enlargement

(d) Job rotation

38. When two HR managers of the same organisation communicate with each other, we call it:

(a) Upward communication

(b) Downward communication

(c) Lateral communication

(d) Diagonal communication

(e) Peer Communication

39. In today's knowledge-based world, organisational success largely depends on:

(a) Cost Control

(b) Quality Control

(c) Efficiency

(d) Innovation

(e) Knowledge, skills and abilities of the employees

(f) All the above

40. Which of the following is not a key trend of today's HR function?
    (a) Globalization
    (b) Managing change
    (c) Developing human capital
    (d) Controlling costs
    (e) Job Security
41. Which of the following is not one of the most important roles for today' s Human Resource Managers?
    (a) Administrator
    (b) Advisor
    (c) Counselor
    (d) Policy formulation
    (e) Employee advocacy
42. Employee productivity and performance is a function of which of the following factors:
    (a) Salaries and benefits
    (b) Recognition and rewards
    (c) Socialization process
    (d) Relationship between the employee, their co-workers and their manager
    (e) Employee's ability, motivation and environment
43. Which of the following are important social issues in Human Resource Management?
    (a) Shrinking pool of entry level workers
    (b) Use of temporary workers
    (c) Increasing use of technology
    (d) Only 'a' and 'c'
    (e) Only 'a' and 'b'
44. Which of the following is not the way for controlling HR costs in organisations?
    (a) Downsizing
    (b) Leasing employees
    (c) Reducing compensation and benefits
    (d) Outsourcing
    (e) Utilizing the contingent workforce
45. Human Resource Management is a set of interrelated functions:
    (a) True
    (b) False

46. The main purpose of core competencies in organisations is to enhance learning and development within the organisation:
    (a) True
    (b) False
47. Knowledge workers' limit their tasks and duties as assigned:
    (a) True
    (b) False
48. Intellectual capital adds economic value to the organisation:
    (a) True
    (b) False
49. Which of the following is not a part of 360 degree appraisal system:
    (a) Multiple sources of feedback
    (b) Customer feedback
    (c) Peer feedback
    (d) Annual Confidential Reports
    (e) Increased validity of feedback
50. E-enabled Balanced Scorecard can ensure regular monitoring of performance of employees!
    (a) True
    (b) False
51. Essay method of performance appraisals facilitates collection of objective performance feedback:
    (a) True
    (b) False
52. Pay Equity was derived from the Equity Theory of motivation.
    (a) True
    (b) False
53. Organisations are concerned with attracting qualified applicants as well as retaining them:
    (a) True
    (b) False
54. Performance based pay includes all elements of compensation except for:
    (a) Bonuses
    (b) Salary
    (c) Salary commissions

(d) Team incentives

(e) Merit based pay

55. Gainsharing is not a part of individual incentive:

(a) True

(b) False

56. Balanced scorecards are yardsticks that:

(a) Focuses on short-term financial results only

(b) Allows companies to focus on building future economic value

(c) Measures inputs and outcomes

(d) All of the above

(e) None of the above

57. Perquisites are special benefits given to executives.

(a) True

(b) False

58. Skill-based pay is regularly used to increase flexibility in compensation in high-performance work systems.

(a) True

(b) False

59. Leadership is typically found in management positions only:

(a) True

(b) False

60. Organisations sustain their competitive advantage through competent human resources:

(a) True

(b) False

61. Which of the following is/are not true activity of job analysis:

(a) The job elements are rated in terms such as frequency of use or amount of time involved

(b) Jobs are broken into elements such as information or relations with other people

(c) The rate of pay for the job is fixed

(d) It aims to describe the purpose of a job and the conditions under which it is performed

(e) Both (a) and (b) above.

62. For a multi-location bank, what could be the appropriate method for training?

(a) E-learning

(b) Discovery learning

(c) Cross-cultural training

(d) Activist learning

63. What is the appropriate term to describe the process of helping new employees to settle into their jobs?

(a) Action learning

(b) Discovery learning

(c) E-learning

(d) induction

64. Which of the following is not a stage in the systematic training cycle:

(a) Evaluation

(b) Assessing training needs

(c) Designing the training

(d) Drawing a training calendar

(e) Individual job instruction

65. Which of the following is the best definition of a learning organisation:

(a) An organisation which facilitates the learning of all its members and continuously transforms itself.

(b) An organisation in which the managers are encouraged to develop

(c) An organisation which facilitates the learning of all its members in order to preserve the status quo

(d) An organisation which does a lot of training on an ad hoc basis

66. Which of the following is the best term to describe people who guide and suggest suitable learning experiences for their protégés:

(a) Human resource managers

(b) Line managers

(c) Coaches

(d) Mentors

67. In the long run, which of the following outcomes would be the most critical result of an effective performance management system?

(a) Higher appraisal scores awarded to employees

(b) Improvement in organisational performance

(c) Lower turnover rates

(d) Fewer errors in production

68. What should be considered the "ultimate" goal of performance appraisal?

(a) To be able to improve performance on the job

(b) To provide performance information in a useful form

(c) To document employment-related decisions based on performance

(d) To determine appropriate rewards

69. Which one of the following items most completely describes a career?

(a) The series of jobs an individual holds within a certain occupational category.

(b) The length of time an individual is employed with a particular company.

(c) The time an individual spends gainfully employed.

(d) The set of work-related experiences that an individual has over their working life

70. How can a company combat mid-career plateauing?

(a) Aid in retirement planning

(b) Create new opportunities for promotion

(c) Terminate lower-level employees

(d) Design special career counseling services for employees

71. What is the most general form of a merit pay plan?

(a) Annual salary increases

(b) Bonuses

(c) Incentives

(d) Gainsharing

72. Which one of the following reward mechanisms provides employees with actual ownership in the organisation:

(a) ESOPs

(b) Profit sharing

(c) Scanlon Plan

(d) Bonuses

73. In HR acquiring of information, storing of information, manipulating information, analysing, retrieving and distributing information are facilitated by:

(a) HRIS

(b) Progressive discipline system

(c) IRS

(d) Contingent workforce system

(e) HR Scorecard

74. Which of these is a major dimension of HRM practices contributing to organisational competitiveness:

(a) Compensating human resources

(b) Acquiring and preparing human resources

(c) Managing the human resource environment
(d) All of the given options

75. Attracting potential employees is a part of:
(a) Indicator analysis
(b) Recruitment
(c) Personnel policies
(d) Selection

76. Designing and delivering efficient HR systems, processes, and practices become possible, when HR managers play the role of:
(a) Administrative Agent
(b) Change Agent
(c) Strategic Partner
(d) Employee Advocate

77. Manpower planning which considers current level of manpower as the basis to decide the future is known as:
(a) Bottom-Up Approach
(b) Forecasting Human Resource Availability
(c) Zero-based Forecasting
(d) Wastage Analysis
(e) None of the given options

78. For HR organizing function pertains to:
(a) Assigning every subordinate with a specific task
(b) Recruiting prospective employees
(c) Training and developing employees
(d) Developing rules and procedures

79. Organisational success largely depends on effectiveness of:
(a) Management by Objectives
(b) Performance Appraisal
(c) Performance Management
(d) Organisational Planning

80. Performance evaluation matching with a list of behavioural descriptions is called:
(a) Forced-Choice Appraisal
(b) Forced Distribution Appraisal
(c) Checklist Appraisal
(d) Behaviorally Anchored Rating Scales

81. Compensation plan that links quantity and quality of work is called:
   (a) Gain-sharing Plan
   (b) Incentive Plan
   (c) Compensation Plan
   (d) Pay for Performance Plan
82. Recognition, positive reinforcement and employees' empowerment can be used to avoid the:
   (a) Turnover
   (b) Conflict
   (c) Accident
   (d) Frustration
83. The first formal stage of the disciplinary procedure is:
   (a) Verbal Warning
   (b) Written Warning
   (c) Employee Separation
   (d) Show-Cause Notice
84. A statement which evokes positive emotional feelings in organisational members is known as:
   (a) Vision
   (b) Mission
   (c) Goal
   (d) Declaration
85. ESOP is not a direct compensation
   (a) Yes
   (b) No
86. Gain sharing is the appropriate method for group rewards based on pay for performance:
   (a) Yes
   (b) No
87. Direct benefits are provided to all cross-sections of employees:
   (a) Yes
   (b) No
88. HR systems that hire management people from the home country for non-home country operation is known as:
   (a) Geocentric Approach
   (b) Ethnocentric Approach
   (c) Polycentric Approach
   (d) Regional-centric Approach

Match the terms with the definitions

a. Core Competencies	a. Process of hiring employees through leasing company.
b. Downsizing	b. Information on people to provide purposes of control and decision making.
c. Employee Leasing	c. Planned elimination of jobs within the organization
d. Globalization	d. Management driven change to take advantage of targeted opportunities.
e. Human Capital	e. Partnering with organizations in other countries.
f. Human Resource Information Systems HRIS)	f. Being acutely aware of characteristics common to employees, while also managing these employees as individuals.
g. Total Quality Management	g. Knowledge base of the organization that distinguishes it from its competitors and delivers value to customers.
h. Knowledge workers	h. Conducting training within the organization.
i. Managing Diversity	i. Holistic approach to develop the organization.
j. Outsourcing	j. Performance Standards.
k. Reactive Change	k. Hiring someone outside the company to perform tasks that could be done internally.
l. Reengineering	l. Principles and practices to understand customer needs, doing things right the first time, and striving for continuous improvement.
m. Organizational Development	m. Aggregation of knowledge, skills, and abilities of employees.
n. In-house Training	n. When performance planning does not consider the effect of external factors.
o. KRA	o. Employees whose responsibilities encompass activities like; planning, decision making, and problem solving.
p. Six-sigma	p. The fundamental rethinking and radical re-creation of business processes to achieve dramatic improvements in cost, quality, service, and speed.
q. Rippling Effect	q. Recruitment
r. Markov Chain	r. Organizational Development
s. Organizational Diagnostics	s. Manpower Planning
t. Successive hurdles	t. Employee election
u. Career Anchor	u. Attrition
v. Rookie Ratio	v. Career Planning
w. Culture	w. Diversity
x. TNA	x. Performance Management
y. Assessment Centre	y. Training
z. Golden Parachute	z. Compensation

(Find the answers from various units of the book)

Set 2

1. TQM and re-engineering programs have been instituted in organisations as a result of:
   (a) Increasing costs
   (b) Responsiveness to customers needs
   (c) Increasing globalization
   (d) Strategic planning
   (e) Advancements in technology
2. In order to achieve organisational goals, HR managers must be aware of the following issues EXCEPT for:
   (a) Economic issues
   (b) Social issues
   (c) Individual issues
   (d) Technological issues
   (e) Legal issues
3. The end result of an effective HRM function is:
   (a) A satisfied workforce
   (b) To attract, retain and motivate employees
   (c) Cost control
   (d) An adequate number of employees
   (e) None of the above
4. Knowledge workers' responsibilities are limited to tasks and duties assigned to them by the position description.
   (a) True
   (b) False
5. The use of Intranet in many companies has resulted in enormous savings.
   (a) True
   (b) False
6. The top issue for managers in balancing work and home is telecommuting arrangements.
   (a) True
   (b) False
7. The only people who should be involved in HR functions in an organisation are HR Professionals.
   (a) True
   (b) False

8. In organisations where employees are viewed as an expense, the role of the HR department is to cut costs by reducing the labour component.
   (a) True
   (b) False
9. Intellectual capital is defined as "the knowledge, skills and abilities of individuals who have economic value to an organisation".
   (a) True
   (b) False
10. The Human Resources framework includes the influences of competitive challenges and employee concerns.
   (a) True
   (b) False
11. TQM refers to the results of quality circles in organisations.
   (a) True
   (b) False
12. Which one of the following depicts the order of the steps in Human Resources Planning?
   (a) Determining supply> forecasting demand> balancing supply and demand
   (b) Forecasting demand> determining supply> balancing supply and demand
   (c) Balancing supply and demand> forecasting demand> determining supply
   (d) It depends on the strategic plan
   (e) None of the above
13. The term "attrition" refers to:
   (a) Retirements
   (b) Resignations
   (c) Termination
   (d) Only " a" and " b"
   (e) Only " b" and " c"
14. Restructuring occurs in an organisation as a result of:
   (a) Mergers
   (b) Acquisitions
   (c) Plant closures or relocations
   (d) All of the above
   (e) None of the above

15. Which one of the following factors does NOT affect the supply of labour?
    (a) Education level of the workforce
    (b) Forecasted needs of the organisation
    (c) Demographic changes in the population
    (d) Demand for specific employee skills
    (e) Governmental policies
16. Which one of the following methods of forecasting future employment needs is considered a "quantitative approach"?
    (a) Delphi technique
    (b) Management forecasting
    (c) Trend analysis
    (d) Scenario planning
    (e) None of the above
17. Methods of internal recruiting include job bidding, skills inventories and job posting.
    (a) True
    (b) False
18. HRP can be considered both reactive and proactive.
    (a) True
    (b) False
19. Which one of the following is NOT one of the ways to obtain information about applicants for selection purposes:
    (a) Application blanks
    (b) Tests
    (c) Interviews
    (d) Background investigations
    (e) Skills inventories
20. The main purpose of "selection" is to:
    (a) Promote the organisation
    (b) Attract applicants to a particular position
    (c) Choose an applicant from one of the disadvantaged groups identified
21. To increase interviewer effectiveness, the interviewer should NOT do which one of the following:
    (a) Develop an interview plan
    (b) Record inferences and judgements about what the applicant says in the interview
    (c) Recognize his/her own bias and stereotypes

(d) Use questions effectively

(e) Be an active listener

22. The formal process of familiarizing new employees with the organisation, their job and their work unit is referred to as:

(a) Team training

(b) Diversity training

(c) Sensitivity training

(d) Orientation training

(e) Management training

23. Which one of the following is NOT one of the key benefits of orientation programs?

(a) Lower turnover

(b) Core competency development

(c) Reduction of employee anxiety

(d) Improved employee morale

(d) Lower training costs

24. The primary reason that organisations train new employees is:

(a) To achieve cultural diversity

(b) To achieve organisational long term goals

(c) To achieve a competitive advantage

(d) To achieve a KSA level of satisfactory performance

(e) All of the above

25. Which training is more relevant for marketing professionals?

(a) Communication skills

(b) Computer applications

(c) Customer service

(d) Management development

(e) Supervisory skills

(f) All the above

26. Which one of the following is NOT a part of the systems approach to training?

(a) Needs assessment

(b) Program design

(c) Orientation effectiveness

(d) Transfer procedures

(e) Evaluation

27. Which of the following is NOT a type of evaluation component in the systems model of training?

(a) Reactions

(b) Behaviour transfer

(c) Results

(d) Person analysis

(e) Learning

28. Which one of the following is NOT one of the factors in successful role playing as a training technique?

(a) Keep it lengthy

(b) Realize that volunteers make better role players

(c) Select and prepare the role players

(d) Guide the role play through its bumps

(e) Discuss the enactment

29. All of the following are "principles of learning" EXCEPT for:

(a) Goal setting

(b) Active practice

(c) Whole versus part learning

(d) Feedback

(e) Reactions

30. The term "training" when referred to in organisations tends to be oriented towards short-term performance concerns.

(a) True

(b) False

31. The purpose of orientation is to enable the new employee to develop career paths for their future in the organisation.

(a) True

(b) False

32. The Human Resources department has the most important role in orienting the new employee to the organisation.

(a) True

(b) False

33. A needs assessment should include organisational analysis, task analysis and person analysis.

(a) True

(b) False

34. "Instructional objectives" are details of the types of training methodologies used in a training session.
    (a) True
    (b) False
35. Modelling can be a useful training technique even if the modelling is of the wrong behaviour and then clarifies appropriate behaviour.
    (a) True
    (b) False
36. Feedback during training serves the two purposes of (1) correcting what is wrong and (2) documenting the learning process.
    (a) True
    (b) False
37. Which one of the following is NOT one of the sources of information needed for employees to plan their career path with an organisation:
    (a) Skills inventories
    (b) Internal postings
    (c) Forecasting
    (d) Succession planning
    (e) Strategic planning
38. Career development programmes can benefit managers in all but which one of the following ways:
    (a) As a reputation as people developers
    (b) Retention of valued employees
    (c) Managing their own careers
    (d) Developing employees who leave to pursue other opportunities
    (e) Increasing employees ability to manage their own careers
39. Which one of the following would NOT be considered a career advancement opportunity for an employee:
    (a) Promotion
    (b) Demotion
    (c) Voluntary exit
    (d) Termination
    (e) Lateral transfer
40. Which one of the following is NOT one of the major issues facing dual career partnerships?
    (a) The need for quality day care
    (b) The need for additional sick leave days

(c) The need for stress management strategies

(d) The need for understanding of emotional stress

(e) The need for spousal assistance when relocating

41. In which of the stages of career development does one fit into a chosen occupation and pursue goals:

(a) Preparation for work

(b) Organisational entry

(c) Early career

(d) Mid career

(e) Late career

42. Which one of the following is NOT one of the factors in self-evaluation for successful career development.

(a) Academic aptitude and achievement

(b) Social skills

(c) Interests and values

(d) Hobbies

(e) Leadership abilities

43. One of the most important roles management can support in individual career planning endeavours is that of "mentoring."

(a) True

(b) False

44. There is an increasing expectation in organisations that individuals will have to take on more responsibility for their own career planning.

(a) True

(b) False

45. A structural career plateau means that the individual is bored with the job.

(a) True

(b) False

46. Job progressions serve as a basis for career paths.

(a) True

(b) False

47. Which one of the following is NOT one of the reasons to conduct a performance appraisal:

(a) To provide an opportunity to discipline an employee

(b) To provide a basis for salary adjustments

(c) To give employees a chance to discuss performance standards with a supervisor

(d) To develop a performance improvement plan

(e) To assist supervisors in discussing strengths and weaknesses of employees performance

48. Which one of the following is NOT one of the reasons for the failure of performance appraisals in organisations:

(a) Rater bias

(b) Too many forms

(c) Forms that are too simplistic

(d) Unclear performance standards

(e) Use of the program for too many purposes

49. In establishing performance standards, "criterion contamination" refers to:

(a) The extent to which standards do not embrace the whole of an employee' s responsibilities

(b) The lack of consistency of a standard

(c) The extensive use of a single criterion

(d) That there are factors outside the employee' s control that influence performance

(e) All of the above

50. Which one of the following is NOT an advantage of a 360 degree appraisal system:

(a) More sources of feedback

(b) Customer feedback

(c) Peer feedback

(d) Time investment

(e) Increased validity of feedback

51. All of the following are safeguards that Intel uses for a 360 degree appraisal system EXCEPT:

(a) Reassuring

(b) Anonymity

(c) Prevention of too-high or too-low evaluations

(d) The use of subjective input as well as objective input

(e) The use of statistical measures

(f) All of the above are safeguards of the system

52. Which one of the following is NOT considered to be a performance appraisal error:

(a) Similar to me error

(b) Distribution

(c) Error

(d) Central tendency error

(e) Contrast error

(f) Polarization error

53. In conducting the appraisal interview, the manager should NOT:

(a) Ask the employee for a self-appraisal

(b) Invite participation

(c) Attempt to change the person to encourage a better " fit"

(d) Focus on solving problems

(e) Be too supportive

54. Managers often avoid conducting performance reviews for all of the following reasons EXCEPT:

(a) They dislike the employee

(b) They do not like to be "the judge"

(c) They are often not trained

(d) They do not have good feedback skills

(e) They lack preparation

55. All of the following are methods of performance appraisal EXCEPT:

(a) BARS

(b) Essay

(c) Graphic Rating Scales

(d) BERS

(e) Mixed Standard Scales

56. Electronic performance monitoring of employees is a relatively new way to assess employee performance in an organisation.

(a) True

(b) False

57. Peer appraisals provide more accurate information than the information provided through appraisals by superiors.

(a) True

(b) False

58. Performance appraisal programs serve two main purposes. They are to identify weaknesses of employees and to improve employees' attitudes towards work.

(a) True

(b) False

59. Self-raters tend to be more lenient on themselves than their managers.

(a) True

(b) False

60. One of the biggest problems with performance appraisals is that of "rater error."

(a) True

(b) False

61. An advantage of the "essay format" of performance appraisals is that it gathers mostly objective information from the evaluator.

(a) True

(b) False

62. One of the problems with the "results appraisals" is that they can be affected by external factors not under the employee's control.

(a) True

(b) False

63. Managers who "lay it on the line" are most likely to enhance an individual's performance through criticism and expectations.

(a) True

(b) False

64. Research shows that "internal attribution errors" often occur when managers assess performance problems.

(a) True

(b) False

65. Value-added compensation is described as:

(a) Indirect compensation

(b) Components of the compensation program that add value to the organisation and to employees

(c) To give employees a chance to discuss performance standards with a supervisor

(d) The value comparison of inputs and outcomes direct compensation

66. Which one of the following is NOT one of the job evaluation systems?

(a) Job rating system

(b) Job ranking system

(c) Job classification system

(d) Factor comparison system

(e) Point system

67. The factors considered in job evaluation systems to determine the worth of a job are: skill, effort, mental activity and working conditions.
   (a) True
   (b) False
68. One of the advantages of a job-based pay system is that it encourages employees to learn new job-related skills.
   (a) True
   (b) False
69. One of the problems with published pay surveys is that they are not always compatible with users' jobs.
   (a) True
   (b) False
70. "Stock Options" can be defined as:
   (a) Opportunities for executives to purchase shares of the organisation at market price
   (b) Grants of units equal in fair market value of a share of stock paid appreciation on a specified date
   (c) Rights granted to executives to purchase shares at an established price for a fixed period of time
   (d) Cash or stock award determined by the increase in stock price during a time chosen by the executive
   (e) None of the above
71. As performance is multidimensional, performance appraisal methods must consider various aspects of a job. The most widely used appraisal approaches focus on employee behaviour or performance results. Listing the ranges of performance values for specified traits is a feature of which of the following performance appraisal methods?
   (a) Behaviourally Anchored Rating Scales (BARS)
   (b) Graphic rating scales
   (c) 360 degree appraisal
   (d) Both (a) and (b) above
   (e) Both (b) and (c) above.
72. Which of the following is a specialized appraisal system wherein a high powered panel constituted by senior persons in the organisation appraises employees by identifying their best capabilities or skills and training them further?
   (a) 360 degree appraisal
   (b) Behaviourally anchored rating scales
   (c) Formal appraisal

(d) Peer assessment

(e) Assessment development centres.

73. Performance appraisal involves the formal evaluation of an individual's job performance. Which of the following guidelines is least likely to improve the effectiveness of the appraisal process?

(a) Stress both performance in the position the individual holds and the success with which the individual is attaining organisational objectives

(b) Emphasize the evaluator's impression of the individual's work habits

(c) Ensure that the appraisal is acceptable to both the evaluator and the evaluated

(d) Ensure that the appraisal provides a base for improving individuals' productivity within the organisation by making them better equipped to produce

(e) Determine standards of effective performance

74. Performance rating can either be behaviour-oriented or results-oriented. Within the behaviour-oriented category, two assessment means are Graphic Rating Scales and Behaviourally Anchored Rating Scales (BARS). Which of the following is not true with regard to BARS?

(a) BARS minimize subjective interpretation inherent in graphic rating scales

(b) BARS make use of 'anchors' (common reference points of performance)

(c) BARS concentrate on job-specific behaviours, and hence, is highly meaningful

(d) BARS are a simple and cost-effective rating method

(e) BARS can be applied in organisations where a large number of people perform similar jobs.

75. Which of the following is/are claim(s) that support self-appraisal?

I. It increases personal commitment of employees.

II. It improves employees understanding of job performance.

III. It provides a great deal of information about the appraisee.

(a) Only (I) above

(b) Only (II) above

(c) Only (III) above

(d) Both (I) and (II) above

(e) All (I), (II) and (III) above

76. Which of the following is not a strength of appraisal against verifiable objectives?

(a) Luck plays an important role in the performance of an individual

(b) It is operational in nature

(c) There is credibility because the appraisal is objective in nature

(d) It is carried out with mutual cooperation from superiors and subordinates

(e) It does not form a separate component from the job

77. Which of the following is the most accurate statement regarding the effect of corporate culture on performance and responsiveness?

(a) Only tangible aspects of the organisation have a real effect on performance and responsiveness

(b) Corporate culture is the sole determinant of organisation performance and responsiveness

(c) Corporate culture affects performance and responsiveness in two main ways-some values support responsiveness and some values act as guide

(d) Only top management and leadership affect an organisation's performance and responsiveness

(e) Top management does not play any role.

78. Which of the following principles of Henry Fayol's administrative theory runs contrary to Taylor's functional foremanship principle?

(a) Division of work

(b) Unity of command

(c) Unity of direction

(d) Centralization

(e) Scalar chain.

79. Which of the following is/are not true of the activity known as job analysis?

(a) The job elements are rated in terms such as frequency of use or amount of time involved

(b) Jobs are broken into elements such as information or relations with other people

(c) The rate of pay for the job is fixed

(d) It aims to describe the purpose of a job and the conditions under which it is performed

(e) Both (a) and (b) above.

80. Which of the following refers to changing a task to make it inherently more rewarding, motivating and satisfying?

(a) Enlargement

(b) Rotation

(c) Enhancement

(d) Enrichment

(e) Horizontal loading

81. The stage of Kurt Lewin's change model where employees need to be helped to integrate changed attitudes and behaviors into their normal ways of doing things is called ___.

(a) Refreezing

(b) Changing

(c) Unfreezing

(d) Benchmarking

(e) Moving

82. Which of the following is not a characteristic of the organisation culture?

(a) Corporate culture is based on certain norms

(b) Promotes dominant and stable values

(c) Leads to observed behavioural regularities

(d) Corporate culture is built overnight

(e) It shapes philosophy.

83. Which one of the following is preferred method of on-the-job training (OJT)?

(a) Structured OJT

(b) Unstructured OJT

(c) Job instruction training

(d) The Meyers-Briggs method

84. Which is not a basis of evaluating jobs?

(a) the nature of the skills required

(b) individual performance on the job

(c) working conditions under which job is performed

(d) job content

(e) culture values/values of the organisation

85. A small group gathered in the conference room to discover the impact they had on others, to explore and express their feelings, and to learn more about them. What is this Organisation Development (OD) application called?

(a) Team building

(b) Hostile confrontation

(c) Strategic intervention

(d) Sensitivity training

(e) Process consultation.

86. Organisational culture is the collection of shared values, beliefs, rituals, stories, myths and specialised language. It fosters a feeling of community among organisation members. Which of the following is not a characteristic of organisation culture?

(a) It differentiates one organisation from another

(b) It defines the internal environment of an organisation

(c) It ensures consistency in the behaviour of organisation members

(d) It remains absolutely stable throughout the life of an organisation

(e) It is perceived by the organisation members as well as by outsiders.

87. Which of the following is the most accurate statement regarding the effect of corporate culture on performance and responsiveness?

(a) Only tangible aspects of the organisation have a real effect on performance and responsiveness

(b) Corporate culture is the sole determinant of organisation performance and responsiveness

(c) Corporate culture affects performance and responsiveness in two main ways-some values support responsiveness and some values act as guide

(d) Only top management and leadership affect an organisation's performance and responsiveness

(e) Top management does not play any role.

88. The difference between the Nominal group technique and the Delphi technique is:

(a) One is a verbal approach, one is written

(b) One is a short term group, the other long term

(c) One is visual, the other is verbal

(d) One is face-to-face, the other keeps group member anonymous

(e) One utilizes a devil's advocate, the other does not.

(Search your answer from the text book)

Source: with permission from the [illegible]

REFERENCES

1. A.J. Walker, 1980, A Brief History of the Computer in Personnel, Personnel Journal Vol. 16, pp. 33-36.
2. Adams, LT., Changing Employment Patterns, American Labour News (Supplement), March-April, 1985, pp. 1-7.
3. Agarwal, K.G. Self, Role and Status; Stratification Theory of Work Motivation, Sterling Publishers, New Delhi, 1976.
4. Agarwal, N.C. (1981). Determinants of Executive Compensation, Industrial Relations, 20: pp. 36-46.
5. Ahluwalia I. J. (1991) "Productivity and Growth in Indian Manufacturing" Centre for Policy Research, Oxford University Press, Delhi.
6. Aikin, O., Promotion Problem, Personnel Management, August, 1981, Vol. 14, P. 48.
7. Alam, Fowler (1999), Managing Redundancy, 2nd edition, Institute of Personnel & Development, London.
8. Alivn Toffler, Power Shift, Bantam Books, New York, 1992.
9. Almsick, G.V., A. Job Opening System, Personnel Journal, December, 1978.
10. Andrews, K.R. 'Ethics in Practice', Harvard Business Review, vol.67 no.,5 1989, pp. 99-104.
11. Anthony, R. and Govindarajan, V., 2007. Management Control Systems, Chicago, Mc-Graw-Hill IRWIN.
12. Anthony, W.P., Get to know your Employees. The Human Resource Information System, in readings in Personnel Management, Greenlaw, P.S. and Saunder, W.B. (editions), Philadelphia, 1979.
13. Antle, M. J.and Capalbo, S.M. (1988) "An Introduction to Recent Development in Production Theory and Productivity Measurement" in Capalbo, S.M. and Antle, M.J. 'Agricultural Productivity: Measurement and Explanation' Resources for the Future, Inc., Washington, DC.
14. Argyris, C., Personality and Organisation, Harper & Row, New York, 1957.
15. Arya, P.P., Worker's Aspirations for promotion in Public Sector Undertaking, Lok Udyog, Vol. 19, No. 11, Februa ry, 1986.
16. Atkinson, J.W., An Introduction to Motivation, Preinceton, New Jersey, 1964.
17. Bailyn, Lottie, Patterned Chaos in Resource Management, Solan Management Review, Winter, 1993, PP. 77-83
18. Ball, Kirstie, 2000, Interface Value, People Management, January 6, pp 40-42
19. Banerjea, S., Total Quality Management and ISO 9000 Series - The Role of The Cost and Management Accountants, Conference Proceedings, 18th Eastern Indian Regional Cost Conference (5-6 June, 1998), The Institute of Cost and Works Accountants of India, Howrah, India
20. Bardwick, J. Quoted in matteches, K, Empowerment: Fact or Fiction? HR Focus (Formerly Personnel), May, 1992.
21. Bardwick, J.M. How Executive Can help Plateaued Employees, Management Review, January, 1987.
22. Bardwick, J.M. The plateauing Trap-Getting Caught (in 2 parts), Personnel, Vol. 63, October, 1986 and November, 1986.
23. Bardwick, J.M., The Plateauing and Productivity, Solan Management Review, Spring, 1983.
24. Barrie, O. Pettman and Genard, Taowernier (1976) Manpower Planning Workbook, Grover Publishing Company, Vermont, US.
25. Barrier, M, Small Firms Put Quality First, Nation's Business, 1992, No. 80 (5), pp. 22-32.
26. Bartlett, C.A. and Ghoshal, S. (1989) Managing Across Borders: Ttie Transnationat Sotution. Boston, MA: Harvard Business School Press.
27. Barzon, J., and Henry, F.G., The Modern Researcher, Harcourt Brace Jovanovich, New York, 1970.
28. Basu, M.K. Managerial Performance Appraisal in India, Vision Books, New Delhi, 1988.
29. Bayo-Moriones, J.A. and Merino-Diaz de Cerio, J. (2001) 'Size and HRM in the Spanish Manufacturing Industry', Emptoyee Retations, 23: 188.
30. Beach, D.S., Personnel: The Management of People at Work, Macmillan Publishing Company, New York, 1975

31. Bear, J.L, Cultural Determinism, Technological Determinism and the Action Approach" Competing Explanations of New Working Class Militancy in Rsearch in the Sopciology of Work (Editors: Simpson, R.L, and Simpson, L.H.), Vol. 1, JAI Press, Inc., Greenwich, Connecticut, pp. 403-433.

32. Becker, B.E., Huselid, M.A. (1998), "High performance work systems and firm performance: a synthesis of research and managerial implications", in Rowland, K.M., Ferris, G.R. (Eds), Research in Personnel and Human Resource Management, JAI Press, Greenwich, CT.

33. Becker, B.E., Huselid, M.A. (2006), "Strategic human resources management: where do we go from here?", Journal of Management, Vol. 32 No.6, pp.898-925.

34. Becker, B.E., Huselid, M.A. and Ulrich, D.A. (2001) The HR Scorecard. Strategy and Performance. Boston, MA: Harvard Business School Press.

35. Beer, M. and Spector, B. (1985) "Corporate-wide transformation in human resource management", in Walton, R.E. and Lawrence, P.R. (eds), Human Resource Management: Trends and Challenges, Harvard Business School Press, Boston, MA, pp. 219-53.

36. Beer, M., Spector, B., Lawrence, P.R., Quinn-Mills, D. and Walton, R.E. (1984). Managing human assets. Free Press, New York.

37. Behrman, D., Perreault, W. (1982), "Measuring the performance of industrial salespersons", Journal of Business Research, Vol. 10 pp.355-70.

38. Behrman, D., Perreault, W. (1984), "A role stress model of the performance and satisfaction of industrial salespersons", Journal of Marketing, Vol. 48 pp.9-21.

39. Belanger, P., Giles, A. and Murray, G. (2002). Workplace innovation and the role of institutions in G. Murray, J. Belanger, A Giles and P. Lapointe (eds) Work and employment relations in the high commitment workplace, Continuum, London.

40. Bell, Chip R (2002), Managers as Mentors: Building Partnerships for Learning, San Francisco, Berrett-Koehler Publishers, Inc., 2002.

41. Benninson, Malcolm, and Jonathan, C, The Manpower Planning Handbook, McGraw-Hill London, 1983.

42. Bernard, B. and Steiner, G.A., Humanb Behaviour, Harcourt, Brace and World, New York, 1964, P. 240.

43. Bernard, Taylor, and Gordon, Lippit, Career Development in Management Development & Training Handbook, Second Edition, McGraw-Hill Book Company, London, 1984.

44. Berned, E. The Internationalisation of Labour Markets: Causes and Consequences, American Economic Review, Vol. 73, No.2, May, 1983

45. Best, M (1990). The new competition: institutions of industrial restructuring. Polity Press, London.

46. Bhatia, S.K., Personnel Function in 21st Century, Personnel (Now Personnel Today),. January-March, 1987.

47. Bhatia, S.K., Career Management - A two way Process, Indian Management, November, 1985, Vol. 24, No. 11, pp.35-38.

48. Bhatnagar, V., Wage-Productivity Relationship in Indian Industries, Productivity, January-March, 1988, pp. 405-412.

49. Bhattacharyya D.K. and Banerjee, S., Evaluation of Corporate Effectiveness Through Multi Factor Productivity Indices, Research Bulletin. The Institute of Cost and Works Accountants of India, Vol. IX, No.1 & 2. January and July, 1992, P.P.57-64.

50. Bhattacharyya, D.K. Quality Management and ISO 9000: India's Problems and Prospects and the Changing Role of the Cost Accountants, Seminar Proceedings, Silver Jublee Seminar (22 November, 1992), The Institute of Cost and Works Accountants of India, Durgapur, India

51. Bhattacharyya, D.K. (2000) Competency Mapping and Manpower Redundancy - A Macro Level Study of India organisations, Management and Accounting Research, October - December, Volume 4, Issue-2, PP. 97105.

52. Bhattacharyya, D.K. (2007), Human Resource Research Methods, Oxford University Press, New Delhi.

53. Bhattacharyya, D.K. (2009), Compensation Management, Oxford University Press, New Delhi.

54. Bhattacharyya, D.K. (2010), Cross Cultural Management, PHI, New Delhi.

55. Bhattacharyya, D.K. (2011), Organisational Change and Development, Oxford University Press, New Delhi.

56. Bhattacharyya, D.K., Impact of Technology on Human Resource Management, Personnel Today, JanuaryMarch,1988.

57. Bhattacharyya, D.K. and Banerjee, S., Learning TQM in Indian Organisations, Published in the Book on Management Research by the University of Calcutta, 1995.

58. Bhattacharyya, D.K. Corporate Research, Total Quality and our Accounting System: Some Organisational Issues, Seminar Proceedings (16 January, 1993), Indian Accounting Association, Habra, India.

59. Bhattacharyya, D.K. Employees Empowerment - A Study of Selected Banking Organisation in India, in HRD Repositioning, National HRD Network, Conference Volume, 1995, pp. 33-48

60. Bhattacharyya, D.K. Employees Leasing and Labour Market Flexibility. An Empirical Study of its Problems in Selected Manufacturing Units, Indian Journal of Labour Economics, Vol. 37, No.4, 1994,549-555.

61. Bhattacharyya, D.K. Workers Participation in Management: A Cross Organisational Case Study. The Chartered Accountant, Vol XLI, No. 12, June, 1993, P.O. 1042-1044.

62. Bhattacharyya, D.K., (2001), Managing Manpower Redundancy - A Strategic Human Resource Manager Approach for rightsizing employees, in, contemporary Trends on Human Resource Management, SAS Consultants, Calcutta, PP. 5-13.

63. Bhattacharyya, D.K., and Banerjea, S. (1994), The Significance of Total Quality Management for Organisational Effectiveness in the Wider Context of Economic Restructuring, in ISO: 9000 and Indian Business Environment - Application and Adoption, Department of Business Management, University of Calcutta.

64. Bhattacharyya, D.K., and Banerjee, S., Quality Performance of Some Selected ISO Certified Manufacturing Units. A Third Party Evaluation, International Conference on Manufacturing Excellence, Indian Institution of Production Engineers, August 3-5,1994.

65. Bhattacharyya, D.K., Career Planning & Development, IIMS, 1995.

66. Bhattacharyya, D.K., Corporate Body Builder. The Emerging Role of HRD Professionals. A Prescriptive Model for Success, Indian Journal for Training and Development, April-June, 1995, New Delhi.

67. Bhattacharyya, D.K., Economic Restructuring, Total Quality Management and the Indian Labour: Some Organisational Issues, Conference Proceedings, 34th Labour Economics Conference (2-4 January, 1993), Indian Society of Labour Economics, New Delhi, India.

68. Bhattacharyya, D.K., Employment Relations in CommerCial Banking Organisations. A study of selected branches, Indian Journal of Labour Economics. Vol. 38, No.4, 1995.

69. Bhattacharyya, D.K., Human Resource Development, HMS, 1997.

70. Bhattacharyya, D.K., Impact of Labour Earnings on Productivity, Management and Change, January - July issue, 2001.

71. Bhattacharyya, D.K., Labour Economics & Productivity, IIMS, 1995.

72. Bhattacharyya, D.K., Managing People, Excel Books, New Delhi, 1999.

73. Bhattacha:yya, D.K., Manpower Obsolescence. A study in Indian Ordnance Factories, International Congress on Economic Transition with Human Face, Indian Industrial Relations Association, New Delhi, September 36,1995.

74. Bhattacharyya, D.K., Practical Guide toResearch on Commerce and Management, Kitab Mahal, New Delhi, 1989.

75. Bhattacharyya, D.K., Production and Operations Management, Excel Books, New Delhi, 1999.

76. Bhattacharyya, Dipak Kumar (2000), Production and Operations Management, Excel Books, New Delhi.

77. Bilodeau, E.B., International Encyclopedia of the Social Sciences (editor: Sills, D.L.), Vol. 9, Macmillan, New York, 1968, pp. 173-176.

78. Birkinshaw, J.M. and Hood, N. (1998) 'Multinational Subsidiary Evolution: Capability and Charter Change in Foreign-owned Subsidiary Companies', Academy of Management Review, 23: pp. 773-96.

79. Blom, M.L., and Naylor, J.e, Industrial Psychology: Its Theoretical and Social Foundations, Harper and Row, New York, 1968, p. 353.

80. Bloom, M., Milkovich, G. (1995), "The relationship between risk, performance-based pay, and organisational performance", Working paper 95-01, Center for Advanced Human Resource Studies, Cornell University, Ithaca, NY.

81. Bowen, D.A, How the Baldrige Award Really Works? Harvard Business Review, 1991,69(6), 80-95.

82. Bowen, D.E., and Laeler II, E.E. Total Quality Oriented Human Resources Management, Organisational Dynamics, Vol. 20, No.4, Spring, 1992.

83. Boxall, P. (1996). The strategic HRM debate and the resource-based view of the firm. Human Resource Management Journal, 6:3. Pp. 59-75.

84. Boxall, P. and Purcell, J. (2003). Strategy and human resource management. Palgrave Macmillan, London.

85. Brahmananda, P.R., Productivity in the Indian Economy, Himalaya Publishing House, Bombay, 1982.

86. Brahmananda, P.R., Productivity Growth in Commercial banking, Paper Presented at the Conference of Bank Economists, Calcutta, November 17-18, 1982.

87. Braverman, H., Labour and Monopoly Capital, Monthly Review Press, New York, 1974.

88. Braverman, H., Labour and Monopoly Capital: The Degradation of Work in theTwentieth Century, Monthly Review Press, New York, 1974.

89. Brinkerhoff, R.J. and Dressler, E.E. Productivity Measurement: A Guide for Managers and Evaluation, Sage Publications, California, 1990.

90. Brock, W.E., A Reflection on Tomorrow's Labour Force, American Labour News, January-February, 1987, pp. 4-6

91. Burnard, P. (1995). Counselling Skills Training, Viva Books, New Delhi.

92. Byrne, J.A, and Cowan, AL., Should Companies Groom New Leaders or by Them? Business Week, September 22,1986.

93. Cable, D., & Parsons, C.K. (2001). Socialization Tactics and Person-Organisation Fit. Personnel Psychology, 54, pp. 1-23.

94. Caldwell, D., & O'Reilly, C. A., III (1990). Measuring Person-Job Fit with a Profile-Comparison Process. Journal of Applied Psychology, 75, pp. 648-658.

95. Campbell, J., and eta I., Managerial Behaviour, Performance and Effectiveness, McGraw-Hill Book Company, Inc., New York, 1970.

96. Carl, C. Hoffmann, Kathleen, P., Hoffmann and Emily, D., Eason (1992), complexities of the "Simple". Report Request, HR Masgazine, November issues, PP. 49-57.

97. Carmichael, L.H. and MacLeod B.W. (1993)' Multiskilling, technical change and the Japanese firm.' Economic Journal, vol. 103, pp. 142-160.

98. Carnegic Mellon Univerisyt, Software Engineering Institute (1995), The capability Maturity Model, Addison Wesley Longman, Inc.,

99. Chakraborty, S.K., Managerial Effectiveness and Quality of Worklife: Indian Insights, Tata McGraw-Hill Publishing Company Limited, New Delhi, 1987, pp. 236-237.

100. Challagalla, G., Shervani, T. (1996), "Dimensions and types of supervisory control: effects on salesperson performance and satisfaction", Journal of Marketing, Vol. 60, pp.89-105.

101. Chang, W., Huang, T. (2005), "Relationship between strategic human resource management and firm performance: a contingency perspective", International Journal of Manpower, Vol. 26 No.5, pp.434-49.

102. Chatman, J.A. and Cha, S.E. (2003) 'Leading by Leveraging Culture', California Managemenl Review, 45(4): 20-34.

103. Chatman, J.A., (1991). Matching people and organisations: Selection and socialization in public accounting firms. Administrative Science Quarterly, 36, pp. 459-484.

104. Chatterjee, N.N., Management of Personnel in Indian in Enterprises (2nd Edition), Allied Book Agency, Calcutta, 1980.

105. Chen, A. Y. S., Sawyer, R.B., & Williams, P.F. 1997, 'Reinforcing Ethical Decisions Through Corporate Culture', Journal of Business Ethics, vol. 16, 1997, pp. 855-865.

106. Child, J. (1973) 'Strategies of Control and Organisational Behavior', Administrative Science Quarterly, 18(1): pp. 1-17.

107. Child, J. (1974) 'Predicting and Understanding Organisation Structure', Administrative Science Quarterly, 19: pp. 168-85.

108. Chris Hendry, Human Resource Managemet - A Strategic Approach to Employments, Btt Contemporary Business Series, London, 1995.

109. Churchill, G., Ford, N., Hartley, S., Walker, O. (1985), "The determinants of salesperson performance: a meta-analysis", Journal of Marketing Research, Vol. 22 No.May, pp.103-18.

110. Churchill, G., Ford, N., Walker, O. (2000), Sales Force Management, 7th ed., Irwin, Burr Ridge, IL.

111. Clutterbuck, D. (2004) Everyone needs a mentor: fostering talent in your organisation. 4th ed. London: Chartered Institute of Personnel and Development.

112. Cofer, C.N. and Appley, M.H., Motivation Theory and Practice, John Wiley, New York, 1964

113. Coleman, CJ., Personnel- As open system approach, Wintrop Publishers, Inc., Massachusetts, 1979, pp. 61

114. Conion, E.J. & Parks, J.M. (1990). Effects of monitoring and tradition on compensation arrangements: An experiment with principal-agent dyads. Academy of Management Journal, 33(3): pp. 603-622.

115. Coughlan, A., Sen, S. (1989), "Salesforce compensation: theory and managerial implications", Marketing Science, Vol. 8 No.4, pp.324-42.

116. Coughlan, A.T. & Schmidt, R.M. (1985). Executive compensation management turnover and firm performance - an empirical investigation. Journal of Accounting and Economics, 7(1): pp. 43-66.

117. Cravens, D., Ingram, T., LaForge, R., Young, C. (1993), "Behavior-based and outcome-based sales force control systems", Journal of Marketing, Vol. 57 No.October, pp.47-59.

118. Dalvi, G.R. Benaji, PJ. Joseph, K.J., and Murthi, G.N. Merit Rating Procedures and Promotion Policies, Administrative Staff College of India, Hyderabad, 1969.

119. Darmon, R. (1998), "The effects of some situational variables on sales force governance system characteristics", Journal of Personal Selling & Sales Management, Vol. 18 pp.17-30.

120. David, A, Garvin, (1993), Building a Learning Organisation, Harvard Business Review,July- August, 1993, PP. 78 - 91.

121. David, A., Decenzo and Stephen, P, Robbins, Human Resource Management, Sixth Edition, John Wiley & Sons, Inc. 1999.

122. Davis, K., Human Relations in Business, McGraw-Hill Book Company, Inc. New York, 1957.

123. Dayal, I & Aggarwal, V (1995), Modernising Organisations., New Concepts, New Delhi.

124. Dayal, I, Sahgai, P, Jain, R, Gupta, P & Sen, A K (1996) .Successful Applications of HRD: Case Studies of Indian Organisations:, New Concepts, New Delhi.

125. Delery, J., Doty, D. (1996), "Modes of theorizing in strategic human resource management: tests of universalistic, contingency, and configurational performance predictions", Academy of Management Journal, Vol. 39 pp.802-35.

126. Denova, C Transfer/Promotion System. A two-way Street, Supervision, Vol. 45, January, 1983.

127. Department of Personnel & Administrative Reforms, Workshop on Cadre review of Groups C and D Cadr Participative Research Programme-3, Proceeding and Recommendations, May 17-18, 1982, Ne_ Delhi, Pol and Planning Wing, Department of Personnel and Administrative Reforms, Ministry of Home Affairs, N, Delhi, 1982.

128. Desai, CJ., Analysing Productivity in Banking:Concept and Methodology, Prajanan, July-September, 1983.

129. Deshpande, KR, Role of Employee Motivation in Productivity and Economic Development of India in 7th Plan, Southern Economist, December 1, 1985, pp. 11-12.

130. Deshpande, S. et al., Census of 1981 and the Structure of Employment, Economic an Political Weekly, June 1, 1985, pp. 969-979.

131. Dev, N., Structure of Working Classes in India, Economic and Political Weekly, May 2, 1987, pp. 799-809.

132. Diewert, W. E (1985) "Productivity Management: Planning, Measurement and Evaluation, Control and Improvement" John Wiley and Sons, New York.

133. DiMaggio, P.J. and Powell, W.W. (1993) 'The Iron Cage Revisited: Institutional Isomorphism and Collective Rationality in Organisational Fields', American Sociological Review, 48: pp. 147-60.

134. Dolke, A.M., Factors in Job Satisfaction of Indian Workers in Motivation and Organisational Effectivenl (editors: Roy, S.K, and Menon, A.S.K), Shri Ram Centre For Industrial Relations & Human Resources, N Delhi, 1974, pp. 75-103.

135. Doyle, Gr., People Power: The Global Human Resource Challenges for the 1990s. Columbia Journal of World Business, Spring/Summer, 1990, Vol. XXV, Nos. 1 & 2, PP.36-45

136. Doyle, P.P., People-Power: The Global Human Resource Challenge for the '90s, Columbia Jou'rnal of World Business, Spring/Summer, 1990, pp.36-45.

137. Dreher, George, and Ronald Ash. "A Comparative Study of Mentoring Among Men and Women in Managerial, Professional, and Technical Positions." Journal of Applied Psychology 75 (1990): 539-546.

138. Dreyfuss, J., 1988, Catching the Computer Wave, Fortune, Sept. 26, pp. 77-82. Drucker, P.F., 1989, The New Realities, Harper & Row., New York, p. 175.

139. Dukes, C.W., Skills Inventories and Promotion System in Handbook of Modern Personnel Administrati (editor-in-chief:Joseph.J.), McGraw-Hill book Company, Ine., New York, 1972.

140. Eatwell, J.M. and Newman, P. (1991) "The New Palgrave: A Dictionary of Economics" vols. 3, 4 .& 12, Macmillan, Tokyo.

141. Edward, E. Gordon (2000), Skill Wars - Winning the Battle for Productivity and Profit, Butterworth-Heinemar Boston.

142. Eisenhardt, K. (1988), "Agency- and Institutional-theory explanations: the case of retail sales compensation", Academy of Management Journal, Vol. 31 No.3, pp.488-511.

143. Eisenhardt, K. (1989), "Agency theory: an assessment and review", Academy of Management Review, Vol. 14 No.1, pp.57-74.

144. Ellen, Enst, Kossek, Willard Young, Debra C, Gash, and Victor, Nichol, 1994, Waiting for Innovation in the Human Resource Department. Godot Implements a Human Resource Information System, Human Resource Management, Vol. 33, No.1, pp. 135-159.

145. Eric, G. Flamholtz (1974), Human Resource Accounting, Dicken Son Publications Co., Ine., California.

146. Etzioni, A. (1961) /4 Comparative Anatysis of Comptex Organisations. New York: Free Press.

147. Falicia Nathan (1987), Analysing Employers, Costs for Wages, Salaries and Benefits, Monthly Labour Review, October, 1987, PP. 3 - 10.

148. Ferner, A. (2000) 'The Underpinnings of "Bureaucratic" Control Systems: HRM in European Multinationals', Journat of Management Studies, 37(4): pp. 521-40.

149. Filter, J.H., The Jobs Challenge, Pressures and Possibilities, edited by Burton, D.P., J.R, et aI., Ballinger Publishing Company, 1986, pp. 3-9.

150. Finley, E. The Personnel Man and his job, D.B. Taraporevala Sons & Co. Private Limited, Bombay, 1970.

151. Fisher, C.D. (1989). Current and Recurrent Challenges in HRM. Journal of Management, 15, 2, pp. 157-180.

152. Flamholtz, E., Randle, Y., and Sackmann, S., Personnel Management: The Tone of Tomorrow, Personnel Journal, July, 1987.

153. Flamholtz, E.G. Human Resource Accounting Dickenson Publishing Co., California, 1974.

154. Foley, CD., and Balok, R, When Career Panic Strikes, Personnel, September, 1991, Vol. 68, No.8, p.13.

155. Foley, G.N. (1962) "Planning for Increased Productivity in Industries" Butterworths, Sydney, London.

156. Fombrum, C, Noel, M.T., and Marry, AD. Strategic Human Resource Management, John Willey, New York, 1984.

157. Fombrun, C.J., Tichy, N.M. and Devanna, M.A. (1984), Strategic Human Resource Management, John Wiley & Sons, New York, NY.

158. Foulkes, F.K. (1986), Strategic Human Resource Management: A Guide for Effective Practice, Prentice-Hall, Englewood Cliffs, NJ.

159. Frangner, B.N. Affirmative Action Through Hiring and Promotion: How Fast a Rate? Personnel, November, December, 1979.

160. French, W.L., The Personnel Management Process, Human Resources Administration & Development (L Edition), Houghton Mifflin Company, Boston, 1979.

161. Fulmer, W.F., Supervisory Selection: The Acid Test of Affirmative Action, Personal, November, 1976.

162. Gaba, A., Kalra, A. (1999), "Risk behavior in response to quotas and contests", Marketing Science, Vol. 18 pp.417-34.

163. Gary Dessler, Human Resource Management, Seventh Edition, PHI, New Delhi, 1998

164. George T. Milkovich and Johri W. Boudrequ, Human Resource Management, Chicago, Irwin, 1997.

165. Gerhart, B., Milkovich, G. (1990), "Organisational differences in managerial compensation and financial performance", Academy of Management Journal, Vol. 33 pp.663-91.

166. Germnil, G., and Desaliva, D., The Promotional Beliefs of Managers as a Factor in Career Progress: An Exploratory Study, Solan Management Review, Winter, 1977.

167. Ghalye, B.R, and Malhotra, N., Employment - its Terms and Condition (reprint), Eastern Book Compa! New Delhi, 1979.

168. Ghoshal, S. and Nohria, N. (1989) 'Internal Differentiation within Multinational Corporations', Strategic Management Journat, 10: pp. 323-38.

169. Giber, D., Carter, L., and Goldsmith, M. (2000) (eds.), Linkage Inc.'s Best Practices in Leadership Development Handbook, San Francisco: Jossey-Bass.

170. Goleman, D. (1995), Emotional Intelligence: Why It Can Matter More than IQ, New York: Bantam.

171. Gomez, C. and Ranft, A. (2003) 'The Influence of Organisational Variables on the Transferability of Management Practices; An Examination of Traditional and Learning Manufacturing Environments in Mexico', Journal of Business Research, 56: pp. 989-97.

172. Gómez-Mejía, L., Balkin, D. (1992), Compensation, Organisational Strategy, and Firm Performance, South-Western Publishing, Cincinnati, OH, .

173. Gomez-Mejia, L.R, Tosi, H. & Hinkin, T. (1987). Managerial control, performance, and executive compensation. Academy of Management Journal, 30: pp. 51-70.

174. Gong, Y. (2003) 'Subsidiary Staffing in Multinational Enterprises: Agency, Resources, and Performance', Academy of Management Journal, 46(6): pp. 728-39.

175. Gopal, AS., Employee Motivation and Productivity, Financial Express, November 30, 1986, p. 3

176. Govindarajan, V. & Fisher, J. (1990). Strategy, Control Systems, and Resource Sharing: Effects on Business-Unit Performance. Academy of Management Journal, 33, 259-285.

177. Greenlaw, P.S., and Biggs, W.D., Modern Personnel Management, W.B. Saunders, Philadelphia, 1979, pp. 94.

178. Grosskopf, S. (1993) "Efficiency and Productivity" in Fried, H.O,

179. Grote, RC, Implementing Job Enrichment, California Management Review, Vo.. XV, No.1, pp. 16-23.'

180. Guest, D (1999). Human resource management - the workers' verdict. Human Resource Management Journal, 9:4, pp. 5-25.

181. Guest, D. (2002). Human resource management, corporate performance and employee well-being: building the worker into HRM. The Journal of Industrial Relations, 44:3, pp. 335-358.

182. Guest, D. (2001). Industrial relations and human resource management in J. Storey (ed) Human resource management: a critical text (2nd Edn), Thomson, London.

183. Guest, D.E. (1987), "Human resource management and industrial relations", Journal of Management Studies, Vol. 24 No. 5, September, pp. 503-21.

184. Guest, D.E. (1999), "Human resource management and performance: a review and research agenda", in Schuler, R.S. and Jackson, S.E. (Eds), Strategic Human Resource Management, Basil Blackwell, Oxford, pp. 177-90.

185. Guha, B.P. (1996), Voluntary Retirement., Shri Ram Centre for Industrial Relations and Human resources, New Delhi.

186. Gupta, A.K. and Govindarajan, V. (1991) 'Knowledge Flows and the Structure of Control within Multinational Corporations', Academy of Management Review, 16: pp. 768-92.

187. Gupta, R.K., Human Resource Accounting, Anmol Publications, New Delhi 1988.

188. Hackman, J.R, Is Job Enrichment Just A Fad? Harvard Business Review, May-June, 1973.

189. Hair, J.F. Jr, Anderson, R.E., Tatham, R.L. and Black, W.C. (1998) Multivariate Data Anatysis, 5th edn. Upper Saddle River, NJ: Prentice Hall.

190. Hal, Glatzer (1995), HR Systems get re-engineering, HR Magazine, July issue, PP. 44-47.

191. Hall, D.T, and Hall, P.S., What is New in Career Management, Dynamics, Organisational, Summer, 1976.

192. Hamel, G. and Prahalad, C.K. (1994). Competing for the future. Harvard Business School Press, Boston, Mass.

193. Hamilton, R.D. and Kasklak, R.J. (1999) 'National Influences on Multinational Corporation Control System Selection', Management International Review, 39: pp. 167-89.

194. Hammer, M. and Champy, J. (1993), Re-engineering the Corporation, HarperCollins, New York, NY.

195. Hannon, J.M., Huang, I. and Jaw, B. (1995) 'International Human Resource Strategy and its Determinants: The Case of Subsidiaries in Taiwan', Journat of Internationat Business Studies, 26: pp. 531-54.

196. Harris, R.G. 1999, December. "Determinants of Canadian Productivity Growth: Issues and Prospects." Discussion paper # 8. Ottawa: Industry Canada.

197. Hendricks, W. (1996) (ed.), Coaching, Mentoring and Managing, New York: Career Press.

198. Hendry, C and Pettigrew, A (1986). The practice of strategic human resource management. Personnel Review, 15:5, pp. 3-8.

199. Hendry, C. and Pettigrew, A. (1992), "Patterns of strategic change in the development of human resources management", British Journal of Management, Vol. 3 No. 3, pp. 137-56.

200. Hess, H., Real Peter Principle: Promotion to Pain, Harvard Business Review, July-August, 1976.

201. Hitt, M. A., L. Bierman, K. Shimizu, & Kochhar, R. (2001). Direct and Moderating Effects of Human Capital on Strategy and Performance in Professional Service Firms: A resource-Based Perspective. Academy of Management Journal, 44, 1, 13-28.

202. Horn, J.L., Concise Encyclopedia of Psychology, edited by Corsini, R.J., John Wiley & Sons, New York, 1987, p.1046.

203. Horngren, C., Sundem, G. and Stratton, W., 2005. Introduction to Management Accounting, New Jersey, Pearson.

204. Hoyda, L., Promotions form within Decline, Academy of Management Journals, Vol. 47, August, 1986, pp.6-7.

205. Hudson, Frederick M (1999), The Handbook of Coaching, San Francisco: Jossey-Bass.

206. Hunt, J.M. and Weintraub, J.R. (2002). The Coaching Manager, Response Books, New Delhi.

207. Huselid, M. (1995), "The impact of human resource management practices on turnover, productivity, and corporate financial performance", Academy of Management Journal., Vol. 38 pp.635-72.

208. Huselid, M.A., Jackson, S.E. and Schuler, R.S (1997). Technical and strategic human resource management effectiveness as determinants of firm performance. Academy of Management Journal, 39: pp. 949-969.

209. International Labour Office (1990), Job Evaluation, International Labour Organisation, Geneva.

210. International Labour Officer, Higher Productivity in Manufacturing Industries. International Labour Organisation, Geneva, Third impression, 1967.

211. International Organisation for Standardisation (ISO), International Standards:8402, 9000-9004, 10011 (ir parts), ISO, Geneva. 1987.

212. Iyaniwura, O. and Osoba, A.M. (1983) "Measuring Productivity; Conceptual and Statistical Problems: Improvement of Statistics" in Osoba A.M. (ed.) 'Productivity in Nigeria' Proceedings of a National Conference' NISER, Ibadan.

213. Jackson, S., Schuler, R. (1995), "Understanding human resource management in the context of organisations and their environments", Annual Review of Psychology, Vol. 45 pp.237-64.

214. Jackson, S.E., Schuler, R.S. & Rivero, J.C. (1989). Organisational Characteristics as Predictors of Personnel Practices. Personnel Psychology, 46, 569-592

215. Jackson, S.E., Schuler, R.S. and Rivero, J.C. (1989) 'Organisational Characteristics as Predictors of Personnel Practices', Personnet Psychotogy, 42: pp. 727-86.

216. Jaeger, A. (1983) 'The Transfer of Organisational Culture Overseas: An Approach to Control in the Multinational Corporation', Journal of International Business Studies, 14: pp. 91-114.

217. Jarillo, J.C. and Martinez, J.I. (1990) 'Different Roles for Subsidiaries: The Case of Multinational Corporations in Spain', Strategic Management Journal, 11: pp. 501-12.

218. Jensen, M., & Meckling, W. (1976). Theory of the firm: Managerial behaviour, agency costs, and ownership structure. Journal of Financial Economics, 3, pp. 305-360.

219. Jensen, M., Murphy, K. (1990), "Performance pay and top management incentives", Journal of Labor Economics, Vol. 4 pp.606-28.

220. Jiménez-Jiménez, D., Sanz-Valle, R. (2005), "Innovation and human resource management fit: an empirical study", International Journal of Manpower, Vol. 26 No.4, pp.364-81.

221. John, Bramham (1994), Human Resource Planning, University Press (India) Limited, Hyderabad.

222. John, Edwards, Chris, Leck, Ray Loveridge, Roger Lumley, John, Morgan and Mick (1983) Silver, Manpo" Planning, Joh Wiley & Sons, New York.

223. Johnston, W.B., Global Work Force: The New World Labour Market, Harvard Business Review, March-April, 1991, pp. 115-127.

224. Joseph, K., Kalwani, M. (1995), "The impact of environmental uncertainty on the design of salesforce compensation plans", Marketing Letters, Vol. 6 No.3, pp.183-97.

225. K.N. Subramarian, Wages in India, TMH, New Delhi, 1979.

226. Kanungo, RN., and Misra, S., Declining Work Motivation in India, Indian Management, May, 1985, Vol. 24, No.5, pp. 6-14.

227. Kilmoski, R.J., & Jones, R.G. (1995). Staffing for effective group decision making: Key issues in matching people and teams. In Guzzo, R., & Salas, E. (Eds), Team effectiveness and decision making in organisations, San Francisco: Jossey-Bass.

228. Kleiman, L.S., and Durham, R.L., Performance, Performance Appraisal, Promotion and the Courst, a Critical Review, Personnel Psychology, September, 1981, Vol. 34, pp. 103-121.

229. Klitgaard, R. (1989) " Incentive Myopia" World Development, vol. 17, no. 4 pp. 477-459.

230. Kono, T. (1984). Strategy and Structure of Japanese Enterprises. New York: M. E. Sharpe.

231. Krafft, M. (1999), "An empirical investigation of the antecedents of sales force control systems", Journal of Marketing, Vol. 63 pp.120-34.

232. Krafft, M., Albers, S., Lal, R. (2004), "Relative explanatory power of agency theory and transaction cost analysis in German salesforces", International Journal of Research in Marketing, Vol. 21 pp.265-83.

233. Kristies, Ball (2000), Interface Value, People Management, January, PP. 40-41.

234. Kristof, A.L. (1996). Person-organisation fit: An integrative review of its conceptualizations, measurement, and implications. Personnel Psychology, 49, pp. 1-49.

235. Krugman, P. (1990) "The Age of Diminished Expectations" MIT Press., Mass., Cambridge

236. Kulkarni, S.S., Prakasan, R, and Nagia, R, Personnel Policies in Banks: and Employee Opinion SurVI National Institute of Bank Management, Bombay, 1983.

237. Kundu, Gorachand, A New Technique of Attitude Measurement, Annapurna Publishing House, Calcutta, 1975.

238. Lal, R., Srinivasan, V. (1993), "Compensations plans for single- and multi-product salesforces: an application of the Holmstrom-Milgrom model", Management Science, Vol. 39 pp.777-93.

239. Lawler, E.E. (1986) High Involvement Management. San Francisco, CA: Jossey-Bass.

240. Lawler, E.E., and Porter, L.W., The Effects of Performance on Job Satisfaction, Industrial Relations, Vol. 1, October, 1967, p.5.

241. Lawlor, A. (1985) "Productivity Improvement Manual" Aldershot, United Kingdom.

242. Legge, K. (1995), Human ResourcesManagement: Rhetorics and Realities, Macmillan, London.

243. Legge, K. (2001). Silver bullet or spent round? Assessing the meaning of the high commitment management/ performance relationship in J. Storey (ed) Human resource management: a critical text (2nd Edn), Thomson, London.

244. Leonard, D. (1998). Well-springs of knowledge: building and sustaining the sources of innovation. Harvard Business School Press, Boston, Mass.

245. Leong, S.M. and Tan, CT. (1993) 'Managing Across Borders: An Empirical Test of the Bartlett and Ghoshal (1989) Organisational Typology', Journal of Internationat Business Studies, 24: pp. 449-65.

246. Lepak, D.P. & Snell, S.A. (2002). Examining the Human Resource Architecture: The Relationships among Human Capital, Employment, and Human Resource Configurations. Journal of Management, 28, 4, 517-543

247. Lewin, K., Group Decisions and Social Change in Readings in Social Psychology, Maccoby, E., et aI, (editors), Holt, Rinehert & Winston, New York, 1958.

248. Liao, Y.S. (2005). Business Strategy and Performance: The Role of Human Resource Management Control. Personnel Review, 34, 3, pp. 294-309.

249. Likert, R., Motivation: The Core of Management, American Management Association, Personnel Series, No 155,1933, p. 16.

250. Likert, R., The Human Organisation, McGraw-Hill Book Company, Inc. New York, 1967, pp. 4-10.

251. Lipman-Blumen, Jean (1996), The Connective Edge: Leading in an Interdependent World, San Francisco: Jossey-Bass Publishers.

252. Lloyd L Byars and Leaslie W. Rue, Human Resource Management, Chicago, Irwin, 1997.

253. Lundy, O. and Cowling, A. (1996), Strategic Human Resource Management, Routledge, London.

254. Luo, Y. and Peng, M.W. (1999) 'Learning to Compete in a Transition Economy: Experience, Environment, and Performance', Journal of International Business Studies, 30: pp. 269-95.

255. M.P., Srivastava (1999), Human Resource Planning, Institute of Applied Manpower Research, New Delhi.

256. MacCrimmon, K.R., Wehrung, D.A. (1986), Taking Risks: The Management of Uncertainty, The Free Press, New York, NY.

257. MacDuffie, J.P. (1995). Human Resource bundles and manufacturing performance: Organisational logic and flexible production systems in the world auto industry. Industrial and Labor Relations Review, 48: pp. 197-221

258. Maciariello, J. and Kirby, C., 1994. Management Control Systems - Using Adaptive Systems to Attain Control, New Jersey, Prentice Hall.

259. Madsen, P. and Shafritz, J. M., (Eds.), (1990). "Essentials of Business Ethics". New York: Penguin Books.

260. Mahajan, T.R., Structure and Growth of Central Government Employees, Yojajna, October, 16-31, 1986.

261. Maheshwari, B.L Management by Objectives (2nd Reprint), Tata McGraw Hill Publishing Company, New Delhi,1985.

262. Mamoria, C.B. Personnel Management, 6th Edition, Himalaya Publishing House, Bombay, 1988.

263. Mantrala, M., Krafft, M., Weitz, B. (2000), "An empirical examination of economic rationales for companies", Documento de trabajo 00-07, Discussion paper series in economics and management, German Economic Association of Business Administration - GEABA, .

264. Martin, Godfrey (1997, edited), Skill Development for International Competitiveness, Edward Elgar Publishing Company, Cheltenham, U.K.

265. Martinez, J.I. and Jarillo, J.C (1989) 'The Evolution of Research on Coordination Mechanisms in Multinational Corporations', Journal of International Business Studies, 19: pp. 489-514.

266. Martinez, J.I. and Jarillo, J.C. (1991) 'Co-ordination Demands of International Strategies', Journal of International Business Studies, 21: pp. 429-44.

267. Maslow, A.H., Motivation and Personality, Harper and Brothers, New York, 1954, p.83.

268. Matthes, K., Empowerment: Fact or Fiction? HR Focus (formerly Personnel), 1992,69 (8), 1 & 6.

269. Mayo, E., The Human Problem of Industrial Civilisation, Macmillan, New York, 1933.

270. McCall, Morgan W., Jr. (1998), High Flyers: Developing the Next Generation of Leaders, Boston: Harvard University Press, 1998.

271. McCausland, W., Pouliakas, K., Theodossiou, I. (2005), "Some are punished and some are rewarded: a study of the impact of performance pay on job satisfaction", International Journal of Manpower, Vol. 26 No.7/8, pp.636-59.

272. McGrath, J. E. (1991). Time, interaction, and performance (TIP): A theory of groups. Small Group Research, 22, pp. 147-174.

273. Megginson, D., and Clutterbuck, D. (2009), Further techniques for coaching and mentoring. Oxford: Butterworth Heinemann.

274. Megginsoon, L.C. Personnel and Human Resource Administration (3rd Edition), Richard W. Irwin, Homewood, Ilinois, 1977.

275. Melian-Gonzalez, S., Verano-Tacoronte, D. (2006), "Is there more than one way to manage human resources in companies?", Personnel Review, Vol. 35 pp.29-50.

276. Michael, J Kavanagh, Hall, G. and Scott 1. Jannenbaum, 1990, Human Resource Information Systems: Development and Applications, PWS-KENT Publishing Company, Boston, Massachusetts.

277. Miles, R. and Snow, C. (1984). Designing strategic human resources systems, Organisational Dynamics, Summer, pp. 36-52.

278. Milkovich, G., Newman, J. (1996), Compensation, 5th ed., Irwin, Burr Ridge, IL,

279. Miller, D. & Friesen, P.H. (1984). A Longitudinal Analysis of the Corporate Life Cycle. Management Science, 30,10, 1161-1183.

280. Miller, D. & Friesen, R.H. (1982). The Longitudinal Analysis of Organisations: A Methodological Perspective. Management Science, 28, 9, 1013-1033.

281. Mills, D.Q., Seniority Versus Ability in Promotion Decisions, Industrial labour Relations Reviews Review, Vol. 38, No.3, April 1985.

282. Mintzberg, H. (1994). The rise and fall of strategic planning. Prentice Hall International, Hemel Hempstead.

283. Monappa, A., and Salyadain, S., Personnel management, Tata McGraw-Hill Publishing Company, New Delhi 1979.

284. Mukherjee, M., and Chatterji, S., Merit as Promotion Criterion for Performance, Productivity, Vol. 27, No.2, July-September, 1986, pp. 163-168.

285. Murray, B.J., Motivation and Emotion, Englewood Cliffs, Prentice-Hall, New Jersey, 1964, p.9.

286. Myers, S. & Marquis, D.G. (1969). Successful Industrial Innovations. National Science Foundation, Washington, DC.

287. National Productivity Council, Personnel Management in Japan, USA and Britain, National Productivity Council, New Delhi 1963.

288. Near, J.P., Career Plateau: Causes and Effects, Business Horizons, October, 1980, Vol. 23, pp. 53-57.

289. Neff, T.J., Bridging the Promotion. Gap, Management Review, January, 1978.

290. Nobel, R. and Birkinshaw, J. (1998) 'Innovation in Multinational Corporations: Control and Communications Patterns in International R&D Operations', Strategic Management Journal, 19(5): pp. 479-96.

291. Nohria, N. and Ghoshal, S. (1994) 'Differentiated Fit and Shared Values: Alternatives for Managing Headquarters-Subsidiary Relations', Strategic Management Journal, 15: pp. 491-503.

292. Nonaka, I. and Takeuchi, H. (1995). The knowledge-creating company. Oxford University

293. Nunnally, J.C. and Bernstein, I.H. (1994) Psychometric Theory, 3rd edn. New York: McGraw-Hill.

294. Odiorne, G.5., Personnel Management for the 80's, The Personnel Administrators, Vol. 22, No.6, 1977.

295. Olaoye, A. O. (1985) " Total Factor Productivity Trends in Nigerian Manufacturing" Nigerian Journal of Economic and Social Studies, vol. 27, no. 3, pp.317-345.

296. Oliver, R.L., Anderson, E. (1994), "An empirical test of the consequences of behavior-and outcome-based sales control systems", Journal of Marketing, Vol. 58 No.October, pp.53-67.

297. Oliver, R.L., Anderson, E. (1995), "Behavior- and outcome-based sales control systems: evidence and consequences of pure-form and hybrid governance", Journal of Personal Selling & Sales Management, Vol. 15 No.Fall, pp.1-15.

298. Oliver, R.L., Weitz, B. (1991), "The effects of risk preference, uncertainty and incentive compensation on salesperson motivation", Report No. 91-104, Marketing Science Institute, .

299. Orth, C.D., Wilkinson, H.E., and Benfari, R.C (1987), "The Manager's Role as Coach and Mentor," Organisational Dynamics, Vol. 15, Issue 4, pp. 66-74.

300. Osterman, P (1994). How common is workplace transformation and who adopts it? Industrial and Labor Relations Review, 47:2, pp. 173-188.

301. Ouchi, W. (1977). The relationship between organisational structure and organisational control, Administrative Science Quarterly, 21, pp. 173-192.

302. Ouchi, W.G. (1977) 'The Relationship Between Organisational Structure and Organisational Control', Administrative Science Quarterly, 22(2): pp. 129-41.

303. Ouchi, W.G. (1982). Theory Z, Avon Books, New York.

304. P. Webb, "Business Ethics: A View from the Trenches," California Management Review 37:2 (Winter 1995): pp. 8-28.

305. Padaki, R, Job Enrichment, Theory into Practice, Indian Management, August, 1985, Vol. 24, No.8, pp.3-10.

306. Pareek, U. and Rao, T.Y. Designing and Managing Human Resource System, Oxford & IBH Publishing Co., New Delhi 1986.

307. Paul, O., Internal labour Market, the MIT Press, Massachusetts, 1984.

308. Paul, Miller (1992), Integrating Strategy and Human Resource Management in Brian Towers edited. The Handbook of Human Resource Management, Blackwell Publishers, Cambridge.

309. Penrose, E. (1959). The theory of the growth of the firm. Blackwell, Oxford.

310. Perrow, C. (1967). A Framework for the Comparative Analysis of Organisations. American Sociological Review. April, 194-208.

311. Perrow, C. (1970). Organisational Analysis: A Sociological View. New York: Tavistock publications.

312. Peter, Bamberger and 11 am, Meshoulam, Human Resource Strategy, Sage Publications, Inc., California, 2000.

313. Peter, J., Dowling, Denice, E., Welch and Randall, S., Schuler (1999), International Human Resource Management, South-Western College Publishing, Cincinnati.

314. Peters, T.J. and Waterman, R.H. Jr (1982). In search of excellence: Lessons from America's best run companies. Harper and Row, New York.

315. Pfeffer, J. (1994). Competitive advantage through people. Harvard Business School Press, Boston, Mass.

316. Pfeffer, J. (1998). The human equation: building profits by putting people first. Harvard Business School Press, Boston, Mass.

317. Piercy, N., Cravens, D., Morgan, N. (1999), "Relationships between sales management control, territory design, salesforce performance and sales organisation effectiveness", British Journal of Management, Vol. 10 pp.95-111.

318. Pigors, P., and Charles, A.M., Personnel Administration, 4th edition, McGraw-Hill Book Company, Inc., New York, 1961.

319. Pil, F.K. and MacDuffie, J.P. (1996). The adoption of high involvement work practices. Industrial Relations, 35: pp. 423-455.

320. Pinnington, A. and Edwards T. (2000), Introduction to Human Resource Management, Oxford University Press, Oxford.

321. Poe, R, and Courter, C.L, Quality Busters, Across the Board, 1992 XXIX (7 & 8), 5

322. Porter, M (1985). Competitive advantage: creating and sustaining superior performance. Free Press, New York.

323. Prakash, R, and Preeti, J., Class Differences and Achievement Motivation: Indian Journal of Industrial Relations, July, 1984, pp. 65-72.

324. Procter, L.W., and Lawler, E.E., Managerial Attitudes and Performance, Richard W. Irwin, Inc. Homewood, Illinois, 1968.

325. Prokopenko, J. (l987) "Productivity Management: A Practical Handbook" International Labour Organisation, Geneva.

326. Pucik, v., Promotion Patterns in a Japanese Trading Company, The Columbia Journal of World Business, Vol. 20, Fall, 1985, pp. 73-79

327. Quinn, J.B. and Cameron, K. (1983). Organisational Life Cycles and Shifting Criteria of Effectiveness: Some Preliminary Evidence. Management Science, 29, pp. 33-51.

328. Rajiv, R, Employment and Structural Change, The Indian Worker, February 29,1988, p. 5.

329. Ramaswami, N., Motivation & Inter-Personal Relations, The Economic Times, October 22,1987, p. 8.

330. Ramsay, H., Scholarios, D.and Harley, B. (2000). Employees and high-performance work systems: testing inside the black box. British Journal of Industrial Relations, 38:4, ll. 501-531.

331. Reddy, B.B., Industrialisation, Employment in India, Southern Economist, March 1, 1988, pp. 9-12

332. Reddy, T.S., and Ramesh, B., Produtivity in Banks, Indian Management, May, 1985, Vol. 24, No.5, pp. 35-40. 100.

333. Reich, R.B. (1990). Who Is Us? Harvard Business Review, (January-February), 53-64

334. Rensis, Likert (1967), The Human Organisations- Mangement and Value, McGraw Hill.

335. Rice A K (1958) .Productivity and Social Organisation., Tavistock, London.

336. Robert, E., Sibson (1992), Strategic Planning for Human Resources Management, American Management Association, New York.

337. Rolf, P, Lynton and Udai Pareek (1999), Training for Development, Vistaar Publications, New Delhi.

338. Rosenzweig, P.M. and Nohria, N. (1994) 'Influences on Human Resources Management Practices in Multinational Corporations', Journal of International Business Studies, 25: pp. 229-251.

339. Ross, W.T. (1991), "Performance against quota and the call selection decision", Journal of Marketing Research, Vol. 28 pp.292-306.

340. Roth, K. and Nigh, D. (1992) 'The Effectiveness of Headquarters-Subsidiary Relationships: The Role of Coordination, Control, and Conflict', Journal of Business Re.search, 25: pp. 277-301.

341. Rousseau, D.M. and Arthur, M.B. (1999) 'The Boundary less Human Resource Function: Building Agency and Community in the New Economic Era', Organisational Dynamics, 27(4): pp. 7-18.

342. Rudrabasavraj, M.N. Dynamics of Personnel Administration, Indian Institute of Personnel Management (IIPM), Coimbatore, 1967.

343. Rynes, S., & Gerhart, B. (1990). Interviewer assessment of applicant "fit": An exploratory investigation. Personnel Psychology, 43, pp. 13-22.

344. S K Chakraborty, Managerial Transformation by Values - A corporate Pilgrimage, Sage Publications, New York, 1993.

345. Sandara, E., O'Connel, 1994, Planning and Setting up a New HRIS, HR Magazine, February, pp. 36-40

346. Sandesara, J.C. and Bishnoi, T.R., Factor Income shares in Indian Economy, 1960-61 to 1981-82 - A Statistical Analysis, Economic & Political Weekly, August 9,1986.

347. Sandra, E. O'Connel (1994), Planning and Setting up a New HRIS, HR Magazine, February Issue, PP. 36 -40.

348. Sarkar, K.K., Commentary on Awards & Settlements in Banks, Gemini Book House, Calcutta, 1986, pp. 159160.

349. Schachter, S., The psychology of Affiliation, Standard University Press, Stanford, California, 1959.

350. Schaefer, M.E., et al., Peter Principle Revisited, Human Resource Management, Winter, 1979, Vol. 18., pp. 1-5.

351. Schaeffer, D., Counseling the Unpromotable, Supervision, August, 1980.

352. Schein, Edgar. H. The Art of Managing Human Resources, Oxford University Press, New York, 1987.

353. Schneider, B. (1987). The people make the place. Personnel Psychology, 40, pp. 437-453.

354. Schuler, R. (1987), Personnel and Human Resource Management, 3rd ed., West Publishing Co., St Paul, MN.

355. Schuler, R. S. and MacMillan, I. C. (1984). Gaining Competitive Advantage Through Human Resource Management Practices. Human Resource Management, 23, 3, pp. 241-255.

356. Schuler, R.S. & Jackson, S.E. (1987). Linking Competitive Strategies with Human Resources Management Practices. Academy of Management Executive, 1, 207-219

357. Schuler, R.S. (1989). Strategic Human Resource Management and Industrial Relations. Human Relations, 42, pp.157-184.

358. Schuler, R.S. (1996). Market-focused management: human resource management implications. Journal of Market-focused Management, 1: pp. 13-29.

359. Schuler, R.S., Budwar, P.S. and Florkowski, G.W. (2002) 'International Human Resource Management: Review and Critique', International Journal of Management Review, 4: pp. 41-70.

360. Schuler, R.S., Dowling, P. and DeCieri, H. (1993) 'An Integrative Framework of Strategic International Human Resource Management', International Journal of Human Resource Management, 4: pp. 717-764.

361. Scrott, W.B., Clotheir, R.C., and Spriegel, W.B., Personnel Management Principles, Practices and a point of View, Tata McGraw-Hill Publishing Company Ltd., New Delhi, 1982.

362. Shah, K.R., Education-Impact on Employment, The Economic Times, October 24, 1986, p. 5.

363. Sharifzadeh, M., Internal Hiring: The Sensible Approach to Filling Positions, Supervisory Management, August, 1990, Vol. 35, p. 4.

364. Sikula, A.F., and Mckenna, J.F., The Management of Human Resources, John Wiley, New York, 1984.

365. Singh, B.P.c., Power Motivation - A Factorial Study, Indian Journal of Industrial Relations, Vol. 3, January, 1986, pp. 287-296.

366. Singh, P.N. Developing and Managing Human Sources, Suchandra Publications, Bombay, 1992. 101.

367. Skineer, B.F., Behaviour of Organism, Appleton-Century Crofts, New York, 1938.

368. Snell, S.A. (1992). Control Theory in Strategic Human Resource Management: The Mediation Effect of Administrative Information. Academy of Management Journal, 35, 2, 292-327

369. Snell, S.A., Youndt, M. (1995), "Human resource management and firm performance: testing a contingency model of executive controls", International Journal of Human Resource Management, Vol. 21 pp.711-37.

370. Srinivasan, K., Developmental and Demographic changes in Indian Since Independence, Journal of Institute of Economic Research, January, 1986, pp. 33-42.

371. Srivastava, S.K Motivation and Job Satisfaction, Indian Management, October, 1985, Vol. 24, No.9, pp.29-31.

372. Steers, R. & Ungson, G.R. (1987). Strategic issues in executive compensation decisions. pp. 315-327 in D.B. Balkin & L.R. Gomez-Mejia (Eds.), New perspectives on compensation. Englewood Cliffs, N J: Prentice-Hall

373. Steven, A., Larson (1993), Selecting a new payroll/HRIS, Management Accountant, October issue, PP. 28-31.

374. Stewart, G.L. & Barrick, M.R. (2000). Team Structure and Performance: Assessing the Mediating Role of Intrateam Process and the Moderating Role of Task Type. Academy of Management Journal, 43, 135-148.

375. Stewart, L.P. and Gudykunset, W.B., Differential Factors Influencing the Hierarchical Level and Number of Promotions of Males and Females within an Organisation, Academy of Management Journal, September, 1992, Vol. 25, pp. 586-597.

376. Stone, E.F. & Hollenbeck, J.R. (1989). Clarifying some Controversial Issues surrounding Procedures for Detecting Moderator Variables: Empirical Evidence and Related Matters. Journal of Applied Psychology, 74, 3-10.

377. Storey, J (1989). New perspectives in human resource management. Routledge, London.

378. Storey, J (2001). Human resource management today: an assessment in J. Storey (ed) Human resource management: a critical text (2nd Edn), Thomson, London.

379. Storey, J. (1994), Developments in the Management of Human Resources, Basil Blackwell, Oxford.

380. Strauss, G. and Sayless, L.R. Personnel: The Human Problems of Management (3rd Edition), Prentice-Hall of India Private Limited, New Delhi, 1977.

381. Subha Rao, A (1994) .Management of Technology Change., Global Business Press, New Delhi.

382. Sumangala, K, Writings on the Wall: Narasimham Committee Implications, Monthly Review, Punjab National Bank, June, 1992, pp. 351-365.

383. Suri, G.K and Singh, Ajit, (editors), Role of Trade unions iri Productivity Movement, National Productivity Council, New Delhi, 1990.

384. Suzuki, H. Age, Seniority and Wages, International Labour Reviews, Vol. 113, No.1, January-February, 1976.

385. Sweeney, J.J. and Teel. K.S., A New Look at Promotion from within, Personnel journal, August 1979.

386. T.V. Rao (1999), HRD Audit, Response Books, New Delhi 105.

387. T.V. Rao, Readings in HRD, New Delhi, Oxford & IBH, 1991.

388. Tannenbaum, A.S. (1968), The Social Psychology of Work Organisation, Brooks-Cole, Belmont, CA.

389. Taylor, F.W. (1911). The principles of scientific management. Harper and Row, New York.

390. Teece, D., Pisano, G. & Shuen, A. (1997). Dynamic Capability and Strategic Management. Strategic Management Journal, 18, 7, 509-533.

391. The Indian Institute of Personnel Management (IIPM), Personnel Management in India. The Practical approach to human relations in industry (2nd revised edition), Asia Publishing House, Bombay, 1973.

392. Thomas, C., Greble (1997), A leading role for HR in Alternative Staffing, HR Magazine, February issue.

393. Thomas, David (1990) "The Impact of Race on Managers" Experiences of Developmental Relationships (Mentoring and Sponsorship): An Intra-Organisational Study." Journal of Organisational Behavior, Vol. 11, pp. 479-492.

394. Thompson, P (2003). Disconnected capitalism: or why employers can't keep their side of the bargain. Work, Employment and Society, 17:2, pp. 359-378.

395. Tidd, J., Bessant, J. & Pavitt, K. (1997). Managing Innovation, Chichester, John Wiley.

396. Torrington, D. and Hall, L. (1998), Human Resource Management, 4th ed., Prentice-Hall Europa, Hemel Hempstead.

397. Truss, C. (1999), "Soft and hard models of human resource management", in Gratton, L., Hailey, V.H., Stiles, P. and Truss, C. (Eds), Strategic Human Resource Management: Corporate Rhetoric and Human Reality, Oxford University Press,Oxford, pp. 40-58.

398. Tumin, M.M., Social Stratification, the forms and functions and inequality, Second Edition, Prentice-Hall of India.

399. Tyre, M.J., Managing Innovation on the Factory Floor, Technology Review, October, 1991, Col. 94, No.7, pp. 59-65.

400. Tyson, S. (1995), Human Resource Strategy: Towards a General Theory of Human Resource Management, Pitman, London.

401. Udai Pareek, and T.v. Rao, Designing and Managing Human Resource Systems, Oxford and IBH Publishing Co., New Delhi, 1997.

402. Ulrich, D (1997). Human resource champions: the next agenda for adding value and delivering results. Harvard Business School Press, Boston.

403. V.S. Mahesh, Thresholds of Motivation - The Corporation as a Mursery for Human Growth, TMH, New Delhi,1993.

404. Vaid, D.K., Compensating Your Field Sales Force, Indian Management, August, 1985, Vol. 24, No.8, pp. 28-34.

405. Valentine, R.I., Performance Objective for Managers, D.P Taraporevala & Sons (P) Ltd., New York, 1972.

406. Venkata Ratnam, C.S., Srivastava, B.K., Personnel Management and Human Resources, Tata McGraw-Hill Publishing Company Limited, New Delhi, 1991.

407. Verma, P Personnel Management in Indian Organisations, Oxford IBH Publishing Co., Pvt. Ltd, New Delhi, 1988.

408. W.J. Paul and K.B. Robertson, Job Enrichment and Employee Motivation, Gower Press, London, 1970.

409. Walton, R.E (1985). From control to commitment in the workplace. Harvard Business Review, 63:2, pp. 77-84.

410. Walton, R.E. (1985), "Toward a strategy of eliciting employee commitment based on policies of mutuality", in Walton, R.E. and Lawrence, P.R. (Eds), Human Resource Management: Trends and Challenges, Harvard Business School Press, Boston, MA.

411. Ward, P.T. & Duray, R. (2000). Manufacturing Strategy in Context: Environment, Competitive Strategy and Manufacturing Strategy. Journal of Operations Management, 18,2, 123-138.

412. Watkins, G. McNaughton, D., and Parsow, P. The Management of Personnel and Labour Relations (2nd Edition), McGraw-Hill Bokk Company, Inc. New York, 1950.

413. Wayne F. Cascio, Managing Human Resources, Mc Graw-Hill, New York, 1995.

414. Welbourne, T., Cyr, L. (1997), "Human resource management in initial public offering firms: validation of a control orientation typology", Advances in Entrepreneurship, Firm Emergence and Growth, Vol. 3 pp.249-96.

415. Whitmore, J. (2002). Coaching for Performance, Nicholas Brealey, London.

416. Wickens, P (1987). The road to Nissan. MacMillan, London.

417. William B. Werther, Jr. and Keith Davis, Human Resources and Personnel Managemet, Mc-Grawl Hill, 1994.

418. William P. Antony, et al. Strategic Human Resource Management, Dryden Press, 1991.

419. William, E., Berry (1994), The Human Resource Information System, Management Accountant, January Issue, PP. 56-57.

420. Wiseman, R.M., Gómez-Mejía, L.R. (1998), "A behavioral agency model of managerial risk taking", Academy of Management Review, Vol. 23 No.1, pp.133-53.

421. Womack, G., Jones, D and Roos, D (1990). The machine that changed the world. Rawson-MacMillan, New York.

422. Wood, S (1999). Human resource management and performance. International Journal of Management Review, 1:4, pp. 367-413.

423. Wret, J.E., et al., Statistical Methods in Educational and Psychological Research, Appleton Century-Crofts, Inc., New York, 1954.

424. Wright, P.M. (2003), "Next generation SHRM research: from covariation to causation", Working Papers Series 03-01, CARHS, Cornell University.

425. Wright, P.M., Gardner, T.M., Moynihan, L.M. (2003), "The impact of Human Resource practices on business-unit operating and financial performance", Working Papers Series 02-12, CARHS, Cornell University, Ithaca, NY.

426. Wright, P.M., McMahan, G., Snell, S., Gerhart, B. (2001), "Comparing line and HR executives' perceptions of HR effectiveness: services, roles, and contributions", Human Resource Management Journal, Vol. 40 pp.111-24.

427. Yoder, D., Henceman, H.C. Tumbull, J., and Store, C.H. Handbook of Personnel Management and Labour Relations, Mc Graw-Hill Book Company, New Delhi, 1958.

INDEX